THE HISTORIES

HERODOTUS

The Histories

Translated by
ROBIN WATERFIELD

with an Introduction and Notes by
CAROLYN DEWALD

Oxford   New York
OXFORD UNIVERSITY PRESS
1998

Oxford University Press, Great Clarendon Street, Oxford OX2 6DP
Oxford New York
Athens Auckland Bangkok Bogota Bombay Buenos Aires
Calcutta Cape Town Dar es Salaam Delhi Florence Hong Kong Istanbul
Karachi Kuala Lumpur Madras Madrid Melbourne Mexico City
Nairobi Paris Singapore Taipei Tokyo Toronto Warsaw
and associated companies in
Berlin Ibadan

Oxford is a trade mark of Oxford University Press

British Library Cataloguing in Publication Data
Data available

Library of Congress Cataloging-in-Publication Data
Herodotus.
[History. English]
The histories / Herodotus; translated by Robin Waterfield; with
an introduction and notes by Carolyn Dewald.
(Oxford world's classics)
Includes bibliographical references and index.
1. History, Ancient.   2. Greece—History.   I. Waterfield, Robin,
1952– .   II. Dewald, Carolyn.   III. Title.   IV. Series: Oxford
world's classics (Oxford University Press)
D58.H3313   1998   930—dc21   97-34379
ISBN 0-19-212609-1 (hardback).
ISBN 0-19-282425-2 (pbk.)

1 3 5 7 9 10 8 6 4 2

Typeset by Best-set Typesetter Ltd., Hong Kong
Printed and bound in Great Britain by
Mackays of Chatham PLC, Chatham, Kent

For Michael F. Brown
and for Phyllis H. Jones

CONTENTS

INTRODUCTION

IN the earliest years of the fifth century BCE, the dominant power in the Greek world was the Persian empire, which stretched from the Mediterranean Sea eastward to India, and from Egypt northward through the Near East to Thrace and modern Afghanistan. The Greeks of the mainland were in comparison a small, disunited, and quite poor people scattered in little towns through the southern Balkan peninsula. In 490 BCE the Athenians repulsed a Persian naval invasion at Marathon on the north coast of Attica; in 481 Xerxes, the Great King of Persia, led a massive invasion by both land and sea to conquer all of Greece and open the western Mediterranean to Persian rule. To the great surprise of everyone (most of all, the Greeks themselves), in about two years the Greeks—few in number, poor, and disunited as they were—managed to thwart Xerxes' ambitions. The Greeks, not the Persians, won the Persian Wars.

The fifty years that followed saw something as surprising and as important for the course of later history: Athens, the largest town on the Greek mainland, and with Sparta one of the two leaders of the Greek defence against Persia, became the dominant cultural and political centre in Greece. In the middle of the fifth century Athens was a city of thirty or forty thousand adult Greek male citizens. It was by this time a powerful participatory democracy; through the power of its citizen navy, it controlled and taxed large parts of the Greek world to the east and north of it. Its inhabitants, both citizens and foreigners drawn to Athens because of its power, created out of traditional Greek cultural materials a new set of ideas about what it was to be a member of a human community. They acted these ideas out in dramas for the stage, they spoke and wrote about them in the new medium of argumentative prose, they put some of them into practice in the democratic government of Athens, and— perhaps in the long run most important of all—they developed a form of professional secondary schooling that taught the young both how to think in these new ways and how to transmit their new habits of thought in writing to the next generation. We call this period of intellectual ferment in Athens the first sophistic, or the Greek enlightenment.

The Athenians themselves did not always like these new developments. Aristophanes' *Clouds*, originally written in 423 BCE, is a very funny play, but it also testifies to the tensions inherent in such massive cultural change. Aristophanes' play makes clear the disgust and fear felt by some of the Athenians themselves, as they moved from being a traditional culture, honouring and duplicating the achievements of their fathers, to a critical and rational one, questioning the past and willing to subject its values to outside standards of rational evaluation. In the play the young man Pheidippides, fresh from Socrates' 'thinkateria', ends up deciding it is perfectly all right to beat his father—and his mother too! This is Aristophanes' comic assessment of the new education. But once the genie was out of the bottle it could not be put back. The intellectual revolution of the middle and later Athenian fifth century changed how educated Greeks thought about culture. It is not overstating the case to say that it also changed the course of western civilization. We ultimately owe to this remarkable period many of our most basic ideas about democracy, about the importance of the individual, the importance of rational political discourse, about how we think education works and what it is for, as well as many of our basic genres of literary expression: drama, philosophy, rhetoric—and, thanks to the achievement of Herodotus himself, the writing of history.

Herodotus was not a native of Athens. He was born in Halicarnassus (the modern Turkish city of Bodrum), about the time of the Persian Wars. Halicarnassus was a Dorian town with substantial intermarriage among its Greek, Carian, and Persian populations. Judging from the names of some of Herodotus' older relatives, his own family probably contained a Carian element. If the later ancient reports that have come down to us are correct, his family was exiled during the troubled years after the Persian Wars, and as a very young man Herodotus may have lived on the island of Samos. His occasional comments in the *Histories* show us that he travelled widely around the world of the east Mediterranean. We do not know when and how the *Histories* were first written down; very likely, however, they arose out of recitations or readings that he gave over a number of years both in other Greek cities and in Athens at the height of its imperial power, about things he had seen and found out on his travels. People Herodotus might have encountered in Athens included the playwrights Sophocles and Euripides, the visiting Ionian thinkers Protagoras and Anaxagoras, Pericles the great Athenian general and statesman, Phidias the sculptor, Socrates the philosopher, Hippodamus the town planner, and perhaps also Hippocrates the father of medicine (and a native of Cos, an island city just off the coast near Halicarnassus). Herodotus himself joined the Panhellenic colony that under Athenian sponsorship was sent to Thurii, in southern Italy, in the late 440s. He shows some knowledge of events in Greece during the early years of the Peloponnesian War, but the *Histories* do not mention anything that took place after 425, and he may have died in the 420s, well before the war's conclusion. His tomb was identified at Thurii, but there is also an ancient report that he died at Pella, in Macedonia.

In one of his audiences, if a late ancient biography does not mislead us, was the young Athenian aristocrat, Thucydides. Thucydides went on to do one of the things that Herodotus had also done, that is, to tell the story of great events of the recent past, but what Thucydides wrote could not have been delivered as lectures to a general audience. In austere and analytic prose Thucydides concentrated on events he himself had lived through, recording the course of the Peloponnesian War between Athens and Sparta that ended the fifth century and Athens' hopes for political dominance in Greece. The works of Herodotus and Thucydides together created an intellectual field that we still call by the name Herodotus gave his own investigations: *historiē*, or history. The magnitude of Herodotus' achievement as the first historian is hard to appreciate, however, precisely because the genre that he invented became so important a contribution to our own thought-world in the hands of Thucydides and later historians after him. Part of what we are obliged to do as we read Herodotus' work is to try to see it through the lens of the time in which he thought and wrote, so that we begin to grasp the intellectual sweep and boldness of his initial accomplishment. What Herodotus had in mind as he wrote up his *Histories* remains very much an open question.

No doubt one major subject of Herodotus' lectures as he travelled around the Greek world was the victory the Greeks had achieved a generation earlier over the Persians. Herodotus begins his massive *Histories* by alluding to it. The questions he starts with are fairly basic: how did the war between Greeks and barbarians happen? what were the causes and explanations for it? Herodotus

was not the first person to ask such questions; there were very likely
essays about the war and about Persians and other eastern peoples already circulating among educated Greek audiences. Ionian
savants like Dionysius of Miletus, Charon of Lampsacus,
Hellanicus of Lesbos, Xanthus of Lydia, and especially Hecataeus
of Miletus may have contributed more than we now realize to
Herodotus' text, both in content and in style. None the less,
Dionysius of Halicarnassus, a Greek literary critic in the Roman
empire, was right to emphasize that Herodotus was the first to see
many different stories of the past as parts of a single whole story—
to see the immensity of the known human world that was opened
up by his intent: to tell, really to tell, the story of the Persian Wars.
The *Histories* are not the chronicle of a single rule or a single
people's contract with its god, but a 'polycentric' narrative that
moves easily among the different voices, stories, and points of view
of many individuals from many different lands.

Herodotus tells us in his first sentence that his purpose is to
record great and wonderful deeds of Greeks and barbarians, both
other matters and *di' hēn aitiēn epolemēsan allēloisi*, 'the cause of
their hostilities'. The work as we have it now consists of nine
books; although the book divisions were not created by Herodotus
but by later Hellenistic editors, we retain them for their convenience. The last three books, 7 to 9, give us a detailed account of
Xerxes' invasion of Greece in 481–479 BCE. The first six books give
the background that allows us to understand the larger implications of what we read in Books 7 to 9. They sketch out the peoples
and places encountered by the Persians in the course of their imperial expansion from the time of Cyrus the Great, and they trace
the growth of the Persian empire from its beginning under Cyrus
in the 550s through the brief reign of his son Cambyses and then
through the much longer reign of a third Achaemenid king, Darius.
The last three books concern the reign of Darius' son Xerxes. Thus
Herodotus' long work has a structural organization that is at its
simplest genealogical and dynastic: the successive stories of the
deeds of conquest of four Persian kings:

Cyrus (557–530 BCE)   Book 1
Cambyses (530–522 BCE)   Book 2 and the first third of Book 3
Darius (521–486 BCE)   the rest of Book 3 and Books 4–6
Xerxes (486–479 BCE)   Books 7 to 9

Brief synopsis of the *Histories*

When we look at the *Histories* in this largest and simplest frame, we find in its overall sweep a story more dark than light in colour: we trace the way that the Persians developed a *nomos*, or custom, of conquest (7.8), and how their habits of thinking about the world and acting in it betrayed them finally in Greece. This is something that was not widely realized until Felix Jacoby's careful outline of the *Histories* in 1913; before that, many dismissed Herodotus for his charm, regarding him only as a skilled raconteur and not understanding the architectonic scope of the work as a whole.

Book 1 opens not with the Persians but with Croesus, the famous sixth-century king of Lydia and closest eastern neighbour of the Ionian Greeks of Asia. After a brief and rather humorous retelling of four mythic abductions of women, Greek women by barbarians and barbarian women by Greeks, Herodotus begins his narrative proper by saying that he is starting with Croesus, as the man who first committed injustice against the Greeks, by conquering the Greeks of Asia Minor and making them a part of his kingdom. This is the first statement of a theme that will reappear in many of the *Histories'* subsequent narratives: initial injustice gives rise to reciprocal violence, which may be called *tisis* or 'retribution' if one is theologically inclined, but which Herodotus sees as part of the natural order of the human world. The narrative that follows concerns Croesus the Lydian; about half-way through Book 1 Croesus is conquered in turn by his eastern neighbour, Cyrus the Persian (546 BCE), and this begins the Persian narrative thread that will last through the rest of the *Histories*. Backtracking in time, we see Cyrus first conquering his own Median grandfather, Astyages, and then, after defeating Croesus, conquering a variety of other eastern peoples, including most importantly Greek Ionia, but also Caria, Caunia, Lycia, and Babylon. Cyrus dies dreadfully at the end of Book 1, his head stuffed into a bag filled with blood. He has overreached himself trying to conquer the Massagetae, a nomad people on Persia's north-east borders. He leaves the kingdom to his son, Cambyses (530 BCE).

Cambyses' reign is the briefest and the most briefly treated in the *Histories* (2.1–3.66). In Herodotus' account, Cambyses conquers Egypt but in the process also overreaches himself. He goes mad, outraging Egyptian custom and religion, murdering members of his own family, and finally dying while trying to wrest his throne back from Median usurpers who have established themselves as rulers during his absence in Egypt. At the outset of Cambyses' reign, before narrating his Egyptian campaign, Herodotus inserts into the narrative of Persian imperial conquest an enormous essay, comprising all of Book 2, that focuses on Egypt itself: its geography, flora and fauna, customs, architectural wonders, religion, and history. At the end of Cambyses' eight-year reign (522 BCE; 3.66), we are left with a paradoxical picture of Persian power. On the one hand, the king dies in disgrace and the Persian government is in disarray; on the other, Persia itself is stronger than ever, since it possesses Egypt, and Herodotus has used Book 2 to make it clear that Egypt is the oldest and in many respects the most impressive country in the whole of the east Mediterranean.

The third Persian king, Darius son of Hystaspes, is also an Achaemenid and thus from the clan that provides the royal family of Persia, but he is not a direct descendant of Cyrus. In Herodotus' account, he becomes almost accidentally part of a seven-man conspiracy to unseat the Medes who have usurped Cambyses' throne. He persuades the other conspirators to choose monarchy again as their form of government (3.80–3), and through a trick created by his faithful groom becomes king himself. Herodotus comments that while the Persians call Cyrus their father, they call Darius a 'retailer' (3.89), and the story of his reign begins with a description of the scope of the vast and complex administrative structure that Darius governs and the taxes he collects. In the rest of Book 3 we read about how Darius' empire worked, and some of his campaigns, including the conquest of Samos and the quelling of a revolt in Babylon. The next three books also concern Darius' reign. Most of Book 4 is taken up with his abortive campaign in Scythia c.513 BCE (like Book 2, the first half of Book 4 describes the land and the people before proceeding to the story of the campaign proper). Books 5 and 6 focus on the Ionian revolt, the unsuccessful attempt of the eastern Greeks, who live in Ionia or the west coast of Asia Minor, to throw off Persian domination in 499–494 BCE. Darius defeats the Ionians at the battle of Lade. Because Athens has sent help to the Ionians, Darius in retaliation sends a naval expedition to attack Athens, and Book 6 ends with the battle of Marathon on the Attic coast in 490 BCE. Darius' generals are repulsed at Marathon, in an encounter that Herodotus says left 192 dead on the Greek side, 6,400 dead on the Persian. All of this sets the stage for and explains the massive Persian campaign of 481–479 BCE that will occupy the last three books of the *Histories*.

Darius' decision to march against the mainland Greeks in general and Athens in particular opens Book 7. He busies himself in preparation for several years, but is obliged to turn his attention instead to Egypt, now (486 BCE) also in revolt. Even the narrative of Darius, however, the most successful and long-ruling of the kings whose reign Herodotus narrates, concludes on a note of pessimism, since Herodotus expressly comments at the end that Darius dies without exacting retribution from either Egypt or Greece (7.4). It is Darius' son, Xerxes (486–465 BCE), who resubdues Egypt and then turns to the conquest of Greece. A sequence of five major battles defines the major stages of Xerxes' campaign in Books 7 to 9: Thermopylae, Artemisium, Salamis, Plataea, and Mycale. Herodotus brings events just past the battle of Mycale (479 BCE), and then stops with a brief story about Xerxes' bad judgement concerning his family and a capping anecdote, a flashback to the time of Cyrus the Great, and some good advice Cyrus had given the Persians as they began their career of world conquest.

In the earlier books of the *Histories*, the 'red thread' of Persian imperial conquest, though clearly underlying and giving shape to Herodotus' account, seems at times almost a narrative convenience. Certainly (as we shall see at greater length below) Herodotus departs from it often, to tell many other kinds of stories, about different Greek communities, other peoples encountered by the Persians in their military campaigns, and an odd assortment of fascinating material only very tenuously related to the theme of Persian military aggression. In contrast, the narrative of the last three books is a focused single story, structured until after the battle of Salamis around the aggressive moves of Xerxes' army. Herodotus rarely overtly preaches. But by the time we have read to the end of Book 9, we understand that, although Greek valour was necessary to resist the Persians, what really undid the Persians at the end were certain habits of thought that their long experience in imperial conquest had ingrained in them. Kings and other powerful people in the *Histories* tend to assume that their power is more far-reaching than it is, and the Persian kings exemplify this trait particularly clearly. Information was available to Xerxes from his Greek advisers that could have made his invasion of Greece much more successful than it was, but, insulated by his ambitious courtiers and his own assumptions, he did not take advantage of it.

Narrative habits

It is possible to read the *Histories* as though they convey only what I have just described: the growth of Persian power and its check in Greece; if one were forced to a single-sentence description of Herodotus' work as a whole, this one would do better than most. It is also, however, a complete distortion of Herodotus' actual accomplishment. For the reader proceeding through the *Histories* as a continuous narrative, it is a more accurate description of his or her experience to say that at many points the Persian story appears merely as the backdrop against which Herodotus does something much more complicated and interesting: he constructs a huge road-map of the known human world, past and present, in which everything is linked through story to everything else. He weaves a dense web of causal connections created in large part by personal reciprocities that span generations and cultures. Thus in Book 1, Croesus of Lydia loses his kingdom both because of decisions made by his ancestor Gyges four generations earlier and also because of his own perceived obligations to one of Cyrus' defeated enemies, Astyages the Mede. In Book 7, Xerxes attacks the mainland Greeks because they have aided the Ionians in an attempted revolt about twenty years earlier, and also because his father, Darius, has provided a model for success through conquest that he must build on. Again and again, choices made by individual actors in the *Histories* are portrayed as the consequences of previous actions, while their own acts in turn have enormous and often unintended consequences. John Gould puts this aspect of the interconnectedness of the *Histories* particularly well:

Herodotus' model of a world which is structured spatially and socially by patterns of reciprocity . . . is the key to understanding his work as a proto-historian. It both gives Herodotus a means of sorting and recalling information he has accumulated in vast quantities, and provides a model which can generate narrative on a historical scale, because the network of obligations flows through time by the mechanism of inheritance from one generation to another. It is not a closed system, since there is no reason why

spatial and social reciprocities cannot be indefinitely extended, which is
why Herodotus' world is both so open and expansive and so rich.
(*Herodotus*, 110)

Within the doubled pattern of Persian imperial expansion and
interconnected spatial and social reciprocities, occurs a third distinctive narrative move. In 4.30 Herodotus makes the apparently
disingenuous comment that his work 'seeks out digressions', and
indeed this is so. No matter where in his ongoing story Herodotus
finds himself, he is always willing to pause to note interesting and
astonishing phenomena that occur almost as afterthoughts, or parenthetical remarks only tangentially related to the topic at hand.
Distracting and amusing details about Herodotus' world emerge:
the problems of mule breeding unique to Elis (4.30), ants almost
the size of dogs in India, busy digging gold (3.102), sheep in Arabia
with tails so large and flat that little wagons have to be built for
them to carry their tails around in (3.113), flying snakes whose
skeletons Herodotus claims to have seen himself on his trip to
Egypt (2.75), people in Libya who live in caves and chirp like bats
(4.183), or a doughty Athenian warrior who brings into battle with
him an anchor tied around his middle that he drops so as not to
give ground before the enemy (9.74). Hundreds of such observations dot the narrative throughout, although in the latter books
they tend more strictly to concern people and places germane to
the war with Greece. They give us information both about what a
fifth-century Greek would find to be of interest in the world around
him and about the social and natural outlines of a world otherwise
largely inaccessible to us.

In the human sphere, Herodotus also includes details about the
lives of important political figures that intrigue us as much for their
folk-tale panache or novelistic human interest as for their historical importance. In a tragic family quarrel between Periander, the
wealthy tyrant of Corinth, and his angry young son, the boy, to
spite his father, becomes a homeless street-person (3.50–2); the
Persian nobleman Zopyrus conquers Babylon by cutting off his
own nose and ears, and then going to the besieged Babylonians and
convincing them that King Darius had done it to him (3.154–9).
Unlike many of his successors in the art of history writing,
Herodotus takes us not only into the council chambers and on to
the battlefields but also into the agora, the streets and fields, and

the ordinary anecdotal life of the east Mediterranean world of the sixth and fifth centuries. He loves a good story and recounts *thōmata*, astounding facts, but also witty retorts (3.119, 7.120, 7.226) and even bedroom conversations (3.134). I am going to argue that this does not, if properly understood, make Herodotus' achievement less impressive or vitiate its usefulness as history. It does sometimes make it harder for us to figure out his authorial intent, beyond that of providing enormous entertainment. Plutarch, a later Greek writer with a bias of his own, likens Herodotus as a narrator to a drunken young man in Herodotus' own text: 'It seems to me that, just like Hippoclides doing his headstand upon the table, Herodotus would dance away the truth and say, "Herodotus doesn't care"' (*On the Malice of Herodotus* 867b).

How does Herodotus manage to make a long work composed of so many variegated elements appear coherent? Important here, although not I think ultimately decisive, is the fact that he is the only substantial extant Greek prose author whose own intellectual formation antedates the rhetorical and educational revolution in Athens discussed at the beginning of this essay. He was the contemporary and perhaps the friend of the first great generation of sophistic teachers, not (like Thucydides) their student. Thus his idea of how to organize written prose did not come from the guidelines fashioned for clear and persuasive rhetorical narrative by teachers aiming their students at success in the lawcourts and assembly and still followed, in the main, today; it had its roots instead in Ionian epic and sixth-century intellectual life.

Later rhetorically trained writers, including Thucydides, organized their work so that the author remains firmly and conspicuously in control at all times of the overall argumentative direction; this still forms the basis of a good non-fictional prose style. Herodotus, however, goes to considerable lengths to disguise his authorial control of the text, and rarely specifies why a particular narrative segment is placed where it is. As Plutarch's critical comment suggests, if we simply read through the whole casually, it can look to our later taste chaotic, as though Herodotus the narrator has lost control and has become a mere rambler, a raconteur and anecdotalist. Odd as it seems, however, the style of the *Histories* must not simply be dismissed as an aberrant curiosity. If one takes the trouble to see what it accomplishes, and how it fits into

Herodotus' larger understanding of how *ta anthrōpeia*, the human world, works, one begins to understand that even if Herodotus had been able to write according to the canons invented in Athens' first sophistic, he might well have chosen not to do so. Several aspects of his style (defined in its largest sense, as opposed to content) can be isolated that are both crucial to his ability to shape his text and also alien to our normal assumptions about a good continuous and coherent prose style. Particularly important are parataxis; the shaping and focus of the individual narrative account; associative thinking; and, finally, a feature that is somewhat inappropriately named 'ring composition'. These stylistic features interlock with one another to produce a narrative so different from most later history writing that they are worth briefly discussing here; properly understood they add not just to the *Histories'* charm but to its power as a text reflecting on *ta anthrōpeia*.

Parataxis

Aristotle in the *Rhetoric* (1409[a]24) comments that Herodotus was the foremost practitioner of the 'old strung-along style' of writing, as opposed to the newer, more tightly and logically organized prose. Aristotle was actually thinking about the structure of the sentence; we use the same contrast, however, to define Herodotus' largest formal narrative structures. In what we call paratactic or the 'old-style' prose, fairly short, self-contained narrative units are not obviously integrated into a larger conceptual whole but follow each other in a sequence of discrete segments, like beads on a string. Even if, as in Herodotus' case, the string—the organizing 'red thread' of Persian imperial aggression—is there, it often remains hidden.

   An advantage of this style is that in the hands of a master narrator like Herodotus, the general effects of a sequence of self-contained prose units of variable length can be complex, subtle, and profound, more like those of poetry than those of a conventional modern prose essay. Many more different kinds of interpretive patterns can simultaneously be sustained, interwoven in various ways with one another, since the author is not constrained to define one theme as dominant or to follow one overall topic or logical train of thought throughout. The result can look something like the drawings of W. Escher: as one reads through a longish stretch of narrative, foreground and background are in the process of continuous redefinition, as the main theme of one account gives way and becomes merely a supporting background detail to the next.

Shaping and focus of the individual account

What is highlighted in a prose like Herodotus' is not an overall thematic continuity, but rather the integrity of the immediate individual narrative unit. Some units continue for more than a score of pages, while others are only a paragraph long, and either are inserted as fillers between longer units or appear as isolated parenthetical remarks suddenly interrupting a larger ongoing narrative. Generally, whatever the length of the unit, a strong opening sentence states its initial focus, and almost always a concluding sentence wraps it up, often restating a variant of the introductory sentence. For instance, the story of Croesus, one of the longest and most elaborately composed in the *Histories*, begins: 'Croesus was a Lydian by birth. He was the son of Alyattes and ruled over all the various peoples who live west of the River Halys. . . . Croesus was the first non-Greek we know of to have subjected Greeks to the payment of tribute. . . . ' (1.6). Some fifty pages of Greek text later, the Croesus episode concludes: 'That is the story of Croesus' reign and the first conquest of Ionia' (1.92). Much of the intervening narrative of Croesus wanders far from the theme of his conquest of the eastern Greeks, but Herodotus has used that theme as the framing topic to set off the beginning and end of the account and to mark it as a single narrative unit.

Individual narrative accounts differ enormously in their pacing, their structure, their narrative focus, and their subject-matter. Some are dramatic, some annalistic, some might have been written up as tragedies, complete with dialogue, some are straightforward catalogues, or descriptions of battles, political and diplomatic negotiations, or ethnographic surveys. Particularly in the first four books, the interpretive thrust of the individual account is distinctive, and does not extend in an obvious way beyond its own confines. Whatever interpretive connections may be drawn linking one unit to others occurring at other points in the *Histories*, Herodotus generally lets us draw on our own. It is up to us to notice structural analogies, thematic echoes, or similarities in language or tone that suggest possible comparisons or contrasts to be drawn.

This leaves us, as modern students of Herodotus and ancient Greek history, with a problem. We often want more guidance, more global constructions of authorial judgement and interpretation, than Herodotus as narrator is willing to advance. For instance, sometimes an individual is of great importance historically and appears in a number of different narrative units in the *Histories* but does not always play the same role or kind of role, and Herodotus does not unify the various aspects of him revealed by different units into a single picture. In the long first narrative account about Croesus' reign and loss of power, Croesus changes from an arrogant king to the generous host and protector of Adrastus, to the wise adviser of his captor, Cyrus. So far so good. Later, however, he again reappears giving Cyrus disastrously bad and even ignoble advice (1.207); finally, we see him as a comic and rather pathetic figure scuttling from the room to avoid Cambyses' mad attack (3.36). Does Herodotus expect us as readers to construct a larger picture of Croesus' moral disintegration here, or is the trajectory one we invent and impose on a collection of discontinuous incidents? Herodotus does not tell us; the same kinds of problems dog our wish to understand other important historical figures in the *Histories*, like the Spartans Cleomenes and Pausanias, or Themistocles the Athenian.

Associative thinking

We have considered both the way narrative units discretely follow one another and the way the individual narrative unit is constructed. What are the principles by which one unit is linked with the next, if they are not systematically subsumed into one larger thematic and argumentative whole? Most obvious is the narrative sequence that is roughly chronological and therefore also causally linked: the events of one Persian king's reign lead down into those of the next, from Cyrus' conquest of Lydia down to the Persian Wars of Xerxes' day (546–479 BCE). This is the structure that Thucydides took up from Herodotus to tell the history of the Peloponnesian War, and other historians to tell other stories about empirically ascertainable political events thereafter; Herodotus' invention of this kind of narrative is a large part of why Cicero called him the 'father of history' and the title has stuck.

Within that ordering by causal and chronological sequence (which seems normal, familiar, and reasonable to us), occur the sudden detours that are, to our modern taste, quite surprising. The ongoing narrative comes to a new name or event interesting in its own right and often stops to give this new topic pride of place. Sometimes a clearly demarcated new unit is formed, while at other times the interrupting material remains only a longish parenthesis within the account already in progress. Whatever its length, at the conclusion of the interruption the earlier narrative takes up exactly where it left off, so that the digression becomes a self-contained pendant hanging on the larger ongoing narrative thread.

This procedure is a reasonable one, given the constraints that attended the initial construction and delivery of Herodotus' narrative. If a modern writer wants to include material that is relevant and useful but a distraction from the main point of his or her essay, it is always possible to write a footnote; Herodotus did not have footnotes available to him. Moreover, his initial deliveries of the *Histories* were probably oral; he read his material aloud to a variety of audiences scattered widely throughout the Greek world. One of his most important tasks as a travelling savant would have been to make connections, to add material, to show linkages between things his audiences had not known were connected. Thus, when he came to something relevant that his immediate audience might not know, he simply stopped, added it, and went on. The result, for us as students of the world of the sixth and fifth centuries, has been of inestimable value: much information has been preserved simply because Herodotus thought it would interest one or another of his audiences. But the effect on the narrative is odd: as I have said, the main narrative thread looks at times as though it is merely a formal device that Herodotus exploits so as to pursue his real goal, the addition of new, extraneous material—rather as a clothes-line's principal function is to provide support for the various articles suspended from it.

'Ring composition'

The three narrative habits I have just described—parataxis, the integrity of the individual narrative unit, and associative thinking—all contribute to an overall narrative pattern that is often called ring composition. The name comes from the fact we have already noted, that the beginning and end of each narrative unit repeat the same information, more or less, and by this repetition they show us that a new topic is being introduced and then that it is being concluded. If a unit is interrupted, the beginning and end of the digression mark their own presence in the same way. An *a–b–a* pattern results that is often repeated, sometimes in elaborate interlocking forms, throughout the *Histories*, since the units themselves often display the same sandwiching formation: *a*(main narrative)/*b*(digression)/*a*(main narrative resumed). As Henry Immerwahr has well observed: 'It is a basic feature of early prose that the principles underlying large units of composition are equally applicable to smaller entities down to a short phrase, a sentence, a brief remark, or a story' (*Form and Thought in Herodotus*, 47).

The same pattern is used in a looser thematic way as well; it even marks the way Herodotus brings the *Histories* as a whole to their end. In Book 9, at the end of the Persian Wars, the narrative focuses on an image that recalls both the beginning of Xerxes' invasion in Book 7 and the beginning of the *Histories* themselves in Book 1. Artayctes, the wicked Persian governor of Sestus, is crucified at the spot where Xerxes first crossed over into Greece (9.120). Moreover, Artayctes' punishment is so severe because he has violated the temple of Protesilaus in nearby Elaeus, even using it for sexual encounters (9.116). Protesilaus was the first Greek ashore at Troy in the mythic Trojan expedition, killed as the Greeks first landed; in effect, he had begun the Trojan War. The vengeance exacted by the Greeks for Protesilaus in 9.120 returns us thematically not only to the beginning of the Persian Wars but also to the theme of the *Histories*' proem, the hostile separation of Greeks from barbarians created by the Trojan War (1.4). Both the chain of reciprocities set in motion by Protesilaus' death at the very beginning of the Trojan War and the one created by Xerxes' invasion of Greece are completed in 9.120 by the account of the punishment meted out to Artayctes, the Asiatic violator of Protesilaus' temple.

Even simple versions of the *a–b–a* pattern, encountered almost at random throughout the narrative, have interesting interpretive consequences. In Book 3, for instance, the ongoing narrative describes Darius' kingdom and the first acts of his rule, in particular his efforts to limit the encroachments of his former fellow conspirators (3.88–119). It is interrupted by a brief account of the death of the Greek tyrant of Samos, Polycrates (3.120–5). After the digression about Polycrates the narrative resumes its description of Darius' efforts to extend his royal control. Oroetes, the Persian governor of Phrygia, Lydia, and Ionia, had used the time of chaos at the end of Cambyses' reign to overreach his power; Darius has Oroetes killed (3.126–8). The main narrative thread concerns Darius' extension and consolidation of his power.

The intervening little story about the murder of Polycrates starts as an interruption that backtracks in time (3.120): 'Here is something that happened round about the time that Cambyses became ill.' With no preparation or overt linkage to the Darius story, the story starts with the wickedness of Oroetes, the Persian satrap at Sardis, and goes on to describe how Oroetes had once tricked Polycrates of Samos into travelling to the mainland to meet him in Persian territory. When Polycrates was in his power, Oroetes had him murdered shamefully, 'in a way that does not bear mentioning'. The story of Polycrates is presented as an unmotivated digression interrupting the main narrative about Darius. It turns out, however, also to be thematically directly relevant to the resumption of the '*a*' theme, Darius' establishment of control over his kingdom. Since we have just read the Polycrates story, as readers we see that the misbehaviour for which Darius afterwards punishes Oroetes the rebellious governor has longer and more complex roots than those indicated in the major narrative thread alone. Although the connection is not made explicit, Darius is avenging the death of Polycrates as well as punishing Oroetes' other misdeeds.

Nor does the pattern end there. Polycrates' death will also ultimately have causal consequences for the 'red thread' of the *Histories*, the theme of Persian imperial expansion. For, as the story of Darius continues, we learn that Democedes of Croton, a Greek physician whom Polycrates had brought with him to Oroetes' court, ends up by chance as Darius' slave and doctor (3.129). In that role Democedes gains access to Atossa, Darius' most powerful wife. Indirectly, because he wants to get home again, Democedes uses Atossa to interest Darius in sending a scouting expedition to Greece. This means that one of the trivial and unintended consequences of Oroetes' murder of Polycrates—the servitude of one insignificant Greek physician, itself the result of an accidental feud among squabbling potentates on the Ionian coast— turns out to be important to the main theme of the *Histories*, because it begins the process through which Persian eyes are first turned westward (3.138). In tracing somewhat obscure causal connections like this through the use of *a–b–a* narrative patterning, Herodotus uses the narrative style itself to indicate that it is not always easy to tell main narrative threads from digressions, or historically insignificant facts from important ones. That is one reason why he has decided to tell as much as he can of each (1.5).

Herodotus does not always tell us why a given account is important to the larger narrative, but no matter how complicated the backtracking and apparent interruptions get, he never loses control of how the various pieces of his narrative fit together. To give some idea of how extensive the interlocking of different small thematic narrative units can be, I would like briefly to outline an exceptionally interesting and complicated passage from the account of the Ionian revolt in Book 5. It begins (5.55) and ends (5.97) at precisely the same moment: with Aristagoras the Milesian arriving in Athens in 499 BCE, to seek the Athenians' help in the Ionian rebellion just getting under way against Darius. What Herodotus then backtracks to tell is the story of how Athenian democracy began.

He begins with the murder of Hipparchus, the brother of the Athenian tyrant, in 514 BCE. The basic outline of the next forty-one chapters brings the story down to 499 and includes Hipparchus' murder; the final expulsion of the tyrants by the Lacedaemonians four years later (5.65); the political struggles that result in Athens between Cleisthenes the Alcmaeonid and his political rival Isagoras (5.66); Cleisthenes' democratic reorganization of the Athenian tribal system (5.69); and Isagoras' response, to summon Sparta (5.70). War ensues for the Athenians against the Spartans, and the Athenians first request help from Persia but then decide that the price of Persian support is too high, since the Persians have demanded acknowledgement of Persian sovereignty. Chalcis and Thebes join Sparta in attacking Athens (5.74). The Lacedaemonians try to bring in their allies from the rest of the Peloponnese but the Corinthians pull out (5.75), leading to tensions between the two Spartan kings. More fighting occurs between the Athenians and their neighbours, now including the Aeginetans. The Lacedaemonians call a council, to try to involve the other Peloponnesians more deeply in reinstating Hippias, the deposed Athenian tyrant (5.91); they are again rebuffed by the Corinthians. At this point the narrative has brought us back to the point at which it began, the arrival of Aristagoras in Athens in 499 BCE.

Inserted into the chronological and causally linked stages of this relatively straightforward digression on Athenian history is a series of smaller background digressions: the origins of the family of the tyrannicides (5.57–61); the story of Cleisthenes' grandfather, the tyrant of Sicyon (5.67–8); the story of how the Alcmaeonidae came by the name of 'accursed' (5.71); why Aegina was hostile to Athens in 510 BCE and ready to help Thebes, unrolling a complicated history of previous Aeginetan–Athenian enmity (5.82–9); and finally, a long speech by the Corinthian delegate to the Spartan meeting, explaining through a history of Corinthian tyranny why tyranny should not be reinstated in Athens (5.92).

Both the story of Polycrates' murder in Book 3 and the story of Athens' first steps on the road to democratic self-rule in Book 5 are introduced as digressions to the main account; both are vital in helping us understand why the main account subsequently unrolls as it does. The main story in Book 5 concerns how the mainland Greeks, through Athens, are drawn into enmity with Persia; the explanation achieved in the long digression reaches far back into the complicated inter-city relations of Athens, Sparta, Chalcis, Thebes, Aegina, and Corinth, and into the intra-city rivalries and anxieties of Athens' first steps as a democracy. Herodotus does not make the connections explicit; as often, he merely provides the necessary background information and expects us to construct out of it our understanding of Athens' self-confidence stemming from her recent achievements and also her sense of isolation in 499. When we resume the story of Aristagoras (5.97), and we see the Athenians voting to support the Ionian revolt, the previous forty-one chapters of digression, and digression within digression, help us to understand why it is 'easier to persuade thirty thousand Athenians than one Lacedaemonian'. Story itself, starkly juxtaposed to other stories, has served as explanation.

We do not know why Herodotus chose to write his *Histories* in this way, but we should beware of assuming that he simply didn't know any better. We have already noticed, in discussing his treatment of Persian imperial accomplishments, the tendency for powerful men—men like Croesus, Cyrus, or Xerxes—to ignore the limitations that the world has placed on their power, and in particular to fail to hear information that would be useful but does not fit their own notions of the scope of their personal control over events. Herodotus' choice of narrative structure is a surprisingly sophisticated vehicle for making the same point stylistically. For Herodotus has adopted a paratactic, associative style that itself avoids the kinds of assumptions about what is important that kings and other powerful people inside the narrative display. In this narrative everything is potentially important and interconnected, but Herodotus rarely tries as author to dominate the connections, or tell us which ones he thinks relatively more important. His tendency to construct discrete episodes in interlocking *a–b–a* ring patterns, with numerous pendants that are independent from the main narrative, instead sets all of his material out for us so that we can take what we think important from it.

The *Histories* as history

In one very obvious sense, Herodotus' *Histories* are certainly history, since stories from the past provide their basic content. On the other hand, we expect historians (as opposed to historical novelists) to interrogate their stories from the past: 'Is it true? How do we know that it is true?', and Herodotus, the first historian, does not present the results of his interrogation in the same way that narrative historians after him do. Since Herodotus himself is by far our richest early narrative source for the Greek history of the late archaic and early classical period, it is incumbent on us to gain as clear an idea as possible of the ways in which he does interrogate his material, and the likelihood that what his text preserves is real information about the past.

The longer, more polished stories, or *logoi*, in Herodotus' *Histories* certainly retell past events, both Greek and barbarian, but they do so with much included that is not today customarily found in historical narrative. Conversations from foreign lands in the distant past are recounted that neither Herodotus nor his informants probably knew about, motives are described, stories are told from the imagined points of view of their actors, vivid details are supplied that are almost certainly the product of someone's invention rather than of actual memory. Most of this would have seemed natural both to Herodotus' fifth-century interlocutors and his audiences as the normal way to hear about things from the past (it was the way Homer did it, after all), but to us such narrative practices seem suspect.

Herodotus himself does not expect us to believe everything we read. For him the word *historiē* continued to carry its Ionian meaning of 'research' or 'investigation, enquiry', and he often emphasizes that what he gives us is provisional information, the best that he has been able in his researches to discover. He sometimes interrupts the ongoing account in his first-person voice as the narrator, precisely to remind us not to treat the ongoing narrative as definitively true. In 7.152, discussing the thorny issue of whether the Argives went over to the Persian side in the Persian Wars, he adds: 'I am obliged to record the things I am told, but I am certainly not required to believe them—this remark may be taken to apply to the whole of my account.' We do not know if by 'the whole account' he means only this particular story, or the whole narrative of his *Histories*; he does, however, say much the same thing in 2.123: 'Anyone who finds such things credible can make of these Egyptian stories what he wishes. My job, throughout this account, is simply to record whatever I am told by each of my sources.'

In one way this makes the *Histories* a profoundly historical text. Where later narrative historians like Thucydides, Tacitus, Gibbon, or the Durants broke down their informants' reports into data, and from that data constructed their own authoritative version of events, Herodotus takes a different approach. What he claims, at least, to give us is in each case the best version or versions of past events and the distant reaches of the present that he has been able to hear, taken from the most qualified informants he could find. Thus he narrates, for instance, the most credible of the many versions available to him of Cyrus' death (1.214). He strings these stories together to form the ongoing narrative of his *Histories*. Clearly the initial selection of stories, the pacing, the structuring, and much in the literary presentation reveal Herodotus' own interests, values, and gifts as a narrator; he insists, however, that the contents of the *logoi* are not his, but have been gathered from others.

The phrases 'it is said' or 'they say' occur hundreds of times in the narrative, as Herodotus reminds us that he owes his *logoi* to others who have told them to him. He names a handful of his informants. Some, especially priests at temple sites, he identifies without naming; several hundred times he cites unnamed speakers by their cities: Spartans, Corinthians, Athenians, and many other mainland Greeks; Greeks and non-Greeks from the north and Asia Minor like Macedonians, Thracians, Scythians, Taurians, Samians, Carians, Phoenicians, and Syrians; and non-Greek interlocutors from farther off as well: Egyptians of course, but also Chaldeans,

Arabians, Ethiopians, and many others. On his extensive travels Herodotus talked with a wide variety of people; in most instances we can only guess where he spoke to them, what problems he might have had in communicating cross-culturally or through an interpreter, and how accurately he remembered or transcribed what they told him. What he repeatedly emphasizes is that his *logoi* contain real information, but he remains aware, and wants us to be aware too, of the fact that as data they are only as good as the quality of his sources allows.

Herodotus does not merely uncritically transcribe on to his pages what he has been told by others and then cover his own doubts with a blanket authorial caveat. The main narrative structure of the *Histories* is built out of the *logoi* that have been told to him, but the active, first-person intervention of Herodotus as narrator also shapes our readerly understanding of the text. Herodotus intervenes in his own voice on almost every page, often expressly as an investigator in order to deliver a variety of critical comments on the information he has gathered. Several hundred times he comments on the likelihood of some detail being correct within a particular story. More than fifty times he assures us that he knows something to be so: he says that he knows (*oida*) that a certain prophecy was not about the Persians, as the *logos* asserts, but about Illyrians (9.43); he knows that people who claimed to have buried Mardonius' corpse were given gifts by Mardonius' son (9.84). Much more common are various expressions of doubt, ranging from qualified belief to outright disbelief. He provisionally accepts that a silver bowl at Delphi was the work of Theodorus of Samos (1.51); Scyllias of Scione probably did not swim to Artemisium but came by boat instead (8.8); and, despite what the Scythians and Greeks in Scythia say, the Neurians are not in Herodotus' opinion werewolves (4.105). Sometimes Herodotus disbelieves something we know to be true: the Phoenicians' claim that they saw the sun on their right as they sailed around the southern tip of Africa, although disbelieved by Herodotus, is for us good evidence that the Phoenicians probably did what they said they did (4.42).

Most of the longer discussions of this type occur in Books 2 and 4 and concern details of natural history or ethnography. Beyond Book 4, Herodotus speculates in his own voice about someone's motivations for action (7.24, 8.30), about the correct calculation of numbers (7.184, 9.32), or about matters of religion or gnomic judgement (7.137). Sometimes (especially in Book 2) he will tell us directly about efforts he has made to ferret out or investigate a particular problem, including eyewitness investigation (*opsis*) (2.29, 44, 6.47). Sometimes he tells us about the grounds on which he doubts or accepts a story, especially if it is a question of general probability (2.56, 4.195); more often, he simply notes his own reservations or the limitations to his knowledge and moves on with the story (4.45, 8.128).

We receive from Herodotus' first-person interjections the impression of a careful, critical distance maintained towards his data, but he also has other means at his disposal to note the limitations of the version of events the *logoi* convey. Sometimes he gives two or more variant versions of the same account, or includes particles or adverbs of doubt ('so they say, at any rate'), or suddenly shifts into reported speech when something particularly improbable is being recounted. He sometimes notes when an informant may be speaking from self-interest, or for some other reason should not be believed (1.70, 6.14). In all these ways, although Herodotus' reasoning is not technical and is never encapsulated into a chapter of self-conscious methodology, he often uses his *Histories* not just to tell stories, but also to tell us what kinds of reasoning should be brought to bear on them, if we are to reach an informed judgement on the quality of the information they contain. Even if the narrative of events is sometimes not history as we now normally use that term, by paying attention to Herodotus' first-person comments we can read his text as an ongoing workshop on how to think historically about *logoi*. We learn this by watching the movements of the narrative voice in the text, and especially the interjections of Herodotus as the first-person narrator. Donald Lateiner sums it up succinctly: 'Impelled by his desire to record the accomplishments of the previous generation, he developed a method that tested assertions when it could and recorded untestable assertions where it had to, complete with warnings to the reader. Herodotus the historian closes in on, and distances himself from, events and their reporters' (*The Historical Method of Herodotus*, 58).

This way of reading the *Histories* assumes that we take at face value Herodotus' own account of what he has done as an honest one. Despite his apparent ingenuousness and the openness of his stated aims and procedures, however, readers right from ancient times have refused to find him trustworthy as an author.

Thucydides (1.20–2) did not mention him by name but both expressly criticized two details of fact found in Herodotus and more generally eschewed investigation of the past as the realm of *to muthōdes*, the mythic. Aristophanes seems to have made fun of the beginning of the *Histories* in the *Acharnians*, and within a generation the unreliable Ctesias had written a Persian history that systematically contradicted Herodotus' version of events. Plutarch, the Boeotian writer of the early Roman imperial period, attacked Herodotus for 'malice' and in particular for his portrait of Boeotians as medizers; in the *Laws* (1.1.5) Cicero mentioned that although Herodotus was the father of history, his work was 'full of legends'. Arnaldo Momigliano has shown us that it was not until the era of European exploration in the fifteenth century that Herodotus' text again became respectable and was read as a serious attempt to describe the real improbabilities the world contained. It was then used as a literary model by Europeans struggling to describe new continents and peoples to their compatriots back at home.

In contemporary scholarship, questions about Herodotus' reliability as a historian tend to come in two forms. The more reasonable is not directed against Herodotus himself but follows Thucydides' pessimistic lead in doubting the degree to which solid factual data can be recovered from the kinds of stories that Herodotus preserves. Scholars of this persuasion emphasize that as modern readers we must remain aware of the vast gulf that separates our own sense of what it means to preserve the past from those that prevailed in the mid-fifth century BCE. Modern students of oral history, drawing on the comparative study of other oral cultures, claim that three generations is the outside limit to be placed on the accurate oral transmission of past events; judged by this standard, much of the information included in the first four books of the *Histories* would not be considered historical. In assessing ancient traditional stories, moreover, two particular sources of error must also be kept in mind, apart from the accidental distortions created by the passage of time: first (something Herodotus himself was acutely aware of), stories preserved orally from the past are by definition particular and tendentious in nature—the people who remembered and told them have always told them from their own (limited) funds of information, and for their own reasons; second, ancient social memory habitually supplied highly personal motives as explanations for events that modern historians would consider largely the product of impersonal economic or social forces. To take a couple of concrete examples drawn from the *Histories*: assuming that there really was an alliance in the 520s between Amasis of Egypt and Polycrates of Samos, modern historians would expect that the international balance of political power in general, and calculations about the newly powerful role of Persia in the Mediterranean in particular, played far more of a part in the cessation of that alliance than did Amasis' anxiety about what happened to Polycrates' favourite ring; they would also think it more likely that Polycrates ended the alliance than that Amasis did, and that Herodotus heard a Samian version that from local patriotism exonerated Polycrates from responsibility for its end (3.40–3). Similarly, modern historians assume that trading rivalries played a far greater role in creating the sixth-century ill will between Epidaurus, Aegina, and Athens than did the particular fate of a couple of olive-wood cult statues named Damia and Auxesia (5.83–9); Herodotus himself comments that different versions of the final Athenian attack on Aegina exist, depending on whether the source of the story is an Aeginetan or an Athenian (5.86).

Sceptical source criticism can be useful. As we have seen, Herodotus himself often practises it—arguably he most richly deserves the title 'father of history' because of his own authorial insistence on reminding us as readers that what we are reading has been told by different informants, each of whom has a particular point of view. To the modern historian extremely sceptical of Herodotus, however, we are entitled to retort that one should distinguish the orality of a fifth-century Greek from the orality of contemporary peoples studied by anthropologists or sociologists. Herman Strasburger has pointed out how much genuine historical impulse is to be found already in Homer; one of the reasons the Greeks developed writing as a way to preserve records from the past was that they were already interested in memory and in a truthful preservation of their past through memory. By the nature of the evidence we can independently validate relatively little of what Herodotus tells us from the seventh and sixth centuries BCE— but it is also true that details culled from archaeology or the chance preservation of fragmentary written material often corroborate what Herodotus has told us. The surprising extent to which archaeology in southern Russia and Ukraine has confirmed Herodotus' description of Scythian burial practices in Book 4 is one example. Or, on a smaller scale, recently archaeologists have discovered in the Greek sanctuary at Gravisca, north-west of Rome, a sixth-century dedication by one Sostratus of Aegina, otherwise unknown except through Herodotus' passing mention of him in 4.152 as the richest Greek merchant of all. Because of the nature of Herodotus' material we are often unable within an individual account to distinguish accurate data from what has become 'erased by time' (to use the language of Herodotus' proem). But it is still worth stressing that both Herodotus and those in whom he reposed confidence might have been quite likely themselves to set some store by accuracy—and that, without Herodotus' *Histories*, we would know comparatively little of Greek history as a coherent narrative of events before *c*.450 BCE.

Our dependence on Herodotus for archaic Greek history lends a particular urgency to a second set of issues involving Herodotus' own credibility as a historian. Some scholars have scrutinized the text of the *Histories* and have come to the conclusion not merely that it is unhistorical, but that it was intended by Herodotus to mislead us by persuading us through its rhetoric to read it as history. Detlev Fehling in particular argues that Herodotus' use of source citations—something I have discussed above as an important element in Herodotus' bona fides as a collector of empirical data—is simply too good to be true. According to Fehling, sources cited in the *Histories* always improbably support a partisan version of events put forward by their own city; moreover, Herodotus more than once claims two or more widely removed and thus apparently independent sources for obviously fictive 'information'; both the systematic tidiness and the harmonious meshing of (invented) information show us that the informants themselves have been invented by the author. According to this view, Herodotus is not at all a historian, or someone with any respect for data, but on the contrary a gifted narrator who has virtually made up the whole of what he recounts. In particular he has made up the version of his own investigative efforts that the first-person authorial interjections convey.

Because of Herodotus' peculiar position as the first historian and the sweeping nature of the charges, it is difficult to rebut them succinctly. None the less, arguments from probability can be made that are certainly no weaker than Fehling's own. One may ask whether Herodotus' work would have been preserved by his contemporaries if it were recognized from the outset as fabricated for the occasion; did ordinary fifth-century Greeks know so little of their own past or that of their neighbours that deceit or invention on such a massive scale as Fehling suggests was possible? There was, moreover, extensive travel between ancient cities, especially religious centres, in the late archaic and early classical period. For this reason it is likely that even ahistorical legends were accepted as received truth in several different places in Herodotus' day, and that Herodotus might well have heard the same highly improbable story from more than one source.

Every reader must in the end assess for him- or herself how earnest or trustworthy Herodotus is as a reporter of genuine information. One final observation might be germane here, however. In the first part of this essay I noted how often in Herodotus' narrative people in power come to grief because they have not paid attention to facts about the world that would ultimately defeat their plans. Sometimes it is a generalized set of ethical or philosophical truths they ignore: Croesus cannot hear Solon's warnings that no man can be counted fortunate until his life has ended; Cambyses despises the religious traditions of others and comes to grief in consequence; Xerxes flogs the Hellespont (1.33, 3.38, 7.35). Sometimes they commit errors that simple enquiry would have avoided: Apollo himself after Croesus' disastrous campaign against Cyrus tells Croesus that his defeat was his own fault because he did not ask enough questions of the oracle; Cambyses sends his army off on a mad march across the desert against the Ethiopians without sufficient information about the terrain; even Darius, the cleverest of the Persian kings, is tricked by his wife into sending a scouting expedition against Greece, and lets Histiaeus, the ringleader of the Ionian conspiracy, go home without interrogating him carefully (1.91, 3.25, 134, 5.107). Xerxes does not listen to the good advice of Demaratus and Artemisia, two Greeks in his own forces, but to his ambitious cousin Mardonius instead (7.235–6, 8.68, 100).

People in the *Histories* who do possess knowledge and understanding often have no power of their own. In 9.16, an unnamed Persian analyses the Persian cause on the eve of the battle of Plataea and declaims, in tears: 'an event which has been decreed by the god cannot be averted by man. . . . There's no more terrible pain a man can endure than to see clearly and be able to do nothing.' An assumption permeates Herodotus' narrative that it is better to know more, to see more clearly, and to find information out, but it is also true that people with power often fail in this respect. A few individuals, like Solon the Athenian or Xerxes' Spartan adviser Demaratus, act as 'warners' or wise advisers, but they are rarely heeded by their interlocutors. Both times that Herodotus' illustrious predecessor, Hecataeus the Ionian logographer, figures as an actor in the narrative proper, he acts as such an adviser. He takes part in a group that Aristagoras the Milesian tyrant has assembled to advise him about the likelihood of success, if Ionia revolts from Persia. Hecataeus tries to bring Aristagoras and the others to their senses, 'listing all the nations and tribes subject to Darius, and all his resources' (5.36; cf. 5.125)—in other words, telling them information much like that found in the *Histories* themselves. Like most sensible pieces of advice given to others, this one is ignored and, as Hecataeus predicts it will, the revolt ends in failure.

In sum, Herodotus portrays a world in the narrative in which accurate information is a valuable commodity (though often very difficult to get and neglected when it is available), and that fact in itself is perhaps a useful clue to Herodotus' basic stance towards his material. Could a narrative repeatedly and deeply striking the note of the painful importance of accurate information also be making up most of the data that it deploys? If so, the *Histories* are an even more consummately brilliant perversity than Herodotus' modern critics claim.

Herodotus as thinker: underlying assumptions and patterns

Herodotus begins his introduction: 'Here are presented the results of the enquiry carried out by Herodotus of Halicarnassus . . .' He goes on to give two reasons why he has written the *Histories*: so that astonishing deeds performed by both Greeks and barbarians should not become *aklea*, without fame, and so that great and wonderful *erga*, perhaps best translated as 'achievements', should not vanish; he will write about other things, to be sure, but also about why the Greeks and barbarians went to war with one another. The force of this declaration should not be underestimated: finishing his work on the *Histories* in the early years of the Peloponnesian War, Herodotus intends to save the memory of a moment in the recent past when Greeks for once worked together to repel the invader. This is a memory in danger of being lost in his own day, when Athenians and Peloponnesians seem bent on destroying Greece between them.

As we have seen, he gives us a huge series of stories culled over numbers of years from both Greeks and barbarians, in the service of this bitter-sweet commemoration. Some of these stories may stretch back a century or more, some may tap Egyptian or Persian archival material or transmit the direct words of powerful Greek political insiders, some may be idle, fantastic, or malicious gossip, or vivid novelistic embellishment. But in any case, as one reads through them, one notices certain assumptions that, while not often the point of a particular narrative, none the less colour almost all of what is recounted throughout. I would like to end this essay by briefly mentioning a handful of these governing assumptions, thematic or cultural grids, that organize the way the narrative of the *Histories* looks at the world.

Many of them are widely shared Greek assumptions, and Herodotus would have been surprised to learn that modern readers think of them as representing his own sensibility or even interest. The most obvious is the role that the gods play in the *Histories*. Herodotus uses a fairly conventional fifth-century set of religious beliefs. He himself incorrectly etymologizes the word 'gods' (*theoi* in Greek) as the 'powers that set the world in order' (from the Greek verb 'to set', one of whose stems is also *the-*), and for him this wordplay is a largely self-evident tautology (2.52). He is interested in religious practices only as an aspect of human culture; he is not interested in gods *per se* as actors, and avoids mentioning them in his narrative of events unless the account of significant human doings requires it. When their powers become manifest, it is almost always through the agency of a portent, an oracle, or a dream. The gods and fate represent for Herodotus a second and superpersonal strand of causation that occasionally impinges on the interplay of ordinary human choice and the various kinds of secular causation unrolling at the same time in the narrative. Thus, although the gods have destined Croesus to pay for his fifth-generation ancestor's misdeeds, it is Croesus' serious human miscalculations that lose his kingdom to Cyrus—a fate that Apollo is able to mitigate slightly but not erase. Concerning religious institutions, both Greek and foreign, Herodotus is respectful but not unduly credulous; he makes it clear that false oracles can be written and even the Delphic priestess can be bribed (7.6, 6.66).

Another basic Greek set of assumptions that shapes Herodotus' text links freedom with poverty and smallness, and autocracy with wealth and bigness, whether of resources, land, or numbers of subject peoples. Solon the Greek enrages King Croesus by refusing to call him the happiest man in the world and choosing an Athenian of moderate status instead; more than fifty years later, Demaratus lectures King Xerxes on the power that freedom holds over the imagination and will of the average Spartan soldier—a hold so strong that three hundred Spartans will resist to the death an invading army of several hundred thousand at Thermopylae. The very end of the *Histories* is a flashback to the time of Cyrus the Great giving the Persians good advice: 'soft lands tend to breed soft men. It is impossible . . . for one and the same country to produce remarkable crops and good fighting men.' The later books of the *Histories* show that the Persians might have taken this observation more seriously than they did.

A third and more general Greek nexus of ideas is an interest in balance and order, comparison and contrast, and a deep sense of natural limits that pervades the *Histories*. Antithesis, the notion of two contrasting ideas, is built deeply into the Greek language, and Herodotus repeatedly uses comparison and contrast to describe foreign peoples, places, flora, and fauna to his Greek audiences. The Crimea is compared both to south-eastern Attica and to the heel of Italy for good measure (4.99; cf. 2.7); Lydian customs on the whole are like Greek ones (1.94); Scythians are the youngest people in the world, while the Egyptians say that they are among the oldest (4.5, 2.2); the supposedly old-fashioned and xenophobic Spartans resemble foreigners in some of their most basic customs (2.167, 6.58).

The gods set limits and do not allow human beings to go beyond them; Herodotus makes it clear that the Persians have to fail in their plan to conquer Greece, because they have overreached their natural boundaries. Xerxes announces his campaign by telling his advisers that he intends to conquer Greece so that 'we will make Persian territory end only at the sky' (7.8). Rivers and water in general are for Herodotus natural boundaries, and dire things happen to those who heedlessly transgress them. The spheres of biology, geography, ethics, and politics are all governed by a deep-seated underlying reciprocity and balance. Animals who breed too abundantly are short-lived; while the most exotic products of the earth lie at its extremities, the most harmonious climate occurs at its centre, in Greece (3.106–8). People who become too grandiose in their thinking trigger regulatory mechanisms that eventually deflate them; this is true whether they are simply too prosperous for their own good (2.182, 3.40–3 and 126) or, like Cyrus or Xerxes, are too ambitious politically (1.204, 7.8). The world for Herodotus is a single interlocking grid whose underlying self-regulatory mechanisms preserve its natural balance.

In articulating such themes, Herodotus is most likely reflecting his culture's beliefs as well as his own personal convictions. But we can also form some tentative opinions about Herodotus himself; certain kinds of narrative recur strikingly enough to make us feel we are seeing the idiosyncratic taste of the narrator emerging—that he enjoys a particular kind of story and, given the option, includes it when possible. Herodotus is fascinated by the interplay of nature and culture; the Scythians, living in a treeless land, invent a way of cooking meat in which the animal's bones and fat provide the fire, and the stomach provides the pot in which the meat is cooked (4.61). He also singles out clever individuals and great achievements; he enjoys noting the 'first inventor' of something, or a particularly striking building, or boat, or custom, or other cultural achievement. In this, as in some passages of paradoxical argument, like the investigation of the Nile's mysterious habits in Book 2, or the Persian constitutional debate in Book 3, we are reminded that Herodotus might have been himself a full-fledged member of the Athenian cultural revolution (2.19–27, 3.80–3). It would not be difficult to imagine him engaging Pericles or Protagoras in an all-day debate about how to assign blame when a javelin accidentally hits someone.

On the other hand, absent from Herodotus' text are the confidence and brilliant political rationalism of imperial Athens as the first two or three books of Thucydides depict it. Herodotus is acutely aware of the horror of war and the even greater horror of civic infighting (1.87, 6.98, 8.3); Mardonius' sneer at Greek habits of warfare, though self-serving and wrong in the immediate event, is not stupid (7.9). This is part of a larger coloration that critics early in this century often termed 'melancholy': loss and the pain that attends it are woven into many stories. Some lose status and honour: Hermotimus of Pedasa loses his Greek manhood, Demaratus loses the kingship of Sparta through an enemy's trick, Psammenitus the defeated king of Egypt must watch his captured family paraded before him, by the order of his new master, King Cambyses (8.105, 6.66, 3.14). Others lose family members: Harpagus' son is killed and served up to him as dinner, Croesus' son and heir is accidentally killed by the man Croesus had generously befriended (1.119, 1.44). Even the man who grows wealthy on the spoil of the shipwreck of the Persian fleet off Cape Sepias is called unlucky by Herodotus because of the death of his child shortly thereafter; Herodotus praises the Persian habit of not letting a father get to know his child before he is 5 years old, since the loss suffered if the child dies is so acute (7.190, 1.136). Some in the *Histories* lose homelands, like the Paeonians, removed by Darius *en masse* to central Asia, or the Phocaeans, who swear terrible oaths to leave their homeland for ever but some of whom, drawn back by longing, break their oaths and return (5.15, 1.65). The loss of culture leads to suffering of other, subtler kinds. The Lydians, after their conquest by Cyrus, survive, but they do so by being forced to become soft and effeminate (1.155–6); their poor female children must now become prostitutes to pay for their dowries (1.93; cf. 1.196, on the Babylonians). Egypt fascinates Herodotus because so much about it is seemingly fixed and orderly, including its history—but even Egypt has been defeated by the Persians, and both its king and its religion are outraged by Cambyses. Cannibalism occurs in 1.73, 1.119, 3.25, 4.18, and 4.26, and is advanced as an Indian custom in 3.38 and 3.99 and one practised by some neighbours of the Scythians in 4.106; more idiosyncratic instances of brutality figure in numerous stories, although perhaps reports of savage excess stem in part from Herodotus' fascination with all things that reach the limits of the ordinary.

Herodotus also enjoys narrating a sudden shift of view, and the revelation of an incommensurability of viewpoint between people who must deal with one another. The Scythians shake their heads at how slavish Ionians are, but they have not really understood that they are not talking to Ionians, but to Ionian tyrants (4.137–42). Hermotimus the eunuch achieves the most satisfying revenge Herodotus knows of against his enemy, because his enemy has been assuming the absence of normal male values in a eunuch (8.106). At the end of the story of Cyrus' conquest of the Medes, Astyages, the cruel old king, is revealed to have had the interests of his people in mind, where his victim and opponent Harpagus has been so selfishly obsessed with his personal loss that he has helped a Persian enslave his own people, the Medes (1.129). Both the wife of Candaules at the beginning of the *Histories* and the wife of Xerxes at the end are brutally successful at protecting their own interests largely because their husbands have underestimated them (1.12, 9.112). This ironic pleasure in observing misperception and miscommunication shades at times into broad humour. When the wordy Samians are rejected in their long plea for aid from Sparta and return with a new and more laconic effort—'this bag needs grain'—the Spartans, according to Herodotus, stay true to form, retorting that the word 'bag' is unnecessary (3.46).

Herodotus is unimpressed by power and status in themselves, and his cavalier attitude and enjoyment of a good story against even Greeks in power makes Plutarch, the later encomiast of Greek glory, very unhappy. Alcmaeon, the founder of the powerful dynasty of the Alcmaeonidae, waddles out of Croesus' treasury with his clothes, shoes, hair, and mouth stuffed with gold dust (6.125); Demaratus listens to his mother's involved and rather unlikely tale of his conception, covers his head, and goes silently into exile (6.68–70). Cleomenes has committed so many outrages that at the end everyone thinks his horrible death is the punishment for a different crime, while the Spartans themselves think he is just an alcoholic (6.75, 84). Megacles the Alcmaeonid has successfully intrigued to marry his daughter to the tyrant Pisistratus, because he wants his own descendants to be tyrants, but Pisistratus outmanœuvres him by refusing to make love to her 'in the usual way', in order to avoid having children by her. This, Herodotus says, is the real reason why Megacles the Alcmaeonid makes common cause with the tyrant's enemies (1.61).

Conversely, nobodies in the *Histories* often speak up and sometimes make very good sense; sometimes their acts also lead to important consequences. Often enough these nobodies are women. Apries' daughter, in one version, is sent by her father's conqueror to Persia when Cambyses requests a royal Egyptian princess to marry. As soon as she can speak Persian she points out what has happened and brings the wrath of Cambyses down on Egypt (3.1). Because Cyno the cowherd's wife rescues Cyrus, he will later be able to found the Persian empire (1.112). Insignificant men too end up important. Syloson of Samos, in Egypt as a tourist, gives Darius a cloak when Darius is just one of Cambyses' retinue, and is later rewarded with the Persian conquest of Samos and installation as its tyrant (3.139–40). Croesus' dumb son speaks out in time to save his father's life (1.85). As I have already noted, Democedes the Crotoniate physician is responsible for turning the attention of Darius westwards, in his desire to escape slavery and get home to Croton (3.129–34).

One could go on at length with this kind of commentary, for the pleasure in thinking of these highly charged little *logoi* is very great; the stories themselves become much-loved objects, not to be analysed but rather experienced. The neurologist Oliver Sacks tells of autistic twins whose communication with each other consists entirely of listing prime numbers of increasing size to each other. Lovers of Herodotus when they get together become a little bit like this—one reader has only to mention his or her favourite story for the other person to cap it with another that is even better. Herodotus himself would have understood: repeatedly, the stories he recounts contain symbolic patterns that he does not as an author explain, but merely points at, for us to observe also. At the end of the *Histories*, the Athenians, led by Pericles' father, crucify Artayctes the cruel Persian, at the spot on the Hellespont where the Persians first crossed over into Greece. As he dies they stone his son to death before his eyes. Is this a final and just punishment from the gods for Persian hubris, or does it also indicate the beginning of a period where the Athenians in turn begin to exhibit the characteristic flaws of the Persians? Here and in many other places in the *Histories*, Herodotus stands aside and lets us draw our own conclusions. He does not determine what we are to take from his text, but has generously laid out before us the material that will allow us to make whatever meaning we need.

TRANSLATOR'S NOTE

I HAVE translated the Oxford Classical Text of C. Hude (3rd edn., Oxford, 1927), except at the places marked in the translation with an obelus (†), which refer the interested reader to a note in the Textual Notes. Specialist readers will be able to see that as well as the Oxford Classical Text, I have also profited from the Teubner (both the old edition and the new one, of which at present only the first volume exists), the Budé, and Loeb texts. Among the various textual notes that appear in academic journals, I still find much to commend in the articles by J. Enoch Powell in the *Classical Quarterly* for 1935 and 1938. His suggestions and conjectures are also implicit in his absolutely indispensable *Lexicon to Herodotus* (Cambridge, 1938; repr. Hildesheim, 1966).

Where the translation is concerned, my policy, guided at every stage by the expert advice of my co-author, Carolyn Dewald, has been to achieve as much fluency as possible, while not disguising the fact that Herodotus was an *early* prose writer—which is to say that he was writing before many of the 'tricks of the trade' had been introduced by, initially, the orators later in the fifth century. It seems to me that other recent translations have not achieved this balance of fluency and fidelity to the original: they have either tended to go too far in the direction of modern English fluency, or have adopted a stilted and awkward style to get across Herodotus' lack of rhetorical flair. But to say that Herodotus was an early writer is not to say that he was an awkward writer. Far from it— he is immensely readable and enjoyable. I can only hope that I have done him some justice.

After considerable agonizing, rather than transliterating names in their original Greek forms, I chose to adopt the familiar Latinized-English forms of proper names, in order to keep the work as accessible as possible to modern English readers. So, for instance, I have 'Pisistratus' rather than 'Peisistratos', 'Thrace' rather than the disyllabic 'Thrake', 'Aeschylus' rather than 'Aiskhylos', and so on. It is to be hoped that what the reader gains in accessibility will more than offset what he or she loses in authenticity.

SELECT BIBLIOGRAPHY

Texts and Commentaries

Asheri, D., *Erodoto, Le Storie: Libro I, La Lidia e la Persia* (Milan, 1989–93).
—— *Erodoto, Le Storie: Libro III, La Persia* (Milan, 1991).
Corcella, A., *Erodoto, Le Storie: Libro IV, La Scizia e la Libia* (Milan, 1993).
How, W. W., and Wells, J., *A Commentary on Herodotus*, 2 vols. (Oxford, 1913; repr. with corrections, 1928) = H & W.
Hude, C., *Herodoti Historiae*, 2 vols. (Oxford, 1927).
Legrand, Ph.-E., *Hérodote: Histoires*, 11 vols. (Paris, 1945–56).
Lloyd, A. B., *Herodotus: Book II*, 3 vols. (Leiden, 1975–88).
Macan, R., *Herodotus: The Fourth, Fifth and Sixth Books*, 2 vols. (London, 1895; repr. New York, 1973).
—— *Herodotus: The Seventh, Eighth, and Ninth Books*, 2 vols. (London, 1908; repr. New York, 1973).
Nenci, G., *Erodoto. Le Storie: Libro V, La rivolta della Ionia* (Milan, 1995).

Bibliographic Surveys

Bergson, L., 'Herodotus 1937–1960', *Lustrum*, 11 (1966), 71–138.
Bubel, F., *Herodot-Bibliographie 1980–88* (Hildesheim, 1991).
Dewald, C., and Marincola, J., 'A Selective Introduction to Herodotean Studies', *Arethusa*, 20 (1987), 9–40.
Hampl, F., 'Herodot: Ein kritischer Forschungsbericht nach methodischen Geschichtspunkten', *Grazer Beiträge*, 4 (1975), 97–136.
Lachenaud, G., 'Les Études hérodotéennes de l'avant guerre à nos jours', in *Storia della Storiografia*, 7 (1985), 6–27.
MacKendrick, P., 'Herodotus, 1954–1963', *CW* 56 (1963), 269–75.
—— 'Herodotus, 1963–1969', *CW* 63 (1969), 37–44.
Verdin, H., 'Hérodote historien? Quelques interprétations récentes' *Ant. Class.* 44 (1975), 668–85.

General Studies

Boedeker, D. (ed.), *Herodotus and the Invention of History, Arethusa*, 20 (1987).
—— (ed.), *The New Simonides, Arethusa*, 29 (1996).

Burn, A.R., *Persia and the Greeks* (London, 1962; repr. with a post-script by D. M. Lewis, Stanford, Calif., 1984).

Cambridge Ancient History, vol. iii, pt. 1, *The Prehistory of the Balkans; and the Middle East and the Aegean World, Tenth to Eighth Centuries B.C.*, ed. J. Boardman, I. Edwards, N. Hammond, and E. Sollberger (Cambridge, 1982) = *CAH* iii/1.

——vol. iii, pt. 2, *The Assyrian and Babylonian Empires and Other States of the Near East, from the Eighth to the Sixth Centuries B.C.*, ed. J. Boardman, I. Edwards, N. Hammond, E. Sollberger, and C. Walker (Cambridge, 1991) = *CAH* iii/2.

——vol. iii, pt. 3, *The Expansion of the Greek World, Eighth to Sixth Centuries B.C.*, ed. J. Boardman and N. Hammond (Cambridge, 1982) = *CAH* iii/3.

——vol. iv, *Persia, Greece and the Western Mediterranean c.525 to 479 B.C.*, ed. J. Boardman, N. Hammond, D. Lewis, and M. Ostwald (Cambridge, 1998) = *CAH* iv.

——vol. v, *The Fifth Century B.C.*, ed. D. Lewis, J. Boardman, J. Davies, and M. Ostwald (Cambridge, 1992) = *CAH* v.

Cartledge, P., *The Greeks: A Portrait of Self and Others* (Oxford and New York, 1993).

Cook, J. M., *The Persian Empire* (London, 1987).

Drews, R., *The Greek Accounts of Eastern History* (Cambridge, Mass., 1973).

Evans, J. A. S., *Herodotus: Explorer of the Past. Three Essays* (Princeton, 1991).

Fehling, D., *Herodotus and his 'Sources'* (Leeds, 1989).

Flory, S., *The Archaic Smile of Herodotus* (Detroit, 1987).

Fornara, C., *Herodotus: An Interpretative Essay* (Oxford, 1971).

——(ed. and trans.), *Archaic Times to the End of the Peloponnesian War*, 2nd edn. (Cambridge, 1983) = Fornara.

Gould, J., *Herodotus* (London, 1989).

Grimal, N., *A History of Ancient Egypt* (Oxford, 1992).

Hartog, F., *The Mirror of Herodotus* (Berkeley and London, 1988).

Immerwahr, H., *Form and Thought in Herodotus* (Cleveland, 1966).

Jacoby, F., 'Herodot', in *Realenkyclopädie der klassischen Altertums-wissenschaft*, Suppl. ii (1913), 205–520.

——*Die Fragmente der griechischen Historiker*, i² (Leiden, 1957) = *FGH*.

Kuhrt, A., *The Ancient Near East* (*c.3000–330 BC*), 2 vols. (London, 1995).

Lateiner, D., *The Historical Method of Herodotus* (Toronto, 1989).

Lazenby, J. F., *The Defence of Greece 490–479 BC* (Warminster, 1993).

Meiggs, R., and Lewis, D. (eds.), *A Selection of Greek Historical Inscriptions to the End of the Fifth Century B.C.* (Oxford, 1969) = M–L.

Momigliano, A., 'The Place of Herodotus in the History of Historiography', in *Studies in Historiography* (London, 1966), 127–42 (repr. from *History,* 43 (1958), 1–13).

Pearson, L., *Plutarch's Moralia,* xi: *On the Malice of Herodotus* (Cambridge, Mass. and London, 1965).

Pritchett, W. K., *Studies in Ancient Greek Topography,* i (Berkeley and Los Angeles, 1965).

——*Studies in Ancient Greek Topography,* v (Berkeley and Los Angeles, 1985).

——*The Liar School of Herodotus* (Amsterdam, 1993).

Rolle, R., *The World of the Scythians* (Berkeley and Los Angeles, 1989).

Sasson, J. (ed.), *Civilizations of the Ancient Near East,* 4 vols. (New York, 1995).

Strasburger, G., *Lexikon zur frühgriechischen Geschichte, auf der Grundlage von Herodots Werk verfasst* (Zurich and Munich, 1984).

Strasburger, H., *Homer und die Geschichtsschreibung,* Sitzungsberichte der Heidelberger Akademie der Wissenschaften, Jahrgang 1972/1 (Heidelberg, 1972).

West, M., *Greek Lyric Poetry* (Oxford and New York, 1994).

West, S., 'Herodotus' Epigraphical Interests', *CQ* 35 (1985), 278–305.

TIMELINE FOR HERODOTUS' HISTORIES

THE GREEKS

*c.*1200 Trojan War.
*c.*900 Dorian Invasion of Greece (so-called 'return of the Heraclidae').

*c.*750–700 The Homeric poems.
*c.*700 Lelantine War.
*c.*700–650 Reforms at Sparta.
*c.*683/2 Annual archonship in Athens begins.

THE REST OF HERODOTUS' WORLD

*c.*700 Deioces founds the Median dynasty.
*c.*680–645 Gyges' reign in Lydia—founder of the Mermnad dynasty, which lasts until 546 and the fall of Croesus.

664–526 Saite Dynasty (26th Dynasty) in Egypt:
  664–610 Psammetichus I in Egypt
  (660s onwards Greeks settle in Egypt. *c.*620 Greek settlement at Naucratis.)
  610–595 Nekos II of Egypt
  595–589 Psammetichus II
  589–570 Apries of Egypt
  570–526 Amasis

*c.*657–587 Cypselid tyranny at Corinth:
  657–627 Cypselus
  627–587 Periander
*c.*650–620 Spartan conquest of Messene in Second Messenian War.
*c.*632 Cylon attempts to seize the Athenian Acropolis. Origin of the 'Alcmaeonid curse'.
*c.*630 Foundation of Cyrene. Dynasty of Battiads rule until *c.*440.

625–585 Cyaxares' reign in Media.

THE GREEKS	THE REST OF HERODOTUS' WORLD
	612 Cyaxares captures Nineveh—Fall of the Assyrians.
	580s War between Cyaxares and Alyattes of Lydia.
c.612–550 Sappho, poet of Lesbos.	597–538 'Jewish Captivity' in Babylon.
c.600–570 Tyranny of Cleisthenes of Sicyon.	
594/3 Solon archon of Athens.	
	585–550 Astyages' reign in Media.
c.561 Pisistratus' first tyranny at Athens.	
c.560–550 Sparta successful in war with Tegea. Spartan–Tegean alliance.	560–546 Croesus' reign in Lydia—conquest of the Ionian Greeks.
c.546 Battle of the Champions between Argos and Sparta (at Thyreatis) further consolidates Sparta's place as leading Peloponnesian state.	c.547–6 Croesus disastrously attacks Persia. End of the Lydian empire.
c.555 Elder Miltiades in Chersonese.	
546–527 Pisistratus' third tyranny in Athens.	557–530 Reign of Cyrus of Persia.
	c.550 Cyrus and Persians revolt and conquer Medes under Astyages.
c.545 Ionians revolt from Cyrus. Revolt suppressed by Harpagus.	547–6 Cyrus conquers Croesus of Lydia.
	539 Cyrus conquers Babylon, the great Assyrian city.
	c.530 Cyrus attempts to conquer the Massagetae but fails and dies.
	c.535 Battle of Alalia between Carthage and the Etruscans.
535–522 Polycrates tyrant of Samos. Alliance of Samos and Amasis of Egypt. Sparta and Samian exiles attack Samos unsuccessfully. Polycrates murdered by Oroetes.	530–522 Reign of Cambyses Conquest of Egypt by Persians. Abortive Persian invasion of Ethiopia. Madness of Cambyses.

THE GREEKS	THE REST OF HERODOTUS' WORLD
521–515 Syloson and Maeandrius in Samos.	522/1 Revolt of Magi. Death of Cambyses. Conspiracy of the seven nobles and accession of Darius.
527–510 Tyranny of Hippias in Athens. 514 Murder of Hipparchus.	521–486 Reign of Darius. Reorganization of Persian Empire and administration. Reconquest of Babylon following its revolt.
c.520–490 Reign of Cleomenes in Sparta.	
	c.513 Darius' expedition against Scythia. c.513 Persian expedition against Cyrene. 512–510 Megabazus subdues parts of Thrace. c.510 Persians demand submission of Macedon—Persian ambassadors are killed.
510 Dorieus in Italy. Destruction of Sybaris in southern Italy by Croton. c.510 Athenian–Aeginetan war begins—lasts intermittently until 481.	
510 Expulsion of Hippias from Athens thanks to help from Cleomenes and Alcmaeonid plotting. 508/7 Reforms of Cleisthenes at Athens. 507 Isagoras appeals to Cleomenes; Cleisthenes briefly driven out, but soon returns. Athens sends envoys to Sardis. 506 Attempt by Cleomenes to overthrow Cleisthenes blocked by Demaratus and Corinth. c.506 Athens is successful against Thebes and Chalcis, which had helped Cleomenes. Thebes now joins Aegina against Athens.	

THE GREEKS	THE REST OF HERODOTUS' WORLD
505/4 Spartans attempt to reinstate Hippias in Athens—fail because of Corinthian opposition.	
c.500 Hippias stirs Persia against Athens. Enmity of Athens and Persia.	
c.500/499 Failed expedition of Artaphrenes and Persians against Naxos.	
499–494 The Ionian Revolt.	
499 Aristagoras appeals to Sparta and Athens. Athens sends aid to rebels (as does Eretria).	
498 Burning of Sardis by rebel Ionians. Athens leaves the rebel alliance.	
494 Ionian defeat at battle of Lade. Fall of Miletus.	
493 Persian reprisals against Ionians. Persians encroach upon Chersonese, previously governed by Miltiades, who flees to Athens. Earlier Miltiades had taken Lemnos for Athens.	
c.492 Prosecution of Phrynichus for production of his *Fall of Miletus*.	493/2 Mardonius unsuccessfully attempts Persian military advance into Europe—storm off Mount Athos.
c.498–454 Reign of Alexander I of Macedon.	
c.491 Gelon to power in Gela in Sicily.	
485 Gelon takes Syracuse.	
c.494 Spartan victory under Cleomenes against Argos at Sepeia.	
c.491 Cleomenes plots to remove other Spartan king Demaratus. Demaratus flees to Persia.	

THE GREEKS

Leotychidas becomes king in his
place (491–469).
491 Athens refuses demand to
submit to Persia and appeals to
Cleomenes against Aegina.
c.490 Madness and death of
Cleomenes of Sparta. Leonidas
becomes king (490–480).

490 Datis and Artaphrenes head
Persian expedition against
Greece. Fall of Eretria. Persians
land in Attica. Athenian victory
at Marathon.
490/489 Miltiades fails to capture
Paros.
489 Death of Miltiades.

483/2 Athenian fleet built by
Themistocles with silver from
mines at Laurium.

481 Greek League formed. Athens
and Aegina put an end to their
hostilities.
480–479 Xerxes' expedition
against Greece.
480 Battles of Thermopylae and
Artemisium. Destruction of
Athens. Greek victory at
Salamis. Xerxes returns to
Persia. Mardonius remains.
479 Greek victories at Plataea
and Mycale. Persians leave
Greece.

THE REST OF HERODOTUS'
WORLD

490 Persian attack on Greece;
aimed at Eretria and Athens
which had helped Ionians in
their revolt.

c.486 Egypt in revolt from Persia,
delaying Persian retaliation
against Greece. Death of
Darius.

486–465 Reign of Xerxes.
c.485 Xerxes puts down
Egyptian revolt.
c.484 Babylon in revolt from
Persia.
484–1 Xerxes prepares for
invasion of Greece.

THE GREEKS

**THE REST OF HERODOTUS'
WORLD**

480 Gelon of Syracuse defeats
Carthage at Himera.

479 Ionian islands join Greek
League.
Greeks take Sestus.
478 Athenians rebuild walls.
478/7 Foundation of the Delian
League under Athenian
leadership.
472 Aeschylus' *Persians*.

465 Xerxes dies amid palace
intrigue.
465–424 Reign of Artaxerxes in
Persia.

459–446 The First Peloponnesian
War.
c.444/3 Foundation of Thurii.
431–404 The Second
Peloponnesian War.

THE HISTORIES

BOOK ONE

Here are presented the results of the enquiry carried out by Herodotus of Halicarnassus. The purpose is to prevent the traces of human events from being erased by time, and to preserve the fame of the important and remarkable achievements produced by both Greeks and non-Greeks; among the matters covered is, in particular, the cause of the hostilities between Greeks and non-Greeks.

[1] According to learned Persians, it was the Phoenicians who caused the conflict. Originally, these people came to our sea from the Red Sea, as it is known. No sooner had they settled in the land they still inhabit than they turned to overseas travel. They used to take Egyptian and Assyrian goods to various places, including Argos, which was at that time the most important state, in all respects, in the country which is now called Greece. Once, then, the Phoenicians came to Argos and began to dispose of their cargo. Five or six days after they had arrived, when they had sold almost everything, a number of women came down to the shore, including the king's daughter, whose name (as the Greeks agree too) was Io, the daughter of Inachus. These women were standing around the stern of the ship, buying any items which particularly caught their fancy, when the Phoenicians gave the word and suddenly charged at them. Most of the women got away, but Io and some others were captured. The Phoenicians took them on to their ship and sailed away for Egypt.

[2] According to the Persians, that is how Io came to Egypt (the Greek version is different), and that was the original crime. Later, some Greeks landed at Tyre in Phoenicia and abducted the king's daughter, Europa. The Persian sources are not in a position to name these Greeks, but they were presumably Cretans. So far the scores were even, but then, according to the Persians, the Greeks were responsible for a second crime. They sailed in a longship to Aea in Colchis, to the Phasis River, and once they had completed the

business that had brought them there, they abducted the king's daughter Medea. The king of Colchis sent a herald to Greece to ask for compensation for the abduction and to demand his daughter back, but the Greeks replied, 'You have never compensated us for your abduction of the Argive princess Io, so we will not make amends to you either.'

[3] A generation later, the Persians say, Alexander the son of Priam heard about this and decided to steal himself a wife from Greece. He was absolutely certain that he would get away with it, without incurring any penalty, since the earlier thefts had gone unpunished—and that is how he came to abduct Helen. The Greeks' initial reaction, it is said, was to send men to demand Helen's return and to ask for compensation for her abduction. Faced with these demands, however, the others brought up the abduction of Medea and said, 'Do you really expect compensation from others, when you paid none and did not return Medea when you were asked to?'

[4] Now, so far it had only been a matter of abducting women from one another, but the Greeks were basically responsible for the next step, the Persians say, since they took the initiative and launched a military strike against Asia before the Asians did against Europe. Although the Persians regard the abduction of women as a criminal act, they also claim that it is stupid to get worked up about it and to seek revenge for the women once they have been abducted; the sensible course, they say, is to pay no attention to it, because it is obvious that the women must have been willing participants in their own abduction, or else it could never have happened. The Persians claim that whereas they, on the Asian side, did not count the abduction of their women as at all important, the Greeks raised a mighty army because of a woman from Lacedaemon, and then invaded Asia and destroyed Priam and his forces. Ever since then, the Persians have regarded the Greeks as their enemies. They think of Asia and the non-Greek peoples living there as their own, but regard Europe and the Greeks as separate from themselves.

[5] That is the Persian account; they date the origin of their hostility towards Greece from the fall of Ilium. However, where the Io incident is concerned, the Phoenicians do not agree with the Persians. The Phoenicians say that they did not have to resort to kidnapping to take her to Egypt. According to them, she slept with

the ship's captain in Argos, and when she discovered that she was pregnant, she could not face her parents, and therefore sailed away willingly with the Phoenicians, to avoid being found out.

So this is what the Persians and Phoenicians say. I am not going to come down in favour of this or that account of events, but I will talk about the man who, to my certain knowledge, first undertook criminal acts of aggression against the Greeks. I will show who it was who did this, and then proceed with the rest of the account. I will cover minor and major human settlements equally, because most of those which were important in the past have diminished in significance by now, and those which were great in my own time were small in times past. I will mention both equally because I know that human happiness never remains long in the same place.

[6] Croesus was Lydian by birth. He was the son of Alyattes and ruled over all the various peoples who live west of the River Halys, which flows from the south (between where the Syrians and the Paphlagonians live) and in the north issues into the sea which is known as the Euxine Sea. Croesus was the first non-Greek we know of to have subjected Greeks to the payment of tribute, though he made alliances with some of them. The ones he made his tributaries were the Ionians, Aeolians, and Asian Dorians, while he allied himself with the Lacedaemonians. Before Croesus' reign, all Greeks were free; the Cimmerian expedition which reached Ionia before Croesus' time was a raiding party, intent on pillage, and not a conquest of the communities there.

[7] Here is how the kingdom passed from the Heraclidae, who had been the Lydian royal family, to Croesus' family, who were called the Mermnadae. There was a man, Candaules by name (although the Greeks call him Myrsilus), who was the ruler of Sardis and a descendant of Alcaeus the son of Heracles; the Heraclid dynasty in Sardis started with Agron (who was the son of Ninus, grandson of Belus and great-grandson of Alcaeus) and ended with Candaules (who was the son of Myrsus). Before Agron, this region had been ruled by descendants of Lydus the son of Atys—the one who is the reason for the whole population being called 'Lydian', when they had previously been known as Maeans. The Heraclidae, whose ancestors were Heracles and a slave girl belonging to Iardanus, gained the kingdom of Lydia, which they had been entrusted by Lydus' descendants, thanks to an oracle. The

kingship passed down from Heraclid father to son for twenty-two generations, or 505 years, until the time of Candaules the son of Myrsus.

[8] Now, this Candaules became enamoured of his own wife and therefore thought she was the most beautiful woman in the world. One of the members of his personal guard, Gyges the son of Dascylus, was an especial favourite of his, and Candaules used to discuss his most important concerns with him; in particular, he used to keep praising his wife's appearance, because he thought she was so beautiful. Candaules was destined to come to a bad end, and so after a while he said to Gyges, 'Gyges, I don't think you believe what I tell you about my wife's looks—and it's true that people trust their ears less than their eyes—so I want you to find a way to see her naked.'

Gyges cried out and said, 'Master, what a perverse thing to say! How can you tell me to look at my mistress naked? As soon as a woman sheds her clothes, she sheds her modesty as well. There are long-established truths for us to learn from, and one of them is that everyone should look to his own. I believe you: she *is* the most beautiful woman in the world. Please don't ask me to do anything wrong.'

[9] He was afraid of disastrous consequences, but Candaules replied to these protestations of his by saying, 'Don't worry, Gyges. You needn't be afraid that this suggestion of mine is designed to test you, and you needn't be afraid of my wife either, because no harm will come to you through her. I'll contrive the whole business from start to finish in such a way that she won't even know she's been seen by you. I'll get you to stand behind the open door of our bedroom, and I'll be there already, before my wife comes to bed. There's a chair near the entrance to the room on which she'll lay her clothes one by one as she undresses, so that will make it very easy for you to watch her. When she leaves the chair and goes over to the bed, you'll be behind her back, and then you just have to make sure that you get out through the doorway without her spotting you.'

[10] Because he could not get out of it, Gyges agreed. When Candaules thought it was time for bed, he took Gyges to the bedroom, and very shortly afterwards his wife arrived too. Gyges watched her come into the room and put her clothes on the chair. When he was behind her back, as she was going over to the bed, he set about slipping out of the room—but the woman spotted him

on his way out. She realized what her husband had done; despite
the fact that she had been humiliated, she did not cry out and she
did not let him see that she knew, because she intended to make
him pay. The point is that, in Lydia—in fact, more or less throughout the non-Greek world—it is a source of great shame even for a
man to be seen naked.

[11] Anyway, she kept quiet at the time and gave nothing away.
As early as possible the next morning, however, she had those
of her house-slaves who she could see were the most loyal to her
stand by, and then she summoned Gyges. He had no idea that she
knew anything about what had happened and so he responded
to her summons by going to her, just as he had always gone in
the past, whenever the queen summoned him. When he arrived she
said to him: 'Gyges, there are now two paths before you: I leave
it up to you which one you choose to take. Either you can kill
Candaules and have me and the kingdom of Lydia for your own,
or you must die yourself right now, so that you will never again do
exactly what Candaules wants you to do and see what you should
not see. Yes, either he or you must die—either the one whose idea
this was or the one who saw me naked when he had no right to
do so.'

At first, Gyges was too astonished to reply, but then he begged
her not to force him to make such a choice. She could not be
moved, however. He saw that he really was faced with choosing
between killing his master or being killed himself by others—and
he chose to survive. So he had a question for her. 'It's not as if
I want to kill my own master,' he said, 'but since you're forcing me
to do so, please tell me how we're going to attack him.'

'The place from where he showed me to you naked', she replied,
'will be the place from which to launch the attack against him. The
attack will happen when he's asleep.'

[12] So they made their plans. There was no way out for Gyges,
no escape: either he or Candaules had to die. When night came, he
followed the woman to the bedroom, where she gave him a dagger
and hid him behind the same door. And after this, while Candaules
was sleeping, he slipped out and, by killing him, gained both
Candaules' wife and his kingdom. Archilochus of Paros (who lived
at the same time) commemorated Gyges in a poem of iambic
trimeters.†

---

† An obelus indicates that there is a note in the Textual Notes, pp. 736–9.

[13] So he gained control of the kingdom—and he retained power thanks to the Delphic oracle. What happened was that the Lydians armed themselves in anger at what had happened to Candaules, but Gyges' supporters made a deal with the rest of the Lydians; the agreement was that if the oracle pronounced Gyges king of Lydia, he would rule, but if not, power would be restored to the Heraclidae. In fact, the oracular pronouncement was favourable and so Gyges became king of Lydia. However, the Pythia qualified her declaration by saying that for the Heraclidae vengeance would come on the fourth in descent from Gyges. But neither the Lydians nor their kings took any notice of this prediction until it was fulfilled.

[14] That is how the Mermnadae deprived the Heraclidae of the rulership of Lydia and gained it for themselves. Once Gyges was king, he sent a fair number of votive offerings to Delphi. In fact, no one has dedicated more silver offerings at Delphi than him, and apart from the silver, he dedicated a huge amount of gold there. The six golden bowls dedicated by him are particularly worth mentioning. They weigh thirty talents and stand in the Corinthian treasury—although strictly speaking it is not the treasury of the Corinthian people as a whole, but of Cypselus the son of Eëtion. As far as we know, Gyges was the first non-Greek to dedicate offerings at Delphi since the Phrygian king Midas the son of Gordias had done so. For Midas made an offering too, of the throne on which he had used to sit to deliver verdicts on legal matters, and it is worth seeing. It can be found in the same place as Gyges' bowls. The Delphians call the gold and silver which Gyges dedicated 'Gygian', after its dedicator.

It is true that, during his reign, Gyges too attacked Miletus and Smyrna, and took the city of Colophon, but he achieved nothing else of significance during the thirty-eight years of his kingship, so I will say no more about him, beyond what I have already said.

[15] I move on now to Ardys, who was Gyges' son and succeeded him to the kingdom. Ardys captured Priene and attacked Miletus, and it was during his rule in Sardis that the Cimmerians (who had been driven out of their homeland by the nomadic Scythians) reached Asia and captured all of Sardis except the acropolis.

[16] Ardys' reign lasted forty-nine years, and then his son Sadyattes succeeded him and reigned for twelve years. Sadyattes

was succeeded by Alyattes, who fought a war against the Medes under Cyaxares, the descendant of Deioces. He also drove the Cimmerians out of Asia, took Smyrna (the colony of Colophon), and attacked Clazomenae, although matters did not turn out there as he wished; in fact, he suffered a major defeat. Otherwise, the most notable achievements of his reign are as follows.

[17] He inherited from his father a war between Lydia and Miletus. This is how he used to conduct the invasion of Milesian territory and the siege of the city. He would invade at the time when the crops were ripe, with his troops marching to the sound of wind-pipes, harps, and treble and bass reed-pipes. When they reached Milesian land, they left all the houses in the countryside standing, throughout the territory, without razing them or burning them or breaking into them; instead, they would destroy the fruit-trees and the crops, and then return home. The point is that the Milesians controlled the sea, and so the Lydian army could achieve nothing by a siege. The reason the Lydian king did not raze their houses was to ensure that the Milesians would have a base from which they could set out to sow seed and work the land, so that he—as a result of their work—would have some way to hurt them during his invasions.

[18] This is the way the Lydian king conducted the war for eleven years. During this time the Milesians suffered two major defeats, once in a battle in their own territory, at Limeneium, and the other time on the plain of the Meander River. For six of the eleven years Sadyattes the son of Ardys was still the Lydian ruler and it was he who invaded Milesian territory each year; in fact, he had been the one who had started the war with Miletus, but for the next five years, it was Alyattes the son of Sadyattes who carried on the war. As I have already explained, he inherited the war from his father, and he put a lot of energy into it. Out of all the Ionian Greeks, none except the Chians helped the Milesians with the burdens of this war. In doing so, they were repaying them for similar aid, because some time earlier the Milesians had supported the Chians in their war against the Erythraeans.

[19] Here is an account of an event which happened to take place in the twelfth year of the war, while the crops were being burnt by the army. As soon as the crops were alight, the wind drove the flames on to a temple of Athena (called the temple of Athena of Assesus), which caught fire and burnt to the ground. At first, no

account was taken of it, but later, when the army was back in
Sardis, Alyattes became ill. The illness went on for rather a long
time, and so—perhaps because he had been recommended to do
so, or perhaps because he himself thought it was a good idea—he
sent emissaries to Delphi, to consult the god about his illness. When
the men reached Delphi, however, the Pythia refused to let them
consult her until they had rebuilt the temple of Athena which they
had burnt down at Assesus in Miletus.

[20] I know that this is what happened, because I heard it from
the Delphians; but the Milesians add certain details. They say that
Periander the son of Cypselus, who was a very close guest-friend
of Thrasybulus (the tyrant of Miletus at the time), heard about the
response the oracle had given Alyattes and sent a messenger to tell
Thrasybulus about it, to enable him to plan for forthcoming events
with foreknowledge.

[21] That, then, is the Milesian account. As soon as Alyattes
received the report from his emissaries, he sent a herald to Miletus
because he wanted to arrange a truce with Thrasybulus and
the Milesians for however long it would take to build the temple.
So the man set off for Miletus. Meanwhile, armed with reliable
advance information about the whole business and with foreknowledge of what Alyattes was going to do, Thrasybulus devised
the following plan. He had all the food there was in the city,
whether it was his own or belonged to ordinary citizens, brought
into the city square; then he told the Milesians to wait for his signal,
which would let them know when to start drinking and making
merry with one another.

[22] Thrasybulus did this and gave these instructions in order to
ensure that the herald from Sardis would report back to Alyattes
about the huge stockpile of food he had seen and about how people
were living a life of luxury. And this is in fact exactly what happened. When the herald had seen all this (and once he had given
Thrasybulus the message the Lydian king had told him to deliver),
he returned to Sardis; and, as I heard it, the end of the war occurred
for this reason and no other. The point is that Alyattes expected
there to be a severe shortage of food in Miletus, and he thought
that the people would have been ground down to a life of utter
hardship—and then the report the herald gave on his return from
Miletus contradicted these expectations of his! After that, they

entered into a peace treaty with each other, according to which they
were to be friends and allies; also, Alyattes built not one but two
temples to Athena in Assesus, and recovered from his illness. This
is what happened during the war Alyattes fought with the Milesians and Thrasybulus.

[23] This man Periander, the one who told Thrasybulus about
the oracle's response, was the son of Cypselus and the tyrant of
Corinth. Now, the Corinthians say (and the Lesbians agree) that
a really remarkable thing happened during his lifetime—that Arion
of Methymna was carried to Taenarum on a dolphin. Arion was
the leading cithara-player of his day, and was the first person we
know of who not only composed a dithyramb and named it as such,
but also produced one, in Corinth.

[24] They say that Arion, who was based for most of the time
at Periander's court, wanted to visit Italy and Sicily and, while he
was there, he earned a great deal of money and then decided to sail
back to Corinth. He set out from Tarentum, and since he trusted
no one more than Corinthians, he hired a crew of Corinthian
sailors. But they hatched a plan to throw him overboard when they
were out in the open sea and take his money for themselves. When
he found out what they were up to, he bargained with them by
offering them his money but begging them to spare his life. The
sailors were unmoved by his pleas and they told him either to take
his own life, if he wanted to be buried on land, or to stop wasting
time and jump overboard into the sea. In this desperate situation,
since that was their decision, Arion asked their permission to stand
on the thwarts in his full ceremonial costume and sing; when he
had finished singing, he said, he would do away with himself. They
liked the idea of having the opportunity to hear the best singer
in the world, so they pulled back from the stern into the middle of
the ship. Arion put on his full ceremonial costume and took hold
of his cithara. He stood on the thwarts and sang the high-pitched
tune all the way through; and at the end of the song he threw
himself into the sea as he was, in his full ceremonial costume. The
sailors then continued their voyage to Corinth, but they say that
a dolphin picked Arion up and carried him to Taenarum. When he
disembarked from the dolphin he went to Corinth, still in his
costume, and once he was there he gave a full report of what had
happened. Periander did not believe him, and kept him confined

and under guard, while keeping a sharp eye out for the sailors. When they arrived (the story continues), they were summoned to his presence and interrogated about what they could tell him of Arion; they told him that Arion was safe and sound somewhere in Italy and that they had left him doing well in Tarentum. At that point Arion appeared, just as he had been when he had jumped into the sea. The sailors were so astonished that, when examined further, they could no longer hide the truth. So that is the story the Corinthians and Lesbians tell, and there is in fact in Taenarum a small bronze statuette dedicated by Arion, of a man riding a dolphin.

[25] Some time after the end of the war he had waged against Miletus Alyattes of Lydia died, after a reign of fifty-seven years. On recovering from his illness, he had made a dedicatory offering at Delphi—he was the second of his line to do so—consisting of a large silver bowl and a stand of welded iron. Delphi is full of offerings, but this one is still worth seeing; it was made by Glaucus of Chios, who was the man who single-handedly invented iron-welding.

[26] After Alyattes' death, his son Croesus succeeded to the kingdom; he was 35 years old at the time. The first Greeks he attacked were the Ephesians. It was during his siege that the Ephesians dedicated the city to Artemis by running a rope to the outside wall from the temple; the distance between the old town (which was the part under siege on that occasion) and the temple is seven stades. So the Ephesians were the first Greeks Croesus attacked, but afterwards he attacked all the Ionian and Aeolian cities one by one. He always gave different reasons for doing so; against some he was able to come up with more serious charges by accusing them of more serious matters, but in other cases he even brought trivial charges.

[27] Once the Greeks in Asia had been subdued and made to pay tribute, his next project was to build ships and attack the Aegean islands. But just when the shipbuilding programme was poised to begin, Bias of Priene came to Sardis (at least, that is what some say, but others say it was Pittacus of Mytilene), and when Croesus asked what news there was of Greece, the reply caused him to cancel his shipbuilding programme. The reply was: 'My lord, the islanders are jointly buying ten thousand horses, since they plan to make a strike against you at Sardis.'

Croesus, supposing he was telling the truth, said, 'If only the gods *would* put it into the islanders' minds to come against the sons of Lydia with horses!'

'My lord,' came the response, 'your prayer shows that you're eager to catch the islanders on horseback on the mainland, and there are sound reasons for you to hope that this is what happens. But as soon as the islanders heard that you were planning to build ships for your campaign against them, what else do you think their prayer was for except the chance to catch Lydians out at sea, so that they can repay you for your enslavement of the Greeks living on the mainland?'

Croesus was very pleased with the man's point and, since he thought he spoke very shrewdly, he was persuaded by him to stop the shipbuiliding programme. And that is how Croesus came to make a pact of friendship with the Ionian Greeks living on the islands.

[28] After a while, almost all the people living west of the Halys River had been subdued. Except for the Cilicians and the Lycians, Croesus had overpowered and made all the rest his subjects—the Lydians, Phrygians, Mysians, Mariandynians, Chalybes, Paphlagonians, the Thynian and Bithynian Thracians, the Carians, Ionians, Dorians, Aeolians, and Pamphylians.

[29] When these peoples had been subdued and while Croesus was increasing the Lydian empire, Sardis was at the height of its prosperity and was visited on occasion by every learned Greek who was alive at the time, including Solon of Athens. Solon had drawn up laws for the Athenians, at their request, and then spent ten years abroad. He claimed to be travelling to see the world, but it was really to avoid the possibility of having to repeal any of the laws he had made. The Athenians could not do it by themselves, since they were bound by solemn vows to try out for a period of ten years whatever laws Solon would set for them.

[30] So that—as well as seeing the world—is why Solon was abroad from Athens. In the course of his travels, he visited Amasis in Egypt and, in particular, Croesus in Sardis, where Croesus put him up as his guest in his palace. Two or three days after his arrival, Croesus had some attendants give Solon a thorough tour of his treasuries and show him how magnificent and valuable everything was. Once Solon had seen and examined everything, Croesus found an opportunity to put a question to him. 'My dear guest from

Athens,' he said, 'we have often heard about you in Sardis: you are famous for your learning and your travels. We hear that you love knowledge and have journeyed far and wide, to see the world. So I really want to ask you whether you have ever come across anyone who is happier than everyone else?'

In asking the question, he was expecting to be named as the happiest of all men, but Solon preferred truth to flattery and said, 'Yes, my lord: Tellus of Athens.'

Croesus was surprised at the answer and asked urgently: 'What makes you think that Tellus is the happiest man?'

'In the first place,' Solon replied, 'while living in a prosperous state, Tellus had sons who were fine, upstanding men and he lived to see them all have children, all of whom survived. In the second place, his death came at a time when he had a good income, by our standards, and it was a glorious death. You see, in a battle at Eleusis between Athens and her neighbours he stepped into the breach and made the enemy turn tail and flee; he died, but his death was splendid, and the Athenians awarded him a public funeral on the spot where he fell, and greatly honoured him.'

[31] Croesus' attention was engaged by Solon's ideas about all the ways in which Tellus was well off, so he asked who was the second happiest person Solon knew; he had absolutely no doubt that he would carry off the second prize, at least. But Solon replied, 'Cleobis and Biton, because these Argives made an adequate living and were also blessed with amazing physical strength. It's not just that the pair of them were both prize-winning athletes; there's also the following story about them. During a festival of Hera at Argos, their mother urgently needed to be taken to the sanctuary on her cart, but the oxen failed to turn up from the field in time. There was no time to waste, so the young men harnessed themselves to the yoke and pulled the cart with their mother riding on it. The distance to the temple was forty-five stades, and they took her all the way there. After this achievement of theirs, which was witnessed by the people assembled for the festival, they died in the best possible way; in fact, the god used them to show that it is better for a person to be dead than to be alive. What happened was that while the Argive men were standing around congratulating the young men on their strength, the women were telling their mother how lucky she was in her children. Their mother was overcome with joy at what her sons had done and the fame it would bring,

and she went right up to the statue of the goddess, stood there and prayed that in return for the great honour her children Cleobis and Biton had done her, the goddess would give them whatever it is best for a human being to have. After she had finished her prayer, they participated in the rites and the feast, and then the young men lay down inside the actual temple for a rest. They never got to their feet again; they met their end there. The Argives had statues made of them and dedicated them at Delphi, on the grounds that they had been the best of men.'

[32] Croesus was angry with Solon for awarding the second prize for happiness to these young men, and he said, 'My dear guest from Athens, do you hold our happiness in utter contempt? Is that why you are ranking us lower than even ordinary citizens?'

'Croesus,' Solon replied, 'when you asked me about men and their affairs, you were putting your question to someone who is well aware of how utterly jealous the divine is, and how it is likely to confound us. Anyone who lives for a long time is bound to see and endure many things he would rather avoid. I place the limit of a man's life at seventy years. Seventy years make 25,200 days, not counting the intercalary months; but if you increase the length of every other year by a month, so that the seasons happen when they should, there will be thirty-five such intercalary months in the seventy years, and these extra months will give us 1,050 days. So the sum total of all the days in seventy years is 26,250, but no two days bring events which are exactly the same. It follows, Croesus, that human life is entirely a matter of chance.

'Now, I can see that you are extremely rich and that you rule over large numbers of people, but I won't be in a position to say what you're asking me to say about you until I find out that you died well. You see, someone with vast wealth is no better off than someone who lives from day to day, unless good fortune attends him and sees to it that, when he dies, he dies well and with all his advantages intact. After all, plenty of extremely wealthy people are unfortunate, while plenty of people with moderate means are lucky; and someone with great wealth but bad fortune is better off than a lucky man in only two ways, whereas there are many ways in which a lucky man is better off than someone who is rich and unlucky. An unlucky rich man is more capable of satisfying his desires and of riding out disaster when it strikes, but a lucky man is better off than him in the following respects. Even though he is not as capable of coping with disaster and his desires, his good luck protects him, and he also avoids disfigurement and disease, has no experience of catastrophe, and is blessed with fine children and good looks. If, in addition to all this, he dies a heroic death, then he is the one you are after—he is the one who deserves to be described as happy. But until he is dead, you had better refrain from calling him happy, and just call him fortunate.

'Now, it is impossible for a mere mortal to have all these blessings at the same time, just as no country is entirely self-sufficient; any given country has some things, but lacks others, and the best country is the one which has the most. By the same token, no one person is self-sufficient: he has some things, but lacks others. The person who has and retains more of these advantages than others, and then dies well, my lord, is the one who, in my opinion, deserves the description in question. It is necessary to consider the end of anything, however, and to see how it will turn out, because the god often offers prosperity to men, but then destroys them utterly and completely.'

[33] These sentiments did not endear Solon to Croesus at all, and Croesus dismissed him as of no account. He was sure that anyone who ignored present benefits and told him to look to the end of everything was an ignoramus.

[34] After Solon's departure, the weight of divine anger descended on Croesus, in all likelihood for thinking that he was the happiest man in the world. Soon afterwards, while he was asleep, he had a dream which accurately foretold the calamities that were going to happen to his son. Croesus had two sons, one of whom was handicapped by being deaf and dumb, while the other, whose name was Atys, was easily the most outstanding young man of his generation in all respects. The dream was about Atys, and its message was that he would die from a wound caused by an iron spearhead. When Croesus woke up, he reflected on the dream and it made him afraid. First, he found a wife for his son, and second, although Atys had regularly commanded the Lydian army, Croesus stopped sending him anywhere on that kind of business. He also had all javelins, spears, and similar weapons of war removed from the men's quarters and piled up in the bedrooms, in case any of them fell from where it hung on to his son.

[35] While he was busy with his son's wedding, a man arrived in Sardis who was oppressed by misfortune and had blood on his

hands; he was a Phrygian by birth, from the royal family. He came to Croesus' home and asked if he could obtain a purification in accordance with local custom, and Croesus purified him (the rite is nearly the same in Lydia as it is in Greece). Once he had done it in the customary fashion, Croesus asked the man who he was and where he was from. 'What is your name, sir?' he asked. 'You have come here from Phrygia to seek refuge at my hearth, but whereabouts in Phrygia are you from? And what man or woman did you kill?'

'My lord,' he replied, 'Gordias the son of Midas is my father, and my name is Adrastus. It was my own brother that I killed, by accident. I'm here because I've been expelled from my home by my father, and stripped of everything.'

Croesus' response was as follows: 'You are among friends now: your family and mine are friends. As long as you stay here in my house, you will have everything you want. Try to let the burden of your misfortune weigh you down as little as possible, because that will do you the most good.'

[36] So Adrastus lived in Croesus' house. While he was there, a huge monster of a boar arrived on Mount Olympus in Mysia and kept coming down from his mountain base and ruining the Mysians' fields. The Mysians often went out after him, but they failed to inflict the slightest injury on him, although he hurt them. In the end a Mysian delegation came to Croesus to tell him about it. 'My lord,' they said, 'an enormous monster of a boar has appeared in our land and is wreaking havoc on our farmlands. All our attempts to get him have failed. So please could you send us your son with some of your élite young fighting men, and dogs too, so that we can drive the beast from our land.'

Faced with this request, Croesus remembered his dream and replied as follows: 'No, I won't let my son go to you, so you had better forget about him. He has only just got married, and he's busy with that. But I will send you some of my élite troops, and you can have the whole pack of my hunting-dogs, and I will give them strict instructions to do their very best to help you drive the beast out of your land.'

[37] That was good enough for the Mysians, but then Croesus' son, who had heard the Mysians' request, came in to see his father. When Croesus insisted that he was certainly not going to send his son to help them, the young man said, 'Father, in times past I used

to perform the most admirable and noble deeds; I used to go to war or go out hunting, and win distinction there. But these days you've been keeping me from both these activities, even though you have no evidence of any cowardice or faint-heartedness on my part. What impression do you think I must give as I come and go in the city square? What kind of a man will my fellow citizens take me to be? What will my new bride think of me? What kind of a husband will she think she is living with? Please, either let me go on the hunt or persuade me that this course of action is better for me.'

[38] 'Son,' Croesus answered, 'I'm certainly not doing this because I've noticed a cowardly streak in you, or any other defect for that matter. But an apparition came to me in a dream while I was asleep and told me that you didn't have long to live, and that an iron spearhead was going to cause your death. It was because of this apparition that I was anxious for your wedding to take place, and that is also why I am refusing to send you on this mission. I'm taking these precautions in case there's a way for me to hide you away while I am alive. You are in fact my one and only son; the other one, with his ruined hearing, I count as no son of mine.'†

[39] 'What a dream!' the young man said. 'I don't blame you for trying to protect me. But there's something you don't under-stand about the dream, something you haven't noticed, and it's only fair to let me explain it to you. You say that the dream told you that an iron spearhead was going to cause my death. But does a boar have hands? Where is its iron spearhead for you to worry about? If the apparition had told you that a tusk or something like that was going to cause my death, then of course you should have taken these precautions. But in fact it was a spear. So since it's not men we're going up against, please let me go.'

[40] 'All right, son,' Croesus replied, 'I give in. Your explana-tion of the dream does make a kind of sense. I'll change my mind and let you go on the hunt.'

[41] After this conversation, Croesus sent for Adrastus, the Phrygian. When he arrived, Croesus said, 'Adrastus, when you had been brought low by grim misfortune—not that I'm holding it against you—I purified you and took you into my house. I have covered all your expenses. I have done you a lot of good, and now you ought to return the favour. I'd like you to be my son's body-

guard when he goes out on this hunt, in case any bandits ambush
you on the road and try to do you harm. And besides, you too
should be seeking out opportunities for distinguishing yourself: you
come from a distinguished family and you're endowed with physical strength.'

[42] 'My lord,' Adrastus said, 'I wouldn't normally have anything to do with this kind of task; it isn't appropriate for someone
who has met with the kind of misfortune I have to associate with
those of his peers who are successful, nor do I want to. In fact, I'd
have found plenty of reasons for not going. But you are insistent
and I have to do what you want, because I ought to repay you for
the favours you have given me. I'm ready to do it, then, and you
can expect your son, whom you are putting into my care, to return
home unharmed. As his bodyguard, I'll see to it.'

[43] This was his reply to Croesus. Some time later they set out,
along with the élite young fighting men and the dogs. Once they
had reached Olympus, they started searching the mountain for the
beast. They found it, stood in a circle around it, and began to throw
their spears at it. This was the point at which Croesus' guest-friend,
the one who had been purified of manslaughter and whose name
was Adrastus, threw his spear at the boar, missed it, and hit
Croesus' son. Since it was a spear that hit him, he fulfilled the
prophecy of the dream. A runner set out to let Croesus know what
had happened, and when he reached Sardis he told him about the
encounter with the boar and his son's death.

[44] Croesus was devastated at his son's death and was all the
more aggrieved because he himself had purified the killer of
manslaughter. He was so terribly upset that he called on Zeus as
the god responsible for purification to witness what his guest-friend
had done to him, and he also called on the same god in his capac-
ities as god of the hearth and god of friendship—as god of the
hearth because he had taken the visitor into his home without realizing that he was feeding his son's killer, and as god of friendship
because he sent as a bodyguard for his son the man who turned
out to be his worst enemy.

[45] Later the Lydians arrived carrying the body, with the killer
following along behind them. He stood in front of the corpse,
stretched out his arms towards Croesus and gave himself up to him.
He told Croesus to take his life over the corpse, because now, on
top of his earlier misfortune, he had destroyed the life of the one

who had purified him, and there was no point in his going on living. Croesus heard him out and felt pity for Adrastus, even though he had troubles enough of his own. 'My friend,' he said, 'your declaration that you deserve death is all the compensation I want from you. You are not to blame for the terrible thing that has happened to me; you were just an unwitting instrument. Responsibility lies with one of the gods, who even warned me some time ago what was going to happen.'

So Croesus gave his son a proper burial. But Adrastus, the son of Gordias and grandson of Midas, who had killed his own brother and now his purifier as well, waited until it was quiet around the tomb and then, realizing that there was no one in his experience who bore a heavier burden of misfortune than himself, he took his own life at the graveside.

[46] For two years Croesus sat in deep grief over the loss of his son, but then, when Cyrus the son of Cambyses deprived Astyages the son of Cyaxares of his power, the growing might of the Persian caused Croesus to put aside his grief and he began to wonder whether there might be a way for him to restrain the growing power of the Persian before it became too great. Once the idea had taken hold, he immediately devised a way to test the oracles—the one in Libya as well as the Greek ones. He sent men off to the various locations—to Delphi, to Abae in Phocis, to Dodona, and others to Amphiaraus and Trophonius, and to Branchidae in Miletus. These were the Greek oracles he sent men to consult, and then he dispatched others to consult Ammon in Libya. The reason he sent men all over the place like this was to test the wisdom of the oracles; then he planned to send men a second time to any which proved accurate, to ask whether he should undertake an invasion of Persia.

[47] The instructions he gave the men before sending them out to test the oracles were as follows. They were to keep track of the number of days from the time they left Sardis, and on the hundredth day they were to consult the oracles and ask what the Lydian king, Croesus the son of Alyattes, was doing. They were to have the response of each of the oracles written down and then they were to bring them back to him. Now, no one records what the rest of the oracles said, but at Delphi, as soon as the Lydian emissaries had entered the temple to consult the god and asked the question Croesus had told them to ask, the Pythia spoke the following lines in hexameter verse:

I know the number of grains of sand and the extent of the sea;
I understand the deaf-mute and hear the words of the dumb.
My senses detect the smell of tough-shelled tortoise
Cooked in bronze together with the flesh of lambs;
Beneath it lies bronze, and bronze covers it.

[48] The Lydians wrote down this prophecy delivered by the
Pythia and returned to Sardis. The other emissaries also arrived
with their oracular responses, and as they did so Croesus unfolded
each one and read what had been written down. None of them
satisfied him, but on hearing the one from Delphi, he offered up
a prayer and accepted it; in his opinion, only the oracle at Delphi
was a true oracle, because it had realized what he had been doing.
For once he had sent his emissaries to the oracles, he had waited
for the critical day and then put into effect the following plan. His
idea was to come up with something unthinkable and unimagin-
able, so he chopped up a tortoise and some lamb's meat and cooked
them together in a bronze pot with a bronze lid on the top.

[49] That was the response the Delphic oracle gave Croesus. I
am not in a position to give details of the response given by the
oracle of Amphiaraus to the Lydians when they had performed the
traditional rites at the temple, because there is in fact no record of
it either; all I can say is that in Croesus' opinion this oracle too
gave him an accurate response.

[50] Croesus' next step was to set about propitiating the Delphic
god with the generosity of his sacrifices. He offered three thousand
of every kind of sacrificial animal; he heaped a huge pyre out of
couches overlaid with gold and silver, golden cups, and purple
cloaks and tunics, and burnt them to ashes. He thought he stood
a better chance of winning the god over by doing this. He also told
all the Lydians that every one of them was to sacrifice whatever he
could.

When he had finished sacrificing, he melted down an enormous
amount of gold and beat it out into 117 ingots. Each ingot was six
palms long, three palms wide, and one palm high. Four of them
were made out of pure gold, each weighing two and a half talents,
while the rest of the ingots were white gold, each weighing two
talents. He also had made out of pure gold a statue of a lion, which
weighed ten talents. When the temple at Delphi burnt down, this
lion fell off the ingots which were acting as its base; it now sits in
the Corinthian treasury, weighing six and a half talents, because
three and a half talents of gold melted off it.

[51] Once these items were finished, Croesus sent them to Delphi; he also sent other things at the same time. First, there were two huge bowls, one of gold and one of silver. The gold one used to stand on the right of the entrance to the temple, with the silver one on the left. They too were relocated when the temple burnt down; the gold bowl sits in the Clazomenaean treasury, weighing eight and a half talents and twelve minas, and the silver one in the corner of the temple porch. It has a capacity of six hundred amphoras, because the Delphians use it as a mixing-bowl at the festival of the Theophania. The Delphians claim that it was made by Theodorus of Samos, and I see no reason to disagree, since it strikes me as an extraordinary piece.

In addition, Croesus sent four silver jars, which stand in the Corinthian treasury, and he sent a votive offering of two aspergilla too, one of gold and one of silver. On the golden one there is an inscription 'from the Lacedaemonians', and they claim that it was they who dedicated it. They are wrong, however, because it was one of Croesus' offerings, and it was a Delphian who wrote the inscription in order to please the Lacedaemonians; I know who it was, but I refrain from mentioning his name. The statue of the boy through whose hand water trickles is Lacedaemonian in origin, but neither of the aspergilla is. Croesus sent plenty of other dedicatory offerings at the same time, none of which is inscribed, including some round, cast bowls of silver and also a golden statue of a woman which is three cubits tall, and which according to the Delphians is a statue of the woman who was Croesus' baker. Croesus also dedicated his wife's necklaces and belts.

[52] So much for the items Croesus sent to Delphi. As for Amphiaraus, once Croesus had found out about his courage and his misfortune, he dedicated to him a shield made entirely of gold, and a spear which was made of solid gold from its shaft to its head. Both these items were still lying in Thebes in my day—in the temple of Ismenian Apollo, to be precise.

[53] Croesus instructed those of his men who were to take the gifts to the sanctuaries to ask the oracles whether he should make war on the Persians and whether he should make an ally of any other military force. When they reached their destinations, the Lydians dedicated their offerings and then approached the oracles with their question: 'Croesus, king of the Lydians and of other peoples, is of the opinion that yours are the only true oracles in the

world. Accordingly, he has given you the gifts you deserve for your insight, and now his question to you is whether he should make war on the Persians and whether he should make an ally of any other military force.' The answers both oracles gave to the question were perfectly consistent with each other: they told Croesus that if he made war on the Persians, he would destroy a great empire, and they advised him to find out which was the most powerful Greek state and ally himself with it.

[54] When Croesus heard the answers his men brought back, he was delighted with the oracles and was convinced that he would destroy Cyrus' empire. First he found out how many people lived at Delphi, and then he sent agents there once again to give every man two gold staters. The Delphians repaid Croesus and the Lydians by giving them precedence in consulting the oracle, exemption from taxes, front seats at festivals, and the right, granted in perpetuity to any Lydian, to become a citizen of Delphi.

[55] Since he now knew that the oracle was accurate, Croesus intended to drink deep of it, and after giving this present to the Delphians he consulted it a third time. This time he wanted a statement on the question whether his rule would last a long time. The Pythia's response was as follows:

> When a mule becomes Persian king, it is time,
> Tender-footed Lydian, for you to flee beside the pebbly Hermus
> Without delay, and without worrying about cowardice.

[56] When this response reached Croesus, it afforded him far more pleasure than anything else the oracle had told him, because he was sure that a mule would never replace a man as the Persian king, and that in consequence he and his descendants would rule for ever. He next turned his mind to investigating which was the most powerful Greek state, so that he could gain them as his allies. As a result of his enquiries, he discovered that Lacedaemon and Athens were the outstanding states, and that Lacedaemon was populated by Dorians while Athens was populated by Ionians. For these two peoples†—the one Pelasgian, the other Hellenic—had been pre-eminent in the old days. The Pelasgians never migrated anywhere, but the Hellenes were a very well-travelled race. When Deucalion was their king, they were living in Phthia, but in the time of Dorus the son of Hellen they were in the territory around Mounts Ossa and Olympus, known as Histiaeotis. Then they were

evicted from Histiaeotis by the Cadmeans and settled on Mount Pindus, where they were called Macedonians. Next they moved to Dryopis, and from Dryopis they finally reached the Peloponnese and became known as the Dorians.

[57] I am not in a position to say for certain what language the Pelasgians used to speak, but if it is appropriate to judge by those Pelasgians who still exist today—the ones who live in the town of Creston north of Tyrrhenia (who used to inhabit the country which is now called Thessaliotis and so shared a border with the people now known as Dorians), the ones who founded Placia and Scylace on the Hellespont (who used to be inhabitants of Attica along with the Athenians) and all those other places which were Pelasgian settlements but have changed their names—judging by them, the Pelasgians spoke a non-Greek language. So if the whole Pelasgian race was like them too, the Attic people (which used to be Pelasgian) must also have learnt a new language at the time when they became Hellenized. For the fact that neither the Crestonians nor the Placians speak the same language as any of their neighbours, but do speak the same language as each other, shows that they retained the form of language they brought with them when they moved to the places they now inhabit.

[58] It seems clear to me, however, that the Hellenes have always spoken the same language, ever since they began. Although when they were separate from the Pelasgians they were weak, they expanded from these origins until instead of being small they encompassed a great many peoples, once the Pelasgians in particular had combined with them, along with quite a few other non-Greek peoples. It is also my view that when the Pelasgians spoke a non-Greek language they never grew to any great size.

[59] Anyway, Croesus discovered that, of the two peoples in question, the one in Attica had been oppressed and fragmented by Pisistratus the son of Hippocrates, who was in those days the tyrant of Athens. Once, when Hippocrates was a spectator at the Olympic Games (he was an ordinary citizen at the time), a really extraordinary thing had happened to him. He had finished sacrificing, and the pots full of meat and water were standing there, when they boiled and started overflowing, even though they were not on a fire. Chilon the Lacedaemonian happened to be on hand to see the miracle. He advised Hippocrates either not to get married—that is, not to bring a child-bearing wife into his house—or, failing that, if

he happened to have a wife already, to get rid of her and to disown any son he had. Hippocrates refused to listen to these suggestions of Chilon's, and some time later Pisistratus was born. When there was a factional dispute between the people of the coast, whose leader was Megacles the son of Alcmaeon, and the people of the plain, led by Lycurgus the son of Aristolaïdes, Pisistratus—with his mind set on tyranny—formed a third party. He gathered his supporters together and made himself appear to be the leader of the hill people. Then he put the following plan into effect. He wounded himself and his mules and drove his cart into the city square, making it seem as though he was trying to escape from some enemies who had set upon him with murderous intent (or so he said) as he drove out of town. He asked the Athenian people to provide him with personal guards; he had already won their respect as a military commander during the campaign against Megara, during which not the least of his important achievements was the capture of Nisaea. The Athenian people were completely taken in by his trick and chose from among the citizen body some men to give him—that is, those who became his club-carriers, if not his spear-carriers, because they followed him around carrying wooden clubs. Pisistratus started an uprising with their help and together they took control of the Acropolis. After that, Pisistratus ruled Athens, but he did not interfere with the existing structure of offices or change the laws; he administered the state constitutionally and organized the state's affairs properly and well.

[60] Not long afterwards, though, Megacles and Lycurgus united their supporters into a single party and expelled him. That was how Pisistratus came to take control of Athens the first time, but his rule was not yet secure enough to prevent him losing it. However, now that they had got rid of him, Megacles and Lycurgus fell out with each other all over again. Megacles was coming off worst in the dispute, and so he sent a message to Pisistratus, asking him whether he would consider marrying his daughter in order to become tyrant. Pisistratus accepted the offer and agreed to his terms. Now, the trick that he and Megacles played in order to bring about his return was by far the most simple-minded one I have ever come across, given that Greeks had long been distinguished from non-Greeks by being more clever and less gullible— assuming that, even at this late date, they really did play this trick on the Athenians, who are supposed to be the most intelligent of

the Greeks. There was a woman called Phya in the deme of Paeania who was only three fingers short of four cubits tall and was also very good-looking. They dressed this woman up in a full set of armour, put her on a chariot, and, after showing her how to hold herself in order to give the most plausible impression, set out for the city with her. Runners were sent ahead to act as heralds, and they, on arriving in the city, made the announcement they had been told to make. 'Men of Athens,' they said, 'Athena is giving Pisistratus the singular honour of personally escorting him back to your Acropolis. So welcome him.' They took this message from place to place, and word soon reached the country demes that Athena was bringing Pisistratus back. Meanwhile, the city-dwellers were so convinced that the woman was actually the goddess that they were offering prayers to her—to a human being—and were welcoming Pisistratus back.

[61] So this is how Pisistratus became tyrant again. He married Megacles' daughter, as he had promised Megacles he would, but because he already had grown-up sons, and because the Alcmaeonidae were supposed to be under a curse, he did not want to have children by his new wife, so he did not have sex with her in the usual way. At first his wife kept it secret, but later she told her mother (who may or may not have questioned her about it), and the mother told her husband. Megacles was furious at the slight and, in an angry frame of mind, he made peace with his political rivals. When Pisistratus heard about the actions that were being taken against him, he got right out of the country and went to Eretria. Once he was there, he consulted with his sons, and Hippias won the day by arguing that they should regain power. They set about collecting contributions from all the communities which were under some kind of obligation to them and, although a number of communities were extremely generous with their financial support, the Thebans were the most generous of all with their money. Eventually, to cut a long story short, they were fully equipped for their return. Argive mercenaries had come from the Peloponnese, and a volunteer from Naxos, whose name was Lygdamis, came and raised morale a great deal by bringing both money and men.

[62] They set out from Eretria and came home after ten years of exile. The first place in Attica that they took was Marathon. While they were camped there, they were joined by supporters from

the city and there was also an influx of men from the country demes
who found the rule of a tyrant more pleasant than freedom. So
their ranks were swelling. Now, the Athenians in the city had taken
no account of Pisistratus while he was collecting money, or even
afterwards, when he had taken Marathon; but when they found
out that he was marching on the city, they came out to defend the
city against him. On the one hand there were the Athenians, proceeding with full strength against the returning exiles; on the other
hand there were Pisistratus' troops, proceeding against the city
from their base at Marathon. The two sides met at the sanctuary
of Athena in Pallene and took up positions opposite each other. At
this juncture, a seer called Amphilytus of Acarnania came up to
Pisistratus—it was divine providence that he was there—and delivered the following prophecy in hexameter verse:

> The net has been cast, the mesh is at full stretch,
> And the tuna will dart in the moonlit night.

[63] These were Amphilytus' inspired words to Pisistratus. Pisistratus understood the meaning of the prophecy, told Amphilytus
he accepted its validity, and led his army to battle. The Athenians
from the city were actually busy with their midday meal just then,
if they had not already finished, in which case they were playing
dice or sleeping. Pisistratus and his men fell on the Athenians and
routed them. Then Pisistratus thought up a very clever plan to stop
the fleeing Athenians from regrouping and to make sure they stayed
scattered. He had his sons mount their horses and ride up ahead.
Whenever they caught up with a group of fugitives they followed
Pisistratus' instructions and told them that they need not worry and
that each man should return to his own home.

[64] The Athenians followed this suggestion, and so Pisistratus
took control of Athens for the third time. This time he planted his
tyranny firmly, with the help of large numbers of mercenary troops
and a substantial income, partly gained locally and partly coming
in from the Strymon River area. He also took the children of those
Athenians who had stood their ground without immediately
running away and sent them to Naxos, where he had put Lygdamis
in charge; here too, the island's opposition to him had been suppressed by military means. Another thing he did, as the oracles
advised, was purify the island of Delos. The way he performed the
purification was to dig up all the land that was visible from the

sanctuary, remove the corpses and transfer them to another part of the island. And so Pisistratus was the tyrant of Athens. Some Athenians had fallen in the battle, and others, including the Alcmaeonidae, were in exile from their homeland.

[65] So Croesus gathered that the Athenians were currently in this state of oppression. Where the Lacedaemonians were concerned, however, he discovered that they had got through a time of great difficulty and now had the upper hand over the Tegeans in the war. The Lacedaemonians had been at war with the Tegeans before, during the reign of Leon and Hegesicles in Sparta, but they always came to grief against them, even though they were successful against all their other opponents. Also, the Lacedaemonians had previously had just about the worst customs in the whole of Greece; not only were their domestic policies no good, but they also had no dealings with foreigners. But they changed their constitution for the better, and this is how it happened.

Lycurgus, a Spartiate of some eminence, went to consult the oracle at Delphi and as soon as he entered the temple the Pythia said:

> Lycurgus, here you are. You have come to my rich temple,
> Beloved of Zeus and all who dwell on Olympus.
> Should I address you, in my prophecy, as a god or as a man?
> I think it would be better to call you a god, Lycurgus.

There are those who say that the Pythia did not stop there, but also taught him the organizational structure which the Spartans currently have. This is not what the Lacedaemonians themselves say, however. They say that when Lycurgus became the guardian of Leobotes (who was his nephew, and was one of the two Spartan kings), he imported their current constitution from Crete. As soon as he became Leobotes' guardian, he changed the whole constitution and took measures to ensure that these new laws were not broken. It was also Lycurgus who subsequently instituted their military organization—the sworn companies, the divisions of thirty, and the communal messes—and established the ephors and the council of elders as well.

[66] These were the changes that altered their system for the better. When Lycurgus died they built a shrine to him and they hold him in great reverence. Because their land was good and the population quite large, they soon grew and flourished—and then they

stopped being content with peace. Convinced that they were stronger than the Arcadians, they put a question to the Delphic oracle which referred to the whole of Arcadia. The Pythia's response was as follows:

> You ask for Arcadia? You ask a lot; I will not give it to you.
> There are many men in Arcadia, toughened by a diet of acorns,
> And they will stop you. But I do not want to be niggardly.
> I will give you the dance-floor of Tegea; you can caper there
> And measure out her beautiful plain with a rope.

Faced with this response, the Lacedaemonians left the rest of Arcadia alone and attacked Tegea. They took chains with them, because they expected to reduce the people of Tegea to slavery, as the Pythia's ambiguous response had led them to believe they would. In fact, however, they came off worst in the engagement and those of them who were taken prisoner wore the chains which they themselves had brought, and measured out the Tegean Plain with a rope as labourers on the land. The actual chains with which they were tied up were still preserved in Tegea in my time, hanging in the temple of Athena Alea.

[67] Anyway, although this earlier war of theirs against the Tegeans never went well for them, in Croesus' time, during the reign of Anaxandridas and Ariston in Lacedaemon, the Spartiates gained the upper hand in the war, and this is how they did so. Since they were constantly being beaten by the Tegeans, they sent emissaries to Delphi to ask which god they should propitiate in order to start winning the Tegean War, and the Pythia replied that they had to bring the bones of Orestes the son of Agamemnon back home. They could not discover Orestes' grave, however, so they sent emissaries again, this time to ask the god to tell them where Orestes was buried. The Pythia's response to this question of theirs was as follows:

> On the Arcadian plain there is a place called Tegea
> Where strong necessity drives the blast of two winds,
> Where there is blow and counter-blow, grief piled on grief.
> There the life-giving earth holds the son of Agamemnon,
> Whom you must bring home if you would be overlord of Tegea.

Despite a thorough search, however, even this response brought the Lacedaemonians no closer to discovering Orestes' burial-place,

until it was found by Lichas, who was one of those Spartan officials they call 'Benefactors'. The Benefactors are the citizens—five
every year—who are passing out of the ranks of the Knights
because they are the oldest; they have to spend the year of their
withdrawal from the Knights in constant travel here and there on
missions for the Spartan authorities.

[68] It was one of these Benefactors, Lichas, who made the
discovery, and he did so through a combination of luck and intelligence. It was possible at that time for Lacedaemonians to have
dealings with Tegea, and Lichas arrived at a forge there. He
watched the smith beating iron and was impressed by his work.
The smith saw that he was impressed, stopped what he was doing
and said, 'So you think I do amazing work with iron, do you, my
Laconian friend? I tell you, if you'd seen what I'd seen, you'd really
be amazed. You see, I decided to make a well here in this yard. As
I was digging, I came upon a coffin which was seven cubits long!
Since I didn't believe that people were really taller in the past than
they are nowadays, I opened it up—and the corpse I saw inside was
exactly the same size as the coffin! I measured it before putting it
back in the ground.'

Lichas thought about the smith's description of what he had seen
and came to the conclusion that the description matched what the
oracle had said about Orestes. He reached this conclusion by realizing that the 'winds' referred to the two bellows he could see the
smith had, that 'blow and counter-blow' referred to the hammer
and the anvil, and that 'grief piled on grief' referred to the iron the
smith was beating, since (on his interpretation of the metaphor) the
discovery of iron brought grief to men.

Once he had reached this conclusion, he returned to Sparta. He
explained the whole thing to the Lacedaemonians, and they faked
a charge against him which led to his banishment. He went to
Tegea, told the smith about his misfortune, and tried to rent the
yard from him. At first, the smith would not let him have it, but
eventually Lichas won him over and moved in. Then he dug up the
grave, collected the bones, and took them with him to Sparta. And
ever since then, whenever there was a military trial of strength
between the two sides, the Lacedaemonians easily won. In fact, by
the time in question most of the Peloponnese was under their
control.

[69] On the basis of all this information, then, Croesus sent agents to Sparta, to take gifts and to ask for an alliance. He had told them what to say, and when they arrived in Sparta they said, 'These are the words we bring from Croesus, king of the Lydians and other peoples: "Lacedaemonians, the oracle advised me to make the Greek my ally and now I have learnt that you are the leading Greek people. You, therefore, are the ones to whom I am extending the invitation the oracle recommended. I want to be on good terms with you and to enter into an alliance with you without treachery or deceit." '

This was the declaration Croesus made through his agents to the Lacedaemonians, who had in fact already heard of the oracle's answer to Croesus. They were pleased that the Lydians had approached them, and they swore solemn oaths of friendship and alliance with Croesus. Actually, they were already indebted to Croesus for certain favours he had done them in the past, because the Lacedaemonians had once sent men to Sardis to buy gold, which they wanted to use for a statue of Apollo (the one which now stands in Thornax in Laconia), but although they came to buy it, Croesus gave it to them for free.

[70] For this reason, and also because he had chosen them rather than any other Greeks as his friends, the Lacedaemonians accepted Croesus' offer of alliance. They were ready if he ever called on them. They also wanted to give him something in return, so they made a bronze bowl which was extensively decorated with pictures on the outside of its rim and which had a capacity of three hundred amphoras. They sent this bowl on its way, but it never arrived at Sardis, and there are two alternative reasons given for this. The Lacedaemonians say that when it was off the island of Samos on its way to Sardis, the Samians found out about it, sent longships after it, and stole it; but the local Samian account is that the Lacedaemonians who were taking the bowl to Sardis were too late, and when they found out that Sardis had fallen and that Croesus had been taken prisoner, they sold the bowl in Samos, where the people who had bought it—they were just ordinary citizens—set it up as a dedication in the temple of Hera. And perhaps it might make sense that when those who sold it got back to Sparta they would claim that it had been stolen by the Samians.

[71] So that is what happened to the bowl. Meanwhile, due to his misunderstanding of the oracle, Croesus invaded Cappadocia, on the assumption that he would depose Cyrus and destroy the Persian empire. While Croesus was mobilizing his troops for the attack on Persia, he received some advice from a Lydian called Sandanis. Now, Sandanis had been regarded as clever even before this, but the opinion he expressed on this occasion gave his reputation in Lydia an enormous boost. 'My lord,' he said, 'you are getting ready to attack the kind of men who wear nothing but leather, including their trousers. Their food consists of what they can get, not what they might want, because of the ruggedness of their land. They drink no wine, just water, and figs are the only good things they have to eat.† They have nothing, so if you win, what will you gain from them? But if you're defeated, think of all the good things you will lose. Once they have experienced the benefits of our way of life, they will cling to them and it will be impossible to dislodge them. For my part, I am thankful that the gods do not give the Persians the idea of attacking Lydia.' Although this speech of his did not convince Croesus, it is true that before the Persians conquered Lydia, they had no delicacies or anything good.

[72] The Greeks call the Cappadocians Syrians. At this time, Cyrus was their ruler, but before being part of the Persian empire, the Syrians had been the subjects of the Medes. For the boundary between the Median and Lydian empires was the Halys, which rises in the mountains of Armenia, flows through Cilicia, and then continues with Matiene to the north and Phrygia to the south; after leaving these countries behind, its course takes it north, where it skirts the territory of the Syrian Cappadocians and to the west that of the Paphlagonians. The Halys, then, makes a separate region out of almost all the lands in coastal Asia from that part of the sea between Cyprus and the mainland to the Euxine Sea. This region is the neck of the whole continent, and its extent is such that a man travelling light would take five days to cross it.

[73] The main reasons for Croesus' invasion of Cappadocia, in addition to the fact that his desire for land led him to want to increase his share of territory, were his faith in the oracle and his wish to punish Cyrus for what had happened to Astyages. Astyages the son of Cyaxares was Croesus' brother-in-law and the king of the Medes, and Cyrus the son of Cambyses had defeated him and was holding him captive. This is how Astyages became Croesus'

brother-in-law. A rebel band of nomadic Scythians slipped into Median territory, which was ruled at the time by Cyaxares, who was the son of Phraortes and grandson of Deioces. At first Cyaxares treated the Scythians well, on the grounds that they had come to him as suppliants; in fact, he thought highly enough of them to entrust some teenage boys to them, to learn their language and their skill at archery.

Time passed. Now, the Scythians used to go out hunting all the time and they always brought something back for Cyaxares. One day, however, they were unlucky and failed to catch anything. When they returned empty-handed, Cyaxares (who was obviously a hot-tempered man) treated them in an extremely harsh and humiliating manner. They felt that this treatment from Cyaxares was unwarranted, and they decided after consideration to chop up one of their young pupils, prepare him for the table in the way that they had usually prepared wild animals, and serve him up to Cyaxares as if he were really game from their hunting; they planned to make their way then as quickly as possible to Alyattes the son of Sadyattes in Sardis. This is exactly what happened. Cyaxares and his guests in feasting ate some of this meat and the Scythians who had done the deed sought refuge with Alyattes.

[74] After this, Cyaxares demanded the return of the Scythians, but Alyattes refused to hand them over, so war broke out between the Lydians and the Medes. The war lasted for five years and although plenty of battles went the Medes' way, just as many went the Lydians' way too. They even once fought a kind of night battle. In the sixth year, when neither side had a clear advantage over the other in the war, an engagement took place and it so happened that in the middle of the battle day suddenly became night. Thales of Miletus had predicted this loss of daylight to the Ionians by establishing in advance that it would happen within the limits of the year in which it did in fact happen. When the Lydians and the Medes saw that night had replaced day, they did not just stop fighting; both sides also more actively wanted an end to the war. Peace between them was brokered by Syennesis of Cilicia and Labynetus of Babylon, who were anxious that the two sides should enter into a formal peace treaty and arranged for there to be mutual ties of marriage between them. That is, they decided that Alyattes should give his daughter Aryenis in marriage to Cyaxares' son Astyages, on the grounds that strong treaties tend not to last in the absence

of strong ties. These peoples formalize their treaties in the same way the Greeks do, with the extra feature that when they cut into the skin of their arms, each party licks the other's blood.

[75] So this was the Astyages whom—for reasons I shall explain in a later narrative—Cyrus had defeated and was holding captive, despite the fact that Astyages was his mother's father. It was because Croesus had this complaint against Cyrus that he sent emissaries to the oracle to see if he should attack Persia. And so, when he received the ambiguous response from the oracle, he assumed that it was favourable to him and invaded Persian territory.

When Croesus reached the Halys he next used existing bridges to get his army across. At least, that is what I think, but the usual account of the Greeks is that Thales of Miletus got the army across. The story goes that Croesus did not know how his troops were going to cross the river, since the bridges I mentioned were not in existence at the time. But Thales was in the camp, and he helped Croesus by making the river flow on both sides of the army, instead of only to the left. This is how he did it, they say. He started upstream, above the army, and dug a deep channel which was curved in such a way that it would pass behind the army's encampment; in this way he diverted the river from its original bed into the channel, and then, once he had got it past the army, he brought it back round to its original bed again. The immediate result of this division of the river was that it became fordable on both sides. There are those who go so far as to claim that the original river-bed completely dried up, but I find this implausible, because if it were true, how would they have crossed the river on their way back?

[76] Once Croesus and his army were across the river, they found themselves in the part of Cappadocia called Pteria, which is the most impregnable region of Cappadocia and lies more or less on a line with the town of Sinope on the Euxine Sea. Croesus established a camp there and set about destroying the Syrians' farms. He captured the capital of Pteria and reduced the inhabitants to slavery, and he also overran the outlying settlements, forcing the Syrian population to become refugees, even though they had not offered him any provocation. Meanwhile Cyrus mustered his army and went to meet Croesus, conscripting all the inhabitants of the regions he passed through on the way. Before setting off with his

army on this expedition, he had sent messengers to the Ionians and tried to incite them to rebel against Croesus, but the Ionians had refused to listen. Anyway, Cyrus reached Pteria and positioned his army opposite Croesus' camp, so Pteria was the site of the trial of strength between the two armies. A fierce battle took place, with heavy losses on both sides, but by nightfall, when the two armies separated, neither side had won.

[77] Now, the army with which Croesus had gone into battle was much smaller than that of Cyrus, and he blamed his lack of success on the number of troops he had. So when Cyrus did not come out to engage him the next day, Croesus pulled his army back to Sardis. What he planned to do was this. He had made an alliance with the Egyptian king Amasis, which preceded his alliance with Lacedaemon, and he had also entered into a similar treaty with the Babylonians too (whose ruler at the time was Labynetus). He intended to send for the Egyptians and the Babylonians, according to their sworn promises, as well as telling the Lacedaemonians to come at a specified time; then, once they were all present and he had mustered his own army too, he would let the winter go by and attack the Persians as soon as it was spring. With these thoughts in mind, when he got back to Sardis he dispatched heralds to his various allies, calling on them to assemble in Sardis in four months' time. As for the army he already had, the one which had engaged the Persians, he dismissed the foreign element in its entirety and let them return to their various homes, because he never actually expected Cyrus to march on Sardis after they had been so evenly matched in their first contest.

[78] While Croesus was making these plans, all the outskirts of the city became infested with snakes, and as they appeared the horses used to stop grazing in their pastures, walk over to where the snakes were, and eat them. This struck Croesus as ominous— as indeed it was—and he immediately sent emissaries to Telmessus, to the shrine where omens were interpreted. The emissaries arrived and were told by the Telmessians what the omen meant, but they could not make their report to Croesus, because he was in enemy hands before they completed their voyage back to Sardis. However, the Telmessians' interpretation was that Croesus should expect a foreign army to invade his land and overcome the local inhabitants; a snake, they said, is a child of the earth, while a horse is a hostile intruder. So this was the reply the Telmessians gave to Croesus'

question; although he had already been captured, at the time they had not heard what had happened in Sardis and to Croesus.

[79] As soon as Croesus withdrew his troops after the battle in Pteria, Cyrus learnt that he intended to disband his men. After some thought, he realized that he had better march as quickly as possible on Sardis, before the Lydian forces could gather for the second time. No sooner had he come to this decision than he put it into action and marched into Lydia. He himself was the messenger through whom Croesus heard of his arrival. This put Croesus into an impossible situation, because things had not gone according to his expectations; nevertheless, he led his troops out to battle. The Lydians were the most courageous and warlike race in Asia at that time; they fought on horseback, carried long spears, and were superb horsemen.

[80] The two sides met on the plain in front of the city of Sardis. This plain is broad and bare, with a number of rivers flowing through it, including the Hyllus. All these rivers are tributaries of the largest river, the Hermus, which rises in the mountain sacred to Mother Dindymene and issues into the sea by the town of Phocaea. When Cyrus saw the Lydians forming up for battle on this plain, he realized that the Lydian cavalry was a threat, so he adopted the following tactics, which were suggested to him by a Mede called Harpagus. There were camels with the army, used to carry food and baggage. Cyrus had them all collected and unloaded, and then he mounted men on them in full cavalry gear. Once the men were ready, he ordered them to advance against Croesus' cavalry with the rest of the army following them—first the infantry behind the camels, and then his entire regular cavalry bringing up the rear. When all his troops had taken up their positions, he commanded them to kill every Lydian they came across without mercy, but to spare Croesus, even if he was resisting capture. These were his instructions. He had the camels positioned to confront the cavalry because horses are afraid of camels and cannot stand either their sight or their smell. In other words, the reason for the stratagem was to disable Croesus' cavalry, which was in fact exactly the part of his army with which Croesus had intended to make a mark. So battle was joined, and as soon as the horses smelled and saw the camels, they turned tail and Croesus' hopes were destroyed. However, this did not turn the Lydians into cowards; when they realized what was happening, they leapt off

their horses and engaged the Persians on foot. Losses on both sides were heavy, but eventually the Lydians were pushed back to the city, where they were trapped behind their walls and besieged by the Persians.

[81] So the Persians were besieging the city. Croesus expected the siege to last a long time, so he sent men out of the city with further dispatches for his allies. Whereas the men he had sent before had taken messages requesting the allies to gather in Sardis in four months' time, this current lot of messengers were to ask them to come and help as quickly as possible, since he was under siege.

[82] The men were dispatched to all his allies, including the Lacedaemonians. Now, it so happened that the Lacedaemonians themselves were at that time engaged in a dispute with Argos about the region known as Thyreae. The Lacedaemonians had taken over this place Thyreae, which had been part of Argive territory, and were occupying it. (Argive territory extended as far west as Malea and included not only the mainland but also the island of Cythera and the rest of the islands there as well.) When the Argives came to reclaim the land the Lacedaemonians had taken, the two sides got together and agreed that three hundred men from each army would fight and that whichever side won would keep the land. The bulk of each army, however, would disperse and return to within its own borders and not stay during the fight; this was to prevent either side being in a position to come and help their own men, if they saw them being beaten. Once these terms had been agreed, the two armies dispersed except for the selected men who were left behind to fight, which they proceeded to do. The contest between them was so evenly matched that eventually only three men remained out of the six hundred—Alcenor and Chromius for the Argives and Orthryades for the Lacedaemonians. They were the only survivors at nightfall. At that point, the two Argives assumed that they were the winners and hurried away to Argos, while Orthryades the Lacedaemonian stripped the Argive corpses, carried their weapons back to his own camp, and held the position he had been assigned. The next day both sides came to find out what had happened. At first, they each claimed the victory for themselves: the Argives argued that more of their men had survived, while the Lacedaemonians pointed out that although the others had fled the battlefield, their own man had stayed and stripped the Argive

corpses. In the end, the quarrel spilled over into fighting. Losses on both sides were heavy, but the Lacedaemonians won.

Ever since then, the Argives have cut their hair short, although they had previously been required to wear it long. They made it a rule, sealed with a curse, that no Argive man should grow his hair and that the women were not to wear gold until they had recovered Thyreae. The Lacedaemonians, however, instituted the opposite custom; although they had previously kept their hair short, they now started to wear it long. They also say that Orthryades, the sole survivor of the three hundred, was too ashamed to return to Sparta when all his comrades had died, and committed suicide right there in Thyreae.

[83] That was the situation facing the Spartiates when the herald arrived from Sardis to ask them to come and help Croesus lift the siege. Despite their problems, the Spartiate response to the man's news was to set about providing help. But in the middle of their preparations, when their ships were ready, another message came, this time with the news that the Lydian city had fallen and that Croesus had been taken prisoner. So, with a sense of deep regret, the Spartiates called off their preparations.

[84] This is how Sardis fell. On the fourteenth day of the siege, Cyrus sent riders to the various contingents of his army and announced that there would be a reward for the first man to scale the wall. This induced his men to try, but without success. Then, when everyone else had given up, a Mardian called Hyroeades went up to have a go at a particular part of the acropolis where no guard had been posted, because the steepness and unassailability of the acropolis at that spot had led people to believe that there was no danger of its ever being taken there. Even Meles, the past king of Sardis, had omitted this spot when he was carrying around the acropolis the lion to which his concubine had given birth, in response to the Telmessian judgement that Sardis would never be captured if the lion was carried around the walls. Meles carried it around the rest of the wall, where the acropolis was open to attack, but he ignored this place because of its unassailability and steepness. It is on the side of the city which faces Tmolus. Anyway, this Mardian, Hyroeades, had the day before seen a Lydian climb down this part of the acropolis after his helmet (which had rolled down the slope) and retrieve it. He noted this and thought about it, then he led a band of Persians in the ascent. Soon a lot of them had

climbed up, and then Sardis was captured and the whole city was sacked.

[85] As for Croesus himself, here is what happened. As I mentioned earlier, he had a son who was fine in other respects, but could not speak. In the past, when things were going well, Croesus had done everything possible for him; he had tried all kinds of plans, including sending men to Delphi to ask about him. The Pythia's reply was as follows:

> Croesus of Lydia, ruler of many, you are being very foolish.
> You should not desire to hear in your home the sound you
>   have long prayed for
> Of your son speaking. It is far better for you not to,
> For you will hear it first on a day of misfortune.

Now, during the capture of the city, a Persian soldier failed to recognize Croesus and came up to kill him. Croesus saw him coming, but was too overwhelmed by the catastrophe that was taking place to care: it did not matter to him that he might be put to the sword and die. But this son of his, the one who could not speak, was so frightened and upset at the sight of the Persian approaching that he burst into speech and said, 'Man, don't kill Croesus.' These were the first words he ever spoke, but after that he carried on speaking for the rest of his life.

[86] So the Persians took Sardis and captured Croesus himself. His rule had lasted fourteen years, the siege had lasted fourteen days, and as the oracle had foretold he had put an end to a great empire—his own. The Persians took their prisoner to Cyrus, who built a huge funeral pyre and made Croesus (who was tied up) and fourteen Lydian boys climb up to the top. Perhaps he intended them to be a victory-offering for some god or other, or perhaps he wanted to fulfil a vow he had made, or perhaps he had heard that Croesus was a god-fearing man and he made him get up on to the pyre because he wanted to see if any immortal being would rescue him from being burnt alive. Anyway, that is what he did. Meanwhile (the story goes), although Croesus' situation up on top of the pyre was desperate, his mind turned to Solon's saying that no one who is still alive is happy, and it occurred to him how divinely inspired Solon had been to say that. This thought made him sigh and groan, and he broke a long silence by repeating the name 'Solon' three times.

When Cyrus heard him, he told his translators to ask Croesus who it was he was calling on. The translators went up and asked him. At first Croesus made no reply, but then, when he was coerced, he said, 'Someone whom I would give a fortune to have every ruler in the world meet.' This was meaningless to them, of course, so they repeated their question. When they persisted and crowded around him, he told them how Solon had arrived at his court in the first place, all the way from Athens, how he had seen all his wealth and dismissed it as rubbish (or words to that effect), and how in his case everything had turned out as Solon had said it would, although his words applied to the whole of mankind—and particularly to those who thought themselves well off—just as much as they did to him. Now, the pyre had been lit, and as Croesus was telling his story, flames were licking around its edges. But when the translators relayed the story to Cyrus, he had a change of heart. He saw that he was burning alive a fellow human being, one who had been just as well off as he was; also, he was afraid of retribution, and reflected on the total lack of certainty in human life. So he told his men to waste no time in dousing the flames and getting Croesus and the others down from the pyre. When they tried, however, they found it was too late—the fire was out of control.

[87] What happened next, according to the Lydian account, was this. Croesus realized that Cyrus had changed his mind. When he saw that it was too late for them to control the fire, despite everyone's efforts to quench it, he called on Apollo. 'If any gift of mine has pleased you,' he cried, 'come now and rescue me from this danger.' Weeping, he called on the god, and suddenly the clear, calm weather was replaced by gathering clouds; a storm broke, rain lashed down, and the pyre was extinguished.

As a result of this, Cyrus realized that Croesus was in the gods' favour and was a good man. So once he had got Croesus down from the pyre he asked him who had persuaded him to invade his country and be his enemy rather than his friend. 'My lord,' Croesus replied, 'it was my doing. You have gained and I have lost from it. But responsibility lies with the god of the Greeks who encouraged me to make war on you. After all, no one is stupid enough to prefer war to peace; in peace sons bury their fathers and in war fathers bury their sons. However, I suppose the god must have wanted this to happen.'

[88] That is what Croesus said. Cyrus untied him and had him seated near by. He was very impressed with him, and he and his whole entourage admired the man's demeanour. But Croesus was silent, deep in thought. Then he turned and at the sight of the Persians looting the Lydian city he said, 'My lord, shall I tell you what just occurred to me or is this an inappropriate time for me to speak?'

Cyrus told him not to worry and to say whatever he wanted, so Croesus asked, 'What are all these people rushing around and doing so eagerly?'

'They are sacking your city,' Cyrus replied, 'and carrying off your property.'

'No,' Croesus replied. 'It's not my city and property they are stealing; none of it belongs to me any more. It is your property they are plundering.'

[89] Cyrus was intrigued by Croesus' words, so he dismissed everyone else and asked Croesus what, in his opinion, the situation held for him. Croesus answered, 'Since the gods have given me to you as your slave, I consider it my duty to pass on to you any special insights I have. Persians are naturally aggressive, and they are not used to possessions. So if you just stand by and let them loot and keep all this valuable property, you should expect the one who gets hold of the most to initiate a coup against you. However, I have a suggestion to make, which you might like. Put men from your personal guard on sentry duty at all the city gates and have them take the spoils away from those who are trying to bring them out of the city, on the pretext that a tenth of it has to be offered to Zeus. Under these circumstances, you won't be hated for the forcible removal of their property; they will appreciate the rightness of what you're doing and willingly hand it over.'

[90] Cyrus was delighted with what Croesus was saying; he thought the suggestion was excellent. He was full of praise for Croesus and told his personal guards to put Croesus' idea into practice. Then he said to Croesus, 'Your royal background, Croesus, has not affected your ability to do good deeds and offer sound advice. Whatever you would like me to give you will be yours straight away; you have only to ask.'

'Master,' Croesus replied, 'nothing would give me more pleasure than to be allowed to send these shackles of mine to the god of the

Greeks, whom I revered more than any other god, and to ask him if it is his normal practice to trick his benefactors.'

Cyrus asked what wrong he thought the god had done him, that he was making this request, and Croesus told him the whole story of his plans and the oracle's replies; he emphasized the offerings he had dedicated and told how he had marched against the Persians because of the oracle's encouragement. He concluded by repeating his request for permission to go and make this complaint against the god. Cyrus laughed and said, 'Yes, of course you have my permission, Croesus, and the same goes for future requests of yours too.'

Croesus took Cyrus at his word and sent a delegation of Lydians to Delphi. He told them to lay the shackles on the threshold of the temple and ask the god if he was not ashamed to have used his oracles to encourage Croesus to march against the Persians by leading him to believe that he would put an end to Cyrus' empire—an empire which produced victory-offerings like *these*, they were to say, pointing to the shackles. And they were also to ask whether Greek gods were normally so ungrateful.

[91] The Lydians went to Delphi and said what Croesus had told them to say. The Pythia's reply, we are told, was as follows: 'Not even a god can escape his ordained fate. Croesus has paid for the crime of his ancestor four generations ago, who, though a member of the personal guard of the Heraclidae, gave in to a woman's guile, killed his master, and assumed a station which was not rightfully his at all. In fact, Loxias wanted the fall of Sardis to happen in the time of Croesus' sons rather than of Croesus himself, but it was not possible to divert the Fates. However, he won a concession from them and did Croesus that much good: he managed to delay the fall of Sardis for three years. Croesus should appreciate, then, that his capture has happened that much later than was ordained. In the second place, Loxias came to his help when he was on the pyre. Moreover, Croesus has no grounds for complaint as regards the oracle. Loxias predicted that if he invaded Persia, he would destroy a great empire. Faced with this, if he had thought about it he would have sent men to enquire whether Loxias meant Cyrus' empire or his own. Because he misunderstood the statement and failed to follow it up with another enquiry, he should blame no one but himself for what happened. Then again, in response to his final question Loxias told him about a mule, but Croesus misunderstood

this too. The point is that Cyrus is this mule, because he comes from parents of different nationalities. His mother was of nobler lineage, since she was a Mede and a daughter of Astyages the Median king, but his father was of baser blood, since he was a Persian and a subject of the Medes—so it was his own mistress he married, despite being her inferior in all these ways.'

This was the Pythia's response to the Lydians. They took it back to Sardis and relayed the statement to Croesus. When he heard it he realized that the fault was his and not the god's.

[92] That is the story of Croesus' reign and the first conquest of Ionia. Greece holds plenty of other votive offerings made by Croesus besides the ones already mentioned. In Boeotian Thebes, for instance, there is a golden tripod which he dedicated to Ismenian Apollo; in Ephesus the golden cows and most of the pillars were set up by Croesus; in the temple of Athena Before the Temple at Delphi there is a huge golden shield. These offerings of his were still surviving in my day, although others have perished. In Branchidae in Miletus there are, I hear, offerings made by Croesus which are equal in weight and similar in kind to those he made at Delphi. The ones he dedicated at Delphi and at the shrine of Amphiaraus were his own property (in fact, they were a proportion of the estate he inherited from his father), but the rest came from the estate of one of his enemies, a man who had become an adversary of Croesus by supporting Pantaleon's bid for power before Croesus became king. Pantaleon was the son of Alyattes, but Croesus and he were only half-brothers, since Croesus was born to Alyattes from a Carian wife, while Pantaleon's mother was Ionian. Once his father had bequeathed control of the kingdom to him, Croesus tortured this opponent of his to death by having him hauled over a carding-comb. Then, as I have already said, he sent the man's property (which he had previously consecrated) to the places mentioned. So much for his dedicatory offerings.

[93] Compared with other countries, Lydia does not really have any marvels which are worth recording, except for the gold-dust which is washed down from Mount Tmolus. However, there is one edifice in Lydia which is by far the biggest in the world, with the exception of those in Egypt and Babylon, and this is the tomb of Alyattes, Croesus' father. The base of the tomb is made out of huge blocks of stone, and the rest of it is a mound of earth. It was built by traders, artisans, and prostitutes. Even in my day there were five

plaques at the top of the tomb, engraved with a written record of
what each of these three groups had done, which prove, when the
figures are added up, that the prostitutes made the greatest contribution. The point is that the daughters of every lower-class Lydian
family work as prostitutes so that they can accumulate enough of
a dowry to enable them to get married, and they arrange their own
marriages. The circumference of the tomb is six stades and two
plethra, and it is thirteen plethra in breadth. Near the tomb there
is a large lake called Lake Gyges, which never dries up, according
to the Lydians. That is what Alyattes' tomb is like.

[94] Apart from this practice of having their female children
work as prostitutes, Lydian customs are not very different from
Greek ones. They were the first people we know of to strike gold
and silver coins and use them, and so they were also the first to
retail goods. According to native Lydian tradition, the games which
both they and the Greeks at present have in common were invented
by them. They claim that the invention of these games coincided
with their colonization of Tyrrhenia, and here is what they say
about it. During the reign of Atys the son of Manes there was a
severe famine throughout Lydia. At first, the Lydians patiently
endured it, but as it went on and on they tried to find some ways
to alleviate the situation, and a number of different ideas were proposed by different people. Anyway, according to them, that was
how they came to invent all sorts of games, including dice, knuckle-
bones, and ball games. The only game the Lydians do not claim to
have invented themselves is backgammon. Once they had invented
all these games, they say, their procedure with regard to the famine
was as follows. They spent the whole of every alternate day playing
games, so that they would not want food, and then on the days in
between they would stop playing and eat.

Eighteen years passed in this way, and there was still no end to
their troubles; in fact, they just got worse. Then their king divided
the whole population into two groups and drew lots to decide
which group would stay in Lydia and which would emigrate. He
appointed himself the ruler of those who were to stay there, and
he put his son, who was called Tyrrhenus, in command of the
emigrants. The group whose lot it was to leave their country
made their way down to Smyrna, where they built ships for themselves. They put on board all the equipment they might need and
sailed away in search of land and livelihood. Their journey took

them past a number of peoples, but eventually they reached the Ombricians, where they founded settlements and still live to this day. But they changed their name and instead of 'Lydians' they named themselves after the king's son, who had led them there—that is, they made up a name for themselves based on his and called themselves Tyrrhenians. So the Lydians were reduced to slavery under the Persians.

[95] The next task of this account of ours is to learn more about Cyrus, the man who destroyed Croesus' empire, and about how the Persians came to be the leading race in Asia. My version will be based on what certain Persians say, those who seek to tell the truth rather than exalt Cyrus' achievements. But I know of three other versions of the Cyrus story.

Assyrian dominance of inland Asia had lasted for 520 years when the Medes first rebelled against them. In fact, their war of independence against the Assyrians improved them; they cast off the yoke of slavery and became free men. Their example was later followed by all the rest of the peoples who made up the Assyrian empire.

[96] After gaining their independence, however, the mainland peoples all returned to a state of tyranny. There was a clever Mede called Deioces (whose father's name was Phraortes), who had designs on becoming a tyrant. This is what he did. Deioces was already a person of some standing in his village (the Medes used to live in village communities), and now he began to practise integrity in a more wholehearted and thorough fashion—and did so, what is more, even though there was at the time considerable lawlessness throughout Media, because he was well aware of the incompatibility of lawlessness and justice. The Medes from his village noticed his conduct and appointed him their judge, and he did in fact behave with integrity and honesty, since he was courting power. This conduct of his earned him a great deal of praise from his fellow citizens—so much so that his reputation for being the only man to give fair judgements spread to the other villages. When people there heard about Deioces, they began to go to him and let him judge their cases too, and they were happy to do so, because they had previously met with unfair judgements; eventually, he was the only one they ever turned to.

[97] The number of people coming to him was constantly increasing, as they heard that the truth determined the outcome of

the cases he tried. When Deioces realized that everything was being referred to him, he started to refuse to take the seat where he had previously sat to deliver his verdicts, and he said that he would no longer try cases, on the grounds that it was doing him no good to spend his days hearing others' cases to the neglect of his own affairs. When theft and lawlessness returned to the villages, and on a far greater scale than before, the Medes met and considered what action to take under the circumstances. I suspect that Deioces' supporters played a major part in this debate. 'The country is ungovernable', they said, 'on our current system, so let's make one of us king. Then the country will be well governed and we'll be able to concentrate on our jobs instead of losing our homes thanks to lawlessness.' That was more or less the argument which convinced them of the need for monarchy.

[98] They were immediately faced with the question of whom to appoint as king. Everyone was full of praise for Deioces and wholeheartedly endorsed his nomination, until at length they agreed that he should be their king. He ordered them to build him a palace fit for a king and to assign him personal guards for his protection, and the Medes did so: they built him a large, secure residence in a part of the country he designated, and they let him pick his personal guards from among the whole Median population. Once power was in his hands, Deioces insisted that the Medes build a single city and maintain this one place, which involved caring less for their other communities. The Medes obeyed him in this too; they built the place which is now known as Ecbatana—a huge, impregnable stronghold consisting of concentric circles of defensive walls. This stronghold is designed so that each successive circle is higher than the one below it just by the height of its bastions. This design is helped, of course, to a certain extent by the fact that the place is on a hill, but it was also deliberately made that way. There are seven circles altogether, and the innermost one contains the royal palace and the treasuries. The largest of the walls is approximately the same size as the wall around Athens. The bastions of the outer five circles have all been painted various colours—first white, then black, red, blue, and orange. But as for the bastions of the last two circles, the first are covered in silver and the second in gold.

[99] So Deioces had this stronghold built for himself, surrounding his own residence, but he told the whole population to

build their houses outside the stronghold. Once the building programme was completed, Deioces was the first to establish the following rules: no one was to enter into the king's presence, but all
business was to be conducted through messengers; the king was to
be seen by no one; and furthermore absolutely no one was to
commit the offence of laughing or spitting in the king's presence.
The reason he instituted this grandiose system of how to behave in
relation to himself was to prevent any of his peers seeing him. They
had been brought up with him, their lineage was no worse than
his, and they were just as brave as he was, so he was worried that
if they saw him they might get irritated and conspire against him;
on the other hand, if they could not see him, they might think that
he had changed.

[100] Once he had established this system and had used his position as tyrant to protect himself, he became a harsh champion of
justice. People used to write their suits down and send them in to
him, and then he would assess them and send his verdicts back out.
That was how he dealt with lawsuits. Another system he instituted
was that if he heard that an offence had been committed, he would
have the perpetrator brought to him and then inflict on him the
punishment the crime deserved. And he had people spying and listening for him throughout his kingdom.

[101] Anyway, Deioces united the Median people (but only
the Median people) and ruled over it. The Medes consist of the
following tribes: the Busae, Paretacenians, Struchates, Arizanti,
Budians, and Magi. These are all the tribes of the Medes there
are.

[102] Deioces ruled for fifty-three years and then, after his
death, his son Phraortes succeeded to the kingdom. Phraortes,
however, was not satisfied with ruling Media alone. He made war
on Persia, which was only the first country he attacked—and the
first he made a subject state. Afterwards, with two strong peoples
under his command, he conquered Asia tribe by tribe. Eventually
his campaigns brought him into conflict with Assyria, and in particular those of the Assyrians who held Ninus. Although these
Assyrians had formerly controlled the whole country, they had subsequently been abandoned by their allies, who all rebelled from
them. Nevertheless, they were still prosperous, and in his war
against them a major part of Phraortes' army was wiped out, and
he himself was killed, having reigned for twenty-two years.

[103] After Phraortes' death, Cyaxares became king; he was Phraortes' son and Deioces' grandson, and to judge by the stories, he was far more warlike than even his predecessors. He was the first to divide his Asian troops into regiments and to make separate units out of the spearmen, archers, and horsemen, who had previously all been jumbled up indiscriminately. He is the one who was fighting with the Lydians when the eclipse occurred, and who united the whole of inland Asia—the part beyond the River Halys—under his control. Then he gathered all his subjects together and marched on Ninus, to take revenge for his father's defeat. He intended to destroy Ninus, and he did defeat the Assyrians in battle, but during his siege of the city he was attacked by a huge Scythian army, led by their king Madyes the son of Protothyes. The Scythians had driven the Cimmerians out of Europe and, as the Cimmerians fled into Asia, the Scythians followed them. That is how they came to invade Asia and in due course to reach Median territory.

[104] From Lake Maeetis to the River Phasis and Colchis is a thirty-day journey for a man travelling light, and then it does not take long to cross over from Colchis to Median territory. There is only one race in between, the Saspeires, and Median territory begins immediately after theirs. However, this was not the path of the Scythian invasion; they turned aside and took the much longer upper route, with the Caucasian mountains on their right. Then the Medes and the Scythians clashed; the Medes lost the battle, their empire crumbled and the Scythians occupied the whole of Asia.

[105] From there they marched on Egypt. When they reached Syrian Palestine, the Egyptian king Psammetichus came to meet them. With a combination of bribery and entreaty he persuaded them not to go any further and they turned back. On their way back they came to the town of Ascalon in Syria. Most of the Scythians bypassed the town without doing it any harm, but a few of them, who had fallen behind the main body, plundered the sanctuary of Heavenly Aphrodite. As I learnt by enquiry, this sanctuary is the oldest of all the sanctuaries of Heavenly Aphrodite. Even the temple on Cyprus was founded from this one, as the Cyprians themselves acknowledge, and the one on Cythera was founded by Phoenicians who came from this part of the world—that is, from Syria. The goddess afflicted the Scythians who plundered her temple in Ascalon and all their descendants for ever with

hermaphroditism. And so, as well as admitting that this is why they suffer from this disease, the Scythians also tell visitors to their country that they can see the condition of these people, whom the Scythians call *enareis*.*

[106] The Scythian domination of Asia lasted twenty-eight years, and their expulsion came about because of their abusive and disdainful attitude. It was not just that they used to exact a tax which they imposed on every single individual, but also that, as if the tax was not enough, they used to ride around and plunder people's belongings. Cyaxares and the Medes invited a great many of them to a feast, got them drunk, and then killed them. So the Medes regained their empire and took control again of the same peoples as before. They also took Ninus (I will explain how elsewhere) and subdued all of Assyria except for Babylon and its territory. Some time later Cyaxares died, after a reign of forty years (including the years of Scythian domination).

[107] Cyaxares' son Astyages succeeded to the kingdom. Now, he had a daughter called Mandane, and he dreamt that she urinated so much that she not only filled his city, but even flooded the whole of Asia. He described this dream to some of the Magi who could interpret dreams, and the details of what they told him frightened him. The time came when Mandane was old enough to marry. Although there were Medes of his rank, his fear of the dream made him refuse to marry her to any of them; instead, he gave her to a Persian called Cambyses, whom he found to be of noble lineage and peaceful behaviour, although he regarded him as the social inferior by far of a Mede of the middle rank.

[108] A few months after Mandane married Cambyses, Astyages had another dream in which a vine grew from Mandane's genitals and overshadowed the whole of Asia. He told the dream-interpreters what he had seen and then had his daughter, who was pregnant, sent from Persia. When she came, he kept a close watch on her, because he wanted to kill the child she was carrying; for the Magi had interpreted his dream to mean that his daughter's offspring would rule in his place. So that was what Astyages was guarding against. When Cyrus was born, Astyages summoned a relative of his called Harpagus; there was no one among the Medes

---

* For *enareis* and other words foreign to Herodotus, see the Glossary of Foreign Words Used by Herodotus on pp. 742–4.

he trusted more, and Harpagus was the steward of all his property. 'Harpagus,' he said, 'you should never disregard any job I ask you to do for me, nor should you betray me and side with others rather than me: you would be encompassing your own downfall later. I want you to get the baby Mandane bore, take him to your own home, and kill him. How you bury the body is up to you.'

'My lord,' Harpagus replied, 'you have never detected the slightest fault in me in the past, and I am constantly alert to the danger of offending you at any time in the future too. If this is what you would like to happen, it is my duty to serve and obey.'

[109] That was the reply Harpagus gave. The child was handed over to him, dressed for its death, and he set off weeping for home. When he got there he told his wife everything that Astyages had said.

'And what do you think you're going to do?' she asked him.

'Not what Astyages told me,' he replied. 'Even if he gets even more deranged and demented than he is now, I won't go along with his plan or serve him in this kind of murder. There are plenty of reasons why I won't kill the child, not the least of which is that he's a relative of mine. Also, Astyages is old now, but has no male offspring. Suppose, when he dies, that the tyranny devolves on to Mandane, whose son he is now using me to kill. The only possible outcome for me will be that my life will be in danger. Still, for the sake of my own safety, the child has to die, but it must be one of Astyages' men who commits the murder and not one of mine.'

[110] No sooner said than done. He sent a message to a man called Mitradates, who of all Astyages' herdsmen was the one who, Harpagus knew, pastured his cattle in countryside that particularly suited his purpose—that is, in mountains full of wild animals. He lived with another slave, his wife, whose name, translated into Greek, was Cyno or 'bitch', because her Median name was Spaco, and the Median word for a female dog is *spaka*. The foothills of the mountains, where this herdsman grazed his cattle, are north of Ecbatana in the direction of the Euxine Sea. That part of Media, where it borders on the territory of the Saspeires, is very mountainous, high, and wooded, whereas the whole of the rest of the country is flat. The herdsman responded to Harpagus' summons very promptly, and when he arrived Harpagus said, 'Astyages wants this child dead as quickly as possible, so it is his command

that you take it and leave it in the most remote part of the mountains. He also told me to tell you that if you do not kill the child,
but keep it alive in some way, he will put you to death in the
most terrible fashion. And I have been ordered to see the child
exposed.'

[111] The herdsman listened to what Harpagus had to say,
picked up the child, and retraced his steps back to his hut. Now,
this same herdsman's wife was in fact due to go into labour any
day, and by a kind of providence she gave birth while the herdsman was travelling to the city. Each of them was concerned for the
other: the herdsman was worried about his wife going into labour
and she was worried about the unusual summons her husband had
received from Harpagus. When he got back and she saw him unexpectedly standing there, she was the first to speak; she asked him
why Harpagus had been so eager to send for him. He replied, 'My
dear, the things I've seen and heard while I was in the city! I wish
I hadn't. It should never have happened to our masters. The whole
of Harpagus' household was given over to weeping and wailing.
I didn't know what to make of it, but I went inside. As soon as I
was inside, I saw a baby lying there wriggling and bawling, wearing
golden jewellery and fancy clothes. Harpagus saw me and told me
to pick the baby up straight away and to take it with me and leave
it somewhere in the mountains, wherever there are the most wild
animals. He said that these orders came to me from Astyages, who
had also threatened me, repeating over and over what would
happen to me if I didn't carry them out. So I picked the baby up
and took it with me. I imagined that the mother was one of the
house-slaves; I certainly couldn't have guessed where it really came
from. But I was surprised to see the gold and clothes it was wearing,
and then there was the open weeping and wailing in Harpagus'
house. Anyway, an attendant escorted me out of the city and
handed the baby over to me, and as soon as we set out he told me
the whole story. It turns out that it is actually the child of Mandane
the daughter of Astyages and Cambyses the son of Cyrus, and
Astyages told him to kill it. And now here it is.'

[112] With these words, the herdsman uncovered the child and
showed it to his wife. When she saw the healthy, good-looking
baby, she burst into tears, flung her arms around her husband's
knees and begged him not to expose it on the mountainside under
any circumstances. He said that he had no choice in the matter,

because Harpagus was going to send people to check up on them, and that he would die a horrible death if he did not carry out his instructions. The woman could not win her husband over, so she tried a different approach and said, 'Since I can't persuade you not to expose the child, here's what I suggest you do, if it's absolutely inevitable that the exposed infant is to be seen. You see, I gave birth too, but it was stillborn. So why don't you take my baby and leave it out there, and we can bring up the son of Astyages' daughter as if he were our own? If you do this, you won't be caught deceiving our masters, and the plan also works well for us because the baby which is already dead will receive a royal burial and the one which is still alive will not lose his life.'

[113] The herdsman thought that his wife's suggestion was excellent, under the circumstances, and he immediately set about putting it into practice. The child he had brought to kill he handed over to his wife, while he took his own dead child and put it in the container he had used to carry the other one. Then he dressed it up in all the other baby's clothes, took it to the most remote part of the mountains, and left it there. Two days after exposing the child, the herdsman travelled to the city, leaving one of the under-herdsmen to guard it; he went to Harpagus and said that he was ready to show the baby's body to him. Harpagus sent his most trusted personal guards, and they carried out an inspection on his behalf and buried the herdsman's child. So the one child lay in its grave, while the other—the one who was later called Cyrus—was adopted and brought up by the herdsman's wife, although she called him something else, not Cyrus.

[114] Now, the boy's identity was revealed when he was 10 years old. This, or something like this, is what happened. He was in the same village, the one where the royal herds were, playing with other boys his age in the road. The game involved the boys choosing someone to be their king, and they chose him—the one they called the herdsman's son. He gave them various jobs to do: some built houses, some formed his bodyguard, one of them was the King's Eye, and one of them was privileged enough to be allowed to bring messages in to him. To each of them he assigned a task. Now, one of his playmates, who was the son of an eminent Mede called Artembares, refused to carry out one of Cyrus' orders, so Cyrus told the other boys to grab him. They did so, and Cyrus gave the boy a very severe thrashing. The boy was furious at having

received what he regarded as a humiliating punishment, and as soon as he was free he went to the city and complained to his father of the way Cyrus had treated him—except that he did not say it was Cyrus, because that was not yet his name; he said that it was the son of Astyages' herdsman. Artembares went in an angry frame of mind to Astyages and told him about the horrific treatment his son—whom he had brought with him—had received. He showed Astyages the boy's shoulders and said, 'My lord, look at the insolent way we have been treated by one of your slaves, the son of a herdsman.'

[115] Astyages listened to him and saw the evidence. He decided to punish the boy because of Artembares' position in society, and so he sent for the herdsman and the child. When they both arrived, Astyages fixed his gaze on Cyrus and said, 'So did you assault this boy? Did you—and we know what your father is—did you assault this man's son, the son of the principal man in my kingdom?'

'Yes, master, I did,' Cyrus replied, 'and I was right to do so. You see, some of the village boys, including him'—Cyrus pointed to Artembares' son—'were playing a game and made me their king, since they thought I had what it takes to do the job. All the other boys did what I told them to do, but he went on refusing to do what he was told and ignoring me, until he was punished for it. If that was wrong and I deserve to get into trouble for it, here I am.'

[116] While the boy was speaking, Astyages began to feel that he knew who he was. The boy's features seemed to resemble his own, he spoke like a free man rather than a slave, and his age fitted in with the amount of time that had passed since the exposure of the infant. He was so astonished that for a while he could not speak, but at last, with some difficulty, he pulled himself together. He wanted to send Artembares away in order to get the herdsman by himself and interrogate him, so he said: 'Artembares, I will take care of this matter, and I will do so in a way that will leave you and your son no grounds for complaint.' So he dismissed Artembares and told his attendants to take Cyrus inside. When he and the herdsman were alone, just the two of them together, Astyages asked how he came to have the boy and who it was who gave him to him. The herdsman replied that the boy was his own son and that the boy's mother was still with him. Astyages told him that he was stupid to want to bring terrible punishment down on himself,

and at the same time he gave his guards the signal to seize the man. As he was being led away to torture, he began to tell the truth. Starting from the beginning, he gave an honest and thorough account of what had happened, and finally begged and beseeched Astyages to pardon him.

[117] Astyages was not particularly concerned with the herdsman, now that he had explained what had actually happened, but he was extremely displeased with Harpagus and he told his personal guards to summon him. When Harpagus arrived Astyages asked, 'Harpagus, how exactly did you kill that child I entrusted to you—I mean the one born to my daughter?'

When Harpagus saw the herdsman inside, he decided that his best course was not to lie, in case further questioning caught him out. 'My lord,' he said, 'once I had taken charge of the baby, I got to wondering whether there was a way for me to carry out your wishes and yet, without giving you any reason to find fault with me, to avoid being branded an assassin by your daughter and by myself too. This is what I did. I summoned that herdsman there, gave him the baby, and told him that it was you who had ordered it killed. This at least was no more than the truth, since those were your instructions. But I handed the baby over to him with express instructions to expose it in a remote part of the mountains and to stay there and watch over it until it was dead, and I accompanied these instructions with all kinds of threats against him if he failed to do what he had been told. Once he had carried out my orders and the child was dead, I sent my most trusted eunuchs and they examined the corpse for me and buried him for me. That is what happened in this matter, my lord; that is how the child met his death.'

[118] Harpagus had told him the truth, but Astyages was furious at what at happened. He did not let Harpagus know how angry he was with him, however. First, he repeated for Harpagus' benefit the herdsman's side of the story, and then, once he had been through the whole sequence of events, he finished by telling him that the boy was still alive and that it was all for the best. 'You see,' he said, 'I didn't feel at all good about what I'd done to the boy, and my daughter's hostility towards me was very upsetting. But as it happens, everything has turned out fine. So why don't you send your son to meet this young newcomer, and then join me for dinner? We will celebrate the sacrifice of thanksgiving I am

going to make to the gods who are responsible for keeping the boy safe.'

[119] At these words, Harpagus prostrated himself before the king. He was encouraged by the thought that his offence had turned out to be useful and that in view of the fortunate results he had been invited to dinner, and in this frame of mind he set off home. Now, he had just the one son, a boy of about thirteen years, and as soon as he got home, he sent him to Astyages, with instructions to go there and do whatever he was told. Then in his delight he gave his wife the good news.

However, when Harpagus' son arrived, Astyages murdered him and dismembered him. He baked some of his flesh, stewed the rest, prepared it all for the table, and kept it ready. The time for the meal arrived, and Harpagus and all the other guests presented themselves. The tables were laden; Astyages and the others were served with mutton, but Harpagus was given his own son's flesh to eat—everything except the head, hands and feet, which were lying covered up in a dish elsewhere. When he thought that Harpagus had eaten his fill, Astyages asked him if he had enjoyed the meal. Harpagus said that he had, very much so. Then the servants who had been given the job brought in the boy's head, hands, and feet, all still covered up. Standing before Harpagus, they asked him to take the lid off the dish and to help himself to anything he wanted. Harpagus did as they suggested; he uncovered the dish and saw his son's remains. However, he did not allow the sight to disconcert him, but he retained his self-control. Astyages asked him if he recognized the creature whose flesh he had eaten. Harpagus replied that he did and that the king could do no wrong. Then he picked up what was left of his son's body and returned home—in order to gather the remains together and bury them all there, I suppose.

[120] That was how Astyages punished Harpagus. What should he do with Cyrus, though? He summoned exactly the same Magi who had given him the earlier† interpretation of his dream and when they came he asked them what they made of the dream for him. Their response was the same as before: they said that if the boy had remained alive rather than having already died, he would inevitably have become king. 'The boy is alive,' Astyages replied. 'He didn't die, and he lives out in the country. The boys in his village made him their king, and he accomplished everything by acting just like a real king. He gave everyone their various jobs to

do—as his bodyguards, porters, heralds, and so on—and ruled over them. Now, what does this seem to you to suggest?'

The Magi said, 'If the boy is alive and ruled as a king, although everyone concerned was acting in ignorance, that need not worry you. In fact, it should give you grounds for confidence, because he won't gain power a second time. It is not unknown for even our prophecies to be fulfilled in trivial matters, and things like dreams may come true in an insignificant manner.'

Astyages replied as follows: 'That's very much what I think too. Now that the boy has been called a king, my dream has come true and this child is no longer a threat to me. All the same, I'd appreciate your advice, once you've given the matter due consideration, as to what course of action will best preserve my house—and keep you safe too.'

'My lord,' the Magi said, 'it's true that the prosperity of your rule is very important to us as well, because the alternative is for power to fall into foreign hands. If it devolves on to this boy, who is Persian, we Medes will be enslaved by the Persians and will become worthless outcasts. But you are one of us. As long as you are king, then, power is partly ours too, and we have important standing in society thanks to you. We are bound to do all we can to look out for you and your rule. If we had seen anything alarming in the present situation, we would have told you all about it in advance. In fact, though, we ourselves are encouraged by the fact that the dream has spent itself in an insignificant way, and we see no reason why you shouldn't have the same attitude too. So send this boy out of your sight; dismiss him to Persia and to his parents.'

[121] Astyages was very pleased when he heard this advice and he sent for Cyrus. 'Child,' he said, 'once I saw something in a dream. Now, what I saw didn't come to pass, but I was worried enough about it to have tried to wrong you. Still, it was your destiny to survive. So now go in peace to Persia, and I will detail an escort to accompany you. There you will find a father and mother who are quite different from Mitradates the cowherd and his wife.'

[122] With these words, Astyages dismissed Cyrus. He returned to Cambyses' house, where his parents took him in. When they found out who he was, they were overjoyed, because they had been certain that he had died all that time ago. They asked him how he

had survived. 'Until just now,' he said, 'I wouldn't have been able to answer. I would have been way off the mark, but while travelling here I heard all about my personal misfortunes. I mean, I was convinced that I was the son of Astyages' herdsman, but on the way here the people who were escorting me told me the whole story.' He explained that he had been brought up by the herdsman's wife, and he went on praising her throughout his story and referring to Cyno, the bitch. His parents seized on this name and, because they wanted the Persians to think of their son's survival as even more miraculous than it was, they started spreading the rumour that after his exposure Cyrus had been reared by a bitch.

[123] That was how this rumour started. Now, Cyrus grew up to be the bravest and best-liked man of his generation, so Harpagus made overtures to him by sending him gifts. Harpagus wanted to make Astyages pay for what he had done, but he did not think that he, an ordinary citizen, had the resources to bring about his punishment by himself. He watched Cyrus growing up, however, and set about cultivating an alliance with him, because he thought Cyrus' treatment at Astyages' hands was comparable with his own. Even before this, though, he had taken certain steps: in view of Astyages' oppression of the Medes, Harpagus had met with all the most important Medes, one by one, and had tried to convince them of the necessity of setting up Cyrus as their leader and bringing Astyages' reign to an end. Once he had successfully accomplished this and all was ready, he wanted to let Cyrus know his plan. Cyrus was living in Persia, however, where the roads were guarded, so there was only one way for Harpagus to get the message through. The method he devised involved the clever use of a hare. He slit open its stomach and, leaving it just as it was, without removing any of its fur, he inserted a letter in which he had written down his ideas; then he sewed up the hare's stomach again. He gave his most loyal house-slave nets, to make him look like a hunter, and sent him off to Persia, with verbal instructions to give Cyrus the hare and to tell him to open it up himself, when there was no one else with him.

[124] Everything went according to plan; Cyrus received the hare and slit it open. He found the letter inside, took it out, and read it. The message was as follows: 'The gods must be watching over you, son of Cambyses, or else you would not have been so lucky. You should make your murderer Astyages pay. I call him

your murderer because that is what he wanted you—dead—and only the gods and I kept you alive. Anyway, I'm sure you've known for a long time all about what happened to you and about how I suffered at Astyages' hands because I refused to kill you and gave you to the herdsman instead. If you take my advice, you will rule all the territory that Astyages now rules. Persuade the Persians to revolt and march on Media. It will all work as you want, whether the commander appointed by Astyages to take charge of the forces ranged against you is myself or some other eminent Mede, because they will be the first to desert from him, come over to your side, and try to bring about his downfall. Everything is ready here, then, so do as I suggest—and don't delay.'

[125] Once he had received this message, Cyrus began to think up a subterfuge to persuade the Persians to rebel, and he came up with a very neat plan, which he proceeded to put into effect. He wrote what he had in mind in a letter and called the Persians to a meeting, where he unrolled the letter and read out that Astyages had appointed him commander of the Persian forces. 'And now, men of Persia,' he said, 'I command you all to present yourselves here with scythes.'

That was Cyrus' order. Now, a large number of tribes go to make up the Persian race, and not all of them were convened by Cyrus and persuaded to rebel from Median rule—only those on whom all the other tribes depended, namely the Pasargadae, the Maraphians, and the Maspians. The Pasargadae are the noblest of these peoples and include the clan of the Achaemenidae, which provides Persia with its kings. The other Persian tribes are as follows: the Pan-thialaei, Derusiaei, and Germanii (who all work the land), and the Daï, Mardians, Dropici, and Sagartians (who are nomadic).

[126] So they all came, bringing their scythes with them. Now, there was a patch in that region of Persia, about eighteen or twenty stades on each side, which was full of thorny shrubs. Cyrus ordered them to clear this area in one day. Once the Persians had completed their assigned task, he next told them to present themselves on the following day fresh from bathing. Meanwhile, Cyrus collected all his father's goats, sheep, and cattle, slaughtered them, and got ready to entertain the Persian army; he also supplied them with wine and the most enjoyable food available. Next day, when the Persians arrived, he provided couches for them in the meadow to lie on and treated them to a feast.

When they had finished eating, Cyrus asked them whether they preferred yesterday's programme or today's. They replied that there was an enormous difference between the two: yesterday's events held nothing but trouble, while today's were nothing but good. Cyrus seized on this remark and revealed his plan in its entirety. 'Men of Persia,' he said, 'this is the situation you're in. If you choose to take my advice, you can enjoy the advantages you have enjoyed today and thousands of others too, without having to work like a slave to get them. If you choose not to take my advice, however, your life will consist of countless chores like yesterday's. So do as I suggest: free yourselves from slavery. I believe that I was destined by providence to undertake this task, and I am sure that you are at least the equals of the Medes in everything, including warfare. Since this is so, there is no time to waste: rise up against Astyages!'

[127] The Persians had hated Median rule for a long time, so now that they had found a leader, they enthusiastically went about gaining their independence. When Astyages found out what Cyrus was up to, he sent a message ordering him to appear before him. Cyrus told the messenger, however, to inform Astyages that he would come sooner than Astyages wanted. When he received this message, Astyages armed all the Medes and, in his delusion, appointed Harpagus the commander of his forces, forgetting what he had done to him. So the Medes marched out and engaged the Persians, but only some of them—those who were not privy to the conspiracy—began to fight, while others deserted to the Persians, and the majority deliberately fought below their best and fled.

[128] As soon as Astyages found out that the Median army was in shameful disarray, he sent a threatening message to Cyrus, which read: 'Cyrus will still regret it.' His next actions were first to impale the Magian dream-interpreters who had persuaded him to let Cyrus go, and then to arm the Medes who were left in the city, however young or old they were, and to lead them out against the Persians. In the ensuing battle, the Medes were defeated. Astyages himself was captured, and he lost all the men he had led out against the Persians.

[129] Harpagus came to where Astyages was being held prisoner to gloat over him and mock him. He lashed him with his tongue in a number of ways, and also, remembering the dinner-party at which he had served him with his son's flesh, he asked him

what it was like being a slave rather than a king. Astyages looked at him and asked him in return whether he was taking credit for what Cyrus had achieved. Harpagus replied that since he had written the letter, the result could fairly be attributed to him. Astyages pointed out that he had just admitted to being the most stupid and unjust person alive—the most stupid because if he really was responsible for what had happened, he could have become king himself instead of presenting someone else with the power, and the most unjust because if it was absolutely necessary for him to confer the kingship on someone else and not to take it for himself, it would have been more just to confer this blessing on a Mede rather than a Persian, yet because of that dinner he had enslaved the Medes. The result was that the Medes had through no fault of their own exchanged mastery for slavery, while the Persians, who had previously been the slaves of the Medes, had now become their masters.

[130] So this is how Astyages' reign came to an end, after he had ruled for thirty-five years. Thanks to his cruel behaviour the Medes became subject to the Persians after having dominated that part of Asia which lies beyond the River Halys for 128 years, not counting the period of Scythian control. Later, they regretted what they had done and rebelled against Darius, but the rebellion was put down again when they were defeated in battle. At the time in question, however, during Astyages' reign, the Persians under Cyrus rose up against the Medes, and they have ruled Asia ever since. Cyrus did no further harm to Astyages, but kept him at his court until his death.

So that is the story of Cyrus' birth and upbringing, and that is how he came to be king. Later, he defeated Croesus (who was the aggressor in the affair, as I have already explained), and so gained control over the whole of Asia.

[131] Now, the Persians, to my certain knowledge, have the following practices. It is not one of their customs to construct statues, temples, and altars; in fact, they count those who do so as fools, because (I suppose) they do not anthropomorphize the gods as the Greeks do. Their worship of Zeus consists in going up to the highest mountain peaks and performing sacrifices; they call the whole vault of heaven Zeus. They also sacrifice to the sun and the moon, and to earth, fire, water, and the winds. Originally, these were the only deities to whom they offered sacrifices, but since then

they have also learnt from the Assyrians and Arabians to sacrifice to the Heavenly Aphrodite. Aphrodite is called Mylitta by the Assyrians, Alilat by the Arabians, and Mitra by the Persians.

[132] The way the Persians sacrifice to these deities is as follows. They do not construct altars or light fires when they are going to perform a sacrifice, nor do they use libations, reed-pipes, garlands, or barley. Whenever anyone decides to perform a sacrifice to one of the gods, he takes the animal to a purified place and invokes the deity, wreathing his *tiara* (usually with myrtle). He† is not allowed to exclude others and pray for benefits for himself alone; he prays for the prosperity of the king and the whole Persian race, since he is, after all, a member of the Persian race himself. Once he has chopped up the limbs of the sacrificial victim into pieces and boiled the meat, he spreads out the freshest grass he can find—usually clover—and places all the meat on it. When this arrangement is in place, a Magus comes up and chants a theogony—at least, that is what they say the song is about. There always has to be a Magus present in order for a sacrifice to take place. After a short pause, the person who has performed the sacrifice takes the meat away and does whatever he wants with it.

[133] It is Persian custom to regard a person's birthday as the most important day of the year for him. They consider it their duty to serve larger quantities at dinner on their birthday than they do on any other day. Well-off Persians serve an ox, a horse, a camel, or a donkey, roasted whole in an oven; poor Persians serve some smaller creature from their flocks. They do not eat many main courses as a rule, but they eat a lot of extra courses, and not all together. That is why the Persians say that Greeks are still hungry at the end of a meal: it is because nothing worth while is served as an extra after a meal; if it were, the Persians say, the Greeks would not stop eating. They are extremely fond of wine, and they are not supposed to vomit or urinate when anyone else can see. Although they have to be careful about all that, it is usual for them to be drunk when they are debating the most important issues. However, any decision they reach is put to them again on the next day, when they are sober, by the head of the household where the debate takes place; if they still approve of it when they are sober, it is adopted, but otherwise they forget about it. And any issues they debate when sober are reconsidered by them when they are drunk.

[134] There is a way of telling whether or not two Persians who meet on the street are of the same social standing. If they are, then instead of saying hello to each other, they kiss each other on the lips; if either of them is from a slightly lower rank, they kiss each other on the cheeks; and if one of them is the other's inferior by a long way, he falls to the ground and prostrates himself in front of the other person.

After themselves, they hold their immediate neighbours in the highest regard, then those who live the next furthest away, and so on in order of proximity; so they have the least respect for those who live furthest away from their own land. The reason for this is that they regard themselves as by far the best people in the world in all respects, and others as gradually decreasing in goodness, so that those who live the furthest away from them are the worst people in the world. During the period of Median dominance, there was even a hierarchy of rulership among the various peoples. The Medes ruled all of them at once, including their immediate neighbours, who ruled *their* neighbours, who in turn ruled the people next to them. The same principle governs the way the Persians assign respect, because their race consists of a series of rulerships and mandates.

[135] Nevertheless, the Persians adopt more foreign customs than anyone else. For example, they wear Median clothes because they consider them to be more attractive than their own, and they wear Egyptian breastplates for fighting. Also, they learn and then acquire the habit of all kinds of *divertissements* from various parts of the world, including the practice of having sex with boys, which they learnt from the Greeks. Every Persian man has a number of wives, but far more concubines.

[136] After bravery in battle, manliness is proved above all by producing plenty of sons, and every year the king rewards the person producing the most; they think that quantity constitutes strength. Their sons are educated from the time they are five years old until they are twenty, but they study only three things: horsemanship, archery, and honesty. Until they are five years old, they are not taken into their fathers' sight, but live with the women. This is to prevent a father being grieved by the death of a son during the period of his early upbringing.

[137] I think this custom of theirs is very good, and I also approve of the fact that no one, not even the king, can execute anyone who has been accused of only a single crime, nor can any

other Persian do irreversible harm to any of his house-slaves for committing a single crime. But if after due consideration he finds that the crimes committed outweigh in number and in gravity the services rendered, then he can give way to anger.

They say that no one has ever killed his own father or mother. They insist that all such incidents would inevitably be found on examination to have been the work of a child substituted for a genuine child, or of a bastard; they simply deny the plausibility of a full parent being killed by his own child.

[138] Anything they are not allowed to do they are also forbidden to talk about. The most disgraceful thing, in their view, is telling lies, and the next most disgraceful thing is being in debt; but the main reason (among many others) for the proscription of debt is that, according to the Persians, someone who owes money is obliged to tell lies as well.

If any town-dweller contracts any form of leprosy, he is not allowed back inside the town and he is forbidden to have any dealings with other Persians. They say that the disease is a result of having offended the sun. Any foreigner who contracts it is driven out of the country by crowds of people, and so are white doves, which are accused of the same offence.

Because rivers are objects of particular reverence for them, they do not urinate or spit into them, nor do they wash their hands there or allow anyone else to either.

[139] It also happens to be the case—as I have noticed, even though the Persians themselves have not remarked on it—that their names (which reflect their physical characteristics and their prestige) all end with the same letter—the one the Dorians call 'san' and the Ionians 'sigma'. Anyone who looks into the matter will find that it is not merely common for Persian names to have the same ending, but universal.

[140] I can mention these Persian customs with confidence because I know about them, but there are others, to do with the dead, which are talked about obliquely, as if they were secrets. It is said that the body of a Persian man is not buried until it has been mauled by a bird or a dog. I know for certain that the Magi do this, because they let it happen in public; but the Persians cover corpses in wax before burying them in the ground.

Magian customs are very different from everyone else's, and especially those of the priests in Egypt, in that while the latter avoid the contamination of killing any living thing (except for the purposes of ritual sacrifice), Magi with their own hands kill everything except dogs and people; in fact, they turn it into a major achievement and indiscriminately kill ants, snakes, and anything else which crawls on the ground or flies in the air. As far as this custom is concerned, it has always been that way and we can leave it to continue. I now resume my earlier narrative.

[141] The first thing the Ionians and Aeolians did after the Lydians had been defeated by the Persians was send a delegation to Cyrus at Sardis, since they wanted the terms of their subjection to him to be the same as they had been with Croesus. Cyrus listened to the delegation's suggestions and then told them a story. A pipe-player once saw some fish in the sea, he said, and played his pipes in the hope that they would come out on to the shore. His hopes came to nothing, so he grabbed a net, cast it over a large number of the fish, and hauled them in. When he saw the fish flopping about, he said to them, 'It's no good dancing now, because you weren't willing to come out dancing when I played my pipes.' The reason Cyrus told this story to the Ionians and Aeolians was that the Ionians had in fact refused to listen to Cyrus earlier, when he had sent a message asking them to rise up against Croesus, whereas now that the war was over and won, they were ready to do what he wanted. So that was his angry response to them. When his message got back to the Ionians in the cities, they all built defensive walls and met in the Panionium—all of them, that is, except the Milesians, who were the only ones whose treaty with Lydia Cyrus renewed. The rest of the Ionians, however, agreed unanimously to send a message to Sparta to ask for help.

[142] In terms of climate and weather, there is no fairer region in the whole known world than where these Ionians—the ones to whom the Panionium belongs—have founded their communities. There is no comparison between Ionia and the lands to the north and south, some of which suffer from the cold and rain, while others are oppressively hot and dry.

They do not all speak exactly the same language, but there are four different dialects. Miletus is the southernmost Ionian community, followed by Myous and Priene; these places are located in Caria and speak the same dialect as one another. Then there are the Ionian communities in Lydia—Ephesus, Colophon, Lebedus,

Teos, Clazomenae, and Phocaea—that share a dialect which is quite different from the one spoken in the places I have already mentioned. There are three further Ionian communities, two of which are situated on islands (namely, Samos and Chios), while the other, Erythrae, is on the mainland. The Chians and Erythraeans speak the same dialect, but the Samians have a dialect which is peculiar to themselves. So these are the four types of dialect spoken there.

[143] Of these Ionian communities, then, the Milesians were out of harm's reach because of the treaty they had made with Cyrus, and the islanders were in no danger because the Phoenicians were not yet under Persian control and the Persians themselves were not a seafaring race. The split between these Ionians and the rest came about for a single reason and a single reason only. There was a time when the whole Greek race was weak, and the Ionians constituted by far the weakest and most insignificant part of it. Apart from Athens, there was no other city of any distinction. The majority of the Ionians, including the Athenians, avoided the name and did not want to be called 'Ionian'; even now, in fact, I think most of them feel that the name is degrading. However, these twelve communities were proud of the name and founded for their own exclusive use a sanctuary which they called the Panionium and which they decided not to let any other Ionians use—not that any of them even asked to do so, except the Smyrnans.

[144] The Dorians from the region now known as Five Towns (though it used to be called Six Towns) do much the same. They too make sure that none of their Dorian neighbours are admitted into the Triopian sanctuary; indeed, they even excluded those of their own number who abused the customs of the sanctuary from making use of the place. It has long been the rule that winners in the games sacred to Triopian Apollo were awarded bronze tripods, and that the recipients of these tripods were not allowed to take them out of the sanctuary but had to dedicate them there to the god. Once, however, a man from Halicarnassus, whose name was Agasicles, disregarded the rule after his victory and took his tripod back home, where he nailed it down. For this offence, the five towns—Lindos, Ialysus, Camirus, Cos, and Cnidos— excluded the sixth town, Halicarnassus, from making use of the sanctuary. So that was the penalty imposed by the five towns on the Halicarnassians.

[145] I think that the reason the Ionians formed a league of twelve communities and refused to admit more is that they were also twelvefold when they lived in the Peloponnese, just as the Achaeans (who drove them out of the Peloponnese) are now. The twelve Achaean communities, counting westward from Sicyon, are as follows: Pellene, Aegeira, Aegae (through which flows the River Crathis, which never runs dry and which the river in Italy was named after), Bura, Helice (where the Ionians took refuge after they had been defeated by the Achaeans), Aegium, Rhypes, Patrae, Pharae, Olenus (which is on the River Peirus, a river of some size), Dyme, and finally Tritaeae, which is the only one of these towns which is inland.

[146] These are the twelve divisions of the present-day Achaeans, and they were formerly the twelve divisions of the Ionians, which is why the Ionians created twelve settlements. It is sheer stupidity to say that they did so because they are somehow more Ionian than the rest of the Ionians or have a nobler origin than the others. In the first place, a not insignificant proportion of the citizens of the twelve communities are Abantians from Euboea, who have no right to the name 'Ionian'; then there is an admixture of Minyans from Orchomenus, Cadmeans, Dryopians, Phocian expatriates, Molossians, Pelasgians from Arcadia, Dorians from Epidaurus, and a number of other peoples. As for those who came from the town hall of Athens and who consider themselves to be the noblest Ionians—well, they did not bring wives with them on their voyage of colonization, but murdered some Carians and took their daughters to be their wives. It is because of this massacre that the women made it a rule (a rule they bound themselves to by oaths and passed on from mother to daughter) never to share a meal with their husbands and never to call out to them by name—these were, after all, the men who had gained them as their wives by murdering their fathers, husbands, and children. These events took place in Miletus.

[147] Moreover, some of these Ionians were ruled by Lycians descended from Glaucus the son of Hippolochus, some by Caucones from Pylos, who were descended from Codrus the son of Melanthus, and some by both at once. All the same, it is true that they adhere to the name 'Ionian' more than any other Ionians, so let them have their claim to be pure Ionians. In fact, however, the

name applies to everyone who can trace his origin back to Athens and who celebrates the festival of Apaturia, which is celebrated everywhere except at Ephesus and Colophon. The excuse they give for being the only ones not to celebrate the Apaturia is some murder or other.

[148] The Panionium is a sacred place in Mycale; it faces north and is dedicated, by the common consent of the Ionians, to Poseidon of Helicon. Mycale is the west-facing headland jutting out from the mainland towards Samos where the Ionians from the twelve communities used to meet to celebrate a festival to which they gave the name 'Panionia'. It is a feature not just of Ionian festivals, but of Greek festivals in general, that they all end in the same letter, just like the names of Persians.†

[149] So much for the Ionian communities. The Aeolian ones are as follows: Cyme (that is, 'Phriconian' Cyme), Lerisae, New Walls, Temnus, Cilla, Notium, Aegiroessa, Pitane, Aegaeae, Myrina, and Gryneia. These are the eleven original Aeolian communities which remain from the twelve there used to be on the mainland, until one of them, Smyrna, was taken over by Ionians. In actual fact, the land these Aeolians occupy is more fertile than that owned by the Ionians, but it does not have such a good climate.

[150] This is how the Aeolians lost Smyrna. They took in some men from Colophon who had come off worst in a political dispute and had been banished from their homeland. These Colophonian exiles waited until the Smyrnans were involved in a festival to Dionysus outside the town walls, and then closed the gates and took control of the town. Aeolians came from everywhere to help and an agreement was reached whereby if the Ionians returned the Aeolians' personal effects the Aeolians would abandon Smyrna. Once this agreement had been put into effect, the eleven communities distributed the Smyrnans among themselves and enrolled them in their citizen bodies.

[151] So these are the Aeolian communities on the mainland, apart from the ones around Mount Ida, which form a different unit. As for the island communities, there are five on Lesbos (the sixth town on Lesbos, Arisba, the Methymnans enslaved, despite their common ancestry), one on Tenedos, and another one on the so-called Hundred Islands. The inhabitants of Lesbos and Tenedos had

as little to fear as the Ionian islanders, but the rest of the Aeolian communities took a joint decision to fall in behind the leadership of the Ionians.

[152] Matters proceeded apace, and when the messengers sent from Ionia and Aeolis arrived in Sparta, they chose a Phocaean called Pythermus to speak for them all. He wore a purple cloak so as to attract the Spartiates' attention and get as many of them as possible along to the meeting. He gained an audience and spoke at length, requesting help for their people, but he did not convince the Lacedaemonians, who decided against supporting the Ionians. The Ionian delegation left, but, despite having rejected them, the Lacedaemonians still sent men in a penteconter to reconnoitre Cyrus' situation and see what was happening in Ionia—at least, that seems to me to have been the purpose of the mission. When these men reached Phocaea they sent to Sardis their most distinguished member, a man called Lacrines, to deliver a message to Cyrus, telling him not to harm any settlement on Greek soil, since the Lacedaemonians would not tolerate it.

[153] Cyrus' response to this message was reputedly to have asked some Greeks in his entourage who on earth Lacedaemonians were, and how numerous they were, that they addressed him in this way. Once he had been told about them, he is supposed to have replied to the Spartiate agent as follows: 'I have never yet found occasion to fear the kind of men who set aside a space in the middle of their town where they can meet and make false promises to one another. If I remain healthy, their tongues will be occupied with events at home rather than those in Ionia.' This was intended by Cyrus as a slur against Greeks in general, because they have town squares where they buy and sell goods, whereas it is not Persian practice to use such places at all and the town square is entirely unknown among them.

Next, Cyrus entrusted Sardis to a Persian called Tabalus, and put a Lydian called Pactyes in charge of collecting Croesus' gold and that of all the other Lydians, while he himself marched back to Ecbatana, taking Croesus with him. He was not concerned about the Ionians for the time being, because Babylon, the Bactrians, the Sacae, and the Egyptians were all making difficulties for him. These were the people he was intending to lead his army against personally, while he sent another commander against the Ionians.

[154] Once Cyrus had marched away from Sardis, Pactyes led the Lydians in an uprising against Tabalus and Cyrus. He went down to the coast and, since he had all the gold from Sardis, he set about hiring mercenaries and persuading the people living in the coastal region to join his forces. Then he marched against Sardis, trapped Tabalus in the acropolis, and proceeded to lay siege to him there.

[155] The news of these events reached Cyrus on the road and he said to Croesus, 'When will I be free of this business, Croesus? It doesn't look as though the Lydians will ever stop making work for me and trouble for themselves. I'm wondering whether it might not be best to reduce them to slavery. At the moment I suppose I've behaved like someone who has killed the father but spared the children. It's true that I have you here beside me, my prisoner, when you were more than a father to the Lydians, but I did give them back their city, and so I'm surprised to find them rebelling.'

Croesus was afraid that Cyrus would drive his people out of Sardis, so faced with this expression of the king's thoughts he said, 'My lord, what you've said is perfectly reasonable, but you shouldn't be motivated completely by anger. Don't turn an ancient city into an empty ruin when it wasn't to blame for the earlier situation and isn't now either. I was responsible for the first incident and on my head fell the consequences; as for the current situation, it is Pactyes who has done you wrong, since he was supposed to be your representative in Sardis, so let him pay the penalty to you. You can be lenient towards the Lydians and still issue them a directive to ensure that they never rebel and are no threat to you. Send a message that they are forbidden to own weapons of war, that they are to wear tunics under their coats and slippers on their feet, that they are to take up the cithara and the harp, and that they are to raise their sons to be retailers. Before long, my lord, you will see them become women instead of men, and so there will be no danger of them rising up against you.'

[156] There were three reasons why Croesus put these proposals to Cyrus. First, he was sure that the Lydians would be better off this way than if they were reduced to slavery and sold; second, he was aware that if he did not make a cogent suggestion, he would not persuade Cyrus to change his mind; and third, he was afraid that, if the Lydians escaped the danger they were currently facing, they would at some time in the future rise up against the Persians

and be destroyed. Anyway, Cyrus liked the idea; he calmed down and told Croesus that he would do as he suggested. He sent for a Mede called Mazares and told him to repeat Croesus' proposals to the Lydians as directives, and also to sell into slavery everyone who had joined the Lydian attack on Sardis, except for Pactyes himself, who was at all costs to be brought back to him alive.

[157] Cyrus made these arrangements while he was on the road and then completed his journey to the Persian heartlands. As for Pactyes, when he discovered that an army was bearing down on him, he fled in fear to Cyme. Meanwhile, Mazares the Mede marched to Sardis with some of Cyrus' troops (not the whole army). The first thing he did, on finding that Pactyes and his forces were no longer there, was force the Lydians to carry out Cyrus' orders—orders which resulted in a complete alteration of the Lydian lifestyle. Next, he sent men to Cyme to ask the town to surrender Pactyes. The Cymeans decided to seek advice from the god in Branchidae, where there was a long-established oracle which was commonly consulted by all the Ionians and Aeolians. Branchidae is in Milesian territory, overlooking the harbour of Panormus.

[158] So the Cymeans sent emissaries to the priests at Branchidae to ask what the gods would prefer them to do about Pactyes, and the response was that they should surrender him to the Persians. That was the course of action they set in motion, once they had heard the oracle's response. Although that was the preference of the majority, however, an eminent Cymean called Aristodicus the son of Heraclides stopped them from carrying out the plan, because he did not find the oracle credible; in fact, he thought the emissaries were lying. So he wanted to wait until another delegation of emissaries, including himself, had gone and repeated the question about Pactyes.

[159] When the delegation reached Branchidae, Aristodicus took the role of spokesman and put the question to the oracle in the following way: 'Lord, Pactyes of Lydia came and sought refuge with us to escape violent death at the hands of the Persians. They demand his surrender and are telling us to hand him over. Although we are afraid of the power of Persia, we have not dared to give him up so far, since he is a suppliant; we first want you to make absolutely clear to us which of the two possible courses of action we should follow.'

The god gave the same reply to this question of Aristodicus'
as he had given before: he told them to surrender Pactyes to the
Persians. In response Aristodicus put into effect a plan he had
made. He walked all around the temple and evicted the sparrows
and all the other kinds of birds which had made their nests in the
building. The story goes that as he was doing this a voice came
from the temple and addressed itself to Aristodicus by saying:
'Have you no respect? How dare you do this? How can you strip
my temple of its suppliants?'

Aristodicus, it is said, was not stuck for a reply. 'Lord,' he said,
'are you really helping your suppliants like this and at the same
time commanding the Cymeans to surrender theirs?'

'Yes,' answered the god, 'that is my command. Why? To hasten
the impiety and consequent destruction of Cyme, so that you
never again come to consult me on the issue of the surrender of
suppliants.'

[160] When the Cymeans heard the response the oracle had
given to Aristodicus' question, they did not want to surrender
Pactyes and be destroyed, but they also did not want to keep him
and be besieged. They therefore sent him off to Mytilene. So
Mazares sent heralds to the Mytileneans demanding Pactyes' surrender, and the fact that some money was offered as well induced
them to set about complying with the demand. I cannot say for
certain exactly how much money was involved, because the plan
came to nothing. When the Cymeans found out what the Mytileneans were up to, they sent a ship to Lesbos and moved Pactyes to
Chios. However, the Chians hauled him out of the sanctuary of
Athena the Guardian of the Community and handed him over to
the Persians. The reward the Chians received for doing this was
Atarneus, which is located opposite Lesbos in Mysia. Now that the
Persians had been given Pactyes, they kept him under guard, since
they wanted to bring him before Cyrus. For quite a long time afterwards, no Chian would use barley from Atarneus as an offering to
any of the gods nor would he use grain from there to make sacrificial cakes; in fact, nothing from that region was allowed in any
sanctuary.

[161] The next thing Mazares did, once the Chians had surrendered Pactyes to him, was undertake a campaign against everyone
who had been involved in besieging Tabalus. First he reduced
Priene to slavery and then he overran the whole plain of the

Meander River and let his men plunder it. Magnesia received the same treatment, but then Mazares fell ill and died.

[162] After his death another Mede, Harpagus, took over the command. (Harpagus was the one whom Astyages, the king of the Medes, had entertained with that obscene dinner and who had helped win the kingdom for Cyrus.) After he had been put in charge of the army by Cyrus, he marched into Ionia and set about making use of earthworks to capture the towns there. This entailed pinning the inhabitants inside a town, and then building earthworks up against the walls to allow the town to be captured.

[163] The first Ionian town he attacked was Phocaea. The Phocaeans were the earliest Greeks to make long voyages by sea; they opened up the Adriatic, Tyrrhenia, Iberia, and Tartessus. The ships they used for these voyages were penteconters rather than round-bodied ships. When they reached Tartessus they became friendly with the Tartessian king, whose name was Arganthonius. He had ruled Tartessus for eighty years, and lived to be 120 altogether. The Phocaeans got to be on such very good terms with him that he initially suggested that they leave Ionia and settle wherever they liked within his kingdom. The Phocaeans did not want to do that, however, so next—because they had told him about the growth of the Persian empire—he gave them money to build a wall around their town. The amount he gave was extremely generous, because the wall makes a circuit of quite a few stades, and all of it is constructed out of huge blocks of stone which fit closely together.

[164] That is how the Phocaeans' wall came to be built. Harpagus marched his army up to it and the siege of the town began. Harpagus let it be known that he would be satisfied if the Phocaeans were willing to tear down just one of the wall's bastions and consecrate just one building. The Phocaeans, however, could not abide the thought of being enslaved and they requested a single day to debate the matter, after which they would give him their reply; they also asked him to pull his army back from the wall while they were deliberating. Harpagus gave them permission to go ahead with their deliberations, despite the fact that he was, as he told them, well aware of what they intended to do. So while Harpagus led his army away from the wall, the Phocaeans launched their penteconters, put their womenfolk, children, and all their personal effects on board, along with the statues and other dedicatory offerings from their sanctuaries, except those which were made out of

bronze or stone or were paintings—anyway, once everything else
was on board they embarked themselves and sailed to Chios. So
the Persians gained control of a Phocaea which was emptied of
men.

[165] The Phocaeans offered to buy the islands known as the
Oenussae from the Chians, but the Chians refused to sell them,
because they were worried that if the islands became a trading-
centre, their own island would consequently be denied access to
trade. So the Phocaeans made Cyrnus their destination, because
twenty years earlier, on the advice of an oracle, they had founded
a community there called Alalia. Arganthonius was by then dead.
In preparation for the voyage to Cyrnus they first put in at Phocaea
and massacred the Persian contingent which Harpagus had left to
guard the place; once that job was done, they next called down terrible curses on any of their number who stayed behind and did not
take part in the expedition. They also sank a lump of iron in the
sea and swore that they would not return to Phocaea until this iron
reappeared. As they were fitting out their ships for the voyage to
Cyrnus, however, over half of their fellow citizens were so overcome by longing and sorrow for the city and the customs of their
native land that they broke their promises and sailed back to
Phocaea. The ones who kept their promises, however, set sail from
the Oenussae.

[166] For five years after reaching Cyrnus, they lived together
with the earlier settlers and established their sanctuaries there. But
because they were continually raiding all the local settlements, the
Tyrrhenians and Carthaginians joined forces and attacked them,
each providing sixty ships for the venture. The Phocaeans got sixty
of their own ships ready too and went out to meet the enemy in
the Sardonian Sea. A battle ensued in which the Phocaeans gained
a rather Cadmean victory, in the sense that they lost forty of their
own ships and the twenty which survived had bent rams and so
were unfit for active service. They sailed back to Alalia, where they
picked up their women and children and as much of the rest of
their property as the ships could carry; then they left Cyrnus and
sailed to Rhegium.

[167] The Carthaginians and Tyrrhenians ⟨drew lots to divide⟩
the crews of the wrecked Phocaean ships between themselves ⟨and,
among the Tyrrhenians, the Agyllans⟩† gained by far the largest
number of prisoners. They took them to a place outside the town

and stoned them to death. Afterwards, anything connected to
Agylla—whether it was an animal from their flocks or for their
carts, or a human being—which passed through the place where
the Phocaeans were stoned to death and lay buried became crippled, lame, and paralysed. The Agyllans sent men to consult the
oracle at Delphi, to try to find a way to remedy their offence. The
Pythia told them to initiate the practice which is still followed in
Agylla even today—that of making generous offerings to the dead
Phocaeans and holding an athletic contest and a chariot-race in
their honour.

That was how these Phocaeans met their death. The others, the
ones who escaped to Rhegium, used it as a base from which they
set out and gained a site in the land of Oenotria to build a community, which is the one nowadays called Hyele. They established
the town once they had been told by a man from Poseidonia that
the oracle had not been referring to the island Cyrnus, but had
meant them to establish the hero Cyrnus. So that is what happened
to the Ionian town of Phocaea.

[168] The inhabitants of Teos adopted almost exactly the same
course of action too. Once Harpagus had overrun their fortifications with his earthworks, the whole population took to their ships
and sailed away to Thrace, where they founded the city of Abdera.
Abdera had actually been founded earlier by a man from Clazomenae called Timesius, but it had not turned out well for him. In
fact, he was driven out of the country by the Thracians. However,
he is now worshipped as a hero by the Teans in Abdera.

[169] The Phocaeans and the Teans were the only Ionians who
emigrated from their native lands rather than endure slavery. The
rest of them (apart from the Milesians) stood up to Harpagus
just as much as the emigrants did, and every man among them
fought bravely for his own community, but the difference was
that, once they had been defeated and their towns and cities taken,
they stayed in their native land and submitted to Persian government. The Milesians (as I said before) had entered into a treaty
with Cyrus himself and so kept quiet. That was how Ionia came
to be enslaved for the second time, and Harpagus' conquest of the
mainland Ionians frightened the islanders into surrendering to
Cyrus as well.

[170] Despite their defeat, the Ionians still used to meet in the
Panionium, and my information is that Bias of Priene made a very

valuable suggestion to them there—a suggestion which would have
made them the most prosperous Greek people, if they had followed
it. He proposed that the Ionians should pool their resources, set
sail for Sardo, and then found a single city for all Ionians. This, he
said, would enable them not just to avoid slavery, but to thrive,
since they would inhabit the largest island in the world and exercise authority over all the rest. However, he added, if they stayed
in Ionia, he could not foresee freedom for them.

This proposal by Bias of Priene was made to the Ionians after
their defeat, but another good proposal had been put to them, even
before the conquest of Ionia, by Thales of Miletus, a man originally of Phoenician lineage. He suggested that the Ionians should
establish a single governmental council, that it should be in Teos
(because Teos is centrally located in Ionia), and that all the other
towns should be regarded effectively as demes.

[171] So much for the suggestions made by Bias and Thales to
the Ionians. Harpagus followed his conquest of Ionia with campaigns against the Carians, the Caunians, and the Lycians, and he
took contingents of both Ionians and Aeolians along with him.
Now, the Carians came to the mainland from the Aegean islands.
Long ago, when they were subjects of Minos and were called the
Leleges, they had inhabited the islands. As far as I have been able
to gather from my enquiries, they used not to pay Minos any
tribute, but they would man ships for him on demand. So since
Minos was successful in war and conquered a great deal of land,
the Carians were far and away the most important race at this time.
(The Greeks have adopted three practices which were originally
Carian discoveries. It was the Carians who originally started tying
plumes on to their helmets, they were the first to put designs on
their shields, and they were also the first to fit shields with handles.
Previously, no handles had been involved and the universal practice of those who used to wear shields was to manoeuvre them by
means of a leather strap which lay around the neck and left shoulder.) Much later, the Dorians and Ionians made the Carians
abandon the islands and then they arrived on the mainland. At any
rate, that is the Cretan version of what happened to the Carians,
but the Carians themselves disagree. They think they are indigenous mainlanders and have always had the name they have now.
For proof, they point to the antiquity of the sanctuary of Carian
Zeus at Mylasa. Mysians and Lydians are allowed to use this

sanctuary too, on the grounds that they are related to the Carians, because in Carian legend Lydus and Mysus were the brothers of Car. So Mysians and Lydians can use the sanctuary, but no other non-Carians can, even if they speak the same language as the Carians.

[172] In my opinion the Caunians are indigenous, though they say they came originally from Crete. However, their language has come to approximate that spoken by the Carians (or the Carian language has come to approximate that spoken by the Caunians; I would not like to say for certain which alternative is correct), although it is true that their way of life is quite different from everyone else's, including the Carians'. For instance, the best thing of all in their opinion is to get together in groups, formed on the basis of age or friendship, and drink—men, women, and children too. Their religious rituals used to be imported from abroad, but later they turned against this and decided to rely only on their ancestral deities, so the entire male adult Caunian population put on armour and, stabbing the air with their spears, advanced up to the border with Calynda. What they claimed to be doing was expelling the foreign gods.

[173] So much for the Caunians and their customs. The Lycians were originally from Crete; in fact there was a time, long ago, when the whole of Crete was in the hands of non-Greeks. The island became embroiled in a dispute for the kingdom between Sarpedon and Minos, the sons of Europa, which Minos won. He banished Sarpedon and his supporters from the island, and they came to the part of Asia called Milyas. Now, in antiquity Milyas was the region which is nowadays inhabited by Lycians, and the Milyans were in those days called the Solymians. During Sarpedon's reign, the inhabitants were known as the Termilae, which is the name they brought with them from Crete and is what the Lycians are still called even today by the neighbouring peoples. But later Lycus the son of Pandion (who was banished from Athens by *his* brother Aegeus) came to Sarpedon and the Termilae, and eventually the Lycians came to be named after Lycus. Their way of life is a mixture of Cretan and Carian. One custom which is peculiar to them, and like nothing to be found anywhere else in the world, is that they take their names from their mothers rather than from their fathers. Suppose someone asks his neighbour who he is: he will describe himself in terms of his mother's ancestry—that is, he will list all the mothers on his mother's side. Also, if a female citizen and a male

slave live together as a couple, her children are considered legitimate, whereas if a male citizen—even one of the highest rank—
marries a woman from another country or a concubine, his children
have no rights of citizenship.

[174] Anyway, the Carian effort was unremarkable and they
were duly reduced to slavery by Harpagus. Nor was it only the
Carians who were ineffectual: the same also goes for all the Greeks
who live in that part of the country. These include the Cnidians,
who were originally Lacedaemonian emigrants and who occupy a
coastal region known as Triopium. Starting at the Bybassian peninsula, Cnidian territory is—except for a thin stretch of land—
entirely surrounded by water: it is bounded to the north by the Gulf
of Ceramicus and to the south by the sea off Syme and Rhodes.
So while Harpagus was in the process of subduing Ionia, the Cnidians started to dig through that thin bit of land (it is no more than
five stades wide), with the intention of turning their territory into
an island. All of Cnidos was to be included, because the isthmus
through which they were digging was exactly where their territory
ends and the mainland begins. Now, a good many Cnidians set to
work, but the number of injuries caused by shattered stone—particularly affecting the eyes, but elsewhere on the body too—seemed
unexpectedly and even miraculously high, so they sent emissaries
to Delphi to ask what it was that was blocking them. According
to native Cnidian tradition, the Pythia's response, in iambic trimeters, was as follows:

> The isthmus is not to be fortified or dug through;
> If Zeus had wanted an island, he would have made an island.

Faced with this response from the Pythia, the Cnidians stopped
their digging, and when Harpagus and his army arrived they surrendered without offering battle.

[175] The inland country north of Halicarnassus was inhabited
by the Pedasians. Now, whenever they or their neighbours were
threatened by some disaster, the priestess of Athena grew a long
beard. This happened on three occasions. The Pedasians were the
only people living in or around Caria to hold out against Harpagus for any length of time; they caused him a great many problems
with the stronghold they built on a hill called Lida.

[176] Eventually, however, the Pedasians were overcome. As for
the Lycians, when Harpagus and his troops marched into the plain
of Xanthus, the Xanthians came out and engaged him in battle,

despite the fact that they were up against superior numbers. They showed great bravery, but they lost the battle and became trapped inside the city. They brought everything—wives, children, property, and house-slaves—to the acropolis, set fire to it, and burnt it to the ground. Then they pledged terrible oaths, came out of the city, and died fighting. Every single Xanthian was killed there. Almost any Lycian who claims to be a Xanthian today is actually an immigrant, unless he is from one of the eighty families who survived because they happened to be away from Xanthus at the time. That is how Harpagus took Xanthus, and since the Caunians largely followed the example of the Lycians, the fall of Caunus came about in almost exactly the same way too.

[177] While Harpagus was laying waste to coastal Asia, Cyrus himself was doing the same in inland Asia. He systematically defeated every tribe, one after another. I will pass over most of these and mention only those which gave him the most difficult time and were the most noteworthy.

[178] Once he had subdued the rest of the continent, Cyrus launched a strike against the Assyrians. Now, among all the many important cities in Assyria, the most famous and well fortified—and the place where the royal palace was located after the devastation of Ninus—was Babylon. Here is a description of the city. It is situated on a huge plain, and the length of each of its sides (it forms a square) is 120 stades; altogether, then, the circumference of the city is 480 stades long. So much for its size. Its design differs from that of any other city in the known world. First there is a wide, deep moat, full of water, surrounding the entire city. Then there is a defensive wall 50 royal cubits thick and 200 cubits high (a royal cubit is three fingers longer than an ordinary one).

[179] I had better add an explanation of where the earth that was dug out of the moat was used and a description of the construction of the wall. The earth that the excavation of the moat yielded was being made into bricks even while the digging was going on. Whenever they had moulded enough bricks, they fired them in kilns. Then, using a mortar of hot bitumen and inserting a course of reed mats every thirty layers of bricks, they built first the banks of the moat and then, by the same method, the wall itself. Along the edges of the top of the wall they built, facing one another, one-room buildings which were separated by gaps wide enough for

a four-horse chariot to drive through. The wall contains a hundred gates, of solid bronze, with bronze posts and lintels too. Now, there is another place eight days' journey away from Babylon called Is, where there is an insignificant river (also called Is) which is a tributary of the Euphrates. This River Is produces, along with its water, plenty of lumps of bitumen, and the bitumen which was used for the wall of the city of Babylon was fetched from there.

[180] So that is how Babylon's defensive wall was built. The city has two districts, because a river—the Euphrates—divides the city down the middle. The Euphrates is a wide, deep, and fast-flowing river which rises in Armenia and issues into the Red Sea. Each wall, then, curves when it reaches the river and from there angles back along each bank of the river as a low wall of fired brick. The city itself is packed with three-storeyed and four-storeyed houses and criss-crossed by straight streets, some running right through the city and others at right angles to them going down to the river. At the end of each of these transverse streets there are postern gates set into the wall which runs beside the river—one gate for each alleyway. As well as being bronze (like the other gates) these postern gates also afford access to the river.

[181] This wall is a breastplate, then, but another wall runs along inside this first one. It too surrounds the city, and although it is not much weaker than the first one, it is less thick. In the centre of one of the two districts of the city stands the royal palace, surrounded by a tall, strong wall, and in the centre of the other there is a bronze-gated sanctuary to Zeus as Bel, still standing in my day and forming a square with each side two stades long. In the middle of the sanctuary has been built a solid tower, a stade long and the same in width, which supports another tower, which in turn supports another, and so on: there are eight towers in all. A stairway has been constructed to wind its way up the outside of all the towers; halfway up the stairway there is a shelter with benches to rest on, where people making the ascent can sit and catch their breath. In the last tower there is a huge temple. The temple contains a large couch, which is adorned with fine coverings and has a golden table standing beside it, but there are no statues at all standing there. No one is allowed to spend the night there except a single local woman who (according to the Chaldeans, who are the priests of Bel) has been selected from among all the local women by the god.

[182] The Chaldeans also say that the god comes in person to the temple and rests on the couch; I do not believe this story myself, although it is exactly the same as what happens in Thebes (that is, Egyptian Thebes), according to the Egyptians. The parallel even extends to the fact that a woman sleeps in the temple of Zeus at Thebes as well, and it is said that neither of these women has intercourse with any man. The same goes for the prophetess of the god at Patara in Lycia, when there is one. I mean, an oracle is not a constant feature of the place, but when there is a prophetess there, she spends every night shut up inside the temple with the god.

[183] Lower down in the Babylonian sanctuary there is also another temple, where there is a large golden statue of a seated Zeus, with a large golden table beside him; the base of the statue and the throne on which he is seated are both golden too. As the Chaldeans told it, eight hundred talents of gold went into the making of these pieces. Outside the temple there is a golden altar, and also another large altar which is used for sacrificing the pick of the flocks, while they are allowed to sacrifice only unweaned creatures on the golden altar. On the larger altar the Chaldeans also burn a thousand talents of frankincense each year during the festival of this god. At the time of Cyrus' conquest this precinct also contained a statue of solid gold, twelve cubits high. I did not see it myself, but I am repeating what the Chaldeans say. Darius the son of Hystaspes had designs on this statue, but did not have the effrontery to take it; however, his son Xerxes did take it, as well as killing the priest who was telling him not to touch it. Anyway, this is how the sanctuary has been decorated, apart from numerous private votive offerings.

[184] The design and ornamentation of the walls and sanctuaries of Babylon were the work of a number of Babylonian kings (who will feature in my Assyrian narrative), but also of two women. Five generations separated these two queens. The one who ruled first was called Semiramis, and the remarkable dykes on the plain were her work. Before then, the river had used to flood the whole plain.

[185] The second of these two queens was called Nitocris. She was a more intelligent ruler than her predecessor. Apart from the monuments she left to posterity, which I am going to describe, she also noticed the size and restlessness of the Median empire, saw that other places, including Ninus, had been taken by them, and

took all the precautions she possibly could. The first precaution she took was to alter the course of the River Euphrates (the river which flows through the middle of Babylon). Up until then the river had flowed in a straight line, but she had channels dug above the city which made its course so very crooked that it actually flows past one of the Assyrian villages—called Ardericca—at three points. Even today, anyone travelling from our sea to Babylon will come to this village three times, on three separate days, as he sails down the Euphrates.

This was quite a feat she accomplished. Another one was to have an embankment built along both sides of the river; this is well worth seeing for its bulk and height. Some way north of Babylon, she had a lake excavated next to the river and not far away from it; she had it dug down to the water level at each point, and it was broad enough to have a perimeter of 420 stades. She had all the earth that was excavated from this site used for the embankments by the river. Once the lake had been excavated, she had a pavement built around it, made out of stones brought from elsewhere.

The reason for both of these projects—diverting the river and creating by means of the excavation an area of nothing but marshland—was to reduce the speed of the river by having it spend its current against numerous curves, and to force anyone sailing to Babylon to take a meandering course followed by a lengthy circuit of the lake. These works of hers were carried out in the part of the country where there were passes and the shortest route from Media, in order to prevent the Medes mingling with her people and gathering information about her affairs.

[186] So she gave the city this thorough defensive system, and then, with that basis in place, added the following projects. Since the city was divided by the river into two districts, whenever anyone wanted to cross from one district to the other in the time of earlier rulers, they had to be ferried across, which was a nuisance, I am sure. She took care of this problem too. The excavation of the basin for the lake gave her the opportunity to leave another monument to posterity as well, from the same project. She quarried huge long stones, and when the stones were ready and the lake site had been excavated, she completely diverted the river into the excavated site. While it was filling up, the old river bed dried out. This gave her the time to build up the banks of the river in the city and the stairs from the postern gates to the riverside with

fired bricks in the same way as in the construction of the defensive wall. She also used the quarried stones to build a bridge, more or less in the centre of the city, and she joined the stones together with braces of iron and lead. During the day squared-off planks of wood used to be laid on it, so that the Babylonians could walk across on them, but at night these planks would be removed so that people did not cross over and steal from one another. When the excavated lake had been filled by the river and the bridge had been completed down to the last detail, she let the Euphrates flow out of the lake and back to its original bed. So in becoming a marsh the excavated site was thought to serve a useful purpose, and at the same time the Babylonians gained a bridge.

[187] Here is a clever trick which this same queen played. She had a tomb built for herself over the busiest city gates, in a prominent place right above the actual gates, and she had the tomb engraved with the following inscription: 'Any subsequent king of Babylon who is short of money may open my tomb and take as much as he wants. But it will not go well for him if he opens the tomb for any other reason than because he is short of money.' The tomb was undisturbed until Darius became king. He resented the fact that he could not use these gates (because that would have involved his riding under a corpse) and that the money was just lying there with its beckoning inscription, but he could not take it. So he opened the tomb. He found no money, however, but there was the corpse and the following message: 'Only greed and avarice could have led you to open the tomb of the dead.' That is the kind of person this queen is supposed to have been.

[188] Cyrus' strike was launched against this woman's son, who was called Labynetus after his father and had succeeded to the Assyrian kingdom. Now, the Great King goes on his military expeditions well equipped with food and livestock from home, and he also brings water from the River Choäspes (on whose banks the city of Susa is situated), because water from no other river except the Choäspes is allowed to pass the king's lips. This Choäspes water is boiled, and wherever the king might be campaigning on any given occasion, he is accompanied by a large number of four-wheeled wagons, drawn by mules, which carry the water in silver containers.

[189] On his way to Babylon, Cyrus came to the River Gyndes. This river rises in Matiene, flows through the land of the Dardanae

and joins another river, the Tigris, which flows past the town of
Opis and issues into the Red Sea. Now, as Cyrus was negotiating
the crossing of this river, which was deep enough to be navigable,
one of his sacred white horses charged violently into the water and
tried to swim across, but the river submerged it in its current and
swept it away. Cyrus was extremely angry with the river for this
brutal act and he warned it that he would reduce its strength to
such an extent that in the future even women would easily be able
to cross it without getting their knees wet. Having issued this
threat, he abandoned his expedition against Babylon and divided
his army into two halves. Then he marked out a hundred and eighty
plumb-straight channels on either bank of the river, radiating out
in every direction, positioned half of his army on each side and
ordered his men to start digging. He had a considerable work-force
at his disposal, and so the work proceeded well, but they still spent
the whole summer working there.

[190] So Cyrus punished the Gyndes River by dividing it into
three hundred and sixty channels. At the start of the second spring
he resumed his march on Babylon. The Babylonians brought their
army out of the city and awaited Cyrus' arrival. When he drew
near the city, the Babylonians engaged him, but they lost the battle
and were driven back into the city. Now, this was not the first time
that Cyrus' expansionist ambitions had come to their attention;
they had noticed how he attacked every race indiscriminately,
and they had for very many years been stockpiling food in the city.
So they were not at all bothered by the siege. As more and more
time went by and there was no progress in the matter, Cyrus did
not know what to do.

[191] Perhaps it was someone else's suggestion for a way out of
his difficulties, or perhaps he discovered what to do by himself, but
anyway what he did was this. He stationed his army at some distance from† the point where the river entered Babylon, and posted
some other troops behind the city, where the river comes out again.
He told his men to wait until they saw the river become fordable,
and then to enter the city that way. Once he had posted them there
and given them these instructions,† he himself withdrew, along
with that part of his army which was unfit. When he came to the
lake, he did more or less exactly what the Babylonian queen had
done to the river and the lake: that is, he dug a channel to divert
the river into the marshy lake, so that once the river had subsided,

its original bed became fordable. This was what the Persians who had been stationed by the river were there for, and when the Euphrates had subsided until the water reached more or less the middle of a man's thigh, they entered Babylon along the river-bed. If the Babylonians had heard or learnt in advance what Cyrus was up to, they would have allowed the Persians to enter the city and then massacred them. If they had locked all the postern gates that gave on to the river and mounted the low walls which ran along the banks of the river, they would have caught the Persians like fish in a trap. As things were, however, the Persians were upon them before they knew anything about it. And according to local sources, the city is so huge that the Babylonians living in the centre were unaware of the capture of their compatriots from the edges of the city, and in fact, at the time of the city's fall, were dancing and enjoying themselves, since it happened to be a holiday—until they found out the hard way what was going on. So that is how Babylon fell the first time.

[192] I will give a number of examples to illustrate the resources of Babylon, including the following. The whole of the Great King's empire is divided up for the purpose of feeding him and his army (this is apart from tribute-payment, which is a separate obligation). Now, for four of the twelve months of the year, Babylonian territory provides the food, while the whole of the rest of Asia does so for the remaining eight months. In other words, Assyrian territory alone has one third of the resources of the rest of Asia. The administration (or satrapy, to use the Persian word) of this territory is by far the most powerful of all the administrative posts in the Persian empire, as is shown by the fact that while Tritantaechmes the son of Artabazus held this post as the king's deputy, his income was a full *artaba* of silver every day of his satrapy—an *artaba* being a Persian measure equivalent to an Attic medimnus and three choenixes. Over and above the horses he kept for military purposes, he also had his own private herds of eight hundred stud stallions and sixteen thousand mares—one stallion to cover twenty mares. He had so many Indian hunting-dogs to maintain that four sizeable villages from the plain were exempted from any other form of taxation and had to provide food for the dogs. These are the kinds of resources the governor of Babylon has at his disposal.

[193] Assyria has a low rainfall, but it is enough to get the crops' roots to begin growing. However, it is irrigation by the river that

makes the crops ripen and the grain appear. It is not like Egypt, where the river itself rises and floods the fields; in Assyria they use manual labour and swipes to irrigate the crops. For Babylonian territory is completely criss-crossed by canals, just as Egypt is. The largest of these canals, which is navigable, tends south-east and leads from the Euphrates to another river, the Tigris, on which the city of Ninus was built. Cereal crops flourish here far better than anywhere else we know of. While they do not even begin to try to grow other plants, such as figs, vines, and olive-trees, cereal crops grow so well that a yield of 200 times the weight of the seed grain is not unusual and, when the soil is exceptionally fertile, the yield can increase to 300 times the weight of the seed grain. In this country blades of wheat and barley grow to a width of at least four fingers. I am not going to mention the size of the plants that grow from millet-seed and sesame-seed, although I know how big they are, because I am well aware of the sceptical response even my account of the crops has evoked in those who have not been to the Babylonian countryside. They do not use olive oil at all, but they get oil from sesame seeds. Palm-trees grow all over the plain, and the majority of them produce fruit, which people use to make food, wine, and syrup. The method of cultivation of the palm in Assyria resembles the cultivation of the fig in Greece in a number of ways, and not least in the way they tie the fruit of what the Greeks call the 'male' palm-trees to the date-bearing trees, so that the gall-wasp (which is carried by the male trees in their fruit, as is also the case with wild figs, in fact) can penetrate the date and cause it to ripen rather than fall off prematurely.

[194] I will now give a description of what was to me the most amazing thing in Assyria, after Babylon itself. They have boats plying the river down to Babylon which are completely round and are made of leather. In Armenia, which is upstream from Assyria, they cut branches of willow and make them into a frame, around the outside of which they stretch watertight skins to act as a hull; they do not broaden the sides of the boat to form a stern or narrow them into a prow, but they make it round, like a shield. Then they line the whole boat with straw and send it off down the river laden with goods. Their cargo is most commonly palm-wood casks filled with wine. The boats are steered by two men, who stand upright and wield a paddle each; one of them pulls the paddle towards his body, while the other pushes his paddle away from his body. These

boats vary in size from very large downwards; the largest of them can manage cargo weighing five thousand talents. Each boat carries a live donkey—or, in the case of the larger boats, several donkeys. At the end of their voyage in Babylon, when they have sold their cargo, they sell off the frame of the boat and all the straw, load the donkeys up with the skins, and drive them back to Armenia. They do this because the current of the river is too strong for boats to sail up it, and that is why they make these boats out of skins rather than wood. Once they have got back to Armenia with their donkeys, they make themselves more boats in the uⅎual way.

[195] That is what their boats are like. As for their clothing, they wear a linen tunic which reaches down to their feet; on top of this they wear another tunic, made out of wool, and they put a white shawl around their shoulders. Their shoes are of a local design and resemble Boeotian slippers. They wear their hair long and wrap a turban around their heads. They perfume their whole bodies. Every man has a signet-ring and a hand-carved staff, and every staff bears a design of some kind—an apple, a rose, a lily, an eagle, or something. It would be abnormal for any of them to have a staff which was not emblazoned with a device. So much for their outfits.

[196] I now turn to their customs, the most sensible of which, in my opinion, is also practised, I hear, by the Illyrian tribe, the Eneti. Once a year, in every village, this is what they used to do. They used to collect all the young women who were old enough to be married and take the whole lot of them all at once to a certain place. A crowd of men would form a circle around them there. An auctioneer would get each of the women to stand up one by one, and he would put her up for sale. He used to start with the most attractive girl there, and then, once she had fetched a good price and been bought, he would go on to auction the next most attractive one. They were being sold to be wives, not slaves. All the well-off Babylonian men who wanted wives would outbid one another to buy the good-looking young women, while the commoners who wanted wives and were not interested in good looks used to end up with some money as well as the less attractive women. For once the auctioneer had finished selling off the best-looking girls, he used to make the most ugly one stand up, or a handicapped girl if there was one there, and he would proceed to auction her off by announcing that the man who was prepared to take the least money

could have her for his wife, until she was given to whoever named the smallest amount of money. But it was thanks to the good-looking women that there was money available, and so the attractive girls helped the unattractive girls and the handicapped ones find husbands. No one was allowed to arrange his own daughter's marriage to a man of his choice, and no one was allowed to take a girl he had just bought back home without first taking a pledge; he had to pledge that he would indeed live with her, and then he could take her back home. If they did not get on, the rule was that the man returned the money. Anyone who wanted to could legitimately come from another village and take part in the auction. Anyway, this was their finest custom, but it has lapsed and they have recently found an alternative. Since their loss of independence they have been reduced to squalor and economic ruin, and nowadays every commoner who lacks an income has his female children work as prostitutes.

[197] Their next most sensible custom is as follows. Because they do not consult doctors, when someone is ill they carry him to the main square, where anyone who has personal experience of something similar to what the ill person is suffering from, or who knows someone else who has, comes up to him and offers him advice and suggestions about his illness. They tell him what remedy they found effective in their own case, or what they saw working in someone else's case, which enabled them to recover from a similar illness. No one is allowed to walk past a sick person in silence, without asking what sort of illness he has.

[198] They use honey to embalm the dead, and their mourning procedure is similar to that of Egypt. Whenever a Babylonian man has had sex with his wife, he sits and purifies himself with incense, while his wife does the same elsewhere. At daybreak they both wash as well, and they cannot touch any bowls and so on until they have washed. This is exactly the same as what the Arabians do.

[199] The most disgraceful Babylonian custom is that at some point in her life every woman of the land is required to sit in a sanctuary of Aphrodite and have sex with a strange man. It is not unknown for women who are snobbish because of their wealth, and who refuse to associate with the rest of the women there, to drive to the sanctuary in covered carts† and stand there surrounded by a large retinue of attendants. The usual practice, however, is for

a number of women to sit in the precinct of Aphrodite wearing a garland made of string on their heads. New women are constantly coming into the precinct to replace the ones who are leaving. Plumb-straight lanes run this way and that through the women, and men they have never met before walk along these lanes and take their pick of the women. A woman sitting in the sanctuary is not allowed to return home until one of the strangers has thrown money into her lap and had sex with her (which happens outside the sanctuary). The man who throws the money has to say: 'I call on the goddess Mylitta to bless you'—Mylitta being the Assyrian name for Aphrodite. It can be any amount of money: by religious law she is not allowed to refuse it because it becomes sacred. The first man to throw money is the one she has to leave with; she cannot reject anyone. Once she has had sex with him, she has fulfilled her sacred obligation to the goddess and she is free to return home. Afterwards, you can offer her as much money as you like, but you will not get her. Women who are attractive and tall get to go home quickly, while the ugly ones wait for a long time without being able to do their duty. In fact, some of them wait three or four years. Almost exactly the same custom is practised in some parts of Cyprus too.

[200] So much for Babylonian customs. There are also three clans there who eat nothing but fish. Once they have caught them, they dry them in the sun, and then put them in a mortar, grind them up with pestles, and sieve the powder through pieces of muslin. Then they knead the powder into a kind of dough and have it this way, or they bake it like bread, according to their individual preferences.

[201] After having conquered the Assyrians, Cyrus was eager to bring the Massagetae under his rule. They are said to be a large tribe, with a reputation for being warlike. They live in the east, beyond the River Araxes and opposite the Issedones. There are some who claim that they are a Scythian people.

[202] Accounts of the size of the Araxes vary: some make it larger than the Ister, some smaller. There are said to be a great many islands in it which are about as big as Lesbos, and whose inhabitants live during the summer months off all kinds of roots that they dig up, while during the winter they eat the fruit from a kind of tree which, they have discovered, they can put into storage when

ripe and keep for later consumption. They have also discovered a
kind of plant whose fruit they use when they meet in groups. They
light a bonfire, sit around it, throw this fruit on the fire, and sniff
the smoke rising from the burning fruit they have thrown on to the
fire. The fruit is the equivalent there to wine in Greece: they get
intoxicated from the smoke, and then they throw more fruit on to
the fire and get even more intoxicated, until they eventually stand
up and dance, and burst into song.

That is how these people are supposed to live. The Araxes rises
in Matiene (as does the Gyndes, the river Cyrus divided into three
hundred and sixty channels), and it ends in forty mouths, all except
one of which issue into marshes and swamps, which are said to be
the homes of people who eat raw fish and normally wear sealskin
clothing. The one of the mouths which keeps cleanly to its channel
flows into the Caspian Sea. The Caspian Sea is isolated and does
not interconnect with the other sea. I say 'the other sea' because
the whole of the sea the Greeks sail and the one beyond the Pillars
of Heracles which is called the Atlantic and the Red Sea are actually a single sea.

[203] The Caspian, however, is a distinct sea, a sea in its own
right. Its length is such that it would take someone fifteen days to
row across it, and at its broadest point it would take eight days.
To the west of the Caspian spreads the Caucasus, which is the
largest mountain range in the world, with the tallest peaks. The
Caucasus is home to a wide variety of peoples, most of whom live
entirely off wild plants. In this part of the country there are said
to be trees with leaves which are such that people crush them, mix
them with water, and then use the juice to paint figures on their
clothes. These figures do not wash out, but grow old along with
the rest of the cloth as if they had been woven in from the start.
The people here are said to have sex out in the open, as herd
animals do.

[204] So the Caucasus presses in on the western shore of this
sea—the Caspian, as it is called. To the east, however, the sea is
succeeded by a plain which goes on for ever, as far as the eye can
see. The Massagetae, whom Cyrus was eager to attack, occupy
quite a sizeable portion of this huge plain. There were a number
of significant factors tempting and inducing him to undertake this
campaign. The main two were the apparently miraculous nature of

his birth, and the good fortune that attended him in war, in the
sense that any race which Cyrus sent his troops after found it
impossible to escape.

[205] At the time the Massagetae were ruled by a woman, since
her husband had died. Tomyris was her name. Cyrus sent an
ambassador to her with a message ostensibly of courtship, saying
that he wanted her to be his wife. However, Tomyris realized that
it was not her he was courting so much as the Massagetan kingdom, so she rejected his advances. Since Cyrus had got nowhere by
trickery, he next marched to the Araxes and started to wage open
war against the Massagetae. He began by bridging the river to
enable his army to cross and building towers on the boats which
ferried his troops across the river.

[206] While this work was in progress, Tomyris sent the following message to Cyrus: 'King of Persia, abandon your zeal for
this enterprise. You cannot know if in the end it will come out right
for you. Stop and rule your own people, and put up with the sight
of me ruling mine. But no: you are hardly going to take this advice,
since peace is the last thing you desire. If you really are committed
to a trial of strength with the Massagetae, you need not bother with
all the hard work of bridging the river; we will pull back three days'
journey away from the river and then you can cross over into our
land. Or if you would rather meet us in your own land, you withdraw the same distance.'

After hearing this message, Cyrus called all the leading Persians
to a conference, and once the meeting had convened he threw the
matter open for discussion, looking for advice as to what he should
do. They unanimously felt that they should meet Tomyris and her
army on their own ground.

[207] However, Croesus of Lydia was at the meeting and he disapproved of this idea. He argued against the prevalent view. 'My
lord,' he said, 'I told you before, when Zeus gave me to you, that
I would do all I could to avert any catastrophe I saw threatening
your house.† My own experiences have taught me an unwelcome
lesson. If you are think both you and the army under your
command are immortal, there's no point in my telling you my
opinion; but if you are aware that you are a human being and that
your subjects are too, then the first thing you should appreciate is
that human affairs are on a wheel, and that as the wheel turns
around it does not permit the same people always to prosper. Now,

my view of the issue currently before us contradicts the others'. The idea that we should meet the enemy in our own land is risky. Why? Because if you lose the battle you will also lose your whole empire. After all, if the Massagetae win, they're obviously not going to run back home; they'll march on into your provinces. On the other hand, if you win, you won't gain as much as you would if you had crossed into their territory, beaten the Massagetae there, and pursued them as they ran away. This scenario is the opposite of the one I described before, because if you beat the enemy you will march straight into Tomyris' domain. And apart from what I've said, it would be intolerably demeaning for Cyrus the son of Cambyses to withdraw and give ground to a woman. So I think we should cross the river and advance as far as they pull back, and then try to get the better of them by putting the following plan into effect. You see, a Persian-style good life and anything approaching real luxury is, I hear, something with which the Massagetae have no acquaintance or familiarity. Therefore, what I think we should do for these men is slaughter huge numbers of our livestock, prepare them for the table, and serve them up in our camp as a feast—a feast which also includes endless flagons of undiluted wine and a wide assortment of foods. Then we should leave the least important part of the army behind and pull the rest of the men back to the river again. If I am not mistaken, as soon as the Massagetae catch sight of all these good things, they will go for them, and that will give us the chance to achieve a magnificent victory.'

[208] Faced with these conflicting viewpoints, Cyrus abandoned the first one and adopted Croesus' plan. So he told Tomyris to pull her troops back, because he was going to cross over the river into her territory. And that is what she did, just as she had originally said she would. Cyrus handed Croesus over to his son Cambyses, to whom he was intending to leave the kingdom, and told him to treat Croesus with respect and kindness if the crossing and the assault on the Massagetae did not go well. Then he sent Croesus and his son back to Persia and proceeded to cross the river with his army.

[209] So Cyrus crossed the Araxes, and that night, asleep in the land of the Massagetae, he had a dream. He seemed in his dream to see Hystaspes' eldest son with wings growing out of his shoulder-blades; with one wing he cast a shadow over Asia, with the

other he overshadowed Europe. Now, Hystaspes the son of Arsames was an Achaemenid, and his eldest son was called Darius. At that time Darius was about 20 years old, and had been left behind in Persia, because he was still too young to go to war. When he woke up, Cyrus reflected on the dream. It struck him as an important dream, so he called for Hystaspes, took him aside, and said, 'Hystaspes, your son has been caught plotting against me and my empire. I am certain of his guilt, and I will tell you why. The gods care for me and they show me everything that is going to happen in advance. Now, last night, while I was asleep, I saw in a dream the eldest of your sons with wings growing from his shoulders; with one of these wings he was casting a shadow over Asia, and with the other he overshadowed Europe. As a result of this dream there can be absolutely no doubt that he is conspiring against me. I want you to go back to Persia as quickly as possible and make sure that on my return, once I have been victorious here, you bring your son before me for examination.'

[210] Cyrus' assumption in saying this was that Darius was conspiring against him, but in fact the gods were forewarning him of his own impending death there, and telling him that his kingdom would devolve on to Darius. Anyway, Hystaspes replied, 'My lord, there had better not be any Persian alive who is plotting against you. If there is, his death cannot come too soon, as far as I am concerned. After all, you have given the Persians their independence, when formerly they were slaves, and made them rulers of all others, when formerly they were ruled by others. If your dream tells you that my son is conspiring against you, I hand him over to you for you to deal with as you see fit.' With these words, Hystaspes crossed the Araxes and returned to Persia to watch over his son Darius for Cyrus.

[211] Cyrus advanced a day's journey into Massagetan territory from the Araxes and then did as Croesus had suggested. Then Cyrus and those of his men who were in peak condition withdrew back to the Araxes, leaving behind those who were unfit. A third of the Massagetan forces attacked this remnant of Cyrus' army, who put up some resistance, but were slaughtered. Once they had overcome this opposition, the Massagetae noticed the feast, which had been laid out, and they reclined and ate it. When they had eaten and drunk their fill, they fell asleep—and then the Persians fell on them. Many of the Massagetae were killed, but even more

were taken prisoner, including Queen Tomyris' son, who was the commander of the army and whose name was Spargapises.

[212] When news of what had happened to her army and her son reached the queen, she sent a herald to Cyrus with the following message: 'You bloodthirsty man, Cyrus! What you have done should give you no cause for celebration. You used the fruit of the vine—the wine which you swill until it drives you so mad that as it sinks into your bodies foul language rises up to your tongues. That was the drug, that was the trick you relied on to overcome my son, rather than conquering him by force in battle. Now I am giving good advice, so listen carefully: give me back my son, and then you can leave this country without paying for the brutality with which you treated a third of the Massagetan army. But if you do not, I swear by the sun who is the lord of the Massagetae that for all your insatiability I will quench your thirst for blood.'

[213] This was the message that was brought back to Cyrus, but he took not the slightest notice of it. When Spargapises, the son of Queen Tomyris, recovered from the wine and saw the trouble he was in, he begged Cyrus to release him from his chains. Cyrus granted his request, but as soon as Spargapises was free and had regained control of his hands, he killed himself.

[214] That was how Spargapises died. Since Cyrus refused to take her advice, Tomyris mustered all her forces and engaged Cyrus in battle. I consider this to be the fiercest battle between non-Greeks there has ever been, and in fact I have information that this was actually the case. At first, the two sides stood some distance apart and fired arrows at each other, and then, when they had no more arrows left to shoot, they came at each other and fought with spears and daggers. They fought at close quarters for a long time, and neither side would give way, until eventually the Massagetae gained the upper hand. Most of the Persian army was wiped out there, and Cyrus himself died too; his reign had lasted for twenty-nine years. Tomyris filled a wineskin with human blood and searched among the Persian corpses for Cyrus' body. When she found it, she shoved his head into the wineskin, and in her rage addressed his body as follows: 'Although I have come through the battle alive and victorious, you have destroyed me by capturing my son with a trick. But I warned you that I would quench your thirst for blood, and so I shall.' Of all the many stories

that are told about Cyrus' death, this one seems to me to be the
most trustworthy.

[215] The Massagetae resemble the Scythians in both their
clothing and their lifestyle. In battle they may or may not be on
horseback, since they rely on both methods, and as well as using
bows and spears it is normal for them to wield *sagareis*. They make
very extensive use of gold and bronze; they use bronze for the heads
of their spears and arrows and for the blades of their *sagareis*, and
gold to decorate their headgear, belts, and chest-bands. The same
goes for their horses too: they put bronze breastplates on their
fronts, but use gold on their bridles, bits, and cheek-bosses. Iron
and silver play no part in their lives, however, because there is in
fact none to be found in their country, although there is gold and
bronze in abundance.

[216] As for their customs, although each man marries a wife,
they all make their wives available for anyone else to have intercourse with. In Greece this is said to be a Scythian custom, but it
is Massagetan, not Scythian. If a Massagetan desires a woman, he
hangs his quiver outside her wagon and has sex with her, with no
fear of reprisal. The only imposed limit on life there is as follows.
When a person becomes very old, all his relatives come together
and sacrificially kill him and some livestock along with him; then
they stew the meat and eat it. They believe that there is no more
fortunate way to die, whereas anyone who dies after an illness is
buried in the ground rather than eaten, and they regard it as a
calamity that he did not get to be sacrificed. They do not cultivate
the land, but live off cattle and fish, which the Araxes River provides for them in vast quantities. They also drink milk. The only
god they worship is the sun, to whom they sacrifice horses. The
thinking behind this ritual is that they should offer the swiftest
mortal creature to the swiftest of the gods.

BOOK TWO

[1] After Cyrus' death, the kingdom passed to Cambyses, the son of Cyrus and of Cassandane the daughter of Pharnaspes. Cassandane had died while Cyrus was still alive, and as well as grieving deeply for her himself, he had ordered all his subjects to mourn her too. Anyway, with this woman as his mother and with Cyrus as his father, Cambyses thought of Ionians and Aeolians as slaves he had inherited from his father, and when he launched an expedition against Egypt, there were Greek subjects of his in the army, as well as contingents from various other peoples under his yoke.

[2] Before Psammetichus' reign, the Egyptians had regarded themselves as the oldest race on earth, but when Psammetichus became king he decided to settle the issue, and ever since then they have regarded themselves as older than everyone else except the Phrygians. Because his enquiries were unable to elicit an answer to the question which was the oldest race on earth, he devised the following experiment. He gave a shepherd two new-born infants to rear, from ordinary families, and told him to bring them up among his flocks in such a way that no one ever spoke in their hearing; they were to lie in a remote hut by themselves, and he was to bring them she-goats from time to time, give them their fill of milk, and do whatever else needed doing. Psammetichus made these arrangements because he wanted to find out what the children's very first word would be, once they were past the age of meaningless whimpering. And so it happened. One day, when the shepherd had been carrying out this programme for two years, he opened the door and went into the hut, and both children rushed up to him, reaching out their hands, and said '*bekos*'. The first time he heard this word, the shepherd did not do anything, but since it kept recurring on visit after visit, when he went there to tend to them, he passed the information on to his master. Psammetichus told him to bring the children to him, and the shepherd did so. When Psammetichus heard the word for himself, he started trying to find out

which people call something '*bekos*', and he was told that it was the Phrygian word for bread. This is the event which led the Egyptians to conclude that the Phrygians were an older race than themselves. I heard this version of the story from the priests of Hephaestus in Memphis, but the Greek version includes, among its many other absurdities, the detail that Psammetichus cut out some women's tongues and then had the children live with these women.

[3] This is what I heard about the children and their upbringing, and I heard other things as well in Memphis during my conversations with the priests of Hephaestus. The information I gained there led me to travel to Thebes and to Heliopolis, to try to find out whether their accounts would agree with what I had heard in Memphis, because there are said to be no Egyptians more learned than the Heliopolitans. Because I believe that everyone is equal in terms of religious knowledge, I do not see any point in relating anything I was told about the gods, except their names alone. If I do refer to such matters, it will be because my account leaves me no choice.

[4] As far as human matters are concerned, the priests all agreed in what they told me. They claimed that the Egyptians were the first people to discover the year, and to distribute throughout the year the twelve parts into which they divided the seasons. They said that they discovered this from the stars. It seems to me that the Egyptian monthly system is cleverer than the Greek one: the progress of the seasons forces the Greeks to insert an intercalary month every other year, whereas because the Egyptians have twelve months of thirty days and add five extra days on to every year, the seasonal cycle comes round to the same point in their calendar each time.

The priests also told me that the Egyptians were the first to establish the epithets of the Twelve Gods and that the Greeks got these epithets from them, and they claim to have been the first to assign the gods altars, statues, and temples and to carve figures on to stones. They actually demonstrated the validity of most of these claims, but I have only their word for the fact that the first man to rule over Egypt was called Min. In his time, the whole of Egypt, except for the Thebaïd province, was a marsh and the whole present country below the lake of Moeris (which is a seven-day sail up the river from the sea) was under water.

[5] My view is that they are right in saying this about the country. Even someone—a man of intelligence, at any rate—who has not already heard about it, but just uses his eyes, can easily see that the Egypt to which the Greeks sail is new land which the Egyptians have gained as a gift from the river. The same also goes for the land up to three days' sailing upstream from this lake; the priests told me nothing of the kind about it, but it is more of the same. The physical geography of Egypt is such that as you approach the country by sea, if you let down a sounding-line when you are still a day's journey away from land, you will bring up mud in eleven fathoms of water. This shows that there is silt this far out.

[6] The length of the coastline of Egypt proper is sixty schoeni. That is, I take it that the coastline from the Gulf of Plinthine to Lake Serbonis (alongside which is Mount Casius) is Egypt, and from the one place to the other it is sixty schoeni. People with little land use fathoms as their standard of measurement, those who are somewhat better off for land use stades, those with plenty of land use parasangs, and those with an excessively huge amount of land use schoeni. A parasang is thirty stades, and one schoenus, which is the unit of measurement the Egyptians use, is sixty stades. It follows that the Egyptian coastline extends for 3,600 stades.

[7] From the coast to the interior of the country as far as Heliopolis Egypt is a broad country, consisting of plains, water, and marshland. The journey inland from the coast to Heliopolis is more or less as long as the journey from the Altar of the Twelve Gods in Athens to the temple of Olympian Zeus in Pisa. If one were to measure these two routes, one would find that the distance is not exactly the same—that they differ by the slight amount of not more than fifteen stades. The journey from Athens to Pisa is fifteen stades short of 1,500 stades, whereas the journey from the Egyptian coast to Heliopolis is exactly 1,500 stades.

[8] Continuing south from Heliopolis Egypt becomes narrow. On the Arabian side it is bounded by a mountain range which runs from north to south and then continues inland without a break towards what is known as the Red Sea. In these mountains are the quarries where the stone for the pyramids in Memphis was cut. Here the mountains start to decline and the range changes direction, as mentioned, towards the Red Sea. As I myself found out, it

takes two months to traverse the mountains from east to west at their widest point, and the country at their eastern end produces frankincense. That is what this mountain range is like. As for the Libyan side of Egypt, it is bounded by another rocky mountain range, where the pyramids are to be found. These mountains are covered with sand and run parallel to the part of the Arabian range which runs south. So south of Heliopolis there is not much land, in Egyptian terms; in fact, within approximately four† days' sailing upstream from Heliopolis, the land is narrow, for Egypt. Between the two mountain ranges mentioned the land is level, and it seemed to me that, at its narrowest point, there were no more than two hundred stades between the Arabian range and the Libyan mountains. Further upstream, however, Egypt broadens out again.

[9] That is what this part of the country is like. From Heliopolis upstream to Thebes is a voyage of nine days, covering 4,860 stades (or eighty-one schoeni). The total extent of Egypt in stades, then, is as follows. The coastline, as I have already explained, is 3,600 stades long, and now I can indicate how far it is from the coast to the interior of the land, as far as Thebes: it is 6,120 stades. Then from Thebes to the city of Elephantine is another 1,800 stades.

[10] Most of the land in question has been recently gained by the Egyptians; this was my personal impression as well as being what the priests told me. The land south of the city of Memphis, between the mountain ranges mentioned, looked to me as though in times past it was a gulf of the sea, as was the case with the land near Ilium, Teuthrania, Ephesus, and the plain of the Meander. But this is to compare small with large, because none of the rivers whose deposits gave rise to these lands bears comparison in terms of size with one of the mouths of the Nile—and the Nile has five mouths. There are other rivers as well which, though not as large as the Nile, have had substantial results. In particular (although I could name others), there is the Acheloüs, which flows through Acarnania into the sea and has already turned half the Echinades islands into mainland.

[11] In Arabia, quite close to Egypt, there is a gulf which is an extension of the Red Sea; this gulf is very long and narrow, as I shall now describe. Its length is such that if one started from the head of the gulf and rowed right down it to the open sea, the voyage would take forty days; its breadth, however, is half a day's voyage,

at the gulf's widest point. The tide in this gulf ebbs and flows every day. In my opinion, in times past Egypt was another such gulf, so that there was one gulf extending from the northern sea towards Ethiopia, and another (the Arabian Gulf, which I will speak of shortly)† coming from the south towards Syria; the two gulfs almost bored through to join together at their heads, but a little strip of land kept them apart. So if the Nile decided to change its course and flow into this Arabian Gulf, what would stop the gulf from silting up within twenty thousand years? In fact, I expect it would take less than ten thousand years. Now, in all the time which has preceded my own lifetime, would even a much larger gulf than the one I am talking about not have become silted up by such a large and vigorous river?

[12] I am sure that those who give this account of Egypt are right, and I am particularly convinced of its correctness because I have seen that Egypt projects beyond the adjacent landmass, that shells appear in the mountains, that salt forms crusts on the surface of the ground and corrodes even the pyramids, and that the only sandy mountain range in Egypt is the one overlooking Memphis. Besides, I have observed the dissimilarity between Egyptian soil and that of Arabia and Libya, its neighbours, and that of Syria too (which is worth mentioning because the Syrians inhabit the coast-line of Arabia): Egyptian soil is black and friable, which suggests that it was once mud and silt carried down from Ethiopia by the river. Libyan soil, on the other hand, I know to be redder and more sandy, while Arabian and Syrian soil is more clayey and stony.

[13] Another thing the priests told me about the land is an important piece of evidence. They told me that in the time of King Moeris the river had only to rise a minimum of eight cubits and it flooded the country north of Memphis. Now, Moeris had been dead less than nine hundred years, at the time when I was told this by the priests. Nowadays, however, unless the river rises a minimum of fifteen or sixteen cubits, it does not spill over on to the land. It seems to me that if the land continues to increase in height, and similarly expands in extent, at the same rate as it has in the past, until the Nile stops flooding the land, then the Egyptians who live north of the lake of Moeris, and especially those who live in the Delta (as it is called), will some time in the future be permanently in the situation they once said the Greeks would experience. When they found out that the whole of Greece relies on rainfall rather

than its rivers, as Egypt does, to irrigate the land, they commented that the Greeks would one day have their high hopes dashed and would suffer the torments of starvation. What they were getting at was that if the god decides not to rain and maintains a state of drought instead, the Greeks will die of hunger, because Zeus is their only source of water.

[14] In saying this about the Greeks, the Egyptians were right. But now I will state the situation the Egyptians themselves are in. As I said before, if the land north of Memphis (which is the land that is growing) continues gaining height at the same rate as it has in the past, the Egyptians living there will starve, as long as the land is not watered by rain and the river cannot spill over on to their fields. What other possible consequence is there? At the moment, of course, they gather their crops with less effort than anyone else in the world, including the rest of Egypt. They do not work at breaking the land up into furrows with a plough, they do not have to wield hoes or carry out any of the other crop-farming tasks which everyone else does. Instead, the river rises of its own accord and irrigates their fields, and when the water has receded again, each of them sows seed in his own field and sends pigs into it to tread the seed down. Once this has been done, he only has to wait for harvest-time, and then he has his pigs thresh the grain. And that is how he brings in his crops.

[15] Now, if we want to adopt the Ionian view—that Egypt consists of only the Delta, defined as the 40-schoeni stretch of coast-line between the watch-hill of Perseus (as it is known) and the fish-salting works of Pelusium, and as extending inland as far as city of Cercasorus, where the Nile divides and flows respectively to Pelusium and to Canobus, while all the rest of Egypt, on this view, belongs either to Libya or to Arabia—if we choose to follow this view, we can demonstrate that in times past the Egyptians had no country at all. For the Delta is now alluvial and is, so to speak, a brand-new phenomenon; this is what the Egyptians themselves claim, and I agree. If they had no land, then, why do they waste their time with the belief that they were the earliest human race? They would not have had to carry out that experiment with the infants to find out what would be the first language they would speak. The facts of the matter, in my opinion, are that the Egyptians did not come into existence along with the Delta that the Ionians call Egypt,† but that they have always existed, as long as

there have been human beings, and that as their land grew a good number of them stayed behind, but a good number also gradually moved downstream. However, it is true that long ago the Thebaïd (which is 6,120 stades around its borders) was called Egypt.

[16] So if I interpret these matters correctly, the Ionians are not being very intelligent about Egypt. However, if the Ionian view is correct, I can demonstrate that the Greeks and the Ionians themselves do not know how to count. They claim that the whole world is divided into three parts—Europe, Asia, and Libya. But then they should add a fourth part, the Delta of Egypt, if it does not belong to either Asia or Libya. After all, on their account, the Nile does not form the border between Asia and Libya, but divides at the apex of this Delta and flows around it; and it follows from this that the Delta must be between Asia and Libya.

[17] Anyway, let us say no more about the Ionian view. My personal opinion about these matters is as follows. Egypt is the whole land inhabited by Egyptians, just as Cilicia or Assyria are the countries where Cilicians or Assyrians live; and I know of no true boundary between Asia and Libya except the borders of Egypt. If we adopt the Greek view, we will have to regard the whole of Egypt, all the way from the Cataracts and Elephantine, as consisting of two halves, each with a different name—one half being part of Libya, the other part of Asia. After all, from the Cataracts all the way to the sea, the Nile flows right through the middle of Egypt and divides it into two. It flows in a single bed until Cercasorus, where it divides into three branches. One turns east (this one is called the Pelusian mouth), another turns west (this one is called the Canobic mouth), and the third branch of the Nile carries straight on: it continues towards the coast until it reaches the apex of the Delta, and then it divides the Delta in two and issues into the sea. The largest proportion of the river's water is carried by this branch, and it is particularly famous; it is called the Sebennytic mouth. There are also two other mouths which break off from the Sebennytic mouth and carry on to the sea, and the names they have been given are the Saïtic mouth and the Mendesian mouth. The Bolbitine and Bucolic mouths, however, are not natural mouths, but are man-made canals.

[18] Evidence in support of my view that Egypt is the size I show it to be can also be found in an oracle delivered by Ammon, which I heard about after I had formed my own opinions about Egypt.

The citizens of Marea and Apis, which are in the part of Egypt that borders Libya, regarded themselves as Libyans rather than Egyptians and did not like some of the religious observances they had to follow; in particular, they did not want to have to abstain from cow's meat. So they sent emissaries to Ammon, claiming that they and the Egyptians had nothing in common, in the sense that they lived outside the Delta and were completely different, and saying that they wanted to be able to eat everything. But the god refused to let them go ahead. His response to them was to say that any land watered by the Nile in flood was Egypt, and that anyone living north of Elephantine who drank the water of the Nile was an Egyptian.

[19] When it bursts its banks, the Nile inundates not only the Delta, but also some tracts of land which are supposed to be Libyan and Arabian, for as much as two days' journey on either side, though it may be more or less than this. I could not gain any information about the nature of the river from the priests or from anyone else. I was particularly eager to find out from them why the Nile starts coming down in a flood at the summer solstice and continues flooding for a hundred days, but when the hundred days are over the water starts to recede and decrease in volume, with the result that it remains low for the whole winter, until the summer solstice comes round again. No one in Egypt could give me any information about this at all, when I asked them what it was about the Nile that made it behave in the opposite way from all other rivers. My desire to know about these matters led me to make enquiries, and I also tried to find out why it is the only river in the world from which no breezes blow.

[20] Three different theories have been advanced by certain Greek thinkers, who were, however, motivated by a desire to enhance their reputation as clever people. Two of these views would not be worth mentioning, in my opinion, except that I do want to give some idea of what they are. The first claims that the Etesian winds prevent the Nile from flowing out into the sea, and so cause it to flood. However, the fact is that the Nile carries on as usual even when the Etesian winds are not blowing. Moreover, if the Etesian winds were responsible for the Nile's flooding, the same thing that happens to the Nile would also happen to any other rivers which run counter to these winds; in fact, it would happen even more, in so far as, being smaller rivers, they have weaker cur-

rents. But there are plenty of rivers in Syria, and plenty of others in Libya, whose behaviour is nothing like that of the Nile.

[21] The second theory is even more ignorant than the one I have just mentioned, though it is more striking in expression; it claims that it is because the Nile flows from the Ocean that it manages to do what it does, and that the Ocean surrounds the whole world.

[22] The third theory, despite being the most plausible, is also the furthest from the truth. It claims that the water of the Nile comes from melting snow, but this is just as nonsensical as the others. The Nile flows from Libya and through the middle of Ethiopia until it ends up in Egypt. How, then, could it rise in snowy regions, when its course takes it from the hottest places in the world to places which are, by and large, cooler? The idea that it rises in snowy regions makes no sense at all, as anyone capable of rational thought could realize. The first and most convincing piece of evidence is that the winds which blow from these regions are warm. Secondly, it never rains and frost never forms in the regions in question, whereas it is absolutely inevitable that rain will fall within five days of snow, and so if there was snow in these regions, there would also be rain. Thirdly, it is so hot there that the people are black. Also, kites and swallows stay there all the year round without leaving, and cranes flee the winter in Scythia and migrate to these regions to spend the winter there. In short, it necessarily follows that if it snowed even a little bit in the regions through which the Nile flows and where it rises, none of these things would happen.

[23] It is impossible to argue against the person who spoke about the Ocean, because the tale is based on something which is obscure and dubious. I do not know of the existence of any River Ocean, and I think that Homer or one of the other poets from past times invented the name and introduced it into his poetry.

[24] I suppose that, having criticized the theories that have been proposed, I should state my own theory about this obscure issue. So this is why I think the Nile floods in the summer. In winter, the sun is driven by storms out of its original path and into the inland regions of Libya. That sums up my view as briefly as possible. After all, it stands to reason that the nearer the god is to a land, and the closer he passes over it, the more that land will lack water and the more its rivers will dry up.

[25] If I am to express my view in more detail, it is as follows. In inland Libya, the air is constantly clear, the land is exposed to the sun, and there are no cold winds, so as the sun passes over those parts it does exactly what it usually does in summer as it passes through the mid-heaven: it draws the water to itself and then pushes it away inland, where the winds take over, and scatter and disperse the moisture. Just as one would expect, then, the winds that blow from there—the south and south-westerly winds—are by far the most rainy of all the winds. (However, I am sure that the sun does not in fact get rid of the whole of the Nile's annual volume of water each time, but keeps some of it in its own vicinity.) As the winter storms die down, the sun resumes its former course across the mid-heaven, and from then on it draws water equally from all rivers, not just the Nile. Meanwhile, however, all the other rivers have been swollen by plenty of rain-water, and because the land is rainy and full of ravines, they pour down in torrents, whereas during summer, when the rains fail and they are being sucked up by the sun, their currents are feeble. The Nile, on the other hand, is not being fed by rain and is being sucked up by the sun, and so it stands to reason that it is the only river which flows at this time of year at a considerably reduced volume, compared with its volume during the summer. In the summer months, the sun draws water out of the Nile just as much as it does out of all bodies of water, but in winter it is the only one to suffer. And this, I have concluded, is how the sun is responsible for these phenomena.

[26] The sun is also responsible, in my opinion, for the dryness of the air there: it scorches the air as it passes through it. That is why inland Libya is in the grip of constant summer. If the seasons changed position, so that the part of the sky currently occupied by the north wind and winter was occupied by the south wind and noon, and vice versa—if this happened, then when the sun was driven from the mid-heaven by the storms of winter and the north wind, it would go to inland Europe (just as now it goes to inland Libya), and as it passed over Europe I expect it would have the same effect on the Ister as it now does on the Nile.

[27] As for the fact that there is no cool breeze off the Nile, it is in my opinion hardly surprising that no such breeze blows from places that are warm; a cool breeze tends to blow from somewhere cold.

[28] Well, as far as this subject is concerned, it has always been the way it is and we can leave it to continue. As for the question where the Nile rises, no Egyptian or Libyan or Greek I have spoken to claimed to have the definitive answer, except the scribe of the treasury of Athena in the city of Saïs in Egypt—and I got the impression that he was joking when he said that he knew the answer for certain. But what he said was that there were two mountains with sharply pointed peaks between the cities of Syene in the Thebaïd and Elephantine, which were called Crophi and Mophi; between them, he said, rise the springs of the Nile, which are bottomless, and half of their water flows north towards Egypt, while the other half flows south towards Ethiopia. He also told me that King Psammetichus of Egypt found a way to test the fact that the springs are bottomless. He had a rope made, many thousands of fathoms long, and this was let down but did not reach the bottom. Now, if this story of the scribe's was true, all he proved, to my mind, was that there are strong whirlpools and counter-currents there, and because the water was dashing against the mountains, this prevented them reaching the bottom when they let their sounding-line down.

[29] I was unable to get any information from anyone else. However, I myself travelled as far as Elephantine and saw things with my very own eyes, and subsequently made enquiries of others; as a result of these two methods, the very most I could find out was as follows.

After Elephantine the land rises steeply, so that from then on one has to have a rope running from the boat to both banks, as one harnesses an ox, and to proceed like that. If the rope were to break, the boat would be carried downstream by the force of the current. This kind of terrain lasts for four days' travelling, and the Nile here twists and turns as much as the Meander. One has to travel in this fashion for a distance of twelve schoeni, and then you come to a level plain, where the Nile flows around an island called Tachompso. The inhabitants of the country south of Elephantine, and of half the island, are Ethiopians, while the other half of the island is occupied by Egyptians. Near the island is a vast lake (on whose margins Ethiopian nomads live) which you have to sail across to rejoin the Nile, which flows into this lake. At this point you leave your boat and travel by foot by the side of the river for forty days, because there are sharp rocks sticking out of the water and a number of reefs which are unnavigable. Once you have spent the forty days passing through this region, you take another boat and twelve days of travel will bring you to a big city called Meroë, which is said to be the capital city of all Ethiopia. The only gods worshipped by the people here are Zeus and Dionysus, whom they revere greatly; an oracle of Zeus has been established there. They make war when and where Zeus commands them through his oracular pronouncements.

[30] If you continue upriver past this city for the same amount of time again as you spent travelling from Elephantine to the Ethiopian capital, you will reach the Deserters, or *Asmakh* as they are called—a word which, translated into Greek, means 'those who stand to the left of the king'. They were originally 240,000 Egyptian soldiers who deserted to Ethiopia, for the following reason. In the time of King Psammetichus, there were garrisons established in various places: one in Elephantine to afford protection against the Ethiopians, another in Pelusian Daphnae against the Arabians and Syrians, and another in Marea against Libya. (Even in my day there were Persian guard-posts in the same places as there had been in the time of King Psammetichus: the Persians manned garrisons in both Elephantine and Daphnae.) Anyway, the Egyptian troops had been on garrison duty for three years, and no one had come to relieve them. They discussed the matter among themselves and came to the unanimous decision that they should mutiny against Psammetichus and go over to Ethiopia. When Psammetichus found out what they were doing, he came after them. He caught up with them and made a long speech pleading with them and trying to persuade them not to abandon their ancestral deities and their wives and children. At this, one of the soldiers, so the story goes, pointed to his genitals and said that wherever this was he would have wives and children. When they reached Ethiopia, they entrusted themselves to the Ethiopian king, who gave them a gift in return. Some of the Ethiopians had become rebellious, and he told the Egyptians to drive out the disaffected people and then they could have their land to live in. As a result of their living there, the Ethiopians have learnt Egyptian customs and become less wild.

[31] Anyway, the Nile is known to exist for the distance of four months' river and land travel beyond where it enters Egypt; if you add it all up, that is how many months you will find the journey

from Elephantine to these Deserters takes. At this point, the Nile is flowing from the west. But from then there is no reliable information to be had about it: the land is uninhabited because of the heat.

[32] However, I heard from some men from Cyrene how once, in the course of a visit to the oracle of Ammon, they got into conversation with Etearchus the king of the Ammonians. The conversation happened to come around to the Nile and how no one knows about its source, and Etearchus told them about a visit he had once had from some Nasamones, a Libyan tribe who live around the Gulf of Syrtis and the land a little way east of the Syrtis. During the course of their visit, the Nasamones were asked whether they could add to what was known about the uninhabited desert parts of Libya. In response, they told how some high-spirited chiefs' sons of their tribe, once they had reached adulthood, concocted a number of extraordinary schemes, including casting lots to choose five of their number to go and explore the Libyan desert, to find out if they could see more than had ever been seen before. Libyans—many tribes of them—have spread out along the whole of the Libyan coastline of the northern sea, from Egypt to Cape Soloeis (where Libya ends), except for land occupied by Greeks and Phoenicians. Then there is the part of Libya which is inland from the sea and from the people who occupy the seaboard: this is the part of Libya which is infested by wild animals. Further inland from the part full of animals Libya is sandy desert, totally waterless, and completely uninhabited by anyone or anything. So when the young men left their friends, the story goes, they were well equipped with food and water; they first passed through the inhabited region and then reached the part which is infested by wild animals. Next they started to travel in a westerly direction through the desert. After they had crossed a great deal of sandy country, surrounded by nothing but desert, they at last, after many days, saw trees growing on a plain. They approached the trees and tried to pick the fruit that was growing on them, but as they were doing so they were set upon by small men of less than normal human stature, who captured them and took them away. The two groups—the Nasamones and their guides—could not understand each other's language at all. They were taken through vast swamps and on the other side of these swamps they came to a town where everyone was the same

size as their guides and had black skin. The town was on a size-able river, which was flowing from west to east, and in it they could see crocodiles.

[33] So much for my account of what the Ammonian king Etearchus said. The only thing I will add is that, according to the Cyreneans, he said that the Nasamones made it back home and that the people they had reached were all magicians. Also, Etearchus came to the conclusion that the river which the town was on was the Nile. Now, this makes sense, in fact, because the Nile cuts through the middle of Libya before entering Egypt from there, and since we may draw on the familiar to understand the unknown, I reckon that its total length is the same as that of the Ister. The Ister rises in the land of the Celts, at the city of Pyrene (the Celts live beyond the Pillars of Heracles and are neighbours of the Cynesians who are the westernmost European people), and flows through the middle of Europe; its course takes it right through Europe to the Milesian colony of Istria, on the Euxine Sea, where it ends.

[34] Now, since the Ister flows through inhabited lands, it is well known, but no one can state where the source of the Nile is, because the part of Libya through which the river flows is unin-habited desert. I have already given the fullest possible information about its course that my enquiries could gain me. It ends up in Egypt, which is more or less exactly opposite the mountainous part of Cilicia, and the direct route from there to Sinope on the Euxine Sea would take a man travelling light five days. Sinope in its turn is opposite where the Ister issues into the sea. This is why I think the Nile flows through the whole of Libya and is the same length as the Ister. Anyway, that is enough about the Nile.

[35] I am going to talk at some length about Egypt, because it has very many remarkable features and has produced more mon-uments which beggar description than anywhere else in the world. That is why more will be said about it. In keeping with the idio-syncratic climate which prevails there and the fact that their river behaves differently from any other river, almost all Egyptian customs and practices are the opposite of those of everywhere else. For instance, women go out to the town square and retail goods, while men stay at home and do the weaving; and whereas every-one else weaves by pushing the weft upwards, the Egyptians push it downwards. Or again, men carry loads on their heads, while

women do so on their shoulders. Women urinate standing up, while men do so squatting. They relieve themselves indoors, but eat outside on the streets; the reason for this, they say, is that things that are embarrassing but unavoidable should be done in private, while things which are not embarrassing should be done out in the open. There are no female priestesses of any god or goddess; all their gods, and goddesses too, are served in this capacity by men. Sons do not have to look after their parents if they do not want to, but daughters must even if they are reluctant.

[36] Everywhere else in the world, priests have long hair, but in Egypt they shave their heads. In times of mourning, it is the norm elsewhere for those most affected by the bereavement to crop their hair; in Egypt, however, in the period following a death, they let both their hair and their beards grow, when they had previously been shaved. Everywhere else in the world people live separately from their animals, but animals and humans live together in Egypt. Other people live off barley and ordinary wheat, but Egyptians regard it as demeaning to make those grains one's staple diet; their staple is hulled wheat, or 'emmer' as it is sometimes known. They knead dough with their feet and clay with their hands, and they pick up dung with their hands too.† Other people, unless they have been influenced by the Egyptians, leave their genitals in their natural state, but the Egyptians practise circumcision. Men have two cloaks each, but women have only one. In other countries rings and reefing-ropes are attached to the outside of the sail, but in Egypt they are on the inside. As Greeks write and do their sums they move their hands from left to right, but Egyptians move from right to left; although this is their actual practice, they say that they are doing it right, while the Greeks are left-handed. They have two kinds of script, one of which is called 'sacred' or 'hieroglyphic', while the other is called 'demotic'.

[37] Because they are exceedingly religious, more so than any other people in the world, they have the following customs. Everyone, without any exceptions, scrubs clean the bronze cup he uses for drinking every day. The linen cloaks they wear are always freshly washed; this is something they are very particular about. Their concern for cleanliness also explains why they practise circumcision, since they value cleanliness more than comeliness. Priests shave every part of their bodies every other day, to stop themselves getting lice or in general being at all unclean as they

minister to the gods. The priests wear only one garment made out of linen, while their shoes are papyrus; they are not allowed to wear any other kind of clothing or footwear, and they wash with cold water twice every day and twice at night too. It is hardly an exaggeration to say that the priests practise thousands upon thousands of other religious observances. However, they gain plenty of benefits as well: they do not have anything of their own to wear out or to consume, but even their food, which is sacred, is cooked for them; each of them is also provided with a generous daily allowance of beef and goose-meat, and their wine is donated as well. They are not allowed to eat fish. The Egyptians do not cultivate beans in their country at all, and any beans that grow there are not eaten either raw or cooked. Priests cannot even stand the sight of beans, since they consider them to be an impure form of legume. Each deity has a number of priests, not just one, though there is a single high priest in each case; when a priest dies, his son is appointed in his place.

[38] Bulls are thought to be the property of Epaphus and are therefore examined as follows. If even a single black hair is found growing on a bull, he is regarded as unclean. One of the priests is given the job of searching for black hairs on the animal and he has to examine it when it is on its back, as well as when it is standing up. He also pulls out its tongue, to see if it is free from certain prescribed features, which I will describe later. He examines its tail hairs too, to make sure they are growing properly. If the bull is pure in all these respects, the priest marks it by winding papyrus around its horns, which is then sealed with clay and stamped with the priest's signet-ring. The bull is then led away. The penalty for sacrificing a bull which has not been marked in this way is death. So that is how they test the animal.

[39] The way they perform the sacrifice is as follows. They take the marked beast to the altar where the sacrifice is to take place and light a fire. Then they sprinkle wine over the sacrificial victim and on to the altar, invoke the deity, and cut the animal's throat. Once this is done, they cut off its head. They skin the body, but call down many curses on the creature's head and bear it away. In towns which have a square and where there are resident Greek traders, they take the head to the square and sell it, but if there are no Greeks around, they throw it away in the river. The intention expressed in the curses they call down on the victims' heads is to

divert on to the creature's head any evil that might befall either the particular worshippers or Egypt as a whole. The same practice as regards the heads of the sacrificial animals and the sprinkling of wine is followed all over Egypt in all their sacrifices, and as a result of this practice no Egyptian will eat the head of any living creature.

[40] The way the entrails are removed and burnt varies from victim to victim in Egypt. I shall talk about the most important goddess in their religion and about the most important festival they celebrate. After skinning the bull, they offer up prayers and remove all the intestines, but leave the rest of its innards and the fat in the body. Then they cut off its legs, the very end of its rump, its shoulders, and its neck. Next, they fill the remainder of the bull's body with purified loaves, honey, raisins, figs, frankincense, myrrh, and other perfumed spices, and then they burn it all, while pouring over it huge quantities of oil. They fast before performing the sacrifice, and everyone beats his breast in grief as the entrails are being burnt. Once they have finished grieving, they serve up the remaining bits of the entrails as a meal.

[41] It is universal practice in Egypt to sacrifice unblemished bulls and male calves, but they are not allowed to offer cows for sacrifice, because they are sacred to Isis. The way Isis is represented in statuary is as a woman with cow's horns (as the Greeks depict Io), and all Egyptians regard cows as far more sacred than any other herd animal. That is why no Egyptian man or woman will kiss a Greek on the mouth, or use a Greek's knife, skewers, or cooking-pot; in fact they will not eat the flesh of even an unblemished bull if a Greek knife was used to cut it up.

The way they bury their cattle as they die is as follows. They throw cows into the river, but bulls are interred by the local inhabitants on the margins of their community, with one or both horns sticking out of the ground as a marker. When the flesh has rotted and the allotted time has come, a *baris* comes to each community from Prosopitis, which is an island in the Delta with a circumference of nine schoeni. There are various communities on the island, but the one from which the *bareis* come to collect the bulls' bones is called Atarbechis, and it contains a sanctuary dedicated to Aphrodite. People are constantly making trips from this town all over the place to the various other communities, where they dig up the bones, take them back to Atarbechis and bury them in a single spot. They do not kill other dying animals either, but their practice as regards them too is to bury them in the same way that they bury their cattle.

[42] Apart from the fact that Isis and Osiris (whom they identify with Dionysus) are worshipped by everyone throughout Egypt, not all Egyptians worship the same gods. For instance, anyone whose place of worship is a sanctuary of Theban Zeus, or who comes from the Theban province, will have nothing to do with sheep, but uses goats as his sacrificial animals, whereas anyone with a sanctuary of Mendes or who comes from the province of Mendes, will have nothing to do with goats, but uses sheep as his sacrificial animals. Now, Thebans and those who follow them in avoiding the use of sheep explain the establishment of this prohibition in the following way. They say that Heracles' overriding desire was to see Zeus, but Zeus was refusing to let him do so. Eventually, as a result of Heracles' pleading, Zeus came up with a plan. He skinned a ram and cut off its head, then he held the head in front of himself, wore the fleece, and showed himself to Heracles like that. That is why Egyptian statues of Zeus have a ram's head. (Ammonian statues of Zeus are the same; the Ammonians learned the convention from Egypt, because they were originally emigrants from Egypt and Ethiopia, and their language is a hybrid of Egyptian and Ethiopian. It seems to me that we also have here the origin of the Ammonians' name, because the Egyptians call Zeus 'Amun'.) Anyway, that is why rams are sacred to the Thebans and they do not use them as sacrificial animals. However, there is just one day of the year—the day of the festival of Zeus—when they chop up a single ram, skin it, dress the statue of Zeus in it in the way just mentioned, and then bring a statue of Heracles up close to the statue of Zeus. Then everyone in and around the sanctuary mourns the death of the ram and finally they bury it in a sacred tomb.

[43] I was told that Heracles was one of the Twelve Gods, but I could not hear anything anywhere in Egypt about the other Heracles, the one familiar to the Greeks. Now, I could supply a great deal of evidence to support the idea that the Greeks got the name of Heracles from Egypt, rather than the other way round, and that then the Greeks applied the name Heracles to the son of Amphitryon. I have a great deal of evidence pointing in this direction. Here is just one item: both parents of the Greek Heracles, Amphitryon and Alcmene, trace their lineage back to Egypt.

Moreover, the Egyptians claim not to know the names of Poseidon and the Dioscuri, and these gods are not to be found in their pantheon. But if the Egyptians had borrowed the name of any deity from the Greeks, Poseidon and the Dioscuri would not have been overlooked, but would have stuck in their minds more than any other Greek deity—if I am right in my view that even in those days the Egyptians were making sea voyages and so were some of the Greeks. From this it follows that the Egyptians would be more aware of the names of these gods than they would of Heracles. No, in fact Heracles is a very ancient Egyptian god; as they themselves say, it was seventeen thousand years before the reign of King Amasis when the Twelve Gods descended from the Eight Gods, and they regard Heracles as one of the Twelve.

[44] I wanted to understand these matters as clearly as I could, so I also sailed to Tyre in Phoenicia, since I had heard that there was a sanctuary sacred to Heracles there, and I found that the sanctuary there was very lavishly appointed with a large number of dedicatory offerings. In it were two pillars, one of pure gold, the other of emerald which gleamed brightly at night.† I talked to the priests of the god there and asked them how long ago the sanctuary was founded, and I discovered that they too disagreed with the Greek account, because according to them the sanctuary of the god was founded at the same time as Tyre, which was 2,300 years ago, they said. I also saw another sanctuary of Heracles in Tyre, which is called the sanctuary of Heracles the Thasian. I went to Thasos as well, and I found there a sanctuary of Heracles which had been founded by Phoenician explorers who had left their homeland in search of Europa and had colonized Thasos. And this happened as much as five generations before Heracles the son of Amphitryon was born in Greece. These enquiries of mine, then, clearly show that Heracles is an ancient god. So I think those Greeks did just right who established two kinds of cult for Heracles, in one of which they sacrifice to Heracles as an immortal god—Olympian Heracles, as he is known—while in the other they make offerings to him as a hero.

[45] The Greek account of Heracles' birth is far from being the only thoughtless thing they say. Here is another silly story of theirs about Heracles. They say that when he came to Egypt, the Egyptians crowned him with garlands and led him in a procession with the intention of sacrificing him to Zeus. He did nothing for a

while, and began to resist only when they were consecrating him at the altar, at which point he massacred them all. Now, in my opinion, this Greek tale displays complete ignorance of the Egyptian character and customs. For it is against their religion for Egyptians to sacrifice animals (except for sheep, ritually pure bulls and male calves, and geese), so how could they sacrifice human beings? And how could Heracles kill thousands and thousands of people when he was just one person, and (by their own admission) not yet a god either? Anyway, that is all I have to say about this matter; I trust the gods and heroes will look kindly on my words.

[46] The reason the Egyptians I mentioned do not sacrifice goats of either gender is as follows. The Mendesians count Pan as one of the Eight Gods, and according to them the Eight Gods precede the Twelve Gods. Pan's portrait in Egypt, as represented by artists and sculptors, is the same as it is in Greece—that is, with a goat's head and a he-goat's legs. It is not that they think he looks like that; he is no different from any of the other gods, in their view. However, I should prefer not to explain why they depict him that way. Mendesians regard all goats as sacred—he-goats more than she-goats—and goatherds of male goats are held in particular respect. One he-goat is chosen to be an especial object of veneration, and when it dies the whole Mendesian province is given over to mourning. In the Egyptian language the word Mendes means 'he-goat' as well as 'Pan'. A remarkable thing happened in this province in my time: a goat mated with a woman, for all to see. This happened in public view.

[47] Egyptians consider pigs to be unclean animals. In the first place, if someone just brushes against a pig, he goes to the river and immerses himself there, clothes and all. In the second place, swineherds are the only native Egyptians who never enter the grounds of any Egyptian sanctuary; moreover, no one will arrange a marriage between his daughter and a swineherd or marry the daughter of one himself, so swineherds marry only into the families of other swineherds. The only deities to whom the Egyptians are allowed to sacrifice pigs are Selene and Dionysus; both these rituals take place at the same time of the month, at the full moon, and they first sacrifice the animals and then eat the flesh. The Egyptians have a story to explain why although pigs are taboo at all other festivals, they are sacrificed on this one occasion; but although I know it, it is an inappropriate tale to tell. The way pigs

are offered to Selene is that the sacrificer lumps together the tip of
the tail, the spleen, and the omentum, covers them with all the fat
he can get from the region of the creature's belly, and then burns
this mixture in the fire. The rest—that is, the flesh†—is eaten on
the day of the performance of the ritual, the day of the full moon;
on any other day, they would not eat it. The poorer members of
society have the means only to make pigs out of dough, bake them,
and use them as their sacrificial offerings.

[48] On the evening before the festival of Dionysus, everyone
slaughters a pig on the threshold of his home and then gives it to
the swineherd who sold it to him, and who now takes it away. The
rest of the festival of Dionysus the Egyptians celebrate pretty much
as the Greeks do, except that there are no choral dances. Instead
of phalluses, however, they have other contraptions—figurines,
about a cubit tall, which are moved by strings. Women take them
around the villages, and each figurine has a penis which is almost
as big as itself and which moves up and down. The procession
is led by a pipe-player, and the women follow singing hymns to
Dionysus. The Egyptians have a sacred story as to why these figurines have oversized genitals, and why this is the only part of the
body that can move.

[49] Now, it seems to me that Melampus the son of Amytheon
was not ignorant of this Egyptian ritual, but was well aware of it.
In fact, Melampus was the one who introduced the Greeks not only
to the name and worship of Dionysus, but also to the phallic procession. Strictly speaking, he did not combine all the elements and
reveal the whole story: it was more fully revealed by later sages.
But all the same, Melampus was the one who instituted the phallic
procession in honour of Dionysus, and it was he who taught the
Greeks to do what they do. What I am suggesting is that Melampus was a clever person who not only mastered the art of divination, but also introduced into Greece a number of things he learnt
which came originally from Egypt, including the Dionysian rites,
which he hardly changed at all. I mean, I will absolutely deny that
the similarities between the Greek and Egyptian versions of the rites
are coincidental; if there were no influence from Egypt, the Greek
rites would be home-grown and would not have been just recently
introduced. I will also deny that the Egyptians could have learnt
either this or any other practice from the Greeks. The most likely
scenario, in my opinion, is that Melampus learnt these Dionysian

rites from Cadmus of Tyre and those who accompanied him on his journey from Phoenicia to the country now known as Boeotia.

[50] The names of almost all the gods also came to Greece from Egypt. My enquiries led me to discover that they are non-Greek in origin, but it is my belief that they came largely from Egypt. With the exception of Poseidon and the Dioscuri (as I have already mentioned), and also Hera, Hestia, Themis, the Graces, and the Nereids, all the gods and their names have always been found in the country of Egypt. Here I am repeating what the Egyptians themselves say. As for the gods whose names they told me they do not recognize, I think that they were given their names by the Pelasgians—except for Poseidon, whom the Greeks learnt about from Libya. I say this because the Libyans are the only people to have possessed the name of Poseidon from the beginning, and his worship has been a constant there. The Egyptians do not have hero-cults, however.

[51] This is not the sum total of the customs which the Greeks have taken over from the Egyptians, as I shall explain. The Greek practice of making ithyphallic statues of Hermes, however, was not learnt from Egypt, but from the Pelasgians. The Athenians were the first Greeks to take over the practice, and then everyone else got it from them. The point is that the Pelasgians became fellow inhabitants of the land occupied by the Athenians at a time when the Athenians already counted as Greeks; this is how the Pelasgians too began to be regarded as Greeks. Anyone will know what I mean if he is an initiate of the mysteries of the Cabiri—rites which are celebrated on Samothrace and are Pelasgian in origin, since the Pelasgians who came to share land with the Athenians had previously lived on Samothrace and were the ones from whom the Samothracians learnt the rites. Anyway, the Athenians were the first Greeks to make ithyphallic statues of Hermes, and they learnt it from the Pelasgians. The Pelasgians told a sacred story about it, which is revealed during the mysteries in Samothrace.

[52] Originally, as I know from what I was told at Dodona, the Pelasgians used to pray to the gods during every sacrificial ritual they performed, but without giving any of them a name or epithet, because they had not yet heard of such things. They called them 'gods', because they had *set* all things in order and assigned everything its place.† Then a long time afterwards the gods acquired names imported from Egypt, and they learnt these in the case of

all the gods except Dionysus, whom they learnt about much later. After a while they consulted the oracle at Dodona (which is the most ancient oracle established among the Greeks, and was at that time the only one in existence) about these names. The Pelasgians asked the oracle whether they should adopt these names of the gods which had come from abroad, and the oracle told them they should. So from then on they used the gods' names while performing their rituals, and the Greeks inherited the practice from the Pelasgians.

[53] However, it was only yesterday or the day before, so to speak, that the Greeks came to know the provenance of each of the gods, and whether they have all existed for ever, and what they each look like. After all, I think that Hesiod and Homer lived no more than four hundred years before my time, and they were the ones who created the gods' family trees for the Greek world, gave them their names, assigned them their honours and areas of expertise, and told us what they looked like. Any poets who are supposed to have lived before Homer and Hesiod actually came after them, in my opinion. Of the last two opinions, the first is the view of the priestesses at Dodona, but the second—the bit about Hesiod and Homer—is my own opinion.

[54] Here is a tale the Egyptians tell about the oracle in Greece and the one in Libya. According to the priests of Theban Zeus, two women—priestesses, in fact—were abducted from Thebes by some Phoenicians. The priests found out that one of the women had been sold in Libya and the other to Greeks, and they claimed that these women were the original founders of the two oracles in those two countries. When I asked how they could speak with such certainty, they replied that they had held an extensive search for these women, and that although they had failed to find them, they had subsequently discovered what they were telling me about them.

[55] That is what the priests at Thebes told me, but the Dodona oracle's prophetesses say that two black doves took off from Thebes in Egypt, one of which flew to Libya, while the other came to them in Dodona. It perched on an oak-tree and spoke in a human voice, telling the people of Dodona that there ought to be an oracle of Zeus there. The people of Dodona realized that they were hearing a divine command, and they therefore did what the dove had told them to do. The story goes on to say that the dove which

went to Libya told the Libyans to construct the oracle of Ammon—
another oracle of Zeus. This is the story told by the priestesses of
Dodona (who are, from oldest to youngest, Promeneia, Timarete,
and Nicandra), and it is supported by what the other Dodonans
connected with the shrine say too.

[56] I would suggest that this is what happened. If the priestesses really were abducted by Phoenicians and sold in Libya and
Greece, it was the Thesprotians, in my opinion, who bought the
one who came to what is now called Greece (though it is the same
place that was in those days called Pelasgia). Since she was working
as a slave for the Thesprotians, she built a shrine of Zeus under an
oak-tree that was growing there, which is only what one would
expect her to do: after all, she had served in the sanctuary of Zeus
in Thebes, and one would expect her to think of Zeus when she
came to her new home. Then she subsequently founded an oracle
when she had learnt to speak Greek, and she told people about
how the same Phoenicians who had sold her had also sold her sister
in Libya.

[57] I think that the women were called doves by the people of
Dodona because they were foreigners and when they spoke they
sounded like birds. They say that after a while the dove spoke to
them in a human voice, because that was when the woman could
make herself understood by them. As long as she spoke a foreign
language, however, they thought she sounded like a bird. After
all, how could a dove speak in a human voice? When they say that
the dove was black, they are indicating that the woman was
Egyptian. It is in fact the case that the divinatory methods used in
Egyptian Thebes and in Dodona are very similar to one another,
and that the art of divination from entrails did reach Greece from
Egypt.

[58] But anyway, the Egyptians were the first people in the world
to hold general festive assemblies, and religious processions and
parades, and the Greeks learnt from the Egyptians. My evidence
for this suggestion is that these activities have obviously been going
on in Egypt for a very long time, whereas they have only recently
started in Greece.

[59] The Egyptians have a lot of public festivals a year, not just
one. The one that they take the most trouble about is held in
honour of Artemis in the city of Bubastis, and then the second most
important one is celebrated in honour of Isis in the city of Busiris.

Busiris, which is located in the middle of the Delta, has the largest sanctuary of Isis—or Demeter, to translate her name into Greek—in Egypt. They celebrate the third most important festival in honour of Athena in Saïs, and the fourth most important is held in Heliopolis in honour of the sun. After that, the fifth and sixth most important are the one in Buto in honour of Leto and the one in Papremis in honour of Ares.

[60] When people travel to Bubastis for the festival, this is what they do. Every *baris* carrying them there overflows with people, a huge crowd of them, men and women together. Some of the women have clappers, while some of the men have pipes which they play throughout the voyage. The rest of the men and women sing and clap their hands. When in the course of their journey they reach a community—not the city of their destination, but somewhere else—they steer the *bareis* close to the bank. Some of the women carry on doing what I have already described them as doing, but others shout out scornful remarks to the women in the town, or dance, or stand and pull up their clothes to expose themselves. Every riverside community receives this treatment. When they reach Bubastis, they celebrate the festival, which involves sacrifices on a vast scale, and more wine is consumed during this festival than throughout the whole of the rest of the year. According to the local inhabitants, up to 700,000 men and women, excluding children, come together for the festival.

[61] That is what they do there, and I have already described how they celebrate the festival of Isis in Busiris. All the men and women, in their tens of thousands, express grief after the sacrifice, but it would be sacrilegious of me to say who it is that they are mourning. Any Carians resident in Egypt take the mourning to even further extremes and cut their foreheads with knives—which marks them clearly as foreigners and not Egyptians.

[62] As for the festival in Saïs, on a certain night all the people who have gathered there to worship burn lots of lamps in a circle outdoors around their houses. The lamps are saucers filled with salt and oil, with the wick floating on the top. They burn all night long, and the traditional name for the festival is the Lamplight festival. Even those Egyptians who do not actually attend the festival all wait for the night of the rites and burn lamps, so there are lamps alight throughout Egypt, not just in Saïs. There is a sacred story told to explain why this night receives light and honour.

[63] The festivals people go to at Heliopolis and Buto involve nothing more than sacrifices. In Papremis they perform the sacrifices and rites as elsewhere, but there is more besides. As the sun is going down, apart from those few priests who are busy with the cult statue, the majority of them stand in the entrance to the sanctuary carrying wooden clubs. They are confronted by a crowd of more than a thousand men, each of whom also has a stick, in fulfilment of a vow he has taken. Now, the day before, the priests removed the cult statue in a gilded miniature wooden shrine and took it to another sacred dwelling. The few priests who remain with the statue put the miniature temple, with the statue inside it, on to a four-wheeled cart and pull it to the sanctuary. The priests standing in the entrance try to stop them bringing the statue back in, while the votaries take the god's side and wield their clubs against the priests who are defending the sanctuary. A fierce stick-fight ensues. Heads are broken and, I think, a lot of them die from their wounds. However, the Egyptians said that no one dies.

The locals say that this festival was established because Ares' mother used to live in the sanctuary. Ares had been brought up somewhere else, and when he reached manhood he came to the sanctuary with the intention of getting together with his mother. His mother's attendants had never laid eyes on him before, so they refused him entry. They successfully kept him out at first, but he brought reinforcements from another town, beat the attendants, and forced his way in to his mother. And that, the people of Papremis say, is why this confrontation is a traditional part of the festival.

[64] The Egyptians were the first to ban on religious grounds having sex with a woman within a sanctuary and entering a sanctuary after having sex without washing first. Almost everywhere else in the world, except in Egypt and Greece, people do both these things, since they do not differentiate between humans and other animals. They point out that we see animals and birds of all kinds mating in the temples and precincts of the gods, and they argue that this would not happen if the gods disapproved of it. Personally, I take a dim view of this kind of excuse. This is just one example of how extraordinarily scrupulous the Egyptians are in religious matters.

[65] Despite having Libya as a neighbour, Egypt does not have much wildlife. All the animals in Egypt are regarded as sacred.

Some are domesticated, and others are not, but if I were to explain why some animals are allowed to roam free, as sacred creatures, my account would be bound to discuss issues pertaining to the gods, and I am doing my best to avoid relating such things. It is only when I have had no choice that I have touched on them already. However, one of their customs concerning animals is as follows. Each separate species of animal has been appointed a keeper who is in charge of looking after it; the keeper may be an Egyptian man or woman, and children inherit the post from their parents. In the cities people fulfil their vows by praying to the god whose sacred creature a given type of animal is, and shaving their child's head (it might be the whole head, or a half, or a third) and weighing the hair in a pair of scales against some silver. This weight in silver is then given to the keeper of the animals. She cuts up as much fish as the silver buys and gives it as food to the animals. That is how the animals are fed. The deliberate killing of one of these animals is punishable by death, and anyone who kills one of them accidentally has to pay a fine whose amount is determined by the priests. However, the death of an ibis or hawk at someone's hands, whether or not he intended to kill it, is inevitably a capital offence.

[66] Although there are plenty of domestic animals in Egypt, there would be many more if it were not for what happens to the cats. When female cats give birth, they stop having intercourse with the males. However much the toms want to mate with them, they are unable to do so. The toms have therefore come up with a clever solution. They sneak in and steal the kittens away from their mothers, and then kill them (but not for food). The females, deprived of their young, long to have some more, because the feline species is very fond of its young, and so they go to the males.

If a house catches fire, what happens to the cats is quite extraordinary. The Egyptians do not bother to try to put the fire out, but position themselves at intervals around the house and look out for the cats. The cats slip between them, however, and even jump over them, and dash into the fire. This plunges the Egyptians into deep grief. In households where a cat dies a natural death, all the people living there shave off their eyebrows—nothing more. In households where a dog dies, they shave their whole bodies, head and all.

[67] After their death, the cats are taken to sacred chambers in the city of Bubastis where they are mummified and buried. Dogs are buried by each householder in his own community in sanctified tombs, and mongooses receive the same form of burial as well. Shrews and hawks are taken to the city of Buto, and ibises to Hermepolis. Bears (which are rare) and wolves (which are not much larger than foxes) are buried wherever they are found lying.

[68] This is what crocodiles are like. They eat nothing during the four winter months. They are four-footed, and amphibious in the sense that they lay their eggs in the earth, hatch their young there, and spend most of the day on dry land, but spend the whole night in the river since the water is warmer than the clear, dew-laden air. As far as is known, there is no mortal creature which grows so big from such small beginnings. The eggs it lays are not much bigger than a goose's eggs, and the size of a new-born crocodile corresponds to that of its egg, but a fully grown adult can be at least seventeen cubits long, and maybe more. It has eyes the size of a pig's, but huge teeth and tusks. It is the only creature in the world without a tongue, and the only one which does not move its lower jaw but brings its upper jaw down to meet the lower one. It has strong claws and its back is covered with impenetrable scaly skin. It is blind in the water, but has excellent sight in the open air. Because it spends its life in the water, its mouth is filled with leeches. With the exception of the sandpiper, all other birds and animals run away from it. The sandpiper, however, is on good terms with it, because it is of use to the crocodile. When the crocodile climbs out of the water and on to land, it yawns widely (usually when facing west), and then the sandpiper slips into its mouth and swallows the leeches. This does the crocodile good and gives it pleasure, so it does not harm the sandpiper.

[69] Crocodiles are sacred to some Egyptians, but others treat them as enemies. They are especially sacred to the people who live in and around Thebes and the lake of Moeris. In each of these places the people look after one particular crocodile, which has been trained until it is tame. They put glass and gold jewellery in its ears and bangles on its front legs, they feed it with special food and with their sacrificial victims too, and generally pamper it for as long as it is alive. When it dies, they mummify it and bury it in a sanctified tomb. The people living in and around Elephantine, however, go so far as to eat crocodiles, which are not sacred animals in their view.

The Egyptian word is *khampsa* rather than 'crocodile'. It was Ionians who called them 'crocodiles', since they thought they looked like the *krokodeiloi* or lizards which can be found on walls in Ionia.

[70] Crocodiles are hunted in all sorts of different ways, one of which strikes me as particularly remarkable and so I will write it down. The hunter baits a hook with the backbone of a pig and casts it out into the middle of the river; on the riverbank with him he has a live pig, which he hits. The crocodile hears the pig squealing. It sets off in the direction of the sound, encounters the backbone, and swallows it. Then they haul the creature in. Once they have got it ashore, the first thing the hunter does is smear mud over the creature's eyes. This makes it easy for the crocodile to be overpowered, but it would be a struggle to do so otherwise.

[71] Hippopotamuses are sacred in the province of Papremis, but not elsewhere in Egypt. Here is what they look like. They are four-footed, cloven-hoofed (their hoofs are like an ox's), and blunt-nosed; they have a horse's mane, visible tusks, and the tail and voice of a horse; they are more or less as big as the biggest ox. Their hide is so thick that when it is dried people make spear-shafts out of it.

[72] Another river animal which is regarded as sacred is the otter. As for fish, they consider the species they call *lepidotos* and also eels to be sacred. These Nile fish are sacred, and the same goes, among birds, for the fox-goose.

[73] Another sacred bird is the one called the phoenix. Now, I have not actually seen a phoenix, except in a painting, because they are quite infrequent visitors to the country; in fact, I was told in Heliopolis that they appear only at 500-year intervals. They say that it is the death of a phoenix's father which prompts its visit to Egypt. Anyway, if the painting was reliable, I can tell you something about the phoenix's size and qualities, namely that its feathers are partly gold but mostly red, and that in appearance and size it is most like an eagle. There is a particular feat they say the phoenix performs; I do not believe it myself, but they say that the bird sets out from its homeland in Arabia on a journey to the sanctuary of the sun, bringing its father sealed in myrrh, and buries its father there. The method it uses for carrying its father is as follows. First it forms out of myrrh as big an egg as it can manage to carry, and then it makes a trial flight to make sure it can carry the egg. When this has been tested, it hollows out the egg and puts its father inside, and then seals up with more myrrh that part of the egg

which it had hollowed out to hold its father. The egg now weighs the same, with its father lying inside, as it did before it was hollowed out. So when the phoenix has sealed the egg up again, it carries its father to the sanctuary of the sun in Egypt. That is what they say the bird does.

[74] In Thebes there are sacred snakes which never hurt a human being. They are small and have two horns growing from the tops of their heads. When they die, they are buried in the sanctuary of Zeus, since it is Zeus to whom they are sacred.

[75] I went to the part of Arabia fairly near the city of Buto to find out about winged snakes. When I got there, I saw countless snake bones and spines; there were heaps and heaps of spines there—large, medium-sized, and smaller ones. The place where all these backbones are scattered about on the ground is a narrow†pass linking hills to a great plain, which joins the Egyptian plain. The story goes that at the beginning of spring these winged snakes fly from Arabia towards Egypt, but birds—ibises—meet them there at the pass and do not allow them past, but kill them. It is because the ibis does this that the Egyptians value the bird so highly, according to the Arabians, and the Egyptians agree that this is why they value these birds.

[76] Here is a description of the ibis. It is pitch-black all over, and it has the legs of a crane and a very hooked beak. It is about the size of a corncrake. That is what the black ibises are like, which are the ones that fight the snakes, but there are two kinds of ibis and the other kind, which one is more likely to come across in places inhabited by human beings, is different. It has no feathers anywhere on its head and neck, and its plumage is completely white, except for its head, neck, the tips of its wings, and the very end of its tail, all of which are pitch-black. Its legs and beak are like those of the other kind.

The snakes are similar in shape to water-snakes. Rather than proper feathered wings they have winglike membranes, which are not too dissimilar from those of a bat. That completes my account of the sacred animals of Egypt.

[77] As for the actual people of Egypt, those who live in the cultivated part of the country make a particular practice of recording the history of all peoples, and are consequently by far the most learned people I have ever come across and questioned. Here are some aspects of their lifestyle. They purge themselves for three con-

secutive days of every month; they make emetics and douches their
means of pursuing health, because they believe that all human
illness is due to food causing colic.† In fact, the Egyptians are, after
the Libyans, the most healthy people in the world, which in my
opinion is due to the fact that the climate is very stable there. I
mean, we generally get ill when things change—and by 'things' here
I mean especially, but not exclusively, the seasons. The loaves they
eat—which are called *kyllestis* in their language—are made out of
emmer wheat. They have no vines in their country, so they drink
an ale made out of barley. They eat raw sun-dried fish as well as
salted fish. As for birds, they eat quail, duck, and raw salted young
birds. In general, however, they first bake or boil any species of bird
or fish their country provides, except for those which have been
consecrated, before eating them.

[78] After the meal at a party of well-to-do Egyptians, a man
carries round the room in a coffin a corpse made of wood, which
has been painted and carved so as to be as lifelike as possible, and
whose length is about a cubit or two.† The man shows the corpse
to all the guests, one by one, while saying: 'Look on this while you
drink, for this will be your lot when you are dead.' That is what
happens at their parties.

[79] They perpetuate their traditional customs rather than
acquiring new ones. They have a number of remarkable customs,
and in particular a song, the 'Linus'. Linus is also the subject of
songs in Phoenicia, Cyprus, and elsewhere, but he has different
names in different countries. Still, it seems as though the Egyptian
song is about the same person who is called Linus in the Greek
version of the song, and so one of the many puzzles about things
in Egypt is where they got the 'Linus' from. One gets the impression that they have always sung the song. The Egyptian name for
Linus is Maneros. The Egyptians said that Maneros was the only
son of their first king, and that when he died at an early age they
made up this dirge to honour him, which was not only the first
Egyptian song, but at the time the only one.†

[80] There is another Egyptian custom which is similar to a
Greek custom—or to be precise to a Lacedaemonian one. If a
younger person meets an older person in the street, he defers to
him by getting out of his way; young people also stand up when
someone older approaches. Something else the Egyptians do,
however, is not Greek at all: instead of greeting one another when

they meet on the streets, they put their hands down on to their knees and bow down.

[81] They wear linen tunics, fringed at the bottom, which they call *kalasiris* and which come down over their legs. On top of these tunics they wear white woollen cloaks thrown over their shoulders. However, it is against religious law for them to take anything woollen into their sanctuaries or to be buried along with any woollen items. This custom of theirs accords with the Orphic and Bacchic rites, as they are called (though they are actually Egyptian and Pythagorean), because no initiate of these rites either is allowed to be buried in woollen clothing. There is a sacred story told on these matters.

[82] Here are some other Egyptian discoveries. Every month and every day is sacred to a particular deity, and the day of a person's birth determines what will happen to him, how he will die, and what kind of person he will be. This is something Greek poets have made use of. They have discovered more omens than anyone else in the world. When one happens, they write it down and wait to see what the outcome is, and if anything similar ever happens again in the future, they think that the same result will follow.

[83] As for divination, they attribute this ability to some of the gods, but never to a human being. In fact, there are in Egypt oracles of Heracles, Apollo, Athena, Artemis, Ares, Zeus, and—the one which is held in the most honour of them all—of Leto, in the city of Buto. However, the methods of divination vary from place to place.

[84] Medicine is organized as follows. Each doctor specializes in a single illness rather than covering a range of illnesses. So there are doctors all over the place—eye doctors, for example, and others who tend heads, others for teeth or stomachs, and still others for illnesses whose provenance is obscure.

[85] Here is how they mourn and bury their dead. When a man of some standing departs from his house all the womenfolk of the household smear mud on their heads, or even their faces. Then they leave the corpse lying in the house while they and all their female relatives wander here and there in the city beating their breasts, with their clothing loosened and their breasts exposed. Elsewhere, the men are also beating their breasts, and they too have their clothing loosened. After this phase of mourning, they take the corpse to be mummified.

[86] There are professional embalmers who specialize in this work. When a corpse is brought to them, they show those who brought it sample corpses made out of wood, which are painted so as to be lifelike. The best embalming method, I am told, is sacred to the god whose name it would be sacrilegious of me to mention in this context. They also show samples of the second-best method, which is both inferior to and cheaper than the first one, and of the third-best method, which is the cheapest of them all. They explain the procedures and ask which method the relatives want used on the corpse, and then, once they have agreed on a price, the relatives leave, and the others stay behind in their shop and get right to work on the embalming.

Their first job, in the best embalming method, is to extract the brain by passing a hooked iron instrument through the nostrils; part of the brain is extracted in this way, and part of it by pouring in drugs. Next, they cut open the side of the corpse with a sharp Ethiopian stone knife and remove all the intestines. Then they clean out the cavity and rinse it first with palm wine and then with crushed spices. After this, they fill the corpse's belly with crushed myrrh and cassia and other perfumed spices (but not with frank-incense) and sew it back up. The next phase is to pack the corpse in natron and leave it to mummify for seventy days—but they are not supposed to leave it for longer. Once the seventy days are over, they wash the corpse and then wrap the whole of its body in bandages made out of fine linen cloth cut into strips. The bandages have gum (which is usually used in Egypt instead of glue) smeared on their underside. Then the relatives come and collect the corpse. They make a hollow casket in the shape of a man and enclose the corpse inside it. Once the corpse has been shut away inside the casket, they store it upright against the wall in a burial chamber.

[87] That is the most expensive procedure for preparing corpses, but if the next-best procedure is chosen to save money, they prepare the corpse as follows. They fill syringes with oil made from cedars and squirt it into the intestines of the corpse, until it is full. This procedure does not involve them cutting the corpse open or removing its guts; they insert the syringe into the anus and use a stopper to prevent any backflow from the douche. They preserve it for the prescribed number of days, and then on the last day they draw off from the entrails the cedar oil which they had injected in earlier.

The effect of the oil has been to dissolve the guts and the intestines, with the result that they are all drawn off along with the oil. Meanwhile, the natron has dissolved the flesh, so that all that is left of the corpse is the skin and the bones. Then they return the corpse as it is, without putting any more work into it.

[88] The third embalming method is used to prepare the corpses of those who were less well off financially. The entrails are cleaned out with myrrh, the corpse is preserved as usual for the seventy days, and then it is returned to be taken away.

[89] When the wife of an eminent man dies, or any woman who was particularly beautiful or famous, the body is not handed over to the embalmers straight away. They wait three or four days before doing so. The reason for this is to stop the embalmers having sex with the women. They say that one of them was caught having sex with the fresh corpse of a woman, and was denounced by one of his colleagues.

[90] If anyone—it makes no difference whether he is a native Egyptian or a foreigner—has been carried off by a crocodile or has obviously been killed by the river, it is up to the people in the community where his body is washed ashore to embalm him, fit him out as handsomely as possible, and bury him in a sanctified tomb. Not even any of his relatives or friends is allowed to touch him: the corpse is something more than human, so only the actual priests of the Nile can lay hands on him and bury him.

[91] The Egyptians avoid using Greek customs or, by and large, those of any other people either. Everywhere else in Egypt, this rule is followed strictly, but in Chemmis (a large city in the Thebaïd province near Neapolis) there is a square sanctuary of Perseus the son of Danaë, with palm-trees growing around it. The entrance to the sanctuary is an enormous stone gateway, by which there are two tall stone statues. In the outer courtyard there is a temple, inside which is a statue of Perseus. According to the people of Chemmis, Perseus often appears in their country (and frequently inside the sanctuary), and people find one of his sandals, which is two cubits long. The appearance of the sandal signifies prosperity for the whole of Egypt.

This is what they say. They serve Perseus in the Greek fashion, in the sense that they hold an athletic contest covering the whole range of competitive sports, with cattle, cloaks, and hides as prizes. When I asked them why Perseus habitually appeared to them alone and why they were unique in Egypt in holding an athletic contest, they replied that since Danaus and Lynceus were Chemmitans who emigrated to Greece, and since they trace their lineage from Danaus and Lynceus down to Perseus, then Perseus originally came from their city. What brought Perseus to Egypt, according to the Chemmitans, is the same as in the Greek story: it was to collect the Gorgon's head from Libya. But they said that he visited Chemmis and recognized his relatives, and that he had already learnt the name of Chemmis before he came to Egypt, because he had heard it from his mother. It was Perseus, they say, who told them to put on the games for him.

[92] All these customs have been those of the Egyptians living inland from the marshes. Life in the marshes is basically the same as elsewhere in Egypt—for instance, men and women live together in couples, as in Greece—but one difference is that they have found a cheap source of food. When the river is in spate and floods the plains, a large number of lilies grow in the water; the Egyptian name for this water-lily is *lotos*. They pick them, dry them in the sun, and then they crush the poppy-like middle part of the flower and make loaves out of it, which are baked in a fire. The root of the lotus, which is round and apple-sized, is also edible and tastes quite sweet. Another kind of lily, which looks like a rose, also grows in the river; in this one there is, in a separate pod which grows alongside the main one from the root, a fruit which closely resembles the honeycomb of a wasps' nest. Inside the fruit are a great many edible seeds, each about the size of an olive stone, which can be eaten both fresh and dried. When they have pulled up from the marshes the annual crop of papyrus, they cut off the upper part of the plant (which they use for something else), while the remainder, about a cubit's length from the bottom of the plant, they both eat and sell. Those who want to enjoy the papyrus at its very best bake it in a red-hot oven and then eat it. Some of these marsh-dwellers live entirely off fish, which they catch and gut, dry in the sun, and then eat dried.

[93] Fish that swim in shoals are never actually born in the rivers here; they grow to maturity in the lakes and then, when they are seized by the urge to be fertilized, they swim in shoals to the sea. The males lead, dribbling seed behind them, and the females follow, swallow it down, and conceive from it. So they become pregnant in the sea, but then each group makes its way back to its original

location. However, this time they swim in a different order: it is the females who lead the shoal, but they behave in pretty much the same way as the males did, because they dribble eggs out a few at a time as tiny seeds, and the males following behind them swallow them down. These tiny seeds are actually fish, though, and from the ones that are not swallowed come the fish which grow to maturity. Any fish that are caught during the course of their journey to the sea display bruising on the left of their heads, whereas those that are caught during the return journey have bruising on the right. The reason is that as they swim down the river to the sea they keep close to the bank on their left, and during the return journey they again keep close to the same bank; they swim as close to it as they can, and even touch it, so that they do not lose their way through the river's currents.

When the Nile begins to rise, all the low-lying land and the mud-pools next to the river start to fill with the water which trickles through from the river, and as soon as they are flooded they all begin to teem with tiny fish. I think I understand the probable reason for this. When the Nile recedes the year before, the fish lay eggs in the mud before leaving with the last of the water. In due course of time the water returns, and then the fish hatch straight away from these eggs. Anyway, that is what happens with regard to fish.

[94] The Egyptians who live near the marshes use oil made from the fruit of the castor-oil plant, which is called *kiki* by the Egyptians. They sow these plants on the riverbanks and beside the lakes. The plant grows wild in Greece, but when it is sown in Egypt it produces a plentiful, if foul-smelling crop. Once the fruit has been harvested, it can either be sliced and crushed, or roasted and boiled down. The end result is a thick liquid which they collect, and which is just as good as olive oil for lamps, except that it emits a heavy smell.

[95] Here is how they cope with the huge numbers of mosquitoes there. Those who live inland from the marshes have the advantage of sleeping up in tall buildings, which helps because the winds stop the mosquitoes flying high in the air. The marsh-dwellers, however, have come up with an alternative. Every man there has a net which he uses in the daytime for fishing, but at night he finds another use for it: he drapes it over the bed where he spends the night and then crawls in under it and goes to sleep. Mosquitoes

can bite through any cover or linen blanket that a person might wrap himself up in when he is in bed, but they do not even try to bite through the net at all.

[96] Their cargo boats are made out of the wood of the acacia, which is very similar in appearance to Cyrenean lotus and weeps gum. The way they make these boats is to cut planks of this acacia wood, each about two cubits long, and put them together like bricks. They use long, thick pins to fix these two-cubit planks together, and once the hull has been built in this way, they next lay thwarts on top of it. Their boats have no ribbing, but instead they reinforce the fastenings on the inside of the boat with papyrus. They make a single steering-oar, which is plugged in and through the keel. They use a mast of acacia wood and sails of papyrus.

These boats are incapable of sailing upriver without a strong following wind; instead, they are towed along from the bank. Travelling downstream involves the use of a raft made out of tamarisk wood tied together with rush matting, and a stone, weighing about two talents, with a hole bored through it. The raft is let out on the rope which joins it to the boat so that it floats up in front, while the stone, which is held by another rope, is let out astern. Once the raft is taken by the current, it starts to move along rapidly and pull the *baris* behind it (*baris* is the Egyptian word for this kind of boat), while the stone is dragged behind the boat along the river bottom and so keeps the boat straight. There are lots of these boats on the river, and some of them can carry many thousands of talents of goods.

[97] When the Nile covers the land, only the towns are visible above the water, and they look like nothing so much as the Aegean islands. The rest of Egypt becomes open sea, with only the towns rising up out of it. So under these conditions people take ferries not just along the course of the river, but right across the plain! The journey by boat from Naucratis to Memphis becomes one that goes past the pyramids, instead of the normal route via the apex of the Delta and the city of Cercasorus. And sailing over the plain from Canobus on the coast to Naucratis you will pass the town of Anthylla and one named after Archander.

[98] Of these two towns, Anthylla is famous as the place from where the wife of every successive king of Egypt gets her shoes, since the town has been made over to her for that purpose. This has been happening ever since Egypt became part of the Persian

empire. The other town is named, I think, after Danaus' son-in-law, Archander the son of Phthius and grandson of Achaeus. It could also be another Archander, but it is certainly not an Egyptian name, at any rate.

[99] So far my account of Egypt has been dictated by my own observation, judgement, and investigation, but from now on I will be relating Egyptian accounts, supplemented by what I personally saw.

According to the priests, the first king of Egypt was Min. His achievements were, first, the construction of the dyke which protects Memphis. They say that the whole river used to flow past the sandy mountain range towards Libya, but that about a hundred stades upstream from Memphis Min created by means of a dam the southern bend in the river, causing the original bed to dry up and diverting the river through the middle of the mountains. (And even now this bend in the Nile is closely watched by the Persians, to make sure that the river keeps to its bed, and they strengthen the dam every year, because if the river decided to burst its banks and overflow at this point, Memphis would be in danger of being completely inundated.) Once the land separated off by this Min, the first king of Egypt, had dried out, his second achievement was to found there the city which is nowadays called Memphis (for Memphis is also located in the narrow part of Egypt). In the countryside outside the city he is said to have dug a lake, away from the river, to the north and west of the city, because the Nile itself skirts the city to the east. Then his third achievement was to build the sanctuary of Hephaestus in Memphis, which is huge and remarkable.

[100] The priests then read out from a papyrus roll the names of the 330 kings following Min. In all that time, 330 generations, there were eighteen Ethiopian kings and one native Egyptian queen, but all the rest were Egyptian men. The name of the queen was Nitocris—the same as that of the Babylonian queen. They said that she avenged her brother. Despite the fact that he was their king, the Egyptians killed him and then handed the kingdom over to her, but in order to avenge him she killed a lot of them by a trick. What she did was construct a massive underground chamber, and although in reality she had other plans, she claimed to want to hold an inauguration ceremony for it. She invited the Egyptians she knew to have been the ringleaders in her brother's murder—and

there were quite a few of them—to the reception; while they were in the middle of the meal she had the river flood in on them through a large secret passage. That is all the information I was given about Nitocris, except that afterwards she threw herself into a chamber full of ashes, to avoid retribution.

[101] The priests attributed no particularly outstanding achievements to any of the other kings, except for the last one, King Moeris. The monuments he constructed are the northern gateway in the sanctuary of Hephaestus, a lake, and some pyramids in the lake. I will later record how many stades the perimeter of the lake is, and at the same time how large the pyramids are. They said that these were Moeris' achievements, but they had nothing to note for any of the rest.

[102] Passing over them, then, I will mention the person who reigned after them, whose name was Sesostris. The priests told me that he first launched a naval expedition from the Arabian Gulf and subdued the inhabitants of the Red Sea coastline until he reached a part of the sea where shallows made it impossible for him to continue any further. According to the priests' account, what he did next, on his return to Egypt, was raise a great army and march across the mainland, subduing every tribe he came across. Whenever he encountered a brave people who put up a fierce fight in defence of their autonomy, he erected pillars in their territory with an inscription recording his own name and country, and how he and his army had overcome them. However, whenever he took a place easily, without a fight, he had a message inscribed on the pillar in the same way as for the brave tribes, but he also added a picture of a woman's genitalia, to indicate that they were cowards.

[103] Eventually this expedition of his across the mainland brought him from Asia over into Europe, where he defeated the Scythians and the Thracians. I think that this was as far as the Egyptian army came, because pillars erected by them can be seen there, but nowhere further on. So he turned back towards Egypt. When he reached the River Phasis, one of two things happened, but I am not in a position to say for certain which of the two alternatives is correct. Either King Sesostris himself detached a certain portion of his troops and left them there to settle the country, or some of his men had had enough of this circuitous journey of his and stayed behind at the Phasis River.

[104] For the fact is, as I first came to realize myself, and then heard from others later, that the Colchians are obviously Egyptian. When the notion occurred to me, I asked both the Colchians and the Egyptians about it, and found that the Colchians had better recall of the Egyptians than the Egyptians did of them. Some Egyptians said that they thought the Colchians originated with Sesostris' army, but I myself had guessed their Egyptian origin not only because the Colchians are dark-skinned and curly-haired (which does not count for much by itself, because these features are common to others too), but more importantly because Colchians, Egyptians, and Ethiopians are the only peoples in the world who practise circumcision and have always done so. The Phoenicians and Palestinian Syrians are the first to admit that they learnt the practice from Egypt, and the Syrians who live in the land between the Thermodon and Parthenius rivers, and their neighbours the Macrones, say that in their case it is a recent import from Colchis. These are the only places in the world where circumcision is practised, and it is clear that the others do it in the same way it is done in Egypt. The obvious antiquity of the custom in Egypt and Ethiopia prevents me from saying whether the Egyptians learnt it from the Ethiopians or vice versa, but what convinces me that the other peoples learnt it as a result of their contact with Egypt is that any Phoenicians who have come into contact with Greece have stopped copying the Egyptians with respect to their genitalia,† and do not cut off their children's foreskins.

[105] And let me mention one more way in which the Colchians resemble the Egyptians: these two peoples alone work linen, and they do so in the same way. In fact, their lifestyles in general and their languages are similar. The Greeks call Colchian linen Sardonian, while the linen which comes from Egypt is called Egyptian.

[106] Most of the pillars which King Sesostris of Egypt erected in these places no longer appear to be there, but I myself have seen them in Palestinian Syria with the inscriptions I mentioned and the female genitalia. In Ionia, there are also two figures of Sesostris carved in the rock, one on the route from Ephesus to Phocaea and the other between Sardis and Smyrna. In both places a man is carved, four cubits and a span high, with a spear in his right hand, a bow in his left, and the rest of his equipment to match—in fact, it is partly Egyptian and partly Ethiopian. From one shoulder right

across his chest to the other shoulder runs a carved inscription in Egyptian hieroglyphs, saying: 'I took this land with the power of my shoulders.' He does not indicate in this inscription who he is and what country he is from, but it is clear from elsewhere. Some people who have seen these carvings guess that the figure is Memnon, but that does not really correspond to the facts.

[107] Now to return to Sesostris, the Egyptian king: the priests told me that he brought with him on his return from abroad a number of people from the tribes whose lands he had conquered. Arriving back in Pelusian Daphnae, he was invited to a banquet by his brother, to whom he had entrusted the kingdom during his absence. His sons were invited too. But when they came, his brother piled wood around the outside of the house and set fire to it. As soon as Sesostris realized what was going on, he turned to his wife, because he had brought her along with him too, and asked her advice. She suggested that he have two of his six sons lie down over the flames and act as a bridge across the fire, so that the rest of them could walk on them and escape. Sesostris did this, and although it resulted in two of his sons being burnt to death, this made it possible for their father and the others to escape.

[108] Once Sesostris was back in Egypt and had taken vengeance on his brother, he found a use for the horde of people he had brought with him, whose lands he had conquered. It was they who hauled the massive blocks of stone which were collected during his reign for the sanctuary of Hephaestus, and they were also forced to work digging all the canals which now exist in Egypt. As a result of all this, without meaning to, they made horses and carts disappear from Egypt, when there had previously been plenty of horses and the whole land had teemed with cart traffic. For ever since then, despite being a completely flat country, Egypt has been unfit for horses and carts, because of the number of canals and the way they criss-cross the country in all directions. Sesostris had these canals slice up the countryside because all the Egyptians in places which were not on the river but in the middle of the country were short of water when the river went down, and had to make do with rather brackish drinking-water drawn from wells.

[109] The priests also told me that Sesostris divided the country among all the Egyptians, giving each man the same amount of land in the form of a square plot. This was a source of income for him, because he ordered them to pay an annual tax. If any of a person's

plot was lost to the river, he would present himself at the king's court and tell him what had happened; then the king sent inspectors to measure how much land he had lost, so that in the future the man had to pay proportionately less of the fixed tax. It seems to me that this was how geometry as a land-surveying technique came to be discovered and then imported into Greece. But the Greeks learned about the sundial, its pointer, and the twelve divisions of the day from the Babylonians.

[110] Sesostris was the only Egyptian king to rule over Ethiopia. The monuments he left to posterity stand in front of the temple of Hephaestus and consist of two stone statues thirty cubits in height of himself and his wife, and statues of his four sons too, each twenty cubits in height. Many years later the priest of Hephaestus refused to let Darius the Persian erect a statue of himself in front of this group of statues, arguing that his achievements did not match those of Sesostris the Egyptian. 'After all,' he said, 'Sesostris defeated as many peoples as you, and the Scythians as well, whom you were unable to conquer. It would not be right, then, for you to stand out in front of Sesostris' statues, since your achievements do not surpass those of Sesostris.' They say that Darius conceded the point.

[111] The priests told me that after Sesostris' death his son Pheros inherited the kingdom. Pheros has no military exploits to his credit, but it happened that the following event led to his blindness. Once, the volume of water coming down the river was greater than ever before; the river rose to eighteen cubits, and when it flooded the fields, a wind descended and the river became turbulent. The king, they say, committed sacrilege: he seized a spear and hurled it into the middle of the swirling river, and was immediately afterwards afflicted with an eye disease from which he became blind. Sometime in the eleventh year, after he had been blind for ten years, an oracle came to him from the city of Buto that the time of his punishment had come to an end and that he would regain his sight once he had washed his eyes in the urine of a woman who had slept only with her own husband and had never been with another man. He tested out his own wife first, but he still did not regain his sight, so then he tried all kinds of women one after another. When at last he did recover his sight, he had all the women he had tested, except the one whose urine he had washed in to regain his sight, assemble in a single town (the one which nowa-

days goes by the name of Erythrebolus), and once they were all gathered there he burnt the town down, with them inside it. As for the woman whose urine he had washed in to regain his sight, he made her his wife. To mark his deliverance from the eye disease, he dedicated a number of offerings throughout all the famous sanctuaries of Egypt, but the most noteworthy one consists of the remarkable structures he dedicated in the sanctuary of the sun— two monolithic stone obelisks, each a hundred cubits tall and eight cubits thick.

[112] The priests told me that after Pheros the kingdom passed to a man from Memphis whose name in Greek is Proteus. To this day there is in Memphis, south of the temple of Hephaestus, a particularly fine and well-appointed precinct which was his. The houses around this precinct are inhabited by Phoenicians from Tyre, and the whole district is called the Tyrian Camp. Inside Proteus' precinct is a sanctuary sacred to 'the Foreign Aphrodite'. I have come to the conclusion that the person it is sacred to is Helen the daughter of Tyndareus, not only because I am aware of the story that Helen spent some time in Egypt with Proteus, but also, and in particular, because the sanctuary is called the sanctuary of the *Foreign* Aphrodite; no other sanctuary of Aphrodite is called 'foreign'.

[113] On the business concerning Helen, I asked the priests what they knew and this is what they told me. After Alexander had abducted Helen from Sparta, he set sail back to his native land, but while he was in the Aegean, violent winds pushed him off course and into the Egyptian Sea. The winds did not let up and so he ended up landing in Egypt—specifically, at what is nowadays called the Canobic mouth of the Nile and its fish-salting works. Now, there was then, as there still is, a sanctuary of Heracles on the shore there, and there is a custom (which has survived unchanged from its ancient origins right up to my own day), that any house-slave who takes refuge in the sanctuary and brands himself with sacred marks, to signify that he is giving himself to the god, cannot be touched, no matter whose slave he was. So when Alexander's attendants heard about the custom connected to this sanctuary, they left him and installed themselves in the sanctuary as suppliants of the god. They wanted to hurt Alexander and so they made an accusation against him and told the whole story of his treatment of Helen and the wrong he had done Menelaus. They lodged this information

not only with the priests, but also with the officer in charge of this mouth of the Nile, whose name was Thonis.

[114] When Thonis had heard what they had to say, he sent an urgent message to Proteus in Memphis, saying: 'A stranger has arrived, a Teucrian, fresh from committing an unholy deed in Greece. He seduced the wife of his host and has been brought here by the winds to your kingdom with her and with a great many valuable goods as well. Shall we let him sail away unharmed, or shall we confiscate what he brought with him?'

The message Proteus sent in reply said: 'It doesn't matter who this man is: he has committed unholy deeds against his own host. Arrest him and bring him to me, so that I can see what he has to say for himself.'

[115] On receipt of this message Thonis arrested Alexander and impounded his ships. Then he took Alexander, along with Helen, the valuables, and the suppliants as well, to Memphis. When they were all there, Proteus asked Alexander who he was and where he had come from. Alexander gave him the details of his family and his native country, and also told him where he had been sailing from. Proteus next asked him where he had got Helen, but Alexander prevaricated and did not tell the truth, so the suppliants (as they now were) gave all the details of his crime and exposed his lies. When they had finished, Proteus declared: 'You're lucky that I think it important not to take the lives of visitors, especially those who have come to my kingdom after having been driven off course by winds. Otherwise, you scum, on behalf of the Greek I would make you pay for what you have done—for the terrible crime you have committed after accepting his hospitality. You made advances to the wife of your host. As if that were not enough, you gave her the wings to flee with you when you left. But you didn't even leave it at that: you also plundered your host's house before coming here. Well, it is true that I think it important not to take the lives of visitors, but I will certainly not let you leave with this woman and the valuables. I'll look after them for your Greek host, until he decides to come here himself to fetch them. As for you and your companions, I hereby give you three days to leave my shores and find some other haven. If you fail to comply, I will treat you as enemies.'

[116] The priests told me that this was how Helen came to stay with Proteus. Now, I think that Homer had heard this story as well, because although he omitted it on the grounds that it was not as

suitable for an epic poem as the other one (the one that he used),
he still showed that he knew this alternative story too. He makes
this clear, because he was drawing on this version† when he composed in the *Iliad* (and he never corrected himself) the section
describing Alexander's travels—how he was driven off course while
bringing Helen home and how in the course of his wanderings he
landed, among other places, at Sidon in Phoenicia. His mention of
Alexander's travels occurs in 'The Prowess of Diomedes' and goes
like this:

> There were the gorgeous robes, embroidered by women
> Of Sidon, which godlike Alexander himself
> Had carried from Sidon, sailing across the broad sea
> On the journey when he brought back Helen of famous lineage.

†It is clear from these words that Homer knew of Alexander's circuitous journey to Egypt, because Syria (where the Phoenicians, to
whom Sidon belongs, live) is on Egypt's borders.

[117] These words and this passage also make it absolutely clear,
beyond the shadow of a doubt, that someone else, not Homer, is
the author of the *Cypria*. In the *Cypria* it is said that Alexander
reached Ilium with Helen three days after leaving Sparta, because
he met with a favourable wind and a calm sea. In the *Iliad*,
however, Homer says that Alexander's journey home with Helen
was not direct. Anyway, that is enough about Homer and the
Cypria.

[118] I asked the priests whether or not the Greek version of
what happened at Ilium was completely ridiculous, and this is what
they told me (adding that they were sure of the correctness of their
information because they had asked Menelaus himself): after the
abduction of Helen, a large Greek army came to Teucrian territory
to help Menelaus. When they had disembarked and established a
camp, they dispatched messengers to Ilium, and with them went
Menelaus himself. Once the delegation was inside the city, they
called for the return of Helen and of the goods which Alexander
had stolen and carried off, and they also demanded recompense for
the crimes that had been committed. The Teucrians said then what
they consistently said later too, whether or not they were under
oath: that they did not have Helen or the property in question, that
both were in Egypt, and that it would hardly be fair for them to
have to recompense the Greeks for things that King Proteus of

Egypt had.† The Greeks thought the Teucrians were laughing at them and so they besieged the city and eventually took it. When the city was in their hands, however, Helen was nowhere to be found. All they got was the same information as before, but now the Greeks believed what the Teucrians had been telling them all along and so they sent Menelaus himself to Proteus.

[119] So Menelaus came to Egypt and sailed up the river to Memphis, where he told them exactly what had happened. The Egyptians looked after him magnificently, returned Helen to him completely unhurt, and gave him back all his property as well. Nevertheless, after all this good fortune, Menelaus treated the Egyptians unjustly. He was impatient to sail away, but adverse winds were holding him up; after this had been going on for a long time, he found a solution, but it was an abomination. He seized two children from local families and sacrificed them. When the Egyptians found out what he had done, they set sail in hatred after him, but he set a course straight for Libya with his ships, and then they lost his trail. My informants told me that they learnt this as a result of their enquiries, but that they were certain of the events that had happened in their own country.

[120] That is what the Egyptian priests told me; personally, I accept their version of the Helen story, for the following reasons. If Helen had been in Ilium, she would have been returned to the Greeks with or without Alexander's consent. It would have been completely insane for Priam and the rest of his family to choose to put themselves, their children, and their city in danger just so that Alexander could live with Helen. Even if they had chosen this course of action at first, yet in the face of heavy Trojan losses resulting from their encounters with the Greeks, and when (if one must speak using the evidence of epic poets) at least two or three of Priam's own sons died every time battle was joined—under these circumstances, I expect that even if it had been Priam himself who was living with Helen, he would have given her back to the Achaeans in order to end the disasters they were faced with. Nor was Alexander even the heir to the kingdom, so it was not as if he was in charge now that Priam was elderly; no, Hector was not only older than Alexander, but he was more of a man than him. It was Hector who would inherit the kingdom on Priam's death, and he was not the kind of man to let his brother get away with wrong-doing, especially when his brother was responsible not only for

Hector's own personal suffering, but for that of all the other Trojans as well. No, the fact is that they did not have Helen to give back; they were telling the truth, but the Greeks did not believe them. In my opinion, this was because the gods were arranging things so that in their annihilation the Trojans might make it completely clear to others that the severity of a crime is matched by the severity of the ensuing punishment at the gods' hands. That is my view, at any rate.

[121] The priests told me that the kingdom passed from Proteus to Rhampsinitus. Rhampsinitus left as his memorial the western gateway of the sanctuary of Hephaestus; he erected two statues facing this gateway, each of which is twenty-five cubits in height. The Egyptians call the northern one 'Summer' and the southern one 'Winter', and they prostrate themselves in front of 'Summer' and treat it with respect, but do the opposite to 'Winter'.

Now, they say that Rhampsinitus had a huge fortune in silver, more than any of his successors, none of whom even came close. He wanted to store his money in a safe place, so he built a stone chamber as an extension off one of the outside walls of his residence. The builder, however, came up with the following crafty scheme. He cleverly fitted one of the stones in such a way that it would easily be removable from its wall by two men or even one. Anyway, the chamber was finished and the king stored his money in it. Time passed. At the end of his life, the builder summoned his sons (there were two of them) and told them of the plan he had put into effect while building the king's treasure-chamber, so that they would be comfortable for the rest of their lives. He explained precisely to them how to remove the stone and described its position in the wall. He told them that if they remembered his instructions, they would be the stewards of the king's treasury!

He died, and his sons soon set to work. They went by night to the royal residence and found the stone in the building. It was easy for them to handle, and they carried off a lot of money. When the king happened to go into the chamber next, he was surprised to see that the caskets were missing some money, but the seals on the door were still intact and the chamber had been locked up, so he could not blame anyone. But the same thing happened the next couple of times he opened the door as well: his money was obviously dwindling all the time (for the thieves had not stopped their depredations). So the king had traps made, and set them around the caskets which held the money. The thieves came as usual and one of them sneaked into the chamber, but as soon as he approached a casket he was caught in the trap. As soon as he realized how desperate his situation was, he called out to his brother, explained the state of affairs, and told him to come into the chamber as quickly as possible and cut his head off. This was to stop him being seen and recognized and so bringing ruin down on his brother as well. His brother thought that this was sound advice, and he acted on the suggestion. Then he fitted the stone back in its place and went back home, taking his brother's head with him.

The next morning, the story continues, the king went into his treasure-chamber. He was astonished at the sight of the thief's headless body caught in a trap in an undamaged room without any way in or any way out. He did not know what to make of it, but this is what he did. He hung the thief's body on the city wall, and posted guards around it with instructions to arrest and bring to him anyone they saw crying or grieving.

With the corpse hanging there, the mother was very upset, and she told the surviving son somehow to find a way to cut his brother's body down and bring it back home. She warned him that if he did not give the matter his attention, she would go to the king and let him know that he had the money. The mother kept on scolding the surviving son and refusing to listen to all his arguments, and eventually he came up with a plan. He got some donkeys ready, loaded wineskins which he had filled with wine on to them, and then took them out on the road. When he reached the spot where the men were watching over the corpse hanging on the wall, he pulled on the necks of a couple of the wineskins and undid their fastenings. The wine poured out, and the man hit his head and shouted out in dismay, as if he did not know which of the donkeys to go to first.

When the guards saw the wine flooding out, they thought they had struck it lucky. They ran into the road with jars and caught the wine as it poured out, while the thief swore at them all and pretended to be angry. The guards tried to calm him down, however, and he eventually let them think they had succeeded and that he had forgiven them. He drove the donkeys off the road, settled their loads, and carried on talking with the guards. One of the guards even teased him and made him laugh, and he gave them a skin of wine. The guards immediately settled themselves there on the ground and decided to have a drink. They included him and told him to stay and have a drink with them—and of course he was won over and stayed. As a result of their drinking, the guards warmed to the donkey-driver, and he gave them another skin. The huge quantity of wine they had consumed put the guards into a drunken stupor, and they lay down, overcome with sleep, right there on the spot where they had been drinking. The other man waited until the night was well advanced and then cut down his brother's body. Also, in order to mock the guards, he shaved the right cheek of every one of them. Then he loaded the corpse on to the donkeys and drove them home. He had done what his mother had told him to do.

When news of the theft of the thief's corpse reached the king, he was furious. There was nothing he wanted more than to catch whoever it was who had pulled the trick off. So what he did—so the story goes, but I find it unbelievable—was install his daughter in a room with instructions to accept all men indiscriminately; she was not to sleep with them, however, until she had got them to tell her the cleverest and the worst things they had ever done in their lives. As soon as the business with the thief came up in someone's reply, she was to grab him and not let him go.

The king's daughter obeyed her father's instructions, but the thief heard what the king was up to. He wanted to prove himself even more cunning than the king, so he cut an arm off a fresh corpse at the shoulder and went along with the arm under his cloak. He went in to the king's daughter and in reply to the question she was asking everyone, he told her that the worst thing he had done was decapitate his own brother when he was caught in a trap in the king's treasure-chamber, and that the cleverest thing he had done was get the guards drunk and cut his brother's corpse down from the city wall. Hearing this, she seized hold of him, but in the darkness the thief put the corpse's arm in her way. She grabbed the arm and held on to it, thinking that she had the actual thief's arm in her grip. But the thief left it in her grasp and ran out of the door.

When this too was reported to the king, he was impressed with the man's resourcefulness and daring. Eventually, he sent heralds round all the settlements and offered the man immunity and a gen- erous reward if he would present himself before him. The thief believed the offer and went to the king. Rhampsinitus was so taken with him that he gave him his daughter to marry, proclaiming him

the most intelligent man in the world. For the king thought the
Egyptians more outstanding than everyone else, and this man the
most outstanding of the Egyptians.

[122] The next thing Rhampsinitus did, according to the priests,
was go down into the place the Greeks know as Hades and play
dice with Demeter there. He won some games and lost others, and
then he came back up again with a golden scarf which she had
given him. They said that the Egyptians celebrate a festival based
on Rhampsinitus' descent and subsequent return, and I know for
a fact that they were still celebrating it in my time, although I
cannot confirm that it takes place because of Rhampsinitus' descent
and return. On a single day, the priests weave a shawl. One of their
number, with the shawl, then has a headband tied over his eyes.
They take him out into the street which leads to the sanctuary of
Demeter and then retrace their steps. They say that this blindfolded
priest is escorted by two wolves to the sanctuary of Demeter, which
is twenty stades away from the city, and later the wolves bring him
back again to the very spot where they had joined him.

[123] Anyone who finds such things credible can make of these
Egyptian stories what he wishes. My job, throughout this account,
is simply to record whatever I am told by each of my sources. The
Egyptians say that Demeter and Dionysus are the rulers of the
underworld kingdom. The Egyptians were also the first to claim
that the soul of a human being is immortal, and that each time the
body dies the soul enters another creature just as it is being born.
They also say that when the soul has made the round of every creature on land, in the sea, and in the air, it once more clothes itself
in the body of a human being just as it is being born, and that a
complete cycle takes three thousand years. This theory has been
adopted by certain Greeks too—some from a long time ago, some
more recently—who presented it as if it were their own. I know
their names, but I will not write them down.

[124] The priests said that up to the reign of King Rhampsinitus Egyptian society was stable and the country was very prosperous, but that under their next king, Cheops, it was reduced to a
completely awful condition. He closed down all the sanctuaries,
stopped people performing sacrifices, and also commanded all the
Egyptians to work for him. Some had the job of hauling blocks of
stone from the quarries in the Arabian mountain range as far as
the Nile, where they were transported across the river in boats and

then passed on to others, whom he assigned to haul them from
there to the Libyan mountains. They worked in gangs of 100,000
men for three months at a time. They said that it took ten years†
of hard labour for the people to construct the causeway along
which they hauled the blocks of stone, which I would think
involved not much less work than building the pyramid, since the
road is five stades long, ten fathoms wide, and eight fathoms high
at its highest point, and is made of polished stone, with figures
carved on it. So they spent ten years over this road and the underground rooms which Cheops had constructed as his sepulchral
chambers in the hill on which the pyramids stand, which he turned
into an island by bringing water from the Nile there along a canal.
The actual pyramid took twenty years to build. Each of its sides,
which form a square, is eight plethra long and the pyramid is
eight plethra high as well. It is made of polished blocks of stone,
fitted together perfectly; none of the blocks is less than thirty feet
long.

[125] The pyramid was built up like a flight of stairs (others use
the image of staggered battlements or altar steps). When that first
stage of the construction process was over, they used appliances
made out of short pieces of wood to lift the remaining blocks of
stone up the sides. First they would raise a block of stone from the
ground on to the first tier, and when the stone had been raised up
to that point, it was put on to a different device which was positioned on the first level, and from there it was hauled up to the
second level on another device. Either there were the same number
of devices as there were tiers, or alternatively, if the device was a
single manageable unit, they transferred the same one from level to
level once they had removed the stone from it. I have mentioned
two alternative methods, because that is exactly how the information was given to me. Anyway, they finished off the topmost parts
of the pyramid first, then the ones just under it, and ended with the
ground levels and the lowest ones.

There is a notice in Egyptian script on the pyramid about how
much was spent on radishes, onions, and garlic for the labourers,
and if my memory serves me well, the translator reading the notice
to me said that the total cost was sixteen hundred talents of silver.
If that is so, how much more must have been spent, in all likelihood, on iron for the tools, and on food and clothing for the
work-force, considering how much time, as I mentioned, was spent

building the pyramid? And then, I suppose, there was also the not inconsiderable amount of time spent quarrying the stone and bringing it to the site and excavating the underground chambers.

[126] Cheops was such a bad man that when he was short of money he installed his own daughter in a room with instructions to charge a certain amount of money (I was not told exactly how much) for her favours. She did what her father had told her to do, but she also had the idea of leaving behind her own personal memorial, so she asked each of the men who came in to her to give her a single block of stone in the work-site.† I was told that the middle pyramid of the group of three was built from these blocks of stone—the one which stands in front of the large one and the sides of whose base are one and a half plethra long.

[127] The Egyptians said that after a reign of fifty years Cheops died and the kingdom passed to his brother Chephren. He carried on in the same manner as his brother, and not least in the sense that he too built a pyramid, although it did not reach the size of his brother's. I know because in fact I measured them both myself. There are no underground chambers in Chephren's pyramid, nor does a channel come flowing into it from the Nile, as in the case of the other one, where a conduit was built so that the Nile would encircle an island on which, they say, Cheops himself is buried. The bottom layer of Chephren's pyramid was made out of patterned Ethiopian stone and the whole thing is the same size as the other pyramid, but forty feet less tall. Both of them stand on the same hill, which is about a hundred feet high. They said that Chephren's reign lasted fifty-six years.

[128] So by their own reckoning, this terrible period in Egypt lasted 106 years, and the sanctuaries, locked for all these years, were never opened. The Egyptians loathe Chephren and Cheops so much that they really do not like to mention their names. Instead, they say the pyramids belonged to a shepherd called Philitis, who at this time used to graze his flocks on the same land.

[129] The priests said that the next king of Egypt was Mycerinus the son of Cheops, and that he disapproved of what his father had done. He not only reopened the sanctuaries and let the people, who had been ground down to a state of total misery, return to their work and their sacrifices, but he was also the fairest of all the kings in judging their legal cases. Because of this they speak more highly of Mycerinus than they do of any other Egyptian king. And it was not just that his judgements were sound, but also that if

anyone complained after one of his decisions, he gave him from his own treasury whatever extra amount it took to satisfy him. But even though Mycerinus was kind to the people of Egypt and followed these practices, trouble still came his way. His daughter's death marked the beginning of it. She was the only child in his household, and he was terribly upset at the calamity. He wanted to give her an outstanding tomb, so he made a hollow cow out of gilded wood and then he buried his dead daughter inside it.

[130] Now, this cow was not buried in the ground, but could still be seen in my day lying in a decorated room of the royal palace in Saïs. Every day perfumed spices of all kinds are burnt before it, and a lamp is kept alight all night and every night. In another room, near this cow, there are statues which the priests in Saïs identified as Mycerinus' concubines. There are about twenty of these wooden figures, made to represent naked women. As to who these women are, I have nothing to go on except what I was told.

[131] There is also another story, however, about this cow and the figures. It is said that Mycerinus raped his own daughter because he was in love with her. Afterwards, they say, she hanged herself in grief, and he buried her in the cow. Her mother, however, cut off the hands of the serving-maids who had betrayed the daughter to her father, and the same thing has happened to the statues of these serving-maids as happened to their living originals. But this is all nonsense, in my opinion, and not least the part about the statues' hands. I actually saw the statues, and it was obvious that the passage of time was responsible for the loss of their hands, because right up to my day they could still be seen lying on the ground at the statues' feet.

[132] A red cloth has been draped over the whole of the cow, so that it is all hidden except for the neck and head, which are gilded over with a very thick layer of gold plate. Between its horns there is a golden circle representing the sun. The cow is resting on its knees, rather than standing up. Its size is that of a large living cow. It is carried out of the room every year on the occasion when the Egyptians mourn the death of the god whom I will not name in this context. Anyway, that is when they bring the cow into the light, because (so the story goes) the dying girl asked her father Mycerinus to let her see the sun once a year.

[133] After his daughter's death a second disaster struck Mycerinus. He received an oracle from the city of Buto to the effect that he had only six more years to live and would die sometime

within the seventh year. He thought this was dreadful, and he sent emissaries to the oracle with an indignant reproach for the god. He protested the fact that his father and uncle, both of whom had closed the sanctuaries, ignored the gods, and ruined men's lives, had lived a good many years, while a god-fearing man like himself was going to die so soon. A second message came from the oracle, explaining that it was precisely because he was a god-fearing man that his life was being cut short—that he had not behaved as he should. Egypt was supposed to suffer for a hundred and fifty years, and his two predecessors had understood that, while he had not. When Mycerinus received this message and realized that his fate had already been sealed, he had plenty of lamps made, so that he could light them at nightfall, and drink and carouse without stopping all day and all night; he also used to roam through the marshes and groves, and anywhere else that he heard was a particularly good place to take pleasure. His plan was to prove the oracle wrong: by turning his nights into days, he hoped to convert his six years into twelve.

[134] He too left a pyramid as a memorial. His pyramid is much smaller than his father's, each side of the square base being twenty feet short of three plethra, and the bottom half of it is made out of Ethiopian stone. There are Greek writers who say that it was built by Rhodopis, who was a courtesan, but they are wrong. It seems to me that this theory is based on complete ignorance about Rhodopis, otherwise its proponents would not have ascribed the building of a pyramid like this to her, when it is hardly going too far to say that countless thousands of talents must have been spent on it. Besides, Rhodopis was in her prime during the reign of King Amasis, not at the time of Mycerinus. In other words, Rhodopis was alive a great many years later than the pyramid-building kings. She was a Thracian by birth, and was the slave of a Samian called Iadmon the son of Hephaestopolis, another of whose slaves was the writer Aesop. That he too was a slave of Iadmon's is proved above all by the fact that when the Delphians kept on proclaiming, on the advice of the oracle, that anyone who so wanted could claim compensation from them for Aesop's life, no one came forward until Iadmon's grandson, who was also called Iadmon, claimed it. This shows that Aesop belonged to Iadmon.

[135] Rhodopis was brought to Egypt by Xanthes of Samos, and then, so that she could ply her trade, her freedom was bought for

a great deal of money by a man from Mytilene called Charaxus, who was the son of Scamandronymus and the brother of the poet Sappho. Once she had gained her freedom in this way, Rhodopis stayed in Egypt and was so alluring that she earned a fortune—a fortune for a Rhodopis, that is, but not enough to build that kind of pyramid. Since it is possible even today for anyone who so wants to see what a tenth of her fortune amounts to, there is no need for anyone to suggest that she was hugely wealthy. She wanted to leave a tribute to herself in Greece—something that no one else had thought of making and dedicating in a sanctuary—and to dedicate it in Delphi as her memorial. So with a tenth of her fortune she had a quantity of ox-sized iron spits made—as many as she could with that amount of money—and sent them to Delphi, and even today they are still lying in a pile behind the altar which the Chians dedicated and in front of the actual temple. (For some reason, courtesans in Naucratis are particularly beguiling. Not only was there the one we have been talking about, who became so famous that all Greeks are familiar with the name of Rhodopis, but there was also another one later, called Archidice, who became the subject of a popular Greek song, although she is less notorious than Rhodopis.) After he bought Rhodopis' freedom, Charaxus returned to Mytilene, to be much ridiculed in Sappho's poetry. That is all I have to say about Rhodopis.

[136] The priests told me that Asychis succeeded to the Egyptian kingdom after Mycerinus. He built the eastern gateway of the sanctuary of Hephaestus, which is the most magnificent and by far the largest. All the gateways have figures carved on them and countless other marvels of construction, but this eastern one easily outdoes the others. They said that during his reign there was a severe financial recession and so a law was passed that a person might use his father's corpse as security to take out a loan. There was a rider to the law, however, to the effect that the lender also became the proprietor of the whole of the borrower's burial-plot, so that if the mortgagee refused to pay back the loan, as a penalty neither he nor any other member of his family could have access on their deaths to burial in the family tomb (or indeed in any other tomb either). They say that Asychis wanted to outdo the Egyptian kings who came before him, so he built as his monument a pyramid made out of bricks, and had the following words chiselled in stone on it: 'Do not compare me unfavourably with the

pyramids of stone. I surpass the other pyramids as Zeus surpasses the other gods. For I was made out of bricks, which were formed out of mud, which was collected from a pole it had stuck to when the pole was plunged down into a lake.' So much for Asychis' achievements.

[137] The next king was a blind man from the city of Anysis, whose name was Anysis. During his reign Egypt was invaded by a strong force of Ethiopians under their king Sabacos. The blind Egyptian king withdrew into the marshes, and the Ethiopian ruled Egypt for fifty years. The following were the achievements of his reign. The death penalty was abolished, and instead he sentenced every Egyptian wrongdoer, according to the seriousness of his crime, to build a dyke near his native city. In this way, the cities were raised even higher above the water level than they already were. They had first been heaped up by the people who excavated the canals in the time of King Sesostris, and now it happened again during the Ethiopian's reign, with the result that the cities became really quite elevated. Of all the Egyptian cities which were raised in this way, it was Bubastis, I should say, whose level was raised the most. This city also contains a truly remarkable sanctuary of Bubastis (or Artemis in Greek); it may not be the largest or most lavishly appointed sanctuary in Egypt, but is certainly the most beautiful.

[138] This is what the sanctuary of Bubastis is like. Only the entrance stops the whole thing being an island, because there are two canals drawing water from the Nile, one flowing around one side of the sanctuary, the other around the other side, and they both end just by the entrance, without joining. Each canal is a hundred feet wide and is shaded with trees. The gateway is ten fathoms high and has been embellished with remarkable figures, six cubits tall. Because the sanctuary is in the middle of the city, and because the rest of the city has been raised by earthworks, but the sanctuary has been left exactly as it was originally built, one can walk around it and look down into it from any direction. A stone wall, with figures carved on it, surrounds the sanctuary. Inside the wall there is a grove of enormous trees growing around the great temple that houses the cult statue. The whole sanctuary is a stade long and a stade wide as well. A road, which is four plethra wide and paved with stones, starts at the entrance to the sanctuary and runs for about three stades eastwards through the city square. Here and

there along the side of the road, which ends at the sanctuary of Hermes, there are trees growing which seem to touch the sky. Anyway, that is what this sanctuary is like.

[139] The final departure of the Ethiopian king came about, they said, because he had a dream which caused him to flee. The dream was of a man standing over him and advising him to gather together all the priests in Egypt and cut them in half. His response to the dream was to say that, to his mind, the gods had shown him the dream as a kind of intimation, to make him commit sacrilege and suffer terrible consequences at the hands of gods or men. He refused to do it, he said, and in any case the period of his rule over Egypt, as foretold by the oracles, had come to an end and it was time for him to leave. For while he was in Ethiopia the oracles consulted by the Ethiopians had announced that he was to rule over Egypt for fifty years. Now, since his time was up and the dream had disturbed him, Sabacos voluntarily left Egypt.

[140] After the Ethiopian had left Egypt, the blind king returned from the marshes and resumed his reign. He had lived in the marshes for fifty years on an island built up from ashes and earth, because the Egyptians were under orders to bring him food without Sabacos' knowledge, and every time one of them did so, the blind king told him to bring him ashes as well, as a gift. Until the time of King Amyrtaeus, no one knew the location of this island; for more than seven hundred years none of the kings before Amyrtaeus was able to find it. Its name is Elbo, and it has a diameter of ten stades.

[141] The next king, they said, was the priest of Hephaestus, whose name was Sethos. He had no respect or regard for the warrior class of Egyptians, because he thought he had no need of them, and one of the ways he insulted them was by depriving them of their plots of land—each of them having held as a special privilege, during the reigns of earlier kings, twelve arouras of land. Some time later, Egypt was invaded by a huge army of Arabians and Assyrians under their king Sennacherib, and the Egyptian warriors refused to help. In desperation, the priest went into the temple, approached the cult statue and protested about the danger he was facing. And in fact, after he had voiced his complaints, he fell asleep and dreamt he saw the god standing over him and telling him not to worry, since nothing terrible would happen to him if he went out to confront the Arabian army, because he would send him

allies. Sethos put his trust in this dream. He enlisted any Egyptians who were prepared to follow him and established his position near Pelusium, because this is where the routes into Egypt are; his army consisted of no members of the warrior class, but only retailers, artisans, and traders. The opposing army arrived—but at night a swarm of field-mice gnawed through their quivers and their bows, and the handles of their shields as well, so that the next day, weaponless, all they could do was flee, and their losses were heavy. A stone statue of this king can still be seen today standing in the sanctuary of Hephaestus with a field-mouse in his hand, and on the statue is an inscription which reads: 'Let all who look on me reverence the gods.'

[142] So far, my account has relied on what I was told by the Egyptians and their priests. They show in their records that there are 341 human generations between the first king of Egypt and this final one, the priest of Hephaestus, and they have a king and a high priest for each of these generations. Now, three hundred human generations make 10,000 years, because there are three generations in a hundred years, and the forty-one remaining generations, on top of the three hundred, make 1,340 years. So throughout these 11,340 years, they said, no god ever appeared in human form; furthermore, nothing like that happened either earlier or later during the reigns of the subsequent kings of Egypt. However, they did tell me that four times during the period in question, the sun changed its usual procedure for rising: twice it rose from the place where it currently sets, and twice it set in the direction where it currently rises. They told me that nothing in Egypt was altered at these times—nothing growing in the earth or living in the river was any different, and there was no change in the course of diseases or in the ways people died.

[143] Some time ago the writer Hecataeus was in Thebes. He had studied his own lineage and had traced his family history back to a divine ancestor in the sixteenth generation. So the priests of Zeus there did to him what they did to me too (not that I had looked into my family history): they took me into the temple, showed me the wooden figures there, and counted them for me, up to the number I have mentioned, since every high priest sets up his own statue in the temple while he is still alive. The priests started with the statue of the one who had died most recently and went through the whole lot, until they had shown them all, and while

showing me the statues and counting them out, they demonstrated how in each generation the son succeeded his own father. In response to the fact that Hecataeus' studies of his lineage had led him back to a divine ancestor in the sixteenth generation, they established an alternative genealogy on the basis of their counting of the statues, and they refused to accept his idea that a human being could be descended from a god. In constructing their alternative genealogy, they claimed that every one of the figures represented a *piromis* descended from a *piromis* (in Greek this would be a 'man of rank'), and they made this claim for every one of the 345 statues they showed him. In other words, they did not connect any of them to either a god or a hero.

[144] They demonstrated, then, that all the people portrayed by these statues were mortal human beings, bearing no relation to gods. They claimed, however, that before these men gods had been the kings of Egypt—that they had lived alongside human beings and that at any given time one of them had been the supreme ruler. The last of these divine kings of Egypt, they said, had been Horus the son of Osiris, whom the Greeks call Apollo. He had deposed Typhon and become the last divine king of Egypt. In Greek, Osiris is Dionysus.

[145] In Greece the youngest gods are considered to be Heracles, Dionysus, and Pan, but in Egypt Pan is regarded as one of the Eight Primal Gods (as they are called), and therefore as the oldest of the three, because Heracles is thought to belong to the second group (called the Twelve) and Dionysus to the third group, who were descendants of the Twelve. I have stated earlier how many years there are, according to the Egyptians, from Heracles to the time of King Amasis; Pan is supposed to be even earlier, and although the interval between Dionysus and Amasis is the smallest of the three, they calculate it at fifteen thousand years. The Egyptians claim to have precise knowledge of all this, because they have always kept count of and continuously chronicled the passing years. Now, the Dionysus whose mother is said to have been Semele the daughter of Cadmus was born about sixteen hundred years before my time,† Heracles the son of Alcmene was born about nine hundred years ago, and Pan the son of Penelope (following the Greek account which makes Pan the son of Penelope and Hermes) was born after the Trojan War, or about eight hundred years before my time.

[146] Anyone can adopt whichever of these alternative stories he finds more plausible; in any case, I have stated my own opinion. The point is that if Pan, Heracles, and Dionysus had appeared on the earth and grown old in Greece (not just the Heracles who was the son of Amphitryon, but also the Dionysus who was the son of Semele, and the Pan who was the son of Penelope), one might have said that these others too were men who were named after the gods who came before them. In fact, however, the Greeks say that as soon as Dionysus was born, Zeus sewed him up in his thigh and carried him to Nysa (the one in Ethiopia, south of Egypt). As for Pan, they cannot say what became of him after his birth. So I think it is obvious that the Greeks heard the names of Pan and Dionysus later than they did those of the other gods; they take the time when they first heard about them as the date from which to trace their lineage.

[147] So far, then, my account has relied on what the Egyptians alone say, but now I will report views about this country shared by other people as well as by the Egyptians. This will be supplemented as well by what I personally saw.

The Egyptians found it impossible to live without a king, so no sooner had they won their freedom after the reign of the priest of Hephaestus than they divided the whole country into twelve regions and created a system of twelve kings. These twelve kings intermarried with one another's families and made it a rule of their kingship that none of them should try to depose any of the others or attempt to gain more territory than any of the others, but that they should be firm friends and allies. The reason why they made this rule, and resolutely upheld it, is that an oracle had declared, at the very beginning of their reigns, that whichever one of them poured a libation in the sanctuary of Hephaestus from a bronze cup would become king of all Egypt. (They used to meet in all the sanctuaries.)

[148] Now, they decided to build monuments together to leave for posterity, and having reached this decision they constructed a labyrinth just beyond the lake of Moeris, very close to the place called Crocodilopolis. I have personally seen it, and it defies description. If someone put together all the strongholds and public monuments of the Greeks, it would be obvious that less labour and money had been expended on them than on this labyrinth—and I say this despite the fact that the temples in Ephesus and Samos are

remarkable structures. The pyramids, of course, beggar description and each of them is the equivalent of a number of sizeable Greek edifices, but the labyrinth outstrips even the pyramids. It has twelve roofed courtyards, six in a row to the north and six with their entrances directly opposite them in a row to the south. A single outside wall surrounds them all. The labyrinth has rooms on two levels—an underground level and an above-ground level on top of it—and there are three thousand rooms in all, with each level containing fifteen hundred. I myself went through the ground-level rooms and saw them, and so I speak from firsthand knowledge, but the underground ones were only described to me. The Egyptians who are in charge of the labyrinth absolutely refused to show the underground rooms, on the grounds that there lie the tombs of the kings who originally built the labyrinth and those of the sacred crocodiles as well. So as far as the underground rooms are concerned I can only pass on what I was told, but the upper rooms, which I personally saw, seem almost superhuman edifices. For instance, the corridors from chamber to chamber and the winding passages through the courtyards are so complicated that they were a source of endless amazement; we would pass from a courtyard to some rooms, and from the rooms to colonnades, from where we would move on to other chambers and then find ourselves back at a different set of courtyards. The roof of the whole complex is made out of stone, as are the walls; the walls are covered with carvings of figures; and every colonnaded courtyard is made out of blocks of fitted white stone. By the corner where the labyrinth ends there is a pyramid forty fathoms in height, with huge figures carved on its surface. The approach to the pyramid has been built underground.

[149] Even more astounding than this labyrinth is the lake known as the lake of Moeris, on whose shore the labyrinth stands. The perimeter of the lake is 3,600 stades, or sixty schoeni; in other words, it is as long as the coastline of Egypt itself. The lake is elongated along its north–south axis, and at its deepest point it is fifty fathoms deep. It is obvious that it is an artificial lake and was excavated, because right in the middle there are two pyramids, which rise out of the water to a height of fifty fathoms, with the same amount built underwater; each of them is crowned by a stone figure seated on a throne. So the total height of the pyramids is a hundred fathoms, which is equivalent to a stade of six plethra, since

a fathom is six feet (or four cubits, because a foot is four palms and a cubit is six palms). The water in the lake has not come from natural springs (this is a terribly dry region), but has been brought through canals leading from the Nile. For six months of the year the water flows from the Nile into the lake, and for the other six months it flows back out of the lake and into the Nile. Every day, during the six months when the water is flowing out of the lake, the lake deposits a talent of silver into the royal treasury from its fish, but when the water is flowing into the lake, it deposits only twenty minae.

[150] The local inhabitants also said that this lake drains underground into the Gulf of Syrtis in Libya, since the western part of the lake stretches inland along the mountain range which runs south of Memphis. I did not see any earth heaped up anywhere from the excavation of the lake, and that bothered me, so I asked some people who lived right by the lake where the excavated earth was, and they told me where it had been taken. I found their explanation very plausible because I knew by report of something similar happening in the Assyrian city of Ninus. Sardanapallus the son of Ninus, who was the Assyrian king, had great wealth, which he kept in an underground chamber. Some thieves planned to steal the treasure, and they worked out how to tunnel through from their house to the palace. They proceeded to do so; every night they used to carry the earth which they dug out of the tunnel and dump it in the River Tigris on which Ninus stands, and they went on doing this until they had achieved their objective. Something similar, I was told, happened in the case of the soil from the Egyptian lake (except that it was done in the daytime rather than at night): the Egyptians took the earth they dug up and dumped it in the Nile, which would certainly carry it away and disperse it. Anyway, that is how this lake is said to have been excavated.

[151] The time came when the twelve kings (who had been dealing fairly with one another) performed the sacrificial rites in the sanctuary of Hephaestus. On the last day of the festival, when they were due to pour the libations, the high priest brought the usual golden libation cups out for them, but he miscounted and brought out eleven cups for the twelve kings. Since he was without a cup, the one standing at the end of the line—it was Psammetichus—took off his bronze helmet, held it out, and used it for the libation. Now, all the other kings were wearing helmets too and

in fact had them on at the time; Psammetichus had held out his helmet without any ulterior motive. But the others noticed what he had done and remembered that the oracle had said that whichever of them used a bronze cup for pouring the libation would be the sole king of Egypt. They interrogated Psammetichus and found that he had acted without premeditation, so they decided that it would be wrong to kill him, but they resolved to strip him of most of his power, exile him to the marshes, and ban him from setting out from the marshes to have anything to do with the rest of Egypt.

[152] This was not the first time that Psammetichus had been in exile: he had once fled from Sabacos the Ethiopian, who had killed his father Necho. On that occasion he had gone to Syria, and he was brought back from there by the inhabitants of the Egyptian province of Saïs when the Ethiopian left as a result of his dream. And then, when he became king for the second time, the incident with the helmet led to his being forced into exile again, this time in the marshes, banished there by the eleven kings. Anyway, he was aware of how badly he had been treated by them, and he kept trying to think of a way to pay them back for driving him away. When he sent a query to the city of Buto, the home of the most reliable Egyptian oracle, he received in return a prophecy to the effect that his revenge would come in the form of bronze men appearing from the sea. The idea of bronze men coming to help him struck him as extremely implausible, but a short while later some Ionian and Carian raiders, who had left home in search of rich pickings, found that they could not avoid being driven on to the coast of Egypt, and disembarked in their bronze armour. An Egyptian who had never before seen men dressed in bronze armour went to the marshes and told Psammetichus that bronze men had come from the sea and were plundering the plain. Psammetichus realized that the oracle was coming true. He got on friendly terms with the Ionians and Carians and, with promises of generous rewards, persuaded them to support him. Then, with the help of his Egyptian partisans and these allies of his he deposed the kings.

[153] So Psammetichus gained control of all Egypt. He built the southern gateway of the sanctuary of Hephaestus in Memphis, and opposite the gateway of the sanctuary of Apis he built the court-yard where Apis is looked after whenever he appears; this court-yard is surrounded by a colonnade (consisting of figures, twelve

cubits high, rather than pillars) and covered with reliefs. The Greek name for Apis is Epaphus.

[154] As a reward to the Ionians and Carians who had helped him win, Psammetichus gave them each their own land to settle; the Ionians were on one side of the Nile, the Carians on the other; these places were called the Encampments. As well as this land, he also gave them everything else he had promised them. In addition, he arranged for some Egyptian children to live with them and learn Greek from them, and the translators who are currently to be found in Egypt are descended from these children with their knowledge of Greek. The Ionians and Carians stayed for quite a long time in the places they had been given, which are located close to the sea, on the Pelusian mouth of the Nile, with the city of Bubastis lying just inland. Later, King Amasis moved them from there and re-settled them in Memphis, where they acted as his personal guards to protect him against the Egyptians. They were the first foreigners to live in Egypt, and it is thanks to their residence there that we Greeks have had some connection with the country, and that is how we have reliable information about Egyptian history from the reign of Psammetichus onwards. The slipways for their warships and their ruined houses could still be seen in my day in the places they originally occupied, before they were moved on. So that is how Psammetichus gained control of Egypt.

[155] I have already mentioned the Egyptian oracle a number of times, but I shall now give it the proper account it deserves. It is sacred to Leto and is located in a large city (called Buto, as I have already said) on the Sebennytic mouth of the Nile, on the right as one sails upriver from the sea.† Buto contains a sanctuary of Apollo and Artemis, and the temple of Leto, where the oracle is to be found, is quite big too; its gateway, for instance, is ten fathoms in height. I will mention the most amazing thing I saw there: it was a temple within this precinct of Leto which was made out of a single block of stone (at least, its sides were), with each wall forty cubits long and forty cubits high. Its roof was made out of another block of stone, with cornices measuring four cubits.

[156] So the temple was the most amazing thing I saw in this shrine, but the second most interesting thing was an island called Chemmis. The sanctuary in Buto is by a deep, wide lake, and the island is in this lake; it is said by the Egyptians to be a floating island. I myself never saw it floating or moving, and I wondered,

when I was told that it was a floating island, whether it really was. Anyway, on this island is a huge temple of Apollo, and three altars have been set up there as well. There are also a large number of palm-trees growing there, and plenty of other kinds of trees too, both fruit-trees and other sorts. The Egyptians have a story to explain why it is a floating island. The story goes that once upon a time the island was not floating. Leto was one of the Eight Primal Gods and lived in Buto on the site of her oracle. Isis entrusted Apollo to her and when Typhon came, searching everywhere for the son of Osiris, she kept him safe by hiding him on this island, the one that is now supposed to float. They say that Dionysus and Isis are the parents of Apollo and Artemis, and that Leto became their nurse and protector. In Egyptian, Apollo is Horus, Demeter is Isis, and Artemis is Bubastis. It is from this Egyptian version of events—where else?—that Aeschylus the son of Euphorion stole an idea of his which is unique to him (none of the poets who preceded him came up with it): he made Artemis the daughter of Demeter. Anyway, this, according to the Egyptians, is how the island came to float.

[157] Psammetichus' reign lasted fifty-four years. For twenty-nine of these years he maintained a siege of the great Syrian city of Azotus, until the city fell. Of all the cities we know of, none has ever held out against a siege for as long as Azotus did.

[158] Psammetichus' son Necho was the next king of Egypt. It was Necho who made the original attempt to dig a canal through to the Red Sea; Darius of Persia, in a second attempt, completed it. The length of the canal is such that it takes four days to sail it, and it has been dug wide enough for two triremes to be rowed abreast along it. Its water is drawn from the Nile, and it runs from just upriver of Bubastis, past the Arabian town of Patumus, and issues into the Red Sea. The first stage of the excavations took place in the Arabian side of the Egyptian plain, just north of the mountain range by Memphis, where the quarries are. In other words, the canal runs at length from west to east past the foothills of this mountain range; it then passes through gorges until, once past the mountains, it heads south and into the Arabian Gulf. Now, the shortest and most direct route from the northern sea to the southern sea (or the Red Sea, as it is known) is from Mount Casius which is on the border between Egypt and Syria; from there it is exactly one thousand stades to the Arabian Gulf. Although this is the most

direct route, the canal is considerably longer, because its course is quite crooked. During the excavation of the canal that was dug in King Necho's time, 120,000 Egyptians died. Necho's digging of the canal was halted by an adverse oracle to the effect that he was doing the barbarian's work ahead of time. The Egyptians refer to anyone who does not speak the same language as them as a barbarian.

[159] After the halting of his work on the canal, Necho turned to military ventures. He had triremes constructed on the northern sea, and others in the Arabian Gulf by the Red Sea; the slipways are still visible. He used these ships as occasion demanded, and he also engaged the Syrians on land, won a battle at Magdolus, and then took the important Syrian city of Cadytis. He sent to Branchidae in Miletus the clothes which he happened to be wearing during this successful campaign against the Syrians, and dedicated them to Apollo. He died after a reign of sixteen years in all, and was succeeded by his son Psammis.

[160] During King Psammis' reign, a delegation of Eleans came to Egypt to boast that the fairest and finest institution in the world was their own Olympic Games, and to claim that not even the Egyptians, for all their superlative wisdom, could come up with anything comparable. When they arrived in Egypt and stated the purpose of their visit, Psammis convened a meeting of all the Egyptians with the greatest reputation for wisdom, who then put questions to the Eleans on everything that pertained to their management of the games. After their thorough account, they said that they had come to Egypt to find out whether the Egyptians could come up with a fairer system than the current one. The Egyptians thought about the matter for a while and then asked the Eleans whether their own fellow citizens took part in the games. They replied that anyone who wanted to could take part in the games, whether he was from their city or anywhere else in Greece. The Egyptians pointed out that the system was therefore not entirely fair, since there was no provision to avoid bias in favour of one of their own citizens, which was unfair to competitors from elsewhere. They added that if the Eleans wanted to have a fair system and if that was really why they had come to Egypt, they should make the games open to competitors from elsewhere, but ban Eleans altogether. That was the Egyptians' advice to the Eleans.

[161] Psammis' reign lasted only six years; he died shortly after invading Ethiopia and was succeeded by his son Apries. Apart from his forebear Psammetichus, there was no earlier king who was more fortunate than Apries. He ruled for twenty-five years, and in the course of his reign he attacked Sidon and fought a sea-battle against the king of Tyre. However, he was destined to come to a bad end; I will describe the circumstances of this more fully when I come to my account of Libya, but for the moment here is the gist of it. Apries launched a major strike against Cyrene which was a disastrous failure. The Egyptians held him responsible for the disaster and rebelled against him; they believed that Apries had deliberately sent them to certain death, so that after their destruction, with fewer subjects left to rule over, his reign would be more secure. The survivors who returned home from Cyrene took this hard: they combined with the friends of those who had met their deaths and rose up in open rebellion.

[162] When news of the insurrection reached Apries, he sent Amasis to calm the rebels down by negotiating with them. Amasis went to the rebels and set about restraining them from their actions, but his speech was interrupted by one of the men standing behind him putting a helmet on to his head. The man said that he had put it on him as a sign of kingship. Amasis showed that this was not altogether displeasing to him by beginning to prepare a campaign against Apries, once the rebels had set him up as king of Egypt. When Apries found out what was going on, he sent as a herald to Amasis an eminent Egyptian who was loyal to him, whose name was Patarbemis, with instructions to escort Amasis back to him alive. Patarbemis approached Amasis and issued the king's command, but Amasis, who happened to be on horseback at the time, lifted himself up in the saddle, farted, and told him to take that back to Apries. The story goes that Patarbemis persevered and insisted that he should obey the king's summons and go to him; Amasis replied that he would not disappoint Apries—he had been getting ready to pay him a visit for a long time, and he would bring others with him when he came. Patarbemis had listened to Amasis' words and seen the measures he was taking; he was left in little doubt as to his intentions, so he left in a hurry, since he was anxious to let the king know as soon as possible what was happening. When he returned without Amasis, however, Apries did not give him a chance to speak, but flew into a rage and ordered his men to cut

off Patarbemis' ears and nose. But when the rest of the Egyptians, who had so far remained loyal to Apries, saw the shocking brutality with which one of their number—and a particularly eminent person too—was being treated, they wasted no time in defecting to the other side and putting themselves at Amasis' disposal.

[163] When Apries heard about this latest turn of events, he mobilized his mercenary troops and marched against the Egyptians. (He had a personal guard of thirty thousand Carian and Ionian mercenary forces, and a large and remarkable palace in Saïs.) So Apries' troops were fighting Egyptians and Amasis' troops were fighting foreigners. The two sides drew up at the town of Momemphis and prepared for combat.

[164] There are seven classes of people in Egyptian society; they are called priests, warriors, cowherds, swineherds, retailers, translators, and pilots. So each of the seven classes is named after a profession. The warrior class consists of subdivisions called the Calasiries and the Hermotybies, and each of these two subdivisions comes from different provinces (the whole of Egypt being divided into provinces).

[165] The Hermotybies come from the provinces of Busiris, Saïs, Chemmis, Papremis, Prosopitis Island, and half of Natho. When their numbers were greatest, there were 160,000 Hermotybies, all from these provinces. None of them has to learn any manual trade, so that they can dedicate themselves to warfare.

[166] The Calasiries come from the provinces of Thebes, Bubastis, Aphthis, Tanis, Mendes, Sebennys, Athribis, Pharbaethus, Thmouis, Onouphis, Anytis, and Myecphoris (which is situated on an island opposite Bubastis). When their numbers were greatest, there were 250,000 Calasiries, all from these provinces. They are not allowed to practise any trade either and are trained solely in military activities, with son succeeding father.

[167] I cannot say for certain whether or not this is another thing the Greeks learnt from Egypt, because I see that the Thracians, Scythians, Persians, Lydians, and almost every non-Greek people also regard those who learn a trade and their descendants as the lowest stratum of society, as opposed to those who have nothing to do with artisanship and especially those who concentrate on warfare. However that may be, all the Greeks have adopted this attitude, with artisans coming in for the most contempt in Lacedaemon, and the least in Corinth.

[168] The warrior class had certain special privileges, in common only with the priestly caste. Each of them was awarded twelve arouras of land, free of tax. An aroura is a measure of one hundred square Egyptian cubits (an Egyptian cubit being the same length as a Samian cubit). They all received this amount of land as a perquisite, but they farmed it in rotation: the same person never farmed the same piece of land year after year. A thousand Calasiries and another thousand Hermotybies made up the king's personal guard each year. In addition to their plots of land, these guards were also given a daily ration of five minas in weight of cooked grain, two minas of beef, and four arysteres of wine. Every member of the king's guard received this ration.

[169] So the two sides—Apries with his mercenaries and Amasis with all the Egyptians—met and fought at Momemphis. The mercenaries fought well, but the vastly superior numbers they were up against ensured their defeat. Apries is said to have believed that his reign was so securely established that not even a god could depose him. And so when he came to fight this battle, he was defeated, captured, and taken to Saïs, to what had formerly been his own house, but was now the palace of Amasis. For a while Amasis let him stay in the palace and treated him well, but eventually the Egyptians complained that it was wrong of Amasis to look after someone who had been such a bitter enemy of theirs and of his. So Amasis handed Apries over to the Egyptians, who strangled him and buried him in his family tomb. This tomb can be found right next to the temple in the sanctuary of Athena, on the left-hand side as you enter. The people of Saïs buried all the kings who came from this province in this sanctuary. In fact, although Amasis' tomb is further from the temple than the tombs of Apries and his ancestors, it too is still within the courtyard of the sanctuary; his tomb is a huge stone colonnade, lavishly decorated with, for instance, columns made to look like palm-trees. There are two doorways set into this colonnade, and behind these doors is the actual tomb.

[170] Saïs also holds the tomb of the god whose name it would be sacrilegious of me to mention in this context; it is in the sanctuary of Athena, behind the temple, along the entire length of one of the walls of the sanctuary. The precinct contains some tall stone obelisks as well, near which is a pond which has been embellished with a stone border and is well shaped into a circle; the size of the

pond, I should say, is the same as the so-called Round Pond on Delos.

[171] It is on this pond that the Egyptians put on, by night, a performance of the god's sufferings, which the Egyptians call the mystery-rites. Although I am familiar with the details of this performance and how each part of it goes, I will keep silence. And as for the rites sacred to Demeter, which the Greeks call the Thesmophoria, I will again keep silence, except for what it is acceptable to say. It was the daughters of Danaus who brought this rite from Egypt and taught it to the Pelasgian women. Then the rite was lost in the aftermath of the general exodus from the Peloponnese as a result of the Dorian invasion, and its preservation is due entirely to the Arcadians, who were the only Peloponnesians to remain where they were without being driven from their homes.

[172] Following the downfall of Apries, Amasis became king. He came from the province of Saïs, from a town called Siouph. At first the Egyptians despised Amasis and did not rate him very highly, because he had previously been a commoner and from an undistinguished house. But this did not make Amasis vengeful, and eventually he found a clever way to earn their esteem. He had countless possessions, and among them was a golden foot-bath, in which Amasis himself and all his dinner guests used on occasion to wash their feet. He scrapped this foot-bath and had a statue of a god made from it, which he erected in an ideal location, where the Egyptians used to come up and treat it with great reverence. When Amasis found out about their behaviour, he summoned the Egyptians to a meeting. He let them know that the statue had been made out of a foot-bath, in which they had previously vomited and urinated and washed their feet as well, but which they now greatly venerated. He went on to say that he and this foot-bath had had very similar experiences, in the sense that even if he had previously been a commoner, yet now he was their king, and so they should treat him with respect and honour. That was how he convinced the Egyptians that it was reasonable to accept him as their master.

[173] He used to order his affairs as follows. From early until mid-morning he devoted himself to the business matters which were brought to his attention, and then after that he used to drink and joke with his drinking-companions, loaf around, and play games. Some of his friends did not approve of this behaviour and told him off. 'My lord,' they said, 'this frittering away of your time

is not the way to order your life. You should spend your days seated in majesty on your high throne, attending to business. Then the Egyptians would know what a great man they had for a ruler, and your reputation would improve as well. But at the moment you're not behaving like a king at all.'

His response was as follows: 'People with bows string them when they need to use them and unstring them when they've finished with them. If they kept them strung all the time, the bows would break, and then they wouldn't be able to use them when they needed them. It is no different with people's temperaments. Anyone who is serious all the time and never allows himself a fair measure of relaxation will imperceptibly slide into madness or at least have a stroke. I am well aware of this, and that's why I divide my time between the two.' That was his reply to his friends' criticism.

[174] It is said that even when Amasis was an ordinary citizen he was fond of a drink and a joke, and not at all serious, to the point that he would even go around stealing if he ran out of supplies of drink and whatever else he needed to have a good time. The people who claimed he had their property would take him, protesting his innocence, to an oracle, wherever there happened to be one; often the oracles convicted him and often he got off. Now, when he became king, he ignored the sanctuaries of the deities who had acquitted him of theft; he refused to give them anything for their upkeep or to go there to perform the sacrificial rites, on the grounds that these deities were worthless and had deceitful oracles. However, he lavished attention on the gods who had convicted him of theft, on the grounds that they were authentic gods and vouchsafed men true oracles.

[175] He built, in the first place, such a wonderful gateway to the sanctuary of Athena in Saïs that he outdid everyone else by far, considering its height and dimensions, and the quantity and quality of its stone. Then he also erected some huge statues and massive man-headed sphinx figures, and contributed to the repair of the sanctuary by having further blocks of stone taken there, some from the quarries in Memphis, but others, extraordinarily huge in size, from Elephantine, which is as much as twenty days' sailing from Saïs. But by far the most remarkable of his building works, to my mind, is a chamber hewn from a single block of stone that he brought from Elephantine. Transporting it took three years, and two thousand men (all from the pilot class) were assigned to the

task. The external dimensions of this chamber are twenty-one cubits in length, fourteen cubits in width, and eight cubits in height; inside the single block of stone (as opposed to its external measurements) it is eighteen cubits and one pygon long, twelve cubits wide, and five cubits high. This chamber is situated outside the sanctuary, next to the entrance. They say that they did not drag it inside the sanctuary because during the process of hauling it inside the foreman let out a groan at how much time had gone into the project and how weary he was, and Amasis took it to heart† and would not allow the stone to be dragged further. However, there is also an alternative version of the story, according to which one of the workmen was crushed to death under the chapel as he was operating one of the levers, and that is why it was not hauled inside.

[176] Amasis erected remarkably large pieces at all the other notable sanctuaries in Egypt as well. They include the 75-foot figure which is lying on its back in front of the sanctuary of Hephaestus in Memphis. On the same base stand two figures made out of the same stone,† each of which is twenty feet in height and which stand one to either side of the huge figure. There is also another stone figure the same size in Saïs, which is lying just like the one in Memphis. Amasis built the enormous and remarkable sanctuary of Isis in Memphis as well.

[177] Amasis' reign is said to have marked a high point in Egypt's fortunes in terms of what the river gave to the land and what the land gave to the people; there are also said to have been, in all, twenty thousand inhabited cities in Egypt in his time. Moreover, it was Amasis who ordained that every year every Egyptian should divulge how he made a living to the governor of his province, and decreed the death penalty for anyone who failed to do this or who could not show that he made a living in an honest fashion. Solon of Athens took this law over from Egypt and made it part of the legal system in Athens, where they should let it remain in force for ever, because it is an excellent law.

[178] Amasis became a philhellene and one of the ways he showed this, among the various favours he did Greeks, was to give them the city of Naucratis as a place where any Greeks who came to stay in Egypt could live. Moreover, any Greeks who made voyages to the country without wishing to settle were given plots of land where they could set up altars and precincts to their gods. The largest of these precincts, as well as being the most famous and

popular, is called the Hellenium, whose foundation was a joint venture undertaken by a number of Greek communities. The Ionian places involved were Chios, Teos, Phocaea, and Clazomenae; the Dorian communities involved were Rhodes, Cnidos, Halicarnassus, and Phaselis; and the only Aeolian town involved was Mytilene. These are the cities to which the precinct belongs (they also supply the officers who are in charge of the trading-centre), and any other communities which lay claim to it are making a claim to something they have no share in. However, precincts sacred to Zeus, Hera, and Apollo were built separately by Aegina, Samos, and Miletus respectively.

[179] Originally, there was no other trading-centre in Egypt apart from Naucratis. If someone fetched up at any of the other mouths of the Nile, he had to swear that he had not done so deliberately, and then after making this statement under oath bring his ship round to the Canobic mouth. Alternatively, if contrary winds made it impossible for him to take his ship round, he had to transport his goods around the Delta by *baris* and get to Naucratis that way. That is how important Naucratis was.

[180] When the Amphictyons contracted to build the present temple at Delphi, after the earlier one had accidentally burnt down, the Delphians undertook to provide a quarter of the funds. Delphian delegations travelled from place to place on a fund-raising tour, and the most generous response to this appeal of theirs came from Egypt. Amasis gave them a thousand talents of alum, and the Greek community in Egypt gave them twenty minas of alum.

[181] Amasis also entered into a treaty of friendship and alliance with the Cyreneans. He decided to marry someone from there as well, either because he wanted a Greek wife or generally to confirm his good relations with the people of Cyrene. Anyway, the woman he married was called Ladice, and she was the daughter (depending on which account one follows) either of Battus the son of Arcesilaus or of an eminent Cyrenean called Critobulus. Now, whenever Amasis came to her bed, he found himself incapable of having intercourse, although he could do it with his other wives. After this had been going on for a while, Amasis said to Ladice, 'Woman, you have bewitched me. There is no way now for you not to die the most horrible death a woman has ever suffered.'

Ladice denied the charge, but she could not calm Amasis down, so she mentally prayed to Aphrodite and vowed that if Amasis had sex with her then and there, that very night, which would solve the problem, she would send a statue of the goddess to Cyrene. No sooner had she finished her prayer than Amasis had sex with her, and from then on, whenever he came to her, he had sex with her; in fact, he was particularly fond of her after this. Meanwhile, Ladice kept her promise to the goddess. She had a statue made and sent it to Cyrene, and it was still intact in my day at its location outside the town. Another thing that happened to Ladice was that when Cambyses conquered Egypt and found out from her who she was, he sent her back to Cyrene without doing her any harm.

[182] Amasis also dedicated votive offerings in Greece—first, in Cyrene, a statue of Athena overlaid with gold and a painted portrait of himself; second, for Athena in Lindos, two stone statues and a remarkable linen breastplate; third, for Hera in Samos, two wooden statues of himself, which could still be found in my day behind the doors in the great temple. It was because of his guest-friendship with Polycrates the son of Aeaces that he presented these items to Samos, but the gifts to Lindos were not due to any such relationship, but because the sanctuary of Athena in Lindos is supposed to have been founded by the daughters of Danaus when they landed there during their flight from the sons of Aegyptus. These were Amasis' votive offerings. He was also the first person to conquer Cyprus and to make it a tribute-paying subject state.

BOOK THREE

[1] This man Amasis, then, was the one against whom Cambyses the son of Cyrus led an army consisting of contingents from all over his empire, including some Ionian and Aeolian Greeks. The reason for the attack arose out of the fact that Cambyses had sent a message to Egypt to ask Amasis for his daughter. It was an Egyptian man who suggested that he make this request; he was motivated by a grudge against Amasis, because Amasis had chosen him out of all the doctors in Egypt, forced him to leave his wife and children, and dispatched him to Persia, when Cyrus had sent a messenger to Amasis requesting the best eye doctor in Egypt. Because he resented this treatment, then, the Egyptian persuaded Cambyses to ask Amasis for his daughter, so that Amasis would either grant the request and suffer or refuse and make an enemy of Cambyses.

Now, Amasis was troubled and anxious about the might of Persia, and was incapable either of handing his daughter over or withholding her. He knew full well that Cambyses was not about to make her his wife, but his concubine. He weighed the matter up and this is what he did. The previous king, Apries, had a daughter called Nitetis, who was very tall and beautiful, and was the only member of Apries' house left alive. Amasis dressed this girl up in fine clothes and gold jewellery and sent her to Persia as if she were his own daughter. After some time, however, when Cambyses used the girl's patronymic in addressing her, she said to him, 'My lord, you don't realize how Amasis has deceived you. He has dressed me up and sent me to you, as if it were his own daughter he was giving, when in fact I am the daughter of Apries, who was Amasis' master when Amasis and the Egyptians rebelled against him and murdered him.' This news made Cambyses the son of Cyrus furious and gave him his reason for attacking Egypt. At any rate, that is what the Persians say.

[2] The Egyptians, however, claim that Cambyses is one of them.

In their version, he was the son of this daughter of Apries, and it was Cyrus, not Cambyses, who sent the messenger to Amasis to fetch his daughter. But this account of theirs is wrong. They are in fact perfectly well aware—for no one understands Persian customs better than the Egyptians—first that it is not legal for the Persians to let an illegitimate son become king while a legitimate heir is alive, and second that Cambyses' mother was Cassandane the daughter of the Achaemenid Pharnaspes, and not an Egyptian woman. Nevertheless, they distort the story because they want to make out that they are related to Cyrus.

[3] So much for that. There is also, however, a story—albeit one which I find unbelievable—that a Persian woman once came to visit Cyrus' wives, saw Cassandane standing there with her beautiful, tall children, and was so impressed that she paid her lavish compliments. In response, the story goes, Cassandane, who was one of Cyrus' wives, was moved by her resentment of Nitetis to remark, 'Although I have borne him children like these, Cyrus treats me with no respect and prefers the new arrival from Egypt.' The story continues that her eldest son, Cambyses, then said: 'And that, mother, is exactly why, when I grow up, I'm going to turn Egypt upside down.' He was about 10 years old when he said this, and the women were astonished. He remembered, however, and so, when he reached adulthood and became king, he attacked Egypt.

[4] This campaign of his was also helped by something else that happened. One of Amasis' mercenaries was a man called Phanes, from Halicarnassus, who was a resourceful person and a brave fighter. Phanes was disgruntled for some reason with Amasis, so he deserted and escaped from Egypt by sea, with the intention of talking with Cambyses. Now, since Phanes had been a person of some standing among Amasis' mercenary troops, and since he had very reliable information about Egyptian affairs, Amasis made his capture a priority and set about hunting him down. He sent the most trustworthy of his eunuchs after Phanes in a trireme, and the man did actually capture Phanes in Lycia, but failed to bring him back to Egypt, because Phanes outwitted him. He got his guards drunk and escaped to Persia, where he found Cambyses intending to make war on Egypt, but uncertain about the route he should take across the desert. So on arriving Phanes not only gave him general information about how matters stood with Amasis, but also

described the route to him and advised him to send someone to the Arabian king to ask for safe passage across the desert.

[5] The desert affords the only clear way into Egypt. The land from Phoenicia to the borders of the territory of the city of Cadytis belongs to the 'Palestinian' Syrians, as they are called; the trading-centres along the coast from Cadytis (which is not much smaller, I should say, than Sardis) to the town of Ienysus are subject to the king of Arabia; the land from Ienysus to Lake Serbonis, which is flanked by the spur of Mount Casius which goes down to the sea, belongs to the Syrians again; and then the land onwards from Lake Serbonis (where the story goes that Typhon was buried) is Egyptian. The tract of land from Ienysus to Mount Casius and Lake Serbonis, which is large enough to take three days to cross, is utterly without water.

[6] I am now going to explain something which few travellers to Egypt have noticed. Every year Egypt imports from all over Greece, and from Phoenicia as well, clay jars full of wine, and yet it is hardly an exaggeration to say that there is not a single empty wine-jar to be seen there. One might well ask: where do they all disappear to? This is yet another issue I can clarify. Every headman has to collect all the jars from his community and take them to Memphis, and then the people of Memphis fill them with water and take them out into the waterless regions of Syria we have been talking about. That is how every jar that is imported into Egypt is taken, once empty, into Syria to join all the earlier jars.

[7] Anyway, it was the Persians who opened up the journey into Egypt in this way, by supplying the route with water as I have described, immediately following their conquest of Egypt. But at the time in question there was no water to be had. So, when Cambyses had found this out from his Halicarnassian visitor, he sent messengers to the king of Arabia, asked for safe passage, and received it. Pledges were given and received between them.

[8] As much as any race in the world, the Arabians regard such pledges as sacred. The way they make such pledges is that a third person stands between the two parties who want to make a pledge and makes a cut on the palms of their hands, near their thumbs, with a sharp piece of stone. Then he takes a tuft of material from each of their cloaks and smears seven stones, which have been placed between the two parties, with their blood, while calling on Dionysus and Urania. Once this ritual is over, the one who is giving

the pledge recommends the foreigner (or fellow countryman, as the case may be) to his friends, who consider it their duty to regard the pledge as sacred themselves too. The only gods whose existence they acknowledge are Dionysus and Urania, and they copy Dionysus, they say, in the way they cut their hair—that is, they cut it round in a circle, with their temples shaved. Their names for Dionysus and Urania are, respectively, Orotalt and Alilat.

[9] So since the Arabian king had given his pledge to Cambyses' agents, he came up with the following plan. He filled camel-skins with water, loaded them on to all his live camels, drove the camels into the desert, and waited there for Cambyses' army. At any rate, this is the more plausible version; there is also a less plausible version, which I had better recount as well, since it exists. There is a large river in Arabia called the Corys, which issues into the Red Sea. The alternative version of events claims that the Arabian king had the hides of cows and other animals sewn together into a pipe, which was long enough to reach the desert from the river. Then he drew the water from the river through the pipe into big storage-tanks, which had been excavated in the desert to receive and hold the water. It is twelve days' journey from the river to this desert, and he is supposed to have brought the water to three separate parts of the desert, through three pipes.

[10] Psammenitus the son of Amasis stationed his army at the Pelusian mouth of the Nile and waited for Cambyses. Cambyses invaded Egypt to find Amasis no longer alive; he had died after a reign of forty-four years, during which he had avoided any terrible disasters. After his death and mummification he was buried in the sanctuary, in the burial-vault which he himself had built. During the reign of Psammenitus the son of Amasis something quite astounding occurred: it rained in Egyptian Thebes. As the Thebans themselves point out, this had never happened before and has never happened since, up until my own time. It simply does not rain at all in southern Egypt—but there was a light sprinkling of rain on Thebes then.

[11] When the Persians had marched across the desert, they took up a position close to the Egyptian army, in order to join battle. But then the Egyptian king's mercenaries, who were Greeks and Carians, found a way to vent their anger at Phanes for bringing a foreign army into Egypt. Phanes' sons had been left behind in Egypt, so the mercenaries brought them to the Egyptian camp.

They set up a bowl between the two armies, in full view of the boys' father, and then they fetched the children one by one and cut their throats so that the blood spilled into the bowl. When they had finished with all the children, the mercenaries poured wine and water into the bowl, and when they had all drunk some of the blood they joined battle. The fighting was fierce and losses on both sides were very heavy, but in the end the Egyptians were routed.

[12] I saw there something astonishing, which I had heard about from the local inhabitants. The bones of the men from both armies who fell in this battle are strewn over the battlefield, with the bones of the Persians lying on one side and those of the Egyptians on the other, in distinct parts of the battlefield, just as they were originally. Now, the skulls of the Persians are so brittle that if you just hit one with a pebble you would make a hole in it; however, the Egyptians' skulls are so strong that you would find it hard to break one by striking it with a rock. The reason they gave me for this—and I found it very plausible—is that from childhood onwards the Egyptians shave their heads and the bone thickens up in the sun. (This also explains why they do not go bald; I mean, there are fewer bald men to be seen in Egypt than anywhere else in the world.) So this is why they have thick skulls, and it also explains why the Persians have thin skulls, because they wear felt *tiaras* from birth and so shelter their heads from the sun. So much for these matters; I also saw something similar in the case of those who fell along with Achaemenes the son of Darius at the battle of Papremis, killed by Inaros the Libyan.

[13] The Egyptians fled from the battlefield in disarray and shut themselves up in Memphis. Cambyses sent a herald, a Persian, up river to Memphis on a Mytilenean ship, to suggest a truce, but as soon as the Egyptians saw the ship approaching Memphis, they streamed out of the city walls *en masse*, smashed up the ship, tore the crew apart limb from limb, and carried the remains back inside the walls. This led to their being besieged and eventually they surrendered. Meanwhile their neighbours, the Libyans, were so terrified by what had happened in Egypt that they surrendered without a fight, accepted tributary status, and sent gifts to Cambyses. The people of Cyrene and Barca shared the Libyans' fear and followed their example. Cambyses received the gifts the Libyans sent with benevolence, but he was displeased with the Cyreneans' offering—because it was so slight, I suppose; they sent five hundred minas of

silver, and Cambyses picked up the coins with his own hand and
tossed them to his troops.

[14] Psammenitus' reign had lasted six months. Nine days after
he had taken the walls of Memphis, Cambyses had a group of
Egyptians, including Psammenitus, sit at the outskirts of the city,
and he deliberately tormented the Egyptian king, because he
wanted to test his courage. He had the king's daughter dressed as
a slave, and sent her out of the city with a pitcher to fetch water,
along with other young women, also dressed as slaves, whom Cambyses had selected as being the daughters of the leading men of
Egypt. As the young women passed their fathers, they cried out and
burst into tears, and all the men who were there responded with
cries and tears of their own at the sight of their daughters' hu-
miliation. However, when Psammenitus saw the girls coming and
understood what was happening, he bowed his head down to
the ground. Next, once the pitcher-carriers had passed them by,
Cambyses sent out the king's son, along with two thousand other
Egyptians of the same age group, all of whom had ropes tied
around their necks and bits in their mouths. They were being taken
to pay for the murder of the Mytilineans who had been killed along
with their ship at Memphis, because the royal judges had decreed
that for every death ten leading Egyptians were to die. When
Psammenitus saw the young men passing by and realized that his
son was being taken to his death, he did not weep and wail like
the rest of the Egyptians who were sitting there with him, but he
did the same as he had done in the case of his daughter. However,
it so happened that once this procession too had passed by, an
elderly man, who had been a frequent guest of the king's, walked
past Psammenitus the son of Amasis and the other Egyptians who
were sitting there at the edge of the city; this man had lost all his
property and been reduced to the status of a beggar, and was
begging from the army. When Psammenitus saw him, he let out a
loud groan, called out his friend's name, and struck his head in distress. Now, the guards who were there brought back to Cambyses
a report of Psammenitus' reaction to each procession out of the
city, and Cambyses was so surprised at Psammenitus' behaviour
that he sent a messenger to him with the following query: 'Your
master Cambyses wants to know, Psammenitus, why the sight of
your daughter being humiliated and your son being taken to his
death did not move you to protests and tears, whereas a beggar

who, he has been informed, is not related to you at all did receive this mark of respect from you.'

To this question, Psammenitus replied: 'Son of Cyrus, my personal troubles are too immense to cry over, but when a friend on the threshold of old age has lost a fortune and happiness, and been reduced to beggary, his sorrow calls for tears.'

The Egyptians say that this reply of Psammenitus' was well received by Cambyses, who thought he had spoken well, and brought tears to the eyes of Croesus (who had come to Egypt with Cambyses) and to the eyes of the Persians who were there at the time. Cambyses himself felt a certain amount of pity for Psammenitus, so he quickly gave the order that the Egyptian's son was to be rescued from the band of condemned men and that Psammenitus was to be fetched from where he was sitting in the outskirts and brought to his presence.

[15] The people who had gone to fetch Psammenitus' son were too late to save him, because he had been the first to be killed, but they fetched Psammenitus and brought him to Cambyses. From then on Psammenitus lived an easy life; in fact, if he had been able to steer clear of political involvement, he would have regained Egypt and been able to reign as Cambyses' regent, since the Persians tend to honour the sons of kings; they even give the sons of kings who have rebelled against them their kingdom back. One can deduce that this is what they usually do from a number of events, including the cases of Thannyras the son of Inaros, who actually regained his father's kingdom, and Pausiris the son of Amyrtaeus as well, despite the fact that no one ever did the Persians more harm than Inaros and Amyrtaeus. As things turned out, though, Psammenitus conspired against the Persians and reaped the reward: he was caught inciting the Egyptians to rebellion, and when this was made known to Cambyses, he drank bull's blood and died on the spot. And that was the end of him.

[16] There was something Cambyses wanted to do in Saïs, so he next left Memphis and went there. As soon as he got to Amasis' residence, he gave orders that Amasis' corpse was to be taken from its coffin and brought outside. Once these orders had been carried out, he told his men to heap every kind of indignity on the corpse, such as flogging it with their whips, pulling out its hair, and prodding it with their goads. Now, the corpse had been mummified and therefore resisted their efforts and refused to disintegrate at all, so

when they reached the point of exhaustion Cambyses gave them a
sacrilegious order: he told them to burn the corpse, when fire is
considered by the Persians to be a god. In fact cremation of corpses
is not allowed in either Persia or Egypt. The Persians forbid it for
the reason I have given—they declare it wrong to present a human
corpse to a god—and the Egyptians regard fire as a living creature
(one which consumes everything it takes hold of until at last, when
it is sated, it dies along with the object it has been devouring), and
it is absolutely forbidden for them to give a corpse to any kind of
creature. (This also explains why they embalm corpses: it is to stop
them being eaten in their coffins by worms.) So Cambyses' command contravened both Egyptian and Persian beliefs.

According to the Egyptians, the Persians were mistaken in thinking that they were heaping these indignities upon Amasis: it was
in fact not Amasis, but some other Egyptian, similar in build to
Amasis, who was at the receiving end of this treatment. They say
that Amasis found out from an oracle what was going to happen
to him after his death, and so in order to ward off what was coming
he had this other man—the one whose corpse was flogged—buried
inside his tomb, just by the entrance, while he told his son to put
his own body in a recess of the tomb, as far out of the way as possible. In my opinion, Amasis never gave these instructions about
how he was to be buried and about the other man, and it is all just
a story told by the Egyptians to make an impression.

[17] Cambyses next began to contemplate three military expeditions, one against the Carthaginians, one against the Ammonians, and one against the long-lived Ethiopians, who live in
Libya, on the coast of the southern sea. The conclusion he reached
was that he should attack the Carthaginians by sea and the
Ammonians by land with a portion of his land forces, and that his
first move against the Ethiopians should be to send spies there,
ostensibly to take gifts to their king, but in fact to reconnoitre the
general state of affairs, and in particular to see whether or not there
really was such a thing as the Table of the Sun there.

[18] This Table of the Sun is supposed to be a field on the edge
of the town which is covered with the cooked flesh of every kind
of four-footed animal. At night the leading citizens, whoever they
may be, prepare the meat and put it in the field, and during the
daytime anyone who wants to can come and eat. Some of the local
inhabitants, however, claim that the earth spontaneously produces

the meat every time. Anyway, that is what the so-called Table of
the Sun is said to be.

[19] As soon as Cambyses had decided to send spies to Ethiopia,
he summoned from the city of Elephantine some members of the
tribe of Fish-eaters who knew the Ethiopian language. While they
were being fetched, he ordered his navy to set out against Carthage.
The Phoenicians, however, refused to obey; they were bound by
solemn oaths, they said, and it would be wrong for them to attack
their own sons. And without the Phoenicians, the remainder of the
navy was not fit for battle. So that is how the Carthaginians escaped
being enslaved by the Persians. Cambyses decided not to try to
force the Phoenicians to go, because they had joined the Persian
forces of their own accord and the whole navy depended on them.
(The Cyprians also voluntarily supplied men to serve in the Persian
army in the campaign against Egypt.)

[20] When the Fish-eaters arrived from Elephantine, Cambyses
told them what they had to say and sent them off to Ethiopia. He
gave them gifts to take, including a purple cloak, a gold torque,
arm-bands, an alabaster pot of perfume, and a jar of palm wine.
The Ethiopians in question, the ones to whom Cambyses sent the
delegation, are said to be the tallest and most attractive people in
the world. It is said that their customs are quite different from those
of any other people, and this applies particularly to the kingship:
they think that whichever of their countrymen they judge to be
the tallest and to have strength in keeping with his size should be
king.

[21] So when the Fish-eaters reached these Ethiopians, they
offered the gifts to the king and said, 'It is because Cambyses, king
of Persia, wants to be your guest-friend and your ally that he
has sent us with instructions to hold talks with you, and that is
also why he is giving you these gifts, which he particularly enjoys
using.'

The Ethiopian king, however, realized that they had come as
spies, so he said to them: 'The Persian king has not sent you with
gifts because he really wants my friendship. You're lying: the real
reason you are here is to spy on my kingdom. Your master's behaviour is reprehensible too. If he were a good man, he would not have
wanted to possess any land other than his own, and he wouldn't
have enslaved people who have done him no wrong. That is how
things are, so I want you to give him this bow and say to him:

"Here is a word of advice from the king of the Ethiopians. When the Persians can draw bows of this size as easily as I do now, then he can march against the long-lived Ethiopians—with an army that considerably outnumbers ours. In the mean time, he should be grateful to the gods for not making the sons of Ethiopia think of acquiring additional lands besides their own." '

[22] With these words he unstrung the bow and handed it over to the visitors. Then he took hold of the purple cloak and asked what it was and how it was made. The Fish-eaters explained about the murex and the process of dyeing, but he called them liars and said that their clothing was not what it appeared to be either. Next he asked about the gold—the torque and the arm-bands. When the Fish-eaters described how gold was used for decoration, the king laughed and, imagining that the objects were shackles, said that they had stronger shackles than these in his country. Then he asked about the perfume, and when they explained how it was made and applied to the body, the king's response was the same as it had been with the cloak. When he came to the wine, however, and asked how it was made, he was delighted with it. He went on to ask what the king of Persia ate and what was the maximum age a man lived to in Persia. They replied that the king ate bread and described how wheat was grown, and said that eighty years was the maximum extent of a man's life. To this the Ethiopian replied that he was not surprised that their lives were so short if they ate manure; in fact, he said, they would not live even that long if they did not revive themselves with their drink—and he indicated the wine—which was the one thing the Persians did better than them, he said.

[23] Next it was the Fish-eaters' turn to ask the king how long people lived there and what they ate. He replied that it was common for people to live to be 120 years old, although some lived even longer, and that they ate cooked meat and drank milk. When the spies expressed surprise at the length of their lives, the king took them to a spring whose water made anyone washing in it more sleek, as if it had been olive oil, and which gave off a scent like violets. In their report, the spies said that the water of this spring was so soft that nothing could float on it, not wood or even anything lighter than wood; everything sank to the bottom. Assuming the truth of the reports of this water, it would explain why these Ethiopians are long-lived, if they use it for everything. Then they left the spring and were taken to a prison, where all the prisoners

were shackled with golden chains; among these Ethiopians the rarest and most valuable substance of all is bronze. After they had seen the prison, they also saw the so-called Table of the Sun.

[24] Finally, after the Table of the Sun, they saw their coffins, which are said to be made out of transparent stone. What the Ethiopians do is dry the corpse (perhaps in the same way that the Egyptians do, or perhaps by some other method), and then smear the corpse all over with chalk and paint it, making it as lifelike as possible; then they enclose the body in a hollow pillar of transparent stone, which is plentiful there and easily dug out of the ground. The corpse can be seen inside the pillar—in fact, it is as completely visible as if there were nothing but the corpse there— but it does not have any disagreeable odours or anything else unpleasant about it. The dead person's closest relatives keep the pillar in their home for a year, during which time they bring the corpse all their first-fruits and offer it sacrifices; then they remove the pillar from the house and set it up near the town.

[25] Once they had reconnoitred everything, the spies left Ethiopia and returned to Egypt. Their report made Cambyses so angry that he immediately set out to attack the Ethiopians, without having requisitioned supplies or considered the fact that he was intending to make an expedition to the ends of the earth. Instead, the Fish-eaters' report made him so enraged and insane that he just set off with all his land forces, but without the Greek troops who were based in Egypt, who were ordered to stay behind.

When the expeditionary force reached Thebes, he detached about fifty thousand of his men and gave them the job of reducing the Ammonians to slavery and burning down the oracle of Zeus, while he himself marched against the Ethiopians with the rest of the army. However, they completely ran out of food before they had got a fifth of the way there, and then they ran out of yoke-animals as well, because they were all eaten up. Had Cambyses changed his mind when he saw what was happening, and turned back, he would have redeemed his original mistake by acting wisely; in fact, however, he paid no attention to the situation and continued to press on. As long as there were plants to scavenge, his men could stay alive by eating grass, but then they reached the sandy desert. At that point some of them did something dreadful: they cast lots to choose one in every ten men among them—and ate him. When Cambyses heard about this, fear of cannibalism made him abandon his expedition to Ethiopia and turn his men back. He arrived back in Thebes with a severely depleted army, and from there went downriver to Memphis, where he released his Greek troops so that they could sail back home.

[26] That was what happened to Cambyses' expedition to Ethiopia. As for the detachment he had sent to attack the Ammonians, they set out from Thebes with guides, and they clearly arrived at the town of Oäsis. This is a town which is inhabited by Samians who are said to belong to the Aeschrionian tribe, and which is seven days' journey from Thebes across the desert; the name of the place, translated into Greek, is the Isles of the Blessed. So by all accounts the army reached this place, but after that the only information available comes directly or indirectly from the Ammonians themselves; no one else can say what happened to them, because they did not reach the Ammonians and they did not come back either. The Ammonians, however, add an explanation for their disappearance. They say that after the army had left Oäsis and was making its way across the desert towards them—in other words, somewhere between Oäsis and their lands—an extraordinarily strong south wind, carrying along with it heaps of sand, fell on them while they were taking their midday meal and buried them. Anyway, that is what the Ammonians say about this army.

[27] Now, Cambyses' return to Memphis coincided with an appearance of Apis, whom the Greeks call Epaphus. As soon as this happened, the Egyptians put on their best clothes and started their celebrations. Cambyses interpreted these thanksgiving celebrations as being held because of the failure of his expedition, and he summoned the governors of Memphis to his presence. When they came before him he asked them why the Egyptians were behaving in this way now that he was in Memphis after the loss of most of his army, when they had never done anything like it when he had been in Memphis before. They explained that the god had appeared, that there was usually a long interval between one appearance and the next, and that the whole Egyptian population celebrated with a holiday whenever he appeared. But Cambyses accused them of lying and condemned them to death on those grounds.

[28] After he had executed the governors, he next summoned the priests of Apis to his presence. When they gave the same explanation as the governors, Cambyses said that he would see if some

tame god had arrived in Egypt, and then he told the priests to bring
Apis to him, and they went off to comply. Now, this Apis, or
Epaphus, is a calf born from a cow which cannot conceive offspring
from then on. According to the Egyptians, a beam of light descends
from the sky to the cow and from it she gives birth to Apis. This
calf, which is known as Apis, has certain features: it is black, except
for a white diamond on its forehead and the image of an eagle on
its back, its tail hairs are double, and it has a beetle-shaped mark
under its tongue.

[29] When the priests brought Apis to him, Cambyses, who was
more or less insane, drew his dagger, aimed for Apis' stomach, but
missed and hit his thigh. Then he said to the priests with a laugh:
'You poor fools! Is this what gods are like? Are they creatures of
flesh and blood, capable of being wounded by weapons? Well, this
is the god you Egyptians deserve. But you won't get away with
making me a laughing-stock.' He then ordered those of his men
who were in charge of discipline to flog the priests, and to kill any
other Egyptians who were caught celebrating the festival. But in
addition to the dissolution of the Egyptians' festival and the punishment of the priests, Apis lay in the sanctuary wasting away from
his thigh wound. After his death, the priests secretly buried him,
without Cambyses knowing about it.

[30] Because of this crime, Cambyses very soon went completely
mad, according to the Egyptians. He had not been entirely sane
previously, and now his first atrocity was to do away with his
brother Smerdis, born from the same father and mother as himself.
He had already sent him back from Egypt to Persia, because he was
jealous of the fact that he was the only Persian who could draw
the bow which the Fish-eaters had brought back from the Ethiopian
king; Smerdis could draw it only to the breadth of two fingers, but
none of the other Persians could do even that much. While Smerdis
was on his way back to Persia, Cambyses dreamt that a messenger
came to him from Persia to tell him that Smerdis was sitting on
the royal throne with his head touching the sky. The dream made
Cambyses fear for his life; he thought his brother would kill him
and gain power. So he sent Prexaspes, the Persian he trusted most,
to Persia to kill Smerdis, and Prexaspes went to Susa and did so.
The story goes that he took Smerdis out hunting and killed him
there, although there is also an alternative account, that he led him
down to the Red Sea and drowned him.

[31] So this is the first atrocity they say Cambyses committed, and the second was to do away with his sister, who had come with him to Egypt. She was also his wife, as well as being his full sister, despite the fact that previously it was not at all customary for Persians to marry their sisters. Cambyses had been in love with another of his sisters, and had wanted to marry her. Because there was no precedent for this plan of his, he summoned all the royal judges, as they are called, and asked them if there was a law inviting anyone who wanted to marry his own sister to do so. These royal judges are a select band of Persians, who hold office until they die or until they are found to have committed a crime; their job is to adjudicate lawsuits for the Persians and to interpret ancestral laws and customs, and all such matters are referred to them. Anyway, their response to Cambyses' question was safe, as well as being within the letter of the law: they said that they could find no law inviting a man to marry his own sister, but that they found another law that the ruler of the Persians could do whatever he wanted. So by finding a regulation which could support Cambyses' desire to marry his sisters, they did not let fear of Cambyses make them break the law, but they also did not destroy themselves while maintaining the law. So Cambyses married the sister he was in love with then, but a short while later he also took another one of his sisters to be his wife. It was the younger of these two sisters who had gone with him to Egypt and whom he killed.

[32] There are two alternative accounts of her death, just as there are about Smerdis. The Greek version is that Cambyses pitted a lion cub against a young dog, and that this wife of his was one of the spectators at the fight. The puppy was losing, but its brother broke its leash and came to its defence, and then the two of them defeated the lion cub. Cambyses thought it had been a good show, but his wife sat there and cried. When Cambyses noticed, he asked her why she was crying, and she replied that the sight of the puppy helping its brother had moved her to tears because it reminded her of Smerdis and she realized that there was now no one to come to Cambyses' defence. It was because of this reply of hers, according to the Greeks, that she was killed by Cambyses. The Egyptian version is that Cambyses and his wife were sitting at their table for a meal, when she picked up a lettuce, pulled off its leaves, and then asked her husband whether the lettuce was better stripped bare or with its leaves on. When he replied that it was better with its leaves

on, she said, 'But you have stripped the house of Cyrus as bare as this lettuce.' He jumped on her in anger, and this caused her to miscarry the baby she was carrying in her womb and to die.

[33] These were the mad acts Cambyses committed against his closest relatives. It might have been the Apis affair that drove him mad, or it might have been something else, because men's lives are generally beset by many misfortunes. And Cambyses is said to have had a terrible sickness—the sacred disease, as it is sometimes called—ever since he was born. So it is hardly surprising that lack of mental health should accompany such a terrible physical ailment.

[34] He committed mad acts against the rest of the Persians as well. The case of Prexaspes, for instance, is mentioned. Cambyses gave Prexaspes the outstanding honour of bringing messages to him, and Prexaspes' son was Cambyses' wine-server, which was also a distinguished position to hold. It is said that Cambyses once asked him, 'Prexaspes, what sort of man do the Persians think I am? What do they say about me?'

'Master,' Prexaspes replied, 'they have nothing but good to say about you, except in one respect: they say that you are rather too fond of wine.'

Prexaspes' news about what the Persians were saying made Cambyses angry, and he retorted, 'In fact the Persians are saying that my fondness for wine is driving me mad and making me lose my mind. It follows, then, that their earlier statements were false.'

The point is that once before, at a meeting between Cambyses, his Persian advisers, and Croesus, Cambyses asked what sort of man they thought him to be, compared to his father Cyrus. The Persians replied that he was a better man than his father, because he had control over the whole of his father's possessions, while also adding dominion over Egypt and the sea. Croesus was there, however, and the Persians' reply did not satisfy him, so he said to Cambyses, 'In my opinion, my lord, you do not bear comparison with your father, because you do not yet have a son of the calibre of the one he left behind.' Cambyses was delighted with this reply of Croesus' and used to mention it with approval.

[35] This is what he was remembering when he spoke angrily to Prexaspes. 'You'll see whether the Persians are speaking the truth,' he said, 'or whether in saying this they are out of their minds. There's your son, standing on the porch. I'll shoot at him, and if I

hit him right in the heart, that will be proof that the Persians are talking nonsense, whereas if I miss, you can say that the Persians are right and that I am out of my mind.'

With these words, he drew his bow and shot the boy with an arrow. The boy fell to the ground and Cambyses ordered his men to slit him open and examine the wound. When it was found that the arrow had pierced his heart, he turned to the boy's father with a laugh and said delightedly, 'So there you have it, Prexaspes! This proves that I am quite sane, and the Persians are out of their minds. Now, tell me: do you know anyone else in the world who can shoot an arrow with such accuracy?'

Prex   es saw that he was quite mad and was afraid for himself. 'Master,' he said, 'I don't think that even the god could have made such a good shot.'

That is what Cambyses did then, and on another occasion he found twelve of the highest-ranking Persians guilty of a paltry misdemeanour and buried them alive up to their necks in the ground.

[36] Croesus of Lydia considered it his duty to rebuke Cambyses for this behaviour. 'My lord,' he said, 'you shouldn't just give way to your youth and passion; use some self-restraint and control. It is good to exercise forethought, and intelligent to look ahead. You are killing men who are your own countrymen, after convicting them of trivial misdemeanours; you are killing children. If you go on behaving like this, you had better watch out or the Persians will rise up against you. This is me, Croesus, speaking; your father Cyrus often told me to rebuke you and to suggest a good course of action to you, if I saw one.'

Despite the fact that this advice was obviously given with goodwill, Cambyses replied, 'How can *you* have the audacity to give *me* advice? Look how well you ruled over your own country! Look how well you advised my father, when you told him to cross the River Araxes and attack the Massagetae, when they were prepared to cross over into our own territory! You brought about your downfall through your incompetence as a leader of your country, and you brought about Cyrus' death through his trust in you. But you won't get away with it: I've been wanting to find an excuse to have a go at you for a long time.'

With these words, he grabbed his bow and arrows with the intention of using them against Croesus, but Croesus leapt to his feet and ra   of the room. Foiled in his attempt to shoot him,

Cambyses ordered his attendants to find him and kill him. But they knew what Cambyses was like and kept Croesus hidden, so that if he changed his mind and missed Croesus, they could produce him and win a reward for keeping him alive, while if he did not change his mind and never felt in need of him, then they could do him in. In fact, a short while later Cambyses did miss Croesus, and when the attendants realized this they told him that Croesus was still alive. Cambyses replied that he shared their happiness that Croesus was alive, but added that those who had kept him alive would not go unpunished, because he would put them to death—which he did.

[37] These are a few examples of the insanity of his behaviour towards the Persians and his allies. During his time in Memphis he even opened some ancient tombs and examined the corpses. Likewise, he even went into the sanctuary of Hephaestus and made a great deal of fun of the cult statue. Now, the statue of Hephaestus there very closely resembles the Pataïci, which the Phoenicians carry around on the prows of their ships. In case anyone is not familiar with what these Pataïci look like, it will help if I say that they resemble dwarfs. Cambyses also went into the sanctuary of the Cabiri, which no one is allowed to enter except the priest, and went so far as to burn the statues there, after subjecting them to a great deal of ridicule. The statues of the Cabiri also look like those of Hephaestus; in fact, the Cabiri are supposed to be his children.

[38] Everything goes to make me certain that Cambyses was completely mad; otherwise he would not have gone in for mocking religion and tradition. If one were to order all mankind to choose the best set of rules in the world, each group would, after due consideration, choose its own customs; each group regards its own as being by far the best. So it is unlikely that anyone except a madman would laugh at such things.

There is plenty of other evidence to support the idea that this opinion of one's own customs is universal, but here is one instance. During Darius' reign, he invited some Greeks who were present to a conference, and asked them how much money it would take for them to be prepared to eat the corpses of their fathers; they replied that they would not do that for any amount of money. Next, Darius summoned some members of the Indian tribe known as Callatiae, who eat their parents, and asked them in the presence of the

Greeks, with an interpreter present so that they could understand what was being said, how much money it would take for them to be willing to cremate their fathers' corpses; they cried out in horror and told him not to say such appalling things. So these practices have become enshrined as customs just as they are, and I think Pindar was right to have said in his poem that custom is king of all.

[39] At the same time as Cambyses' campaign against Egypt, the Lacedaemonians attacked Samos, where Polycrates the son of Aeaces had overthrown the government and taken power. At first he had divided the town into three parts and shared it with his brothers Pantagnotus and Syloson, but later he had put Pantagnotus to death and banished his youngest brother Syloson, so that he was in complete control of Samos. Then he formed ties of guest-friendship with King Amasis of Egypt, and the relationship was sealed with an exchange of gifts. Before long Polycrates' affairs were prospering and became the subject of conversation throughout the whole of Greece, not just Ionia, because every military campaign he directed was completely successful. He acquired a fleet of a hundred pentecounters and an army of a thousand archers, and raided everyone indiscriminately—even friends, because he claimed that he would be doing a friend more of a favour if he returned what he had taken than if he had not taken it in the first place. He conquered a great many of the Aegean islands, and a number of communities on the mainland too. Among his conquests were the Lesbians, who had sent their whole fighting force to help Miletus, but Polycrates defeated them in a sea battle. The prisoners he took dug the whole trench around the town wall on Samos, even though they were in shackles.

[40] Now, as it happened, Polycrates' remarkable good fortune did not go unnoticed by Amasis. He was concerned about it, and as Polycrates' successes continued to mount he wrote the following letter to him at Samos: 'Amasis to Polycrates: Although I am glad to hear that a man who is a guest-friend and ally is prospering, I worry about your remarkable good fortune, because I know that the gods are jealous of success. In fact, my wish for myself and for those I care about is a mixture of success and failure, and so to spend one's life with varied fortune rather than doing well in everything. Why? Because I have never heard tell of a single case of someone doing well in everything who did not end up utterly

and horribly destroyed. So please do as I suggest. In the face of your success I think you should decide what your most valuable possession is—that is, the one whose loss would upset you most—and throw it away, making sure that it will never reappear among mortal men. If from then on your good luck does not meet with varied disasters, continue to try to cure it in the way I have suggested.'

[41] When Polycrates read this letter and realized the extent of Amasis' goodwill towards him, he thought long and hard about which of his precious possessions it would upset him most to lose, and he came to the conclusion that it was the signet-ring he wore, which was made from an emerald set in gold, and was the work of Theodorus the son of Telecles of Samos. Once he had decided that this was what he would throw away, he manned a penteconter, went on board, and then told them to sail out into the open sea. When they were a long way from the island, he took off his ring and, in plain view of the whole crew, threw it into the sea. Then he sailed back to the island, went home, and mourned his loss.

[42] Four or five days later, it so happened that a fisherman caught a huge, beautiful fish, and decided to present it to Polycrates. He brought it to the entrance of his residence and asked permission to appear before Polycrates. Permission was granted, and he offered Polycrates the fish with the following words: 'My lord, I decided not to take this fish I caught to the town square, even though I make my living as a fisherman, because it seemed to me to be good enough for you and your rule. So I've brought it here as a gift for you.'

Polycrates was delighted with the man's speech and replied, 'That's very good of you. I thank you twice—once for your words and once for the gift. I'd like to invite you to dine with me.'

The fisherman felt very proud and went back home. Meanwhile, Polycrates' attendants cut open the fish and there, inside its stomach, they found his ring! They grabbed hold of it as soon as they saw it, carried it in triumph to Polycrates, and gave it to him, along with the story of its discovery. It occurred to Polycrates that this might be a religious portent, so he wrote in a letter a thorough account of what he had done and what had happened and sent it to Egypt.

[43] When Amasis read the letter from Polycrates, he realized that it was impossible for one person to rescue another from what was going to happen and that, because he was so completely lucky that he even found things he had thrown away, Polycrates was fated to die miserably. He therefore sent a herald to Samos to dissolve their guest-friendship, so that he would not be as upset as he would be at the loss of a friend, when great and dreadful disaster overwhelmed Polycrates.

[44] Polycrates, then, met with success in everything he did. This was the man against whom the Lacedaemonians launched a campaign. They had been asked to help by those Samians who subsequently founded Cydonia in Crete. Polycrates had surreptitiously sent a message to Cambyses the son of Cyrus, who was mustering an army to attack Egypt, asking him to send to him in Samos a request for troops. When Cambyses received Polycrates' message, he was happy to comply, and he sent a message to Samos asking Polycrates to send a naval force to help him against Egypt. So Polycrates selected those citizens who he suspected were most likely to revolt and sent them off in forty triremes, and he told Cambyses not to send them back to Samos again.

[45] There are those who say that the Samians Polycrates sent never reached Egypt, but only sailed as far as Carpathos, where on reflection they decided not to continue with their voyage. In another version, they did reach Egypt, where they were held in custody, but escaped. When they sailed back to Samos, this version continues, Polycrates came out against them with his fleet and engaged them in battle; the returning voyagers won and landed on the island, but they were beaten in a land battle there and so sailed to Lacedaemon. Yet another version claims that these Samians from Egypt overthrew Polycrates, but I do not think this can be right, since they would not have had to send for the Lacedaemonians, if they were capable of bringing Polycrates down on their own. Besides, it also does not make sense to think that someone with vast numbers of mercenaries and native archers at his disposal would have been beaten by the few returning Samians. As a safeguard against his subjects' treacherously helping the homecomers, Polycrates shut their wives and children in the shipyards, which he had prepared for this purpose, so that he could burn them up, sheds and all, if he had to.

[46] When the Samians Polycrates had expelled reached Sparta, they gained an audience with the authorities and spoke at a length commensurate with their need. The Lacedaemonian response to this first audience, however, was to say that they had forgotten the earlier parts of the Samians' speech, and could not follow the later parts. The Samians gained a second audience, however, at which they said nothing at all, except that they brought a bag with them and said, 'This bag needs grain.' The Lacedaemonians replied that the word 'bag' was redundant, but they still decided to help them.

[47] So the Lacedaemonians made their preparations and set out to attack Samos. According to the Samians, the Lacedaemonians undertook this campaign to repay the Samians for the favour they had done them some time before, when they had sent ships to reinforce the Lacedaemonian expedition against Messenia. According to the Lacedaemonians, however, the campaign was undertaken not so much in response to the Samians' request for help as because they wanted to avenge the theft of the bowl which they stole while it was being transported to Croesus, and for the theft of the breastplate which King Amasis of Egypt had been sending as a gift to Sparta. The Samians had stolen this breastplate the year before they had stolen the bowl; it was made out of linen, had a large number of creatures woven into it, and was embellished with gold and cotton thread. What is incredible is that every single thread of the breastplate, for all its fineness, consisted of 360 separate threads, all of which were visible. Amasis dedicated another one like it to Athena in Lindos.

[48] The Corinthians were also happy to contribute towards the realization of the expedition against Samos, because a generation previously (at about the same time as the theft of the bowl) they too had met with offensive treatment at the hands of the Samians. Periander the son of Cypselus had sent to Alyattes at Sardis three hundred male children, the sons of the leading families of Corcyra, for castration. The Corinthians who were taking the boys there put in at Samos, and when the Samians found out the reason why the boys were being taken to Sardis, the first thing they did was teach the boys about making contact with the sacred ground of the sanctuary of Artemis, and then they made sure that no one dragged the boys out of the sanctuary once they had taken refuge there. When

the Corinthians cut off the boys' provisions, the Samians instituted a festival (which is in fact still celebrated in the same way nowadays), which involved unmarried girls and boys dancing every night, for the duration of the Corcyran boys' asylum in the sanctuary, and then they made it a rule of the festival that the dancers had to carry snacks of sesame and honey, so that the Corcyran boys could snatch them out of their hands and get food. This went on until the Corinthians who were guarding the boys gave up and went away; then the Samians took the boys back to Corcyra.

[49] If, after Periander's death, the Corinthians and the Corcyrans had been on good terms with one another, the Corinthians would not have had this pretext for assisting the expedition against Samos. But in fact, despite their kinship,† they have been hostile towards one another ever since Corinth colonized the island, and so the Corinthians retained their grudge against the Samians.

It was revenge that motivated Periander to select and send the sons of the leading families of Corcyra to Sardis for castration; for the Corcyrans had earlier begun by committing, without provocation, an atrocity against him.

[50] What happened was this. Periander killed his own wife Melissa and, as if that was not enough, another disaster befell him, as follows. Melissa had borne him two sons, who were 17 and 18 years old. Procles, the tyrant of Epidaurus, who was the boys' grandfather on their mother's side, invited them to stay and made them as welcome as one would expect, given that they were his daughter's sons. But when he was seeing them off, his parting words were: 'Boys, do you know who killed your mother?'

Now, the elder of the two brothers did not pay any attention to what Procles said, but the younger brother, whose name was Lycophron, was so upset by Procles' words that when he got back to Corinth he refused to speak to his father, on the grounds that he was his mother's killer, and would not join in any conversation Periander started or answer any question he put to him. Eventually, Periander got so angry with him that he threw him out of the house.

[51] Once Periander had banished Lycophron from his home, he asked his older son what their grandfather had said to them. The boy told Periander that Procles had made them welcome, but he could not recall his parting words to them, because he had not taken them in. Periander insisted that he must have made some kind of suggestion to them, and he kept on and on asking his son what

it was. At last the boy remembered and told him about that too. Now Periander understood what was going on. He did not want to show any signs of weakness, so he sent a message to the people in whose house the son he had banished was staying and ordered them not to let him stay there. And so it went on: whenever Lycophron was driven out of one house and found another one to live in, he would be driven out of that one too, with Periander issuing threats to anyone who took him in and ordering them to shut their doors against him. Each time he was driven out of one house, Lycophron would go to another one of his friends' homes, and although they were afraid of the consequences, they would take him in, because he was Periander's son.

[52] Eventually, Periander published an edict that anyone who took his son into his house or even spoke to him was to pay a specified amount of money as a sacred fine to Apollo. So, faced with this edict, no one was prepared to speak to Lycophron or to take him into their homes. Besides, he himself did not think it right to defy the prohibition, but he kept himself going by roaming the porticoes. Three days after the edict, Periander saw him in his unwashed, starving state and felt sorry for him. Letting his anger go, he went over to his son and said, 'Son, what would you rather do? You can either carry on with what you're doing now or become reconciled with me, your father, and inherit my kingdom and all the advantages of my position. You are my son and a member of the royal family of the prosperous city of Corinth, but you have chosen to live like a tramp, because you are feeling hostility and anger towards me, when I am the last person in the world you ought to treat this way. If something terrible has happened to make you suspicious of me, remember that it is me it happened to; it affects me above all, because I was the one who did it. You now know how much better it is to be envied than pitied, and also what it is like for people to be angry with their parents and their betters. So come home now.'

Lycophron, however, made no reply to this attempt by his father to persuade him, except to say that he owed a sacred fine to Apollo for talking to him. When Periander realized how terrible, hopeless, and incurable his son's state was, he had him shipped off to Corcyra (which was part of his empire), so that he would not have to keep seeing him. Then he sent his army against his father-in-law Procles, on the grounds that he more than anyone else was responsible for his present troubles; he took Epidaurus and made Procles his prisoner.

[53] Time passed. When Periander was getting on and began to realize that administering and managing his affairs was starting to be beyond him, he sent a message to Corcyra inviting Lycophron to come back and take over as tyrant; he regarded his older son as rather stupid and did not think that he would be up to the job. Lycophron, however, did not even bother to give Periander's messenger a reply. Periander was reluctant to give up on the young man, so he tried again. This time he sent his daughter, Lycophron's sister, since he thought that he would listen to her, if anyone. Once she arrived on Corcyra, she said, 'Do you want the tyranny to fall into others' hands, child? Do you want your father's house to be torn apart? Wouldn't you rather come home and have it yourself? Come home; stop punishing yourself. Stubborn pride warps a person, and two wrongs don't make a right. There are plenty of precedents for doing what is reasonable rather than what is strictly right—and also plenty of cases where siding with the mother has meant losing a paternal inheritance. Absolute power is difficult and dangerous; there are always lots of people who lust after it, and he is an old man now, past his prime. Don't give others the good things in life which are rightfully yours.'

Her father had taught her what to say to try to win him over, but Lycophron replied that he would never come to Corinth as long as he heard that his father was still alive, and this was the message she brought back to Periander. He tried a third time, however. He sent a message expressing his own willingness to come and live on Corcyra and suggesting that Lycophron come to Corinth to take his place as tyrant. Lycophron agreed to these terms, and the two of them were all set to move, Periander to Corcyra and Lycophron to Corinth. When the Corcyrans heard the details of their plan, however, they killed the young man to stop Periander coming to their island. This was why Periander was taking revenge on the Corcyrans.

[54] A strong force of Lacedaemonians came and blockaded Samos. They attacked the town wall and scaled the tower which stands on the edge of the seaward side of the town, but then Polycrates came in person with a sizeable band of reinforcements and drove them out. At the inland tower, which stands on the ridge of the hill, the Samians and their mercenaries sallied out in large numbers, but after withstanding the Lacedaemonian advance for a

short while, they retreated to the town walls, with the Lacedaemonians harrying them and killing them.

[55] Now, if all the Lacedaemonians there that day had been the
equals of Archias and Lycopes, Samos would have fallen. Archias
and Lycopes were the only ones who followed the retreating
Samians all the way back inside the town walls, where they were
cut off from retreat, and so they died there inside the town of
Samos. Once, in Pitana (which was his native village), I personally
met another Archias, who was the grandson of the Archias I have
just been talking about, since he was the son of Samius the son of
Archias. This Archias honoured the Samians more than any other
foreigners, and he told me that his father had been given the name
Samius because of the heroic death *his* father Archias had died on
Samos. He explained that the reason he thought well of the Samians
was because they had given his grandfather a public funeral.

[56] After forty days, the Lacedaemonian blockade of Samos
was still getting nowhere, so they returned to the Peloponnese. As
a rather silly story has it, Polycrates struck a large quantity of local
coinage in lead, which he then covered in gold and used to bribe
them, and they took it and left Samos. This was the first time
Dorians from Lacedaemon had launched a military strike against
anywhere in Asia.

[57] The Lacedaemonian decision to leave prompted the
Samians who had taken up arms against Polycrates to sail away as
well. They went to Siphnos, because they were short of money, and
Siphnos was at that time at the height of its prosperity; its gold-
and silver-mines had made it the richest of the Aegean islands. The
mines were so productive that from a mere tenth of the wealth
generated by them a treasury at Delphi was established, which was
one of the richest there, and every year they used to distribute the
revenue from the mines among the citizen body. When they were
building the treasury at Delphi, they asked the oracle if their current
good fortune was likely to last for a considerable length of time.
The Pythia replied as follows:

> When on Siphnos the town hall turns white
> And so do the brows of the square, then the wise man must
>   beware
> The ambush of wood and the red messenger.

And at this time the Siphnian town square and town hall were fitted
out with Parian marble.

[58] The Siphnians were unable to interpret this oracle either right at the time or when the Samians arrived. For the first thing the Samians did when they reached Siphnos was send ambassadors to the town on one of their ships. Now, in the old days all ships were painted scarlet; that was what the Pythia was referring to when she warned the Siphnians to beware of 'the ambush of wood and the red messenger'. Anyway, when the messengers arrived in the town, they asked the Siphnians to lend them ten talents. The Siphnians refused, so the Samians set about plundering their land. As soon as they found out, the Siphnians came to the rescue and gave battle, but were defeated, and a considerable number of their men were pinned inside the town by the Samians, who subsequently made them pay a hundred talents.

[59] From the people of Hermione, the Samians accepted instead of money the island of Hydrea, which is off the Peloponnese and which they entrusted to the people of Troezen for safe keeping. They themselves colonized Cydonia in Crete. The original purpose of their voyage to Crete was to expel the Zacynthians from their island, not to found a colony, but they stayed there for five years and formed a prosperous community—so much so that they are the ones who built the sanctuaries which can still be found in Cydonia.† In the sixth year, however, they were defeated at sea by a combined force of Aeginetans and Cretans and were enslaved; the Aeginetans cut off the boar-shaped prows which the Samians had on their ships and dedicated them in the sanctuary of Athena on Aegina. The reason for all this was that the Aeginetans bore a grudge against the Samians, because earlier, while Amphicrates was the king of Samos, the Samians had made war on Aegina and caused a great deal of suffering to the islanders (although there were losses on the Samian side too). Anyway, that was their pretext.

[60] I have gone on about the Samians at some length because three of their achievements are unsurpassed in the Greek world. The first is a tunnel which was dug right through the bottom of a hill 150 fathoms high, so that there is an opening at either end; the tunnel is seven stades long and eight feet in both height and width. Along the whole of its length another channel has been dug, which is twenty cubits deep and three feet wide, and which carries water from a great spring through pipes to the town. The master builder of this tunnel was a Megarian called Eupalinus the son of

Naustrophus. The second of the three achievements is a mole in the sea, over two stades long, enclosing the harbour in water which is as much as twenty fathoms deep. The third thing they built is the largest temple ever seen; its original design was drawn up by Rhoecus the son of Phileas, who was a native of Samos. These achievements of theirs are my justification for going on about them at some length.

[61] While Cambyses the son of Cyrus was spending his time in Egypt insane, two Magian brothers rebelled against him. One of these two rebels was the man Cambyses had appointed steward of his household in his absence. He realized that Smerdis' death had been kept secret, and that few Persians knew about it, and in fact that the majority were sure Smerdis was still alive. Taking advantage of these circumstances he plotted to usurp the kingdom. What he did was this. His brother—who was, as I have said, his accomplice—was very similar in appearance to Smerdis the son of Cyrus, whom Cambyses had killed, despite the fact that he was his own brother. Not only did this Magus' brother look like Smerdis, but his name was Smerdis as well. The Magus, Patizeithes, convinced this brother of his that he would take care of everything for him, and went and seated him on the throne. Then he sent messengers all over the place, including Egypt, to tell the army that in the future they were to take their orders from Smerdis the son of Cyrus, not Cambyses.

[62] So all the messengers made this proclamation, including the one who had been detailed to go to Egypt, although in fact he found Cambyses and his army at Ecbatana in Syria. He took his stand and made a public announcement of the orders he was carrying from the Magus. When Cambyses heard what the messenger had to say, he believed that he was telling the truth; that is, he believed that Prexaspes (the man he had sent to kill Smerdis) had betrayed him and had not done it. So he looked at Prexaspes and said, 'Is this how you carried out the task I set you, Prexaspes?'

'Master,' Prexaspes replied, 'the man must be lying. Your brother Smerdis has certainly not rebelled against you. He'll never defy you over anything, big or small. I personally carried out the mission you gave me and buried the corpse with my own hands—these hands here. If the dead are rising from their graves, you should expect Astyages the Mede to rise against you as well. But if everything is as usual, you need never expect any trouble from that

quarter. Now, it seems to me that we should track down this messenger and get him to tell us who sent him with this announcement
about taking orders from King Smerdis.'

[63] Cambyses approved of Prexaspes' idea and so the hunt was
on straight away for the messenger. When he had been fetched back
to the camp, Prexaspes interrogated him. 'You there!' he said. 'You
say you came here as a messenger from Smerdis the son of Cyrus.
Tell the truth now, and then you can leave without further ado:
was it Smerdis himself who personally gave you your instructions,
or was it one of his retainers?'

'No,' the man replied, 'I haven't laid eyes on Smerdis the son of
Cyrus since King Cambyses set out for Egypt. It was the Magus
whom Cambyses appointed as steward of his household who gave
me my mission and told me that the order to take this message to
you came from Smerdis the son of Cyrus.'

This was nothing but the truth, of course. 'Prexaspes,' Cambyses said, 'you are perfectly innocent. You acted properly and carried
out your orders. But the question is: which of the Persians can it
be who has usurped Smerdis' name and is rising against me?'

'My lord,' Prexaspes replied, 'I think I know what has happened.
It is the Magi who have rebelled against you—Patizeithes, the one
you left behind as steward of your household, and his brother
Smerdis.'

[64] When Cambyses heard the name 'Smerdis' he was struck
by the truth of what Prexaspes had said and saw the true meaning
of the dream, in which someone had brought him a message that
Smerdis was sitting on the royal throne with his head touching the
sky. When he realized that he had pointlessly killed his brother, he
was overwhelmed with grief for him. He was so miserable and
upset at the whole disaster that he leapt on to his horse, with
the intention of setting out for Susa without delay and attacking
the Magus. As he did so, the tip of his scabbard came off and the
exposed sword struck him on the thigh. He was wounded in exactly
the same spot that he had previously wounded the Egyptian god
Apis. Cambyses felt that the wound was fatal; he asked what was
the name of the place where they were, and they told him it was
Ecbatana. Now, the oracle in Buto had earlier† told him that he
would die in Ecbatana. He had supposed that he would die of old
age in Ecbatana in Media, which was the administrative centre of
his empire, but the oracle, as it turned out, had meant Ecbatana in

Syria. When in answer to his question he heard the name of the place, although the troubles the Magus had caused him and his wound had driven him insane, he now came to his senses, understood the oracle, and said, 'This is the place where Cambyses the son of Cyrus is destined to die.'

[65] That is all he said then, but about twenty days later he sent for the most eminent Persians who were there in Syria with him. 'My friends,' he said, 'I have no choice under the circumstances but to disclose something I have done my best to conceal. You see, while I was in Egypt I had a dream—I wish it had never happened! I dreamt that a messenger came from my palace and told me that Smerdis was sitting on the royal throne with his head touching the sky. I was afraid of losing my reign to my brother, so I acted with more haste than wisdom. I mean, a man does not—as I now see— have the resources to deflect his destiny, but I foolishly sent Prexaspes to Susa to kill Smerdis. Once this terrible deed had been done, I lived without fear, never imagining that anyone else would rise up against me now that Smerdis was out of the way. I completely misunderstood what was going to happen, and I killed my own brother, when I had no need to do so, and I have still lost my kingdom. And it turns out that it was Smerdis the Magus whose rebellion my personal deity was warning me about in my dream.

'So that is what I did, and you have to understand that Smerdis the son of Cyrus is no longer alive to help you; my kingdom is in the hands of the Magus I left in charge of my palace and his brother Smerdis; and the person who, if anyone, should punish the Magi for the disgrace I have suffered has died an abominable death at the hands of his closest relative. Since he is no longer alive, I must do the next best thing: it has become imperative that I get *you*, men of Persia, to carry out my dying wishes. And so I call on the gods who oversee kingship as I enjoin you—all of you, but especially those of you here who are Achaemenidae—not to let power fall once more into Median hands. No, whatever part treachery played in their acquisition of power must be matched by treachery on your side in depriving them of it again; whatever part force played in bringing them success must be matched by sheer force on your side in regaining control. If you do this, you will be and remain for ever free men, and I pray that the earth may be fruitful for you and that your wives and flocks may be prolific. However, if you do not regain power or make some attempt to get it back, I pray that exactly the opposite of this may be your lot, and also that every man in Persia may meet a death like mine.' With these words, Cambyses expressed his grief at what he had done.

[66] All the Persians responded to their king's distress by rending the clothes they were wearing and giving themselves over to unmitigated grief. Later, gangrene of the bone and mortification of the thigh quickly brought about the death of Cambyses the son of Cyrus. His reign had lasted a total of seven years and five months, and he was completely childless, since he left no sons or daughters. However, the Persians who were there refused to believe that the Magi had assumed authority; they were sure that Cambyses had said what he said about Smerdis' death in order to embroil all of Persia in a war against him.

[67] They were sure that it was Smerdis the son of Cyrus who had been made king. Prexaspes too was now vehemently denying that he had killed Smerdis, since with Cambyses dead it was dangerous for him to admit that he had been personally responsible for the death of a son of Cyrus. So after Cambyses' death, the Magus had nothing to fear as he ruled under his assumed name of Smerdis the son of Cyrus. His reign lasted seven months, up to the end of what would have been the eighth year of Cambyses' reign. During his reign he acted very generously towards all his subjects, so that after his death he was greatly missed by all the inhabitants of Asia except the Persians. For he sent couriers to every tribe within the empire and proclaimed that they were to be exempt from military service and taxes for three years.

[68] He proclaimed this edict at the very beginning of his reign, but seven months later his hoax was exposed. This is how it happened. One of the noblest and wealthiest Persians was a man called Otanes, whose father was Pharnaspes. Otanes was the first to suspect that the Magus was not Smerdis the son of Cyrus and to guess his true identity. He came to this conclusion because Smerdis never left the acropolis and never called any Persian of standing into his presence.

Now, Cambyses had married Otanes' daughter, whose name was Phaedymia, and at the time in question she was married to the Magus, who had taken not just her but all Cambyses' other wives as well to be his own wives. Once Otanes had begun to be suspicious of Smerdis, he got a message to his daughter, asking her who it was she was going to bed with—whether it was Smerdis the son of Cyrus or someone else. She sent a message in reply saying that she did not know, because she had never seen Smerdis the son of Cyrus and therefore did not know who her husband was. Otanes sent her a second message, which ran: 'Even if you yourself cannot recognize Smerdis the son of Cyrus, you can still find out from Atossa who it is that both she and you are married to. After all, she's bound to know her own brother.'

The message his daughter sent in reply said: 'I can't talk to Atossa or meet any of her handmaidens, because at the very beginning of his reign this man—whoever he is—separated us by assigning each of us different quarters.'

[69] When Otanes heard this message, things started to become clear. He sent his daughter a third message, saying, 'Daughter, your noble birth means that you have to accept any risk I, your father, tell you to run. If this man is not Smerdis the son of Cyrus, but is who I suspect he is, he can't be allowed to get away with taking you to bed and with ruling Persia. No, he should be punished. What you must do is this. When you're in bed with him, wait until you're sure he's asleep, and then feel for his ears. If it's clear that he has ears, you can assume that your husband is Smerdis the son of Cyrus; but if he doesn't have ears, you should conclude that it is Smerdis the Magus.'

In her message back to him Phaedymia pointed out the considerable risks involved for her in carrying out this plan, because if he did not in fact have ears, and she was caught feeling for them, she was sure he would murder her—but she said that she would do it all the same. So she promised her father that she would do his bidding. (Cyrus the son of Cambyses had in the course of his reign punished this Magus Smerdis for some serious crime or other by cutting off his ears.) So this Phaedymia, the daughter of Otanes, kept her promise to her father in all respects. In Persia, wives sleep with their husbands in rotation, so when it was her turn to go to the Magus, she went and lay with him, and when he was fast asleep, she felt for his ears. It was no difficult task for her to discover that he had no ears, and the next day she immediately sent a message telling her father what had happened.

[70] Otanes found Aspathines and Gobryas—eminent Persians who were close and trustworthy friends—and told them the whole business. They too had in fact had their suspicions that this might be going on, and so they accepted Otanes' account. They decided

that each of them should recruit another Persian—the one he trusted most. So Otanes brought in Intaphrenes, Gobryas brought in Megabyzus,† Aspathines brought in Hydarnes, and now they were six. At this juncture, Darius the son of Hystaspes arrived in Susa from Persia, where his father was governor, and the six Persian conspirators decided to recruit Darius too.

[71] The seven of them met and conferred, and exchanged pledges. When it was Darius' turn to express his opinion, he said, 'I thought I was the only one who knew that it was the Magus who was ruling over us and that Smerdis the son of Cyrus was dead. In fact, that's exactly why I was eager to come here—to bring about the Magus' death. But since, as it turns out, you too know what's going on, and I am not alone, I suggest we act immediately. I don't think there's anything to be gained by delay.'

It was Otanes who replied to him. 'Darius,' he said, 'your father was a good man, and it looks as though you are proving yourself to be at least his equal. But I think it would be unwise of you to push this enterprise along too fast, rather than taking a more cautious approach to it. I mean, we should wait until there are more of us before striking.'

'Gentlemen,' Darius said to the assembled company, 'if you follow Otanes' advice, you will die horribly—you can be sure of it. Motivated by the desire for personal profit, someone will denounce us to the Magus. You really ought to have proceeded with this by making the assault on your own, but since you decided to let more people in on it and you've told me about it, then let's either act today or, I have to tell you, if you let today slip by, no one will be quicker than me in turning informer: I'll tell the Magus all about it.'

[72] When he saw how upset Darius was, Otanes said, 'Since you're forcing us to hurry along and allowing us no delay, you had better tell us how we're to get into the palace and attack them. You must have personally seen or at least heard about all the guards who have been posted throughout the palace. How are we going to get past them?'

'Otanes,' Darius replied, 'many things cannot be clarified by words, but can by action. Then again, some things may be clearly describable but lead to nothing spectacular. You know it isn't hard to get past the guards on duty. In the first place, they're bound to let people like us past, out of either respect or fear. In the second place, I myself can provide us with a very plausible excuse for getting in, since I can claim that I've just come from Persia and want to give a message from my father to the king. Where a lie is necessary, let it be spoken. Our objective is the same whether we use lies or the truth to achieve it. People lie when they expect to profit from others' falling for their lies, and they tell the truth for the same reason—to attract some profit to themselves or to gain more room to manoeuvre in. In other words, the means may differ but we're after the same thing. If there's no profit to be gained, our truth-teller might as well lie and our liar might as well tell the truth. Any guard who willingly lets us past will be better off in the long run, and if any of them tries to block our way, we must immediately mark him as our enemy, then push past him and set to our work.'

[73] Gobryas spoke next. 'My friends,' he said, 'will there ever be a better time for us to regain power, or failing that to die in the attempt, than now when we Persians have a Mede, a Magus, as our king—and one who has lost his ears too? Those of you who were with Cambyses while he was ill will have no trouble remembering how on his death-bed he cursed any Persians who failed to try to regain power. At the time we didn't believe him; we thought he was motivated by malice. As things are, then, I vote that we listen to Darius and not disband this meeting except to go and attack the Magus.' This is what Gobryas said and all the other conspirators approved.

[74] Now, while they were making their plans, the Magi were also coincidentally making plans of their own, to win Prexaspes over to their side. They bore in mind, first, the horrific way he had been treated by Cambyses, when Cambyses had shot and killed his son with an arrow; second, the fact that he was the only one who knew about the death of Smerdis the son of Cyrus, because he had been personally responsible for killing him; and third, the great respect in which the Persians held him. So they invited him to a meeting and won his allegiance by exchanging oaths and pledges, which bound him to keep their secret and not tell anyone how they were deceiving the Persians, and by guaranteeing to make him unbelievably wealthy. Once the Magi had won him over, and Prexaspes had promised to comply with their wishes, they put a second proposal to him. They suggested convening the whole Persian population under the palace wall, and that he should climb

up to the top of a tower and address the crowd, telling them that they were being ruled by Smerdis the son of Cyrus, and nobody else. They pretended that they wanted him to be the one to do this because there was no one who was more likely to be trusted by the Persians than him, and because he had often stated that in his opinion Smerdis the son of Cyrus was alive, and had denied that his murder had ever taken place.

[75] Prexaspes said that he was prepared to do this as well, so the Magi convened the Persians, sent Prexaspes up to the top of the tower, and told him to address the crowd. But he deliberately ignored everything they had asked him to say, and instead went through Cyrus' ancestry, from Achaemenes all the way down to Cyrus himself, at which point he described all the benefits which Cyrus had achieved for the Persians. Then after all this he told the truth and explained that there were events which it would previously have been dangerous for him to reveal and so he had kept them secret, but now, he said, circumstances left him no choice but to bring them to light. And so he told them how he had been forced by Cambyses to kill Smerdis the son of Cyrus and that it was the Magi who were ruling the empire. He laid many curses on the Persians if they failed to regain power and take vengeance on the Magi, and then he threw himself head first down from the tower. And that was the end of Prexaspes, who had been throughout his life a man of distinction.

[76] Now, the seven Persians came to the conclusion that they should attack the Magi straight away, without any delay, so they offered up prayers to the gods and set out. They knew nothing of the business with Prexaspes; in fact, it was not until they were halfway there that they found out what had happened to him. They stood at the side of the road and talked things over between themselves once more. Otanes and his supporters were forcefully presenting the case for waiting and not attacking while matters were unsettled, whereas Darius and his supporters were arguing that they should get a move on and carry out their plans immediately, without waiting. But while they were hurling arguments back and forth seven pairs of hawks appeared, chasing and harrying and clawing two pairs of vultures. The sight of the birds made all seven come round to Darius' point of view, and so they carried on towards the palace, encouraged by the birds.

[77] When they reached the gates, everything happened more or less as Darius had predicted. The guards were very respectful of such eminent Persians and, without suspecting them of anything underhand, sent them on their divinely appointed way; not one of them asked the conspirators any questions. They got as far as the courtyard and there they met the eunuchs whose job it was to take messages in to the king. The eunuchs enquired what business had brought them there, began to threaten the guards with punishment for letting them in, and stopped the seven when they wanted to go further in. At a signal, the seven drew their daggers, attacked the eunuchs who were blocking their way, and cut them down on the spot. Then they ran towards the main hall.

[78] The two Magi happened to be inside at the time, discussing the consequences of Prexaspes' actions. When they saw the eunuchs in uproar and shouting, they both leapt to their feet. As soon as they realized what was happening, they set about defending themselves; one of them first snatched up his bow and arrows, while the other took up his spear. Then the fight was on. The Magus who had grabbed the bow found that it was no use at all, since his opponents were close at hand and were crowding in on him; the other wielded his spear and wounded Aspathines in the thigh and then Intaphrenes in the eye. In fact, Intaphrenes lost his eye as a result of this wound, but it did not prove fatal.

While one of the Magi was inflicting these wounds, the other took refuge in a bedroom that was off the main hall, when his bow and arrows proved useless. He intended to bar the doors, but two of the seven, Darius and Gobryas, were hard on his heels and followed him into the room, where Gobryas started grappling with him. Darius stood there in a quandary, because it was dark and he was worried about hitting Gobryas. Gobryas saw that Darius was standing by ineffectively and asked him why he was not lending a hand. 'I'm worried about hitting you,' Darius said.

'Use your dagger,' Gobryas replied, 'even if you run both of us through.' Darius obeyed Gobryas and thrust with his dagger—and somehow managed to hit only the Magus.

[79] Once they had killed the Magi, the conspirators cut off their heads. They left their wounded comrades where they were, because they were incapacitated and because the acropolis needed guarding. Taking the heads of the Magi with them, they ran out of the

palace. They raised the alarm as they went and shouted out their news to all the rest of the Persians, showing them the heads and calling them to arms. Meanwhile, they killed any Magi they came across. When the Persians learnt of the hoax the Magi had prac-tised and realized what the seven had done, they decided to follow their lead; they drew their daggers and began to kill any Magi they could find, and if night had not intervened they would not have left a single one alive. This is now the most important day of the year in the Persian public calendar, and they spend it celebrating a major festival which they call the Magophonia. During the festi-val, no Magus is allowed to appear outdoors; they have to stay inside their houses all day long.

[80] Five days later, when things had settled down, the conspira-tors against the Magi met to discuss the general state of things. There are those in Greece who are not convinced of the authenti-city of the speeches that were delivered there, but they did take place. Otanes recommended entrusting the management of the country to the Persian people. 'It is my view', he said, 'that we should put an end to the system whereby one of us is the sole ruler. Monarchy is neither an attractive nor a noble institution. You have seen how vicious Cambyses became and you have also experienced similar behaviour from the Magus. How can monarchy be an orderly affair, when a monarch has the licence to do whatever he wants, without being accountable to anyone? Make a man a monarch, and even if he is the most moral person in the world, he will leave his customary ways of thinking. All the advantages of his position breed arrogant abusiveness in him, and envy is ingrained in human nature anyway. With these two qualities he has in himself every evil: all his atrocities can be attributed to an excess of abusive-ness or envy. Now, you might think that an absolute ruler is bound to be free from envy, since there is nothing good that he lacks, but in fact his natural attitude towards his people is the opposite of what you would expect. He resents the existence of the best men, while the worst of them make him happy. There is no one better than him at welcoming slander, and there is no one more erratic in his behaviour. I mean, if your admiration for him is moderate, he is offended at your lack of total subservience, and if you are totally subservient, he is angry at you as a flatterer. And now I come to the most important problems with monarchy. A monarch subverts a country's ancestral customs, takes women against their will, and

kills men without trial. What about majority rule, on the other hand? In the first place, it has the best of all names to describe it—equality before the law. In the second place, it is entirely free of the vices of monarchy. It is government by lot, it is accountable government, and it refers all decisions to the common people. So I propose that we abandon monarchy and increase the power of the people, because everything depends on their numbers.' These were Otanes' thoughts.

[81] Next Megabyzus spoke in favour of oligarchy. 'Otanes' arguments for abolishing monarchy', he said, 'represent my own views too. However, in so far as he was recommending the transference of power to the general populace, his argument is flawed. A mob is ineffective, and there is nothing more stupid or more given to brutality. People are hardly going to tolerate escaping from the brutality of a despot only to fall into the brutal clutches of the unruly masses, when any action taken by a despot is the action of someone who knows what he is doing, but knowledge and the masses are incompatible. How could anyone know what is right without either having been taught it or having innate awareness of it? No, the approach of the general populace is that of a river swollen with winter rain: they rush blindly forward and sweep things before them. Let us leave democracy to Persia's enemies, while we choose a number of the best men and put power in their hands. After all, we will be members of such a company, and it is reasonable to assume that the best men make the best decisions.' This was Megabyzus' proposal.

[82] The third person to express his opinion was Darius, and he said, 'I think Megabyzus was right in what he said about the masses, but wrong about oligarchy. There are three choices before us, and let us suppose that each of them is the best of its kind—the best democracy, the best oligarchy, and the best monarchy. In my opinion, the best monarchy far outstrips the others. I mean, if you have a single person, and he is the best person in the world, how could you hope to improve on that? His views are the best there are, he can govern the people blamelessly, and he is particularly good at keeping to himself his plans against hostile opponents. In an oligarchy, however, a number of people are trying to benefit the community, and in this situation violent personal feuds tend to arise, because every one of them wants to come out on top and have his own views prevail. This leads them to become violently

antagonistic towards one another, so that factions arise, which lead
to bloodshed, which leads ultimately to monarchy—which just goes
to show that it is by far the best system. Then again, corruption is
inevitable in a democracy. So, in the context of corruption in the
political sphere, the corrupt ones become firm friends, rather than
opponents, because corrupt practitioners of politics act by forming
alliances. This kind of thing goes on until someone emerges as a
champion of the people and puts an end to these corrupt politi-
cians. But by doing this he wins the admiration of the people, and
then he turns out to be a monarch. So he again is proof that monarchy is the best system. One point sums the whole thing up—where
did we get our independence from and who gave it to us? Was it
the people or an oligarchy or a monarch? My view, then, is that
since we gained our freedom thanks to a single individual, we
should keep to this way of doing things. And I would add that we
should not abolish our ancestral customs, which serve us well. That
is not the way to improve matters.'

[83] These were the three views that were put forward for consideration. Four out of the seven endorsed Darius' view. Finding
that his proposal recommending for Persia the idea of equality
before the law had been defeated, Otanes spoke openly to all of
them. 'My fellow conspirators,' he said, 'whether we choose by lot,
or give the Persian people the chance to elect their preferred candidate, or use some other method, it will obviously be one of us
who is to become king. Under these circumstances, I am not going
to stand against you as a candidate; I have as little desire to be a
ruler as I have to be ruled. However, I renounce my claim to the
kingdom on one condition—that I and my descendants should
never be ruled by any of you.' The other six agreed to his idea, so
he stood down and did not compete against them for the kingdom.
And to this day the house of Otanes is the only house in Persia
which remains free and, while obeying the laws of the Persians, is
subject to the king only to the extent that it wishes to be.

[84] The remaining six conspirators turned to discussing the
fairest way of installing a king. They decided that in the event of
one of them becoming king, Otanes and his descendants in perpetuity should be awarded certain privileges annually, namely a set
of Median clothing and every gift which the Persians find most precious. They decided to give him these things since he had been the
prime mover of the conspiracy and had brought them all together.

These special privileges were reserved for Otanes, but they also decided on certain prerogatives to be shared by all seven of them, namely that any of them should be allowed to enter the royal palace whenever he wanted to, without being announced, except when the king was sleeping with a woman, and that the king was not to marry outside the families of his fellow revolutionaries. As for choosing a king, they decided that they should all mount their horses at the edge of the city and that the kingdom should be given to the rider of the first horse to neigh after sunrise.

[85] Now, one of Darius' slaves was an astute groom called Oebares. When the conspirators' meeting was over, Darius found Oebares and said, 'What we've decided to do as regards the kingdom, Oebares, is give it to the rider of the first horse to neigh at sunrise after we've mounted. So if you know some technique, fix it so that we can be the ones to win this prize, not any of the others.'

Oebares replied, 'Master, if that's all it takes to make you king, you can be perfectly confident that no one will beat you to the kingdom. I have the perfect solution.'

'If you really do have a clever ruse for this,' Darius said, 'now is the time to set it up. There's no time for delay—the contest will take place tomorrow.'

Now, Darius' horse was partial to one particular mare. So what Oebares did in response to Darius' instructions was wait for nightfall and then take the mare to the edge of the city and tie her up there. Then he brought Darius' horse to the spot. At first he walked him around near the mare, bringing him ever closer to her, but eventually he let the stallion mount her.

[86] At daybreak the six met on horseback as they had agreed, and rode around the outskirts of the city. When they approached the spot where the mare had been tied up the previous night, Darius' horse ran up to it and whinnied. And just as the horse did this, there was a flash of lightning and a clap of thunder, even though the sky was clear. These extra phenomena clinched it for Darius; it was as if there were some prior agreement that they should happen. The others jumped off their horses and knelt before him.

[87] There is an alternative version of Oebares' trick; in fact, the Persians tell the story both ways. This account claims that he rubbed the mare's genitals with his hand and then kept his hand hidden in his trousers. At dawn, just as the riders were about

to move out, Oebares brought his hand out and passed it near Darius' horse's nostrils, and the smell made the stallion snort and whinny.

[88] So Darius the son of Hystaspes was made king. Thanks to Cyrus' and later Cambyses' conquests, all the peoples in Asia were his subjects—except for the Arabians, who were never reduced to slavery by the Persians. In fact, the Arabians had an alliance with Persia, because they had given Cambyses safe passage into Egypt, and the Persian invasion of Egypt would have been impossible without Arabian support.

Darius' first marriages were with Persian women. He married Cyrus' two daughters, Atossa (who had previously been married first to her brother Cambyses and then to the Magus) and Artystone (who had not been married before). Then he also married the daughter of Smerdis the son of Cyrus, whose name was Parmys, and the daughter of Otanes, who had exposed the Magus.

Everything was filled with Darius' power. The first thing he did was erect a statue in stone featuring a man on horseback, with the following inscription carved on it: 'Darius the son of Hystaspes gained the Persian kingdom through the prowess of his horse'—he inserted the horse's name—'and that of his groom Oebares.'

[89] Next he established within the Persian empire twenty provinces, or satrapies, as the Persians call them. Once he had established the provinces and appointed governors, he fixed the tribute which each people was to pay—a 'people' being counted as including not only the neighbouring tribes, but also, past the immediate neighbours, certain more remote tribes, which were variously assigned to the various peoples. The provinces and their annual tribute payments were divided as follows. First, however, those who were paying in silver were told to use the Babylonian talent, while those who were paying in gold were told to use the Euboïc talent; the Babylonian talent is the equivalent of seventy Euboïc minas.† Now, during the reigns of Cyrus and Cambyses there was no such thing as a fixed amount of tribute, but the various peoples brought donations. Because he established the tribute system and other related systems too, the Persians describe Darius as a retailer (since he put a price on everything), Cambyses as a master (since he was cruel and restrictive), and Cyrus as a father (since he was kind and everything he set up was for their good).

[90] For the purposes of the payment of tribute, the Ionians, Asian Magnesians, Aeolians, Carians, Lycians, Milyans, and Pamphylians were assessed as a single unit and contributed a revenue of 400 talents of silver. This was the first tax province, and the second consisted of the Mysians, Lydians, Lasonians, Cabalians, and Hytenneans, who contributed a revenue of 500 talents. The third consisted of the Hellespontines on the right as one sails in, the Phrygians, Asian Thracians, Paphlagonians, Mariandynians, and Syrians, whose combined tribute was 360 talents. The Cilicians, who constituted the fourth province, contributed 360 white horses, one for each day in the year, and 500 talents of silver, 140 talents of which went towards the upkeep of the cavalry garrison in Cilicia, and the other 360 to Darius.

[91] The whole region stretching from the town of Posideium (which was founded by Amphilochus the son of Amphiaraus on the border between Cilicia and Syria) to Egypt, excluding Arabian territory (which was exempt) had to pay a tribute of 350 talents; this region, which constituted the fifth province, encompasses the whole of Phoenicia, Palestinian Syria, and Cyprus. The sixth province consisted mainly of Egypt, but the Libyans adjacent to Egypt, and Cyrene and Barca were also assessed as part of the province of Egypt. This province contributed 700 talents, not counting the revenue of silver from the fish of the lake of Moeris and also a fixed amount of grain—120,000 sacks—which was issued to the Persians and their auxiliaries who were based in White Wall in Memphis. The seventh province consisted of the Sattagydae, Gandarians, Dadicae, and Aparytae, who between them contributed 170 talents. The eighth province, consisting of Susa and the rest of the land of the Cissians, contributed 300 talents.

[92] Babylon and the rest of Assyria—the ninth province—contributed 1,000 talents of silver and 500 child eunuchs. Ecbatana, the rest of Media, and also the Paretacenians† and Orthocorybantians, formed the tenth province and contributed 450 talents. The eleventh province consisted of the Caspians, Pausicae, Pantimathi, and Daritae, who together contributed 200 talents. The twelfth province consisted of Bactria, as far as the Aegli, and their tribute was 360 talents.

[93] The thirteenth province, comprising Pactyican territory, Armenia, and their neighbours as far as the Euxine Sea, contributed

400 talents. The fourteenth province consisted of the Sagartians, Sarangae, Thamanaeans, Utians, Mycians, and the inhabitants of the Red Sea islands (where the Persian king settles the people known as 'the Dispossessed'), who together contributed 600 talents. The fifteenth province consisted of the Sacae and the Caspians, and they paid 250 talents. The sixteenth province, consisting of the Parthians, Chorasmians, Sogdians, and Arians, contributed 300 talents.

[94] The seventeenth province consisted of the Paricanians and Asian Ethiopians, and contributed 400 talents. The Matieneans, Saspeires and Alarodians, who made up the eighteenth province, had an assessed tribute of 200 talents. Three hundred talents were required from the Moschians, Tibarenians, Macrones, Mossynoecians, and Mares, who together made up the nineteenth province. The twentieth province consisted of the Indians, who are by far the most numerous people in the known world, and who contributed more than any other province—namely, 360 talents of gold-dust.

[95] If the Babylonian silver is assessed in terms of the Euboïc talent it comes to 9,880 talents, and if gold is calculated as thirteen times more valuable than silver, the Indian gold-dust will be found to be the equivalent of 4,680 Euboïc talents. So the sum total, in Euboïc talents, of the annual tribute paid to Darius, is 14,560 talents. Here I omit any amount smaller than these round numbers.

[96] This was the tribute Darius levied from Asia and a few places in Libya. Later, further revenue was raised from the Aegean islands and from settlements in Europe as far as Thessaly. The Persian king stores this revenue of his by melting it down and pouring it into clay jars; then, when each jar is full, he removes the surrounding clay. Whenever he wants money, he slices off as much as he needs at the time.

[97] So much for the provinces and the tribute assessment. The only part of the empire that I have not mentioned as taxable is Persia itself, because any land occupied by Persians is exempt. There are also some peoples which were not required to pay any tribute, but tended to bring donations. First, there are the Ethiopians who live on the border with Egypt (whom Cambyses conquered while he was on his way to attack the long-lived Ethiopians) and the Ethiopians who live in the region of the holy mountain Nysa and who celebrate festivals sacred to Dionysus. (The seed

used by these Ethiopians and their neighbours is the same as that of the Indians of the Callantiae tribe; also, they live in underground dwellings.) These two peoples together used to—and still do even today—make a donation every other year of two choenixes of unrefined gold, two hundred logs of ebony wood, five Ethiopian boys, and twenty huge elephant tusks. Then there are the Colchians and the other tribes living between Colchis and the Caucasian mountain range, which forms the limit of Persian influence, since north of the Caucasus no one is the slightest bit concerned about the Persians. They were assigned to make a donation every fourth year, as they still do today, of a hundred boys and a hundred girls. Then there are the Arabians, who contributed a thousand talents of frankincense every year. So in addition to tribute, these peoples used to provide the Persian king with these donations as well.

[98] The gold-dust that the Indians bring the Persian king has already been mentioned; here is how they come by such a huge quantity of gold. The Indians live further east in Asia than anyone else—further east than any other known people about whom there is reliable information—because beyond them the eastern part of India is sandy and therefore uninhabitable. There is a large number of Indian tribes, and they do not all speak the same language. Some, but not all, are nomadic; some live in marshes formed by the river and eat raw fish which they catch from cane boats they set out in— each boat being made out of a single piece of cane! These marsh Indians wear clothes made out of rushes; first they cut the plant down and gather it from the river, and then they weave it as one would a basket and wear it like a breastplate.

[99] Another tribe of Indians, called the Padaei, who live to the east of these marsh Indians, are nomadic and eat raw meat. They are said to have the following customs. If any of their compatriots—a man or a woman—is ill, his closest male friends (assuming that it is a man who is ill) kill him, on the grounds that if he wasted away in illness his flesh would become spoiled. He denies that he is ill, but they take no notice, kill him, and have a feast. Exactly the same procedure is followed by a woman's closest female friends when it is a woman who is ill. They sacrifice and eat anyone who reaches old age, but it is unusual for anyone to do so, because they kill everyone who falls ill before reaching old age.

[100] There is another Indian tribe, however, with different habits: they do not kill any living thing or grow crops, nor is it

their practice to have houses. They eat vegetables, and there is a seed, about the size of a millet-seed, which grows by itself in a pod without being cultivated and which they collect, cook—pod and all—and eat. If any of them falls ill, he goes and lies down in some remote spot, and no one cares whether he is dead or ill.

[101] All the Indian tribes I have described have sexual intercourse in public, as herd animals do. Also, they are almost as black in colour as Ethiopians. The semen they ejaculate into their women is as black as their skin, not white like that of other men; the same goes for the semen Ethiopians ejaculate too. These Indians live a very long way south, far from Persia, and they were never ruled by King Darius.

[102] Other Indians live at the border of the town of Caspatyrus and Pactyican territory, to the north of the rest of the Indians. Their way of life closely resembles what one finds in Bactria. They are the most warlike Indians, and it is they who mount expeditions to search for the gold; the region in question is too sandy for human habitation. Now, in the sand of this desert there are ants which are bigger than foxes, although they never reach the size of dogs; there are also some of these ants in the Persian king's palace, which were caught in the desert and taken there. Anyway, these ants make their nests underground, and in so doing they bring sand up to the surface in exactly the same way that ants in Greece do (they are also very similar to Greek ants in shape), and the sand which is brought up to the surface has gold in it. It is this sand that the Indians search for on their expeditions into the desert. Each of them harnesses three camels together—two males, which carry the traces, and a female in the middle, on which the Indian rides, because their female camels can run as fast as horses, as well as being far more capable of carrying loads. The Indian makes sure that the female camel in the team is one with a very recent litter, from which he has had to tear her away.

[103] I will not describe the shape of a camel, because the Greeks already know what one looks like. I will, however, mention what is not widely known about it: it has two thighs and two knees on each of its hind legs, and its genitals turn back through its hind legs towards its tail.

[104] So that is the system the Indians use for the team with which they ride out in search of the gold. They time their trip so that the actual taking of the gold will coincide with the hottest part

of the day, because the heat drives the ants away underground. Whereas the sun is hottest at noon elsewhere, for these people it is hottest in the morning, from dawn until the forenoon. It is so much more hot then than it is at noon in Greece that the Indians are said to soak themselves with water at this time. At midday the heat is more or less the same for the Indians as for other people, and then during the afternoon it is as warm there as it is elsewhere in the morning. As the afternoon wears on, it gets more and more cold, until by the time the sun goes down it is really very cold indeed.

[105] The Indians reach their destination, fill the bags they brought with sand, and make their way back home as quickly as possible, because—as the Persians say—the ants' sense of smell lets them know what is going on and then they give chase. They say that there is no faster creature on earth than these ants, and so the Indians have to get a head start while the ants are gathering, or none of them would survive. Male camels are slower runners than females, so the two males are cut loose when they begin to fall behind, but not both at once. Meanwhile, the females remember their offspring back home and show no sign of weakness. That, according to the Persians, is how the Indians get most of their gold, although a small quantity is also dug out of the ground in their country.

[106] For some reason, the outer reaches of the inhabited world were allotted the most attractive features, just as Greece has gained by far the most temperate climate. India, for example, is the most easterly part of the inhabited world, as I remarked a short while ago, and it contains, in the first place, living creatures, both animals and birds, which are far larger than those to be found in other countries (the only exception being that their horses are inferior to the breed in Media known as Nesaean horses), and in the second place there is also an unlimited quantity of gold there, which is either dug out of the ground, or washed down from the hills by rivers, or taken from the ants in the way I have described. There are also wild trees there which produce a kind of wool which is more attractive and of a better quality than sheep's wool, and which is used by the Indians for their clothing.

[107] Then again, Arabia is the most southerly inhabited land, and it is the only place in the world which produces frankincense, myrrh, cassia, cinnamon, and rock-rose resin. None of these are easy for the Arabians to get, except myrrh. They collect

frankincense by burning storax resin, which Phoenicians export to Greece. Gathering frankincense requires the burning of storax because every single frankincense-producing tree is guarded by large numbers of tiny, dappled, winged snakes (these are the snakes which invade Egypt), and only the smoke of burning storax resin drives them away from the trees.

[108] The Arabians also claim that the whole world would be overrun by these snakes, if they were not liable to something similar to what I know happens to vipers too. Divine providence is wise, as one would expect, and it looks as though it has arranged things so that all timid and edible creatures produce young in large quantities, because otherwise they might be eaten into extinction, while all fierce and dangerous creatures produce young in small quantities. Hares, for instance, are hunted by all wild animals and birds of prey, and by man too, and so they are very prolific. Hares are the only creatures that conceive while pregnant. A hare can be carrying foetuses in her womb at various stages of development—some with fur, some still bald, some in the process of taking shape, and some being conceived. That is what happens in this sort of case, but on the other hand a particularly strong and brave creature like a lioness gives birth only once a lifetime to a single cub, because she expels her womb along with the cub. The reason for this is that while the cub is in the womb it begins to move around, and since its claws are far sharper than those of any other animal it scratches the womb, and eventually, as the cub grows, it rips it to shreds, until by the time it is due to be born the womb has been completely destroyed.

[109] The same goes for vipers and winged Arabian snakes: if they fulfilled their natural potential, so many would be born that they would make human life impossible. As things are, however, when they are mating in couples and the male is in the middle of emission, the female gets a grip on his neck while he is ejaculating and hangs on relentlessly until she has bitten right through it. So the male snake dies in the way I have just described, but the female pays for what she has done to the male, because while their offspring are still in the womb, they avenge their father by eating their way through their mother's belly, which is how they make their entry into the world. By contrast, other snakes are not a threat to human life, so they hatch their young out of eggs in large quantities. In any case, there are not as many winged snakes as there

appear to be: it is just that they are concentrated in Arabia and nowhere else, whereas vipers, for instance, can be found in every country in the world.

[110] Anyway, that is how the Arabians get frankincense. Next, cassia. They wrap their whole bodies and faces, except for their eyes, in oxhide and other leathers, and then go out after cassia. The cassia grows in a shallow lake in and around which roost winged creatures, which most closely resemble bats. These creatures emit a dreadful shriek and are very aggressive. The Arabians have to protect their eyes against them while they gather the cassia.

[111] The way they get cinnamon is even more extraordinary. They cannot even say where it comes from and where in the world it grows (except that some of them use an argument from probability to claim that it grows in those parts where Dionysus was brought up). But they say that the sticks which the Phoenicians have taught us to call 'cinnamon' are carried by large birds to their nests, which are built of mud plastered on to crags on sheer mountainsides, where no man can climb. Under these circumstances, the Arabians have come up with the following clever procedure. They cut up the bodies of dead yoke-animals such as oxen and donkeys into very large pieces and take them there; then they dump the joints near the nests and withdraw a safe distance. The birds fly down and carry the pieces of meat back up to their nests—but the joints are too heavy for the nests. The nests break and fall to the ground, where the Arabians come and get what they came for. That is how cinnamon is collected in that part of Arabia, and from there it is sent all over the world.

[112] The way rock-rose resin (or *ladanon* in Arabic) occurs is even more remarkable. Nothing could smell sweeter than the resin, yet nothing could smell fouler than the place where it is found— in the beards of he-goats, where it has stuck like gum from a tree. It is used in many kinds of perfume, and is the most common incense burnt by the Arabians.

[113] So much for aromatic spices; Arabia gives off a wonderfully pleasant smell. There are also two amazing kinds of sheep which are found nowhere else. First, there are sheep whose tails are so long—three cubits or more—that they would get sore from being dragged along the ground, if the sheep were allowed to trail them behind them. In fact, though, every shepherd knows enough woodwork to make little carts on to which they fasten the sheeps' tails,

one for the tail of each animal. The second kind of sheep have broad tails which are as much as a cubit across.

[114] The most remote country stretching to the south-west of the inhabited parts of the world is Ethiopia, which produces gold galore, elephants in abundance, all kinds of wild trees, ebony, and the tallest, best-looking, and longest-lived men in the world.

[115] These are the most remote countries in Asia and Libya. However, I have no reliable information to pass on about the western margins of Europe, because I at any rate do not accept that there is a river which the natives there call the Eridanus (said to issue into the northern sea and to be the source of amber), and I am not certain that the Cassiterides exist, which are supposed to be the source of our tin. In the first place, the very name 'Eridanus' tells against its existence, because it is not a foreign word, but Greek, made up by some poet. In the second place, despite my efforts, I have been unable to find anyone who has personally seen a sea on the other side of Europe and can tell me about it. Nevertheless, it is true that our tin and our amber come from the outermost reaches of the world.

[116] It seems clear that there is gold in exceedingly large quantities to be found in the north of Europe, but again I have no reliable information to pass on about how it is obtained. It is said that one-eyed people called the Arimaspians steal it from griffins, but another thing I am not convinced about is that there is a race of one-eyed men who are in other respects identical in nature to the rest of mankind. In any case, it is likely that the outermost reaches of the world, which encompass and enclose all the rest, contain things which strike us as particularly attractive and unusual.

[117] There is in Asia a plateau surrounded on all sides by a solid wall of mountains, broken only by five gorges. This plateau used to form part of the territory of the Chorasmians, and formed the boundary between them and the Hyrcanians, Parthians, Sarangae, and Thamanaeans; however, now that the Persians are in power, it belongs to the Persian king. Now, a sizeable river called the Aces rises in the mountains which surround this plateau. This river used to divide into five sub-rivers, each of which passed through one of the gorges and provided water for the land of one of the tribes just mentioned. But now that the Persians are in control of the plateau, the rivers have been treated as follows: the

Persian king dammed up the gorges through the mountains and built sluice-gates in each gorge to prevent the water escaping; with no way for the river to get out of the plateau once it has flowed in, the mountain-locked plateau has become a sea. This has caused a great deal of suffering among the tribes, because they used to rely on this water, and now they cannot use it. It is all right in the winter, when the god sends rain on to their land as he does everywhere else, but in the summer when they are planting their millet and sesame, they need water. Since they receive no supply of water, they make the journey to Persia, taking their wives with them, and there they stand at the entrance to the king's palace and bellow loudly and bitterly. The king then gives orders that the sluice-gates blocking the river which flows into the territory of the tribe which pleads most forcefully are to be opened, and when their land has soaked up enough water to become saturated, these gates are closed, and he gives the order for the next loudest pleaders to have their sluice-gates opened. My information is that he opens the gates only after he has exacted from them a great deal of money, over and above their regular tribute. Anyway, so much for that.

[118] It so happened that one of the seven who had rebelled against the Magus died shortly after their uprising; this was Intaphrenes, and he died because he committed an act of violence. He wanted to enter the palace to do some business with the king; and indeed the rule stated that the conspirators could go in to see the king unannounced, unless he happened to be having sex with a woman. So Intaphrenes thought it his right not to be announced, but because he was one of the seven to go right in as he wanted. But the gatekeeper and the message-bearer would not let him in, on the grounds that the king was having sex with a woman. Intaphrenes thought they were lying, however. He drew his *aki-nakes*, cut off their ears and noses, and threaded them on to his horse's bridle. Then he tied the bridle around their necks and sent them away.

[119] The men showed themselves to the king and explained why they had been treated this way. Darius was afraid that the six might have jointly had a hand in the act, so he sent for them one by one and questioned them to find out whether they approved of what had happened. When he was certain that they had not been involved, he arrested not just Intaphrenes himself, but also his sons

and all his male relatives, since he was sure that Intaphrenes and his relations were plotting to overthrow him. Once he had them all in custody, he put them in prison to await death.

Intaphrenes' wife took to coming to the doors of the palace and breaking down in tears and grief. This behaviour of hers eventually moved Darius to pity, and he sent a messenger out to her. 'Woman,' he said, 'King Darius permits you to choose one member of your imprisoned family to save.'

She thought about it and replied, 'If, thanks to the king, I have to choose the life of one person, out of all of them I choose my brother.'

When Darius heard what her reply had been, he was surprised and sent another message to her, as follows: 'Woman, the king would like to know what your reason was for abandoning your husband and children and deciding to save your brother's life, when he is not as near to you as your children or as dear to you as your husband.'

'My lord,' she replied, 'God willing, I may get another husband and more children, if I lose the ones I have at the moment. But my parents are dead, so there's no way I can get another brother. That was why I said what I said.'

Darius liked the woman's thinking and showed his pleasure by releasing not only her brother, as she had requested, but also her oldest son. However, he had all the others executed. So that is how one of the seven died so soon after the coup.

[120] Here is something that happened round about the time that Cambyses became ill. A Persian called Oroetes, who had been appointed governor of Sardis by Cyrus, conceived a desire to commit a terrible crime. Although he had never had anything bad said or done to him by Polycrates of Samos—although in fact he had never laid eyes on him—he wanted to capture him and kill him. Most people say that his reason for wanting to do this was as follows. Oroetes and another Persian called Mitrobates, who was the governor of the province at Dascylium, were sitting by the entrance to the king's palace talking to each other. Their talk degenerated into a quarrel, however, and they began to compare their achievements. In the course of the argument Mitrobates said cuttingly to Oroetes, 'You call yourself a man? The island of Samos is right next to your province, but you haven't gained it for the king. Look how easy it is to conquer Samos! Its present tyrant

gained control after he and fifteen hoplites started a rebellion.'
Some say that Oroetes was stung by this taunt, but rather than
making Mitrobates pay for voicing it, he decided to exterminate
Polycrates for causing him to be insulted.

[121] An alternative version, though less common, is that
Oroetes sent a messenger to Samos with some request or other (precisely what is not mentioned). As it happened, the messenger found
Polycrates laid up on a couch in the dining-room, in the company
of Anacreon of Teos. Now, it may have been deliberate or it may
have been accidental, but Polycrates treated the matter Oroetes was
asking him about with contempt, because he happened to be facing
the wall, and when Oroetes' messenger approached and began
talking to him, he did not turn around or answer him.

[122] These are the two reasons mentioned for Polycrates'
death; anyone can choose which of them to believe. In any case,
Oroetes, who was based in the city of Magnesia on the Meander
River, sent a Lydian called Myrsus the son of Gyges to Samos with
a message. He did so because he had found out about Polycrates'
plan to rule the sea—a plan which Polycrates was the first Greek
to have conceived, as far as we know. I discount Minos of Cnossus
and anyone earlier than Minos who gained control of the sea;
it remains the case that Polycrates was the first member
of what we recognize as the *human* race to do so, and he fully
expected to gain control of Ionia and the Aegean islands. Oroetes
found out about this idea of his and sent the following message:
'Oroetes to Polycrates: I am aware of your grand designs, but I also
know that you do not have the resources to match your plans.
However, there is something you can do to ensure that you are successful—and to protect me too. I say this because I have reliable
information that King Cambyses is intending to have me killed. So
if you come and rescue me and my money, I will share my fortune
with you. Thanks to this money, you will be the master of all
Greece. You may doubt what I am saying about the money, but if
so, send your most trusted man, and I will show it to him.'

[123] Polycrates was very happy to receive this message. He was
eager to comply, because he was, as it happened, very much in
need of money. He first sent his secretary, a fellow Samian called
Maeandrius the son of Maeandrius, to inspect Oroetes' financial
situation (this was the same Maeandrius who a little later dedicated
in the sanctuary of Hera all the furniture from Polycrates'

dining-room, which is well worth seeing). When Oroetes heard that someone was due to arrive to make an inspection, he filled eight chests with stones almost up to the very top and put a layer of gold on top of the stones. Then he locked the chests up and kept them ready. Maeandrius came and made his inspection, and reported back to Polycrates.

[124] Polycrates now made ready to go there in person, despite the fact that he had often been advised not to by both oracles and friends. Moreover, his daughter had seen her father in a dream high up in the air being washed by Zeus and anointed by the sun. After this dream she tried everything to stop Polycrates travelling to Oroetes; she even went as far as speaking words of ill-omen when he was on his way to the pentecorter. When he threatened to make her stay unmarried for a long time if he came back alive, she prayed that it would come to pass, saying that she would prefer to be single for a long time than to lose a father.

[125] Ignoring all this advice, Polycrates set sail for Oroetes. Included among his sizeable entourage was Democedes the son of Calliphon, a Crotonian by birth, who was the best doctor of his day. Polycrates arrived at Magnesia and there died a horrible death, one which neither he nor his grand plans deserved. After all, leaving aside the Syracusan tyrants, there is no Greek tyrant who bears comparison, for his magnificence, to Polycrates. Once he had killed him—in a way which does not bear mentioning—Oroetes crucified the corpse. He let all the Samians in Polycrates' entourage go, and told them to be grateful to him for their freedom, but he kept all the non-Samians and slaves of those who had come with Polycrates as his own slaves. With Polycrates' crucifixion, his daughter's dream came true in all respects: he was washed by Zeus when it rained and he was anointed by the sun as it drew out the moisture from his body. So for all his good fortune, Polycrates died as King Amasis of Egypt had said he would.†

[126] A short while later, however, retribution for Polycrates' death caught up with Oroetes. After Cambyses' death, during the reign of the Magi, Oroetes remained in Sardis without lifting a finger to help the Persians regain the power stolen by the Medes. He also used the chaos of the times as a cover to murder not only Mitrobates, the governor in Dascylium who had taunted him about the Polycrates affair, but also Mitrobates' son Cranaspes, both of whom were distinguished Persians. He demonstrated his brutality

in all sorts of other ways as well. In one instance, he killed an *angaros* who had come from Darius simply because the message he brought displeased him. What he did was arrange for men to ambush the *angaros* when he was on his way back home, and make sure that his dead body and his horse were never found again.

[127] When Darius came to power, he wanted to punish Oroetes for all his crimes, and especially for the deaths of Mitrobates and his son. He did not think it would be a good idea to make open war on him for several reasons: matters were still unstable, he had just come to power, and he found out that Oroetes was very strong, not just because he had a personal guard of a thousand Persians, but also because the provinces of Phrygia, Lydia, and Ionia were all under his control. So the plan Darius adopted under these circumstances was to summon all the most eminent Persians to a meeting and address them as follows: 'Men of Persia, I am calling for a volunteer for a job which will take cunning rather than brute force or numerical superiority. After all, in a situation that needs cunning, brute force is useless. So which of you will either capture or kill Oroetes for me? He has not lifted a finger to help the Persians, and he has done a great deal of harm besides. In the first place, he has murdered two of us, Mitrobates and his son, and in the second place he kills anyone I send to summon him to a meeting. This is obviously intolerable violence. He must be killed before he does the Persians worse harm.'

[128] In response to Darius' question, thirty men volunteered as agents to carry out the mission. Darius had to stop them squabbling by ordering them to let a lottery decide. They held a lottery and the lot fell on Bagaeus the son of Artontes. Now that the mission was his, Bagaeus had a number of letters written, on various matters, and sealed them with Darius' seal. Then he took these letters with him to Sardis. When he got there and came into Oroetes' presence he opened the letters and gave them one by one to the royal secretary (all the provincial governors of the Persian empire have these secretaries). Bagaeus gave the secretary the letters to read so that he could see whether the members of Oroetes' personal guard might possibly be receptive to the idea of rising up against Oroetes. It was clear that they respected the letters and still more the message they contained, so he gave another letter to the secretary. This time the content of the letter was as follows: 'Men

of Persia, King Darius forbids you to serve as Oroetes' personal guard.'

When the soldiers heard these words, they let their spears fall to the ground, and Bagaeus could see that they were obeying the letters' commands so far. This encouraged him, and he gave the secretary the last of his letters, which read: 'King Darius orders the Persians in Sardis to kill Oroetes.' At these words the guardsmen drew their *akinakeis* and killed him on the spot. And that is how retribution for the death of Polycrates of Samos caught up with Oroetes of Persia.

[129] Oroetes' belongings were sent back to Susa, and not long after they arrived King Darius happened to sprain his ankle dismounting from his horse while out hunting. In fact, it was such a bad sprain that the ankle-bone was dislocated from its joint. Previously, it had always been Darius' practice to have at hand Egyptian doctors whose reputation as healers was unsurpassed. He consulted them, but their forceful wrenching of his foot only made it much worse. For seven days and seven nights the pain was so severe that Darius could not sleep, and then on the eighth day, when he was in a bad way, someone who had been in Sardis and had heard about the skill of Democedes of Croton told Darius about him. Darius told his men to bring Democedes to him straight away. They found him consigned to oblivion among Oroetes' slaves and they took him in to the king, still dragging his chains and dressed in rags.

[130] So there he stood in front of Darius. The king asked him whether he was a professional doctor, but he said no, because he was afraid that if he was found out he would never get back to Greece. It was obvious to Darius, however, that he was a professional doctor, and he told the men who had brought Democedes to fetch up whips and spikes. At this, Democedes confessed, explaining that his knowledge was not precise, but that he had spent some time with a doctor and had a rudimentary grasp of the subject. Darius then put himself in Democedes' hands. By using Greek medical techniques and by applying gentle rather than harsh remedies, Democedes enabled Darius to get some sleep. Before long, contrary to Darius' expectations of never fully recovering the use of his foot, he was completely better. Darius then presented Democedes with two pairs of golden shackles, and Democedes asked him if this was his reward for healing him—deliberately to

double the punishment! Darius was pleased with this remark and
sent Democedes off to the royal wives. The eunuchs took him there
and introduced him as the man who had saved the king's life,
whereupon each of the king's wives dipped a cup into a chest full
of gold and gave the cup to Democedes. The gift was on such a
generous scale that the house-slave who had come with Democedes,
whose name was Sciton, made himself a considerable fortune just
from picking up the staters that fell from the cups!

[131] Here is how Democedes came to leave Croton and live in
Polycrates' court. In Croton he was not getting on with his father,
who had a terrible temper, and eventually he could stand it no
longer, so he left and went to Aegina. He settled there and within
a year, despite the fact that he had no equipment or medical instru-
ments, he proved himself better than all their other doctors. In
his second year there the Aeginetans took him on as their state
physician at a salary of one talent; the year after that the Athenians
hired his services for a hundred minas, and the year after that Polycrates hired him for two talents. So that was how he came to
Samos. It was chiefly because of him that Crotoniate doctors
became famous.

[132] Now, at the time in question, once Democedes had cured
Darius at Susa, he became the owner of a very grand house and
started to hobnob with the king; in fact he had everything—except
for passage back to Greece. On one occasion, the Egyptian doctors
who had formerly tended the king were about to be impaled for
letting a Greek doctor get the better of them, but Democedes
implored the king to have mercy and saved their lives. Then again,
there was an Elean diviner who had been part of Polycrates' entourage and had been consigned to oblivion among the slaves, and
Democedes rescued him too. In short, Democedes was extremely
important to the king.

[133] A short while later, something else happened. Atossa, the
daughter of Cyrus and wife of Darius, developed a growth on her
breast which subsequently burst and then spread further. While it
was small, she hid it and did not tell anyone about it, out of shame,
but later, when she was in pain, she sent for Democedes and showed
it to him. He told her that he would make her better, but made her
swear that in return she would do him any favour he asked of her,
and he added that he would not ask her to do anything which
would cause her shame.

[134] Later, after he had made her better, Atossa and Darius were in bed together and, acting on Democedes' instructions, she put the following proposal to Darius: 'My lord, you have so much power, but you do nothing with it. You aren't trying to gain further territory or increase the Persian empire. One would expect a man with youth and vast material resources at his disposal to make the Persians realize that they are being ruled by a real man, by conspicuously accomplishing some significant achievement. In fact, there are two reasons why it's to your advantage to do this—not just to make the Persians understand that their ruler is a real man, but also to keep them ground down by warfare and too busy to conspire against you. And now is the time for you to act and make your mark, while you are young, because while the body is growing, the mind is growing along with it, but as the body ages, the mind ages too and goes into a general decline.'

That is what she said, following her instructions. 'Wife,' Darius replied, 'your words echo my plans. I've decided to build a bridge from our continent to the next and to invade Scythia. This will be done soon.'

'Wait a moment, though,' Atossa said. 'I don't think you should bother to attack Scythia first. They'll be there whenever you want them. I'd rather you invaded Greece. I've heard people talk about what good servants Laconian, Argive, Attic, and Corinthian girls make, and I'd love to have some. And you already have available the best possible person to explain Greece to you in detail and to be your guide—I mean the man who healed your foot.'

'Since you want us to attack Greece first, wife,' Darius replied, 'I think we should send some Persians to Greece, along with the man you mention, to reconnoitre. They will bring me back a thorough report about everything they see and discover there, and then I'll have reliable information for the invasion.' That is what Darius said, and he put the plan into effect immediately.

[135] At daybreak the next day, he summoned fifteen eminent Persians and told them to go with Democedes and thoroughly explore the coastline of Greece; he added that they were to bring Democedes back at all costs, without letting him escape. After he had given these men their instructions, he summoned the man himself, Democedes, and asked him to give the Persians a thorough tour and description of Greece and then to return. He also suggested that he take, as gifts for his father and brothers, all his per-

sonal effects, on the understanding that he, Darius, would replace
them many times over with other such items; and he said that he
would contribute a cargo ship filled with a variety of valuable
goods to go with him on his voyage. Now, in my opinion, these
offers by Darius were not meant as a trap, but Democedes was
afraid that Darius was testing him, so he did not impetuously
accept everything that was on offer, but said that he would leave
his property behind, so that it would be there for him on his return,
while accepting the cargo ship which Darius was offering to transport the gifts to his brothers. Then Darius gave Democedes the
same instructions he had given the Persians and sent them on their
way down to the sea.

[136] They went down to the coast of Phoenicia. There, as soon
as they reached the city of Sidon, they manned two triremes and
also a huge merchant ship, which they filled with all kinds of valuables. When everything was ready, they set sail for Greece. Sailing
close to the Greek coastline they made their observations and wrote
them up, until they had reconnoitred most of the coastline, and
certainly the most notable places, at which point they went to
Tarentum in Italy. There, as a favour to Democedes, Aristophilides
the king of Tarentum first removed the rudders from the Persian
ships, and then imprisoned the Persians themselves, on the pretext
that they were spies. While the Persians were caught up in all this,
Democedes went to Croton. Once he was safely back in his native
country, Aristophilides released the Persians and gave them back
the gear he had taken from their ships.

[137] The Persians left Tarentum and followed Democedes to
Croton, where they found him walking around and tried to seize
him. The Crotonians were divided: some were willing to let them
take Democedes, because they were afraid of Persian power, but
others grappled with the Persians and hit them with their sticks.
The Persians put up an argument. 'Men of Croton,' they said, 'don't
you see what you're doing? You're robbing the king of Persia of
one of his runaway slaves. Do you think King Darius will be happy
with this offensive behaviour? Do you expect things to go well for
you if you take him from us? Which community in this part of the
world will we attack before yours, do you suppose? Which will be
the first place we will try to reduce to slavery?'

These words of theirs made no impression on the Crotonians,
however, so the Persians set out on their return voyage to Asia

without Democedes and also without the merchant ship they had brought with them. They gave up trying to learn any more about Greece, which is what they had come for, since they had lost their guide. However, Democedes did ask them, just as they were putting to sea, to do something for him—to tell Darius that Democedes was engaged to marry the daughter of Milo. He did this because the name of Milo the wrestler counted for a lot at the Persian court. Now, Democedes paid out a lot of money to arrange this marriage contract, and I imagine that the reason he was anxious to have the wedding take place was to make Darius see that he was an important person in his own country as well.

[138] During their voyage from Croton the Persians were shipwrecked at Iapygia. There they were enslaved, but a man from Tarentum called Gillus, an exile from his place of birth, rescued them and brought them back to King Darius, who asked him to name his reward. Gillus said that he wanted to be returned to Tarentum (he had already explained his unfortunate situation). However, he wanted to avoid plunging Greece into turmoil by launching a massive naval expedition against Italy, so he told Darius that the Cnidians alone would be enough to restore him to Tarentum; his idea was that because the Cnidians were on good terms with the Tarentines this would guarantee his return from exile. Darius gave his word and got busy; he ordered the Cnidians, through a messenger, to return Gillus to Tarentum. The Cnidians tried to carry out Darius' command, but could not persuade the people of Tarentum to take Gillus back, and were unable to force them to do so. So much for these events: these were the first Persians to come to Greece from Asia, and they came as spies under the circumstances just described.

[139] After this King Darius captured Samos. He would go on to capture plenty of places, both Greek and non-Greek, but Samos was the first. This is how it came about. During the Egyptian campaign of Cambyses the son of Cyrus, large numbers of Greeks came to Egypt for various reasons—to do business, naturally, to take part in the fighting, or just to see the country. One of those who came as a sightseer was Syloson the son of Aeaces, who was Polycrates' brother and had been exiled from Samos. Syloson had a very lucky break in Egypt. He picked up a red cloak of his and went for a walk, wearing the cloak, in the streets of Memphis, where Darius, who was at the time a member of Cambyses' personal guard and

not yet a person of any particular importance, caught sight of him. Darius wanted the cloak, so he went over to Syloson and offered to buy it off him. Syloson could see that Darius was very anxious to have the cloak, and in a moment of inspiration he said, 'I wouldn't sell this cloak for any amount of money, but I'll give it to you for free, if it really has to be yours.' Darius thanked him and took the cloak, and Syloson was sure that he had been stupid to lose it.

[140] In due course of time Cambyses died, the seven rebelled against the Magus, and Darius emerged from the seven to gain the kingdom. Syloson heard that the kingdom had gone to the man whose request for his cloak he had once satisfied in Egypt, so he went to Susa. He sat in the porch of the king's palace and claimed to be a benefactor of Darius. The gatekeeper reported his claim to the king, but Darius replied in surprise, 'Who is this Greek? How can I be under an obligation to any Greek, when I have only just become king? Hardly any of them have yet come to Susa, and I'm fairly certain that I don't owe anything to any Greek man. Still, you'd better show him in, so that I can find out what he means by this claim of his.'

So the gatekeeper brought Syloson and stood him in front of the king. The translators asked him who he was and on what grounds he was claiming to be one of the king's benefactors. In reply, Syloson told the whole story of the cloak and explained that it was he who had given it to Darius. Darius then said to him, 'Such generosity! When I still had no power, you were the one who gave me something—and even though it was not much, I still feel as grateful for it† as if I had just now somehow been given a magnificent gift. In exchange for your gift, I will give you limitless gold and silver, so that you will never have cause to regret having done Darius the son of Hystaspes a favour.'

'My lord,' Syloson replied, 'instead of giving me gold or silver, give me back Samos, my homeland. Ever since Oroetes killed my brother Polycrates, it has been in the hands of one of our slaves. Give me Samos, but without bloodshed or enslavement.'

[141] Darius' response to Syloson's request was to dispatch an expeditionary force. He put Otanes, who had been one of the seven, in charge of the army and gave him instructions to do whatever Syloson asked him to do. Otanes went down to the coast and got the army ready.

[142] On Samos Maeandrius the son of Maeandrius was in power; he had been left in charge by Polycrates. He was a man who had been thwarted in his desire to be a paragon of virtue. This is what happened. The first thing he did when news of Polycrates' death reached him was to build an altar to Zeus the Liberator and mark off a precinct around it, which is still there, on the edge of the town. Having done that, he next convened an assembly of the whole citizen body and addressed them as follows: 'As you know, Polycrates' sceptre and power have been entrusted to me, and I can now rule over you. However, in so far as I am able, I will avoid doing the things I criticize others for doing. I did not like the way Polycrates was the master of people who were, after all, no different from himself, and I would not condone such behaviour from anyone else either. Anyway, Polycrates has met his fate. For my part, I put power in the hands of all in common and proclaim a state of equality before the law. The only privileges I claim for myself are that six talents from Polycrates' fortune be set aside for me, and I would also like to reserve for myself and my descendants the priesthood of Zeus the Liberator, for whom I have of my own accord built a shrine and am now conferring freedom on you.'

This was Maeandrius' speech to the Samians, but one of them stood up and said: 'But *you* don't even deserve to be our ruler, since you're a low-born good-for-nothing. In fact, you had better give us an account of the money you have handled.'

[143] The man who said this was called Telesarchus, a person of some standing in Samos. Maeandrius realized that if he relinquished power, someone else would set himself up as tyrant, so he stopped thinking about giving it up. He withdrew to the acropolis and sent for people one by one, as if he was going to give them an account of the money, but when they came he arrested them and threw them in prison. While they were in prison, Maeandrius became ill. A brother of his, whose name was Lycaretus, thought he was going to die, and to make it easier for him to take over the reins of government in Samos, he killed all the prisoners. Apparently, they did not want to be free.

[144] So when the Persians involved in restoring Syloson landed on Samos, no one raised a hand to stop them. Maeandrius and his supporters declared themselves ready to leave the island under a truce, and Otanes agreed to the terms and arranged a truce. During the truce-making process, the most important Persians were sitting in their official seats facing the acropolis.

[145] Maeandrius the tyrant had a brother called Charilaus who was half-insane and who had been imprisoned in a dungeon for some offence or other. Now, on the occasion in question he heard the activity, and he leaned out of his dungeon to see what was going on. When he caught sight of the Persians peacably sitting there, he yelled out that he wanted to have a word with Maeandrius. Maeandrius heard his cries and gave instructions for him to be released and brought to him. As soon as Charilaus was brought in, he laid into his brother and called him names, in an attempt to persuade him to attack the Persians. 'You complete and utter coward!' he said. 'You have me, your own brother, thrown into a dungeon for some trivial misdemeanour which does not warrant imprisonment, while you let the Persians get away with expelling you from your home and country without having the guts to make them pay for it. It's not as if it would be at all difficult to overcome them. If you're so afraid of them, give me your mercenaries, and I will make them regret ever having come here. And I'd be happy to get you safely off the island.' This is what he said.

[146] Maeandrius agreed to Charilaus' suggestion. I think the reason he did so was not because he was crazy enough to imagine that he had the ability to defeat the Persian king, but rather because he resented the effortlessness of Syloson's impending recovery of an intact town. He had no doubt that if the Persians were badly treated, they would vent their anger on Samos, so he wanted to provoke the Persians and weaken the island and its affairs as much as possible, so as to be able to hand it over in an impaired state. He also knew that he could get safely off the island whenever he wanted, because he had built a secret passage from the acropolis to the coast.

So Maeandrius himself escaped from Samos by boat, while Charilaus issued weapons to all the mercenaries, flung open the gates, and gave them access to the Persians, who were taken completely by surprise, since they were under the impression that everyone had capitulated.† The mercenaries fell on the Persians as they were being carried around in their litters—they were all very high-ranking men—and killed them. This brought the rest of the Persian expeditionary force down on them, and the mercenaries were forced back and pinned on the acropolis.

[147] When the commander, Otanes, saw the atrocity which had been committed against the Persians, he ignored the fact that Darius' instructions for the mission had included the order not to

kill or enslave any Samians, but to hand the island over to Syloson in pristine condition, and he told his men to kill anyone they found, whether adult or child. So while some of his troops were engaged in besieging the acropolis, others were busy killing everyone they came across, whether or not they were on sacred ground.

[148] Meanwhile, Maeandrius escaped from Samos and sailed to Lacedaemon. He had taken his belongings with him into exile, and one of the things he used to do in Lacedaemon was this: from time to time, he would set out his gold and silver goblets, and on these occasions he used to have his attendants polish them up while he engaged the king of Sparta, Cleomenes the son of Anaxandridas, in conversation, and tried to bring him to his house. Whenever Cleomenes saw the goblets, he was impressed by them and used to admire them, whereupon Maeandrius would tell him to take as many of them as he wanted. After he had heard this two or three times from Maeandrius, Cleomenes proved his exemplary honesty. Not only did he decide that it was dishonest to accept the gifts, but he realized that others of his countrymen would accept them and help Maeandrius, so he went to the ephors and told them that it would be better for Sparta if their visitor from Samos were to leave the Peloponnese, to prevent him corrupting either himself or some other Spartiate. The ephors followed his recommendation and ordered Maeandrius to leave the country.

[149] The Persians 'trawled' Samos and handed over to Syloson an uninhabited island. However, some time later Otanes was persuaded to repopulate it by a dream and by an infection of the genitals he contracted.

[150] During the course of this naval expedition against Samos, the Babylonians revolted. They were very well prepared. They had spent the whole troubled period of the Magus' rule and the insurrection of the seven getting ready for a siege, and somehow nobody had noticed that they were doing so. Once their rebellion was out in the open, this is what they did. The Babylonian men gathered together all the women of the city—with the exception of their mothers and of a single woman chosen by each man from his own household—and strangled them. The single woman was kept on as a cook, while all the others were strangled to conserve supplies.

[151] When news of the rebellion reached Darius, he mustered his army in full strength and marched against them. Once he reached Babylon he began to besiege the city, but the inhabitants

were not in the slightest bit concerned. They used to climb up to
the bastions of the city wall and strut about there, taunting Darius
and his army. Once one of them called out, 'What are you doing
sitting there, men of Persia? Why don't you just go away? Babylon
will fall into your hands only when mules start bearing young'—
something which the speaker assumed would never happen.

[152] A year and seven months passed, and Darius and his
men were getting frustrated with their inability to overcome the
Babylonians. There were no inventions and devices that Darius
did not use against them, but he still could not capture the city.
He even tried the same method that Cyrus had used to capture the
city, but it was as ineffective as the rest, because the Babylonians
were meticulous in their guarding of the city. He just could not beat
them.

[153] Then in the twentieth month a remarkable thing happened
to Zopyrus the son of Megabyzus (the Megabyzus who had been
one of the seven who had overthrown the Magus): one of his pack-
mules gave birth. Zopyrus was told about it, but had to see it for
himself before he believed it; then he ordered the people who had
witnessed the event to keep it secret. He thought about what had
happened and remembered what the Babylonian had said at the
beginning of the siege—that the city would fall when mules gave
birth. In the context of this prediction, Zopyrus came to the conclusion that Babylon could now be captured; after all, a god must
have guided the man to say what he said, and his own mule to give
birth.

[154] Having come to the conclusion that Babylon was destined
to fall now, he went to Darius and asked him how important the
capture of Babylon was to him. Darius replied that it was very
important to him, so Zopyrus next began to try to find a way
whereby he could be the one to bring about the fall of Babylon, as
his own achievement, because among the Persians a high value is
placed on services to the king, and those who perform them are
greatly honoured. Now, the only plan he came up with which
would enable him to make the city his involved him maiming
himself and defecting to the Babylonians. So he coolly gave himself
crippling, permanent injuries: he cut off his own nose and ears,
roughly shaved his head, and flogged himself. Then he went to
Darius.

[155] Darius was very shocked at the sight of a man of Zopyrus'

standing with such terrible injuries. He jumped up from his throne with a cry and asked who it was who had disfigured him and why. Zopyrus said, 'No one did it to me, my lord; after all, you are the only person who could. I did it to myself, because I think it's dreadful to have Assyrians mocking Persians.'

'No, that won't do at all,' Darius replied. 'To claim that you have given yourself these permanent injuries as a way of doing something about the people we are besieging is to gloss over the utter vileness of your deed. It's just stupid to think that your injuries might hasten our opponents' surrender. You must be out of your mind to have disfigured yourself like this.'

'If I'd told you what I was intending to do,' Zopyrus said, 'you'd have stopped me. Instead, I took it upon myself to act. And the result is that we will now capture Babylon, as long as you don't let me down. Here is the plan. I will go as I am to the city wall as a deserter, claiming that it was you who mutilated me like this. I am confident that, once I have convinced them of the truth of my claims, they will give me a military command. What you have to do is this. Ten days after I have entered the city, post a thousand expendable men opposite the Gate of Semiramis. Then, seven days later, post another two thousand men opposite the Gate of the People of Ninus. After an interval of another twenty days, take another four thousand men and station them opposite the Gate of the Chaldeans. Neither the first two groups nor this last contingent are to have any means of defence except their daggers; that's all you must let them have. Then, the very next day, order the rest of your men to attack the walls from all sides, but post the Persian troops opposite the Belian and Cissian Gates. I think my substantial achievements will have won me the Babylonians' complete confidence—and in particular that they will have given me the keys of the city gates to look after. After that, it will be up to me and the Persians to do what needs doing.'

[156] After issuing these instructions, he made his way to the gates of Babylon, looking over his shoulder all the time as if he really were a genuine deserter. The look-outs posted on the towers spotted him, ran down, opened one of the gates a crack, and asked him who he was and what he had come for. He answered that he was Zopyrus and that he was deserting to their side. At this, the gatekeepers took him to the Babylonian council, where he stood forth and complained to them about his sufferings. He blamed

Darius for his self-inflicted injuries, and claimed that he had
received them as a punishment for advising Darius to draw off
his forces, when there seemed no way to take the city. 'Men of
Babylon,' he said, 'my presence here will be a huge boon to you—
and a huge bane to Darius and his army. He will certainly not get
away with mutilating me like this. I know his plans inside out.'
That, or something like it, is what he said.

[157] The sight of one of the most distinguished Persians
without his nose and ears and covered with blood and welts from
being flogged inclined the Babylonians to believe that he was telling
the truth and had come as their ally, and they were happy to entrust
him with everything he asked of them—and he asked them for
an army. Once they had given it to him, he put into action the
plan he had arranged with Darius. On the tenth day he led his
Babylonian forces out of the city, surrounded the thousand troops
he had told Darius to deploy first, and massacred them. When the
Babylonians realized that he was as good as his word, they were
absolutely delighted and were willing to do anything he told them.
After an interval of the agreed number of days, he again led out a
select body of troops and massacred the 2,000-strong contingent
of Darius' men. Following this second achievement, praise of
Zopyrus could constantly be heard throughout Babylon on everyone's lips. Once again, after an interval of the agreed number of
days, he led his men out to the pre-arranged spot, and surrounded
and massacred the four thousand. This feat, on top of his earlier
exploits, made Zopyrus the leading light of Babylon, and he was
appointed commander-in-chief of the army and also put in charge
of the defence of the city walls.

[158] At the agreed time, Darius had his men attack the city wall
from all sides—and then the full extent of Zopyrus' guile was
revealed. While the Babylonians were busy defending the city from
the walls against the onslaughts of Darius' army, Zopyrus flung
open the Cissian and Belian Gates and let the Persians into the city.
Some of the Babylonians saw what he had done and managed to
take refuge in the sanctuary of Zeus as Bel, but those who did not
remained at their posts until they too realized that they had been
betrayed.

[159] So that is how Babylon fell for the second time. Now that
the Babylonians were in his power, Darius demolished the city wall
and tore down all its gates (both of which were actions Cyrus had

failed to do when he had taken Babylon earlier), and he also had about three thousand of the most prominent men impaled on stakes; however, he returned the city to the remaining Babylonians and let them live there. As was explained earlier, the Babylonians had strangled their wives to ensure that they had enough to eat; so in order to make sure that they would have enough women to have offspring, Darius ordered all the nearby peoples to send women to Babylon, and gave each a quota, which resulted in a grand total of fifty thousand women congregating there. Today's Babylonians are descended from these women.

[160] To Darius' mind, no Persian ever performed a greater act of service than Zopyrus—no one ever did later, and no one ever had before, except Cyrus—no Persian would ever compare himself with Cyrus. It is said that Darius often expressed the opinion that he would prefer to see Zopyrus without his injuries than gain twenty more Babylons. He valued Zopyrus a great deal. Every year he presented him with the most precious items in Persia, and among a number of other gifts, he gave him Babylon to be his own domain, free of taxes, for as long as he should live. The Megabyzus who commanded the forces against Athens and her allies in Egypt was the son of this Zopyrus; and the Zopyrus who deserted from the Persians to Athens was the son of this Megabyzus.

BOOK FOUR

[1] After the capture of Babylon, the next military expedition commanded by Darius in person was against the Scythians. Asia's human resources were now flourishing, revenue was pouring in, and Darius was eager to pay the Scythians back, because they had been the first to commit unprovoked aggression, by invading Media and conquering those who opposed them in battle. As I have described earlier, the Scythians ruled over inland Asia for twenty-eight years. They invaded Asia on the heels of the Cimmerians, who were fleeing before them, and caused the end of the Median empire (the Medes had been the rulers of Asia before the coming of the Scythians). But after twenty-eight years away from their homeland, the Scythians returned—only to be greeted, after so long away, by just as much trouble as the Medes had caused them, because they found a sizeable army opposing them. What had happened was that the long absence of their husbands had induced the Scythian women to resort to their slaves.

[2] The Scythians blind all their slaves, and this is connected with the milk that they drink. The way they get their milk is as follows. They have blow-pipes made out of bones (they look very like our reed-pipes), and while one person inserts one of these pipes into the vagina of a mare and blows into it, someone else is doing the milking. They say that the effect of this is that the mare's veins are pumped up and the udder descends. Once the milk has been extracted, it is poured into deep wooden vessels and then they station their blind slaves around the vessels and have them stir the milk. The milk separates into an upper layer (which is skimmed off and regarded as the best bit) and a lower layer (which is thought to be less good), and that is why the Scythians blind everyone they capture. For they are nomads, not farmers.

[3] So a whole new generation had grown up with these slaves and the Scythian women as their parents, and when they discovered the circumstances of their birth, they set about resisting the

return of the Scythians from Media. The first thing they did was isolate their country, by digging a wide trench all the way from the Taurian mountains to the widest part of Lake Maeetis, and then they took up defensive positions and resisted the attempted invasion of the returning Scythians. Several engagements took place, but military tactics were getting the Scythians nowhere, so one of their number came up with an alternative. 'Fellow Scythians,' he said, 'look at what we're doing. In this war against our own slaves, we can either kill or be killed; if we're killed, there'll be fewer of us, and if we kill them, there'll be fewer of them for us to command. So I think we should abandon our spears and bows, take up our horsewhips instead, and pitch into them. All this time they've been seeing us bearing arms against them, as though they were our equals and sons of men as good as us. But the sight of us bearing whips instead of weapons will teach them that they are our slaves, and when they've learnt this they won't resist us.'

[4] The Scythians put this plan into action. Their opponents were so confused by the turn of events that they forgot about fighting and fled. That is how the Scythians ruled over Asia and, driven out of there by the Medes, returned home. And so it was a desire to pay them back that led Darius to raise an army against them.

[5] According to the Scythians, theirs is the most recent race on earth, and their account of their origins is as follows. The first man to be born in their country, which had previously been uninhabited, was someone called Targitaus, whose parents, according to the Scythians—this is what they say, but I myself do not believe it—were Zeus and a daughter of the Borysthenes River. This is supposed to be Targitaus' lineage, and then he had three sons— Lipoxaïs, Arpoxaïs, and Colaxaïs, who was the youngest. During their reign there fell from the sky on to Scythia four golden implements: a plough, a yoke, a *sagaris*, and a cup. The first one to see them was the eldest son, and he ran up to take possession of them, but at his approach the gold caught fire. He retreated, and the second son approached, but exactly the same thing happened to him—the burning gold drove him back as well. At the approach of the youngest son, however, the fire died down, and he took the golden implements back to his own home. The two older brothers therefore yielded to the youngest brother and handed the whole kingdom over to him.

[6] The Scythian tribe called the Auchatae trace their lineage back to Lipoxaïs, while the Catiari and Traspians trace their lineage back to the middle brother Arpoxaïs, and the kings of Scythia, who are called the Paralatae, are descended from the youngest brother. Their own name for themselves collectively is the Scoloti;† it is the Greeks who called them Scythians. Anyway, that is the Scythian account of their origins.

[7] As for the age of their race, they say that altogether, from the time of their first king Targitaus until the invasion of Darius, roughly a thousand years passed, but no more. It is one of the kings' most important jobs to look after the sacred gold I have mentioned, and there is an annual festival of propitiation at which they placate it with great sacrifices. The Scythians say that anyone who has the sacred gold and falls asleep out in the open during the festival will die within a year, and that is why they give him as much land as he can ride around on horseback in a day. Since the country is so large, they say, Colaxaïs established three kingdoms within it—one for each of his sons—and he made the largest the one in which the gold was to be kept. Beyond the territory of their neighbours to the north there are such piles of feathers, according to the Scythians, that nothing can be seen and the land cannot be traversed either. They say that there are too many feathers filling the land and the air to enable sight to function.

[8] That is what the Scythians say about themselves and about the land to the north, but according to the Greeks who live on the Euxine Sea it was Heracles who first came to the country currently occupied by the Scythians, when it was still uninhabited. He was driving the cattle of Geryon, who lived, they say, beyond the Euxine Sea, on the island known to the Greeks as Erytheia, which is near Gadira—Gadira being beyond the Pillars of Heracles on the shore of the Ocean. (The Ocean is supposed to rise in the east and flow all the way around the world, but there is in fact no evidence for its existence.) The story continues that when Heracles left Geryon and came to the country now known as Scythia, he encountered storms and frost, so when he lay down to sleep he covered himself with his lion skin. While he was asleep, his horses, which had been grazing yoked to his chariot, were miraculously spirited away.

[9] When Heracles woke up, he travelled all over the country looking for his horses, and eventually came to a place called Hylaea, where he found in a cave a being who was half young

woman and half viper; from the buttocks upwards she was a woman, but her lower half was serpentine. He looked at her in astonishment and asked her whether she had seen some horses roaming around anywhere. In reply, she said that she had them and would not give them back to him until he had had sex with her. Heracles had sex with her on these terms. Now, she kept postponing the return of the horses, because she wanted Heracles to stay with her for as long as possible, although he wanted to get his horses and go. But she did finally give them back to him, saying, 'When these horses of yours came here I kept them safe for you, and you have rewarded me by giving me three sons. Tell me what to do with them when they grow up. I have power over the whole of this country, so I can find somewhere for them to live here, if you want, or I can send them to you.'

Heracles' reply to this question of hers (so the story goes) was to say, 'Here's what you should do. When the boys have obviously become men, find out whether any of them can draw this bow here and put on this belt as I do now. If any of them can perform these tasks, you should set them up here in this country, but you should banish any of them who fail. This will not only make you happy, but will also be a way of carrying out my wishes.'

[10] He drew one of his bows—he had previously always carried two—and showed her the belt (which had a golden cup hanging from its tip, where it fastened together), and gave her both the bow and the belt. Then he left. When her offspring had grown up, she called the eldest boy Agathyrsus, the next one Gelonus, and the youngest Scythes. Then, mindful of her duty, she carried out the instructions Heracles had given her. Now, two of her sons, Agathyrsus and Gelonus, failed to accomplish the assigned task and their mother ordered them out of the country; Scythes, however, the youngest son, was successful and stayed there. And so, on this account, every successive Scythian king is descended from Scythes the son of Heracles. Also, Scythians still carry cups on their belts even today, because of Heracles' bowl. His mother found a way for Scythes to be the only one to succeed.† That is what the Greeks who live on the Euxine Sea say.

[11] There is still another version of events, which I personally prefer. It claims that the Scythians were a nomadic tribe living in Asia, and that once, by force of arms, they were driven by the Massagetae across the River Araxes and into Cimmerian land—

that is, the land currently occupied by Scythians, which is said to have belonged originally to the Cimmerians. In view of this Scythian invasion, and especially given that the invading force was so large, the Cimmerians tried to decide what to do. There were two distinct schools of thought, and although they were both vigorously championed, the one proposed by the royal family was better. The opinion of the general populace was that the best course would be for them to leave and not run the risk of staying for the sake of what was no more than dust,† whereas the royal family put forward the view that they should fight the invaders for the land. Neither side was prepared to do what the other side was suggesting. The general populace were in favour of abandoning their country without a struggle and handing it over to the invaders; the royal family, on the other hand, bore in mind what a good life they had had and how much they were likely to suffer if they fled from their homeland, and so decided not to join the people in flight, but to die and be buried in their native soil. Having made this decision, they formed themselves into separate groups, each containing an equal number of men, and fought one another. Then the Cimmerian people of the general populace buried them by the River Tyras (where their grave can still be seen) and emigrated, so that the Scythians invaded and took possession of an empty land.

[12] Even today one can find in Scythia places called Cimmerian Walls or the Cimmerian Straits, and there is also a tract of land known as Cimmeria and a part of the Bosporus that is called Cimmerian. It seems clear that the Cimmerians fled into Asia to escape the Scythians and settled in the peninsula where the Greek town of Sinope is established nowadays. And it is also clear that it was because they took the wrong route that the Scythians entered Median territory during their pursuit of the Cimmerians. For the Cimmerians fled along the coast, whereas the pursuing Scythians kept the Caucasian mountains to their right until they entered Median territory, by turning inland. This, then, is the third version, which is told by Greeks and non-Greeks alike.

[13] Aristeas the son of Caystrobus, who came from Proconnesus, claimed in a poem that he visited the Issedones in a state of inspiration by Apollo, that beyond the Issedones lives a one-eyed race called the Arimaspians, beyond them there is the land of the gold-guarding griffins, and beyond them the Hyperboreans, all the way to the sea. All these people, from the Arimaspians on, except

the Hyperboreans, are constantly attacking their neighbours, according to Aristeas, so that the Issedones were driven out of their territory by the Arimaspians, the Scythians were expelled by the Issedones, and the Cimmerians living on the southern sea were forced to leave their country by the Scythians. So he does not agree with the Scythians either concerning the country in question.

[14] I have already said where Aristeas, the author of this account, came from, but now I will recount a story I was told about him on Proconnesus and in Cyzicus. The story goes that Aristeas, who was as high born as anyone on Proconnesus, died in a fuller's shop he was visiting on the island. The fuller locked up his workshop and went to tell the dead man's relatives what had happened. Word soon spread around the town that Aristeas had died, but then a Cyzican man arrived from the town of Artaca with a contradictory report; he said that he had met Aristeas on the road to Cyzicus, and had had a conversation with him. He was very insistent that he was right and the others were wrong. The dead man's family went to the fuller's workshop with the things they needed to collect the body, but when they opened the door, there was no sign of Aristeas, dead or alive! Seven years later, he reappeared on Proconnesus, composed the poem which is nowadays known in Greece as *On the Arimaspians*, and then vanished a second time.

[15] That is what they say in Proconnesus and Cyzicus. However, I also know of an event that took place in Metapontum in Italy two hundred and forty years after the second disappearance of Aristeas, according to the calculations I made in Proconnesus and Cyzicus. The people of Metapontum say that Aristeas appeared in their country and told them to construct an altar to Apollo and to erect alongside it a statue of Aristeas of Proconnesus inscribed with his name. He told them that Apollo had once singled Metapontum out as the only place in Italy he had visited, and that he had been with Apollo at the time of his visit, although he had been a crow in those days, whereas now he was Aristeas. After telling them this, he disappeared. The Metapontines say that they then sent emissaries to Delphi to ask the god what this apparition was, and the Pythia told them to obey the phantom, and that it would be better for them to do so. They accepted the validity of the oracle and did what they had been told to do. A statue inscribed with the name of Aristeas can still be found even today; it stands

in the main square of the town right next to the statue of Apollo, and is surrounded by laurel-trees. Anyway, that is enough about Aristeas.

[16] No one knows for sure what lies further inland from the region this account has set out to describe. I cannot get information from anyone who claims to have firsthand knowledge. Not even Aristeas (the subject of my recent discussion) claimed in his poem to have actually travelled further than the Issedones; he said that his information about more remote parts came from the Issedones—in other words, that it was based on hearsay. However, I will put down all the reliable information I have been able to gain as a result of my enquiries.

[17] Taking as a starting-point the trading-centre of the Borysthenites, which is right in the middle of the coastline of Scythia, the first tribe is the Callippidae, who are Greek Scythians, and then beyond them there is another tribe called the Alizones. The customs of both these tribes are basically Scythian, except that they cultivate and eat grain, onions, garlic, lentils, and millet. Beyond the Alizones there live Scythian tribes who farm the land, but the crops they cultivate are for them to sell, rather than for their own consumption. Further north live the Neurians, but then the country north of the Neurians is uninhabited, as far as anyone knows. These are the tribes along the River Hypanis to the west of the Borysthenes.

[18] If one crosses the Borysthenes, the first region inland from the coast is Hylaea, and then, if one goes on up north, there are tribes of farming Scythians, called Borysthenites by the Olbiopolites (as the Greeks who live on the River Hypanis refer to themselves). These farming Scythians inhabit a region which extends for three days' journey east, up to a river called the Panticapes, and to the north for eleven days' sailing up the Borysthenes. North of this agricultural region there is a vast uninhabited area, and then there are the Cannibals, who have their own distinct way of life and are not Scythian at all. Further north the land is by this stage genuinely uninhabited; not a single human race lives there, as far as anyone knows.

[19] To the east of these agricultural Scythian tribes, across the Panticapes River, live nomadic Scythian tribes who do not grow crops or cultivate the land; moreover, the whole of this part of the world, except for Hylaea, is entirely bare of trees. The territory

inhabited by these nomadic tribes extends east for fourteen days' journey, up to the River Gerrhus.

[20] Across the Gerrhus is the Kingdom, as it is called, which is inhabited by the largest and most advanced Scythian tribe, who regard all other Scythians as their slaves. Their territory extends south as far as Taurian territory, east up to the trench which was dug by the sons of the blind men and the trading-centre on Lake Maeetis which is called Cremni, and also reaches the River Tanaïs. North of these Royal Scythians lives another non-Scythian tribe called the Black Cloaks, and north of them there are lakes but no human beings, as far as anyone knows.

[21] Across the Tanaïs River one is no longer in Scythian territory. The first tract of land one comes to on the other side of the river is inhabited by the Sauromatae, whose territory extends from the head of Lake Maeetis northward for fifteen days' journey and is entirely bare of both wild and cultivated trees. Beyond them, in the second tract of land, live the Budinians, whose territory is entirely covered with trees and shrubs of every conceivable species.

[22] North of the Budinians there is first a seven-day stretch of empty land, and then, if one turns a little eastward, there are the Thyssagetae, a populous tribe with its own distinct way of life. They live off what they can catch by hunting. Next to them, in this same region, live people called the Iyrcae, who also survive by hunting. Their method of hunting is to climb a tree (there are plenty of trees there) and lie in wait. Each hunter's horse has been trained to lie low with its belly on the ground in a state of readiness, and the same goes for his dog as well. When the hunter spots his quarry from the tree, he shoots at it and then leaps on to the horse and chases it, with the dog close behind. Beyond the Iyrcae, if one turns to the east, there are more Scythians, who once split off from the Royal Scythians and moved to this region.

[23] Up to the land of these Scythians, the terrain of the countries mentioned is uniformly even and has a deep layer of soil, but then it becomes rocky and rugged. Far past this rugged region, in the foothills of a mountain range, live people who are said—men and women alike—to be bald from birth; they are also supposed to have snub noses and large chins, to have a distinct language, to dress like Scythians, and to live off trees. The tree is called *pontikos*, and is about the same size as a fig-tree; its fruit looks like a bean, but has a pit inside. When the fruit is ripe, they strain it

through cloths and extract a thick, dark juice from it, which they call *askhu*. They lick this juice and drink it mixed with milk, and compress the thickest sediment into cakes for eating. They do not have much livestock, because the grazing there is poor. They each live under a tree, and wrap white waterproof felt around their trees in winter, while dispensing with the felt in summer. They are said to be holy, and so no one acts unjustly towards them, and they do not have any weapons of war. When disputes arise between neighbouring tribes, they are the ones who settle them, and any fugitive who takes refuge among them is safe from unjust treatment. They are called the Argippaei.

[24] Now, there is a great deal of good information available about the land and all the tribes up to and including these bald people, because Scythians sometimes reach these parts, as do Greeks from the trading-centre Borysthenes and from other trading-centres on the Euxine Sea, and it is not hard to get information from them. The Scythians who travel to these tribes conduct their business in seven languages, each requiring its own translator.

[25] So accurate information is available up to the bald people, but no one knows enough about what lies to the north of them to speak with confidence, because the mountains are so tall that they form an insurmountable barrier; no one passes over them to the other side. However, the bald people give what I consider to be an untrustworthy report, that there are goat-footed men living in the mountains, and that on the other side of the mountains there are other people, who spend six months of the year asleep. I cannot accept this at all. It is known for certain that the land to the east of the bald tribe is inhabited by the Issedones, but our only source of information about what lies to the north of the bald people or the Issedones is their own reports.

[26] Issedonian customs are said to be as follows. When a man's father dies, all his relatives bring livestock to his house. They sacrifice the animals and chop the meat up into pieces—and then they also chop up their host's dead father, mix all the meats together, and serve them up as a special meal. What they do to the head, though, is pluck all the hair off, clean it out, and then gild it. Then they treat it as if it were a cult statue, in the sense that the dead man's son offers it magnificent sacrifices once a year, just as in Greece sons commemorate the anniversary of their father's death.

In other respects, however, the Issedones too are said to be a moral people, and women have as much power as men in their society.

[27] Anyway, we know about the Issedones too, but for information about what lies to the north of them, we have to rely on their say-so. So it is thanks to the Issedones that we hear of the race of one-eyed men living there, and also about the gold-guarding griffins. When the Scythians talk about these one-eyed men and the griffins they are only repeating what they heard from the Issedones, and then the rest of us believe it and call them, Scythian-style, Arimaspians, because the Scythian words for 'one' and 'eye' are *arima* and *spou*.

[28] All the land I have mentioned experiences very severe winters—so much so that for eight months of the year it is gripped by intolerable frost. During these months you cannot make mud by pouring water on the ground, but only by lighting a fire.† The sea near the coast freezes over, as does the whole of the Cimmerian Bosporus, and the ice can bear the weight of the Scythians living inside the boundary of the trench, who go on military campaigns driving their wagons across it as far as Sindica. So a winter of this severity lasts for eight months, and for the remaining four months it is still cold there. Winter in this part of the world is also different in kind from winters anywhere else in the world, in that it hardly rains at all, as one would expect in this season, but in summer it never stops raining. At the time when thunderstorms occur elsewhere in the world, they do not happen there, but they are frequent during the summer. If a thunderstorm ever occurs in winter, it is regarded as a marvellous omen. The same goes for any earthquakes that might occur as well, at any time of the year: they are regarded in Scythia as omens. Horses can bear winter here, but mules and donkeys cannot do so at all, whereas elsewhere horses develop frostbite if they stand on frozen ground, while donkeys and mules can put up with it.

[29] It seems to me that this is also why the cattle there do not grow horns. This opinion of mine is supported by the line of Homer's in the *Odyssey* which goes: 'And Libya, where sheep bear horns soon after birth.' This is true, because horns grow quickly in hot places, whereas in a bitterly cold climate animals either do not grow horns at all or grow only little stumps.

[30] Anyway, that is what happens as a result of the cold. But there is one thing that puzzles me (this may be a digression, but

then this account has sought out such digressions ever since its beginning): what stops mules being born anywhere in Elis, which is not a cold place? There is no other obvious reason for it. According to native Elean tradition, it is a curse that stops mules being born there. However, when their mares are in season, they take them over the border and let the donkeys mount them there, in their neighbours' territory; and when the mares have conceived, they lead them back to Elis.

[31] What about the feathers with which, according to the Scythians, the air is filled, and which stop them either seeing or travelling over more of the continent? My view is that it is constantly snowing north of the region in question (less in summer than in winter, of course), and that it is the harshness of the winter that makes the northern part of the continent uninhabitable. Now, snow does look like feathers, as anyone who has ever seen snow falling thickly from close up can confirm; so I think that the Scythians and their neighbours are describing the snow metaphorically as feathers. Anyway, so much for what is said about these very remote parts.

[32] None of the tribes living there, including the Scythians, have anything to say about the Hyperboreans. Perhaps the Issedones do, but I do not think so, because if they did the Scythians would have stories about them too, just as they do about the one-eyed people. Hesiod, however, has mentioned the Hyperboreans, and so has Homer in the *Epigoni* (if indeed Homer really is the author of this poem).

[33] The overwhelming majority of the stories about the Hyperboreans come from Delos. The Delians say that sacred objects are tied up inside a bundle of wheat straw and are transported from the Hyperboreans first to Scythia, then westward as far as possible—that is, to the Adriatic—through a chain of successive neighbouring tribes, then south to Dodona (which is the first Greek community to receive them), then to the Gulf of Malia, where they cross over to Euboea, where they are passed from town to town until they reach Carystus, at which stage Andros is omitted, because the Carystians are the ones taking them to Tenos, and from Tenos the objects are conveyed to Delos. So this is how these sacred objects are said to reach Delos. They also say that the first time this happened, the Hyperboreans sent two young women (whose names, according to the Delians, were Hyperoche and

Laodice) to carry the sacred objects, together with five men from their country to act as their escorts and protect them; these are the men who are nowadays known as Perphereis and are greatly revered in Delos. But when these emissaries of theirs failed to return home, the Hyperboreans became upset at the prospect of everyone they ever sent on a mission failing to come back, and so they began to take the sacred objects tied up in a bundle of wheat straw to their border and entrust them to their neighbours, with orders to pass them on to the next tribe. So that is the route by which these sacred objects are said to get to Delos. I myself know of another instance of the same kind of thing happening as happens in the case of these sacred objects: when Thracian and Paeonian women sacrifice to Queen Artemis, the rites involve the use of wheat straw.

[34] So much for what these women do, to my certain knowledge. Now, the death of the young women who came from the Hyperboreans is commemorated on Delos by a hair-cutting ritual performed by the girls and boys of the island. Before they get married, the girls cut off a lock of hair, wind it around a spindle and put it on the tomb (which is inside the sanctuary of Artemis, on the left as one enters, and an olive-tree has grown over it), and the Delian boys wind some of their hair around a twig and put it on the tomb as well. So that is how these Hyperborean women are worshipped by the inhabitants of Delos.

[35] The Delians also say that two other young Hyperborean women, called Arge and Opis, came to Delos by the same route even before Hyperoche and Laodice. The purpose of their visit was to bring Eileithyia tribute they had undertaken to pay in exchange for a quick and easy labour at childbirth. According to the Delians, Arge and Opis were accompanied by the gods themselves to the island, where they have received different honours. What happens is that the women of the island beg gifts for them, while calling on them by name in the words of the hymn that Olen of Lycia composed in honour of Arge and Opis. (The practice of singing the praises of Opis and Arge, naming them and begging gifts for them, has spread from Delos to the rest of the Aegean islands and to Ionia. This man Olen also composed all the other traditional hymns which are sung on Delos, when he came to the island from Lycia.) Also, when thigh-bones are burnt as a sacrifice on the altar, the ashes are scattered on the tomb of Opis and Arge until there are none left. This tomb of theirs is situated behind the grounds of the

sanctuary of Artemis, facing east, right next to the banqueting-hall of the Ceans.

[36] That is enough about the Hyperboreans. I am not going to repeat the story about Abaris, who was supposed to be a Hyperborean, and how he carried an arrow all the way around the world without eating anything. But if there are Hyperboreans, people living beyond the north wind, there should also be Hypernotians, people living beyond the south wind.

I am amused when I see that not one of all the people who have drawn maps of the world has set it out sensibly. They show Ocean as a river flowing around the outside of the earth, which is as circular as if it had been drawn with a pair of compasses, and they make Asia and Europe the same size. I shall now briefly explain how big each of these continents is and what each of them should look like on the map.

[37] Persians live all the way south as far as the sea which is called the Red Sea. Their northern neighbours are the Medes, then come the Saspeires, and then the Colchians, all the way to the northern sea, into which the River Phasis flows. The whole of the land from one sea to the other is occupied by these four peoples.

[38] West of this tract of land come two peninsulas which project out from it into the sea. Here is a description of these two peninsulas. One of them starts in the north at the River Phasis, runs past the Euxine Sea and the Hellespont, and reaches the sea at Sigeum in Troas; in the south, this same peninsula starts at the Myriandic Gulf, which is off Phoenicia, and reaches the sea at the Cape of Triopium. This peninsula is inhabited by thirty different peoples.

[39] So that is one of the two peninsulas, and the other one starts in Persia and goes down to the Red Sea, taking in Persia, then Assyria, and then Arabia. This peninsula ends, but only by convention, at the Arabian Gulf, into which the canal flows which Darius dug from the Nile. From Persia to Phoenicia the land is broad and wide, but after Phoenicia this peninsula breaks into our sea and reaches Egypt (where it ends) via Palestinian Syria. This peninsula is home to only three peoples.

[40] These are the parts of Asia that extend west from Persia, and beyond the Persians, Medes, Saspeires, and Colchians, to the east there lies the Red Sea, and to the north the Caspian Sea and the eastward-flowing River Araxes. Asia is inhabited as far as India,

but east of India it is empty, and no one can describe what the land is like.

[41] That is the nature and extent of Asia. Now, Libya is part of the second peninsula, because it extends from Egypt. At Egypt, this peninsula is narrow, since the distance between our sea and the Red Sea is 100,000 fathoms, or a thousand stades; after this narrow bit, however, the peninsula, which now constitutes Libya, is in fact extremely wide.

[42] I am surprised, therefore, at the ways in which Libya, Asia, and Europe have been demarcated and distinguished. The differences between them are not insignificant. Europe extends lengthwise the same distance as both of the other continents together, and there is no comparison between their widths, in my opinion. After all, Libya is demonstrably surrounded by water, except for the bit of it that forms the boundary with Asia. King Necho of Egypt was the first to discover this, as far as we know; after he abandoned the digging of the canal from the Nile to the Arabian Gulf, his next project was to dispatch ships with Phoenician crews with instructions to return via the Pillars of Heracles into the northern sea† and so back to Egypt. So the Phoenicians set out from the Red Sea and sailed into the sea to the south. Every autumn, they would come ashore, cultivate whatever bit of Libya they had reached in their voyage, and wait for harvest-time; then, when they had gathered in their crops, they would put to sea again. Consequently it was over two years before they rounded the Pillars of Heracles and arrived back in Egypt. They made a claim which I personally do not believe, although someone else might—that as they were sailing around Libya they had the sun on their right.

[43] This was how information about Libya was first gained, and then the next people to claim that the continent was circumnavigable were the Carthaginians. I say that the Carthaginians were next, because the Achaemenid Sataspes the son of Teäspis failed to sail around Libya, even though that was his mission; frightened by the length and loneliness of the voyage he turned back, and so failed to carry out the task his mother had set him. The story is that he had raped the unmarried daughter of Zopyrus the son of Megabyzus. King Xerxes ordered him to be impaled for this crime, and the sentence was due to be carried out, when his mother, who was Darius' sister, begged for his life to be spared and promised to impose a heavier penalty on him than Xerxes had. She said that

she would make him sail all the way round Libya until his route
brought him back into the Arabian Gulf. Xerxes agreed to spare
him on these terms, so Sataspes went to Egypt, procured a boat
and crew there, and set sail for the Pillars of Heracles. He passed
through them, rounded the extremity of Libya, which is called Cape
Soloeis, and sailed south. Some months and a great deal of sailing
later, when there was no sign of any end to the voyage, he turned
around and sailed back to Egypt, and then made his way to King
Xerxes. In his report to Xerxes, he said that at the most southerly
point they reached they had been sailing past a country inhabited
by small people who wore clothes made out of palm leaves, and
that whenever they had beached their ship, these people had abandoned their settlements and run away towards the hills, despite the
fact that they had not approached them aggressively, and had taken
only some livestock from them. The reason he gave for not sailing
all the way around Libya was that his ship could go no further, but
had been stopped. Xerxes, however, realized that he was lying. So,
because he had failed to carry out his mission, he had him impaled
on the original charge. One of Sataspes' eunuchs ran away to
Samos, as soon as he found out that his master was dead, with a
great deal of property, but a Samian man seized it all. I know the
name of the Samian, but I deliberately repress it.

[44] Most of Asia was discovered by Darius as a result of his
desire to find out where the Indus River (the only other river in the
world to have crocodiles living in it) meets the sea. On board the
ships he sent out were people he trusted to bring back an accurate
report, including Scylax, a man from Caryanda. They set out from
the city of Caspatyrus, in Pactyican territory, and sailed downriver
in an easterly direction until they came to the sea, whereupon
they turned west and sailed across the sea for thirty months
before ending up at the place from which, as I related earlier, the
Phoenicians had set out on the instructions of the Egyptian king
to sail around Libya. After this successful circumnavigation, Darius
conquered the Indians and made use of the sea they had crossed.
And so all of Asia except the eastern part has been found to have
the same features as Libya.

[45] No one knows for certain whether or not there is sea either
to the east or to the north of Europe; it is known, however, that
lengthwise it is equal to the other two continents together. I have
no idea why the earth—which is, after all, single—has three

separate names (each of which is the name of a woman), or why the boundaries have been set as the Nile in Egypt and the Phasis in Colchis (or, as some say, the River Tanaïs at Lake Maeetis and the Cimmerian Straits), nor can I find out the names of those who decided upon these boundaries or how the continents got their names. Most Greek authorities claim that Libya is named after a woman called Libya who was a native of that continent, and that Asia is named after the wife of Prometheus. However, the Lydians lay claim to the name too; they say that Asia is not named after Prometheus' Asia, but after Asies the son of Cotys and grandson of Manes, who also gave his name to the tribe at Sardis called Asias. As for Europe, not only does no one know whether it is surrounded by water, but the origin of its name is also uncertain (as is the identity of the man who named it), unless we say that it is named after Europa from Tyre, and that before her time the continent was after all as nameless as the other continents were. But it is clear that Europa came from Asia and never visited the land mass which the Greeks now call Europe; her travels were limited to going from Phoenicia to Crete, and from there to Lycia. Anyway, that is enough about all this; we intend to use the standard names of the continents.

[46] The Euxine Sea—the region Darius invaded—is home to the most ignorant peoples in the world (I exclude the Scythians from this judgement). I mean, there is no tribe living on the sea to whom we could plausibly attribute cleverness (except the Scythians) nor, as far as anyone knows, has a single man of learning been born there (except Anacharsis). Although in other respects I do not find the Scythians particularly admirable, they have come up with the cleverest solution I know of to the single most important matter in human life. The crucial thing they have discovered is how to prevent anyone who attacks them from escaping, and how to avoid being caught unless they want to be detected. Since they have no towns or strongholds, but carry their homes around with them on wagons, since they are all expert at using their bows from horseback, and since they depend on cattle for food rather than on cultivated land, how could they fail to be invincible and elusive?

[47] This discovery of theirs was made in conformity with the terrain and with the assistance of the rivers. The land there is flat, grassy, and well watered, and there are almost as many rivers flowing through it as there are canals in Egypt. I will list the most

notable rivers—that is, those which can be sailed up from
the sea. There is the Ister with its five mouths, then the Tyras,
the Hypanis, the Borysthenes, the Panticapes, the Hypacyris, the
Gerrhus, and the Tanaïs. And here are their courses.

[48] The Ister, which is the westernmost river in Scythia, is the
largest known river in the world. The volume of its water never
changes, whether it is summer or winter. The reason for its great
size is that its waters are swelled by various tributaries. Of the rivers
that contribute to its size, there are five which flow through Scythia.
These are the Porata (that is its Scythian name, but the Greeks call
it the Pyretus), the Tiarantus, the Ararus, the Naparis, and the
Ordessus. The first river on this list is a substantial river which
flows east before joining the Ister; the second one, the Tiarantus,
which is not so large, lies more in the west of the country; and the
Ararus, the Naparis, and the Ordessus run and meet the Ister
between the Porata and the Tiarantus. These tributaries of the Ister
run solely within Scythia, but there is also the River Maris which
rises in Agathyrsian territory, but then joins the Ister.

[49] Three further large rivers—the Atlas, the Auras, and the
Tibisis—rise in the Haemus mountains and flow north before
meeting the Ister. Then there are the Athrys, the Noas, and the
Artanes, which flow through Thrace and the land of the Crobyzan
Thracians before joining the Ister. The River Scius rises in Mount
Rhodope in Paeonian territory, flows through the middle of the
Haemus range, and then joins the Ister. The River Angrus rises in
Illyrian territory and flows north to the Triballic Plain, where it
joins the River Brongus; since the Brongus then joins the Ister, the
Ister incorporates the Angrus as well as the Brongus, and they are
both substantial rivers. Then there are the Carpis and Alpis Rivers,
which rise north of the land of the Ombricians, flow north, and
become tributaries of the Ister. The Ister flows through the whole
of Europe. It rises in the land of the Celts, who live beyond the
Cynesians, further west in Europe than any other race, and then
flows through the whole of Europe before entering Scythia from
the side.

[50] The rivers I have mentioned are not the only ones to add
their water to the Ister; there are plenty of others too, and they all
go towards making the Ister the largest river in the world. I say
they *make* the Ister the largest river, because if we take both it and
the Nile on their own, just as single rivers, by its volume of water

the Nile comes out ahead. After all, no rivers or streams join the Nile and add to the volume of its water. Now, the reason why the volume of water in the Ister never changes, whether it is summer or winter, is, I think, as follows. In the winter, it is its natural size, or at most a little larger, because it does not rain very much at all there in winter. It snows all through the winter, however, and then in the summer the thick snow which fell during the winter melts and pours from all directions into the Ister. So all this snow pouring into it tends to increase its volume, and so do the frequent heavy rainfalls (it rains there in the summer), but the amount of extra water that the sun draws to itself in the summer, as compared with the winter, is exactly the amount of extra water that is added to the Ister in the summer, as compared with the winter. The two amounts cancel each other out, and a balance is reached, with the result that the volume of water in the river appears never to change.

[51] This is the first of the rivers in Scythia, the Ister. The next one is the Tyras, which rises in the north and flows south. Its source is a huge lake which forms the border between Scythia and Neurian country. The Greeks living at its mouth are called Tyritae.

[52] The third river, the Hypanis, rises in Scythia. The source of this river is a large lake on the margins of which live wild white horses. The lake is rightly called the Mother of the Hypanis. For five days' journey by boat downstream from this lake where it rises, the river's water remains shallow and sweet, but for the four days it takes after that to get to the coast, it is terribly brackish. The reason for this is that it is joined by a bitter spring which is so brackish that despite its small size it pollutes the Hypanis, which is one of the largest rivers in the world. This spring is situated on the border between where the farming Scythians live and the Alizones. The name of the spring, which is also the name of the region where it rises, is Exampaeus in Scythian, or Sacred Ways in Greek. The courses of the Tyras and the Hypanis draw close to each other in Alizonian territory, but then they veer away from each other and the gap between the two rivers widens as they continue on their way.

[53] The fourth river is the Borysthenes, which is the largest of these rivers after the Ister, and is, as far as I can tell, not just the most productive river in Scythia, but in the whole world—with the exception of the Nile in Egypt which cannot be compared with any

other river in this respect. But apart from the Nile, the Borysthenes is the most productive river. It not only provides wonderful, lush meadows for cattle, but outstandingly fine fish as well, in very large quantities; its water is clear where other rivers are muddy, and makes lovely drinking-water; the crops that grow on its banks are excellent, and where the land is uncultivated grass grows to a great height. Huge deposits of salt build up at its mouth of their own accord. The river is home to large invertebrate fish called *antakaioi*, which the Scythians preserve by salting, and to many other remarkable creatures. Up until the region of the Gerrhians, which is forty days' journey by boat upstream (since it flows from north to south), its course is known, but no one can say whose lands it runs through north of there. However, it is clear that after running through uninhabited land it reaches the territory of the farming Scythians, because they live on its banks for the distance of a ten-day voyage by boat. This river and the Nile are the only ones whose sources I am unable to tell—but I think no other Greek can either. Near the sea, the Borysthenes is joined by the Hypanis and together they flow into the same area of marshland. Between the mouths of the two rivers there is a headland called Hippolaus' Point, on which there is a sanctuary to Demeter. Beyond the sanctuary, on the River Hypanis, the Borysthenites have built their town.

[54] So much for these rivers. The next one, the fifth, is called the Panticapes. It too rises in a lake and flows from the north. The land between it and the Borysthenes is occupied by the farming Scythians. Once it has passed through Hylaea, it joins the Borysthenes.

[55] The sixth river is the Hypacyris. Its source is a lake, and its course takes it through the territory of the nomadic Scythians, skirting Hylaea and the place called Achilles' Racecourse to the west, and finally ending at the city of Carcinitis.

[56] The seventh river is the Gerrhus. It branches off from the Borysthenes about where the course of the Borysthenes becomes obscure. The district where it branches off is called Gerrhus, and the river has the same name as the place. Then it flows down towards the sea, forming a boundary between the land of the nomadic Scythians and that of the Royal Scythians, and issues into the Hypacyris.

[57] The eighth river is the Tanaïs. The source of this river is a large lake, and then it ends at an even larger lake called Lake

Maeetis, which forms a boundary between the Royal Scythians and the Sauromatae. The Tanaïs has a tributary called the Hyrgis.

[58] It is clear, then, that Scythia is very well off for notable rivers. However, the grass which grows there and is eaten by the cattle is the most bile-producing grass in the known world. It is the opening of the cattle that allows one to make this judgement.

[59] So the most important natural resources are abundantly at their disposal; as for the rest, their customs are as follows. The only gods they worship are Hestia (who is their most important deity), then Zeus and Earth (whom they regard as the wife of Zeus), then Apollo, Heavenly Aphrodite, Heracles, and Ares. All Scythians worship these gods, but the Royal Scythians also worship Poseidon. The Scythian name for Hestia is Tabiti, while Zeus (perfectly appropriately, in my opinion) is called Papaeus, Earth Api, Apollo Goetosyrus, Heavenly Aphrodite Argimpasa, and Poseidon Thagimasadas. However, it is not their custom to make statues or altars or temples for any of their gods, except for Ares; they do have this custom in his case.

[60] The way all the Scythians conduct sacrifices, which is identical whatever the particular rite that is being performed, is as follows. The victim stands there with its front legs tied together, and the person performing the sacrifice stands behind the animal and tugs on his end of the rope, which brings the creature down, and while it is falling, he invokes the god for whom the sacrifice is being carried out; then he wraps a noose around the victim's neck, inserts a stick into the noose and twists it until he has strangled the victim to death. In other words, the procedure does not involve lighting a fire, or consecrating the victim, or pouring libations. Once the worshipper has throttled the victim and skinned it, he turns his attention to cooking the meat.

[61] Now, Scythia is more or less entirely treeless, so they have come up with an unusual method of stewing the meat. Once they have skinned the victim, they strip the meat off the bones and then put the meat into a pot, if they happen to have one; these pots are of a local design and most closely resemble Lesbian bowls, except that they are much bigger. When they have put the meat in the pot, they make a fire out of the victim's bones and cook the meat that way. If they do not have a pot, they wrap all the meat up inside the victim's stomach, add water, and then make a fire out of the bones. The bones burn very well, and the stomachs easily hold the

meat once it has been stripped off the bones. In other words, the cow—or whatever animal the victim is—cooks itself! Once the meat is cooked, the worshipper takes some of the meat and the innards as first-fruits and throws them forward. Their most common sacrificial victims are horses, but domestic animals are also used.

[62] That is how they perform sacrifices to most of their gods, and these are the animals they use, but in Ares' case things are different. In every district, within each province, a sanctuary has been constructed to Ares. The design of these sanctuaries is as follows. Bundles of sticks are piled together into a block about three stades long by three stades wide, but not so high off the ground. On top of this pile of sticks is built a square platform, three of whose sides are sheer, while the other is climbable. Each year they add a hundred and fifty cart-loads of sticks, to make up for the subsidence caused by the winter's storms. On top of this structure the inhabitants of each district place an ancient iron *akinakes*, which is taken to represent Ares. The festival takes place once a year, and at it they offer this *akinakes* more domestic animals and horses as sacrificial victims than all the other gods receive. They also sacrifice prisoners of war to this *akinakes*, though the method is different from when domestic animals are the victims. One prisoner in every hundred is selected; they pour wine over the prisoners' heads, cut their throats so that the blood spills into a jar, and then carry the jars up on to the pile of sticks and pour the blood over the *akinakes*. While the jars are being taken up there, something else is happening down below, by the side of the sanctuary: they cut off the right arms of all the slaughtered men—the whole arm, from shoulder to hand—and hurl them into the air. Then they sacrifice all the rest of the victims and leave. The arms are left lying wherever they fall, detached from the corpses.

[63] So that is how they perform sacrifices. They never use pigs as sacrificial animals, and in fact they prefer not to keep them in their country at all.

[64] Here is how they conduct themselves in war. When a Scythian kills his first man, he drinks some of his blood. He presents the king with the heads of those he kills in battle, because his reward for doing so is a share of the spoils they have taken in the battle, but no head means no spoils. The way a Scythian skins a head is as follows: he makes a circular cut around the head at the

level of the ears and then he picks it up and shakes the scalp off
the skull: next he scrapes the skin with a cow's rib, and then, having
kneaded the skin with his hands, he has a kind of rag, which he
proudly fastens to the bridle of the horse he is riding. The reason
for his pride is that the more of these skin rags a man has, the
braver he is counted. Many of them make coats to wear by sewing
the scalps together into a patchwork leather garment like leather
coats. Another common practice is to skin the right arms of their
dead opponents, fingernails and all, and make covers for their
quivers out of them. Human skin, apparently, is thick and shiny-
white—shinier, in fact, than any other kind of skin. They also often
skin the whole of a corpse and stretch the skin on a wooden frame
which they then carry around on their horses.

[65] So much for these practices of theirs. As for the actual
skulls—the skulls of their enemies, that is, not all skulls—they saw
off the bottom part of the skull at the level of the eyebrows and
clean out the top bit. A poor Scythian then wraps a piece of
untanned cow-hide tightly around the outside of the skull and puts
it to use like that, while a rich Scythian goes further: after wrapping it in cowhide he gilds the inside and then uses it as a cup. Also,
if a Scythian falls out with one of his relatives, they fight to the
death in the presence of their king, and the winner treats the loser's
skull in the way I have just described. When he has important visitors, he produces these skulls and tells how they had once been his
relatives, and how they made war on him, but he defeated them.
This they call courage.

[66] Once a year, each provincial governor is in charge of a ceremony that takes place in his province. He mixes a bowl of wine,
and all the Scythians who have killed an enemy that year have a
drink from it. Anyone who has not managed to do this does not
partake of the wine, but sits to one side in disgrace—which is the
greatest indignity there is for them. Any of them who have killed
large numbers of men are given two cups to drink together.

[67] There are a lot of diviners in Scythia; the divinatory method
they practise involves a large number of willow rods. First they
bring their rods wrapped up in large bundles, put them on the
ground, and unroll the bundles; then they position the rods one by
one and make their prophecies, while simultaneously wrapping the
rods back up again one by one into a bundle. This is the traditional
method of divination in Scythia, but the hermaphroditic *enareis*

have another method which they claim was a gift from Aphrodite. They take some of the inner bark from a lime-tree, divide it into three pieces, and then make their prophecy while plaiting and unplaiting it with their fingers.

[68] If the Scythian king ever falls ill, he sends for the three most respected diviners, who use the divinatory method I have already described. They usually say something to the effect that such and such a person—they identify one of their fellow countrymen—has falsely sworn by the king's hearth, which is the usual form of oath when a Scythian wants to make a particularly solemn oath. The person they named as the liar is immediately arrested and brought to the king, and the diviners then accuse him of having been found by their divinatory skill to have falsely sworn by the king's hearth and so caused the king's illness. He denies that he has perjured himself and vehemently protests his innocence, whereupon the king sends for double the number of diviners. If they too convict him of lying under oath as a result of what they see in their divinations, he is immediately beheaded and his property is divided among the first three diviners; however, if the newly arrived diviners acquit him, more and more diviners come, and if the majority find him innocent, it is the Scythian custom for the orginal three diviners to be executed.

[69] Here is how they kill them. First they fill a cart with sticks and yoke oxen to it, then they tie the diviners' feet together, tie their hands behind their backs, gag them, and confine them in the middle of the pile of sticks; finally, they set the sticks on fire and frighten the oxen into motion. It is not uncommon for the oxen to be burnt to death along with the diviners, but the pole often burns through, which enables the oxen to escape slightly singed. Death by burning in this way is also how they kill their diviners if they find them guilty of other crimes too, calling them false prophets. The children of people executed by the king are not safe either: he has every male child killed, although he leaves the females alone.

[70] The procedure in Scythia for entering into a sworn agreement with anyone is as follows. Wine is poured into a large earthenware cup, and then the people swearing the oath are either jabbed with an awl or cut a little somewhere on their bodies with a knife, so that their blood mingles with the wine in the cup. Then they dip into the cup an *akinakes*, some arrows, a *sagaris*, and a javelin. After that, they offer up a lot of prayers, and then the people enter-

ing into the compact and the most valued members of their retinue drink down the blood-and-wine mixture.

[71] Their kings are buried in the territory of the Gerrhians, at the point where, travelling upstream, the Borysthenes ceases to be navigable. On the death of one of their kings, they dig a huge square pit in the ground there, and when this is ready they take up the wax-covered corpse (which has previously had its stomach opened up, cleaned out, filled with chopped galingale, incense, celery-seeds, and aniseed, and then sewn back up again) and carry it in a wagon to another tribe. The people to whom the corpse has been brought do what the Royal Scythians have already done: they cut one of their ears, shave their heads, slash their arms, mutilate their foreheads and noses, and pierce their left hands with arrows. Then the king's corpse is taken on its wagon to another one of the tribes within the Scythian realm, with its retinue being made up of people from the tribe to which the corpse had previously been transported. Finally, after going around all the tribes with the corpse, they come to the Gerrhians, who are the most remote of the tribes within the Scythian realm, and to the tombs. Here, they lay the corpse in his grave on a pallet. Then they stick spears into the ground on both sides of the corpse and make a roof out of wooden planks covered with rush matting. There is still open space left within the grave, and in it they bury, after throttling them to death, one of the king's concubines, his wine-server, cook, groom, steward, and messenger, and some horses and a proportion of all his other possessions, including some golden cups. They do not put anything of silver or bronze in the grave. Then they cover the grave with a huge mound of earth, and they all eagerly compete with one another to make the mound as big as possible.

[72] After a year has gone by, they choose the fifty most suitable of the dead king's remaining attendants and throttle both them and his fifty finest horses to death. The king's attendants are native Scythians; there are no bought slaves in Scythia, but anyone the king orders to be his attendant complies. Once the fifty servants and the fifty horses are dead, they gut them, clean them out, fill them up with chaff, and then sew them up again. Next they halve a wheel and fix each of the two halves, cut side up, in the ground on two stakes, and repeat this process over and over again. Then they drive a thick pole through each of the horses, all the way up to their necks, and use them to mount the horses on the wheels in

such a way that the front wheels support the horses' shoulders and
the rear wheels support their bellies next to their thighs, and all
four legs are dangling off the ground. The horses are then fitted out
with bridles and bits, and the reins are pulled forward over their
heads and tied to pegs. Then they mount each of the fifty young
men they have strangled to death on one of the horses by driving
a pole upright through his body along his spine as far as his neck;
and they fix the projecting lower end of this pole into a socket
bored into the other pole, the one which goes through the horse.
They set up these horsemen in a circle around the grave, and then
ride off.

[73] That is how they bury their kings. As for the rest of the
Scythian population, when one of them dies, his closest relatives
put his body on a wagon and take it round to his friends, each of
whom makes the entourage welcome and gives them a meal at
which the corpse is served the same food and drink as everyone
else. The corpse of a member of the general populace of Scythia is
taken around to his friends like this for forty days, and then buried.
After burying their dead, Scythians purify themselves. First they
anoint and rinse their hair, then, for their bodies, they lean three
poles against one another, cover the poles with felted woollen blankets, making sure that they fit together as tightly as possible, and
then put red-hot stones from the fire on to a dish which has been
placed in the middle of the pole-and-blanket structure.

[74] Now, there is a plant growing in their country called
cannabis, which closely resembles flax, except that cannabis is
thicker-stemmed and taller. In Scythia, in fact, it is far taller. It
grows wild, but is also cultivated, and the Thracians use it, as well
as flax, for making clothes. These clothes are so similar to ones
made out of flax that it would take a real expert to tell the difference between the two materials. Anyone unfamiliar with cannabis
would suppose that the clothes were linen.

[75] Anyway, the Scythians take cannabis seeds, crawl in under
the felt blankets, and throw the seeds on to the glowing stones. The
seeds then emit dense smoke and fumes, much more than any
vapour-bath in Greece. The Scythians shriek with delight at the
fumes. This is their equivalent of a bath, since they never wash their
bodies with water. Their women, however, pound cypress, cedar,
and frankincense wood on a rough piece of stone, and add water
until they have a thick paste which they then smear all over their

bodies and faces. This not only makes them smell nice, but when they remove the paste the day after they turn out to be all clean and shining.

[76] The Scythians are another people who are absolutely set against adopting customs imported from anyone else, especially Greeks. This is clear from what happened to Anacharsis and then later to Scyles. As for Anacharsis, he visited many countries all over the world and became known for his great wisdom wherever he went. On his way back home to Scythia, he was sailing through the Hellespont and he put in at Cyzicus, where he found the inhabitants in the middle of an extremely impressive festival sacred to the Mother of the Gods. Anacharsis himself prayed to the Mother that if he got back home safe and sound, he would offer the same sacrifices to her that he had seen the Cyzicans offering, and would keep a night vigil in her honour. So after his return to Scythia, he slipped into Hylaea (a thickly wooded region, filled with all kinds of trees, which lies next to Achilles' Racecourse) and performed all the rites to the goddess, since he had a drum and had tied cult images of the goddess on to himself. However, his actions were spotted by a certain Scythian, who reported him to King Saulius. The king came in person, saw Anacharsis performing the rites, and shot him dead with bow and arrow. Even nowadays, if anyone mentions Anacharsis' name, the Scythians claim not to recognize it—and this is all because he travelled to Greece and adopted foreign practices. Now, I was told by Tymnes the steward of Ariapithes that Anacharsis was the paternal uncle of King Idanthyrsus of Scythia (and was the son of Gnurus, grandson of Lycus and great-grandson of Spargapithes). If this is Anacharsis' lineage, he should know that he was killed by his own brother, because Idanthyrsus was the son of Saulius, and it was Saulius who killed Anacharsis.

[77] However, I once heard a different story from the Peloponnesians, to the effect that it was the Scythian king who sent Anacharsis to Greece to find out what he could, and that on his return he told the king who had given him this mission that none of the Greeks had any time for any kind of wisdom, except the Lacedaemonians, who were the only ones with whom it was possible to hold a sensible conversation. But this story is an amusing fiction, made up by the Greeks themselves. In any case, the man was killed, as I mentioned earlier. So that is what interest in foreign practices and contact with the Greeks brought him.

[78] A great many years later, almost the same thing happened to Scyles the son of Ariapithes. Scyles was one of the sons of King Ariapithes of Scythia, but his mother was not a native Scythian; she came from Istria, and she taught Scyles to speak and read Greek. Later, when Ariapithes died (thanks to the treachery of King Spargapithes of the Agathyrsians), Scyles inherited not only the kingdom, but also his father's wife, a Scythian woman named Opoea, who had already borne Ariapithes a son called Oricus. Scyles ruled over the Scythians, but he was not happy with the Scythian way of life; as a result of his upbringing, he was far more inclined towards things Greek. So whenever during the course of a military campaign he came to the Borysthenites (who claim to be Milesians originally), he used to leave his army just outside the town while he himself would go inside the town walls and lock the gates. Once he was inside, he would take off his Scythian clothes and dress himself up in Greek attire. Then, wearing these Greek clothes, he would walk around the town entirely unaccompanied by anyone—not even his personal guards; the gates were guarded, to stop any Scythian seeing him dressed like this. For a month or more, he would adopt a Greek way of life, including worshipping the gods in the traditional Greek way, and then he would put his Scythian clothing back on and leave. He used to do this a lot; he even built a house in Borysthenes, where he kept a local woman he had married.

[79] Now, Scyles was destined to come to a bad end, and this came about under the following circumstances. He wanted to perform the rites of Bacchic Dionysus, but just as he was about to do so, a tremendous omen occurred. As I mentioned just now, he had a substantial and luxurious walled house in the Borysthenite community (which was surrounded by white stone statues of sphinxes and griffins). Zeus struck this house with a bolt of lightning. Despite the fact that the house burnt to the ground, Scyles still completed the ceremony. Now, the Bacchic rites are one of the aspects of Greek culture of which the Scythians disapprove, on the grounds that it is unreasonable to seek out a god who drives people out of their minds. So after Scyles had performed the Bacchic rites, one of the Borysthenites hurried off to the Scythians and said, 'You may mock our Bacchic rites, men of Scythia, and the fact that the god takes hold of us, but now the god has taken hold of your own king, and he is in a state of Bacchic frenzy. If you don't believe me, come and I will show you.'

The leaders of the Scythians went with the Borysthenite, who took them and placed them secretly in a high tower. When the sacred procession went past the building, with Scyles in it, they could see that he was possessed by Dionysus. They thought this was a disaster, and on leaving they told the whole Scythian army what they had seen.

[80] The upshot of all this was that Scyles came home to find that his brother Octamasades (the son of Teres' daughter) had been chosen by the Scythians to lead a rebellion against him. As soon as he became aware of the hostility towards him and the cause of it, he fled to Thrace. When Octamasades heard about this, he marched against Thrace. The Thracians met him when he reached the Ister, but just before battle was joined Sitalces sent a man to Octamasades with the following message: 'You are my sister's son. Why should we fight each other? You have my brother with you. If you give him back to me, I'll hand Scyles over to you, and neither of us need endanger the lives of our men.' This was the message Sitalces sent, because his brother had taken refuge with Octamasades when he fled into exile. Octamasades liked this plan and exchanged his uncle for his brother Scyles. When Sitalces got his brother back, he withdrew his forces, but Octamasades beheaded Scyles on the spot. The Scythians are so conservative, then, that this is how they treat people who adopt foreign ways.

[81] It was impossible for me to find out exactly the size of the Scythian population; I kept receiving conflicting reports of their numbers. Some people said there were huge numbers of Scythians, while others said that there were few of them—few genuine Scythians, that is. However, I was shown something relevant to the issue. Between the Borysthenes and the Hypanis there is a district called Exampaeus, which I mentioned a short while ago, when I was talking about the brackish spring there which flows into the Hypanis and makes its water undrinkable. Now, in Exampaeus there is a bronze vessel which is six times as big as the bowl that Pausanias the son of Cleombrotus set up at the mouth of the Euxine Sea. For the sake of anyone who has not seen Pausanias' bowl, I should explain that the vessel in Scythia easily holds six hundred amphoras of liquid, and that it is six fingers thick. Now, I was told by the local Scythians that this bowl was made out of arrowheads. What happened was that one of their kings, who was called Ariantas, wanted to know how many Scythians there were, so he

issued a proclamation that every Scythian was to bring a single arrowhead, and that anyone who failed to do so would be put to death. A huge quantity of arrowheads were brought, and the king decided to use them to construct a monument for posterity. So he used them to make this bronze vessel, and he chose this place Exampaeus to be its site. That is what I heard about the size of the Scythian population.

[82] The land does not really have remarkable features except for the size and number of its rivers. However, apart from its rivers and the size of its plain, one remarkable phenomenon I should mention is a footprint of Heracles, which they point out imprinted in a rock by the Tyras River. It is just like a normal human footprint, except that it is two cubits long. Having dealt with all this, I will now return to the events I originally set out to narrate.

[83] Darius was getting ready to invade Scythia. He sent out messengers in all directions, ordering some of his subjects to supply him with foot-soldiers, others ships, and others to build a bridge over the Thracian Bosporus. But while these preparations were in progress, his brother Artabanus the son of Hystaspes asked him to cancel his expedition against the Scythians and cited the difficulty of getting at them as the reason for his request. This was sound advice, but he eventually gave up the fruitless task of trying to convince his brother; and when all his preparations were complete, Darius began to move his army out of Susa.

[84] At this point a Persian called Oeobazus, all three of whose sons were in the army, asked Darius whether one of them could be left behind. Darius replied in a friendly fashion, as if the request were reasonable, and said that he would leave all three behind. Oeobazus was overjoyed at the prospect of his sons being released from military service, but Darius ordered those responsible for such things to kill all three of them. So he did leave them there in Susa—with their throats cut.

[85] Darius left Susa and made his way to Chalcedon, to the part of the Bosporus where the bridge had been built. He went on board a ship and sailed from there to the Blue Rocks, as they are known, which according to the Greeks were in the past wandering rocks. There he sat on a promontory and looked out over the Euxine Sea, which is the most remarkable sea in the world, and is a sight well worth seeing. It is 11,100 stades long and, at its widest point, 3,300 stades wide. Its mouth is 4 stades wide, but the straits

which form its mouth† are 120 stades long; these straits are called the Bosporus, and this is where the bridge had been built. At the other end of the Bosporus is the Propontis, which is 500 stades wide and 1,400 stades long; the Propontis joins the Hellespont, which is only 7 stades wide, but 400 long; and then the Hellespont joins the open sea, and this is the Aegean Sea.

[86] The method used to reach these measurements was as follows. In summer, when the days are long, a ship usually sails roughly 70,000 fathoms a day and 60,000 a night. The Euxine Sea is at its longest between its mouth and Phasis, and this journey takes nine days and eight nights to sail, which comes to 1,110,000 fathoms or, converting fathoms into stades, 11,100 stades. Then its widest stretch is from Sindica to Themiscyre, on the River Thermodon, and this is a voyage of three days and two nights, which comes to 330,000 fathoms or 3,300 stades. So this is how I worked out the dimensions of the Euxine Sea we have just been talking about, and also of the Bosporus and the Hellespont; they are as I have stated. The Euxine Sea also has a lake flowing into it which is not much smaller than itself, and which is called Lake Maeetis, or the Mother of the Euxine.

[87] When Darius had finished gazing at the Euxine Sea, he sailed back to the bridge (the chief engineer of which was Mandrocles of Samos). Then he inspected the Bosporus too, and erected two marble pillars by it, on which he inscribed (one in Assyrian, the other in Greek) a list of all the tribes and peoples he had brought with him—and he brought all the ones he ruled. The total number of men—including cavalry contingents, but excluding the fleet—was 700,000, and then there were six hundred ships assembled there too. Later the Byzantians removed these pillars and used them for the altar of Artemis the Saviour in their city, except for one block of stone, which was left by the temple of Dionysus in Byzantium, covered in Assyrian writing. According to my calculations, the place on the Bosporus where Darius built his bridge was half-way between Byzantium and the sanctuary at the mouth of the straits.

[88] Next Darius showed his appreciation of the pontoon bridge by showering the engineer, Mandrocles of Samos, with gifts, tenfold of everything. With a portion of his reward Mandrocles commissioned a painting of the whole bridging of the Bosporus, with King Darius sitting on a dais and his army crossing the bridge. When the

picture had been painted, he dedicated it in the temple of Hera,
and he wrote the following inscription:

> This painting Mandrocles dedicated to Hera, to commemorate
> His bridging of the fish-rich Bosporus with a pontoon;
> His feat won the approval of King Darius,
> And earned a crown for himself and glory for the Samians.

This was how the engineer of the bridge commemorated his
achievement.

[89] So Darius crossed over into Europe. As well as rewarding
Mandrocles, he had also ordered the Ionians to take the navy into
the Euxine Sea and sail to the River Ister, where they were to bridge
the river and wait for him. For the navy was commanded by the
Ionians, Aeolians, and Hellespontine Greeks. So the fleet sailed
between the Blue Rocks and made straight for the Ister. They sailed
up river for two days' journey away from the coast, and then
bridged the neck of the river, where it divides into separate mouths.
Meanwhile Darius crossed over the Bosporus on the pontoon
bridge and made his way through Thrace, until he reached the
springs of the River Tearus, where he pitched camp for three days.

[90] The local inhabitants claim that the waters of the Tearus
have various healing properties, including the ability to cure both
people and horses of scurvy. There are thirty-eight springs there,
all issuing out of a single rock-face. Some of them are cold, but
others are hot. They are equidistant from the town of Heraeum,
which is near Perinthus, and from Apollonia on the Euxine Sea;
in both cases, it takes two days to travel to the springs. The Tearus
joins the Contadesdus, which in turn joins the Agrianes, which
joins the Hebrus, which issues into the sea at the city of Aenus.

[91] Anyway, Darius pitched camp by this river. He liked the
river, so he set up a pillar there too. The inscription on this one
read: 'There is no better or finer water in the world than that of
the springs of the River Tearus. And to them there came, leading
an army against the Scythians, the best and finest man in the world,
Darius the son of Hystaspes, king of Persia and the whole continent.' That was what he had inscribed on the pillar there.

[92] Darius continued on his way, and came next to another
river called the Artescus, which flows through the land of the
Odrysians. Here he had every man in his army pass by a particular spot designated by him and place a single stone there. His men

carried out these orders, and, leaving behind huge mounds of stones, Darius marched on.

[93] Before reaching the Ister, he first conquered the Getae, who believe themselves to be immortal. The Thracians holding Salmydessus and those living inland from Apollonia and Mesambria, who are called the Scyrmiadae and the Nipsaei, surrendered to Darius without a fight. The Getae, however, who are the most courageous and upright Thracian tribe, offered stiff resistance, and were promptly enslaved.

[94] Their belief in their immortality takes the following form. Rather than dying, they believe that on death a person goes to a deity called Salmoxis (or Gebeleïzis, as some of them call him). At five-year intervals, they cast lots to choose someone to send to Salmoxis as their messenger, with instructions as to what favours they want him to grant on that occasion. This is how they send the messenger. They arrange three lances, with men to hold them, and then others grab the hands and feet of the one being sent to Salmoxis and throw him up into the air and on to the points of the lances. If he dies from being impaled, they regard this as a sign that the god will look favourably on their requests. If he does not die, however, they blame this failure on the messenger himself, call him a bad man, and then find someone else to send. They tell him the message they want him to take to Salmoxis while he is still alive. Another thing these Thracians do is fire arrows up into the sky, when thunder and lightning occur, and hurl threats at the god, because they recognize no god other than their own.

[95] I am told by the Greeks who live around the Hellespont and the Euxine Sea that this Salmoxis was a human being—a slave on Samos; in fact, he belonged to Pythagoras the son of Mnesarchus. When he gained his freedom, he amassed a considerable fortune there, and then returned to his native land. Now, Salmoxis had experienced life in Ionia and was familiar with Ionian customs, which are more profound than those of the Thracians, who are an uncivilized and rather naïve people; after all, he had associated with Greeks, and in particular with Pythagoras, who was hardly the weakest intellect in Greece. So they say he furnished a dining-room, where he entertained his most eminent countrymen, and taught them, while he wined and dined them, that he would not die, and neither would they, his guests, and neither would any of their descendants. Instead, he explained, they would go to the

kind of place† where they would live for ever in possession of every blessing. But all the time, while he was holding these meetings and teaching this doctrine, he was building an underground chamber. When this chamber was finished, he disappeared, as far as the Thracians were concerned; he descended into his underground chamber and lived there for three years. The Thracians missed him and mourned him as if he were dead, but after three years he reappeared, and so validated what he had been teaching them. That is what I am told he did.

[96] Personally, I am not entirely convinced by this story about Salmoxis and his underground chamber, but I do not entirely disbelieve it either. However, I do think that Salmoxis lived a long time before Pythagoras. There might have been a human being called Salmoxis, or he might be a local Getan deity—but I am not going to pursue the matter further, beyond saying what I have said about Getan practices. Anyway, once the Getae had been defeated by the Persians, they were conscripted into his army.

[97] Darius and his army eventually reached the Ister, and when all his men had crossed over to the other side, he told the Ionians to dismantle the pontoon bridge and ordered them, and the rest of the men from the ships, to join the main body of the army on their overland march. The Ionians were poised to dismantle the pontoon bridge and do what he said when Coës the son of Erxander, who was the commander of the contingent from Mytilene, made a proposal to Darius, having first checked that he would be willing to receive an opinion from anyone who cared to speak out. 'My lord,' he said, 'you are about to invade a land where agriculture is completely unknown and there are no settlements. I would suggest that you leave this bridge in place, and let the men who built it stay behind to guard it. Then, if we find the Scythians and do what we came for, we have a way out of the country afterwards; alternatively, if we fail to locate them, our return, at least, is ensured. I'm confident that the Scythians will never defeat us in battle, but I still worry in case something untoward happens to us as we roam here and there trying and failing to locate them. Now, it might be argued that I am saying this for myself, so that I can stay behind, but in fact I have come to the conclusion that this plan is the best one for you, my lord, and so I am sharing it with you. As for me, I will not stay behind; I will march with the army.'

Darius thoroughly approved of his idea and he responded by saying, 'When I have got back home safe and sound, my Lesbian friend, come and see me. I want to do you good in return for your good advice.'

[98] He then tied sixty knots on a leather strap and summoned the Ionian rulers to a conference. 'Men of Ionia, I have changed my mind about the bridge,' he announced. 'I withdraw my earlier instructions. What I want you to do instead is take this strap and untie a knot a day, starting from the moment you see me set out for Scythia. If I have not returned by the time the number of days indicated by the knots have passed, you should sail back to your own country. But until then—this is the change of plan—guard the pontoon bridge and do everything you can to keep it intact and safe. If you do so, I will hold you in high favour.' After this speech, Darius rapidly moved matters along.

[99] Thrace projects into the sea beyond Scythia. There is a gulf in Thrace, which is where Scythia begins and also where the Ister issues into the sea, with its mouth facing east. I will now describe the size of the coastline of Scythia from the Ister eastwards. Scythia begins immediately after the Ister† and ends, on its southern coast, at the city of Carcinitis. The hilly land from Carcinitis onwards along the same coast is inhabited by the Taurians up until the peninsula which is known as the Rugged Peninsula, which juts into the sea to the east. The point is that, just like Attica, two sides of Scythia's borders reach the sea, to the south and to the east. The comparison with Attica would be very close if it were some other race, and not Athenians, who inhabited Cape Sunium (which would have to jut out further into the sea) from Thoricus to the village of Anaphlystus, just as Taurians inhabit this part of Scythia. That is what Taurian territory is like—though in saying this, I am comparing something small with something large. However, for the sake of those who have not sailed past this part of the coastline of Attica, I will put it another way. It is as if some other race, and not the Iapygians, were to have taken over the Iapygian headland from the Bay of Brundisium to Tarentum and were to be living there. I mention these two places as examples of a number of other places which Taurian territory resembles.

[100] The land to the north of the Taurians and by the eastern part of the sea is inhabited by Scythians, as is the country west of the Cimmerian Bosporus and west of Lake Maeetis up to the River

Tanaïs, which issues into the head of the lake. Then, starting from
the Ister and moving inland in a northerly direction, Scythia is
bounded first by the Agathyrsians, then by the Neurians, then by
the Cannibals, and finally by the Black Cloaks.

[101] We may take it, then, that Scythia is square, with two of
its sides coming down to the sea, and with its inland perimeter
equal to the length of its coastline. For it is a journey of ten days
from the Ister to the Borysthenes, and from the Borysthenes to Lake
Maeetis takes another ten days; and then it is also a journey of
twenty days inland from the coast up to the Black Cloaks who live
north of Scythia. I calculate a day's journey to be two hundred
stades. Therefore, on its east–west axis Scythia is 4,000 stades long,
and on its north–south axis (that is, tending inland) it is again 4,000
stades long. Anyway, these are the country's dimensions.

[102] The Scythians reflected that they did not have the ability
to repel Darius' army by themselves in a straight fight, so they sent
messengers to their neighbours, whose kings had already convened
a conference and were considering what action to take in the
face of the great army marching against them. At the conference
were the kings of the Taurians, the Agathyrsians, the Neurians, the
Cannibals, the Black Cloaks, the Gelonians, the Budinians, and the
Sauromatae.

[103] Here are some details of the customs and practices of these
tribes. The Taurians sacrifice to the Maiden shipwrecked sailors
and any Greeks they capture at sea. What they do is first consecrate the victim, and then hit him on the head with a club. Some
say that they then push the body off the cliff at the top of which
their shrine is located, but impale the head on a stake; others claim
that the body is buried in the ground, rather than being pushed
off the cliff, although they agree about the head. The Taurians
actually claim that this goddess—the one to whom the sacrifice is
made—is Iphigenia the daughter of Agamemnon. If the Taurians
capture their enemies, each of them cuts off a head and takes it
back to his house, where he sticks it on the end of a long pole and
sets it up to tower high above his house, usually over the chimney.
It is their belief that these heads, hanging there, protect the whole
household. They live off the spoils of war.

[104] The Agathyrsians are the most refined of the tribespeople
we are talking about, and invariably wear golden jewellery. Any
woman is available to any man for sex, to ensure that the men are

all brothers and that they are on amicable and good terms with one another, since they are all relatives. In other respects their way of life is similar to that of the Thracians.

[105] The Neurians use Scythian customs. A generation before Darius' campaign snakes made them completely evacuate the region. In addition to their own country producing large numbers of snakes, even more snakes surged in upon them from the empty lands to the north, until they were forced to leave their own country and began to live with the Budinians. The men may well be magicians, since the Scythians and the Greeks who live in Scythia say that once a year every Neurian becomes a wolf for a few days and then reverts to his original state. Personally I do not believe this, but they make the claim despite its implausibility, and even swear that they are telling the truth.

[106] The Cannibals are the most savage people in the world; they have no sense of right and wrong, and their life is governed by no rules or traditions. They are nomads. The clothes they wear are similar to the ones the Scythians wear, but they speak a distinct language. Theirs is the only one of these tribes to eat human flesh.

[107] The Black Cloaks all wear black clothing, which is how they got their name. Their way of life is Scythian.

[108] The Budinians are a large and populous tribe, with piercing grey eyes and bright red hair. There is a town in their country called Gelonus, which is made out of wood. Each side of its high outer wall is thirty stades long, made entirely of wood, and wood has been used for all its houses and shrines too. They have sanctuaries there which are dedicated to the Greek gods and are equipped in the Greek manner with statues, altars and buildings of wood; and every third year they celebrate a festival to Dionysus and become possessed by the god. This is because the inhabitants of Gelonus were originally Greeks from the trading-centres, who moved away from there and settled among the Budinians. Their language is a mixture of Scythian and Greek.

[109] The Budinians, however, differ from the Gelonians in both language and lifestyle. The Budinians, who are nomadic, are the indigenous inhabitants of the country, and they are the only race there to eat lice, whereas the Gelonians are farmers, grain-eaters, and gardeners; moreover, the two sets of people are altogether dissimilar in appearance and colouring. However, the Budinians as well as the Gelonians are incorrectly called Gelonians by the

Greeks. The land is entirely covered with forests of every conceivable species of tree. In the largest forest, there is a large, wide lake,
surrounded by a reedy marsh. They capture otters and beavers in
this lake, and also a square-faced creature whose skin they sew as
trimming on to their jackets, and whose testicles are good for
healing diseases of the womb.

[110] Here is a story about the Sauromatae. It is set during the
war between the Greeks and the Amazons, for whom the Scythian
name is Oeorpata, which, translated into Greek, means 'killers of
men', because *oior* is 'man' in Scythian, and *pata* means 'to kill'.
So the story goes that after their victory over the Amazons at the
battle of Thermodon, the Greeks sailed away in three ships, taking
with them all the Amazons they had been able to capture alive.
When they were out at sea, the women set upon the men and killed
them, but they did not know anything about ships or how to use
the rudders, sails, or oars; consequently, having done away with
the men, they began to drift at the mercy of the waves and winds.
They fetched up in Lake Maeetis, at the place called Cremni, which
is in country inhabited by the free Scythians. The Amazons went
ashore there and made their way to inhabited territory. The first
thing they came across was a herd of horses, which they promptly
seized, and then they began to ride about on these horses robbing
the Scythians of their property.

[111] The Scythians could not understand what was going on.
They could not make out the newcomers' nationality from
their unfamiliar language and clothing; in short, they were puzzled
as to where they had come from. Taking them to be young men,
however, they fought against them. After the battle, the Scythians
were left in possession of the corpses, and so they realized that
they were women. They discussed what to do, and came to the conclusion that they should not make any further attempts at all to
kill the women. Instead they decided to send a band of their
youngest men to the women, approximately the same number of
men as there were women. These young men were to pitch camp
near where the women were, and do exactly what the Amazons
did. If the women chased them, they were to run away without
putting up a fight, and when the women stopped chasing them,
they were to return and set up camp near by again. The point of
the Scythians' plan was that they wanted to have children by the
women.

[112] So the detachment of young men carried out their orders. When the Amazons realized that they had not come to harm them, they let them be, and day by day the distance between the two camps grew less. Just like the Amazons, the young men had nothing except their weapons and their horses; they lived in exactly the same way as the women, by hunting and raiding.

[113] In the middle of every day the Amazons used to split up into ones or twos and go some way apart from one another in order to relieve themselves. When the Scythians noticed this, they did the same thing. One of them approached one of the women who was all alone, and the Amazon did not repulse him, but let him have intercourse with her. She could not speak to him, because they did not understand each other, but she used gestures to tell him to return the next day to the same place and to bring someone else with him; she made it clear to him that there should be two of them, and that she would bring another woman with her too. The young man returned to his camp and told the others the news. He kept the appointment the next day, taking someone else along too, and found another Amazon there as well, waiting for them. When the other young men found out, they joined in and tamed the remaining Amazons.

[114] After that the two sides joined forces and lived together, forming couples consisting of a Scythian man and the Amazon with whom he had first had sex. The men found the women's language impossible to learn, but the women managed the men's language. When they were in a position to understand one another, the men said to the Amazons: 'We have parents and property back home. So let's stop living like this from now on; let's return to the rest of our people and live with them. We will have you and no other women as our wives.'

The women, however, replied as follows: 'We would find it impossible to live with your women, because our practices are completely different from theirs. We haven't learnt women's work. We shoot arrows, wield javelins, ride horses—things which your women never have anything to do with. They just stay in their wagons and do women's work; they never go out hunting or anywhere else either. We would find it impossible to get along with them. No, if you want us to be your wives, and to appear really fair, you should go to your parents and get your share of your property, and then when you come back we can form our own community.'

[115] The young men thought this was a good idea and went and put it into practice. When they had obtained their due share of their property they returned to the Amazons, and the women said, 'We're very anxious about having to live here. It's not just that we've separated you from your parents, but also that we've done a lot of damage to this country of yours. Since you want us to be your wives, let's move together away from here and find somewhere to live on the other side of the Tanaïs River.' The young men were convinced by this plan as well.

[116] So they crossed the River Tanaïs and travelled east for three days away from the river, and then they turned north and travelled for three more days away from Lake Maeetis. In the end they came to the country where they now live and settled there. And ever since then the Sauromatian women have kept to their original way of life: they go out hunting on horseback with or without their husbands, they go to war, and they wear the same clothes as the men do.

[117] The Sauromatae speak Scythian, but ungrammatically, as they always have done, because the Amazons never learnt it properly. One of their marriage customs is that no young woman may marry until she has killed a male enemy. Inability to fulfil this condition means that some of them die of old age without being married.

[118] Anyway, the rulers of all the tribes I have mentioned were in a conference when the Scythian messengers arrived. The messengers told them that the Persian king, who was already master of the whole of the other continent, had built a bridge across the neck of the Bosporus by which he had crossed over into their continent, and was now demonstrating his desire to gain control of everything there too, first by having defeated the Thracians, and then by building a bridge across the Ister. 'You absolutely must not stand idly by and watch us being destroyed,' they went on. 'We should form a common plan and resist the invasion together. Don't you agree? Otherwise we Scythians will be forced either to evacuate our country or, if we stay, to make some kind of deal with the Persians. For what would become of us if you refuse to support us? And that won't make it any easier for you either, because you are the Persian's target just as much as we are, and once he has defeated us he is not going simply to ignore you. We have good evidence to demonstrate the truth of what we're saying. If we were the only objects of Darius' warlike intentions—if all he wanted to do was

make us pay for our time as masters of his country—he should have ignored everyone else and just invaded *our* territory. That way he would have made it clear that he was marching against the Scythians and no one else. But as it is, no sooner has he entered this continent of ours than he sets about subjugating everyone in his path. He has made himself the master of the whole of Thrace, including our neighbours, the Getae.'

[119] After hearing the messengers' proposal, the kings who had come from the various tribes tried to decide what to do, but their views were divided. The Gelonian, Budinian, and Sauromatian kings unanimously promised to support the Scythians, but the kings of the Agathyrsians, the Neurians, the Cannibals, the Black Cloaks, and the Taurians made the following response to the Scythians: 'It was you who started the war by your unjust aggression against the Persians. If you hadn't done that, we would consider this request of yours to be fair; we would agree with your proposal and join in any action you took. But in fact it was you who invaded Persia and ruled over the inhabitants for as long as the god permitted it; we had nothing to do with it. And now that the Persians have been stirred by the same god into action, they are paying you back. We did nothing wrong to them then and we are not now going to be the first to do wrong either. However, if Darius invades our land as well and initiates hostilities against us, we will punish him.† But until this is what we see, we will stay within our own borders. We are not convinced that the Persians have come to attack us; we think they are only after those who are guilty of past wrongdoing.'

[120] In response to this retort, seeing that these allies, at any rate, would not join them, the Scythians decided against straight fighting and open warfare, and in favour of retreat. The plan was that as they rode back in retreat they would fill in any wells and springs they passed, and destroy any vegetation they found growing in the ground. They also decided to divide their forces into two. One detachment, which was ruled by Scopasis, would be reinforced by the Sauromatae, and if Darius turned in their direction, they were to pull back along a route that would take them past Lake Maeetis and straight towards the Tanaïs River; however, if Darius withdrew, they were to pursue him and attack him. So this was one of the Royal Scythians' detachments, and their job was to take the route just mentioned. The other two divisions of the Royal Scythians—a large one ruled by Idanthyrsus and another one ruled

by Taxacis—were to combine forces and, reinforced by the Gelonians and the Budinians, were also to retreat, keeping one day's
march ahead of the Persians, and to carry out the plan as they retreated. They were first to make straight for the territories of those
who had refused them military support, so as to get them involved
in the fighting as well (the idea being to force them to fight the
Persians, since they were not prepared to enter the war of their own
free will). Then they were to turn back towards their own country
and attack the Persians, if that was the plan they came up with.

[121] Having come to this decision, the Scythians went out to
meet Darius' army, and sent their best horsemen ahead of the main
body of their forces as an advance guard. The wagons in which all
their women and children lived were sent off with orders to keep
heading north, and all their livestock was sent with the wagons,
except for whatever they needed for their own provisions.

[122] So off went their wagons and flocks. Meanwhile, the
Scythian advance guard found the Persians about three days'
journey away from the Ister. They then camped a day's journey in
front of the Persians and set about destroying the vegetation. When
the Persians saw that Scythian horsemen had appeared, they
tried to get at them, following the trail the constantly retreating
Scythians led them down. Now, this route took the Persians straight
towards the first of the Scythian divisions, so next they chased the
retreating horsemen east, in the direction of the Tanaïs. When the
horsemen crossed the river, the Persians crossed over after them,
passed through Sauromatian country and eventually reached
Budinian territory.

[123] The Persians' passage through Scythian and Sauromatian
lands had provided them with no opportunities to damage anything, because the land was bare. When they came to Budinian
territory, however, they found the wooden-walled town, which
had been abandoned and evacuated by the Budinians, and they set
fire to it. Then they continued along the trail of the retreating
Scythians, until they left Budinian land behind them and reached
uninhabited territory. This seven-day stretch of empty land, completely uninhabited by human beings, lies to the north of Budinian
territory, and beyond it live the Thyssagetae. Four sizeable rivers
(called the Lycus, Oärus, Tanaïs, and Syrgis) rise in their country
and flow through the land of the Maeetians until they issue into
Lake Maeetis.

[124] When Darius came to this empty region, he stopped chasing the Scythians and had his men pitch camp on the banks of the Oärus. Then he built eight large forts spaced at equal intervals about sixty stades apart from one another, which have survived, though as ruins, right up to my day. While he was busy with these projects, the Scythians he had been pursuing circled back to Scythia by a northern route. They disappeared completely, but Darius believed that they were escaping west back to Scythia, because he was sure that they were all the Scythians there were, and so when he had no further sightings of them, he left his forts half finished and he too turned west.

[125] After a forced march he arrived back in Scythia and met up with the combined force of the other two Scythian detachments, who then proceeded to keep a day's journey in front of him. Because he did not give up his pursuit, the Scythians retreated, in accordance with their plan, into the territory of those who had refused them military support, starting with the Black Cloaks. The arrival of the Scythians and the Persians in their country threw the Black Cloaks into confusion, and then the Scythians led the Persians into the Cannibals' country, creating turmoil there too, and then on to Neurian territory, and finally towards the Agathyrsians. Everywhere they went, they left chaos and confusion in their wake. The Agathyrsians, however, had seen how their neighbours had been forced into flight and thrown into disarray by the Scythians, so before the Scythians reached them they sent them a herald. Through the herald they told the Scythians not to set foot over their borders, and warned them that if they tried to invade they would have to fight them first. Having issued this warning, the Agathyrsians set out to defend their borders, with the intention of repelling the invaders. (The Black Cloaks, Cannibals, and Neurians, however, had not offered any resistance to the joint invasion of the Persians and Scythians; they forgot their earlier threats and fled in disarray ever further northwards into the uninhabited region.) In the face of the Agathyrsians' stand, the Scythians stopped trying to enter their territory, and led the Persians out of Neurian territory and back to Scythia.

[126] The whole business was dragging on endlessly, so Darius sent a rider to King Idanthyrsus of Scythia and said: 'What is this extraordinary behaviour? Why do you keep on running away, when you could do something different? For instance, if you think

you have the ability to resist my power, then stop this aimless wandering, stay in one place and fight. But if you recognize that you are weaker than me, you can still stop running: come and discuss terms with me instead, acknowledging me as your master with gifts of earth and water.'

[127] Idanthyrsus, king of the Scythians, replied as follows: 'Persian, this is how things stand with me: I have never fled from any man in fear—I never have in the past and that is not what is happening now. What I am doing now is not far removed from my usual way of life during peacetime. I'm not going to fight you, and I'll tell you why. If we had towns we might worry about the possibility of them being captured, and if we had farmland we might worry about it being laid to waste, and then we might engage you in battle quite quickly; but we don't have either. If you feel you have to get to fighting soon, there are our ancestral burial grounds. Go on, find them and try to ruin them, and then you'll see whether or not we will fight. But until then, unless it seems like a good idea, we won't join battle with you. I have no more to say on the subject of fighting. As for my masters, the only ones I recognize are Zeus, who is my ancestor, and Hestia, the queen of the Scythians. You won't be getting gifts of earth and water from me, but only what you deserve; as for this "master" business, you'll suffer for it.'

[128] So his messenger went to deliver this message to Darius. The mention of slavery made the Scythian kings furious. They sent the joint Scythian–Sauromatian division (the one commanded by Scopasis) to the Ionians—the ones who were guarding the bridge over the Ister—with instructions to hold discussions with them, and meanwhile those of them who were to stay in Scythia decided to stop leading the Persians all over the place, but to attack them whenever they were foraging for food. So they used to watch for when Darius' men were gathering supplies of food and carry out their scheme. The Scythian horsemen would always rout the enemy cavalry, and the Persian horsemen would retreat until they met up with their infantry, who would come to their assistance. At this point the Scythians used to turn back, because they were afraid of the Persian infantry, despite the fact that they had hurled themselves at the Persian cavalry. Even at night, the Scythians kept up this kind of assault.

[129] There was something I should mention—something quite remarkable—which helped the Persians and hindered the Scythians

during their attacks on Darius' positions. This was the sound of the donkeys and the sight of the mules. As I explained earlier, Scythia produces no donkeys or mules; in the whole country there is not a single donkey or mule, because it is too cold. So the donkeys' braying threw the Scythian cavalry into confusion. Often the Scythians would be in the middle of charging at the Persians when their horses would hear the donkeys braying and would turn back in disarray, with their ears pricked in astonishment at the sounds they were hearing and sights they were seeing for the first time. So this was something that gave the Persians a slight military advantage.

[130] When the Scythians realized that they had the Persians worried, they came up with a way of prolonging their stay in Scythia, which would mean that eventually they would get into serious difficulties as a result of shortage of supplies. What they used to do was leave some of their livestock behind (and the herdsmen too), while they themselves rode off elsewhere. The Persians would come and take the animals, and the incident would boost their morale.

[131] After this had happened a number of times, things were starting to go very badly for Darius. The Scythian kings realized this and sent a herald with gifts for him—a bird, a mouse, a frog, and five arrows. The Persians asked the man who had brought the gifts what the kings meant by them, but he said that all he was supposed to do was hand over the gifts and leave straight away—he had received no further instructions. However, he told the Persians that if they were clever they would work out what the gifts meant. So the Persians talked the matter over among themselves.

[132] Darius' opinion was that the Scythians were giving him earth and water and tokens of their surrender. His reasoning was as follows: a mouse is born in the ground and eats the same food as human beings, a frog lives in water, a bird closely resembles a horse, and they gave arrows as symbols of their own military might. This was the view that Darius expressed, but Gobryas (who was one of the seven who had overthrown the Magus) challenged this view of Darius' and came up with an alternative. This is how he explained the message of the gifts: 'Listen, men of Persia: if you don't become birds and fly up into the sky, or mice and burrow into the ground, or frogs and jump into the lakes, you'll never return home, because you'll be shot down by these arrows.'

[133] So the Persians were trying to work out what the gifts meant. Meanwhile, the first Scythian division—the one which had been detailed originally to retreat† past Lake Maeetis, but subsequently to talk with the Ionians on the Ister—reached the bridge. Once they were there, they said, 'Men of Ionia, the gift we have come to bring you is freedom from slavery, if you are prepared to do as we suggest. Our information is that your orders from Darius were to guard the bridge only for sixty days, after which, if he still hadn't appeared, you were to go back home. All you have to do, then, to avoid his censure, is wait the prescribed number of days and then leave; if you do that, we won't blame you either.' Having gained the Ionians' promise to do as they suggested, the Scythians lost no time in returning to their country.

[134] Once Darius had the gifts, the Scythians who had stayed in Scythia drew up their infantry and cavalry and prepared to attack the Persians. They were ready and waiting in their ranks when a hare ran across the open space between the two sides, and one after another all the Scythians spotted it and gave chase. Seeing the Scythians in disarray and hearing their cries, Darius asked why his opponents were in such a state of commotion. When he heard that they were chasing a hare, he told his confidants, 'These Scythians certainly hold us in contempt. I now think that Gobryas' interpretation of their gifts was right, and what we need is a good plan for getting safely back home.'

'My lord,' Gobryas replied, 'I had a pretty fair idea of how hard it would be to get at the Scythians just from hearing about them, but since we've been here I have come to know a lot more, through watching them toy with us. So I now think we should light our camp-fires at nightfall, as we usually do, tether all our donkeys—and then deceive those of our troops who are least able to endure hardship and slip away. Otherwise it will be too late: either the Scythians will head straight for the Ister and destroy the bridge, or the Ionians will decide on a course of action which will finish us off.'

[135] That was Gobryas' proposal, and after nightfall Darius acted on it. He tethered all the donkeys and left behind in the camp those of his men who were sick and those whose loss would have the least impact. He left the donkeys because he wanted them to bray, and he left the weaker elements among his troops because of their weakness, but the reason he actually gave them was that he

and the unimpaired elements of his army were going to launch an attack against the Scythians, and that in the mean time they were to guard the camp. This was the explanation Darius gave the men he was leaving behind, and then he lit the fires and raced away as quickly as possible towards the Ister. As for the donkeys, on finding themselves abandoned by the bulk of the army they brayed far more than normal, and when the Scythians heard them they were convinced that the Persians were where they expected them to be.

[136] At daybreak those who had been left behind realized that they had been betrayed by Darius, so they threw themselves on the Scythians' mercy and explained the situation. When the Scythians heard what they had to say, they lost no time in combining into a single force not only the two detachments which were already there, but also the one which was reinforced by the Sauromatae, and the Budinians and the Gelonians as well; then they immediately set out for the Ister after the Persians. Now, the Persian army consisted mainly of foot-soldiers and did not know the way, since there were no ready-made roads, whereas the Scythians were on horseback and knew the shortest routes. Consequently the Scythians reached the bridge long before the Persians. The two armies had missed each other on the way, and when the Scythians realized that the Persians had not yet arrived, they addressed the Ionians (who were on board their ships) as follows: 'Your sixty days are up, Ionians, so it's wrong of you to be here still. Previously it was fear that kept you here, but if you dismantle the bridge now, you can leave straight away without any worries, with the gods and the Scythians to thank for your freedom. As for your former master, we will inflict such a defeat on him that he will never again make war on anyone.'

[137] In response, the Ionian leaders talked things over among themselves. Miltiades of Athens, the tyrant of the Hellespontine Chersonese, who was one of the military commanders, was of the opinion that they should do as the Scythians were suggesting and free Ionia from Persian rule. Histiaeus of Miletus, however, took the opposite line; he argued that every one of them owed his position as tyrant of his community to Darius, and that if Darius were to fall, he would not be able to rule Miletus and none of them would remain in power either, because there was not one of their communities which would not prefer democracy to tyranny. Histiaeus' argument immediately won everyone at the meeting over

to his point of view, although they had previously been in favour of Miltiades' proposal.

[138] All the people who voted at this meeting were highly valued by the Persian king. Present at the meeting were the Hellespontine tyrants Daphnis of Abydus, Hippoclus of Lampsacus, Herophantus of Parium, Metrodorus of Proconnesus, Aristagoras of Cyzicus, and Ariston of Byzantium. As well as these Hellespontine tyrants, there were also some from Ionia: Strattis of Chios, Aeaces of Samos, Laodamas of Phocaea, and Histiaeus of Miletus, who came up with the counter-proposal to Miltiades'. The only noteworthy Aeolian present was Aristagoras of Cyme.

[139] So they voted in favour of Histiaeus' proposal, and also decided to make their actions match their words by dismantling as much of the Scythian side of the bridge as could be reached by an arrow shot from the bank. They did this in order to give the Scythians the impression that they were helping when they were in fact not helping one bit, and also to forestall any attempt on the part of the Scythians to force their way across the bridge. They also decided to tell the Scythians, while they were dismantling the Scythian side of the bridge, that they would go on to do everything that the Scythians wanted them to do. So in addition to approving Histiaeus' proposal, they also made these plans. Then they chose Histiaeus to act as their representative and respond to the Scythians' suggestion. 'Men of Scythia,' he said, 'you have come here with valuable information, and thanks to your speed you have arrived just in time. Your suggestions are progressing well in our hands; we are serving you properly. As you can see, we are dismantling the bridge, and our desire for freedom will ensure our continued commitment to your cause. But while we are dismantling the bridge, you should seize the opportunity to track down the Persians and, for our sakes as well as yours, make them pay the penalty they deserve.'

[140] The Scythians once again believed that the Ionians were telling the truth. They turned back inland and began to look for the Persians, but they completely failed to find any traces of their route. Actually, it was the Scythians' own destruction of grassland on which horses might have fed, and their filling in of pools, which was responsible for this lack of success. If they had not done this, tracking down the Persians whenever they wanted would have been straightforward. In fact, however, this apparently good idea was

the cause of their failure. The route the Scythians followed in their hunt for the enemy took them through a part of Scythia where there were still pools to be found, and fodder for the horses as well, because they assumed that the Persians too would retreat along a route with these resources. But the Persians kept to the course they had used before. This did not make their journey easy, but they did at last reach the bridge—only to arrive at night and find the bridge dismantled, which made them absolutely terrified in case the Ionians had deserted them.

[141] However, one of Darius' men was an Egyptian who had the loudest voice in the world. On Darius' orders, he stood at the edge of the Ister and shouted out for Histiaeus of Miletus. Histiaeus heard him the first time he called, and, as well as rebuilding the bridge, he got the whole fleet to start ferrying the army over the river.

[142] This is how the Persians managed to escape, and how the Scythians failed once again to locate the Persian army. The Scythian opinion of Ionians is that they make the worst and most cowardly free people in the world, but that if they were to think of them as slaves, they would have to say that no master could hope to find more loyal and submissive captives. That is the kind of insult Scythians have hurled at Ionians.

[143] Darius next marched through Thrace and came to Sestus on the Chersonese, where he took ship for Asia, leaving a Persian called Megabazus in command of his troops in Europe. Something Darius once said in front of some other Persians was hugely complimentary to Megabazus. He was about to eat some pomegranates, and he had just opened the first of them when his brother Artabanus asked him what he would like to have as many of as there are seeds in a pomegranate. Darius replied that he would rather have that many men like Megabazus than be master of Greece. That was the compliment he paid him in front of some Persians once, and at the time in question he left him in command of his army of eighty thousand men.

[144] Something Megabazus said has never been forgotten by the people of the Hellespont, and it never will. He happened to be in Byzantium and he found out that settlers had arrived in Chalcedon seventeen years before the Byzantine settlers had come. 'In that case,' he said, 'the Chalcedonians must have been blind for all that time, because otherwise they wouldn't have chosen to settle

in a worse place when a more attractive one was available.'
Anyway, Megabazus was left behind on the Hellespont on the occasion in question, and he set about subjugating any settlements
which were not collaborating with the Persians.

[145] While Megabazus was engaged in this, another huge military expedition took place, this time against Libya. I will explain
the reason for this expedition later, but first there are other matters
to go through. After the descendants of the Argonauts were driven
out of Lemnos by a force of Pelasgians—the same Pelasgians who
had abducted the Athenian women from Brauron—they sailed
from Lemnos to Lacedaemon, where they established themselves
on Mount Taygetus and lit a fire. The Lacedaemonian response to
their arrival was to send a messenger to find out who they were
and where they were from. In answer to the messenger's questions
they told him that they were Minyans and were descended from
the heroes who had sailed on the *Argo*, who had put in at Lemnos
and founded their line. The Lacedaemonians listened to the report
about the family history of the Minyans and then sent another messenger, this time to ask what the reason was for their visit to
Lacedaemon and why they had lit a fire. They said that they had
come because they had been expelled by the Pelasgians and so had
turned to the land of their fathers; they said that it was only fair
for them to do so, and that they wanted to live there with them,
sharing their rights and privileges and having land allocated to
them. The Lacedaemonians, influenced especially by the fact that
the Tyndaridae had sailed on the *Argo*, were pleased to accept the
Minyans on their chosen terms. So they took the Minyans in, gave
them some land, and divided them up into tribes. The Minyans
immediately set about marrying local women and arranging marriages between Lacedaemonians and the women they had brought
from Lemnos.

[146] Only a short while later, however, the Minyans started to
behave aggressively, demanding a share in the kingship and doing
wrong in various other ways as well. The Lacedaemonians decided
to kill them, so they arrested them and threw them into prison.
Now, when the Lacedaemonians carry out an execution, they do
so at night, never during the daytime. Just when they were due to
kill them, then, the wives of the Minyans, who were local women,
the daughters of eminent Spartiates, asked permission to enter the
prison and talk to their husbands in private. The Lacedaemonians

let them in, never suspecting them of any underhand behaviour. But when they were inside the prison, they swapped clothes with their husbands. So the Minyans walked out of prison dressed in women's clothing, and were taken to be women. After escaping in this way they re-established their base on Mount Taygetus.

[147] Now, it so happened that at the same time as all this was going on preparations were being made for a colonizing expedition from Lacedaemon, under the leadership of Theras the son of Autesion (whose own father was Tisamenus the son of Thersander and grandson of Polynices). Despite being a Cadmean by descent, Theras had once been the regent of Sparta, since he was the maternal uncle of Eurysthenes and Procles, the sons of Aristodamus, and had ruled while they were still under age. When his nephews grew up and took over the kingdom, the fact that Theras had tasted power made him resent being ruled by others, so he said that he would not stay in Lacedaemon, but would return to his relatives on the island which is now called Thera, but which was previously known as Calliste and was inhabited by descendants of a Phoenician called Membliaraus the son of Poeciles. What happened was that Cadmus the son of Agenor put in at the island which is nowadays known as Thera during his search for Europa, and for some reason—perhaps because he liked the place—he decided to leave a party of Phoenicians on the island, including Membliaraus, one of his own kinsmen. These Phoenicians had been living on Calliste for eight generations when Theras went there from Lacedaemon.

[148] So these were the people to whom Theras was preparing to travel, along with a body of emigrants drawn from the Lacedaemonian tribes, with the intention of claiming kinship with them and sharing the island with them, not of dispossessing them. When the Minyans broke out of prison and established a base on Mount Taygetus, and the Lacedaemonians made up their minds to kill them, Theras interceded, in order to avoid bloodshed, and promised to take them with him out of the country. The Lacedaemonians agreed to his plan, and he took three triaconters and sailed away to the descendants of Membliaraus. He only took a few Minyans with him, however, not the whole lot, because most of them made their way to the Paroreatae and the Caucones and drove them out of their territories. Then they divided themselves into six groups and founded the following towns there: Lepreum, Macistus, Phrixae, Pyrgus, Epium, and Nudium. In my day, most

of these towns were sacked by the Eleans. Meanwhile, Calliste was named Thera after the leader of this band of emigrants.

[149] Theras' son, however, refused to accompany his father, and so Theras said that he would leave him 'as a sheep among wolves'. As a result of this quip, the young man was nicknamed Oeolycus, and somehow he became stuck with this name rather than his original one. Oeolycus was the father of Aegeus, who gave his name to the Aegeidae, an important clan in Sparta. Children born to the men of this clan were always dying young, so on the advice of an oracle they built a sanctuary dedicated to the Avenging Spirits of Laius and Oedipus, and after this they survived. The same thing also happened on Thera to the descendants of those who had built the original sanctuary.†

[150] So far, the Lacedaemonian and the Theran accounts agree, but for subsequent events we have to rely on the Therans alone. This is what they say happened. Grinnus the son of Aesanius, who was a descendant of Theras and king of the island of Thera, arrived in Delphi with a hecatomb. He was accompanied by a number of ordinary citizens, including a descendant of one of the Minyans called Euphemus, whose name was Battus the son of Polymnestus. King Grinnus of Thera was consulting the oracle on other matters when the oracle declared that he would found a community in Libya. 'Lord,' he replied, 'I am already too old and weighed down to take off like that. Please give the job to one of these younger men here.' As he was saying this, he waved in the direction of Battus. That was all that happened then, and later, after their return home, they took no account of the oracle. They did not know where Libya was, and they were not so foolhardy as to send a colonizing expedition off to some unknown destination.

[151] For the next seven years, however, no rain fell on Thera, and all their trees, with a single exception, withered. The islanders consulted the oracle, and the Pythia reminded them that they were supposed to colonize Libya. Since they could not find a cure for their troubles, they sent messengers to Crete to find out if any of their countrymen or resident aliens had ever gone to Libya. These agents of theirs went from place to place on Crete and eventually visited a town called Itanus too, where they met a man called Corobius, who made a living from collecting murexes, and he told them that he had once been driven off course by winds and had ended up on the Libyan island of Platea. They paid him to come back with them to Thera, and an initial small reconnoitring party

set out from Thera. With Corobius' guidance they found the island
he had mentioned, Platea, and they left him there with enough supplies to last him a certain number of months, while they themselves
sailed back to Thera as quickly as possible to tell the Therans about
the island.

[152] However, they were away longer than they had agreed
with Corobius, and he completely ran out of food. But then a
Samian ship, captained by Colaeus, was blown off course on its
way to Egypt and fetched up at Platea. Corobius told the Samians
the whole story and they left him enough food for a year. Then
they put to sea from the island with the intention of sailing to
Egypt, but they were again driven off course by an adverse east
wind. The wind was relentless and drove them through the Pillars
of Heracles until, providentially, they reached Tartessus. This
trading-centre was virgin territory at the time, and consequently
they came home with the biggest profit any Greek trader we have
reliable information about has ever made from his cargo—apart
from Sostratus of Aegina, the son of Laodamas, of course. No one
can rival him, but the Samians withdrew six talents—a tenth of
their profit—and commissioned a bronze vessel, in the style of an
Argive bowl. There were protruding griffin heads around it; they
dedicated the bowl in the temple of Hera, and supported it on a
group of three kneeling bronze figures, each seven cubits high.
Anyway, the help the Samians gave Corobius proved to be the start
of a strong bond of friendship between them and the Cyreneans
and Therans.

[153] After they had left Corobius on the island, the reconnoitring party of Therans returned to Thera and announced that
they had founded a settlement on an island off Libya. The Therans
resolved to send one in every two brothers (which one went was
to be decided by lot), to draw the men who went from every one
of their seven districts, and to send Battus as the expedition leader
and king of the future colony. And so they sent two penteconters
to Platea.

[154] That is the Theran version of events. Now, although the
Cyrenean and Theran versions are in agreement about subsequent
events, they are quite different where Battus is concerned. What the
Cyreneans say about Battus is as follows. There once was a man
called Etearchus, who was the king of the Cretan town Oäxus.
Etearchus had a daughter called Phronime, but her mother had

died, so he married another woman to look after her. She came along and took it upon herself to be a true stepmother to Phronime, by making her life a misery and constantly intriguing against her. Eventually she accused her of promiscuity and convinced her husband that she was telling the truth. Since he believed his wife, he came up with a wicked plan for his daughter. He befriended a Theran trader called Themison, who lived in Oäxus, and made him swear that he would perform any service he asked him. Themison swore that he would, and then Etearchus took him to his daughter. He handed her over to Themison and told him to take her out to sea and drown her. Themison was so furious about being tricked into swearing an oath that he broke off his guest-friendship with Etearchus. He did take the girl and sail off, but when he was out in the open sea, he fulfilled his oath to Etearchus by tying ropes around the girl and lowering her into the water, but then he pulled her back on board and sailed to Thera.

[155] On Thera, an eminent Theran called Polymnestus acquired Phronime and kept her as his concubine. After a while she gave birth to a son who had a speech impediment and a lisp, and so he was given the name Battus, the stammerer. At any rate, that is what both the Therans and the Cyreneans say, but I think he was originally called something else and then changed his name to Battus when he came to Libya. He would have been led to do so, first, because of the oracle he received in Delphi, and, second, because of the prestige he got by taking on the name. The Libyans call a king *battos*, and that, I think, is why in her prediction the Pythia called him by that name: she was using the Libyan word, because she knew that he was going to be a king in Libya. When he became a man he went to Delphi to ask what could be done about his speech. However, the response he got to his question from the Pythia was as follows:

> Battus, you came for a voice, but the Lord Phoebus Apollo has a
>   mission for you:
> You are to go to sheep-breeding Libya and found a colony there.

This is as if she had said, in Greek: 'King, you came for a voice.' Anyway, he replied, 'Lord, I came to consult you about my speech, but in response you are telling me to colonize Libya, which is an impossible task. Where are my resources? Where are my men?' However, this plea of his did not win a different response. He left the Pythia while she was repeating the same prediction as before, and returned to Thera.

[156] Later, things started to go badly for him personally and for Thera in general. The Therans were unaware of the reason for this, so they sent emissaries to Delphi to ask about the problems that were afflicting them. The Pythia replied that things would improve for them if they helped Battus found Cyrene in Libya. They subsequently fitted Battus out with two penteconters and sent him off. The explorers sailed to Libya, but they did not know what else to do, so they left and returned to Thera. The Therans refused to let them land, however; they shot at them every time their boats got close to shore and told them to sail back to Libya. Since they had no choice in the matter, they returned and founded a settlement on an island off Libya; the name of the island, as already stated, was Platea. The island is said to be the same size as the city of Cyrene is nowadays.

[157] They lived on this island for two years, but nothing went right for them, so they left one of their number there and all the rest of them sailed away to Delphi. When they got there, they said that they had been living in Libya and things still had not improved for them, and asked for the oracle's advice. The Pythia replied as follows:

> I am most impressed with your knowledge, if you know
>   sheep-breeding Libya
> Better than I, when you have not been there and I have.

So Battus and his men sailed back again, because Apollo was not going to release them from founding a colony until they reached Libya itself. They got back to the island, picked up the man they had left behind, and founded a settlement actually in Libya itself, directly opposite the island in a place called Aziris, which is skirted by beautiful valleys, and has a river flowing past it.

[158] They lived in Aziris for six years, but in the seventh year some Libyans pretended† that there was a better place they could take them to and persuaded them to leave. Having got them to move, the Libyans led them west of Aziris, and carefully arranged the timing of the journey so that it would be night-time when they took the Greeks through a particularly beautiful spot—a place called Irasa—and too dark for the Greeks to see it as they passed. They brought them to the place called Apollo's Spring and said,

'This is a good place for you Greeks to live, because a hole has been made in the sky here.'

[159] Battus, the founder of the colony, ruled for forty years, and his son Arcesilaus for sixteen years. In their lifetimes the Cyrenean population remained at pretty much the level it had been when they first set out to colonize Libya. During the reign of their third king, however, who was called Battus the Prosperous, the Cyreneans invited settlers to come and share their land, so the Pythia urged all the Greek states to sail and help the Cyreneans in their project of colonizing Libya. The declaration the Pythia made was as follows:

> There is land on offer in lovely Libya;
> Anyone who arrives too late will surely regret it.

Soon a considerable mass of people gathered in Cyrene and took over plots of the surrounding land. The local Libyans and their king, whose name was Adicran, resented being robbed of their land and pushed around by the settlers; a message was sent to Egypt and the Libyans put themselves under the protection of the Egyptian king Apries. He mobilized a huge army of his men and sent it to assault Cyrene. However, the Cyreneans came out to meet them at Irasa; battle was joined near a spring called Thestes, and the Cyreneans were victorious. The Egyptians, who had never come across Greeks before, underestimated them and were so thoroughly annihilated that hardly any of them found their way back to Egypt. Looking for someone to blame for this disaster, the Egyptians added it to their list of grievances against Apries and rose up against him.

[160] Battus was succeeded by his son, Arcesilaus; the first thing Arcesilaus did on becoming king was fall out with his brothers. Eventually they left and went to another part of Libya where they founded, from their own resources, a city called Barca (that was its name then, and still is now). While they were still in the process of settling there, they persuaded the Libyans to rebel against the Cyreneans. Later, then, Arcesilaus launched a strike against these Libyans, who had taken his brothers in and then revolted. The Libyans fled in fear to the eastern Libyans, but Arcesilaus followed them all the way to Leucon, where the Libyans decided to attack him. Battle was joined and the Libyans thoroughly defeated the Cyrenean forces, who lost seven thousand hoplites. After this

catastrophe, Arcesilaus was strangled by his brother Learchus when he was indisposed by sickness and the medicines he had taken. But Arcesilaus' wife, whose name was Eryxo, then set a trap for Learchus and killed him.

[161] The kingdom passed to Arcesilaus' son Battus, who had a club-foot which made him lame. In view of the disaster that had overwhelmed them, the Cyreneans sent emissaries to Delphi to ask what kind of government they should establish to guarantee their future welfare, and the Pythia told them to bring in an arbitrator from Mantinea in Arcadia. The Cyreneans approached the Mantineans, and the Mantineans sent their leading citizen, a man called Demonax. Demonax came to Cyrene and, after a detailed examination, the first thing he did was divide them into three tribes, along the following lines: he made one division consist of the Therans and the local Libyan population, another of the Peloponnesians and Cretans, and the third of everyone from the Aegean islands. In the second place, he reserved certain priesthoods and sacred precincts for Battus as king, but gave the general populace all the other rights and possessions which had previously belonged to the king.

[162] This constitution lasted throughout Battus' reign, but in the time of his son Arcesilaus the issue of the king's prerogatives proved very troublesome. What happened was that Arcesilaus (who was the son of Battus the Lame and Pheretime) refused to accept Demonax of Mantinea's arrangements and demanded the return of his hereditary privileges. There was civil strife, but Arcesilaus came off worst and fled to Samos, while his mother fled to Salamis in Cyprus. Now, the ruler of Salamis at this time was Euelthon (the man who dedicated the remarkable censer in Delphi, which can be found in the Corinthian treasury). So Pheretime went to Euelthon and asked him to supply her with an army, to restore her and her son to Cyrene. Euelthon proceeded to give her everything—except an army. She accepted his presents and said that they were all very well, but it would be even better for him to give her the army she was asking for. Every time he gave her something, this is what she said, until in the end Euelthon presented her with a golden spindle and distaff, and gave her some wool as well. When Pheretime gave her usual response to the gifts, Euelthon replied that these were the kinds of things he would give a woman, but he would never give a woman an army.

[163] Meanwhile in Samos Arcesilaus was collecting all the men
he could by the promise of land redistribution. Once he had a sizeable army in the making, he set out for Delphi to consult the oracle
about his return to Cyrene. The Pythia replied as follows: 'Loxias
grants the kingship of Cyrene to your dynasty for eight generations—for four kings called Battus and four kings called Arcesilaus.
But he advises you not to try to extend that period. As for you,
once you have returned to Cyrene, keep quiet. If you find a kiln
full of amphoras, don't fire the amphoras, but send them off with
a fair wind; if you do fire the oven, don't enter anywhere that is
surrounded by water. If you disregard this warning, you will die,
along with the best-looking bull.'

[164] This was the Pythia's prediction to Arcesilaus. Taking
along the men he had gathered in Samos, he returned to Cyrene,
where he regained control of affairs. But then he forgot the oracle,
and insisted that his opponents pay for forcing him into exile. Some
of them fled clean out of the country. Others were captured by
Arcesilaus and shipped off to Cyprus for execution, but were blown
off course to Cnidos, where the inhabitants rescued them and
shipped them to Thera instead. Still others, however, took refuge
in a tall tower owned by Aglomachus—but Arcesilaus heaped
wood around the building and burnt it to the ground. Afterwards,
when it was all over, he realized that this was what the Pythia had
been referring to when she had forbidden him in her prophecy to
fire any amphoras he might find in an oven. From then on he took
care to stay out of Cyrene, because he thought that it might count
as 'surrounded by water' and he was worried about dying as predicted. His wife (who was also related to him) was the daughter of
the king of the Barcaeans, whose name was Alazeir. Arcesilaus went
and stayed with Alazeir, then, but some Barcaeans, along with some
of the exiles from Cyrene, saw him out and about in the streets of
the town and killed him. They also killed his father-in-law Alazeir.
Whether or not he did so intentionally, then, Arcesilaus fulfilled his
destiny by missing the point of the oracle.

[165] While Arcesilaus was living in Barca, having already
encompassed his own downfall, his mother Pheretime took over
and enjoyed all her son's duties and privileges in Cyrene, including
his seat in the Council. When news reached her of her son's death
in Barca, she fled to Egypt, because Arcesilaus had served
Cambyses the son of Cyrus well—it was he who had surrendered

Cyrene to Cambyses and had undertaken to pay tribute. When Pheretime reached Egypt she threw herself on the mercy of Aryandes and asked him to help her, claiming that her son had been killed because he was pro-Persian.

[166] Aryandes was the man Cambyses had made governor of Egypt. Later, he was to be executed for trying to claim equal status with Darius. What happened was that he realized—it was obvious—that Darius wanted to leave as a memorial to future generations something which no other king had achieved, and he proceeded to do likewise, until he received his reward for doing so. Darius had refined gold until it was as pure as it possibly could be and then struck coinage with it; when Aryandes was in charge of Egypt he did the same with silver. In fact, Aryandic silver is the purest silver even today. When Darius found out what Aryandes was doing, he brought a different charge, that of sedition, against him, and had him executed.

[167] Anyway, at the time in question, Aryandes was sympathetic to Pheretime's pleas and put all the Egyptian armed forces— both the land army and the navy—at her disposal. He made a Maraphian called Amasis commander of the land army, and he put Badres from the tribe of the Pasagardae in charge of the navy. Before sending the army off to war, however, he dispatched a herald to Barca to find out who it was who had killed Arcesilaus. The Barcaeans unanimously claimed responsibility, and said that they had killed him because they had suffered terribly at his hands. When Aryandes heard this, he sent his men off straight away, and Pheretime went with them. This charge was the pretext for the expedition, but I think that the real reason was to conquer Libya. After all, a great many different tribes lived in Libya, and hardly any of them were subjects of the Persian king; in fact most of them were not concerned in the slightest about Darius.

[168] Here is how the Libyans live. Starting from Egypt, the first Libyans are the Adyrmachidae, whose way of life is basically Egyptian, except that they wear the same kinds of clothes as are worn everywhere else in Libya. Their women wear a bronze band around each of their ankles and have long hair. When a woman of this tribe finds a louse on her body, she cracks it with her teeth and then throws it away. They are the only Libyan tribe to do this. Another unique custom of theirs is that when their young women are about to get married they parade them in front of their king, and

whichever one of them pleases him the most is deflowerd by him. Adyrmachidan territory runs from Egypt up to a bay called Plynus.

[169] The next tribe are the Giligamae, whose territory extends west as far as an island called Aphrodisias. Platea (the island where the Cyreneans settled) lies about half-way along the stretch of coastline occupied by this tribe, and on the mainland is a bay called Menelaus, and also Aziris, where the Cyreneans lived. Silphium starts growing here; it grows from Platea to the mouth of the Gulf of Syrtis. Their way of life is not markedly different from that of other Libyan tribes.

[170] The next tribe to the west after the Giligamae are the Asbystae, whose territory lies inland from Cyrene and does not come down to the sea, because the coastal region is Cyrenean territory. No Libyan tribe relies on four-horse chariots more than them. By and large, they try to imitate the Cyreneans.

[171] The next tribe to the west after the Asbystae are the Auschisae, whose territory lies inland from Barca, and comes down to the sea at Euesperides. In the middle of their territory live the Bacales, a tribe with a small population, whose land comes down to the sea at Taucheira, a town in Barcaean country. The Auschisae have the same way of life as those who live inland from Cyrene.

[172] The next tribe to the west after the Auschisae are the Nasamones, a populous tribe. In the summer they leave their livestock by the sea and travel inland to a place called Augila to pick dates from the palm-trees. There are a great many flourishing palm-trees there, and they are all the fruit-bearing kind. They catch locusts, dry them in the sun, grind them up, and then sprinkle the powder on to milk and drink it. It is their custom for each man to have a number of wives, but as in the case of the Massagetae any woman is available to any man for sex; a staff set up in front of a house indicates that sexual intercourse is taking place inside. When a Nasamonian man gets married, first it is the custom for the bride to have sex with all the guests one after another on her wedding night; every man she has sex with gives her something he has brought with him from his house as a gift. When they want to swear an oath they place their hands on the tombs of the men who are said to be most moral and brave men from the tribe's past and swear by these men. And their divinatory practice is to go to the graves of their ancestors and sleep there, after saying prayers; whatever they see in their dreams is taken to be prophetic. When two

Nasamones exchange pledges, they each offer the other something to drink out of their hands; if they do not have anything to drink, they get some dust from the ground and lick that.

[173] The neighbours of the Nasamones are the Psyllians—a tribe that met with extinction. This is how it happened. The south wind dried up their water-holes and there was no water to be found anywhere in their territory, which all lay to the east of the Gulf of Syrtis. They deliberated and unanimously decided—I am repeating what the Libyans say—to march against the south wind. When they reached the sandy desert, the south wind blew and buried them. After their extinction, the Nasamones took over their land.

[174] Further inland, to the south of this region, in the part of Libya that is teeming with wild animals, are the Garamantes, who shun all human intercourse and contact. They have no weapons of war and no knowledge of ways to defend themselves.

[175] The Garamantes are the neighbours of the Nasamones inland, while the next tribe west along the coast is the Macae, who wear their hair in the style of a crest; that is, they shave the hair to either side of their heads down to the skin, but leave the middle part to grow long. When they go to war, they carry ostrich-skin shields. The River Cinyps, which rises from the so-called Hill of the Graces, flows through their land and issues into the sea. This Hill of the Graces is thickly wooded, whereas no trees grow in any of the other parts of Libya so far described. The distance from this hill to the sea is two hundred stades.

[176] Next to the Macae are the Gindanes, whose women each wear many leather anklets; it is said that they tie on an anklet for each man they have had sex with. The woman with the largest number of anklets is considered to be the most outstanding, because she has been loved by the largest number of men.

[177] On a headland which juts out into the sea from the territory of the Gindanes live the Lotus-eaters, who exist on a diet of nothing but the fruit of the lotus plant. This fruit is about the size of a mastic berry, and is as sweet as a date. The Lotus-eaters also make wine out of it.

[178] The next tribe along the coast from the Lotus-eaters are the Machlyes, who also make use of the lotus, but not to the extent that the people just mentioned do. Their territory runs all the way to a great river called the Triton, which issues into a large lake called Tritonis. In the lake there is an island called Phla,

which, they say, the Lacedaemonians were told by an oracle to colonize.

[179] There is also a story that after the *Argo* had been built on the coast by Mount Pelium, Jason was sailing round the Peloponnese on his way to Delphi (he had a hecatomb on board, consisting of various objects, including a bronze tripod), and at Cape Malea a north wind arose which carried him off to Libya. Before he had sighted land, he found himself in the shallows of Lake Tritonis. He did not know how to get out of them, but just then—so the story goes—Triton appeared and told Jason to give him the tripod, and then he would show him the channel and send him and his crew on their way safe and sound. Jason obeyed, and Triton showed him the way through the shallows. Then he put the tripod in his own sanctuary. He also made a prediction over the tripod and told it all to Jason and his men. The prediction was that when a descendant of a member of the crew of the *Argo* carried off the tripod, it was absolutely inevitable that a hundred settlements would be founded around Lake Tritonis. When the local Libyans heard about this prophecy, they hid the tripod.

[180] Next to the Machlyes are the Auseës. They also live around Lake Tritonis, like the Machlyes, but the River Triton forms a boundary between the two tribes. The Machlyes grow their hair long at the back, the Auseës at the front. The Auseës celebrate a festival to Athena once a year at which the unmarried young women of the tribe divide into two groups and fight one another with sticks and stones; the women say that this is how they fulfil their ancestral duties to their native goddess, the one we call Athena. They say that any women who die of their wounds were not true virgins. Before they let them fight, they join together to dress up the prettiest of the current generation of young women at public expense in a Corinthian helmet and a set of Greek armour, mount her on a chariot, and take her around the lake.† I am not in a position to say what they used to dress their young women in originally, before any Greeks came to live near by, but I suspect that it may have been Egyptian armour, since in my opinion the shield and the helmet reached Greece from Egypt. The Auseës claim that Athena is the daughter of Poseidon and Lake Tritonis, but that she got angry for some reason with her father and put herself in Zeus' hands, and he made her his daughter. That is their story, anyway. They have intercourse with women promiscuously; rather

than living in couples, their sex life is like that of herd animals. When a woman's baby is grown, in the course of the third month the men all convene and the child is taken to be the son or daughter of whichever of the men it resembles.

[181] These tribes of nomads I have been talking about all live in the coastal region of Libya. Further inland is the part of Libya which is infested by wild animals, and then beyond that is a sandy ridge that runs all the way from Thebes in Egypt to the Pillars of Heracles. Along this ridge, at intervals of roughly ten days' journey, there are hills made out of salt broken up into huge chunks; at the top of each hill, cold, sweet-tasting water wells up from deep inside the salt and makes the place habitable by human beings. No one lives closer to the desert, beyond the part of Libya that is filled with wildlife, than the people who live around these hills. Starting from Thebes, the first tribe is the Ammonians, who live ten days' journey away from Thebes. They have a sanctuary there that is an offshoot of the sanctuary of Zeus in Thebes; I have already mentioned how the statue of Zeus in Thebes has a ram's head. There is in fact another spring of water there, which is tepid at dawn, cool by the middle of the morning, and very cold at noon (which is when they use it to water their gardens); as the afternoon progresses, the water gradually gets less cold, until by sunset it has become tepid; it gets warmer and warmer as midnight approaches, by which time it is boiling furiously; then, as the night moves on towards dawn, the water cools down. This spring is called the Spring of the Sun.

[182] Another ten days' journey further west along the sandy ridge after the Ammonians there is another hill of salt, like the Ammonian one, again with its water. The place is called Augila, and is inhabited. This where the Nasamones come on their date-picking expeditions.

[183] Another ten days' journey after Augila there is a third hill of salt, with water and a great many fruit-bearing palm-trees, just like the other two places. A very large tribe called the Garamantes live here. They put a layer of soil on top of the salt and so have land to cultivate. This is the place from which the Lotus-eaters are the shortest distance away; it is only a 30-day journey to reach the Lotus-eaters from here. It is also the place where the cows walk backwards as they graze; the reason for this habit is that their horns curve forwards—so much so that if they walk forwards as they

graze, the horns stick into the ground in front of them, and so they move backwards. In other respects they are no different from cows anywhere else in the world, except that leather made from their skin is exceptionally thick and durable. The Garamantes use four-horse chariots to hunt the cave-dwelling Ethiopians, because the cave-dwelling Ethiopians are the fastest people of any of whom we have been brought a report. These cave-dwellers eat reptiles such as snakes and lizards; the language they speak is completely different from any other language, and sounds like bats squeaking.

[184] Another ten days' journey further on from the Garamantes is another hill and water, again with people living in the vicinity. This is a tribe called the Atarantes, and they are the only people we know of who do not have names. They have a collective name—the Atarantes—but individuals do not have names. The Atarantes curse the sun when it is excessively hot, and also heap all kinds of vile abuse on it, because its blazing heat wears down both them and the land.

The next hill of salt, and spring of water, is another ten days' journey further on, and also has people living around it. Near by is a narrow, round mountain called Mount Atlas. It is said to be so tall that clouds hide its peaks from sight throughout the year, winter and summer. The local inhabitants (who are called Atlantes after the mountain) say that it is a pillar supporting the sky. The Atlantes, according to my sources, never eat any living thing, and never dream either.

[185] Up to these Atlantes I can give the names of those living on the sandy ridge, but no further. Nevertheless, the ridge runs all the way to the Pillars of Heracles and beyond, and continues to contain salt-mines at intervals of ten days' journey, each with people living around them. All these tribes have houses made out of lumps of salt, because it never rains in this part of Libya; salt walls could not survive if it rained. The salt that is dug out here is white and purple in colour. Further inland, south of the sandy ridge, the land is sheer desert, without water, wildlife, rain, or vegetation—without the slightest trace of moisture.

[186] All the way from Egypt to Lake Tritonis, then, the Libyans are nomads who eat meat and drink milk, although they never eat cows' meat (their reason for this is the same as the Egyptians') and they do not keep pigs. Cyrenean women also refrain from eating

cows' meat because of the Egyptian goddess Isis, but they hold fasts
and festivals in her honour. And Barcaean women also abstain from
both pigs and cows.

[187] That is the way of things in this part of the world. The
nomadic life stops at Lake Tritonis, and west of there the Libyans
live quite differently. In particular, there is something the nomadic
tribes do to their children which is not done west of the lake. I
cannot say for sure that this is what *all* the nomadic tribes do, but
certainly very many of them cauterize the veins on the top of their
children's heads (or, in some cases, the veins at their temples) when
they are 4 years old with hot grease extracted from sheeps' wool.
This is to stop them ever in their lives coming to harm from the
downflow of phlegm from the head. They attribute their great good
health to this practice of theirs—and the Libyans are in fact the
healthiest people in the known world. I cannot actually confirm
that this practice of theirs is the reason for it, but they are certainly
very healthy. If a child goes into convulsions while they are performing the cautery, they have a way of curing him: they sprinkle
goat's urine on him, and that makes him better. I am only repeating what the Libyans themselves say.

[188] The way the nomads perform their sacrifices is as follows.
They begin by taking the victim's ear as first-fruits and throwing it
over their home, and then they twist the creature's neck back. The
sun and the moon are the only deities to whom they offer sacrifices, and this form of worship is common to all the Libyan tribes;
however, the tribes in the vicinity of Lake Tritonis also offer sacrifices to Athena in particular, but also to Triton and Poseidon.

[189] Now, the Greeks derive the clothing and the aegis of
Athena's statue from the clothes worn by Libyan women. After all,
Libyan women's clothing is identical, apart from being made out
of leather and having thongs rather than snakes as the tassels on
the edge of their aegises. Besides, the name shows that the costume
worn by statues of Athena comes from Libya, because Libyan
women wear tasselled goatskins, de-fleeced and dyed with madder,
as their outer clothes, and the Greeks have only changed the name
aigeai or goatskins to 'aegis'. I also think that the *ololuge* or cry of
praise emitted during the worship of Athena started in Libya,
because it is often employed by Libyan women, who do it extremely
well. The Greeks also learnt to harness four horses to their chariots from the Libyans.

[190] These nomadic tribes all bury their dead in the same way that the Greeks do, except for the Nasamones, who bury their corpses in a sitting position and take care to sit a dying man up rather than have him lying down when he breathes his last. Their houses, which are portable, are made out of asphodel stalks woven on to a reed framework. So much for the customs of these tribes.

[191] West of the Triton River, next to the Auseës, is a Libyan tribe called the Maxyes who cultivate the land and whose custom it is to have houses. They shave their hair off the left side of their heads, but let it grow long on the right side, and they smear ochre on their bodies. They claim to be descendants of the men of Troy. Their land—and the same goes for this western part of the country as a whole—has far more wildlife and many more trees than the rest of Libya. I mean, the eastern part of Libya, where the nomads live, is flat and sandy; but then the land of the farmers west of the River Triton is very hilly and thickly wooded, and teems with wildlife. There are enormous snakes there, and also lions, elephants, bears, asps, donkeys with horns, dog-headed creatures, headless creatures with eyes in their chests (at least, that is what the Libyans say), wild men and wild women, and a large number of other creatures whose existence is not merely the stuff of fables.

[192] These species are unknown in the territory occupied by the nomads, but there are others there—white-rumped impalas, gazelles, elands, donkeys (not the horned but a non-drinking variety, because they never drink), antelopes which are the size of oxen and whose horns are used to make the sides of lyres, foxes, hyenas, porcupines, wild sheep, fennecs, jackals, panthers, addaxes, three-cubit-long land crocodiles which look very like lizards, ostriches, and tiny one-horned snakes. These animals are peculiar to this part of Libya, but there are also creatures which occur elsewhere in the world (except for deer and wild boar, which are completely absent from Libya). There are three species of mice in this part of Libya. One species is called the two-footed mouse, another is called *zegeries* in Libyan (which translates into Greek as 'hill mice'), and the third species is the spiky-haired mouse. There are also weasels living in the silphium, which are very similar to the weasels found in Tartessus. So much for the fauna of the part of Libya where the nomadic tribes live; I have given the fullest possible information that my enquiries could gain me.

[193] The next Libyan tribe after the Maxyes are the Zaueces, whose women drive their chariots when they go to war.

[194] Next to the Zaueces are the Gyzantes. Bees produce a great deal of honey in their country, but even larger quantities are produced of a syrup, which is said to be the local speciality. Anyway, all the people there smear ochre on themselves and eat monkeys, which throng the hills in huge numbers.

[195] According to the Carthaginians, there is an island called Cyrauis off the bit of the coast where the Gyzantes live; they describe the island as being two hundred stades long, but narrow, accessible on foot from the mainland, and full of olive-trees and vines. On the island there is supposed to be a pool where unmarried native women use birds' feathers smeared with pitch to draw gold-dust up from the mud. I cannot vouch for the truth of this story; I am simply recording what is said. Still, it might all be true, since I have personally seen pitch being brought out of the water to the surface of a pool in Zacynthos. There are quite a number of pools there, the largest of which is seventy feet across in all directions and two fathoms deep. What they do is tie some myrtle on to the end of a pole, let the pole down into the water, and then bring the pitch up to the surface on the myrtle. Zacynthian pitch smells like bitumen, but in other respects it is superior to pitch from Pieria. They pour it into a basin they have hollowed out of the ground near the pool, and when they have collected a lot, they drain it from the basin into amphoras. Anything that falls into this pool travels underground and reappears in the sea, which is four stades away from the pool. So this information about the island off the coast of Libya may come close to the truth.

[196] The Carthaginians also say that there is within Libya a land, with people living there, beyond the Pillars of Heracles. They say that they go there, unload their cargo, and put it in a row along the beach, and then get back on board and make a smoky fire. When the natives see the smoke they come to the sea-shore, put some gold on the ground for the goods, and then pull back away from the goods. At that point the Carthaginians return to shore and have a look, and if they think there is enough gold to pay for the cargo, they take it and leave, whereas if they do not think it is enough, they return to their boats and sit there. The natives then approach and add more gold, until the Carthaginians are satisfied. Neither side cheats the other, the Carthaginians say, for they do not

touch the gold until it is equal in value to the cargo, and the natives do not touch the goods until the Carthaginians have taken the gold.

[197] These are all the Libyan tribes I can put a name to. Most of them are not now and were not then concerned in the slightest about the Persian king. On the subject of Libya I can also say that there are four (and, as far as anyone knows, no more than four) nations living in it, two of whom—the Libyans and the Ethiopians, respectively in the north and the south of the continent—are indigenous, whereas the other two, the Phoenicians and the Greeks, are immigrants.

[198] It seems to me that, in general, the soil of Libya is too poor to stand comparison with that of Asia or Europe. The only exception is the part of Libya called Cinyps (which has the same name as its river), which is as good as anywhere in the world in terms of its yield of cereal crops, and is quite different from everywhere else in Libya, because the soil is black and is so well irrigated by springs that there is no need to worry about drought or about torrential downpours (for it does rain in this part of Libya) making it too waterlogged to be any good. On average its crop yield is equal to that of Babylon. The soil in the part of Libya where the Euesperitae live is also good; when it is exceptionally fertile, it can yield a crop of 100 times the weight of the seed grain—but in Cinyps the yield is 300 times the weight of the seed grain.

[199] The land around Cyrene, which is the highest area in the part of Libya that is inhabited by the nomads, has, incredibly, three harvest-times. First the coastal crops ripen and become ready for cutting and gathering; once they have been collected, the crops inland from the coast, in the area known as the hills, become ripe enough to collect; and after this second crop has been harvested, the grain in the highest part of the country ripens and matures. As a result, just when the first crop has been consumed as food and drink, the final crop arrives. In fact, harvesting occupies the people of Cyrene for eight months of the year. Anyway, that is enough on these matters.

[200] The Persians Aryandes had sent from Egypt to avenge Pheretime came to Barca and began to besiege the city. They demanded the surrender of those responsible for the murder of Arcesilaus, but the Barcaeans refused, on the grounds that every single one of them was partly responsible. So the Persian siege of Barca lasted nine months, during which time they tried tunnelling

underground up to the wall and launching a series of fierce assaults. A metalworker invented a way to detect the tunnels. He took a bronze shield around the inside of the city wall and kept holding it against the ground; where there was digging going on, the metal of the shield gave off a ringing sound, but everywhere else he laid it there was no sound. The Barcaeans then dug down there to meet the tunnelling Persians and killed them. So the tunnels were detected in this way, and meanwhile the Barcaeans beat off the Persians' assaults on the city.

[201] For a long time, then, the siege wore on with heavy losses on both sides (the Persians no less than the Barcaeans), until Amasis, the commander of the Persian land army, realized that the city would never fall to brute strength, but that a ruse might succeed, and so came up with the following plan. Under cover of darkness he had a wide trench dug; he laid flimsy planks over the trench, and then he put soil on top of the planks, until it was level with the surrounding ground. At daybreak, he invited the Barcaeans to a meeting—an invitation which they were delighted to accept—and the result of the meeting was that they decided to come to terms with the Persians. The confirmation of the pact involved both sides swearing an oath over the concealed trench; they swore that the oath would stay firm 'as long as this earth lasts', and the Barcaeans promised to pay a suitable tribute to the Persian king, while the Persians promised not to do any harm to the Barcaeans from then on. With these solemn promises in place, the Barcaeans trustingly emerged from their city and threw the gates open to let the Persians come inside at will. The Persians broke the hidden planking and ran inside the city. They broke the planking they had made so that they would not be perjuring themselves. They had promised the Barcaeans that the oath would last for as long as the earth stayed as it was at the time—and now that they had broken the planking, the oath became null and void.

[202] The Barcaeans who had played the biggest parts in her son's death were handed over to Pheretime by the Persians, and she had them impaled at intervals all around the city walls. She also had their wives' breasts cut off and displayed here and there on the city walls too. She told the Persians to treat the rest of the inhabitants as spoils of war, except for any who were members of the house of Battus and were not implicated in the murder. These Pheretime put in charge of the city.

[203] The Persians reduced the rest of the Barcaeans to slavery and then set off back to Egypt. When they came to Cyrene, the Cyreneans let them pass through the city, as they had been directed to by some oracle. Badres, the commander of the Persian fleet, insisted that the army's passage through the city was an opportunity for them to capture it, but Amasis refused to let him have his way, on the grounds that the only Greek city they had been sent to attack was Barca. Afterwards, however, once they had passed through the city and were encamped on a knoll sacred to Zeus Lycaeus, they regretted not having taken Cyrene. So they tried to enter the city again, but the Cyreneans would not let them. Although there was no danger of a battle, the Persians were overcome by panic and they beat a hasty retreat to a site about sixty stades from the city, where they pitched camp. While they were there, a message arrived from Aryandes recalling them. The Persians asked the Cyreneans to give them provisions for their journey; their request was granted, and when they had taken possession of the supplies they set out for Egypt. But even after that the Libyans killed any Egyptian strays or stragglers who fell into their hands, for the sake of their clothes and equipment, and went on doing so until the Persians got back to Egypt.

[204] This Persian army penetrated Libya as far as Euesperides. The Barcaeans they had enslaved were taken out of Egypt and sent to King Darius, who gave them a village in Bactria to settle in. They called this village Barca, and it still existed as an inhabited community in Bactria in my day.

[205] Pheretime came to a bad end as well. As soon as she had made the Barcans pay, she left Libya and returned to Egypt, where she died a horrible death. She became infested with a mass of worms while still alive, as if to show people that excessive vengeance earns the gods' displeasure. So much for Pheretime the daughter of Battus, and so much for the revenge she exacted from the Barcaeans.

BOOK FIVE

[1] Perinthus was the first place in the Hellespont conquered by the Persians Darius had left in Europe under Megabazus' command, because the inhabitants had refused to acknowledge Darius as their ruler. Once, in the past, the Perinthians were savaged by the Paeonians. What happened was that the Paeonians, from the Strymon River, were advised by their god in an oracle to march against the Perinthians, but actually to attack them if, and only if, while they were encamped there opposite them the Perinthians shouted out their name. So that is what the Paeonians did, and the Perinthians took up a position opposite them in the outskirts of the city. At this juncture, the two sides challenged each other to three duels, pitching man against man, horse against horse, and dog against dog. The Perinthians won two of the contests and were so pleased that they started to sing a victory paean. The Paeonians assumed that this was exactly what the oracle had meant and said to one another, perhaps, 'Now the oracle should come true! Now is the time to act!' And so, because the Perinthians had cried out 'Paean!', the Paeonians launched an attack, won a significant victory, and left few of the Perinthians alive.

[2] So that is what had happened earlier to the Perinthians at the hands of the Paeonians. Now, however, the Perinthians fought bravely for their freedom, and the Persians under Megabazus defeated them only because they outnumbered them. After the fall of Perinthus, Megabazus marched through Thrace and brought every settlement and tribe living there under the Persian king's rule. For that was what Darius had told him to do—to conquer Thrace.

[3] The population of Thrace is the largest in the world, after the Indians, of course. If they were ruled by a single person or had a common purpose, they would be invincible and would be by far the most powerful nation in the world, in my opinion. This is completely impossible for them, however—there is no way that it will ever happen—and that is why they are weak. The various tribes

have different names in the various lands they inhabit, but their customs and practices are more or less the same in all respects, except that the Getae, the Trausians, and the tribes north of Crestonia have some special practices of their own.

[4] Of these, I have already described the customs of the Getae, with their belief in their own immortality. Trausian customs are basically identical with those found elsewhere in Thrace, except for what they do at birth and death. Whenever a baby is born, its relatives gather around and grieve for the troubles it is going to have to endure now that it has been born, and they recount all the sufferings of human life. When anyone dies, however, they bury him in high spirits and with jubilation, on the grounds that he has been released from so many ills and is now in a perfectly happy state.

[5] The tribes to the north of Crestonia practise polygyny, and when a man dies, his wives are subjected to searching tests (which their friends take very seriously), to see which of them was loved the most by the husband. When a decision has been reached and one of the wives has been singled out for this distinction, her praises are sung by men and women alike, and then her throat is slit over the grave by her nearest male relative, and she is buried along with her husband. All the other wives consider it a huge misfortune, because there is nothing more disgraceful for them than not being chosen.

[6] Elsewhere in Thrace they have the practice of selling their children for export abroad. They do not restrict the behaviour of their young women, but let them have sex with any men they want; however, they keep a very strict eye on their wives. They buy their wives from the woman's parents for a great deal of money. Being tattooed is taken by them to be a sign of high birth, while it is a sign of low birth to be without tattoos. They consider it best not to work, and working the land is regarded as the most dishonourable profession. The best way to make a living, in their judgement, is off the spoils of war. These are their most remarkable customs.

[7] The only gods they worship are Ares, Dionysus, and Artemis. Thracian rulers, however, differ from ordinary citizens in this respect and worship Hermes above all other gods; Hermes is the only god they swear by, and they also claim to be descended from him.

[8] Well-to-do Thracians are buried as follows. They lay out
the corpse for three days, while they slaughter and consume a wide
variety of victims, after a period of public mourning. Then they
either cremate and bury the corpse, or simply bury it, and after
they have heaped up a mound of earth over it, various athletic competitions are held, and the biggest prizes are awarded in the category of one-to-one combat. That is how funerals are conducted in
Thrace.

[9] No one can offer a reliable description of the people who
live to the north of Thrace, but the land beyond the Ister seems to
be vast and desolate. The only people I have been able to hear about
who live north of the Ister are called the Sigynnae. Their clothing
is Median in style, and they have small, short-faced, long-haired
horses; the hair, which grows all over these horses' bodies, is up to
five fingers long. These horses are incapable of carrying people, but
they are very fast in harness, and so the local tribesmen travel
around in carts. They say that Sigynnan territory extends nearly as
far as the land of the Eneti on the Adriatic, and that they themselves are emigrants from Media; I myself would not like to hazard
a guess as to how they can be Median emigrants, but anything is
possible given enough time. Anyway, in the language of the Ligyes,
who live north of Massalia, *sigynnae* means 'retailers', and on
Cyprus it means 'spears'.

[10] According to the Thracians, the land beyond the Ister is
infested by bees, and that is why it is impossible to travel further
inland. Personally, I find this story implausible, because bees appear
to be intolerant of the cold. In fact, I think it is the cold that has
stopped people from settling in these northern regions. That is what
I was told about this part of the country, but whatever the facts of
the matter Megabazus was bringing its coastline under Persian
control.

[11] Meanwhile, Darius crossed back over the Hellespont and
went to Sardis. The first thing he did once he was there was remember how Histiaeus of Miletus had helped him and how Coës of
Mytilene had given him good advice, and he summoned them to
Sardis and offered them whatever they wanted. Histiaeus was
already the tyrant of Miletus, so he did not want to become tyrant
of anywhere else, but he asked for Myrcinus in Edonia, because
he wanted to found a settlement there. Coës, however, was not
a tyrant but a commoner, so he asked to become the tyrant of

Mytilene. Both these requests were granted, and the two men left for the places of their choice.

[12] Now, Darius happened to see something that made him decide to order Megabazus to round up the population of Paeonia and deport them from Europe to Asia. There were two Paeonians called Pigres and Mastyes, who wanted to rule Paeonia as tyrants. When Darius returned to Asia, Pigres and Mastyes went to Sardis, bringing their sister, who was a tall, beautiful woman. They waited until Darius had established himself just outside the Lydian city, and then they dressed their sister in the best clothes they had and sent her to fetch water; as well as carrying a jar on her head, she was leading a horse with the reins around her arm, and was also spinning flax. As the woman passed by, she attracted Darius' attention, because her actions were not typically Persian or Lydian, or indeed Asian in general. Since his interest was aroused, he sent some of his personal guards after her, with orders to observe what the woman did with the horse. So they followed her. When she got to the river, she watered the horse, filled the jar with water, and then retraced her steps, carrying the water on her head, using her arm to lead the horse, and constantly turning her spindle.

[13] Darius was impressed with what his men told him they had seen her doing, on top of what he had seen with his own eyes, and he gave orders for her to be brought into his presence. His men fetched her, and her brothers (who had been watching the proceedings from somewhere close by) arrived as well. Darius asked where she was from, and the young men answered that they were Paeonians and that she was their sister. 'But who are Paeonians,' Darius asked, 'and whereabouts do they live? And why have you come to Sardis?' They replied that they had come to submit themselves to him, that Paeonia was a settled country on the River Strymon, not far from the Hellespont, whose inhabitants were originally Teucrian emigrants from Troy. When he had got these details from them, Darius asked them if all the women there were as industrious as their sister. Since all their actions had in fact been designed to lead precisely to this point, Pigres and Mastyes eagerly replied that they were.

[14] Darius next wrote a letter to Megabazus, the military commander he had left in Thrace, ordering him to uproot the people of Paeonia—men, women, and children—from their native land and bring them to him. A man raced off on horseback to the

Hellespont with the message, crossed over into Europe, and delivered the letter to Megabazus. He read it, got hold of some guides, and led his army out of Thrace and towards Paeonia.

[15] When the Paeonians found out that the Persians were coming against them, they mobilized an army and marched off in the direction of the sea, because they expected the Persian invasion and attack to come from that direction. The Paeonians were ready to repel Megabazus' invading army, then, but the Persians found out that they had formed themselves into an army and were guarding the coastal approaches into their country, and got their guides to show them an inland route. They got past the Paeonians without being spotted and fell on their towns, which were now empty of men. So it was no problem for them to capture the towns, because there was no one to defend them against their assaults. As soon as the Paeonians heard that their towns were in enemy hands, the army fell apart as each group of men looked to its own safety and surrendered to the Persians. This is how several Paeonian tribes— the Siriopaeonians, the Paeoplae, and other tribes as far north as Lake Prasias—came to be uprooted from their native land and taken to Asia.

[16] The tribes living by Mount Pangaeum, those on the borders of the territory of the Doberes, the Agrianes, and the Odomantians,† and those living around Lake Prasias itself, were not subjugated by Megabazus at all, although he did try to crush them, and the lake-dwellers too. These people manage to live on the lake by constructing a platform of boards fixed on to high posts in the middle of the lake, with only a single bridge providing a narrow causeway to and from the mainland. Originally, the erection of the posts to support the platforms used to be a joint enterprise undertaken by the whole population, but later it became the practice for each man to fetch from the nearby mountain (its name is Orbelus) three posts for every woman he married—and in this tribe a man may have lots of wives—and set them up in the lake. The way they live, then, is that each man has a hut which constitutes his home on the platform and a trapdoor which leads down through the platform to the lake. They tie a cord around their babies' ankles, because they worry about them rolling off into the lake. They feed their horses and their yoke-animals on fish. There are so many fish there that if someone opens the trapdoor and drops an empty basket on a rope into the lake, in no time at all he has a basketful

of fish to pull back up. There are two species of fish in the lake, whose local names are *paprax* and *tilon*.

[17] Anyway, the Paeonian tribes who were defeated were to be taken to Asia. After his victory over the Paeonians, Megabazus sent to Macedonia a delegation consisting of the seven most important Persians in his army after himself. The purpose of their mission to Amyntas was to demand earth and water for King Darius. There is a good short cut from Lake Prasias to Macedonia: first, next to the lake, there is a mine (which later was to provide Alexander with a talent of silver a day), and then after the mine one only has to cross the mountain called Dysorum to reach Macedonia.

[18] When the Persian delegation arrived at Amyntas' residence, they gained an audience with him and demanded earth and water for King Darius, which Amyntas gave them. He then invited them to dine with him, prepared a magnificent banquet, and entertained the Persians generously. After the meal, over the wine, the Persians said, 'Macedonian ally, in Persia it is customary for us to bring in our concubines and wives to join us at the close of important meals. You have made us so very welcome, you are entertaining us so lavishly, and you have given King Darius earth and water—let's see you observe this custom of ours.'

'My friends from Persia,' Amyntas replied, 'that is not the way we do things here: we keep men and women separate. But since you are our masters, if that's what you want, you shall have it.' And with these words Amyntas sent for the women.

The women came in response to his summons and sat in a row opposite the Persians. When the Persians saw how beautiful the women were they told Amyntas that what he had done was quite stupid; it would have been better, they said, for the women not to have come in the first place than to come and not sit next to them, but opposite them, where they were a torment to the eyes. Amyntas had no choice but to tell the women to go and sit next to the Persians. As soon as the women did so, the Persians, who were exceedingly drunk, began to touch their breasts, and one or another of them would even try to embrace them.

[19] The sight of this made Amyntas angry, but he was too afraid of the Persians to do anything about it. However, his son Alexander was there and when he saw what was going on, his youth and innocence made him incapable of holding back. In his anger he said to Amyntas, 'Father, why don't you give in to your

age? You can go and rest; you don't have to carry on drinking. I'll stay here and attend to our visitors' needs.'

Amyntas realized that Alexander was up to no good and said, 'You're burning with indignation, son, and I'm pretty sure that these words of yours are meant to get rid of me so that you can cause trouble. I beg you not to harm these men; if you do, you will bring about our destruction. Try not to let the sight of what is going on upset you. But as for my going to bed, I will take your advice.'

[20] With this request to his son, Amyntas left the room. Then Alexander said to the Persians, 'Sirs, these women are at your disposal. They are all available for sex, and you can pick as many of them as you want. You need only indicate your wishes. For the time being, however, since it's nearly time for you to go to bed, and you're obviously pretty well drunk, I suggest that you let these women go and bathe, if that suits you, and then you'll get them back afterwards.'

The Persians approved of this suggestion. Once the women were out of the room, Alexander sent them back to their quarters; then he personally chose the same number of beardless men as there were women, dressed them in the women's clothing, and armed them each with a dagger. He brought them into the room and said to the Persians, 'Sirs, it seems to me that you have had the perfect banquet. You have had the benefit of everything we have, and everything we could get for you as well, and now, to crown it all, we are making you a present of our own mothers and sisters. All this should leave you in no doubt that we honour you as you deserve, and you can also make it clear to the king who sent you on this mission how welcome you were made by a man of Greece, his governor in Macedonia, and how generous he was with bed and board.' With these words, Alexander had every Macedonian man, disguised as a woman, sit down next to a Persian man, and when the Persians tried to fondle them, the Macedonians killed them.

[21] That is how these Persians met their end. Their servants were killed as well, because the Persians had come with carriages, attendants, and a great deal of baggage, so all these things had to disappear, as well as the men themselves. Not long afterwards, however, a thorough search was undertaken by the Persians for the missing men, and Alexander had to use cunning to make sure that they did not get anywhere. What he did was give a lot of money

and also his sister, whose name was Gygaea, to Bubares, the Persian who was in command of the search-party. By means of these gifts, Alexander ensured that the search for the dead Persians would fail, and so their death was concealed and kept secret.

[22] I can personally vouch for the correctness of the claim of these Macedonians, who are descendants of Perdiccas, to be Greeks, and I will prove in a later part of my work that they are Greeks. Besides, the officials in charge of the Greek games at Olympia have acknowledged that this is so. After all, once when Alexander decided to compete in the games and came down to Olympia for that purpose, the Greeks who were drawn against him in the foot-race tried to prevent him from taking part, on the grounds that non-Greeks were not allowed to compete in the games, which were exclusively for Greeks. However, Alexander proved that he was actually an Argive and was therefore judged to be Greek; so he competed in the sprint and came equal first. Anyway, that is what happened then.

[23] Megabazus took the Paeonians to the Hellespont, crossed over, and went to Sardis. By now, Histiaeus of Miletus was fortifying Myrcinus, the place on the River Strymon that Darius had given him, at his request, as a reward for protecting the pontoon bridge. Megabazus found out what Histiaeus was doing, and the first thing he did on arriving in Sardis with the Paeonians was go and speak to Darius. 'My lord,' he said, 'what have you done? You have allowed a Greek—and a cunning and clever Greek at that— to found a settlement in Thrace, where there is a limitless supply of timber for shipbuilding, where there are plenty of spars for oars, and where there are silver mines too. Moreover, now that the local population there, which consists of huge numbers of Greeks as well as non-Greeks, have found a leader, they will do whatever he commands them to do, day and night. I think you should put an end to Histiaeus' enterprise now, if you want to avoid being embroiled in a war in your own territory. Send for him—but tactfully—and then restrain him. Once you have him here in your control, make sure that he never goes anywhere there are Greeks.'

[24] Darius needed no further argument to convince him that Megabazus' predictions were accurate, and he sent a man to Myrcinus to deliver the following message: 'A dispatch from King Darius to Histiaeus: "After thinking the matter over, I have come to the conclusion that there is no one who cares more for me

and my affairs than you do; you have proved your loyalty to me by your actions, not by mere words. I have great plans for the future, and I want you here, no matter what, so that I can tell you about them." '

Histiaeus believed that this message was sincere and he felt important at the prospect of being the king's adviser, so he went to Sardis. Once he was there Darius said, 'Histiaeus, the reason I sent for you is that soon after my return from Scythia, which meant that you were no longer in my sight, I very quickly found that there was nothing else I wanted so much as that you should see and talk things over with me. I realized that the most valuable possession in the world is an intelligent, loyal friend, and I have proof enough to know that you have both these qualities and apply them to me and my affairs. So thank you for coming, and I have a suggestion to make: forget about Miletus and this new settlement of yours in Thrace, and come with me to Susa, where everything I have will be yours and you will be a constant companion at my table and my adviser.'

[25] After this speech, Darius appointed Artaphrenes (who was his half-brother on his father's side) governor of Sardis, and then marched back to Susa, taking Histiaeus with him. He also made Otanes the military commander of the coastal peoples. Otanes' father Sisamnes had been one of the royal judges, but he had taken a bribe to deliver an unfair verdict, and so King Cambyses slit his throat and flayed off all his skin. He had thongs made out of the flayed skin, and he strung the chair on which Sisamnes had used to sit to deliver his verdicts with these thongs. Then he appointed Sisamnes' son to be a judge instead of the father whom he had killed and flayed, and told him to bear in mind the nature of the chair on which he would sit to deliver his verdicts.

[26] So now Otanes, the one with this chair to sit on, became the successor to Megabazus' command, and captured Byzantium, Chalcedon, Antandrus in Troas, and Lamponium. Taking a fleet from the Lesbians, he captured Lemnos and Imbros, both of which were still inhabited by Pelasgians at the time.

[27] After a brave and well-fought defence, the people of Lemnos were eventually defeated. Lycaretus, the brother of Mae-andrius (the former ruler of Samos), was the Persian choice for governor of the survivors. Lycaretus died while governing Lemnos ⟨after incurring a great deal of unpopularity⟩,† the reason for which

was that he enslaved all the inhabitants and kept them crushed, accusing some of desertion to the Scythian side, and others of inflicting casualties on Darius' army as it was returning after the Scythian campaign.

[28] Anyway, these were Otanes' achievements as a military commander. There was a brief respite, but soon troubles began again for the Ionians, this time as a result of Naxos and Miletus. It should be said, first, that Naxos was the most prosperous of the Aegean islands, and second that this coincided with the time when Miletus was at a particular peak and was, moreover, the pride of Ionia. Two generations earlier, however, Miletus had been stricken with a violent period of civil war, until the Parians had sorted things out for them. In fact, from the whole of Greece the Milesians had chosen the Parians as their arbitrators.

[29] The Parians sent their best men to Miletus, and the way they settled the dispute was as follows. It was obvious to them that the Milesians were facing complete economic ruin, so they said they wanted to visit the whole territory, and proceeded to do so. They travelled throughout Milesian territory, and wherever they saw, in the devastated countryside, a well-worked field, they had the name of the owner of the field written down. By the time they had completed their tour of the territory, they had found few such fields. As soon as they got back to the city, they gathered all the people together and put the government of the city in the hands of the owners of the well-worked fields they had found, on the grounds that these men would presumably manage the city's business as well as they did their own; and they ordered the rest of the population, who had previously been at one another's throats, to do as their new leaders commanded.

[30] So that is how the Parians sorted out the Milesians' affairs. At the time in question, however, these cities were responsible for a troubled period in Ionian history. What happened was that certain men of substance were banished from Naxos by the common people and ended up in Miletus. The acting governor of Miletus at the time was Aristagoras the son of Molpagoras, who was the son-in-law and cousin of Histiaeus the son of Lysagoras, whom Darius was detaining in Susa. Histiaeus was in fact the tyrant of Miletus, but he was in Susa at the time of the arrival of the Naxians, who had previously been his allies. Once they were in Miletus, the Naxians asked Aristagoras to lend them some

military assistance and help them return home. It occurred to Aristagoras that if he were instrumental in their return, he would become the ruler of Naxos, and so, using their friendship with Histiaeus as the pretext, he put the following proposal to them. 'I do not myself have the capability', he said, 'to provide you with a force great enough to restore you in the face of opposition from the Naxians who are currently in possession of the city, because my information is that they have eight thousand men-at-arms and plenty of longships. However, I will do everything I can to make this work, and I have a plan. Artaphrenes—who is, as you know, the son of Hystaspes and the brother of King Darius—happens to be a friend of mine. Now, he is in charge of the whole Asian coastline, and he has a sizeable army and a powerful fleet. I think that he will do whatever we ask.'

Hearing this, the Naxians enjoined Aristagoras to do the best he could, and told him to offer gifts and to undertake to pay the military expenses, which, they said, they would defray themselves. They did this because they fully expected their appearance on Naxos to cause the inhabitants to submit to them, and they had high hopes that the same would happen on all the other islands too, none of which was yet under Darius' control.

[31] Aristagoras went to Sardis and told Artaphrenes that although Naxos was not a large island, it was exceptionally beautiful and fertile, lay close to the Ionian coast, and was rich in property and slaves. 'You should mount an expedition against it,' he said, 'and bring back the exiles who have been banished. I should tell you, first, that I've got a great deal of money set aside for you once you've completed such an expedition, enough to cover everything except the military expenditure, which it is only right that those of us who are directing the expedition should provide. The second point to note is that you will also be gaining for the king not just the island of Naxos itself, but also further islands which are dependent on it—Paros, Andros, and the others called the Cyclades. Then these islands would make an excellent base from which you could launch an attack on Euboea, which is a large, prosperous island, at least as big as Cyprus and easy to take. A fleet of a hundred ships would be enough to subdue all these islands.'

'You bring good news for the royal house,'† Artaphrenes replied. 'The only flaw in your otherwise excellent suggestion is the number of ships. Instead of one hundred ships, two hundred will be ready for you at the beginning of spring. However, the king himself must also approve the plan.'

[32] Aristagoras was delighted with this response, and returned to Miletus. Meanwhile Artaphrenes sent a message to Susa to tell Darius about Aristagoras' proposal. Darius himself approved the plan, and so Artaphrenes not only got two hundred triremes ready, but also mobilized a sizeable force of Persians and their allies. He gave the command of the expedition to a Persian called Megabates, who was an Achaemenid, and was his and Darius' cousin. (Years later—if there is any truth to the story—Pausanias of Lacedaemon, the son of Cleombrotus, wanted to become the tyrant of all Greece, and he got himself betrothed to Megabates' daughter.) Artaphrenes then dispatched the expeditionary force, now with Megabates in command, to Aristagoras.

[33] At Miletus, Megabates was joined by Aristagoras, the Ionian contingent, and the Naxian exiles, and then he set sail, ostensibly for the Hellespont. When he reached Chios, however, he anchored off Caucasa, with the intention of making the crossing over to Naxos on a north wind. But Naxos was not destined to fall to this expedition. What happened was that once, when Megabates was making his rounds of the sentries posted to watch the ships, he found that no guards had been set on board a Myndian ship. He angrily told his personal guards to find the ship's captain, whose name was Scylax, to haul him through one of the ship's oar-holes, and tie him there, with his head outside and his body inside. When Scylax was tied up, someone told Aristagoras that Megabates had mistreated and tied up his guest-friend from Myndus, and Aristagoras went to the Persian and asked him to reconsider. He got nowhere, however, so he went and untied him himself. When Megabates found out, he was furious and raged against Aristagoras. Aristagoras replied, 'What has any of this business got to do with you? Didn't Artaphrenes send you to obey my commands and to sail wherever I tell you to? Why don't you mind your own business?' Megabates was so angry at what Aristagoras had said that during the night he sent men in a boat to Naxos to tell the islanders everything that was going on.

[34] Now, the Naxians had in fact had no idea that they were the targets of this expedition, but as soon as they heard the news they brought everything from the fields within the town walls, equipped themselves with food and water for a siege, and

reinforced the wall. So they prepared themselves for an enemy attack. Meanwhile, the fleet crossed from Chios to Naxos—and they arrived to find themselves up against opponents who were securely defended. Four months later they were still besieging the town. By this time they had spent all the money the Persians had brought with them, and Aristagoras himself had used up a great deal of money too, and the siege was constantly needing more, so they built a stronghold for the Naxian exiles and returned to the mainland. They had failed.

[35] Aristagoras could not keep his promise to Artaphrenes; he was also under a lot of pressure from the expenses required for the expedition, and he was afraid that the military failure and his quarrel with Megabates would result in the rulership of Miletus being taken away from him. Driven by all these fears, he began to contemplate rebellion, and it also so happened, in fact, that a man with a tattooed head arrived from Histiaeus in Susa with a message telling Aristagoras to rebel against the king. Histiaeus could find no other safe way to communicate to Aristagoras the message he wanted to get through to him, because the roads were guarded, so he shaved the head of his most trustworthy slave, tattooed the message on his scalp, and then waited for his hair to grow back. As soon as it had, he sent him to Miletus with just the one task— to tell Aristagoras, when he got to Miletus, to shave his hair off and examine his scalp. And as I have already said, the tattooed message was that Aristagoras should revolt. The reason Histiaeus took this step was because he hated being kept in Susa; he expected to be let go and sent to the coast in the event of a rebellion by Miletus, but he reckoned that unless the city created trouble he would never again get to see it.

[36] That was Histiaeus' plan in sending the messenger, and it happened that all these things came together at the same time for Aristagoras. So what he did was seek the advice of his supporters. He told them his own thoughts and explained about Histiaeus' message. All of them expressed their agreement with him and urged him to revolt, except for the writer Hecataeus, who first tried to stop him embarking on hostilities with the Persian king by listing all the nations and tribes subject to Darius and all his resources; then, when this argument met with no success, he next recommended that they make the attempt to gain control of the sea. He knew that Miletus was weak just then, so he went on to say that

the only way for them to achieve this, as far as he could see, was to take from the sanctuary at Branchidae all the valuable property Croesus of Lydia had dedicated there. This would give them a reasonable hope of gaining control of the sea, and he pointed out that the money would then be theirs to make use of, and that otherwise it would be stolen by the enemy. (There was in fact a great deal of valuable property there, as I showed in the first of my narratives.) This proposal of Hecataeus' did not carry the day, but they still decided to revolt against Persia. They also decided that the first step would be for one of their number to sail to Myous, where the expeditionary force had stopped on the way back from Naxos, and try to seize the commanders, who were on board the ships.

[37] Iatragoras was dispatched on this mission and, with the help of a ruse, he captured Oliatus of Mylasa, the son of Ibanollis, Histiaeus of Termera, the son of Tymnes, Coës the son of Erxander (the man whom Darius had rewarded with Mytilene), Aristagoras of Cyme, the son of Heraclides, and many more. So Aristagoras' rebellion was out in the open, and he did all he could to damage Darius' interests. The first thing he did was relinquish his position as tyrant and convert Miletus to a theoretical state of equality before the law, so that the citizens of Miletus would voluntarily join in the rebellion. He then proceeded to do the same throughout Ionia. He expelled some tyrants from their states, and he handed over to the various states they were from the tyrants he had seized from the ships that had sailed with him to Naxos, because he wanted to get on good terms with the people in those places.

[38] As soon as the Mytileneans got Coës back, they took him out and stoned him to death, but the Cymeans let their tyrant go, as did most of the other states. And so the tyrants were deposed throughout the states. Once Aristagoras of Miletus had deposed the tyrants, he told the people in the various states to appoint military commanders, and then he set off as an envoy in a trireme for Lacedaemon, because he needed to find some powerful military support.

[39] In Sparta, Anaxandridas the son of Leon had died and passed the kingdom on to his son Cleomenes, though it was his lineage rather than excellence that gained it for him. What happened was that Anaxandridas had married his sister's daughter, and although he was pleased with her, they had no children. The ephors

therefore summoned him to a meeting and said, 'Even if you do not look out for yourself, we cannot just let Eurysthenes' line die out. Your present wife is not bearing you children, so we suggest you let her go and marry someone else. That will make you popular among the Spartiates.'

'I refuse to do either of these things,' he replied. 'It's wrong of you to advise me to get rid of my present wife, who is blameless as far as I am concerned, and marry someone else. I shall not do as you suggest.'

[40] At this point, the ephors and the elders talked things over and then put the following proposal to Anaxandridas: 'All right. We can see that you want to keep your present wife, but here is an alternative course of action for you. We recommend that you don't refuse, otherwise the Spartiates might come to an unpleasant decision in your case. We're not going to ask you to dismiss your present wife, or to change the way you treat her at the moment, but you must bring in another woman, one who is not barren, and treat her in exactly the same way too.' Anaxandridas agreed with this idea of theirs, and subsequently had two wives and divided his time between two households, which was completely contrary to Spartiate practice.

[41] Not long afterwards, his new wife gave birth to Cleomenes. By a remarkable coincidence, just as she produced a Spartiate heir apparent, his first wife, who had previously been childless, also became pregnant. When the relatives of Anaxandridas' new wife heard the news, they began to make a nuisance of themselves; although she really was pregnant, they made out that it was a vain boast and that she was intending to adopt a child. They made such a lot of fuss about the matter that when her time drew near, the ephors were uncertain enough to gather around the woman and watch her labour. She gave birth to Dorieus, and then immediately became pregnant with Leonidas and immediately after that with Cleombrotus (although there is also an alternative account which makes Cleombrotus and Leonidas twins). Meanwhile, Cleomenes remained the only child of Anaxandridas' new wife, who was the daughter of Prinetadas the son of Demarmenus.

[42] The story goes that Cleomenes was not in possession of all his faculties, but was on the verge of insanity; Dorieus, however, was the outstanding man of his generation, and was sure that if excellence were the criterion, he would become king. Because of

this conviction of his, when Anaxandridas died and the Lacedaemonians made the eldest son Cleomenes king, as their constitution demanded, Dorieus was angry and refused to be ruled by
Cleomenes. He asked the Spartiates for a band of settlers and led
them off on a colonizing expedition. However, he failed to carry
out any of the prescribed preliminaries, and did not even consult
the Delphic oracle about where he should go and found his colony;
he just angrily sailed straight for Libya, with men from Thera to
guide him. He came to a very beautiful part of Libya, which was
on the River Cinyps, and founded a settlement there, but after two
years he was driven out by a combined force of Carthaginians and
a Libyan tribe called the Macaes, and returned to the Peloponnese.

[43] At this juncture a man from Eleon called Antichares advised
him, on the strength of the oracles of Laius, to colonize Heraclea
in Sicily. He claimed that the whole region around Mount Eryx
belonged to the descendants of Heracles, because Heracles had
taken possession of it. Dorieus listened to what Antichares said,
and then travelled to Delphi and asked the oracle whether he would
capture the land he was heading for. The Pythia gave him a positive reply, so Dorieus enlisted the same body of people he had taken
to Libya and set off for Italy.

[44] At the same time as Dorieus' emigration Sybaris, under the
command of its king Telys, was about to go to war against Croton.
The people of Croton—this is the Sybarite version of events—were
so terrified that they asked Dorieus to help them, and he agreed.
So Dorieus joined forces with the Crotonians and together they
captured Sybaris. That is the Sybarite account of what Dorieus and
his followers did, but the Crotonians claim that they had no outside
help in the war against Sybaris apart from Callias of Elis, a diviner
who was one of the Iamidae. He came to be with them, according
to the Crotonians, because he deserted to them from the Sybarite
tyrant Telys when he kept receiving unfavourable omens about the
attack on Croton from the entrails of his sacrificial victims. That
is the alternative account given by the Crotonians.

[45] Both sides produce evidence to support their version. The
Sybarites point to the existence of a precinct and temple by the dry
bed of the River Crathis, which they say Dorieus built after having
captured Sybaris and dedicated to Athena under the name of
Athena of Crathis. They also point, as their most telling piece of
evidence, to the circumstances of Dorieus' death, and claim that he

died because he was contravening the oracle's prophecy. If he had kept to the original purpose of his expedition and not been side-tracked, they say, he would have captured and held the land around Mount Eryx, without the loss of his own life and those of his men. The Crotonians, for their part, point out that while Callias of Elis was granted a number of special plots of land within Crotonian territory—plots which were still inhabited by Callias' descendants in my own time—there is no evidence of Dorieus or his descendants having received anything at all. And yet, they argue, if Dorieus had helped them in the war against Sybaris, he would have been given far more than Callias. So this is the evidence produced by either side; anyone can agree with whichever of the two accounts he finds plausible.

[46] Among the settlers who sailed with Dorieus were the Spartiates Thessalus, Paraebates, Celeës, and Euryleon. The expedition reached Sicily in full strength, but then they were defeated in battle by the Phoenicians and Segestans, and all died except for Euryleon, who was the only one to survive this catastrophe. He gathered together the remnants of the army and took Minoa, a colony of Selinous, and helped free the Selinians from their ruler Peithagoras. Having deposed Peithagoras, he next tried to set himself up as the tyrant of Selinous, and ruled for a short while, but then the people of Selinous rose up against him and killed him, despite the fact that he had taken refuge at the altar of Zeus the Protector of the Town Square.

[47] Another person who went to Sicily with Dorieus, and died with him, was Philippus of Croton, the son of Butacides, who had been banished from Croton because of his betrothal to the daughter of Telys of Sybaris. With his marriage plans foiled, Philippus sailed off to Cyrene and set out from there to join Dorieus' expedition. He provided his own trireme, and paid all his men's expenses himself. He was an Olympic victor and the most handsome man of his generation in Greece. His good looks have earned him a unique accolade from the people of Segesta: they offer propitiatory sacrifices at his tomb, where they have erected a hero's shrine.

[48] So that is how Dorieus died. If he had patiently stayed in Sparta and submitted to Cleomenes' rule, he would have become the king of Lacedaemon, because Cleomenes did not reign for very long, and died without a leaving a son, only a daughter, whose name was Gorgo.

[49] In any case, Aristagoras the tyrant of Miletus came to Sparta during Cleomenes' reign. The Lacedaemonian account of his visit is that he held discussions with Cleomenes, and brought with him a bronze chart on which was engraved a map of the whole earth, showing every stretch of sea and all the rivers. Aristagoras arrived for the meeting and said, 'Cleomenes, don't be surprised at how eager I am to have this meeting. This is the situation: the sons of the Ionians are slaves, when they should be free. But it isn't only we Ionians who should feel the terrible ignominy and pain; more than anyone else, you should feel it too, because you are the champions of Greece. I beg you, then, by the gods of the Greeks, to liberate your kinsmen in Ionia from slavery. Success in this matter will come easily to you, because these non-Greeks aren't formidable fighters and you have attained the highest achievement of all in military prowess. They fight with bows and short spears; they wear trousers and *kurbasias* into battle. This is how easy they are to beat.

'And there is real wealth there; the inhabitants of that continent are better off in material terms than the rest of the world put together. I'm talking about the amount of gold they have for a start, and silver, bronze, gorgeous clothing, yoke-animals, and slaves. You can have as much of all this as you like.

'I should go on to explain that they live next to one another. Here are the Ionians, and next to them—here—are the Lydians, whose land is fertile and rich in silver.' As he spoke, Aristagoras pointed to the map of the earth engraved on the chart he had brought with him. 'And here,' he went on, 'just to the east of the Lydians are the Phrygians, who have more flocks of animals, and richer harvests, than any other country I know of. Next to the Phrygians are the Cappadocians—or Syrians, as we call them. Their neighbours are the Cilicians, whose territory stretches down to this sea here, where Cyprus is—that's this island here. The Cilicians pay five hundred talents of tribute to the Persian king every year. Next to the Cilicians are the Armenians, and these people too have many herds. Then these people here, next to the Armenians, are the Matieneans. The next country along is Cissia, and Susa itself lies on the banks of this river here in Cissia, which is called the Choäspes. Susa is where the Great King usually lives, and where the treasuries are, with all his wealth. All you have to do is capture Susa, and your wealth will then undoubtedly challenge that of Zeus!

'Now take your land here. It is not very big or particularly fertile; and since it has a limited amount of space, you have to take the

risk of fighting with your equals the Messenians, not to mention
the Arcadians and the Argives. Desire for gold and silver can certainly move a man to fight and die, but your enemies here don't
have any gold or silver at all. When you could easily make yourselves the rulers of all Asia, how could you choose another option?'

When Aristagoras had finished speaking, Cleomenes told him
that he would not give his response straight away, but in two days'
time.

[50] That is as far as they got then. The day chosen for the
response arrived and they met as agreed. Cleomenes asked
Aristagoras how many days' journey it was from the Ionian coast
to the king's palace, and at that point Aristagoras, who up till then
had been so clever and had been successfully taking Cleomenes in,
made a mistake. In pursuit of his aim of seducing the Spartiates to
Asia, he should not have told the truth, but he did: he told him
that the journey inland would take three months. He was going on
to say more about the journey, but Cleomenes interrupted him. 'Sir,'
he said, 'I order you to leave Sparta before sunset. You are not
saying anything attractive to the Lacedaemonians, if you want them
to travel three months' journey away from the sea.'

[51] With these words Cleomenes returned home. Aristagoras
went to Cleomenes' home with a branch of supplication and, as a
suppliant, gained entry and asked Cleomenes to listen to what he
had to say, but first to dismiss the child: Cleomenes' only child, his
daughter Gorgo, who was 8 or 9 years old, was standing next to
him. Cleomenes told him to go ahead and say whatever he wanted
without holding back because of the child. Then Aristagoras began
by promising him ten talents if he did what he was asking him
to do. When Cleomenes refused the bribe, Aristagoras gradually
increased the amount of money he was offering, until he had
promised him fifty talents. At this point the child spoke. 'Father,'
she said, 'your visitor is going to corrupt you, if you don't get up
and leave.' Cleomenes was pleased with his daughter's advice, and
went into another room. Aristagoras left Sparta altogether and he
never got another chance to describe the journey inland to the king
of Persia.

[52] In fact, here is a description of the route. There are royal
staging-posts and excellent inns all along it, and every region the
road passes through is inhabited and safe. There are twenty staging-
posts strung along it as it goes through Lydia and Phrygia, which

is a journey of 94½ parasangs. Phrygia ends at the River Halys, where there is a pass, and it is only after getting through this pass that one crosses the river; there is also a substantial guard-post at the Halys. Across the river one continues on into Cappadocia, and along the road between the river and the border with Cilicia, a distance of 104 parasangs, there are twenty-eight staging-posts. At this border there are two passes to get through and two guard-posts to get by. Then there are three staging-posts on the journey through Cilicia of 15½ parasangs. The border between Cilicia and Armenia is formed by a river—the Euphrates—which is deep enough to be navigable. In Armenia there are fifteen staging-posts where one can break one's journey, and the road covers 56½ parasangs. There is a guard-post on this stretch of road. The road then enters Matiene, where there are thirty-four staging-posts along a route of 137 parasangs.† Matiene has four navigable rivers flowing through it, which have to be crossed by ferry; the first is the Tigris, the second and the third are both called the Zabatus (despite the fact that they are not the same river, not even at their source, since the first one rises in Armenia, while the further one rises in Matiene), and the fourth is the Gyndes, which is the river that Cyrus once divided into three hundred and sixty channels. Across the Gyndes into Cissia, there are eleven staging-posts on this stretch of road, which covers 42½ parasangs and goes up to the Choäspes (another river which is deep enough to be navigable), where Susa has been built. So there are 111 staging-posts in all—111 places to break one's journey inland from Sardis to Susa.

[53] If these distances in parasangs along the Royal Road are correct, and if a parasang is equal to thirty stades (which it is), then from Sardis to the Memnonian Palace, as it is known, is a distance of 13,500 stades, or 450 parasangs. So, supposing one travels 150 stades a day, the whole journey would take exactly ninety days.

[54] It follows that when Aristagoras of Miletus told Cleomenes the Lacedaemonian that it would take three months to reach the king, he was right. If even greater precision is required, I will provide that too, because the journey from Ephesus to Sardis needs to be taken into account as well. My conclusion is that the sum total of stades from the Greek sea to Susa (or the Memnonian city, as it is called) is 14,040, since it is 540 stades from Ephesus to Sardis. This would add three days on to the three-month journey.

[55] After being thrown out of Sparta, Aristagoras went to

Athens, which had become free of its tyrants. This is how it happened. Two members by descent of the family of the Gephyraei, Aristogiton and Harmodius, killed Hipparchus, the son of Pisistratus and brother of the reigning tyrant Hippias, despite the fact that Hipparchus had had a dream which referred unmistakably to his own fate.† The assassination did not improve the situation; in fact, for four years Athens had to endure an even more harsh tyranny than before.

[56] Hipparchus' dream, which occurred to him on the night before the Panathenaea, was that a tall, attractive man stood over him and spoke the following enigmatic words:

> Submit, lion: bear in your suffering heart the insufferable end;
> No one can avoid the penalty for his crimes.

Early the next morning, he was seen telling the dream-interpreters about his dream, but then he dismissed it from his thoughts, joined in the procession—and died during it.

[57] The Gephyraei—the family to which Hipparchus' assassins belonged—came originally, according to their account, from Eretria. However, my own researches have led me to conclude that they were Phoenicians, and were among the Phoenicians who accompanied Cadmus to the region now known as Boeotia, where they lived in Tanagra, the district allotted to them. The Cadmeans were driven out of this region by the Argives, and then later the Gephyraei were expelled by the Boeotians and made their way to Athens. The Athenians took them in and allowed them to join the citizen body with the proviso that they should be debarred from a number of insignificant rights.†

[58] The Phoenicians who came to Greece with Cadmus, among whom were the Gephyraei, ended up living in this land and introducing the Greeks to a number of accomplishments, most notably the alphabet, which, as far as I can tell, the Greeks did not have before then. At first the letters they used were the same as those of all Phoenicians everywhere, but as time went by, along with the sound, they changed the way they wrote the letters as well. At this time most of their Greek neighbours were Ionians. So it was the Ionians who learnt the alphabet from the Phoenicians; they changed the shapes of a few of the letters, but they still called the alphabet they used the Phoenician alphabet, which was only right, since it was the Phoenicians who had introduced it into Greece. The Ionian term for papyrus rolls—namely 'skins'—also goes back

a long way, to when they used goatskins and sheepskins to write on, because they did not have any papyrus. In fact even today many non-Greeks use such skins for writing.

[59] I have actually seen some examples of Cadmean writing myself in the sanctuary of Ismenian Apollo at Thebes in Boeotia; the writing was engraved on three tripods, and was basically similar to Ionian script. One of the tripods is inscribed with the line 'Amphitryon dedicated me out of spoils taken from the Teleboae'.† This must date from the time of Laius the son of Labdacus, grandson of Polydorus, and great-grandson of Cadmus.

[60] Another tripod has the following hexameter lines:

> After his victory in the games Scaeus the boxer dedicated me to you,
> Far-shooting Apollo, to be a beautiful decoration for your temple.

Scaeus must be the son of Hippocoön (unless the dedicator is actually someone else with the same name as the son of Hippocoön), from the time of Oedipus the son of Laius.

[61] The third tripod has the following lines, again in hexameter verse:

> King Laodamas himself dedicated this tripod to you,
> Clear-sighted Apollo, to be a beautiful decoration for your temple.

It was during the reign of this King Laodamas, who was the son of Eteocles, that the Cadmeans were uprooted by the Argives and made their way to the Encheleis, while the Gephyraei were left behind and then later were forced by the Boeotians to withdraw to Athens. They have their own rituals established in Athens, which no one else in the city is allowed to share; in particular, among other unique rituals of theirs, there is the rite of Demeter Achaea, and the mysteries performed there.

[62] Anyway, now that I have described Hipparchus' dream and the origins of the Gephyraei, the family to which Hipparchus' assassins belonged, I had better return to the story I started out to tell, about how the Athenians freed themselves from their tyrants. Hippias' rule over the Athenians had become even more harsh because of Hipparchus' murder, when the Alcmaeonidae, an Athenian family who had been banished by Pisistratidae, made an unsuccessful attempt, assisted by other Athenian exiles, to get back to Athens by force of arms and to liberate the state from Hippias' tyranny. They succeeded in fortifying a place called

Leipsydrium, which is above Paeonia, but then they suffered a heavy defeat. After that, the Alcmaeonidae did all they could to damage the Pisistratidae. One thing they did was gain the contract from the Amphictyons to build the present temple in Delphi, which did not exist then. Now, the Alcmaeonidae had been a prominent family for generations, and they were not short of money; the temple they built improved on the plan in a number of respects, including the fact that whereas the contract called for the use of tufa as the building-material, they used Parian marble for the front.

[63] The Athenians claim that while the Alcmaeonidae were based in Delphi they used to bribe the Pythia to advise any Spartiates who came, whether they were there on personal or public business, to liberate Athens. Since they were constantly receiving the same message, then, the Lacedaemonians sent a task force under one of their foremost citizens, a man called Anchimolius the son of Aster, to expel the Pisistratidae from Athens; they did this despite the fact that they and the Pisistratidae were close guest-friends and allies, because for them divine matters took precedence over human ones. Ships were provided to transport the task force.

Anchimolius put in at Phalerum and his men disembarked, but the Pisistratidae had found out in advance that they were coming and had sent for a mercenary force from Thessaly, with whom they had entered into a treaty of alliance. In response to their request, the Thessalians all agreed to send a thousand horsemen under their king Cineas of Conda. The plan the Pisistratidae adopted, once they had gained their reinforcements, was to clear the plain of Phalerum to make it suitable for cavalry, and then send the horsemen against the enemy troops. Losses among the Lacedaemonians from this cavalry attack were heavy, and included Anchimolius; the survivors were forced back to their ships. So that was the end of the first expedition from Lacedaemon. Anchimolius' tomb is in Attica, at Alopecae near the temple of Heracles at Cynosarges.

[64] The Lacedaemonians next prepared and sent a larger force to attack Athens, and put King Cleomenes, the son of Anaxandridas, in command of the expedition. This time they sent the army by land rather than sea. The Thessalian cavalry engaged them as soon as they entered Attic territory, but they were routed after a brief battle, with the loss of about forty men. The survivors wasted

no time in heading straight back to Thessaly. After this victory, Cleomenes and the Athenian partisans of freedom made their way to the city, where they pinned the tyrants inside the Pelasgian Wall and began to besiege them there.

[65] Under normal circumstances, there is no way in which the Lacedaemonians would have got the Pisistratidae out of there. The Pisistratidae had plenty of food and water, and the Lacedaemonians had not planned on a siege, so they would have kept up the blockade for a few days and then gone back to Sparta. What happened, however, was a piece of luck which was as bad for one side as it was helpful to the other: the children of the Pisistratidae were captured as they were being secretly taken out of the country. This threw the Pisistratidae into complete disarray, and in order to recover the children they were forced to surrender on whatever terms the Athenians wanted, which were that they should be out of Attica within five days. And so they left and went to Sigeum on the Scamander River. They had ruled over Athens for a total of thirty-six years. Originally, this family came from Pylos and were descendants of Neleus, from the same stock as Codrus and Melanthus, who had become kings of Athens despite being immigrants. This is why Hippocrates had called his son Pisistratus, to recall Pisistratus the son of Nestor.

So that is how the Athenians rid themselves of tyrants. But now I shall first give an account of all the notable events that happened to them, whether instigated by them or by others, between the time they gained their freedom and the arrival of Aristagoras of Miletus in Athens to ask them to help the Ionians in their rebellion against Darius.

[66] Athens had been an important state before, but once it had rid itself of tyrants it began to grow in stature. There were two particularly powerful men in Athens: Cleisthenes, who was an Alcmaeonid (and was the one, reputedly, who bribed the Pythia), and Isagoras the son of Tisander, who came from a distinguished house, but one whose origins I have been unable to discover. (However, relatives of his offer sacrifices to Carian Zeus.) Now, a power struggle took place between these two men, which Cleisthenes lost. He then allied himself with the common people and instituted the system of ten tribes in Athens, when there had been only four before. The four tribes had been named after the sons of Ion—Geleon, Aegicores, Argades, and Hoples—but

Cleisthenes abolished these names and came up instead with the names of local heroes, except in the case of Ajax, whose name was added to the list on the grounds that despite being a foreigner, he had been a neighbour and an ally.

[67] It seems to me that in this Cleisthenes was copying his maternal grandfather, Cleisthenes the tyrant of Sicyon. This Cleisthenes had been at war with Argos, and then he suspended the rhapsodic contests in Sicyon, because they involved the Homeric epics, which constantly celebrate Argos and the Argives. Now, there was (and still is) a shrine in the main square of Sicyon to Adrastus the son of Talaus, and, because he was an Argive, Cleisthenes also wanted to banish this hero from the country. He went to Delphi and asked if it would be all right to banish Adrastus, but the Pythia's response was that Adrastus had been the king of Sicyon, whereas he was a nobody. Since the god was not letting him take this course, on his return to Sicyon he began to devise a plan for getting rid of Adrastus. When he thought he had found a way to do it, he sent a messenger to Boeotian Thebes asking for permission to introduce Melanippus the son of Astacus into Sicyon. The Thebans gave him permission, and so Cleisthenes introduced Melanippus into Sicyon. He consecrated a precinct in the actual town hall and built it in the most impregnable spot. Now, it should also be explained that the reason Cleisthenes brought Melanippus to Sicyon was that Melanippus and Adrastus had been implacable enemies, because Melanippus had killed Adrastus' brother Mecisteus and his son-in-law Tydeus. So, having dedicated his precinct, Cleisthenes deprived Adrastus of his sacrifices and festivals and gave them to Melanippus—and Adrastus had always been a particular object of reverence in Sicyon, ever since Polybus, the king of Sicyon, who had no children, bequeathed his kingdom after his death to Adrastus, who was his daughter's son. One of the ways in which the Sicyonians used to worship Adrastus was by commemorating his sufferings with tragic choruses, who performed in honour of Adrastus rather than Dionysus. But Cleisthenes assigned his choruses to Dionysus, and the rest of his rites to Melanippus.

[68] So that is what Cleisthenes did about Adrastus. However, the Sicyonians and the Argives had the same tribes—the Dorian tribes—and he also wanted to avoid that, so he changed the names of the Sicyonian tribes. In doing so, he made the people of Sicyon laughing-stocks, because he changed the tribal names to 'Swine',

'Donkey', and 'Pig', and just added the usual ending. The only exception was his own tribe, which he named the Rulers of the People after his own rule. The others, however, were called the Swineans, the Donkeyans, or the Pigeans. These tribal names were used in Sicyon not only in Cleisthenes' time, but for sixty years after his death as well. But then the issue came up and they changed the names to the Hylleis, the Pamphylians, and the Dymanatae, and added a new name for the fourth tribe—the Aegialians, named after Adrastus' son Aegialeus.

[69] These were the reforms of Cleisthenes of Sicyon. As for his daughter's son and namesake, Cleisthenes of Athens, I think he was another person with a low opinion of others—in his case the Ionians—and that is why, in imitation of the other Cleisthenes, he wanted the Athenians not to have the same tribes as the Ionians. So when he had won over to his side the ordinary people of Athens, who had previously been discounted, he changed the names of the tribes and increased their number. He created ten tribal leaders, then, where there had formerly been four, and divided the whole population between these ten tribes. And once he had won the ordinary people over, he was far more powerful than his political opponents.

[70] So now it was Isagoras' turn to lose in the power struggle. His response was to ask Cleomenes of Lacedaemon to help; Cleomenes had been his guest-friend and ally ever since the blockade of the Pisistratidae (and Cleomenes had been accused of having an affair with Isagoras' wife). At first, Cleomenes sent a messenger to Athens to try to get Cleisthenes and a number of other Athenians banished, on the grounds that they were under a curse. It was Isagoras who told him to say this in the message he sent. For although the Alcmaeonidae and their supporters had been accused of murder (as I shall explain), Isagoras and his allies had not had anything to do with it.

[71] Here is how the 'accursed' Athenians came to get their name. An Athenian called Cylon, an Olympic victor, saw himself as the tyrant of Athens. He made himself the leader of a band of young men his own age and tried to seize the Acropolis. When this attempt failed, he and his men took refuge as suppliants at the base of the statue of Athena. The presidents of the naucraries, who constituted the governing body of Athens in those days, persuaded them to leave with assurances that, whatever punishment they

faced, they would not be put to death. The Alcmaeonidae were accused of murdering them, however. All this happened before the time of Pisistratus.

[72] When Cleomenes made his attempt, through his representative, to banish Cleisthenes and the Athenians who were under a curse, Cleisthenes slipped out of Athens. Nevertheless, Cleomenes subsequently came to Athens with a small force and, on the advice of Isagoras, expelled seven hundred Athenian families. He next tried to dissolve the Council and to transfer its functions to three hundred of Isagoras' supporters. When the Council resisted and refused to comply, Cleomenes, with the help of Isagoras and his supporters, occupied the Acropolis. The rest of the Athenians joined forces and besieged them on the Acropolis. The siege lasted for two days and then on the third day the Lacedaemonian contingent were allowed to leave the country under a truce. So the warning Cleomenes had received came true. In the course of occupying the Acropolis, when he reached the top, he was in the process of entering the temple of Athena to pray, but the priestess got up from her chair before he had passed through the doorway and said, 'Go back, Lacedaemonian. You are not to enter the sanctuary. It is unlawful for Dorians to enter here.'

'I'm no Dorian, woman,' he replied. 'I'm an Achaean.' So he ignored the omen, carried on with the venture, and was expelled on this occasion, as he had been before, along with the rest of the Lacedaemonians. The Athenians condemned the non-Lacedaemonians to death and threw them into prison. Among those taken was Timesitheus of Delphi, whose extraordinary feats of strength and courage I could describe.

[73] After the prisoners had been executed, the Athenians recalled Cleisthenes and the seven hundred families who had been banished by Cleomenes. Then they sent a delegation to Sardis, because they knew that Cleomenes and the Lacedaemonians were up in arms against them, so they wanted to enter into an alliance with the Persians. The delegation reached Sardis and was in the middle of delivering its message when Artaphrenes the son of Hystaspes, who was the governor of Sardis, asked the Athenians who they were and where they were from that they sought an alliance with the Persians. The Athenian delegates gave him the information he had asked for, and then he curtly stated his position as

follows: 'If the Athenians give King Darius earth and water, he will enter into an alliance with them; otherwise, they will have to leave.' The delegates wanted to conclude the alliance, so of their own accord they agreed to offer the king earth and water. This got them into a lot of trouble on their return home.

[74] Meanwhile Cleomenes, who felt deeply injured by the Athenians' actions and their words, was mobilizing an army from all over the Peloponnese. Although he did not explain why he was mustering an army, his intention was to punish the Athenian people and to make Isagoras, who had left the Acropolis with him, the tyrant of Athens. So Cleomenes attacked Eleusis at the head of a large army, and at the same time the Boeotians, by prior arrangement, took Oenoe and Hysiae, which were the most remote villages in Attica, while the Chalcidians invaded and began devastating Attic territory elsewhere. Although the Athenians were being attacked on all sides, they decided to forget about the Boeotians and Chalcidians for the time being, and they went and took up a position facing the Peloponnesians at Eleusis.

[75] Battle was just about to be joined when the Corinthians came to the conclusion that they were perpetrating a miscarriage of justice, so in a complete volte-face they set off back home. Then Demaratus the son of Ariston, who was the other Spartan king and the joint leader of the invading army, followed suit, even though he and Cleomenes had previously been on good terms. (As a result of this rift, a law was passed in Sparta to the effect that both kings were not to take to the field together, as they had up till then. Moreover, since one of the two kings was relieved from active service, one of the two Tyndaridae could be left behind as well, both of whom had also previously gone with the army to support the effort.) Anyway, back in Eleusis, when the remainder of the allies saw that the kings of the Lacedaemonians were at odds and that the Corinthians had abandoned their position, they decamped as well.

[76] This was the fourth time that Dorians had come to Attica. Two of the occasions were hostile invasions, and the other two were for the good of the Athenian people. The first time was when they had also founded Megara (an expedition which should be dated to the time when Codrus was the king of Athens); the second and third times were when they set out from Sparta to get rid of the

Pisistratidae; and the fourth time was when Cleomenes attacked
Eleusis at the head of a Peloponnesian army. So this was the fourth
time that Dorians attacked Athens.

[77] With this army in ignominious tatters, the Athenians, bent
on revenge, set out first to take on the Chalcidians. The Boeotians,
however, advanced up to the Euripus to support the Chalcidians,
and when the Athenians saw the relief force, they decided to attack
it before the Chalcidians. So they engaged the Boeotians and
won a considerable victory, killing large numbers of the enemy
and taking seven hundred prisoners. On the very same day the
Athenians crossed the strait to Euboea and fought another battle
against the Chalcidians, which they also won. Then they left four
thousand smallholders on the land of the Horse-farmers (as men
of substance are called in Chalcis). They took prisoners in this
battle too, whom they kept bound and under guard with the
Boeotian prisoners. Eventually, all the prisoners were released, once
a ransom of two minas each had been paid. The Athenians hung
the chains they had used to shackle them on the Acropolis, and
they were still there in my day, hanging on walls scorched in the
fire started by the Persians, opposite the west-facing temple. They
set aside a tenth of the ransom and had a bronze four-horse chariot
built as a dedicatory offering, which is the first thing one comes
across on the left as one enters the Propylaea on the Acropolis.
There is an inscription on it which reads as follows:

> Crushing the Boeotians and Chalcidians,
> The sons of Athens fought well,
> Quenched their pride in grievous† bondage of iron,
> And made these horses from a tenth of the spoils
> As an offering to Pallas Athena.

[78] So Athens flourished. Now, the advantages of everyone
having a voice in the political procedure are not restricted just to
single instances, but are plain to see wherever one looks. For
instance, while the Athenians were ruled by tyrants, they were
no better at warfare than any of their neighbours, but once they
had got rid of the tyrants they became vastly superior. This goes to
show that while they were under an oppressive regime they fought
below their best because they were working for a master, whereas
as free men each individual wanted to achieve something for
himself.†

[79] So this is how the Athenians were occupied. Some time later, the Thebans sent emissaries to Apollo at Delphi, because they wanted to take revenge on Athens. The Pythia told them that they would not gain revenge from their own resources, and that they should inform 'that which has many voices' of her response and then 'apply to the nearest'. So the emissaries returned home, convened an assembly and reported the oracle's response to the assembled people. On hearing the emissaries say that they should 'apply to the nearest', the Thebans said, 'Aren't our nearest neighbours the people of Tanagra, Coronea, and Thespiae? But they are always committed fighters, and help us in our wars. So why should we apply for help to them? It doesn't look as though that is what the oracle meant.'

[80] These were the lines along which they were thinking, when someone at last got the point and said, 'I think I understand what the oracle means. Asopus is supposed to have had two daughters, Thebe and Aegina. Aegina was Thebe's sister, then, so I think Apollo is telling us to ask the Aeginetans for help.' No one could come up with a better idea than this, so they lost no time in sending a message to the Aeginetans to solicit their help, according to the oracle, on the grounds that they were their 'nearest'. In response the Aeginetans agreed to send the Aeacidae to help them.

[81] The Thebans made an attack, then, with the help of the Aeacidae, but they were badly mauled by the Athenians. So they sent another delegation to Aegina, to return the Aeacidae and ask for men. Now, Aeginetan morale was high, because of their great prosperity, and they also remembered the long-standing antagonism between them and Athens, so they responded to the Thebans' request by launching an unannounced war against Athens. While the Athenians were attacking the Boeotians, the Aeginetans sent their longships against Attica and weakened Athens a great deal by ravaging Phalerum and a number of coastal villages.

[82] The origin of the grudge the Aeginetans owed the Athenians was as follows. The crops failed at Epidaurus, so the Epidaurians consulted Delphi about this calamity. The Pythia told them to erect statues of Damia and Auxesia and said that matters would then improve for them. The Epidaurians asked whether they should make the statues out of bronze or stone, but the Pythia said neither, and told them to use the wood of a cultivated olive-tree instead. So the Epidaurians asked the Athenians for permission to cut down

an olive-tree, because they assumed that Athenian olives would be best suited for religious purposes (though according to another version of the story Athens was the only place in the world where olive-trees grew in those days). The Athenians gave them permission to go ahead, provided that they undertook to bring offerings every year for Athena the Guardian of the Community and for Erechtheus. The Epidaurians agreed to these terms, got the olive wood they wanted, and put up statues made out of this wood. Their land became fertile again and they kept to the terms of their contract with Athens.

[83] Now, both at the time in question and earlier, Aegina was a dependency of Epidaurus. Apart from anything else, this involved their crossing over to Epidaurus to settle the lawsuits that arose among them. After a time, however, the Aeginetans built themselves a navy, adopted an uncompromising attitude, and seceded from Epidaurus. The Aeginetans had control of the sea, so in the ensuing hostilities it was the Epidaurians who suffered, and the Aeginetans also managed to steal these statues of Damia and Auxesis from Epidaurus. They took them to Aegina and set them up in the interior of the island, in a place called Oea, which is about twenty stades from the town. Then they instituted a form of worship which involved sacrificing to the statues and abusive choruses performed by women; each of the deities had ten men appointed to produce the choruses. The abuse in the choruses was reserved for local women, never men. The Epidaurians had the same rituals too, as well as some secret rites.

[84] Now that these statues had been stolen, the Epidaurians stopped fulfilling their obligations to Athens. The Athenians sent an angry message to the Epidaurians, who tried to justify their actions by pointing out that they had kept to the terms of the contract as long as the statues were in their country, and that with the loss of the statues it was unfair for them to have to continue with the offerings; they told the Athenians that they should get what was due to them from those who had the statues—namely the Aeginetans. Under these circumstances, the Athenians sent representatives to Aegina to demand the return of the statues, but the Aeginetans told the Athenians to mind their own business.

[85] Now, according to the Athenians, the next thing that happened, after this demand of theirs, was that the Athenian authorities sent a few of their number to Aegina in a single trireme. When

this band of men got to Aegina, they tried to lift the statues off their bases, so that they could take them back to Athens, since they were made out of Athenian wood. However, they could not manage the job this way, so they next threw ropes around the statues and tried to pull them off. But while they were pulling on the ropes, a thunderstorm occurred, and at the same time the earth shook with a tremor. These phenomena drove the crew of the trireme, who were doing the pulling, out of their minds, and in their insanity they mistook members of their own party for enemies and killed one another. Eventually, there was just one person left out of the whole band, and he made his way back to Phalerum.

[86] That is the Athenian version of events, but according to the Aeginetans the Athenians did not come in just one ship; if a single ship had been involved, or just a few, the Aeginetans argue, they would easily have kept them at bay, even without having a fleet of their own. In fact, they say, the Athenians sent a large number of ships to attack the island, and so they gave in and did not engage them at sea. They do not make it perfectly clear in their account whether they gave in because they realized they would be beaten in a sea battle, or because they had decided on the course of action they did in fact take. Anyway, according to the Aeginetans, when the Athenians met with no resistance, they disembarked and made their way to the statues. They tried and failed to drag them off their bases, and so they tied ropes on to them and started to pull. They went on pulling until both the statues did the same thing—something which I find incredible, but others may not. In any case, they claim that the statues fell to their knees and have remained in that position ever since. That is what the Athenians did, according to the Aeginetans, and for their part, they say, as soon as they found out that the Athenians were intending to launch an expedition against them, they had the Argives stand by. So when the Athenians landed on Aegina, the Argives came to help the islanders. They secretly sailed out of Epidaurus over to the island, fell on the Athenians, who had no prior warning of their arrival, and cut them off from their ships. It was at this point that the thunder and the tremor occurred.

[87] That is the Argive and Aeginetan version of events, and it agrees with the Athenian account in saying that only one man got back alive to Attica. The difference is that the Argives claim that it was they who annihilated the Athenian force from which this one

man survived, whereas the Athenians claim that it was a divine
act. In fact, however, even this sole survivor died, according to the
Athenians. Back in Athens he told everyone about the disaster, and
when the wives of the men who had gone on the expedition to
Aegina heard the news they were furious that he should be the only
one to survive. They surrounded him, grabbed hold of him, and
stabbed him to death with the brooches which fastened their
clothes, while each of them asked him where her husband was.
That was how he met his death. The Athenians found what the
women had done even more shocking than the disaster on Aegina,
but the only punishment they could come up with for the women
was to make them change over to the Ionian style of clothing. Previously, women in Athens had dressed in the Dorian fashion (which
is very similar to the Corinthian style), so they made them change
over to a linen tunic, which did not need fastening with a brooch.

[88] In actual fact, however, the style of clothing they changed
to was Carian in origin rather than Ionian, because in the old days
women's clothes throughout Greece, including Ionia, were in the
style that we nowadays call Dorian. Anyway, this is also the context
in which the Argives and Aeginetans made it customary in each of
their countries for brooches to be made half as long again as was
normal at the time. (Other customs dating from these events are
that women should make a particular point of dedicating their
brooches to these two deities, and that no Attic pottery or anything
else from Attica was to be taken into their sanctuary, but that in
the future locally made cups should be used as drinking-vessels
there.) So from then on, thanks to the dispute with Athens, the
women of the Argives and the Aeginetans have worn larger
brooches than they did before, and this practice still survives today.

[89] That, then, is the origin of the hostility between Aegina and
Athens. So when the Thebans applied for help, the memory of what
had happened with the statues made the Aeginetans only too glad
to come to the Boeotians' assistance, and they began to devastate
the coastal areas of Attica. The Athenians were poised to march
against the Aeginetans when they received an oracular reponse
from Delphi to the effect that they should do nothing about the
Aeginetans' aggression for thirty years, and in the thirty-first year
they should consecrate a precinct to Aeacus and then declare war
on Aegina, and everything would go according to plan; however,
the oracle said, if they fought the Aeginetans straight away, they

would suffer as many troubles as they inflicted throughout that thirty-year period, even though they would ultimately be victorious. In response to this information, the Athenians *did* consecrate a precinct to Aeacus (the one which is now situated in the city square), but they ignored the part about how they were supposed to wait thirty years, because they had already suffered such horrific treatment at the hands of the Aeginetans.

[90] However, the Athenian preparations for revenge against Aegina were checked by fresh trouble from Lacedaemon: the Lacedaemonians had found out about the trick the Pythia had played on them and the Pisistratidae, and how the Alcmaeonidae had engineered it. They were doubly upset, first because they had driven men who were their friends and allies out of their homeland, and second because the Athenians had never shown them any gratitude for having done so. They were also motivated by oracles which spoke of the terrible things that would be done to them by Athens. They had previously been ignorant of these oracles, but Cleomenes had now brought them to Sparta from the Athenian Acropolis, where he had got them, and they became aware of their content. Originally, these oracles had been in the possession of the Pisistratidae, but when they were banished from Athens they left them in the sanctuary of Athena, where Cleomenes picked them up.

[91] It was not just that the Lacedaemonians had the oracles by then; they could also see that Athenian power was on the increase and that there was no way in which Athens was going to accept their hegemony. They realized that the Attic people, given its freedom, would become a match for them, whereas if it was oppressed by tyranny, it would be weak and submissive. Once they fully appreciated this, they summoned Hippias the son of Pisistratus from Sigeum on the Hellespont. Hippias came in answer to their summons, and then they also invited their other allies to send representatives.

When all their allies were there, the Spartiates addressed them as follows: 'Friends, we are conscious of having done wrong. At the instigation of false oracles we expelled from their homeland men who were very good friends of ours and who were undertaking to make the Athenians subject to us, and then we handed the state over to a mob of people who are so ungrateful that they had no sooner won their freedom, with our help, than they threw us and

our king out in a most insolent manner. Their arrogance has grown
along with their power; this is something that their neighbours,
the Boeotians and Chalcidians, have learnt to their great cost, but
it may well be that others will learn the same lesson too, if they are
not careful. So we have made mistakes, but with your help we want
to try to remedy them now. The reason we invited Hippias and the
rest of you to make the journey to this conference was so that we
could reach agreement and join forces to restore him to Athens and
return to him what we had taken away.'

[92] Although this plan did not go down well with most of the
allies, the only one to speak up was Socleas of Corinth. 'Whatever
next?' he said. 'Will the heavens be under the earth and the earth
up in the sky on top of the heavens? Will men habitually live in the
sea and fish live where men did before? It's a topsy-turvy world if
you Lacedaemonians are really planning to abolish equal rights and
restore tyrants to their states, when there is nothing known to man
that is more unjust or bloodthirsty than tyranny. If you think it's
such a good idea for states to be ruled by tyrants, you should take
the lead and set up a tyrant for yourselves before wanting to do so
for others. As things are, however, you have never experienced
tyranny, and in fact you take extreme precautions to ensure that it
never happens in Sparta, while being indifferent to what happens
to us, your allies. No, if you had the firsthand experience of tyranny
that we have, your proposals on this issue would be better than
they now are.

'Take the situation in Corinth, for instance. It used to be an oligarchy, with a family called the Bacchiadae,† who married only
within their own clan, ruling the city. One of these Bacchiadae,
whose name was Amphion, had a daughter called Labda, who was
lame. Since no one from within the family wanted to marry her,
Eëtion the son of Echecrates married her; Eëtion was a commoner
from Petra, but traced his ancestry back to the Lapithae and
Caeneidae. Now, Eëtion had no children by Labda or anyone else,
so he travelled to Delphi to ask whether he would have an heir.
The moment he entered the shrine, the Pythia spoke the following
lines to him:

> Eëtion, no one honours you, though you are full of honour.
> Labda will conceive and give birth to a boulder—
> One that will fall on the rulers and punish Corinth.

News of what the oracle had told Eëtion somehow reached the Bacchiadae, who had failed to understand an earlier oracle about Corinth which had the same meaning as the one given to Eëtion. The text of this earlier oracle was:

> An eagle conceives in a rocky place and will bear a lion—
> A strong, savage lion which will loosen the knees of many.
> Beware, Corinthians, beware, you inhabitants
> Of craggy Corinth, near fair Peirene.

'The Bacchiadae had been unable to decipher this earlier oracle, but as soon as they found out about Eëtion's oracle, they realized that the two of them fitted together. But even so, they did nothing; they preferred to wait for Eëtion's child to be born and then kill it. As soon as his wife gave birth, they sent ten members of their family to the village where Eëtion was living to kill the baby. The Bacchiadae came to Petra, arrived in Eëtion's courtyard, and asked to see the baby. Labda had no idea why they had come; she thought they wanted to see the baby because they were friends of her father's, so she fetched him and put him in the arms of one of the men. Now, on the way to Petra they had decided that whichever of them was the first to get hold of the baby should dash him to the ground. But when Labda brought the baby and handed him over, he providentially happened to smile at the man, and this sight filled the would-be assassin with pity and stopped him killing the child. Feeling sorry for the baby, the first man passed him on to the second—who passed him on to the third, and so on, until he had been passed around all ten, none of whom could bring himself to do the deed. So they handed the baby back to his mother and went outside. Standing near the doorway of the house, they laid into one another, and were especially critical of the one who had been the first to take hold of the child, because he had failed to carry out their plan. After a while, they decided to go back inside the house and make sure that they *all* played a part in the murder.

'It was fated, however, that Eëtion's son would be the source of suffering for Corinth. You see, Labda was standing right by the doors and overheard everything the men said. She was afraid that they'd change their minds the second time they got hold of her baby, and would kill him, so she took him and hid him in the most unlikely place she could think of—a chest, in fact—because she knew that the house would be thoroughly searched if the men came back inside to look for the baby. And that's exactly what happened. They came into the house and looked around, and when they couldn't find the baby, they decided to leave and to tell the people who had given them the mission that they had carried out their orders to the letter.

'So that's what they said when they got back to Corinth. As the years passed, Eëtion's son grew, and because it was a chest that had enabled him to escape danger on that occasion, he gained the nickname Cypselus. As an adult, he once consulted the oracle at Delphi. The response was ambiguous, but on the strength of it he attacked Corinth and gained control there. The oracle was as follows:

> Happy is the man who is now descending into my dwelling,
> Eëtion's son Cypselus, the king of far-famed Corinth.
> Happy is he and happy his children—but no longer his
>   children's children.

That was the oracle Cypselus received. As a tyrant, this is what he was like: large numbers of Corinthians were forced into exile by him, large numbers had their property confiscated, but by far the largest number lost their lives.

'His reign lasted for thirty years, and his death was easy. He was succeeded in the tyranny by his son Periander. At first, Periander was less cruel than his father, but after he had corresponded with Thrasybulus, the tyrant of Miletus, he became far more bloodthirsty than Cypselus. He sent an agent to Thrasybulus to ask what was the safest kind of government for him to establish, which would allow him to manage the state best. Thrasybulus took the man sent by Periander out of the city and into a field where there were crops growing. As he walked through the grain, he kept questioning the messenger and getting him to repeat over and over again what he had come from Corinth to ask. Meanwhile, every time he saw an ear of grain standing higher than the rest, he broke it off and threw it away, and he went on doing this until he had destroyed the choicest, tallest stems in the crop. After this walk across the field, Thrasybulus sent Periander's man back home, without having offered him any advice. When the man got back to Corinth, Periander was eager to hear Thrasybulus' recommendations, but the agent said that he had not made any at all. In fact, he said, he was surprised that Periander had sent him to a man of that kind—a lunatic who destroyed his own property—and he described what he had seen Thrasybulus doing.

'Periander, however, understood Thrasybulus' actions. He realized that he had been advising him to kill outstanding citizens, and from then on he treated his people with unremitting brutality. If Cypselus had left anything undone during his spell of slaughter and persecution, Periander finished the job. One day, moreover, he had all the women in Corinth stripped naked. He did this because of his wife, Melissa. You see, Periander had sent emissaries to the oracle of the dead on the River Acheron in Thesprotia to ask about the location of a friend's funds. The ghost of Melissa appeared and said that she wouldn't indicate or reveal where the money was, because she was cold and naked; the clothes Periander had buried her in were no use, the ghost explained, unless they were burnt. As proof of the fact that she really was who she said she was, she said that Periander had put his loaves into a cold oven.

'Now, this coded information convinced Periander, because he had had sex with Melissa's corpse, so as soon as the message had been delivered, he issued a proclamation that every woman in Corinth was to leave her home and go to the temple of Hera. The women all put on their finest clothes, because they assumed they were going to a festival, but Periander had secretly posted members of his personal guard there, and he forced them to strip regardless of their station, free women and servants alike. Then he had all the clothing collected and taken to a pit, where he burnt it all up while invoking Melissa. Afterwards, he sent another emissary to the oracle, and this time Melissa's ghost told him where she had put his friend's money.

'That's what tyranny is like; these are the kinds of deeds it performs. We Corinthians were astonished to find you Lacedaemonians sending for Hippias, and now we're even more surprised to hear this speech from you. We solemnly implore you, in the names of the gods of Greece, not to turn our states into tyrannies. Will you desist, or will you continue with your unjustifiable attempt to restore Hippias? If you continue, you should know that you do so against the wishes of the people of Corinth.'

[93] This was the speech made by Socleas, the Corinthian representative. In reply, Hippias invoked the same gods and swore that the Corinthians would be the first to miss the Pisistratidae when the time came, as it surely would, for them to suffer at Athenian hands. This reply of Hippias' was based on his unrivalled and precise knowledge of the oracles. The rest of the Lacedaemonian allies had kept quiet up till then, but after hearing Socleas speak

out so freely, every single one of them burst into speech to express their approval of the Corinthian position, and implored the Lacedaemonians not to meddle in the affairs of a Greek state.

[94] So the Lacedaemonians' plans were thwarted and Hippias was sent packing. Amyntas of Macedonia offered him Anthemous, and the Thessalians gave him permission to live in Iolcus, but Hippias refused both offers and went back to Sigeum. Pisistratus had taken Sigeum from Mytilene by force of arms, and having gained control of the place he set up as tyrant there his illegitimate son Hegesistratus, whose mother was a woman from Argos. However, Hegesistratus had to fight to keep this gift of Pisistratus': the Mytileneans based in the town of Achilleum and the Athenians in Sigeum became embroiled in a long, drawn-out war. The Mytileneans demanded the return of the land they had lost, and the Athenians refused to acknowledge their claim to the land and argued that Aeolians had no more right to the land of Ilium than themselves or any other Greeks who had helped Menelaus avenge the abduction of Helen.

[95] Among the incidents that occurred in the battles during this war was the occasion when the poet Alcaeus had to make his escape by retreating from an engagement which the Athenians were winning, and the Athenians took possession of his armour and hung it in the temple of Athena in Sigeum. Alcaeus made up a poem about the episode and sent it to Mytilene as a way of telling his friend Melanippus what had happened to him. It was Periander the son of Cypselus who negotiated an end to the hostilities between the Mytileneans and Athenians, after they had asked him to arbitrate. The terms of the peace were that each side was to retain possession of the land they already had. This is how Sigeum came to be subject to Athens.

[96] Once Hippias was back in Asia after leaving Lacedaemon, he started to do everything he could to blacken the Athenians in the eyes of Artaphrenes, and to try to find a way get Athens within his and Darius' control. When the Athenians found out what Hippias was up to, they sent a message to Sardis advising the Persians not to listen to these exiles from Athens. However, Artaphrenes told them that their future security depended on their taking Hippias back. When this message was brought back to Athens, the Athenians rejected it—and thereby they had effectively decided on open hostility towards Persia.

[97] It was at exactly this juncture—just when the Athenians were in this frame of mind and had fallen out with Persia—that Aristagoras of Miletus arrived in Athens after he had been thrown out of Sparta by the Lacedaemonian king Cleomenes. He chose to come to Athens because after Sparta it was the most powerful Greek state. He presented himself before the Assembly and gave substantially the same speech as he had given in Sparta, emphasizing how rich Asia was and how easy it would be to beat the Persians, since they did not use either shields or long spears when fighting. He went on, however, to point out that Miletus was an Athenian colony, and that therefore it was reasonable to expect Athens to use its considerable power to protect them. His need was so desperate that there was nothing he did not promise, and in the end he did win them over. It seems to be easier to fool a crowd than a single person, since Aristagoras could not persuade Cleomenes of Lacedaemon, who was all alone, but he succeeded with thirty thousand Athenians. So now that they had been won over, the Athenians voted to send a fleet of twenty ships to help the Ionians, and they put Melanthius—an extremely distinguished Athenian—in command of the expedition. These twenty ships proved to be the beginning of misfortune for Greeks and non-Greeks alike.

[98] Aristagoras sailed ahead of the Athenian fleet. Back in Miletus, he came up with a plan which was bound not to help the Ionians in the slightest, nor did he adopt it for this reason; all he wanted to do was annoy Darius. He sent a man to Phrygia, to the Paeonians from the River Strymon who had been captured by Megabazus and transplanted to Phrygia, where they had some land and a village of their own. When Aristagoras' messenger arrived, he said, 'Men of Paeonia, Aristagoras, the tyrant of Miletus, has ˙sent me to offer you protection if you decide to do what he suggests. For all Ionia has risen up against the king, and this gives you the opportunity to get safely back to your homeland. If you can get as far as the coast on your own, from there on we will look after you.'

The Paeonians found this idea very much to their liking. Almost all of them (a few stayed behind out of fear) gathered together their women and children, fled to the coast, and then sailed over to Chios. They had just made it to Chios when a large troop of Persian horsemen arrived hard on their heels. Discovering that they had missed their quarry, the Persians sent a message to the Paeonians on Chios, ordering them to return—an order the Paeonians refused to obey. In fact, the Chians took them from Chios to Lesbos, and the Lesbians transported them to Doriscus, and from there they made their way back to Paeonia on foot.

[99] So the Athenian fleet of twenty ships arrived in Miletus, supplemented by five Eretrian triremes. Miletus itself, not Athens, was the reason the Eretrians had joined the expedition: they were repaying a debt. Some time earlier, the Milesians had helped the Eretrians in their war against the Chalcidians (whose resistance to the Eretrians and Milesians was also supported by a force from Samos). Anyway, once the Athenians and Eretrians had arrived, and so had the other allies, Aristagoras launched an attack on Sardis. He did not accompany the army in person, in fact. He stayed in Miletus and gave the command to other Milesians—his own brother Charopinus, and another Milesian, Hermophantus.

[100] This was the army with which the Ionians went to Ephesus. There they left the fleet at Coresus, in Ephesian territory, and started inland in considerable force, using Ephesians as guides. They marched beside the River Cayster, turned north to cross Mount Tmolus, and reached their destination. No one offered them any resistance, and they captured the whole of Sardis except the acropolis, which was defended by Artaphrenes in person, along with a substantial body of men.

[101] They were prevented from looting Sardis, even though they had captured it, because most of the houses there were made out of reeds, and even the ones which were made out of bricks had roofs thatched with reeds. Consequently, as soon as one of the houses had been set alight by a soldier, the fire spread from house to house and engulfed the whole city. With the city on fire, the Lydians and however many Persians there were on the acropolis were surrounded and trapped. The fire was consuming the outskirts all around them, and there was no way out of the city. They poured into the city square and towards the River Pactolus, which is the river that brings gold-dust down from Mount Tmolus; it flows through the middle of the square and then joins the River Hermus on its way down to the sea. Anyway, the Lydians and Persians congregated in the square, by the side of the Pactolus, and had no choice but to make a stand there. But when the Ionians saw some enemy troops putting up a fight, and others bearing down on them

in considerable numbers, they became afraid and withdrew back to Mount Tmolus. They left there during the night and returned to their fleet.

[102] During the conflagration of Sardis a sanctuary of the local goddess Cybebe burnt down, and later the Persians made this their excuse for the retaliatory burning of sanctuaries they did in Greece. But now the Persians in the provinces west of the Halys River received word of all this, mobilized their troops and went to help the Lydians. In fact, by the time they got there, the Ionians had left Sardis, but the Persians followed their trail and caught up with them in Ephesus. The Ionians formed up to meet the attack, but in the ensuing battle they were severely defeated. The heavy casualties included some famous people, among them Eualcides, the commander of the Eretrian forces, who had been a successful athlete in major competitions, and who was often celebrated by Simonides of Ceos. The Ionians who survived the battle split up and returned to their various states.

[103] That was how the fighting went. Afterwards, the Athenians abandoned the Ionians altogether; Aristagoras sent messages with urgent requests for help, but the Athenians consistently refused. However, the Ionians had already gone so far in their actions against Darius that despite the loss of the Athenian support they still carried on readying themselves for war against the king. They sent a fleet to the Hellespont and gained control of Byzantium and all the other settlements there, and then the fleet sailed back out of the Hellespont and gained the support of most of Caria. Even Caunus, which had not been prepared to join the alliance earlier, was induced by the burning of Sardis to come in with them.

[104] The whole of Cyprus readily joined the alliance, except for the Amathousians. Here is how the people of Cyprus came to revolt against Persia. There was a man called Onesilus, who was the younger brother of King Gorgus of Salamis; he was the son of Chersis, grandson of Siromus, and great-grandson of Euelthon. Now, he had often tried to persuade Gorgus to break away from Persia in the past as well, but once he heard that even the Ionians were rebelling, he redoubled his efforts at persuasion. He failed to win him over, however, so he waited until Gorgus was out of town and then, with the help of his fellow conspirators, closed the gates against him. The now stateless Gorgus took refuge with the Persians, while Onesilus took over as king of Salamis and set out

to persuade the whole of Cyprus to join him in rebellion. The only place he failed to win over to this plan was Amathous, so he proceeded to besiege it.

[105] Meanwhile, news reached King Darius of the Athenian and Ionian capture and burning of Sardis, and he was told that the man who had gathered the troops together, and was therefore the instigator of the whole affair, had been Aristagoras of Miletus. It is said, however, that his first reaction to the news was to discount the Ionians, because he was confident of punishing them for their rebellion, and to ask who the Athenians were. On hearing the answer, he is said to have asked for his bow; he took hold of it, notched an arrow, and shot it up towards the sky. And as he fired it into the air, he said, 'Lord Zeus, make it possible for me to punish the Athenians.' Then he ordered one of his attendants to repeat to him three times, every time a meal was being served, 'Master, remember the Athenians.'

[106] After issuing these instructions, he summoned Histiaeus of Miletus (who had been detained in Susa for a long time by then) and said, 'Histiaeus, I hear that the person you left in charge of Miletus has been making trouble for me. He has persuaded men from the other continent to join the Ionians, who will pay for their actions, and at the head of this combined force has robbed me of Sardis. What do you think of that? Do you approve of what has happened? And how could they have succeeded without your involvement in their plans? You had better be careful, because otherwise you'll be sorry later.'

'My lord,' Histiaeus replied, 'how can you say such a thing? How could I be involved in planning anything that would cause you even the slightest amount of distress? What possible motive could I have for doing so? What do I have to be dissatisfied about, when everything that is yours is mine and I have the honour of being privy to all your plans? No, if my deputy has done what you say he has, or anything like it, you can rest assured that he acted on his own. Actually, I can't quite believe the report that the Milesians and my deputy are making trouble for you, but if your information is correct, my lord, and they really are, then perhaps you can see the effects of your removal of me from the coast. I mean, in all probability the Ionians have simply used the opportunity of being out of my sight to carry out long-cherished plans. If I had been in Ionia, not a single state would have rebelled. So now let me go as quickly as possible to Ionia, so that I can restore order out of all the chaos in your affairs there and deliver into your hands this man I left in charge of Miletus, who is responsible for all this. When I have done everything to your satisfaction, I swear by the gods who protect your majesty that I will not take off the tunic I shall wear on my journey to Ionia, until I have also made Sardo, which is the largest island there is, into a tribute-paying subject state of yours.'

[107] This speech of Histiaeus' was hardly truthful, but Darius believed him and let him go. He told him to do everything he had promised to do, and then to return to Susa.

[108] So the news about Sardis had reached the king, Darius had done the thing with the bow, he had met with Histiaeus, and Histiaeus had been released by Darius and was on his way to the coast. Meanwhile, Onesilus of Salamis was besieging the Amathousians when he received a report that a Persian called Artybius was on his way to Cyprus by sea with a sizeable army of Persians. This information prompted Onesilus to send messages all over Ionia to ask for help, and it did not take the Ionians long to decide to send a substantial body of troops, who duly arrived in Cyprus. So there were Ionians in Cyprus, and the Persians had sailed across from Cilicia and travelled to Salamis by land, and the Phoenicians were in the process of sailing around the headland which is known as the Keys of Cyprus.

[109] This was the situation when the Cyprian tyrants called the Ionian military commanders to a conference and said, 'Men of Ionia, we Cyprians are going to give you the choice of which of the two enemy forces to fight. If you decide to position your troops on land and engage the Persians, now is the time for you to leave your fleet and form up on land, while we board your ships and oppose the Phoenicians. On the other hand, you may prefer to take on the Phoenicians. Whichever of the two courses of action you take, you should do your very best to ensure the freedom of both Ionia and Cyprus.'

The Ionians responded by saying, 'The Ionian authorities sent us here to guard the sea, not to hand our ships over to Cyprians and meet the Persians on land. So we will carry out our mission—and of course we will try to do it well. And you for your part should let the memory of your sufferings as slaves of the Persians encourage you to bravery.'

[110] That was the Ionian response. When the Persian army reached the plain of Salamis, the kings of the Cyprians disposed their troops. They placed their élite troops, the fighting men of Salamis and Soli, opposite the Persians, while the contingents drawn from other Cyprian towns faced other elements of the Persian army. Onesilus deliberately chose a position opposite the Persian commander Artybius.

[111] Now, Artybius used to ride a horse which had been trained to rear up at soldiers in heavy armour. When Onesilus found out about this, he consulted an esquire of his, who was a Carian by birth, a famous fighter, and generally full of courage. 'I hear', he said, 'that Artybius' horse rears up and uses its hoofs and mouth to kill anyone it attacks. So what do you think? Do you want to face and strike the horse or Artybius himself?'

'My lord,' his retainer replied, 'I am ready to do both or either, just as you command, but I'll tell you what I think will be best for you. As a king in command of an army you should meet your opposite number, because if you do away with him, another military commander, it's a significant achievement, and alternatively if he should kill you—which I pray may not happen—death at the hands of a worthy opponent is not an unmitigated disaster. By the same token, then, as your servants, we should take on others of the same rank, even when it's a horse. Don't worry about his horse's tricks; I guarantee that it will never again rear up against anyone else.'

[112] Right after this discussion battle was joined, on land and at sea. At sea, the Ionians proved themselves to be first-rate fighters that day, with the Samians taking the honours as the Phoenicians were defeated. On land, the two armies came together and during the ensuing battle this is what happened to the two commanders. When Artybius came charging down on horseback, Onesilus carried out the plan he had formed with his esquire and aimed at the actual assailant, Artybius;† at the precise moment when the horse brought its hoofs down on to Onesilus' shield, the Carian lashed out with a billhook and sheared off the horse's feet. So both Artybius, the Persian commander, and his horse fell there on the field.

[113] Meanwhile, elsewhere in the battle, Stesenor, who was the tyrant of Curium and had a considerable body of fighting men under his command, turned traitor. Curium is said to be a colony of Argos. The treachery of the Curians was immediately copied by

the contingent of war chariots from Salamis, and the upshot of this was that the Persians overcame the Cyprians. As the Cyprian army was forced back, casualties were heavy, and included Onesilus the son of Chersis, who was the instigator of the Cyprian revolt, and the king of Soli, Aristocyprus the son of Philocyprus. (This was the Philocyprus who was praised above all other tyrants in a poem which Solon of Athens composed during his visit to Cyprus.)

[114] The people of Amathous took revenge for Onesilus' siege of their town by cutting off his head, taking it to Amathous, and hanging it above the main entrance to the town. After the head had hung there for a while and had become hollow, a swarm of bees took up residence inside it and filled it with their honeycomb. Faced with this unusual event, the Amathousians consulted an oracle and were told to take the head down and bury it, and to institute a hero-cult of Onesilus, involving annual sacrifices; then, the oracle said, things would improve for them. This cult of Onesilus is still practised in Amathous even today.

[115] Now, as soon as the Ionians who had taken part in the battle off Cyprus heard about Onesilus' death and found out that all the major towns in Cyprus were under siege (all except for Salamis, that is, which had been returned to Gorgus, its former ruler, by its inhabitants), they sailed back to Ionia. The Cyprian town which held out the longest against its besiegers was Soli; the Persians finally captured it in the fifth month of the siege by tunnelling under its defensive wall.

[116] So the Cyprians, after a year of freedom, were reduced once more to a fresh term of slavery. Meanwhile, three Persian military commanders, Daurises, Hymaees, and Otanes (all of whom were married to daughters of Darius), went after the Ionians who had been involved in the attack on Sardis. They forced them to take to their ships, defeated them in a battle, and then divided up the cities among themselves and proceeded to plunder them.

[117] Daurises made the settlements on the Hellespont his target, and captured Dardanus, Abydus, Percote, Lampsacus, and Paesus, each in a single day.† As he was *en route* for Parium, after leaving Paesus, he received a message to the effect that Caria had joined in the Ionian rebellion against Persia, so he turned away from the Hellespont and marched his men towards Caria.

[118] Now, the Carians somehow heard that Daurises was on his way before he arrived, so they congregated at White Pillars, by

the River Marsyas, which flows from Idrias and joins the Meander.
Once they had all gathered there, they discussed what to do. A
number of different views were expressed, but the best one, in my
opinion, was that of Pixodarus the son of Mausolus, a man from
Cindye who was married to the daughter of King Syennesis of
Cilicia. His suggestion was that they should cross the Meander and
keep the river to their rear while engaging the enemy, so that, with
their line of retreat cut off, they would have no choice but to stand
firm, and would thereby enhance their natural bravery. However,
this proposal of his did not find favour; instead they decided to
arrange things so that the Persians, rather than them, had the
Meander behind them, the idea being that if the Persians came off
worst in the battle and were routed, they would be driven into the
river and never return home.

[119] Later the Persians arrived. Once they had crossed the
River Meander, the Carians engaged them at the River Marsyas.
The battle was long and fierce, but in the end the Carians were
beaten by sheer numbers. Persian casualties numbered about two
thousand, while about ten thousand Carians fell. The Carians who
escaped from the battlefield became trapped in the sanctuary of
Zeus the God of War at Labraunda, which consists of a large sacred
grove of plane-trees. The Carians are the only known people who
sacrifice to Zeus as the God of War. Anyway, finding themselves
caught in a trap, they tried to decide whether their chances of safety
would be improved if they surrendered to the Persians, or if they
evacuated Asia altogether.

[120] They were still undecided when the Milesians and their
allies arrived to help them, with the result that the Carians abandoned their earlier deliberations and prepared to join battle all over
again. The Persians attacked, battle was joined, and the Carians
suffered an even worse defeat than before. Casualties were very
heavy indeed, particularly among the Milesian troops.

[121] Some time after this disaster, however, the Carians
regrouped and renewed the struggle, when they found out that the
Persians were setting out on a campaign against their cities. They
set an ambush on the road at Pedasa, the Persians walked into it
at night, and were wiped out. They lost not only three of their high-
ranking officers—Daurises, Amorges, and Sisimaces—but also
Myrsus the son of Gyges. The leader of the Carian troops involved

in the ambush was Heraclides the son of Ibanollis, who came from Mylasa. So that was how this Persian army was lost.

[122] Meanwhile Hymaees, another of the Persian commanders engaged in the pursuit of the Ionians who had attacked Sardis, had made his way to the Propontis and taken Cius in Mysia. Subsequently, however, he learnt that Daurises had left the Hellespont and was marching against Caria, so he pulled out of the Propontis and took his army to the Hellespont. There he subjugated all the Aeolians living around Ilium, and also the Gergithes, the remnants of the ancient Teucrians. However, Hymaees himself never left Troas; in the course of annexing these tribes, he became ill and died.

[123] So that is how Hymaees met his end. Artaphrenes, the governor of Sardis, and Otanes, the remaining one of the three Persian military commanders, were then detailed to march on Ionia and the neighbouring Aeolian territory. They captured Clazomenae in Ionia and Cyme in Aeolis.

[124] Once these cities had fallen, Aristagoras of Miletus proved himself to be somewhat of a coward. He had caused all the commotion in Ionia and had stirred up a great deal of trouble, but seeing the current situation, and because he now despaired of ever defeating King Darius, he began to contemplate flight. He therefore convened a meeting of his supporters and, claiming that they should have a bolt-hole available in case they were ever thrown out of Miletus, he asked them whether they thought Sardo or Myrcinus in Edonia (the place which Histiaeus had been in the process of fortifying, after he had been given it by Darius) was the best place for him to found a colony.

[125] Hecataeus the son of Hegesander, who was a writer, argued against sending such an expedition to either of the places Aristagoras had asked about; instead, he recommended that Aristagoras should build himself a stronghold on the island of Leros so that he would have somewhere to lie low if he was ever forced out of Miletus. He pointed out that Leros would make a good base for Aristagoras to return to Miletus at a later date.

[126] That was Hecataeus' advice, but Aristagoras was strongly in favour of making Myrcinus his destination. So he left an eminent Milesian called Pythagoras in charge of the city, recruited a band of volunteers, and set sail for Thrace. There he gained control of

the land he had set out for and made it his military headquarters. However, while he was investing a town (even though the Thracian inhabitants were perfectly prepared to leave it under a truce), the Thracians destroyed his army, and Aristagoras himself was one of the casualties.

BOOK SIX

[1] So that was how Aristagoras, the initiator of the Ionian rebellion, died. Meanwhile, however, Histiaeus, the tyrant of Miletus, had been released by Darius and arrived in Sardis from Susa. Once he was there, Artaphrenes, the governor of Sardis, asked him what, in his opinion, had caused the Ionians to revolt. Histiaeus feigned complete ignorance of the situation, saying that he had no idea and expressing surprise at the turn of events. But Artaphrenes realized that he was putting on a false front—in fact, he knew the truth about the revolt—so he said, 'I'll tell you what actually happened in this business, Histiaeus: it was *you* who stitched the shoe, while Aristagoras merely put it on.'

[2] This comment about the revolt made Histiaeus afraid of what Artaphrenes knew, so the very next night he slipped away to the coast. He had tricked King Darius with the promise that he would conquer Sardo, the largest island in the world, when what he intended to do was try to gain the leadership of the war against Darius. He crossed over to Chios, but was imprisoned by the Chians on suspicion of being up to no good and of working for Darius against them. When they found out the whole story, however, and realized that he was hostile to Darius, they set him free.

[3] Histiaeus was next asked by the Ionians why he had been so anxious to encourage Aristagoras to revolt from the king—and thus to cause so much trouble for Ionia. He did not give them the real reason, however: he told them that King Darius had been planning to relocate the Phoenicians in Ionia, and to move the Ionians to Phoenicia, and that was why he had sent the message to Aristagoras. He was trying to alarm the Ionians, even though Darius had not been planning anything of the kind.

[4] Later, Histiaeus used a man called Hermippus, from Atarneus, to take a letter to Sardis; there were Persians there with whom Histiaeus had already spoken about rebellion against Darius. But

Hermippus did not deliver the letter to its addressees; instead he went and put it in Artaphrenes' hands. When Artaphrenes found out what was going on, he told Hermippus to take Histiaeus' letter and give it to the people to whom he was supposed to deliver it, but then to give *him* the reply they sent back to Histiaeus. With the discovery of this plot Artaphrenes put to death a large number of Persians.

[5] So Sardis was in turmoil, and Histiaeus' plan came to nothing. Next, at Histiaeus' own request, the Chians tried to engineer his return to Miletus; the Milesians, however, were glad to have got rid of Aristagoras, and, now that they had tasted independence, they were in no great hurry to welcome another tyrant into their land. In fact, when Histiaeus tried to bring about his restoration by force and under cover of darkness, he was wounded in the thigh by one of the Milesians. Banished from his native city, he returned to Chios. He tried to persuade the Chians to give him a fleet, but they refused, so he went over to Mytilene, where he persuaded the Lesbians to give him some ships. They manned eight triremes and sailed with Histiaeus to Byzantium, where they set up a base and proceeded to seize all ships sailing out of the Euxine Sea, unless the crews promised to recognize Histiaeus as their leader.

[6] While Histiaeus and the Mytileneans were occupied with this, Miletus was in imminent danger of being attacked in strength by both land and sea. The Persian military commanders had combined their forces into a single army, and were marching against Miletus, which they considered the most important of the Ionian states. As for their navy, the Phoenicians formed the most willing contingent, and they were supported by the Cyprians (who had recently been conquered), the Cilicians, and the Egyptians.

[7] When the Ionians learnt of this expedition against Miletus and the rest of Ionia, they sent delegations to the Panionium. When they got there, the matter was debated and the Ionians concluded that they should not raise a land army to oppose the Persians; instead they decided that while the Milesians protected their walls by themselves, every available Ionian ship should be manned, and that this navy should then assemble at the earliest possible opportunity at Lade (a small island off the city of Miletus) and engage the enemy at sea in defence of Miletus.

[8] Later, then, the Ionians came to Lade with their ships manned; they received Aeolian support too, in the form of a contingent from Lesbos. They arranged themselves as follows. The Milesians alone formed the eastern wing, with their 80 ships; next to them came the Prieneans with 12 ships and the contingent from Myous, which consisted of 3 ships; next to the Myesians were the men of Teos with 17 ships, and then the Chians with 100; alongside them were positioned the Erythraeans and Phocaeans, with their squadrons of 8 and 3 ships respectively; and next to the Phocaeans were 70 ships from Lesbos. Finally, the western wing was formed of the Samians, with 60 ships. The whole fleet amounted to a force of 353 triremes.

[9] So this was the Ionian fleet, but there were six hundred ships in all on the foreigners' side, which in due course reached Miletus, as did the whole of their land army as well. At that point, the Persian commanders found out how many ships the Ionians had and they were worried at the prospect of failing to defeat them, because without control of the sea they would be unable to take Miletus and they would also probably be punished by Darius. Bearing all this in mind, they invited to a conference the Ionian tyrants who had taken refuge with the Persians after Aristagoras of Miletus had deposed them, and who had in fact joined the Persian expedition against Miletus. So they convened any of these tyrants who were at hand and said, 'Men of Ionia, now is the time for each of you to show himself to be a benefactor of the king's house, by trying to detach his fellow citizens from the general Ionian alliance. Put it to them that, if they comply, we will not punish them for their rebellion, their sanctuaries and private property will be spared the torch, and their lives will be no harder than they were before. However, if they refuse to comply and insist on fighting, you can threaten them with the dire consequences which will certainly be their lot. Defeat in battle will be followed by enslavement, and we will castrate their sons for eunuchs, send their daughters to serve as slaves in Bactra, and give their land to others.'

[10] That is what the Persians said. One by one, the Ionian tyrants used the cover of darkness to get the message to their fellow citizens. But the Ionian recipients of these messages (each group of whom supposed that they were the only ones to be approached by the Persians) remained committed to their chosen course and

refused to countenance treachery. These events took place immediately after the arrival of the Persians at Miletus.

[11] Later, when the Ionians were assembled at Lade, they held
public meetings. They were addressed on various occasions by
various speakers, but in particular the Phocaean commander
Dionysius spoke as follows: 'Men of Ionia, our affairs are balanced
on a razor's edge. We can remain free or we can become slaves—
and runaway slaves at that. If you are prepared to accept hardship,
then in the short term there'll be work for you to do, but you will
defeat the enemy and be free; if, on the other hand, you choose
softness and lack of discipline, I am quite sure that you'll be punished for rebelling against the king. No, you must do as I suggest.
Put yourselves into my hands, and I can assure you that, if the gods
are impartial, the enemy will either not engage us or, if they do,
they will suffer a severe defeat.'

[12] Dionysius' speech persuaded the Ionians to entrust their
future to him. Each time he took the ships out in a column formation, he had the rowers practise the diecplous, with the marines
armed, and then for the rest of the day he would keep the fleet at
anchor. He made the Ionians work all day long. For seven days
they were obedient and did as they were told, but they were unused
to this kind of hard work, and the hardship and heat exhausted
them. So then they said to one another, 'Why do we have to put
up with this? Have we offended one of the gods? We must have
been crazy, out of our minds, to have put ourselves in the hands of
a Phocaean windbag, with only three ships. Now that he has taken
over, he is inflicting intolerable hardships on us. Many of us have
already become ill, and it looks as though more are about to. Anything in the world is better than this misery, even so-called slavery
in the future, since it's slavery we're enduring at the moment. So
come on: let's stop obeying him from now on.'

This line of thought immediately made them ungovernable. They
stayed on the island as if they were a land army; they pitched tents
and kept to the shade, and refused to board their ships or practise
their manoeuvres.

[13] The Samian commanders found out what the Ionians were
doing, and it was just at this point that a message came from Aeaces
the son of Syloson—the same message he had been sending earlier,
in obedience to the Persians, asking them to leave the Ionian
alliance. This time the Samians gave the request a hearing, not only

because they could see the degree to which discipline had broken down in the Ionian camp, but also because they thought it would be impossible to defeat the Persian king with all the resources at his command; they were convinced that even if they defeated his current fleet, he would get another one, five times as big. The Ionians' evasion of duty gave them an immediate excuse, then; they regarded it as a good opportunity to ensure the survival of their sanctuaries and their private property. Aeaces, the person from whom they received the messages, was the son of Syloson and grandson of Aeaces; he had been the tyrant of Samos until he had been deposed by Aristagoras of Miletus along with all the other Ionian tyrants.

[14] When the Phoenician fleet set sail against them, the Ionians reacted by launching their ships as well, formed into a column. The two fleets drew near each other and battle was joined, but I cannot say for sure what happened next—which of the Ionians proved brave or cowardly in this battle—because everyone blames everyone else. The Samians are said to have hoisted their sails, deserted their post, and sailed back to Samos (which was what they had contracted with Aeaces to do)—all except for eleven ships, whose captains refused to obey the Samian commanders, and stayed to join the battle. For this action the Samian authorities later granted them the privilege of having their names inscribed, with their fathers' names, on a column (which stands in the town square) as men of honour. But when the Lesbians saw the Samian contingent next to them turning tail and fleeing, they copied them, and under these circumstances most of the Ionians did the same thing.

[15] Of those who stayed and fought, the Chians came off worst, because of the conspicuous valour of their actions and because they refused to fight below their best. Their contingent consisted, as reported earlier, of a hundred ships, and on each ship there were forty men, specially picked from the citizen body, serving as marines. Seeing the treachery of their allies all around them, they resolved not to sink to their level of worthless cowardice. With hardly any support they engaged the enemy by means of the diecplous, and kept on fighting until, although they had captured large numbers of enemy ships, they had lost most of their own. Then the remaining Chian ships withdrew and headed for home.

[16] With the enemy in pursuit, all the disabled Chian ships made for the safety of Mycale, where they beached their ships and

left them, and set out by foot across the mainland. Their journey brought them in due course to Ephesian territory. It was dark when they arrived there, and the local women were celebrating the Thesmophoria. The men of Ephesus had no warning of the Chians' situation; all they saw was that an armed band had invaded their territory. Under these circumstances they were absolutely sure that the Chians were bandits who had come to carry off their women, so they came out in full strength to protect their women and proceeded to kill the Chians. That was the misfortune the Chians encountered.

[17] When Dionysius of Phocaea saw that the Ionian cause was lost, he sailed away from the area, with the three enemy ships he had captured. He did not make for Phocaea, however, because he was well aware that it would be enslaved along with the rest of Ionia. Instead he headed straight for Phoenicia, just as he was, where he made himself rich by sinking merchant ships. Then he went to Sicily and set himself up as a pirate with his base there; he used to attack Carthaginian and Tyrrhenian ships, but left Greek shipping alone.

[18] After their naval victory over the Ionians, the Persians blockaded Miletus by land and sea. They used all kinds of stratagems, such as undermining the walls, until the city fell into their hands, acropolis and all, in the sixth year after Aristagoras' revolt. They reduced the city to slavery, and so events confirmed a prediction the oracle had made about Miletus.

[19] What happened was that the Argives once consulted the oracle in Delphi about the safety of their city. They received a shared response, some of which was relevant to the Argives themselves, but there was also an appendix with a prediction about Miletus. I will record the lines that referred to the Argives later, when I come to that part of my account. In the mean time, the statement the oracle made about the Milesians, even though they were not there, was as follows:

> And listen, Miletus, perpetrator of evil deeds: that is when
> Many will feed off you and take you as their gleaming prize.
> Your wives will wash the feet of a host of long-haired men,
> And others will have charge of my temple at Didyma.

This is the fate that overtook Miletus on the occasion in question. Most of the male population was killed by the Persians (who did have long hair), their women and children were reduced to slavery, and the shrine at Didyma—both the temple and the oracle—was plundered and burnt. Elsewhere in this account I have often mentioned the valuables that were to be found in this sanctuary.

[20] Those Milesians who remained alive were taken to Susa. King Darius did them no further harm, except to relocate them on the Red Sea, in the town of Ampe (which is on the mouth of the Tigris River, where it issues into the sea). As for Milesian territory, the Persians kept for themselves the city, the land immediately around the city, and the plain, but gave the hill country to Carians from the town of Pedasa.

[21] On the occasion of these misfortunes, inflicted on the Milesians by the Persians, the people of Sybaris, who had been robbed of their city and were living in Laus and Scidrus, failed to repay a debt. The point is that when Sybaris was captured by the Crotonians, the whole Milesian population, old and young alike, shaved their heads and signalled their deep grief, because there are no known states which have closer ties than Miletus and Sybaris. Even the Athenians behaved better than the Sybarites. They found many ways to express their sorrow at the fall of Miletus, and in particular, when Phrynichus composed and produced a play called *The Fall of Miletus*, the audience burst into tears and fined him a thousand drachmas for reminding them of a disaster that was so close to home; future productions of the play were also banned.

[22] So Miletus was left empty of Milesians. But there were some Samians—the wealthy ones—who found their commanders' behaviour *vis-à-vis* the Persians highly unsatisfactory. They talked things over straight after the battle and decided to sail away on a colonizing expedition before the tyrant Aeaces reached their country, without waiting to become the slaves of the Persians and Aeaces. The people of Zancle in Sicily had coincidentally sent a message to Ionia inviting the Ionians to Fair Cape, since they wanted to found an Ionian settlement there. Fair Cape is the part of Sicily which faces Tyrrhenia and was inhabited by Sicelians. The Samians were the only Ionians to take up the invitation and set out, and they were joined by refugee Milesians.

[23] The outcome of their journey was as follows. On their way to Sicily, the Samians reached the Western Locrians; meanwhile, the Zancleans, under their king (whose name was Scythes), were

besieging a Sicelian settlement which they wanted to take over. Anaxilaus, the tyrant of Rhegium, found out what was going on. Now, at that point of time he was on bad terms with the Zancleans, so he met with the Samians and persuaded them to ignore Fair Cape, their destination, and take control of Zancle, which was undefended. The Samians agreed to the plan and took Zancle.

When the Zancleans discovered that their town had been captured, they set out to its aid, and they called on Hippocrates, the tyrant of Gela, to support them, on the grounds that he was their ally. But when Hippocrates arrived with his army to help them, he threw Scythes, the ruler of Zancle, into chains for having lost his town, treated Scythes' brother Pythogenes in the same way, and sent them off to the town of Inyx. Then, after consulting the Samians, he exchanged oaths of friendship with them, and so his betrayal of the rest of the Zancleans was complete. The price the Samians agreed to give him was that he should have all the movable property, half the slaves in the town, and all the slaves from the farms. He took it upon himself to cast most of the inhabitants of Zancle into chains and keep them in a state of slavery, but he handed the three hundred leading citizens over to the Samians, for them to murder. But the Samians did no such thing.

[24] Scythes, the king of the Zancleans, escaped from Inyx to Himera, and from there he made his way to Asia and travelled inland to King Darius. In Darius' view, Scythes was the most honest man who had ever come to him from Greece, since although he returned with Darius' permission to Sicily, he came back to the king again, and eventually died in Persia a very wealthy man, when he was well on in years. So the Samians escaped Persian rule and effortlessly acquired the wonderful town of Zancle.

[25] After the battle for Miletus the Persians got the Phoenicians to restore Aeaces the son of Syloson to Samos in gratitude for the very valuable and important service he had done them. Because they had withdrawn their ships from the battle, the Samians were the only ones out of all those involved in the rebellion against Darius whose city and sanctuaries were not burnt down. Straight after the fall of Miletus, the Persians occupied Caria too, where some of the communities submitted of their own accord, and others had to be reduced by force.

[26] So much for these events. Off Byzantium, Histiaeus of Miletus was continuing to intercept Ionian merchant ships as they

sailed out of the Euxine Sea. While he was there, though, he received a report about what had happened to Miletus, so he left Bisaltes of Abydus, the son of Apollophanes, in charge of matters in the Hellespont and sailed off to Chios with a force of Lesbians. On Chios, a garrison of islanders at a place called Coela refused to let him pass; battle was joined and a great many of the Chians died. Then, with the help of his Lesbians, he gained control of the rest of the island, which was, after all, weakened as a result of the sea battle. He made Polichne his headquarters on Chios.

[27] There are invariably warning signs given when disaster is going to overwhelm a community or a race; the Chians, for instance, had received extensive indications in advance of these events. In the first place, out of a chorus of one hundred young men they had sent to Delphi, only two returned home, while an outbreak of illness carried off the other ninety-eight. In the second place, at much the same time, shortly before the sea battle, a roof collapsed on a group of children learning their letters, and out of a hundred and twenty children only one survived. After these advance warnings, sent by the god, the battle brought the town to its knees, and then the sea battle was followed by Histiaeus and his Lesbians. In their weakened state, it was no problem for him to conquer the island.

[28] Histiaeus used Chios as his base to mount a campaign against Thasos with a large force of Ionians and Aeolians. But while his blockade of Thasos was in progress, a message reached him that the Phoenicians were sailing out of Miletus against the rest of Ionia. When he heard this news, he left Thasos unsacked and set off in a hurry for Lesbos, taking his whole force with him. His army became very short of food on Lesbos, so he left there and crossed over to the mainland, with the intention of harvesting the crops from Atarneus and from the plain of the Caïcus River in Mysia. However, a Persian, Harpagus, happened to be in that part of the country, with a sizeable army under his command. He engaged Histiaeus just as he disembarked, captured him alive, and wiped out most of his troops.

[29] This is how Histiaeus was captured. The battle between the Greeks and the Persians at Malene, which is in Atarneus, went on for a long time, until the Persian cavalry, which had been held in reserve, launched an attack on the Greeks and so won victory. The Greek forces were routed. Histiaeus thought that the offence he

had committed would not lead Darius to put him to death, so he found a way of hanging on to his life. As he was running away from the battlefield, a Persian soldier caught up with him and was just about to stab him to death when Histiaeus spoke in Persian to him and let him know that he was Histiaeus of Miletus.

[30] It is my opinion that if after his capture he had been taken to King Darius, he would have come to no harm: the king would have pardoned him. But that was exactly why Artaphrenes the governor of Sardis and Harpagus, Histiaeus' captor, had Histiaeus brought to Sardis and then impaled his body on a stake right there in the city, and sent his embalmed head to King Darius in Susa. They did this because they wanted to make sure that he did not survive and become influential with the king again. When Darius found out what they had done, he castigated them for not bringing Histiaeus alive to him; he ordered them to wash Histiaeus' head, dress it appropriately, and bury it with the honour due to such a major benefactor of himself and Persia. So that is what happened to Histiaeus.

[31] The Persian fleet wintered at Miletus and then put to sea again the following year. The islands near the mainland—Chios, Lesbos, and Tenedos—were easily subdued. Whenever the Persians took one of the islands, they 'trawled' for the inhabitants. 'Trawling' involves forming a chain of men with linked arms across the island from the northern coast to the southern coast, who then traverse the whole length of the island hunting people down. They also captured the Ionian settlements on the mainland just as easily; trawling for the inhabitants was not feasible, however, so that manoeuvre was not carried out.

[32] At this point the Persian commanders did indeed carry out the actions they had threatened the Ionians with when the Ionians had pitched camp opposite them. That is, when they had conquered the settlements, they picked the best-looking boys and castrated them, cutting off their testicles and turning them into eunuchs; they also took the most attractive girls and sent them to the king as slaves. In addition, they burnt the settlements, sanctuaries and all. And so the Ionians came to be enslaved for the third time—first by the Lydians, then twice in succession by the Persians.

[33] The Persian fleet then left Ionia and conquered the whole region to the north of the Hellespont; the mainland area to the south of the Hellespont had already been conquered by the

Persians themselves. The places on the Hellespont on the European side are the Chersonese (which contains a great many towns), Perinthus (and the other strongholds on the coast of Thrace), Selymbria, and Byzantium. The people of Byzantium and the Chalcedonians who live opposite Byzantium did not wait for the Phoenician fleet to arrive, but abandoned their homeland and migrated further along the coast of the Euxine Sea, where they settled in Mesambria. Once the Phoenicians had burnt all these places to the ground, they turned towards Proconnesus and Artaces, which they also put to the torch. Then they sailed back to the Chersonese to eradicate any last settlements they had not destroyed on their previous visit. They left Cyzicus completely alone, because the place was already subject to the king, and had been before the Phoenician fleet's campaign, ever since they entered into a treaty with the governor of Dascylium, Oebares the son of Megabazus. But all the other towns and cities in the Chersonese, except Cardia, were subdued by the Phoenicians.

[34] Until then Miltiades the son of Cimon and grandson of Stesagoras had been the ruler of these communities. It was Miltiades the son of Cypselus who acquired this overlordship, and this is how it happened. A Thracian tribe called the Doloncians were in control of this Chersonese. A war with the Apsinthians was not going at all well for these Doloncians, and they sent their kings to Delphi to ask about the war. The Pythia's reply was that they should invite over to their land the first person to extend them hospitality after they had left the shrine, and make him their Founder. The Doloncians took the Sacred Way through Phocis and Boeotia, but no one offered them hospitality, so they turned off towards Athens.

[35] Athens at that time was an autocracy, under Pisistratus, but Miltiades the son of Cypselus was a man of influence, at any rate. His household was wealthy enough to maintain a four-horse chariot and he traced his ancestry back to Aeacus and Aegina, although since then his family had become Athenian—the first Athenian of the house being Philaeus the son of Ajax. Now, Miltiades was sitting on the porch of his house, and when he saw the Doloncians approaching, wearing non-Athenian clothing and carrying spears, he called them over. When they came near he offered them a place to rest and hospitality. They accepted the invitation, and afterwards they told him all about the oracle, and asked whether he would comply with Apollo's plan. Miltiades found their

suggestion immediately appealing, because he was chafing under Pisistratus' rule and wanted to get out from under it. He lost no time in setting out for Delphi to ask the oracle whether he should go along with the Doloncians' request.

[36] The Pythia told him too to go ahead, and so Miltiades the son of Cypselus (who was an Olympic victor from an earlier games in the four-horse-chariot race) recruited from the Athenian popu-lace everyone who wanted to join the expedition, set sail with the Doloncians, and took control of their country. The Doloncians who had invited him made him tyrant of the place. The first thing he did was build a defensive wall across the isthmus of the Cherson-ese from Cardia to Pactya, to stop the Apsinthians' damaging incur-sions. This isthmus is thirty-six stades wide, but beyond the isthmus the total length of the Chersonese is 420 stades.

[37] Next, after building a wall across the neck of the Cher-sonese and so keeping the Apsinthians at bay, Miltiades turned his attention elsewhere. He started by making war on the people of Lampsacus, but they ambushed him and took him prisoner. However, Croesus of Lydia knew about Miltiades, and when he found out what had happened, he ordered the Lampsacenes to let Miltiades go, or else, he said, he would wipe them out 'as if they were a pine-tree'. The Lampsacenes came up with various inter-pretations of this threat of Croesus', but at last one of their older citizens got the point and told them that the pine was the only tree which produced no shoots after it had been cut down, so that it was utterly destroyed, with no hope of regeneration. Afraid of what Croesus would do, then, the Lampsacenes freed Miltiades and let him go.

[38] So thanks to Croesus Miltiades escaped. He was killed later, however, and he died without an heir, so his kingdom and his prop-erty passed to Stesagoras the son of Cimon, who was his half-brother on his mother's side. Since Miltiades' death, the people of the Chersonese have offered him the sacrifices traditional for a founder, and have instituted in his honour games involving both chariot-racing and athletic competitions. No one from Lampsacus is allowed to take part in these games. Stesagoras too, as it hap-pened, died during the war with Lampsacus, and he left no heir. He died from a blow to the head which was delivered, while he was in the town hall, by a man with a battleaxe; the man was pre-tending to be a deserter, but was really an enemy nursing a grudge.

[39] After Stesagoras had died in this way, power in the Chersonese passed into the hands of his brother Miltiades the son of Cimon. He was sent to the Chersonese in a trireme by the Pisistratidae, who had treated him well in Athens too, as if they had no knowledge of the death of his father—I will explain what actually happened elsewhere in my account. When Miltiades arrived in the Chersonese he stayed at home, ostensibly as a way of honouring his brother Stesagoras. Once the people of the Chersonese found out what he was doing, the chief men from all over the region convened from their various towns and came together to join him in mourning—whereupon he imprisoned the whole lot of them. Miltiades maintained power in the Chersonese with the help of a force of five hundred mercenaries he kept, and he married Hegesipyle, the daughter of the Thracian king Olorus.

[40] Now, Miltiades the son of Cimon had not been in the Chersonese long when he was overtaken by events that were even worse than what had happened before. The point is that two years before the events we are talking about he had fled the country in the face of the Scythians. The nomadic Scythians had been chafing under King Darius, so they banded together and came as far as the Chersonese. Miltiades did not wait for them to invade, but fled the country, and it was only when the Scythians left that the Doloncians brought him back again. Anyway, all that took place two years before the events engaging him at the time in question.

[41] So Miltiades now heard that the Phoenicians had reached Tenedos. He manned five triremes, put all his property on board, and set sail for Athens. Starting from Cardia, his course took him through the Black Gulf, and he was just about to leave the Chersonese behind when the Phoenician fleet attacked. Miltiades himself managed to escape to Imbros with four of his ships, but the fifth ship was captured by the Phoenicians during the chase. It so happened that this ship was under the command of Metiochus, who was Miltiades' eldest son (and whose mother was not the daughter of Olorus of Thrace, but another woman). So Metiochus fell into the Phoenicians' hands along with his ship. When they found out that he was Miltiades' son, they took him up to the king at Susa. They were sure that they would get a great deal of substantial gratitude, since it had, after all, been Miltiades who had advised the Ionians to fall in with the Scythians' request that they should dismantle the pontoon bridge and sail back home. But when the

Phoenicians arrived with Miltiades' son Metiochus, so far from doing him harm, Darius heaped him with benefits. He gave him a house, property, and a Persian wife. This Persian wife bore him children who are regarded as Persians. Meanwhile, Miltiades left Imbros and reached Athens.

[42] That year, the Persians initiated no further hostilities against the Ionians other than what has already been mentioned. In fact, there were some developments that year which were extremely beneficial for the Ionians. Artaphrenes, the governor of Sardis, sent for representatives from the states and forced the Ionians to negotiate agreements with one another whereby they would submit their disputes to arbitration instead of raiding and plundering one another. As well as forcing them to do this, he also found the area of their territories in parasangs (a parasang is what the Persians call thirty stades), and then assigned each of them their tribute in accordance with the area of their territory. And Artaphrenes' assessment of how much tribute each region was to pay remained in force from then on, right up to my day. In fact, however, Artaphrenes' assessment was not hugely different from the previous assessment.

[43] These, then, were some peaceful measures the Persians took. In the spring of the following year, when Darius had dismissed all his other commanders, Mardonius the son of Gobryas (a young man who had recently married Darius' daughter Artozostra) came down to the coast at the head of a very large combined land and sea force. When Mardonius and his troops reached Cilicia, he put various people in charge of the army and left them to make their way to the Hellespont, while he set off by sea with the fleet. On his way past Asia, he came to Ionia, and at this point I have something to report which those Greeks who do not believe that Otanes recommended to the seven Persian conspirators that Persia should become a democracy will find very hard to believe— that Mardonius deposed all the Ionian tyrants and instituted democracy in the cities of Ionia. Afterwards, he pressed on towards the Hellespont. Once a vast number of ships and a huge land army had congregated there, the Persians crossed the Hellespont by ship and began to march through Europe, making for Eretria and Athens.

[44] These places were the ostensible targets of the expedition, but in fact the Persians intended to conquer as many Greek towns

and cities as they could. First they used the fleet to subdue the Thasians, who did not even raise a hand against them, and then they used the land army to add the Macedonians to the body of slaves they already had in the area—they already dominated all the tribes closer than the Macedonians.

The fleet crossed over from Thasos to the mainland, where it hugged the coast and sailed up to Acanthus. From Acanthus they set out to round the headland at Athos, but they were caught there in a northerly gale against which it proved impossible to make headway. The storm wrought havoc with them and wrecked a large number of ships on Athos. It is said that about three hundred ships were destroyed, and over twenty thousand men. The men died in various ways: some were seized by the sharks that infest the sea around Mount Athos, others were dashed on to the rocks, others drowned because they did not know how to swim, and others died of cold. So that is what happened to the fleet.

[45] Meanwhile, on land, a Thracian tribe called the Brygi launched a night attack on Mardonius and the army while they were encamped in Macedonia. They succeeded in killing large numbers of the Persians, and wounded Mardonius himself. Nevertheless, even the Brygi did not manage to avoid being enslaved by the Persians, because Mardonius refused to leave those parts until he had conquered them. However, once they had submitted, he pulled the army back, because of his disastrous encounter on land with the Brygi, and the catastrophe at sea off Athos. And so this force returned to Asia after its inglorious campaign.

[46] In the following year Darius started by dealing with the Thasians, because their neighbours had falsely reported that they were planning to revolt. He ordered them, through his envoys, to demolish their defensive walls and to bring their fleet to Abdera. He did this because the Thasians were using their money—and their revenue was considerable—to build longships and strengthen their walls, on the grounds that they had already been besieged by Histiaeus of Miletus. Their revenue came from the mainland and their mines. From the gold-mines at Scapte Hyle they usually gained an income of eighty talents, and although the gold-mines on Thasos itself contributed less than that, it was so much that the usual annual income from the mainland and the mines gained by the Thasians (who paid no taxes on their crops) was two hundred talents, and three hundred at its peak.

[47] I myself have seen these mines. The most remarkable ones, by a long way, were those discovered by the Phoenicians who came with Thasus and colonized the island, which is now named after this Phoenician, Thasos. These Phoenician mines on Thasos are situated between the places called Aenyra and Coenyra, facing Samothrace; a large hill there was completely excavated in the search for gold. So much for this subject.

[48] Anyway, the Thasians obeyed the king's command, demolished their walls, and brought their whole fleet to Abdera. Darius' next step was to try to find out whether the Greeks intended to resist or surrender. Accordingly, he sent heralds here and there throughout Greece, with orders to demand earth and water for the king. As well as sending these heralds to Greece, he also sent others to the coastal states which were already his tributaries, to transmit his instructions to arrange for the building of longships and of transport ships for horses.

[49] So the tribute-paying states began this construction work. Meanwhile, many of the mainland towns and cities did give the Persian heralds who went to Greece what the king was demanding, and so did all the islanders who received the demand. Among the islanders who gave earth and water to Darius were the Aeginetans. This provoked an immediate reaction from the Athenians, who accused the Aeginetans of having Athens in mind when they gave earth and water to Darius; they did so, the Athenians assumed, in order to accompany the Persians when they came to attack Athens. The Athenians made the most of this plausible pretext; they sent a delegation to Sparta and formally accused the Aeginetans of betraying Greece by their actions.

[50] In view of this charge, the Spartan king Cleomenes the son of Anaxandridas sailed across to Aegina with the intention of arresting the ringleaders. But his attempt to make the arrests met with opposition from a number of Aeginetans, especially Crius the son of Polycritus, who threatened Cleomenes with retaliation if he tried to remove anyone from Aegina, on the grounds that he was not acting with the permission of the Spartan authorities, but had been bribed by the Athenians; otherwise, Crius said, Cleomenes would have brought the other king with him to carry out the arrests. It was in fact a letter from Demaratus that put Crius up to making these allegations. So Cleomenes was sent packing from Aegina, but before he went he asked Crius what his name was.

Crius told him the truth and Cleomenes replied, 'Well then, Crius, you had better have your horns coated with bronze, because a great deal of trouble is coming your way.'

[51] Meanwhile in Sparta Demaratus the son of Ariston was blackening Cleomenes' name. Demaratus was also a king of Sparta, but was from the lesser house. In fact, since both families share a common ancestry, the only respect in which this house is inferior is in order of birth, so that the house of Eurysthenes has a touch more honour because of that.

[52] There is no authority in poetry for this, but the Lacedaemonians claim that Aristodamus (who was the son of Aristomachus, grandson of Cleodaeus, and great-grandson of Hyllus) brought them to the land they currently occupy while he was king—that is, they deny that it was Aristodamus' *sons* who did so. Not long afterwards, they continue, Aristodamus' wife (whose name was Argeia, the daughter of Autesion, who was the son of Tisamenus, grandson of Thersander and great-grandson of Polynices) gave birth to twins, and Aristodamus lived to see his children, but then grew ill and died. The Lacedaemonians of the time decreed that the kingdom should pass, as was traditional, to the elder of the two boys, but they did not know which of them to choose, because they were identical twins, with no difference between them. Since they were unable to decide, they consulted the boys' mother (or perhaps they had consulted her at an earlier stage), but she claimed to be just as incapable of telling which was older and which was younger. Despite saying this, she knew perfectly well, but she wanted to find a way for both of them to become kings. So the Lacedaemonians were stuck, and under these circumstances they sent emissaries to Delphi to ask the oracle how to resolve the situation. The Pythia told them to treat both sons as kings, but to honour the elder one more. This reply of the Pythia's did not make things easier for the Lacedaemonians, who still did not know how to tell which of the boys was the elder.

At this juncture, so the story goes, a Messenian called Panites came forward with an idea. He suggested that the Lacedaemonians should watch the mother and see which of the two children she washed first and fed first. If it turned out that she always followed the same routine, they would have all the information they needed to resolve their difficulty; however, if she varied her routine and alternated, it would be clear that she knew just as little as them, and they would have to find some other approach. So the Spartiates put the Messenian's plan into effect and watched the mother of Aristodamus' sons. She had no idea why she was being watched, and they noticed that she always picked the children up in the same way, giving preference to one of them when it came to washing and feeding them. The Lacedaemonians took the child which had been the object of the mother's preferential treatment, who was in fact the elder, and brought him up at public expense. His name was Eurysthenes, and his brother was called Procles. According to the Lacedaemonians, they spent the whole of their adult lives quarrelling with each other, despite the fact that they were brothers, and their descendants continue to do likewise.

[53] This version of events is unique to the Lacedaemonians, but I will now write down the usual account told by the Greeks. This is that the accepted Greek list of the kings of the Dorians back as far as Perseus the son of Danaë, but omitting the god, is correct. The list also proves, they say, that the Dorian kings were Greeks, because they were already being counted as Greeks as far back as then. I said 'as far as Perseus', but took the lineage no further back, because no human being is named as Perseus' father (as Amphitryon is for Heracles, for instance). So I was right to say 'as far as Perseus'. However, if one were to trace back, generation by generation, the lineage of Danaë the daughter of Acrisius, the chiefs of the Dorians would turn out to be true-born Egyptians.

[54] This is the Greek version of their genealogy, but there is a Persian account to the effect that Perseus was an Assyrian whose ancestors were not Greek, but who became Greek of his own accord. The forebears of Acrisius, they say, were not blood-relatives of Perseus at all, but came from Egypt (which agrees with the Greek account).

[55] Enough has been said about all this. Others have explained how and through what achievements they became kings over the Dorians, despite being Egyptians, and so I will not go into that. I will record things which others have not picked up.

[56] The kings have the following privileges, assigned to them by the Spartiates. They have two priesthoods, one of Zeus of Lacedaemon and one of Heavenly Zeus; they have the right to wage war against any country they choose, and no Spartiate is allowed to obstruct them in this, or he will be placed under a curse; on campaign, they must go first on the way out and last on the way back;

they have a hundred picked men to guard them out on campaign; during military expeditions they can have as much of the livestock as they wish for their own use, and whenever any of these animals are sacrificed they get the skins and the backs.

[57] These are their prerogatives in times of war, but they have been granted a different set of rights in times of peace. On the occasion of a public sacrifice, the kings are the first to take their places at the feast, and the servers have to start with them and give each of the kings a double helping of everything, twice what the other diners receive. They have the right of pouring the first libation and the right to the skins of sacrificed animals. Every new moon, and on the seventh day of every month, each king is given, at public expense, an unblemished sacrificial victim for use in the temple of Apollo, a medimnus of barley, and a Laconian fourth of wine; and they have special seats of honour reserved for them at all the games. It is their privilege to appoint any citizen they like to act as the state's diplomatic representatives, and each of them also gets to choose two Pythians. These Pythians act as emissaries to Delphi and are maintained along with the kings at public expense. If the kings do not come to the communal meals, two choenixes of barley and a cotyle of wine are sent to each of them at their private residences; if they do come, they are given a double helping of everything, and they receive the same preferential treatment when they are invited to a meal at someone's house as well. They look after any oracles the state receives, although the Pythians are aware of their content too. The kings have the sole authority to decide who should marry an heiress whose father has died without having betrothed her to anyone, and to adjudicate in cases concerning the public highways. Also, if anyone wants to adopt a son, they have to do so in the presence of the kings. They attend the council meetings of the twenty-eight Elders; at any session they choose not to attend the Elders who are most closely related to them take on their privileges and cast two votes for the kings they are representing and then one for themselves.

[58] These are the rights the kings are granted by the Spartan government during their lifetimes. After their deaths, they gain further privileges. Horsemen ride all over Laconia announcing the news of a king's death, while women beat on cauldrons as they parade through the city. At this signal, two people from each household (one man and one woman, neither of whom can be a slave)

have to disfigure themselves in mourning, or else face a heavy fine. Lacedaemonian practice on the occasion of a king's death can also be found outside of Greece in Asia; in fact, most non-Greeks there follow the same custom when their kings die. That is, when a king of the Lacedaemonians dies, a certain number of the perioeci, in addition to Spartiates, are required to come from all over Lacedaemon to attend the funeral. When they and the helots and the Spartiates are all gathered in their thousands in the one spot, men and women together passionately beat their foreheads and give way to endless lamenting, based on the claim, which they make each time, that this latest king to die was the best there ever was. They make statues of any king who dies in war, and carry the statue around on a lavishly covered bier. For ten days after the funeral the city square is closed for business and there are no sessions of electoral bodies; instead they devote the whole period to mourning.

[59] There is another respect in which Lacedaemonian custom resembles what happens in Persia. After a king's death, another king succeeds him, and this new king frees any Spartiate who was in debt to the king or to the state. In Persia too the newly appointed king cancels the outstanding tribute owed by any community.

[60] There is also a respect in which Lacedaemonians resemble Egyptians. Town-criers, pipe-players, and cooks inherit their work from their fathers; each of them is the son of a father who carried on the same trade. They cannot be displaced by others coming along and taking up town-crying, for instance, on the basis of possessing a strong, clear voice: these jobs are inherited. Anyway, that is enough on these matters.

[61] To resume: Cleomenes was on Aegina, working for the common good of Greece, but Demaratus, motivated not by any concern for Aegina, but by malice and envy, was blackening his name. On his return from Aegina, Cleomenes began to think about deposing Demaratus, and he found a pretext for attacking him in something his father Ariston had done. When Ariston was king of Sparta he had married twice, but without producing any children. Because he refused to entertain the idea that he was responsible, he took a third wife. The circumstances of this third marriage were as follows. His closest friend was a Spartiate whose wife happened to be by far the most beautiful woman in Sparta—and what is more she had become that beautiful after having been repulsive! She was an ugly girl, but she had a nurse and the nurse had an idea. The

nurse was motivated not just by the fact that the girl was ugly, but also by the wealth of the girl's family; besides, it was clear to her that the girl's parents thought her looks a catastrophe. So she took her every day to the shrine of Helen in Therapne, which overlooks the sanctuary of Phoebus Apollo. Every time the nurse brought her there, she would put her in front of Helen's statue and ask the goddess to take away the child's ugliness. And at last, the story goes, just as the nurse was leaving the shrine one day, a woman appeared and asked her what she was carrying in her arms. When the nurse replied that it was a child, the woman asked her to uncover it, but the nurse refused, and explained that the child's parents had told her not to show the child to anyone. The woman insisted on seeing the child anyway, and eventually, seeing that the woman made so much of seeing the child, the nurse showed it to her. The woman stroked the child's head and said that she would be the most beautiful woman in Sparta. From that day on, the girl's looks changed, and when the time came for her to have a husband, Agetus the son of Alcidas married her—and it was this Agetus who was Ariston's friend.

[62] Ariston was, as it turned out, tortured by a passionate longing for this woman, and so he came up with a plan. He promised his friend, the husband of the woman in question, that he would give him as a present anything he wanted, any single item he owned, and he asked his friend to give him a similar present as well, on the same terms. Agetus was not worried about his wife at all, because he could see that Ariston already had a wife, so he agreed to the suggestion. They sealed the bargain with oaths. Ariston gave Agetus whatever it was that Agetus requested from among his valuables, and then it was Ariston's turn to ask for a present in return from him, so he tried to take his friend's wife. Agetus said that she was excluded from the deal—that Ariston could have anything else except for her—but the oath he had sworn and Ariston's deceitful trick left him no choice, and he let him take his wife.

[63] So Ariston divorced his second wife and married for the third time. Before very long—in fact, before ten months were up—his new wife gave birth to a child, who was Demaratus. Ariston was in session with the ephors at the time, and a house-slave brought the news of the child's birth. On the basis of knowing the date of his marriage, Ariston calculated on his fingers the number

of months that had passed and then exclaimed with an oath: 'He can't be mine!' The ephors heard him say this, but they did not make anything of it at the time. The boy grew, and Ariston came to regret his remark, because he became convinced that Demaratus was his son. The reason he called him Demaratus, the people's prayer, was that some time before these events the whole Spartiate population had offered up a prayer for the birth of a son to Ariston, whom they regarded as the most outstanding king there had ever been in Sparta. That is how Demaratus came by his name.

[64] Time passed. Ariston died and Demaratus became king. But apparently it was fated that these things would become general knowledge and would lead to Demaratus losing his kingdom, thanks to the fact that† there was a great deal of bad feeling between him and Cleomenes; this had manifested itself earlier, when Demaratus withdrew the army from Eleusis, and in particular now, when Cleomenes went over to Aegina to deal with the Persian collaborators on the island.

[65] Now that he was determined to take revenge, Cleomenes made a deal with Leotychidas, the son of Menares and grandson of Agis, who was of the same lineage as Demaratus. Their arrangement was that in return for being made king in Demaratus' place, Leotychidas would join Cleomenes' expedition against Aegina. What had made Leotychidas such a bitter enemy of Demaratus was that when Leotychidas was betrothed to Percalus the daughter of Chilon the son of Demarmenus, Demaratus had deliberately robbed Leotychidas of his marriage by carrying Percalus away first and making her his wife instead. That is what had turned Leotychidas against Demaratus. At the time in question, Leotychidas, at Cleomenes' instigation, swore a complaint against Demaratus to the effect that he was not a legitimate king of Sparta because he was not the son of Ariston; then he followed up this affidavit by prosecuting Demaratus in court. During the trial he resuscitated the old remark Ariston had made in response to the house-slave's news of the child's birth, when he had calculated the number of months and exclaimed with an oath that the child was not his. Leotychidas took his stand upon this remark and argued that Demaratus was not Ariston's child and had no right to rule Sparta. He had the ephors who had been at the meeting and had heard Ariston's words come forward to testify in support of his case.

[66] The legal battle raged back and forth, and in the end the Spartiates decided to ask the Delphic oracle whether Demaratus was Ariston's son. The issue was referred to the Pythia by Cleomenes, because this suited his plan; he next got the most influential person in Delphi, Cobon the son of Aristophantus, on to his side, and Cobon persuaded the oracle's prophetess, Periallas† to give the answer Cleomenes wanted to hear. So when the emissaries put their question to the Pythia, she pronounced in favour of Demaratus *not* being Ariston's son. Later, however, word leaked out about what had gone on; Cobon was banished from Delphi and Periallas the prophetess was deprived of her office.

[67] That is how Demaratus came to be deposed. He ended up in Persia, in exile from Sparta, but that was due to an insult. What happened was that after he had been deposed, he held an elected office. During the Festival of Unarmed Dancing Demaratus was looking on, and Leotychidas (who had by then taken his place as king) sent an attendant with a mocking, sarcastic question: he asked Demaratus what it was like to be an official after having been king. Stung by the question, Demaratus replied, 'I have experienced both; you have not. Lacedaemon, however, will meet with either a great deal of misery or a great deal of happiness as a result of your question.' With these words he covered his head, left the theatre, and went home. Then he immediately got everything ready and set about offering an ox to Zeus. Once he had finished performing the sacrifice, he asked his mother to come and see him.

[68] When she arrived, he put some of the entrails into her hands and solemnly asked her to help him. 'Mother,' he said, 'I beg you in the name of all the gods, especially Zeus the guardian of our house, to tell me the truth. Who, in all honesty, is my father? Leotychidas claimed during the court case that you were already pregnant by your former husband when you went to Ariston, and others tell the even stupider tale that you went to bed with one of the house-slaves—the muleteer—and that he is my father. So I implore you in the name of the gods to tell me the truth. After all, if you did do any of the things you are supposed to have done, you certainly weren't the first. And Ariston is commonly rumoured in Sparta to have been sterile, because otherwise his other wives would have had children.'

[69] This is how he spoke, and his mother replied: 'All right, son. If it's the truth you so earnestly want from me, the truth is

what you will hear—the whole truth. On the third night after
Ariston had brought me to his house as his wife, I was visited by
a phantom which looked just like Ariston. After it had slept with
me, it put on me the garlands it was wearing, and then went away.
Later, Ariston came in. When he saw me wearing garlands, he asked
me who had given them to me. I told him that he had, but he
assured me that he hadn't. I swore that he had and said that it was
wrong of him to deny it, because he had given me the garlands just
a short while previously, after he had come and slept with me. It
was obvious that I was serious, and so Ariston realized that this
was the gods' doing. Two further clues pointed in the same direction: first, the garlands turned out to have come from the shrine by
the courtyard door, which is said to be the shrine of the hero Astrabacus, and, second, the diviners we consulted named Astrabacus
as the one who had slept with me. So now you know everything,
my son, that you wanted to hear. That was the night you were
conceived, so either your birth is due to this hero, in which case
Astrabacus is your father, or your father is Ariston. As for the main
piece of evidence your enemies use to attack you—the charge
that at the news of your birth Ariston himself, in front of many
witnesses, said that you were not his son, since there hadn't been
enough time—well, he blurted it out in complete ignorance of these
matters. Not all pregnancies last the full ten months: women give
birth to children after nine months and seven months as well. You
were a seven-month baby. Ariston himself soon came to see that
his remark had been made in ignorance. Now that you know the
whole truth, you needn't listen to any of the other tales about your
birth. As for Leotychidas and his fellow rumour-mongers, let *their*
wives have children by donkey-men!'

[70] His mother's words gave Demaratus all the information he
wanted. He took everything he would need for a journey and set
out for Elis. He told people that he was going to Delphi to consult
the oracle, but the Lacedaemonians suspected that he was trying to
flee the country and started out in pursuit. Somehow he crossed
over to Zacynthos from Elis before they could catch up with him,
but the Lacedaemonians crossed over after him and tried to arrest
him. They succeeded in getting his attendants away from him, but
the people of Zacynthos would not let them have Demaratus, and
he sailed over to Asia and made his way to King Darius, who
received him with great pomp, and gave him land and settlements.

So these were the turns of fortune that brought Demaratus to Asia, after he had won glory among the Lacedaemonians time and time again by his actions and his intelligence. Once, for instance, he gave them a victory at Olympia by winning with his four-horse chariot, which is something no other Spartan king ever achieved.

[71] After Demaratus had been deposed, Leotychidas the son of Menares succeeded to the kingdom. Leotychidas had a son whose name was Zeuxidamus (or Cyniscus, as some Spartiates used to call him) who did not become king of Sparta, because he died before Leotychidas, but he left Archidamus as his son. After the loss of Zeuxidamus, Leotychidas remarried; this second wife of his was called Eurydame, and she was the sister of Menius and daughter of Diactoridas. She bore Leotychidas no sons, but a daughter called Lampito, whom Leotychidas gave in marriage to Archidamus the son of Zeuxidamus.

[72] However, Leotychidas paid for what he did to Demaratus: he did not reach old age in Sparta either. He led a military expedition to Thessaly, and although he could have subdued the whole country, he was bribed with a lot of money not to. He was caught red-handed in the camp, sitting on a glove filled with money, and as a result he was tried and banished from Sparta, and his house was torn down. He went into exile in Tegea, and that is where he died.

[73] But this was all in the future. At the time in question, Cleomenes was still smarting from the insults he had received on Aegina, so as soon as he had the problem with Demaratus well in hand he took Leotychidas and went after the Aeginetans. With both kings coming against them at once, the Aeginetans decided not to resist. Cleomenes and Leotychidas picked out the ten Aeginetans whose wealth and lineage made them the most important members of the community and took them away. Among the ten prisoners were Crius the son of Polycritus and Casambus the son of Aristocrates, who were the most influential men on the island. Cleomenes and Demaratus took their prisoners to Attica and left them in the safe keeping of the Athenians, who were the Aeginetans' worst enemies.

[74] Some time later, however, when information about his dishonest plots against Demaratus leaked out, Cleomenes became afraid of what the Spartiates would do and slipped out of the country to Thessaly. From there he went to Arcadia, where he

proceeded to stir up trouble by uniting the inhabitants against Sparta. He made the Arcadians swear that they would follow his lead come what may, and on top of the other oaths he had them swear, he tried his best to get the leading Arcadians to go with him to the town of Nonacris and swear an oath of loyalty on the waters of the Styx. According to the Arcadians the waters of the Styx are to be found in this town, and in fact it is true that a trickle of water drips out of a rock there and into a basin, which has been encircled by a wall. Nonacris, where this spring is to be found, is a town in Arcadia near Pheneus.

[75] When the Lacedaemonians found out what Cleomenes was up to, they became worried. They brought him home to Sparta† and restored him to his kingship with no change to his former status. Now, Cleomenes had been more or less insane before, and no sooner had he got back to Sparta than he succumbed to an illness† whose symptoms were that he used to poke his staff into the face of any Spartiate he met. Faced with this behaviour and his derangement, his relatives put him in the stocks. While he was in the stocks, he was left with only a single guard, and when he noticed this, he began to ask the guard to give him a knife. At first the guard refused, but Cleomenes intimidated him by threatening him with future punishment, and eventually the guard, who was only a helot, gave him a knife. Cleomenes took hold of the weapon and began to mutilate himself by cutting strips of flesh off his body. He started with his shins and moved up from there to his thighs, and then on to his hips and his sides, until he began slicing into his stomach, at which point he died. The Greeks most commonly attribute the manner of his death to the fact that he had persuaded the Pythia to say what she did about Demaratus, but the Athenians say that it was because during his assault on Eleusis he cut down the trees in the precinct of the gods. According to the Argives, however, it was because he induced the Argives who had taken refuge in the sanctuary of Argos after the battle between Argos and Sparta to come down from the sanctuary, and then massacred them and, showing no respect for the sacred grove, burnt it down.

[76] Cleomenes had consulted Delphi and been told that he would capture Argos. On his way with his Spartiate troops he reached the River Erasinus, which is said to flow from the Stymphalian Lake; to be precise, this lake is supposed to drain into

an immeasurably deep chasm and then re-emerge in Argos, at which point the waters begin to be called the Erasinus by the Argives. Anyway, once Cleomenes reached this river he offered a sacrifice to the river-god, but the omens were not at all favourable for his crossing. In response, however, he said that he admired the god for refusing to betray his citizens, but even so the Argives were not going to get off lightly. Then he pulled his men back to Thyreae, sacrificed a bull to the sea, and transported them by boat to the territory of Tiryns and Nauplia.

[77] When the Argives got wind of this they came down to the coast to meet him. They positioned themselves facing the Lacedaemonians, and not far from their camp, at a place called Sepeia, which is near Tiryns. Now, the Argives were not worried about the prospect of an open battle, but were afraid of falling prey to trickery. The reason for this was that they had an oracle which referred to such an eventuality. It was in a prediction delivered by the Pythia which they and the Milesians shared, and it ran as follows:

> But when female conquers male and expels him,
> When glory in Argos redounds to her name,
> She will set Argive women a-plenty tearing their cheeks;
> And so it will be said by future generations that a fearful
> Thrice-coiled snake fell before the spear and perished.

It was the conjunction of all these events that made the Argives afraid. Under these circumstances they decided to make use of the enemy's crier—that is, to copy the Lacedaemonians every time the Spartiate crier issued an order.

[78] When Cleomenes noticed that the Argives were following every command the Spartiate crier was issuing, he told his men that the next time the crier announced that it was time for them to eat, they should pick up their weapons and attack the Argives. And that is exactly what the Lacedaemonians did. The Argives had followed the crier's command and were busy with their meal when the Lacedaemonians attacked them. Argive losses were heavy, but far more of their troops took refuge in the grove of Argus, where the Lacedaemonians surrounded them and waited.

[79] Cleomenes next questioned the Argive deserters he had among his troops. As a result of what he learnt, he sent a herald calling on the Argives who were shut up in the grounds of the sanctuary to leave; he called them personally by name, and told them

that their ransoms had been paid. (The Peloponnesians have a fixed rate for ransoming a prisoner of war, of two minas per man.) About fifty of the Argives responded one by one to Cleomenes' summons by coming out—and Cleomenes had them killed. Now, for a while the ones who remained in the precinct were unaware of the situation because there were too many trees for those inside the grove to see what was happening to those outside it, but at last someone climbed a tree and saw what was going on. Consequently, of course, they stopped coming out of the grove when their names were called.

[80] Cleomenes then got every single one of his helots to pile up wood around the grove, and once they had carried out his order he set the place alight. The flames had just caught hold when he asked one of the deserters which god the grove belonged to; 'Argus', came the reply. When Cleomenes heard this he gave a great groan and said, 'Apollo, god of prophecy, you seriously misled me when you foretold that I would capture Argos; I think your prediction has now come true.'

[81] Cleomenes next dismissed most of his troops and sent them back to Sparta, while he himself went with a thousand élite soldiers to the temple of Hera, with the intention of offering a sacrifice at her altar. But the priest forbade him from doing so, citing the rule that it is sacrilege for foreigners to perform sacrifices there. So Cleomenes ordered his helots to remove the priest from the altar and whip him, and he carried out the ritual by himself. Then he returned to Sparta.

[82] Back in Sparta, his enemies brought him before the ephors on the charge of having accepted a bribe not to take Argos, which, they claimed, he could easily have taken. I do not know for sure whether or not he was telling the truth, but in any case his response was to say that, in his opinion, the god's prediction had come true once he had captured the sanctuary of Argus and so, under these circumstances, he had decided not to attack the city until he had offered sacrifices and discovered whether the gods would let the city fall into his hands or would block the endeavour. He went on to explain that when he was seeking a favourable omen in the temple of Hera a flame had burst out from the statue's breast, and he had realized the truth, which was that he would not capture Argos. If the flame had burst from the statue's head, he said, he would have captured the city from the top of the acropolis down-

wards; but since it came from the breast he decided that he had
already done everything the gods wanted him to do. The Spartiates
found this defence of his plausible and reasonable, and so he was
acquitted, by a large majority, on the charge his prosecutors had
brought against him.

[83] Argos was so short of men that their slaves took over the
government and administration of the city's affairs at all levels,
until the sons of those who had died grew up, regained control of
Argos, and expelled the slaves. The displaced slaves then fought a
successful battle for the possession of Tiryns. For a while there was
harmony between the two states, but then the slaves were joined
by a diviner called Cleander, a native of Phigalea in Arcadia, who
persuaded them to attack their masters. The resulting war lasted a
long time, but in the end, with great difficulty, the Argives won.

[84] So that is why Cleomenes went mad and died such a horrible death, according to the Argives. The Spartiates themselves
deny, however, that his insanity was of supernatural origin; according to them the time he had spent with the Scythians gave him the
habit of drinking his wine neat and that was what caused his
madness. What happened, on this version, was that the nomadic
Scythians longed to make Darius pay for his invasion of their land,
so they sent agents to Sparta to ask them to become their allies and
to agree to a plan whereby the Scythians themselves would try to
invade Media along the Phasis River, while the Spartiates, they
suggested, would set out inland from Ephesus to join them. So
the story goes that Cleomenes spent a lot of time—an abnormal
amount of time—with this Scythian delegation and acquired the
habit of drinking undiluted wine from them. And that is what drove
him mad, according to the Spartiates. Ever since then, they say that
they want to drink 'Scythian fashion' when they want to drink
stronger wine than usual. So that is the Spartiate explanation of
what happened to Cleomenes. My own view is that it was punishment for what Cleomenes did to Demaratus.

[85] When news of Cleomenes' death reached Aegina, the
islanders sent agents to Sparta to denounce Leotychidas over
the business of the hostages who were being held in Athens. The
Lacedaemonians convened a court which decided that Leotychidas
had treated the Aeginetans over-harshly and sentenced him to
be surrendered to the islanders in compensation for the men who
were being held in Athens. The Aeginetans were poised to take

Leotychidas away when they were addressed by Theasidas the son of Leoprepes, who was a man of distinction in Sparta. 'Men of Aegina,' he said, 'what is this? Are you really planning to remove the king of Sparta? He may have been surrendered to you by his citizens, but if this was a decision taken in anger, you'd better watch out in case sometime in the future they pay you back with the complete destruction of your land.' His words made the Aeginetans stop their removal of Leotychidas. Instead they made a deal with him, that he would come with them to Athens and recover the hostages for them.

[86] When Leotychidas went to Athens and asked the Athenians to return the men left in their safe keeping, he found them reluctant to do so. They came up with various excuses, such as that they had been entrusted with the hostages by *two* kings, so it would be wrong of them to return them to one king without the other one being there too. Faced with their refusal to return the hostages Leotychidas said, 'Men of Athens, it's up to you to choose. You can either return the hostages, which would be right, or not, which would be the opposite. But on the subject of safe keeping, I'd like you to hear a story we Spartiates tell about something that once happened in Sparta. In Lacedaemon, three generations back, there was a man called Glaucus, who was the son of Epicydas. He was the foremost man of his generation in Lacedaemon, and was particularly famous for his integrity. The story we tell concerns something that happened to him in the fullness of time.

'A Milesian came to Sparta to meet Glaucus, with a proposition to put to him. "Glaucus," he said, "I'm a Milesian and I've come all this way because I want to enjoy the benefits of your honesty. You're well known all over Greece, even in Ionia, as a man of integrity. I got to thinking about how risky a place Ionia always is, compared with the stability of the Peloponnese, and about how property never remains in the same hands there, as everyone can see. With these thoughts and ideas in mind, then, I decided to convert half my property into money and to deposit it with you, because I had no doubt that in your hands it would be safe. So please accept this money, and here also are some tokens for you to take and keep. When someone comes to you with the matching tallies and asks for the money, give it to him."

'That was what the visitor from Miletus said. Glaucus agreed to his terms and accepted the deposit for safe keeping. Many years later the sons of the man who had left the money with Glaucus came to Sparta. They spoke to Glaucus, showed him the tallies, and asked for the money back. But his response to their request was to try to put them off. "I have no recollection of this matter," he said. "My mind's a complete blank as regards what you're talking about. Still, if something does occur to me I shall act with total integrity: if I did take the deposit, I will give it back, and if I never had it, my treatment of you will conform to normal Greek practice in such cases. I will therefore postpone settling the matter for three months."

'The Milesians were devastated; they went away convinced that they had been robbed of their money. Meanwhile, Glaucus went to Delphi to consult the oracle. His question was whether he could swear an oath and so get away with stealing the money. The Pythia rebuked him with the following words:

> Yes, Glaucus, Epicydas' son, in the short term you will gain
> If you use an oath to have your way and steal the money.
> Swear an oath: after all, death awaits even an honest man.
> But Oath has a nameless child. Though it has no hands
> Or feet, it is swift in pursuit, until it has seized
> All a man's offspring, all his house, and destroyed them.
> But an honest man's offspring will gain in the long run.

'At this, Glaucus asked the god to forgive him for his question, but the Pythia said that seeking the god's permission for a crime and actually committing the crime amounted to the same thing.

'Glaucus sent for the Milesian visitors and gave them back their money. But here is the point of the story, the reason why I mentioned it to you Athenians: today there is not a single descendant of Glaucus alive, nor is there a single household that is considered to stem from Glaucus. He has been utterly and completely eradicated from Sparta. This just goes to show the advantage of not even *thinking* anything about a deposit with which one has been entrusted except how to give it back when one is asked for it.' Even this story failed to move the Athenians, however, so Leotychidas went home.

[87] Despite the fact that the Aeginetans still had not paid for the wrong they had done Athens earlier as a favour to the Thebans, they put the blame on the Athenians and felt that it was they, the Aeginetans, who were the injured party. Consequently, they

prepared to exact revenge on Athens. Now, once every four years the Athenians held a festival at Sunium, so what the Aeginetans did was ambush the delegates' ship and capture it, and along with it all the important Athenians on board, who became the Aeginetans' prisoners.

[88] After this assault by the Aeginetans the Athenians no longer felt any compunction about doing everything they could to inflict damage on them. Now, there was an eminent Aeginetan called Nicodromus the son of Cnoethus who had once been banished from the island and was still nursing a grudge against his fellow citizens. When Nicodromus realized that the Athenians were serious in their determination to harm the Aeginetans, he arranged to betray the island to them. He told them the day when he would make the attempt and expect them to arrive with reinforcements. Later, then, he occupied what is known as the Old Town (which was his side of the deal with the Athenians), but the Athenians failed to turn up as they were supposed to.

[89] They had asked the Corinthians for some ships, because their own fleet was in fact no match for the Aeginetans in a sea battle, and this delay was enough to ruin the whole enterprise. The Corinthians and the Athenians were on very good terms in those days, so the Corinthians responded to the Athenian request by giving them twenty ships—though actually they charged five drachmas per ship, because there was a law forbidding them from just giving them away for nothing. With these ships as well as their own, the Athenians made up a fleet of seventy ships in all and sailed against Aegina. But they arrived a day later than they had agreed to.

[90] When the Athenians failed to arrive on time, Nicodromus and a number of other Aeginetans fled from the island by boat. The Athenians let them live in Sunium, and they used their new home as a base from which to raid the Aeginetans on their island.

[91] But these raids happened later. The popular uprising on Aegina which had been led by Nicodromus was put down by the men of substance, who then proceeded to lead the captive rebels out of the town to kill them. Ever since then they were under a curse, which they were unable to expiate by ritual means, for all their efforts; instead they were banished from the island before they could win the goddess over. What happened was that they were in the process of taking seven hundred prisoners out of the town for

execution when one of them broke free of his chains and took refuge at the porch of the temple of Demeter the Lawgiver, where he seized the door handles and hung on to them. They could not get him to let go by pulling him away from the door, so they chopped off his hands and took him away for execution like that—while his hands remained gripping the handles.

[92] That is what the Aeginetans did to their own people. In the battle that took place once the Athenians arrived with their fleet of seventy ships, the Aeginetans came off worst and appealed for help to the same people who had responded on an earlier occasion, the Argives. But the Argives refused to help this time, because they were angry with Aegina. Some Aeginetan ships which had been seized by Cleomenes had landed in Argolis, and the crews had helped the Lacedaemonians in a foray ashore—a raid in which the Lacedaemonians also received the support of men from Sicyonian ships. The Argives then imposed a fine of 1,000 talents, 500 talents each. While the Sicyonians acknowledged their guilt and agreed to pay a hundred talents to clear themselves, the Aeginetans stubbornly refused to admit that they were in the wrong. Consequently, no one in Argos was prepared to send official state help in response to the Aeginetan appeal, but they raised a volunteer force of about a thousand men, led by Eurybates, a specialist in the pentathlon. Most of these men did not make it back home again, but died on Aegina in the battle with the Athenians. Eurybates, their commander, specialized in single combat during the fight and killed the first three men who came up against him, but was himself killed by the fourth, who was Sophanes of Decelea.

[93] At sea, however, the Aeginetans caught the Athenians in disarray and won the ensuing engagement. They captured four Athenian ships, crews and all.

[94] So Athens and Aegina were at war. Meanwhile, the Persian king was pursuing his own designs. He had his attendant constantly reminding him to remember the Athenians, and the Pisistratidae by his side turning him against Athens. Moreover, Darius himself wanted to make this into a pretext for conquering the Greek states which had refused to give him earth and water. He relieved Mardonius of his command, because his expedition had been so unsuccessful, and appointed others in his place to command the campaign he was planning against Eretria and Athens. These new military commanders were a Mede called Datis and Artaphrenes

the son of Artaphrenes, who was Darius' nephew. The mission he gave them was to reduce Athens and Eretria to slavery and to bring the captives before him.

[95] These newly appointed commanders left the king's presence and made their way to Cilicia, to the Aleian Plain there, at the head of a huge, well-equipped land army. While they were encamped there they were joined by the whole naval force which the various states had been required to raise, and the horse-transport ships that Darius had ordered his tribute-paying subjects to build the year before. The horses were put on board these transport vessels, the land army embarked, and the fleet of six hundred triremes set sail for Ionia. But they did not then head straight for the Hellespont and Thrace along the Ionian coast; instead they set out from Samos to Icaria, and then sailed from island to island. I imagine that they went this way because they were particularly apprehensive about trying to sail around Athos, because of the disaster they had met with on this route the year before. Besides, the fact that they had left Naxos untaken forced their hand.

[96] After crossing the Icarian Sea, the Persians made for Naxos and landed there, since they had decided to make it the first place they attacked. The Naxians did not stay to fight the Persians, but fled to the hills, mindful of what had happened before. The Persians enslaved any of them they caught, and also burnt their sanctuaries and the town. Then they set off to attack other islands.

[97] In the mean time, the Delians also fled: they abandoned Delos and went to Tenos. As his forces were drawing near the island, Datis sailed ahead and told the fleet to anchor across the straits at Rhenaea, rather than off Delos. Once he found out where the Delians were, he sent a message to them, through a herald. 'Reverend gentlemen, why have you run away?' he asked. 'You must have a mistaken impression of me. Even if it weren't for the king's instructions, I would certainly have enough sense, faced with the birthplace of the two gods, not to inflict the slightest harm on either the land itself or its inhabitants. So why don't you return to your homes and come back to live in Delos?' This was the message Datis delivered to the Delians. He then heaped up three hundred talents of frankincense on the altar and burnt it as an offering.

[98] Datis then sailed away with his army, which included Ionian and Aeolian contingents; the next place he made for was

Eretria. But after he had withdrawn his men from the area, Delos was shaken by an earthquake, which, according to the Delians, had never happened before and has never happened since, up to my day. This was an omen sent by the god, surely, to warn people of the trouble that was to come. After all, for three successive generations—during the reigns of Darius the son of Hystaspes, Xerxes the son of Darius, and Artaxerxes the son of Xerxes—Greece suffered more than it had for twenty generations before Darius, partly as a result of Persian action there, but partly because of power struggles between the leading Greek states. So it was hardly surprising that an earthquake should have struck Delos, even though it had never experienced one before. Moreover, there was on record a prediction about the island, which said, 'I will also shake Delos, previously unshaken.' Translated into Greek the names Darius, Xerxes, and Artaxerxes mean respectively 'doer of deeds', 'man of war', and 'great man of war'. Those would be the correct Greek equivalents of these kings' names.

[99] After they had sailed away from Delos, the Persians stopped off at the Aegean islands, where they rounded up troops for their army and took the islanders' children along with them as hostages. During this voyage from island to island, they also landed at Carystus. The people there refused to hand over hostages or to supply troops for any campaign against neighbouring states (meaning Eretria and Athens), so the Persians proceeded to besiege the place and to devastate their farmlands, until the Carystians too were brought into the Persian fold.

[100] The Eretrians reacted to the news that the Persian forces were sailing against them by asking Athens for assistance, which the Athenians gladly offered in the form of the four thousand smallholders who were occupying the land of the Horse-farmers in Chalcis. As it turned out, however, the Eretrians did not have a sound general strategy. Although they had asked for the Athenians, they were in two minds about what plan to adopt. Some of them were recommending that they should abandon the city and take to the Euboean hill country, while others (motivated by the prospect of being personally rewarded by Darius) were preparing to surrender the city. When Aeschines the son of Nothon, who was one of the Eretrian leaders, saw how things stood with these two factions, he explained the situation to those of the Athenians who had already arrived and begged them to return to their own city, to

avoid being caught up in the destruction of Eretria. The Athenians followed Aeschines' advice.

[101] So these Athenians sailed across to Oropus and saved themselves. Meanwhile, the Persian fleet landed in Eretrian territory, at Tamynae, Choereae, and Aegilia. As soon as they had beached their ships in these places, they proceeded to put the horses ashore and got ready to mount an assault against their enemies. The Eretrian plan was to avoid making sorties and meeting the Persians in battle outside the city; now that the plan not to abandon the city had won out, their concern was to defend their walls, if they could. The attack on the city was fierce, and losses were heavy on both sides. After six days of fighting, however, two eminent Eretrians—Euphorbus the son of Alcimachus and Philagrus the son of Cyneas—betrayed the city to the Persians. Once they were inside the city, the Persians not only plundered the sanctuaries and set them on fire, in revenge for the burning of the sanctuaries in Sardis, but also reduced the population to slavery, just as Darius had commanded.

[102] The Persians waited a few days after the fall of Eretria and then set sail for Attica, pressing on hard, and confident that they would deal with Athens just as they had with Eretria. Now, Marathon was the place in Attica which combined terrain that was admirably suited to cavalry manoeuvres and proximity to Eretria, so this was the place where Hippias the son of Pisistratus directed them.

[103] When the Athenians heard the news, they too marched out to Marathon. There were ten military commanders in charge of the Athenian forces, one of whom was Miltiades, whose father Cimon the son of Stesagoras had been forced into exile from Athens by Pisistratus the son of Hippocrates. It was during his exile that he won a victory at Olympia with his four-horse chariot, thereby matching the victory won by Miltiades, his half-brother on his mother's side. At the very next Olympics, he won again with the same team of horses, but he allowed Pisistratus to be declared the winner—an action which reconciled him to Pisistratus and so enabled him to return to Athens under a truce. The same team of horses gained him victory at a subsequent Olympic Games, but then, as it happened, he was killed by Pisistratus' sons (Pisistratus himself was no longer alive). The Pisistratidae killed him by getting assassins to surprise him one night in the town hall. Cimon is

buried outside Athens, on the far side of the road called 'through Coele'. The mares which won him three victories at Olympia are buried opposite him. This record has also been equalled by the team of horses that belonged to Euagoras of Laconia, but so far they are the only ones to have done so. At the time of the murder, Cimon's eldest son Stesagoras was being brought up in the house of his uncle, Miltiades, in the Chersonese, but the younger son was with Cimon in Athens. He was named Miltiades after the founder of the Chersonese.

[104] So this was the Miltiades who at the time in question was a commander of the Athenian forces. He had come to live in Athens after a period in the Chersonese, and had twice escaped death. In the first place, the Phoenicians who chased him as far as Imbros placed a very high premium on capturing him and taking him to Darius. In the second place, after his escape from these Phoenicians, when he had returned home to apparent safety at last, he found his enemies waiting for him; they prosecuted him for his tyranny in the Chersonese, but he escaped from their clutches too. Later he was appointed by the people of Athens to the post of military commander.

[105] The first thing the commanders did—and this was before they left the city—was send Philippides (an Athenian who was a professional courier) to Sparta with a message. According to Philippides himself, and as he told the Athenians, he had an encounter with Pan near Mount Parthenium, which overlooks Tegea. Pan called out his name, he claimed, and told him to take the following message to the Athenians: 'Why do you ignore me, when I am a friend of Athens? I have often been of service to you in the past, and will be again in the future too.' The Athenians believed in the authenticity of this experience, and later, when their affairs had prospered, they built a sanctuary of Pan under the Acropolis, and on the basis of this message of his they worship him with annual sacrifices and a torch-race.

[106] Anyway, to resume: Philippides was sent by the military commanders on the mission during which he claimed to have had a vision of Pan, and he arrived in Sparta the day after leaving Athens. He went to the leaders and said: 'Men of Lacedaemon, Athens requests your assistance. We beg you not to stand by and watch the most ancient city in Greece be enslaved by a foreign power. Eretria has already been reduced to slavery, thus making

Greece weaker by one notable city than it was before.' This was the message he delivered to the Lacedaemonians, as he had been instructed. The Lacedaemonian decision was to come to Athens' assistance, but they could not do so straight away, because there was a law they were reluctant to break. It was the ninth day of the month, and they said that they would not send an army into the field then or until the moon was full.

[107] So the Lacedaemonians were waiting for the full moon, and the invaders had Hippias the son of Pisistratus as their guide to Marathon. The previous night Hippias had dreamt that he slept with his own mother. He interpreted the dream to mean that he would return to Athens, regain his political position, and die of old age in his homeland. Anyway, that was the meaning he got from the dream. As the Persian guide, first he unloaded the Eretrian prisoners on Aegilia, the island belonging to Styra, and then he beached the ships at Marathon, made them fast there, and disposed the Persian troops once they were on dry land. Now, he was in the middle of arranging the troops when he was seized by an unusually violent fit of sneezing and coughing. Since he was fairly old, most of his teeth were loose, and the force of his sneezing caused one of them to fall out into the sand. He spent a lot of time looking for it. When he failed to find the tooth he groaned and remarked to the people near by, 'This land is not ours. We will never be able to conquer it. The only bit of it that belonged to me has been claimed by my tooth.'

[108] So Hippias concluded that this incident was the fulfilment of his dream. The Athenians had already formed up in the precinct of Heracles when the Plataeans arrived with all their available manpower to reinforce them. They did so because they were subjects of Athens, and the Athenians had often in the past spared no effort on Plataea's behalf. Here is how the Plataeans became Athenian subjects. They were being pressured by the Thebans, and Cleomenes the son of Anaxandridas happened to be in the country with some Lacedaemonian troops. The Plataeans first offered themselves to Sparta, but the Lacedaemonians rejected the offer, saying, 'We live too far away to be anything but feeble help to you. You could be enslaved many times over before any of us even heard about it. But why don't you offer yourselves to the Athenians, who are your neighbours and can provide pretty effective assistance?' This suggestion by the Lacedaemonians was prompted not by

goodwill towards the Plataeans so much as because they wanted
the Athenians to have all the trouble of coming into conflict with
the Boeotians. Anyway, the Plataeans took their advice; they came
and sat as suppliants at the altar while the Athenians were celebrating the Festival of the Twelve Gods, and committed themselves
to become a subject state of Athens. The Theban response to the
news was to march against Plataea, whereupon the Athenians came
to help the Plataeans. Battle was just about to be joined when the
Corinthians, who happened to be near by, intervened. The two
sides accepted Corinthian arbitration, and the Corinthians fixed the
borders between the territories of Plataea and Thebes. They made
it part of the agreement that the Thebans should not put pressure
on any Boeotians who did not want to join the Boeotian League.
After brokering this settlement, the Corinthians left—and as the
Athenians were withdrawing, the Boeotians attacked them, but
they lost the battle. The Athenians crossed over into Theban territory, beyond the border which the Corinthians had fixed for
Plataea, and then went so far as to make the River Asopus the place
where Theban territory ended and that belonging to Plataea and
Hysiae began. That, then, is how the Plataeans came to be committed to the Athenian cause, and so they now came to Marathon
to fight alongside the Athenians.

[109] The Athenian commanders were in two minds as to how
to proceed. Some said that they should avoid fighting, on the
grounds that they were outnumbered by the Persian army; others,
including Miltiades, were in favour of it. Now, there was an
eleventh person there who could cast a vote—the War Archon, who
was selected by lot; the post had long been established at Athens
as having parity with the commanders when it came to voting. At
the time in question it was Callimachus of Aphidnae who was the
War Archon. So since the commanders were divided, and since
the more cowardly view was beginning to gain the upper hand,
Miltiades approached Callimachus and said, 'The future of Athens
lies in your hands now, Callimachus. You can either cast us down
into slavery or win us our freedom—and thereby ensure that
you will be remembered as long as there are people alive on
this earth, with a higher reputation even than Harmodius and
Aristogiton. Athens' position is more precarious now than it ever
has been before, throughout its history. There are two alternatives:
submission to the Persians—and we have seen what will happen

if we fall into Hippias' hands—or victory, in which case we might well become the leading city in Greece. How could that happen, you ask? And why is it up to *you* to determine the course of events? I will explain. The ten generals are evenly divided between those who want to engage the enemy, and those who are advising against it. Failure to take the enemy on will, I'm sure, generate serious civil war, and in the upheaval the Athenians will be disposed to collaborate with the Persians. However, if we engage the enemy before this or any other unsound view infects the minds of some Athenians, and if the gods are impartial, we can get the better of the Persians in the battle. So it is entirely up to you now; it all depends on you. If you support my point of view, your country will be free and your city will become the leader of Greece. But if you side with those who are disinclined to fight, your reward will be the opposite of these benefits.'

[110] These words of Miltiades' won Callimachus over to his side. With the War Archon's support, the view that they ought to engage the enemy prevailed. Subsequently, when each of the commanders who had inclined towards engaging the enemy held the presidency of the board of commanders for the day, he stood down in favour of Miltiades. While accepting the post each time, Miltiades waited until the presidency was properly his before giving battle.

[111] So when it was his turn, the Athenians took up battle positions. The War Archon was in command of the right wing (in conformity with the custom in force in Athens at the time, that the right wing was to be commanded by the War Archon), then the tribes followed, one after another, in their usual order, and finally the Plataeans were positioned on the left wing. And ever since this battle, during the sacrificial rites at the public gatherings in the festival held every four years at Athens, the Athenian crier has prayed for prosperity not just for the Athenian people, but for the Plataeans as well. Anyway, the arrangement of the Athenian army at Marathon was such that it was extended over the same length as the Persian army. It was at its weakest in the centre, which was only a few ranks deep, but each of the two wings was at full strength.

[112] When their battle lines were drawn up and the omens from the sacrifices were favourable, the Athenians were released, and they charged the invaders at a run. The distance between the

two armies was no less than eight stades. When the Persians saw the Athenians running towards them, they got ready to receive them, but they thought the Athenians must be mad—mad enough to bring about their utter destruction—because they could see how few of them there were, and that their charge was unsupported by either cavalry or archers. That was the invaders' assessment of the situation, but when the Athenians came to grips with them all along the line, they fought remarkably well. They were the first Greeks known to charge enemy forces at a run, and the first to endure the sight of Persian dress and the men wearing it. Up until then even the word 'Persian' had been a source of fear in Greece.

[113] The fighting at Marathon was long and drawn out. In the centre, where the Greeks were faced with the Persians themselves and the Sacae, they were beaten; the invaders got the better of the Greeks at this point, broke through their lines, and pursued them inland. However, the Athenians and the Plataeans on their respective wings were victorious. They left the Persians they had routed to flee from the battlefield and concentrated on those who had broken through the centre. The two wings combined into a single fighting unit—and the Athenians won. They harried the retreating Persians and cut them down, until they reached the coast, where they called up fire and began to take over the ships.

[114] During this mêlée the War Archon was killed, fighting bravely, and one of the commanders, Stesilaus the son of Thrasylaus, died as well. It was also at this point that while Cynegeirus the son of Euphorion was grabbing hold of the stern of one of the ships he was fatally wounded when his hand was chopped off by a battleaxe. A number of other famous Athenians fell as well.

[115] The Athenians captured seven of the Persian ships in this way, but the invaders managed to put to sea with the rest of their fleet. They picked up the Eretrian prisoners from the island where they had left them and then set out to sail around Cape Sunium, with the intention of reaching the city of Athens before the Athenian forces could get there. In Athens the Alcmaeonidae were blamed for setting this strategy in motion by raising a shield as a prearranged signal to the Persians when they were out at sea.

[116] While the Persians were sailing around Sunium, the Athenians raced back as quickly as possible to defend the city, which they managed to reach before the Persians got there. On arriving they set up camp at the Heracleum in Cynosarges—thus

exchanging one sanctuary of Heracles, the one in Marathon, for another. The invaders hove to off Phalerum, which was Athens' naval harbour in those days, but then after riding at anchor there for a while they sailed back to Asia.

[117] The losses on either side at the battle of Marathon were as follows: about 6,400 Persian soldiers fell, while only 192 died on the Athenian side. An extraordinary thing happened there: while fighting bravely in the thick of the action an Athenian called Epizelus the son of Couphagoras lost his sight, even though he had not been wounded or struck by a missile anywhere on his body. And from that moment on, for the rest of his life, he was blind. I have it on hearsay that the story he used to tell about the incident was as follows: it seemed to him that he was confronted by a huge man in heavy armour, whose beard overshadowed his whole shield; but this phantom passed him by and killed the man next to him. That is Epizelus' story, according to my informants.

[118] In the course of his voyage back to Asia with the Persian army Datis stopped on Myconos, and while he was there he had a dream. Precisely what he saw in the dream is not recorded, but early the next day he organized a search of the fleet, and a gilded image of Apollo was found in a Phoenician ship. Datis asked, and was told, which sanctuary the image had been stolen from. He then boarded his own ship and made his way to Delos, where he deposited the statue in the sanctuary, told the Delians (who had by then returned to the island) to take it to Delium, a place in Theban territory on the coast opposite Chalcis, and then left the island. The Delians, however, did not return the image, but twenty years later the Thebans fetched it of their own accord and took it to Delium, having been prompted to do so by an oracle.

[119] After landing in Asia, Datis and Artaphrenes took the enslaved Eretrians to Susa. Before their capture, King Darius had been furious with the Eretrians for having been the original aggressors, but he was satisfied with seeing them brought before him in their vanquished state and he did them no further harm. In fact, he settled them in Cissia, in one of his own staging-posts called Ardericca. Ardericca is 210 stades from Susa, and it is also forty stades away from a well which is a source of three different products: bitumen, salt, and oil are all extracted from it. The method used is as follows: water is drawn from it by means of a swipe, to which half a wineskin is attached rather than a bucket. They immerse the wineskin, draw water out with it, and pour it into a tank.

The water is then drained into another container where it is diverted through three channels. The bitumen and the salt immediately harden, but the oil ⟨is collected in vessels⟩.† This oil, for which the Persian word is *rhadinake*, is black and unpleasant smelling. This is the place King Darius gave the Eretrians to live; they were still there in my day, but they have preserved their original language.

[120] So that is what happened to the Eretrians. After the full moon, a force of two thousand Lacedaemonians came to Athens; they were in such a hurry to be on time that they reached Attica two days after leaving Sparta. Although they were too late for the battle, they still very much wanted to see the Persians, so they went to survey the battlefield at Marathon. Afterwards, they expressed their admiration for the Athenians and their achievement, and then returned home.

[121] I find the story about the Alcmaeonidae too implausible to believe—as if they would ever have signalled the Persians by prior agreement with a shield, because they wanted Athens to be controlled by foreigners and Hippias! After all, they were obviously at least as disenchanted with tyranny as Callias (who was the son of Phaenippus and father of Hipponicus), if not even more so. Every time Pisistratus was banished from Athens, Callias was the only person in Athens who dared to buy any of his property when it was offered for sale by the public auctioneer, and that was not the only thing he did to express the depth of his loathing for him.†

[123] The Alcmaeonidae hated tyranny at least as much as Callias, and that is why I find the slander too implausible to accept. It is beyond belief that they could have signalled with the shield, seeing that they spent the whole era of the Athenian tyrants in exile, and were responsible for the Pisistratidae losing their tyranny— and so played a far greater part in winning Athens' freedom than Harmodius and Aristogiton, in my opinion. After all, the assassination of Hipparchus by Harmodius and Aristogiton only served to enrage the surviving Pisistratidae, without checking their tyranny in the slightest. However, if it is really true that, as I explained earlier, the Alcmaeonidae were the ones who persuaded the Pythia to tell the Lacedaemonians to free Athens, it is obvious that they were the liberators of Athens.

[124] It might perhaps be thought, however, that they turned traitors because they had a grudge against the Athenian people. But no men in Athens were respected or admired more than they were,

so it makes no sense to suggest that a shield was held up by them, at any rate, for any such reason. It is impossible to deny that a shield was used to make a signal, because that actually happened, but I can add nothing beyond what I have already said on the matter of who the signaller was.

[125] Although the Alcmaeonidae were a distinguished family in Athens in earlier generations too, from the time of Alcmaeon and then again from the time of Megacles they gained particular prestige. First, Alcmaeon the son of Megacles made himself very useful to the Lydians who were sent by Croesus from Sardis to the Delphic oracle and did everything he could to help them. When the Lydians who had visited the oracle told Croesus how Alcmaeon had furthered his cause, Croesus invited him to come to Sardis and when he was there he offered him as much gold as he could carry away on his person at one time. Alcmaeon considered the nature of this offer and then put a plan into effect: before being taken to the treasury he dressed himself in a large tunic with enough spare material for a deep fold, and put on the biggest pair of boots he could find. In the treasury he fell on a heap of gold-dust. First he stuffed down around his shins as much gold as the boots could take, then he filled the fold of his tunic with gold, sprinkled his hair with the dust, put even more in his mouth, and left the treasury. He could scarcely drag his feet along in their boots, and with his bulging cheeks and extra bulk all over he hardly looked like a human being at all. When Croesus saw him he burst out laughing and gave him not only all the gold he was already carrying, but the same amount again. That is how Alcmaeon's house became extremely wealthy. Alcmaeon could now afford to maintain a four-horse chariot, which he rode to victory at Olympia.

[126] Next, a generation later, Cleisthenes the tyrant of Sicyon elevated the house even further, so that it became far more famous in Greece than it was before. What happened was that Cleisthenes (who was the son of Aristonymus, grandson of Myron and great grandson of Andreas) had a daughter called Agariste, and he wanted to find her the best man in Greece to be her husband. So during the Olympic Games (at which he won in the four-horse-chariot race) he had the criers make the following announcement: 'Any man in Greece who considers himself good enough to become Cleisthenes' son-in-law should come to Sicyon in sixty days' time or sooner, because Cleisthenes will come to a decision about his

daughter's marriage within a year, starting from that date.' So all the Greeks who regarded themselves or their country with pride started going to Sicyon to present themselves as prospective husbands for his daughter, and Cleisthenes had a race-track and a wrestling-ground specially made for them.

[127] From Sybaris in Italy came Smindyrides the son of Hippocrates. Sybaris was at the time at the height of its prosperity, and Smindyrides' lifestyle had reached unsurpassed heights of soft-living luxury. Also from Italy came Damasus of Siris, the son of Amyris the Wise, as he was known. The Ionian Gulf was represented as well: Amphimnestus the son of Epistrophus came from Epidamnus on the Ionian Gulf. From Aetolia came Males, whose brother, Titormus, was the strongest man in Greece, but went to live in the remotest parts of Aetolia to avoid other people. From the Peloponnese came Leocedes the son of the tyrant of Argos, Phidon. It was Phidon who introduced a system of weights and measures into the Peloponnese and whose arrogance was unsurpassed in Greece, in that he ousted the Elean organizers of the Olympic Games and usurped that role for himself. The Peloponnese was also represented by an Arcadian from Trapezus called Amiantus the son of Lycurgus, an Azanian from Paeus called Laphanes the son of Euphorion (it was this Euphorion, according to the tale told in Arcadia, who received the Dioscuri into his house and from then on never turned anyone away), and by an Elean called Onomastus the son of Aegaeus. These men came from the actual Peloponnese, and then from Athens came Megacles the son of Alcmaeon (the one who had visited Croesus) and also Hippoclides the son of Tisander, the most outstanding man in Athens for his wealth and good looks. Lysanias came from Eretria, which was then a prosperous city, but he was the only one to come from Euboea. From Thessaly came one of the Scopadae, Diactorides of Crannon, and the Molossians were represented by Alcon.

[128] All these men came as suitors. On the appointed day, Cleisthenes began by finding out where they were from and what each individual's lineage was. Then he kept them with him for a year, while he tested their courage, character, education, and manners by spending time with each of them on their own and with all of them at once. He would take the younger ones out to the gymnasia, but the most important tests used to take place when they met together to eat. For as well as treating them in all the ways

mentioned, he also entertained them lavishly throughout the period of their stay with him. Now, as it happened, of all the suitors it was the visitors from Athens who pleased him most, and of the two Athenians he had a preference for Hippoclides the son of Tisander, because of his courage and because he was related by his ancestry to the Cypselidae of Corinth.

[129] On the day appointed for the marriage ceremony—the day when Cleisthenes had promised he would make known which one of the suitors he preferred—he sacrificed a hundred cattle and held a feast not just for the suitors themselves, but for the whole city of Sicyon. After the meal, the suitors competed with one another at singing and at public speaking. As the drinking progressed, Hippoclides had a clear lead over the others, but then he told the pipe-player to strike up a tune, and when the musician did so he began to dance. Now, although Hippoclides liked his own dancing a lot, Cleisthenes was beginning to look on the whole business askance. After a while, Hippoclides stopped momentarily and asked for a table to be brought in. When the table arrived there, he first danced a Laconian dance on it, then some Attic figures, and finally stood on his head on the table and waggled his feet around. Hippoclides' uninhibited dancing of the first and second sets of figures had already put Cleisthenes off having him as a son-in-law, but he kept silent because he did not want to scold him. When he saw him waggling his legs around, however, he could no longer restrain himself. 'Son of Tisander,' he said, 'you have danced away your marriage.' The young man replied, 'Hippoclides doesn't care!'—and that is how the proverb arose.

[130] Cleisthenes called for silence and addressed them all as follows: 'Gentlemen, you have come as suitors to try to win my daughter in marriage. I am full of admiration for all of you. If only it were possible for me to gratify you all, instead of having to pick just one of you and reject the rest. But it is of course impossible for me to please all of you, since my plans concern just the one young woman. To each of those whose suit is unsuccessful, I will give a talent of silver in acknowledgement of the honour you have done me in wishing to marry into my family and to recompense you for your absence from home. But I hereby betroth my daughter Agariste to Megacles the son of Alcmaeon, as Athenian custom demands.' Megacles accepted, and the marriage was ratified by Cleisthenes.

[131] So much for the assessment of the suitors, which spread the reputation of the Alcmaeonidae throughout Greece. The marriage of Megacles and Agariste produced the Cleisthenes who fixed the tribes and established democracy at Athens. He was named after his mother's father, the tyrant of Sicyon. As well as Cleisthenes, Megacles also had a son called Hippocrates, who became the father of another Megacles and another Agariste, named after Cleisthenes' daughter. This Agariste, the daughter of Hippocrates, married Xanthippus the son of Ariphron. When she was pregnant she dreamt she gave birth to a lion, and then a few days later she bore Xanthippus a son, Pericles.

[132] After the defeat of the Persians at Marathon, Miltiades' already high reputation in Athens was raised even further. So when he asked the Athenians for seventy ships, an army, and funds, without supporting his request by telling them which country he was planning to attack—in fact, without telling them anything except that they would get rich if they followed him, because he would take them to a country where there was gold in abundance to be had—the Athenians enthusiastically let him have them.

[133] With the forces he was given, Miltiades sailed against Paros. Ostensibly, the strike was in retaliation for Parian aggression in sending a trireme to Marathon in support of the Persian forces. But this was no more than an excuse; in fact he held a grudge against the Parians because one of their number, Lysagoras the son of Tisias, had turned Hydarnes the Persian against him. Having arrived at his destination Miltiades pinned the Parians inside their town walls and proceeded to besiege them there with his troops. After a while he sent in a herald with a demand for a hundred talents, accompanied by the threat that, if they failed to pay up, he would keep his men there until the city had fallen. But the Parians had not the slightest intention of giving Miltiades any money; in fact, they started to work on ways of ensuring the town's safety. Among other plans, they built up any particularly vulnerable parts of the wall under cover of darkness to double their original height.

[134] Up to this point in the story, all the Greek sources agree. As for subsequent events, what follows is the Parian version. Miltiades, they say, did not know what to do. A female prisoner of war of his called Timo asked for a meeting with him; she was a native Parian, and was the under-priestess of the chthonian deities.

When she and Miltiades met, she advised him to do what she suggested, if he really wanted to take Paros. She put forward her proposal, whereupon he made his way to the hill in front of the town, jumped over the fence around the sanctuary of Demeter the Lawgiver, since he could not open the door, and then went to the temple to do whatever it was that he was there for. His intention might have been to interfere with objects which are not supposed to be touched, or something else. When he reached the entrance to the shrine, however, he was suddenly overcome with terror, so he retraced his steps. But as he jumped down from the wall, he wrenched his thigh (or struck his knee, as others say).

[135] So Miltiades sailed back to Athens in a sorry state, without bringing any money for Athens and without having annexed Paros; all he had done was besiege the town for twenty-six days and lay waste to the island. When the Parians found out that their under-priestess Timo had given advice to Miltiades, they wanted to punish her for it. They waited until things had settled down after the siege and then sent emissaries to Delphi to ask whether they should put the under-priestess of the gods to death for having told hostile forces how to bring about the downfall of her country and for revealing to Miltiades matters which men were forbidden to know. The Pythia, however, told them that Timo was not guilty and therefore not to be killed; she explained that since it was fated that Miltiades would die a horrible death, Timo had appeared to him to lure him into evil ways. That was the Pythia's response to the Parians' question.

[136] Following Miltiades' return from Paros, the Athenians began to malign him. His most active detractor was Xanthippus the son of Ariphron, who had him up before the people on the charge, which carried the penalty of death, of having deceived the Athenians. Although Miltiades was present in court, the necrosis of his thigh prevented him from delivering his own defence speech. Instead, his friends spoke in his defence, while he lay there on a litter; they reminded the court at considerable length of the battle of Marathon and how Miltiades had captured Lemnos, made the Pelasgians pay for their crimes, and handed over the island to the Athenians. The Athenian people came down on his side in so far as they exonerated him from the death penalty, but they fined him fifty talents for the wrong he had done them. Afterwards,

Miltiades died from the putrefaction and necrosis of his thigh, and his son Cimon paid the fifty talents.

[137] Here is how Miltiades the son of Cimon came to gain control of Lemnos. At one time, the Pelasgians were driven out of Attica by the Athenians. I am not in a position to comment on the justice or injustice of the act; all I can do is report what is said. Hecataeus the son of Hegesander, in his account of the episode, says that it was not justified. According to him, what happened was that the Athenians cast covetous eyes on the land under Mount Hymettus which they themselves had given the Pelasgians to live in, as a reward for having once built the defensive wall around the Acropolis. Previously, this land had been so poor as to be worthless, but according to Hecataeus, when the Athenians saw how well farmed it had become, they were seized with envy and wanted to possess it, so they expelled the Pelasgians without having any real reason for doing so.

The Athenians, however, claim that the expulsion was justified. They say that the Pelasgians were using their homeland under Hymettus as a base for criminal activities. For instance, in those days the Athenians had no house-slaves (just as no one else in Greece did either), so their own sons and daughters† used to go to fetch water at Nine Springs, but whenever they did so the Pelasgians would assault them—and, not satisfied with this behaviour, they were also caught in the act of plotting to launch an attack against Athens. The Athenian account goes on to point out how much more moral they proved themselves to be, in that although they could have killed the Pelasgians, having discovered their plot, they refused to do so, but told them to leave the country instead. So the Pelasgians left and occupied various places, including Lemnos. These are the two versions, then, the first from Hecataeus, the second from the Athenians.

[138] The Pelasgians who were living on Lemnos at the time in question wanted to pay the Athenians back. They were well aware of the dates of the Athenian holidays, so they got hold of some penteconters and sailed to Brauron, where they ambushed the Athenian women celebrating the festival of Artemis. They abducted a number of women and sailed back to Lemnos, where they kept them as their concubines. Now, these women proved very fertile, and they taught all the children they produced the Attic dialect and Athenian customs. These children would have nothing to do

with the children of Pelasgian women, and they always helped
one another out; for instance, if an Athenian boy was hit by a
Pelasgian child, all the other Athenian boys used to come to help
him. Moreover, the Athenian boys took it upon themselves to wield
power over the other children and were easily the dominant group.
When the Pelasgians found out about this, they tried to decide what
to do. As they thought about the situation, a very disturbing question crept into their minds: if these children had determined to
support one another against the children of their legitimate wives
and were already trying to gain the upper hand over the others,
what would they do when they were actually grown up? The
Pelasgians decided, then, that their best course was to kill the
children of the Athenian women, which is exactly what they did;
they murdered the children's mothers too. This is one of the origins
of the universal Greek practice of describing savage deeds as
'Lemnian'. The other exploit which gave rise to this usage took
place earlier; it was the murder by the Lemnian women of Thoas
and their husbands.

[139] Following the murder by the Pelasgians of their own children and the women, the land became barren and both the human
and animal birthrate declined. Faced with the grim prospect of
starvation and childlessness, the Pelasgians sent to Delphi to ask
how they could obtain relief from their current wretched state.
The Pythia told them they had to submit to any punishment the
Athenians decided to impose on them. So the Pelasgians went to
Athens and expressed their intention of making complete amends
for their crime. The Athenians placed in the town hall a couch
adorned with the finest available coverings and set beside it a table
laden with everything that is good to eat, and told the Pelasgians
to hand over their country to them in a similar condition. In
response the Pelasgians said, 'When a ship makes the crossing from
your land to ours in a single day on the north wind, then we will
give you our country.' They were sure that this was impossible,
because Attica is well south of Lemnos.

[140] That was the end of the matter at the time, but many years
later, when the Hellespontine Chersonese was in Athenian hands,
Miltiades the son of Cimon took advantage of the prevailing
Etesian winds to sail from Elaeus in the Chersonese to Lemnos. He
reminded the Pelasgians of the oracle, which they had never
expected to see fulfilled, and ordered them off the island. The

people of Hephaestia obeyed his command, but the people of Myrina refused to accept that the Chersonese was Attic territory. The Athenians then blockaded them into submission. That is how the Athenians, under Miltiades, came to gain control of Lemnos.

BOOK SEVEN

[1] King Darius, the son of Hystaspes, was already thoroughly displeased with the Athenians because of their attack on Sardis, but the arrival of news of the battle of Marathon made him far more furious, and his determination to launch a strike against Greece increased. He lost no time in sending messengers around to the towns and cities with instructions to raise an army; every community was required to provide considerably more men than they had before, as well as ships, horses, supplies, and transport vessels. Asia was in turmoil for three years as a result of these demands, what with the selection and preparation of the best men for the campaign against Greece. In the fourth year Egypt, which Cambyses had enslaved, rose up in revolt, and this made Darius even more determined to attack both places.

[2] While Darius was preparing to attack Egypt and Athens, a serious dispute arose among his sons over the issue of the kingship, since it is traditional in Persia for the king to appoint a successor before setting out on a campaign. Now, even before he became king, Darius had three sons by his first wife, the daughter of Gobryas, and after his accession he had another four by Atossa the daughter of Cyrus. The eldest of the first three was Artobazanes, and the eldest of the younger four was Xerxes. They would never have fallen out if they had the same mothers, but as it was Artobazanes argued that he was the eldest of all Darius' children and that it was universal practice everywhere for the eldest son to succeed to the kingdom, while Xerxes argued that Atossa was the daughter of Cyrus, who had gained the Persians their independence.

[3] The arrival of Demaratus the son of Ariston in Susa coincided with this situation, when Darius had not yet given his decision. Demaratus had been deposed as king of Sparta and fled Lacedaemon into self-imposed exile. When he found out about the quarrel between Darius' sons, he went to Xerxes (or so the story

goes) and suggested an extra argument, in addition to those he had already used. He should point out, Demaratus said, that by the time he had been born Darius had succeeded to the kingdom and was the supreme commander of Persia, whereas at the time of Artobazanes' birth Darius was still a private citizen; and he should argue that it would therefore be neither right nor proper for preference to be given to anyone except him. Even in Sparta, Demaratus assured him, it was customary for the kingdom to pass to the younger son in cases where the elder sons were born before their father became king but the younger son was born after his accession. Xerxes did as Demaratus suggested, and Darius realized the justice of his claim and made him king. In fact, though, it is my opinion that Xerxes would have become king even without this advice by Demaratus, because Atossa was all-powerful.

[4] After appointing Xerxes as his successor, Darius turned his mind to military matters. But then, a year after the Egyptian rebellion, while he was in the middle of his preparations, it so happened that Darius died, after a reign of thirty-six years in all, before he had the chance to punish either the rebellious Egyptians or the Athenians. After his death the kingdom passed to his son Xerxes.

[5] Now, Xerxes was at first rather reluctant to make war on Greece, although he carried on raising an army to attack Egypt. However, Mardonius the son of Gobryas was at court, and there was no one in Persia who had more influence with Xerxes. Mardonius was his cousin, the son of Darius' sister, and he argued as follows: 'Master, it's wrong for the Athenians to go unpunished for all the harm they've done Persia. It's true that for the time being you had better continue with the business you have undertaken, but once you've curbed the arrogance of Egypt, you ought to march against Greece. It will enhance your reputation, and also make people think twice in the future before attacking your territory.' This was his argument for retaliation, but he also invariably added the rider that Europe was a particularly beautiful place, where every kind of cultivated tree grew and the soil was excellent; it was a place, he said, which no one but the king of Persia ought to own.

[6] He argued in this way because he wanted to stir things up and also because he wanted to become the governor of Greece. Eventually he succeeded in winning Xerxes round to his point of

view. There were other factors which helped him convince Xerxes. In the first place, a deputation arrived from the Aleuadae, the ruling family of Thessaly, offering their complete support and inviting him to invade Greece; in the second place, the Pisistratidae who were resident in Susa not only echoed what the Aleuadae were saying, but also offered him further inducements. They had brought with them to Susa an Athenian called Onomacritus, an oracle-monger who specialized in collecting the oracles of Musaeus. The Pisistratidae had patched up their quarrel with Onomacritus, who had been banished from Athens by Hipparchus the son of Pisistratus when Lasus of Hermione had exposed his insertion into the text of Musaeus of an oracle to the effect that the islands lying off Lemnos were going to sink out of sight into the sea. Hipparchus sentenced him to exile for this, despite the fact that he and Onomacritus had been very close friends before. At the time in question, however, he had gone with the Pisistratidae up to Susa, and whenever he came into the king's presence he would accompany their high-flown compliments of him with a recital of some of his oracles. He never mentioned any oracle in his collection which threatened catastrophe for the Persians, but selected only the most auspicious ones and recited those; in this way he expounded how the Hellespont was fated to be bridged by a man of Persia, and how Xerxes could get his troops to Greece. So Xerxes was being lobbied both by Onomacritus with his oracles and by the Pisistratidae and the Aleuadae with their proposals.

[7] After Xerxes had been persuaded to attack Greece, he first sent an expedition, in the year after Darius' death, against the rebels. Once he had crushed the rebellion and reduced the whole population of Egypt to a state of even worse slavery than they had experienced under Darius, he left his brother Achaemenes the son of Darius in charge of the country. Some time later, during his administration of Egypt, Achaemenes was murdered by a Libyan called Inaros the son of Psammetichus.

[8] After his conquest of Egypt, and just before undertaking the expedition against Athens, Xerxes summoned the pick of the leading Persians to a meeting, because he wanted to hear what they had to say and also to make public his intentions. When the meeting was convened, Xerxes said, 'Men of Persia, I am introducing no new custom here; I am simply drawing on traditional Persian ways. After all, as far as I can gather from our elders, there

has never been a time when we have not been at war, ever since Cyrus deposed Astyages and we took over from the Medes. It is the god who steers us in this direction, and so we prosper as we follow his guidance time and again. There would be no point in recounting all the victories Cyrus, Cambyses, and my father Darius won, and all the peoples they annexed, because you are already well aware of their achievements. But what about me? When I became the king of Persia, I began to wonder how to avoid being left behind by those who preceded me in this position of honour, and how I might increase the Persian empire just as much as they did. And after a lot of thought I found a way for us not only to win glory and gain land which, so far from being smaller or meaner than what we currently have, is in fact more fertile, but also to exact retribution and compensation from our enemies. The reason I have convened this meeting, then, is to tell you my plans.

'I intend to bridge the Hellespont and march an army through Europe and against Greece, so that I can make the Athenians pay for all that they have done to Persia and to my father. Now, Darius was getting ready to march against these men as well, as you know, but he died before he managed to punish them. So on his behalf, and on behalf of all Persians, I will not rest until I have captured Athens and put it to the torch. The Athenians were the original aggressors against me and my father. First they marched against Sardis along with our slave, Aristagoras of Miletus, and burnt its sacred groves and sanctuaries to the ground; then you all know what they did to us when we landed an army in their country under the command of Datis and Artaphrenes.

'That is why I have decided to make war on them. Besides, I have come to the conclusion that we will benefit from the enterprise in a number of ways. If we conquer them and their neighbours—the inhabitants of the land of Pelops of Phrygia—we will make Persian territory end only at the sky, the domain of Zeus, so that the sun will not shine on any land beyond our borders. With your help I will sweep through the whole of Europe and make all lands into a single land. If my information is accurate, once we have eliminated those I have mentioned, there will be nobody left—no town or people—capable of offering us armed resistance. And so the innocent will bear the yoke of slavery along with those who have wronged us.

'Here is what you can do to please me. When I let you know
that the time has arrived for you to come, you should all do so
without hesitation. I will reward the one who brings with him the
best-prepared force with the kinds of gifts which are valued most
highly in our country. So much for what you should do. But I don't
want you thinking that I refuse to take anyone else's views into
consideration, so the matter is now open to debate. Please feel free
to speak your mind.'

[9] After he had finished, Mardonius spoke up. 'Master,' he said,
'you are the greatest Persian there has ever been, nor will there ever
be anyone to equal you in the future either. Throughout your
speech you made some excellent and extremely valid points, but
particularly important was your promise not to let those despic-
able Ionians—the ones living in Europe—get away with making
fools of us. We conquered the Sacae, the Indians, the Ethiopians,
the Assyrians, and plenty of other important races, and we now
hold them in slavery. Why? Not because they did us any wrong,
but just because we wanted to increase our dominion. It would be
a terrible thing, then, for us not to punish the unprovoked aggression of the Greeks.

'What do we have to fear? The number of troops they can
muster? Their wealth and the power it gives them? No, we know
how they fight and we know that their power is limited. We have
overcome and hold subject their offspring—the so-called Ionians,
Aeolians, and Dorians, who settled here on our continent. I myself
already have personal experience of campaigning against these men
at your father's command. I got as far as Macedonia, which is not
far from Athens itself, without meeting any opposition.

'Besides, from all I hear, the Greeks usually wage war in an
extremely stupid fashion, because they're ignorant and incompe-
tent. When they declare war on one another they seek out the best,
most level piece of land, and that's where they go and fight. The
upshot is that the victors leave the battlefield with massive losses,
not to mention the losers, who are completely wiped out. What
they should do, since they all speak the same language, is make use
of heralds and messengers to settle their differences, since anything
would be preferable to fighting. If they had absolutely no choice
but to go to war, they should find a battleground where it is particularly hard for either side to defeat the other and fight it out
there. It's because the Greeks go about things in the wrong way,

then, that I marched as far as Macedonia without them getting to
the point of fighting.

'So, my lord, who is going to oppose you? Who is going to
threaten you with war when you come from Asia at the head of a
massive army and with your whole fleet? I am sure that the Greeks
are not so foolhardy. But suppose I'm mistaken in this opinion;
suppose their rash foolishness encourages them to confront us in
battle. Then they will discover that when it comes to military
matters there is no one in the world to match us. Anyway, we
should leave nothing untried. Nothing comes of its own accord;
people invariably get things as a result of their own efforts.'

[10] There Mardonius stopped, once he had made Xerxes' proposal seem plausible. No one else had anything to say—certainly,
no one dared to voice an opinion contrary to the one before them—
until Artabanus the son of Hystaspes broke the silence, relying on
the fact that he was Xerxes' uncle. 'My lord,' he said, 'unless opposing views are heard, it is impossible to pick and choose between
various plans and decide which one is best. All one can do is go
along with the opinion that has been voiced. However, if opposing
views are heard, it is possible to decide. Think of a piece of pure
gold: taken all by itself it is impossible to tell that it is pure; only
by rubbing it on the touchstone and comparing gold with gold
can we tell which one is best. I told your father, my brother Darius,
not to attack the Scythians, people with no established settlement
anywhere, but he didn't listen to me; he was sure he could defeat
the nomad Scythians. So he launched a campaign against them and
when he came back he had lost a great many brave fighting men
from his army. But this campaign you're planning, my lord, is
against men who are vastly superior to the Scythians; they have the
highest reputation for bravery on both land and sea. There is
danger involved, and it is only right for me to point it out to you.

'You say that you will bridge the Hellespont and march through
Europe to Greece. Now, suppose you suffer defeat in a land or
naval engagement, or even in both. After all, these Greeks do have
a reputation as fighters. In fact, we can assess their abilities from
the fact that the Athenians alone destroyed an army of the size of
the one that invaded Attica under Datis and Artaphrenes. Anyway,
suppose things don't go their way in both spheres, but that they
engage us at sea, defeat us, and then sail to the Hellespont and dismantle the bridge. *That* is where the danger lies, my lord.

'I don't have any special expertise that leads me to this conclusion; it's just that disaster very nearly overwhelmed us once before
under similar circumstances, when your father built a pontoon
bridge across the Thracian Bosporus, bridged the River Ister,
crossed it, and invaded Scythia. On that occasion the Scythians did
everything they could to persuade the Ionians, whose job it was to
guard the bridges across the Ister, to dismantle the causeway. And
if Histiaeus the tyrant of Miletus had gone along with all his fellow
tyrants, rather than opposing their view, that would have been the
end of Persia. However terrifying it is even to hear it said, the whole
of the king's affairs depended on a single man.

'You should not choose to run that kind of risk when you don't
really have to. No, listen to me instead. Dissolve this meeting now,
think things over by yourself and then later, whenever you like,
give us whatever orders you see fit. In my experience, nothing is
more advantageous than good planning. I mean, even if a set-back
happens, that doesn't alter the fact that the plan was sound; it's just
that the plan was defeated by chance. However, if someone who
hasn't laid his plans properly is attended by fortune, he may have
had a stroke of luck, but that doesn't alter the fact that his plan
was unsound.

'You can see how the god blasts living things that are prominent
and prevents their display of superiority, while small creatures don't
irritate him at all; you can see that it is always the largest buildings and the tallest trees on which he hurls his thunderbolts. It is
the god's way to curtail anything excessive. And so even a massive
army may be destroyed by a small force if it attracts the god's
resentment and he sends panic or thunder, until they are shamefully destroyed. This happens because the god does not allow
anyone but himself to feel pride. The offspring of haste in any
venture is error, and error in turn tends to lead to serious harm.
Benefits come from waiting; even if they aren't apparent at first,
one will discover them in time.

'So that is my advice to you, my lord. As for you, son of Gobryas,
you should stop making rude and defamatory remarks about the
Greeks when they don't deserve them. By disparaging the Greeks
you encourage the king to march against them; in fact, I think that
is exactly what all this effort of yours is for. But I hope this campaign never materializes.

'Slander is a truly terrible thing, because it involves two men ganging up to wrong a single victim. The one who casts the aspersions does wrong by accusing someone in his absence, and the other person does wrong by believing the lie before he has found out the truth. Meanwhile, the person who is missing from the discussion is the victim of the situation in the sense that he has been defamed by the one person and has acquired a bad reputation in the other one's mind.

'However, if there is absolutely no help for it and we must make war on these Greeks, then consider this proposal, Mardonius. While the king stays here in Persia, in his homeland, you pick your men, take an army of any size you want, and lead the expedition. Let each of us gamble the lives of our children on the outcome. If matters turn out as you say they will for the king, let my children be put to death, and I will join them; but if things turn out as I am predicting, let your children suffer that fate, and you too, if you make it back home. If you aren't prepared to run this risk, but are still determined to take the army overseas to Greece, I can tell you what news of Mardonius will reach the ears of those who stay behind here: they will be told that Mardonius was the cause of a great disaster for Persia, and that you were then torn apart by dogs and birds somewhere in Athenian territory or somewhere in Lacedaemon—that is, if this doesn't happen earlier, on the way there. Then you will know what kind of men you are trying to persuade the king to attack.'

[11] Xerxes was furious at Artabanus' words. He responded as follows: 'It is only because you are my father's brother, Artabanus, that you are safe from the consequences of your insolence. But for your craven cowardice I will humiliate you by not taking you with me on this expedition to Greece; instead, you will stay here with the women. I will achieve everything I said I would just as well without your help. If I fail to punish the Athenians, may I no longer be descended from Darius, son of Hystaspes, son of Arsames, son of Ariaramnes, son of Teïspes, ⟨and⟩ from Cyrus, son of Cambyses, ⟨son of Cyrus,⟩† son of Teïspes, son of Achaemenes. I am sure the Athenians will do something if we do not; to judge by their past moves, they will certainly mount an expedition against our country, since these are the people who burnt down Sardis and invaded Asia. It is impossible for either side to withdraw now; the only question

at stake is whether or not we actively take the initiative. And in the end either all Persia will be in Greek hands, or all Greece will be in Persian hands; there is no middle ground in this war. It is fair, then, that we should be the ones actively to seek revenge now, since we were the first to suffer, and it will also let me find out about the disaster that is supposed to happen to me if I make war on these men—men whom even Pelops of Phrygia, a slave belonging to my forefathers, defeated so thoroughly that the people and their country still bear the name of their conqueror even today.'

[12] That was the end of the speeches. Later, during the night, Xerxes was still worried by the view Artabanus had expressed. He thought it over during the night and he became quite convinced that it was not in his best interests for him to march on Greece. After this change of heart, he fell asleep, and during the night he had the following dream, or so the Persians say. Xerxes dreamt that a tall, handsome man stood over him and said, 'Are you changing your mind, Persian? Are you deciding against taking an expedition to Greece, although you have already told the Persians to raise an army? You will not benefit from this change of mind, and the one you see before you will not forgive you. No, keep to the course of action you decided on during the daytime.' In Xerxes' dream, after delivering this speech, the man flew away.

[13] In the light of day he dismissed the dream as insignificant, and he convened a meeting, attended by the same Persians who had been at the previous conference, and said to them: 'Men of Persia, forgive me for the fact that I have changed my mind. I have not yet reached the peak of my mental powers, and the people urging me on to the course of action we adopted did not give me a moment's peace. What happened was that when I heard Artabanus' point of view, at first my youthful temper came to the boil, so that the words I blurted out were inappropriate, not the kind of speech which should be addressed to one's elders. But now I concede that he was right, and I am going to adopt his plan. So since I have changed my mind and decided not to attack Greece, you can stop gearing yourselves up for war.' The Persians were delighted with what Xerxes said, and prostrated themselves before him.

[14] That night, however, when Xerxes was asleep, the same figure appeared to him again in a dream and said, 'So, son of Darius, you have gone before the Persians and called off the expedition, have you? You have disregarded my words and treated them

as if they came from a nobody. Well, know this: if you do not go out on this campaign immediately, this is what will happen. You have risen rapidly to a position of prominence and importance, but you will be laid low again just as swiftly.'

[15] This dream terrified Xerxes. He leapt out of bed and sent a messenger to summon Artabanus. When he arrived, Xerxes said, 'Artabanus, I wasn't in my right mind at first, when I responded to your good advice with rudeness, but before too long I changed my mind and came to see that I should act on your suggestions. Yet I find myself unable to do so, even though I want to! You see, ever since I've backed down and changed my mind, I've been haunted by a dream figure who does not approve of what I'm doing at all. In fact he threatened me just now, and then disappeared. If this dream is being sent by a god and he will be satisfied only when the campaign against Greece takes place, the same dream should wing its way to you as well, and give you the same instructions it did me. I think this will happen if you take all these clothes of mine and put them on, sit on my throne, and then later go to sleep in my bed.'

[16] At first Artabanus was reluctant to comply with this command, because he did not think it right that he should sit on the royal throne. In the end, however, he was compelled to do as he was told. But first he said, 'In my opinion, my lord, it is all the same whether one has good ideas oneself or is prepared to listen to someone else who is offering good advice. Though you have both of these qualities, you keep company with bad men and that leads you astray. This is like what they say about the sea: in itself there is nothing more useful for the human race, but the winds that lash it refuse to let it be itself. It wasn't so much that I was upset at being rebuked by you, but that when the Persians were faced with two plans, one of which would increase our abusiveness, while the other would curb it, by pointing out how wrong it is to train the mind to be constantly seeking more than it has at the moment . . . when we were faced with these two points of view, what really upset me was that you chose the one which would be more dangerous not only for yourself, but for Persia too.

'And now, just when you've changed your mind about the expedition to Greece and started preferring the better plan instead, you say that you're being haunted by a dream figure, the emissary of some god, who refuses to let you cancel the expedition. In actual fact, though, dreams don't come from the gods, my son. I have lived many more years than you, so I can explain what these dreams are that drift into us. The visions that occur to us in dreams are, more often than not, the things we have been concerned about during the day. And, you see, we have been extremely occupied with this expedition for some days now.

'However, if I'm mistaken in my assessment of this particular dream, if there is something divine about it, you yourself have already summed the matter up in a few words: let the dream appear to me with the same orders that it has given you. But the chances of its appearing to me are unlikely to be increased whether I am wearing your clothes or my own, or whether I am sleeping in your bed or my own—that is, if it is going to appear anyway. After all, whatever it is that you see in your dream is surely not so naïve as to mistake me for you on the basis of the clothes I am wearing. No, what we have to find out is whether it considers me too insignificant to be worth appearing to, whatever clothes I am wearing, and doesn't appear.† I mean, if it continues to appear, I too would have to admit that it is supernatural. However, if I have to sleep in your bed—that is, if that's the way you want things to be and you are not to be deflected from your purpose—then all right, let's see if it appears to me too when I have fulfilled these conditions. But until then I won't change my mind.'

[17] Without saying any more, Artabanus did as he was told, but he expected to demonstrate that Xerxes' words were without substance. He put on Xerxes' clothes, sat himself down on the royal throne, and then later went to bed. And while he was asleep the same dream figure came to him as had appeared to Xerxes. The figure stood over Artabanus and said, 'So you're the one who has been trying to discourage Xerxes from attacking Greece, are you? And you claim that it is your concern for him that makes you do so? Well, you will not escape punishment, either now or in the future, for trying to deflect the inevitable. And Xerxes has already had the consequences of future disobedience explained to him.'

[18] Artabanus dreamt that as well as making these threats the phantom was about to burn his eyes out with red-hot skewers. He uttered a loud cry, jumped out of bed, and sat himself down next to Xerxes. First he described what he had seen in his dream, and then he said, 'The reason I tried to stop you giving way completely to your youthful impetuousness, my lord, was because I am one

who has in the past often seen mighty powers brought low by relative weaklings. Also, I know what harm can come from excessive
desire: I remember what happened to Cyrus' expedition against the
Massagetae and to Cambyses' campaign against the Ethiopians,
and I myself took part in Darius' attack on the Scythians. Knowing
this, I was of the opinion that happiness for you—and happiness
that everyone would recognize—lay in remaining peacefully at
home. But since your impetuousness is god-given, and since the
destruction overtaking the Greeks is apparently heaven-sent, it is
my turn to back down and change my mind. Let the Persians know
about the visions you have received from the god and tell them to
carry on with their preparations in accordance with the first orders
you issued; and then make sure that, since the god commands it,
you do everything you must.'

This is what Artabanus said. The dream had encouraged them
so much that at daybreak the next day Xerxes told the Persians
what had happened, and Artabanus, who had previously shown
himself to be the only dissenting voice, gave his open and enthusiastic support to the enterprise.

[19] Later, with Xerxes all intent on his campaign, he had a third
dream one night, in which he saw himself wearing a garland made
out of sprigs of an olive-tree whose branches overshadowed the
whole world, but then the garland disappeared from his head. He
described the dream to the Magi and they interpreted its reference
to the whole world as meaning that he would gain dominion over
the whole human race. After the Magi had interpreted the dream
in this way, every one of the Persians who had convened for the
meeting immediately rode back to his own province and devoted
himself wholeheartedly to carrying out his instructions. Each of
them wanted to be the one to win the rewards Xerxes had
promised. In this way Xerxes had every part of the continent
searched in the process of raising his army.

[20] Xerxes spent four whole years after the conquest of Egypt
preparing and equipping his army, and in the course of the fifth
year he set out on his campaign with a huge body of men. Of all
the armies we know of, this was by far the largest. The army with
which Darius attacked Scythia was tiny by comparison; so was the
Scythian army which invaded Media on the heels of a Cimmerian
force and succeeded in conquering and occupying almost the whole
of inland Asia (something for which Darius later tried to punish

them); and so, by all accounts, was the army with which the Atridae attacked Ilium, and the army the Mysians and Teucrians raised—this was before the Trojan War—with which they crossed the Bosporus, invaded Europe, conquered the whole of Thrace, reached the coast of the Ionian Sea, and marched as far south as the River Peneius.

[21] The combined total of all these armies, even with some others included, would not equal Xerxes' expeditionary force. After all, was there any Asian people he did not lead against Greece? And was there any source of water, apart from huge rivers, they did not drink dry? He had ships supplied from here, land forces from there; some were required to provide horsemen, others transport ships for horses (as well as men for the campaign), others longships for the pontoon bridges, others both provisions and ships.

[22] In the first place, because the previous expedition had come to grief while sailing around Athos, he spent about three years making sure he would be ready for Athos when the time came. Elaeus in the Chersonese was made the headquarters, triremes were stationed there, and troops of all different backgrounds were set to work in relays, under the whip, digging a canal. The local inhabitants of Athos worked on the excavation as well. The work was supervised by two Persians, Bubares the son of Megabazus and Artachaees the son of Artaeus. Now, Athos is a large, famous, inhabited mountain jutting out into the sea; where it joins the mainland, it is shaped like a peninsula and forms an isthmus about twelve stades wide, and the terrain there, between the Acanthian Sea and the sea off Torone, is level, with low hills. On this isthmus, where Athos ends, there is the Greek settlement of Sane. Beyond Sane, within Athos itself, are Dion, Olophyxus, Acrothoüm, Thyssus, and Cleonae—places which the Persian king now intended to turn into island instead of mainland communities.

[23] These are the communities on Mount Athos. The way the invaders went about the excavation was to draw a straight line across the isthmus near Sane and then assign each of the various nationalities a section of land to dig. Once the trench had become deep, some men stood at the bottom and carried on digging, while others passed the earth that was constantly being dug out to others who were standing on platforms further up the diggings, who in turn passed it on to others, until it reached the top, where the earth was taken away and disposed of. Everyone else apart from the

Phoenicians found that the steep sides of the trench kept collaps-
ing and doubling their work-load, but then they were making
the width at the top of the trench and at the bottom the same,
which was bound to cause something like that to happen. But the
Phoenicians, who are invariably practical, showed their usual skill
on this occasion: once they had been assigned their plot of land to
work on, they set about making the opening at the top of the trench
twice as wide as the actual canal was to be, and gradually reduced the width as they dug down, until by the time they reached
the bottom they were working to the same width as everyone else.
A local field was turned into a business centre and market-place,
but flour was brought from Asia in large quantities.

[24] On reflection it seems to me that Xerxes ordered the digging
of the canal out of a sense of grandiosity and arrogance, because
he wanted to display his power and leave a memorial. After all, he
could have saved all that hard work and had the ships dragged
across the isthmus, but instead he ordered a channel to be dug for
the sea, wide enough for two triremes to be rowed abreast along
it. The same men who were given the job of digging the canal were
also set to work bridging the River Strymon.

[25] So this is how he was making the canal. Xerxes also had
cables made out of papyrus and white flax for the bridges. This
task was assigned to the Phoenicians and Egyptians, who were also
in charge of leaving the army's provisions in safe storage, to prevent
either the men or the yoke-animals going hungry during the march
to Greece. Xerxes also got detailed information about the places
they would pass through, and then had various people take the provisions from all over Asia in transport vessels and ferries and
deposit them at the various most suitable locations along the way.
They took the largest quantity of provisions† to a place in Thrace
called White Cape, but other places allocated for deposits of supplies were Tyrodiza in Perinthian territory, Doriscus, Eïon on the
River Strymon, and Macedonia.

[26] While these men were getting on with their assigned tasks,
the whole land army assembled at Critalla in Cappadocia and set
out from there with Xerxes for Sardis. He had given orders for
every single contingent that was to join him on the overland route
to assemble there. I cannot say which of the provincial governors
received the king's promised reward for bringing the best-equipped
force; I have no idea if they were even assessed in this respect.

Anyway, they crossed the Halys into Phrygia. On their way through Phrygia they reached Celaenae, where two rivers rise—the Meander and one called the Catarractes, which is just as large as the Meander. The Catarractes rises right in the main square of Celaenae and issues into the Meander. Another feature of the square of Celaenae is that the skin of Marsyas the silenus is hanging there, where it was put, according to local Phrygian legend, after Marsyas had been flayed by Apollo.

[27] A Lydian called Pythius the son of Atys had been waiting for Xerxes to reach Celaenae. He provided lavish meals for the whole of Xerxes' army, as well as for Xerxes himself, and he also said that he would like to help finance the war. Xerxes responded to this offer by asking some of the Persians who were there who this man Pythius was and how he could afford to make such an offer. 'My lord,' they replied, 'he's the one who gave your father Darius the golden plane-tree and vine. He's the richest man in the known world, apart from you.'

[28] Xerxes was surprised to hear this last comment of theirs, so he then put his question directly to Pythius. 'How rich are you?' he asked. 'My lord,' Pythius answered, 'I won't dissemble or try to pretend that I don't know how well off I am. I do know, and I will tell you exactly what I have. You see, as soon as I found out that you were on your way down to the Greek Sea, I checked up on the details of my financial position, because I wanted to give you money for the war. I discovered that, once everything is totted up, I have 2,000 talents of silver and I'm just 7,000 staters short of having 4,000,000 gold Daric staters. I would like to give all of this to you. My slaves and my farms make me enough to live on.'

[29] Xerxes was delighted with this offer. 'My Lydian friend,' he said, 'you're the first person I've met since leaving Persian territory who has been glad to feed my troops, let alone come before me and, of his own accord, offer money to help finance the war. You have not only lavishly entertained my men, but this offer of yours is extremely generous. I'm going to give you something in return. I'd like you to have the honour of being my guest-friend, and I'll give you from my own treasury the 7,000 staters you need to make up the full 4,000,000 staters. Then I'll have rounded the number off nicely to 4,000,000, instead of your being 7,000 short. Please keep what you already have, and do make sure that you never change. For I can tell you that you will never regret this kind of behaviour, now or in the future.'

[30] With these words Xerxes did as he had promised. Then he carried on his way. He passed by the Phrygian town of Anaua and a lake which produces salt, and came to the sizeable Phrygian city of Colossae, where the River Lycus disappears underground into a chasm before reappearing after about five stades and then becoming yet another tributary of the Meander. After Colossae the army proceeded to the border between Phrygia and Lydia and came to the town of Cydrara, where fixed into the ground there is a pillar which was originally set up by Croesus, with an inscription indicating the presence of the border.

[31] Across the Phrygian border and in Lydia, the road forks and one can either turn left towards Caria or right towards Sardis. If one takes the right-hand branch, one is bound to cross the Meander and come to the town of Callatebus, where craftsmen make a local speciality, a sweet syrup of tamarisk and wheat. As he was travelling along this road Xerxes came across a plane-tree which was so beautiful that he presented it with golden decorations and appointed one of the Immortals as guardian to look after it. A day later he reached the capital city of Lydia.

[32] The first thing he did after arriving in Sardis was send heralds to Greece to demand earth and water and to tell them to be ready to provide meals for the king when he came. These heralds were sent everywhere in Greece except Athens and Lacedaemon. This was not the first time the Greeks had received a demand for earth and water: Darius had sent heralds round before. But Xerxes sent the message all over again because he was sure that the places which had refused Darius' demand before would now comply out of fear; so he sent his heralds because he wanted to find out whether or not this was true.

[33] He next got ready to march to Abydus. Meanwhile, his men had been bridging the Hellespont from Asia to Europe. On the Hellespontine Chersonese, between the towns of Sestus and Madytus, a rugged headland projects into the sea opposite Abydus. (This is the place where, not long after the events we are talking about, the Athenians under the command of Xanthippus the son of Ariphron captured a Persian called Artayctes, the governor of Sestus, and nailed him alive to a plank of wood, because he used to have women brought to him in the sanctuary of Protesilaus in Elaeus and commit sacrilege with them.)

[34] The Phoenicians and the Egyptians who had been assigned the task set about building their bridges (the Phoenicians using

white flax and the Egyptians papyrus), taking Abydus as their
starting-point and directing their efforts towards the headland on
the opposite coast—a distance of seven stades. They had just finished bridging the straits when a violent storm erupted which completely smashed and destroyed everything.

[35] This news made Xerxes furious. He ordered his men to give
the Hellespont three hundred lashes and to sink a pair of shackles
into the sea. I once heard that he also dispatched men to brand the
Hellespont as well. Be that as it may, he did tell the men he had
thrashing the sea to revile it in terms you would never hear from
a Greek. 'Bitter water,' they said, 'this is your punishment for
wronging your master when he did no wrong to you. King Xerxes
will cross you, with or without your consent. People are right not
to sacrifice to a muddy, brackish stream like you!' So the sea was
punished at his orders, and he had the supervisors of the bridging
of the Hellespont beheaded.

[36] The men assigned this grotesque task carried out their
orders, and another team of engineers managed to bridge the Hellespont. They made a solid wall of penteconters and triremes, 360
of them to support the bridge on the side nearest the Euxine Sea
and 314 on the other side, with the ships at an angle for the bridge
nearest the Euxine, but aligned with the current for the bridge
nearest the Hellespont, to take the strain off the cables. Once they
had the boats all massed together, they let down anchors on extra-
long hawsers on both sides—from the pontoon on the Euxine side
to counteract the winds blowing from within the Euxine, and from
the westward, Aegean pontoon to counteract the winds from the
west and south. They left a gap in the penteconters and triremes at
two points,† to let small boats sail past at will on their way to or
from the Euxine. Then they attached cables to the land and wound
them taut on wooden windlasses; this time they did not use just
one kind of cable for each bridge, but assigned each pontoon two
cables of white flax and four of papyrus. In thickness and in fineness of quality there was nothing to tell between the two kinds of
cable, but with a weight of a talent per cubit of length the flaxen
ones were proportionately heavier. With these bridges in place
across the straits, they sawed sleepers equal in length to the width
of the pontoon, laid them neatly on top of the taut cables in a row,
and then tied them down.† Next they put brushwood on top of the
sleepers, evened it out, put soil on top of it, and stamped the soil

down. Then they ran a fence along either side, high enough to stop
the yoke-animals and the horses† looking over it and being frightened by the sight of the sea.

[37] At last all the work on the bridges was finished, and also
all the work at Mount Athos—that is, as well as the actual canal
being completed the moles at the mouths of the canal had been
built, to stop the surf from silting up the openings. Once it was
known that these projects had been completed, Xerxes' army
waited out the winter and then early in spring left Sardis fully
equipped and set out for Abydus. Just as they were on their way,
however, the sun abandoned its station in the sky; it disappeared,
despite the fact that there were no clouds and it was a particularly
bright, clear day, and day was replaced by night. Once Xerxes had
realized what he was seeing, he became worried and asked the Magi
to interpret the omen. They said that the god was foretelling the
abandonment by the Greeks of their towns and cities, because in
their view the sun prophetically symbolized the Greeks, and the
moon themselves. Xerxes was very pleased to hear this, and he proceeded with the invasion.

[38] Now, Pythius of Lydia had been terrified by the omen from
the sky. Emboldened by Xerxes' generosity towards him, he went
to the king while he was directing the departure of the army from
Sardis, and said, 'Master, I'd like to ask you a favour—an easy one
for you to grant, but it would mean a great deal to me.'

Xerxes had no idea at all what the favour was that Pythius had
in mind, so he told him he would grant him it and asked him what
it was. Encouraged by Xerxes' words, Pythius said, 'Master, I have
five sons, all of whom have to march with you against Greece.
Please, my lord, take pity on me in my old age and release one of
my sons, the eldest one, from military service, so that he can look
after me and manage my property as well. But take the other four
with you—and may you return home with all your objectives
attained!'

[39] 'Damn you!' Xerxes replied in a rage. 'Look at me: I am
going in person to make war on Greece, and I am taking with me
my sons, brothers, relatives, and friends. How dare you mention
a son of yours, when you are no more than my slave, and should
follow in my train with your whole household, wife and all? A
man's spirit lives in his ears—do you understand what I'm saying?
If a man hears something good, his body is suffused with joy,

whereas if he hears something bad, he loses his temper. Before, your past good deeds and your promises for the future made you my benefactor, and you will not boast that your good deeds surpassed the king's in generosity; now that you have changed, however, and are behaving offensively, you will not get what you deserve, but less. Your hospitality will protect you and those four sons of yours, but you will pay with the life of the fifth son—the one you especially want to keep by your side.' As soon as Xerxes had given Pythius this answer, he ordered those of his men who were responsible for such matters to find the eldest of Pythius' sons and to cut him in half. Then they were to place one half on the right of the road and the other half on the left, so that the army would pass between them.

[40] Once his orders had been carried out, the army filed through. At the front were the baggage-handlers and the yoked animals, and then came a confused mass of soldiers, with all the different peoples and tribes indiscriminately mixed up together. These two groups made up over half of the army, and then there was a break in the formation, which meant that they had no contact with the king. A thousand picked Persian horsemen led the king's retinue, and behind them came a thousand spearmen, also élite fighting men, who marched with their lances pointing down at the ground. Next, magnificently caparisoned, came the ten sacred 'Nesaean' horses, named after the huge Nesaean Plain in Media which produces these tall horses. The place behind the ten horses was taken by the sacred chariot of Zeus, which was drawn by eight white horses. Following them on foot (because no human being is allowed to mount the seat of this chariot) came the charioteer, with the reins in his hands. Behind him came Xerxes himself, seated on a chariot drawn by Nesaean horses. Beside him stood his charioteer, Patiramphes by name, whose father was a Persian called Otanes.

[41] This was how Xerxes left Sardis, but he used to get out of his chariot and into a covered wagon instead, if he felt so inclined. He was followed by the 1,000 bravest and noblest Persian spearmen, who carried their lances in the usual fashion, and then another 1,000 élite Persian horsemen, and after them came the 10,000 best remaining Persian soldiers on foot. The men in this brigade carried spears whose butts ended in pomegranates rather than spikes; 1,000 of them had golden pomegranates on their spears and

enclosed the other 9,000, who had silver pomegranates. (The troops who marched with their lances pointed towards the ground also had golden pomegranates, and the ones who came right behind Xerxes had golden apples.) After this brigade of 10,000 came a 10,000-strong contingent of Persian cavalry, then there was another gap of two stades, and finally the rest of the army brought up the rear, all massed together indiscriminately.

[42] So the army made its way from Lydia to the River Caïcus and Mysia. After the Caïcus they marched, with Mount Cane on their left, through the territory of Atarneus to the town of Carene. Then they crossed the plain of Thebe, bypassing Atramytteium and Antandrus, which is a Pelasgian settlement, and, leaving Mount Ida on their left,† they entered the district of Ilium. While they were spending a night at the foot of Ida they encountered their first thunderstorm, with high winds, and quite a large number of them were killed.

[43] When the army reached the Scamander, which was the first river they had come across since leaving Sardis and setting out on their journey that failed to provide enough water for the men and animals and that they drank dry—anyway, when Xerxes reached the Scamander he wanted to see where Priam had ruled, so he climbed up to the citadel, looked around, and heard the whole story of what had happened there. Then he sacrificed a thousand cattle to Athena of Ilium, and the Magi offered libations to the dead heroes. The following night fear spread throughout the army, but in the morning they left there and continued on their way, passing Rhoeteum, Ophryneum, and Dardanum (whose territory borders that of Abydus) on their left and the territory of a Teucrian tribe called the Gergithes on their right.

[44] While they were in Abydus, Xerxes decided that he would like to survey his whole army. A dais of white stone had already been made especially for him (he had ordered it in advance from the people of Abydus) and set up on a hill there. From this vantage-point he could look down on to the sea-shore and see both the land army and the fleet. As he watched them he conceived the desire to see the ships race; the contest duly took place and was won by the Phoenicians from Sidon. Xerxes took great pleasure in the race, and indeed in the whole army.

[45] The sight of the Hellespont completely covered by his ships, and the coast and plains of Abydus totally overrun by men first

gave Xerxes a feeling of deep self-satisfaction, but later he began to weep.

[46] When his uncle Artabanus (the one who had at first freely expressed his opinion and advised Xerxes not to attack Greece) noticed that Xerxes was crying he said, 'My lord, a short while ago you were feeling happy with your situation and now you are weeping. What a total change of mood!'

'Yes,' Xerxes answered. 'I was reflecting on things and it occurred to me how short the sum total of human life is, which made me feel compassion. Look at all these people—but not one of them will still be alive in a hundred years' time.'

'That's not the saddest aspect of life,' Artabanus replied. 'It's not just that life is short, but also that there's no one on earth, including these men, whose happiness is such that he won't sometimes wish he were dead rather than alive—and this is a thought that occurs frequently during one's lifetime, not just once. We are so overwhelmed by tragic accidents and illness that, however short life actually is, it seems long. So people look forward to dying, as an excellent way to escape from life with all its troubles. And this just goes to show how grudging the god is, because all we get is a taste of how sweet life may be.'

[47] Xerxes' response to this was as follows: 'Let's hear no more about human life, Artabanus; you have described it well. We shouldn't talk about bad things when involved in good things like our current project. But tell me this: if your dream hadn't been so unambiguous, would you have kept to your original point of view and been reluctant for me to march on Greece, or would you have changed your mind? Tell me the truth.'

'My lord,' Artabanus replied, 'I pray that the final outcome of the dream is in accord with what we both want. But it's true that I am still, even now, out of my mind with fear. There are a number of reasons for this, but the main difficulty I see is the presence of precisely those two factors which are your worst enemies.'

[48] 'What an extraordinary thing to say!' Xerxes retorted. 'What can you mean? What are these two worst enemies of mine? Do you find anything wrong with the size of my land army? Do you expect it to be outnumbered to any extent by the Greek forces? Or perhaps you think our fleet, or our infantry and navy combined, will prove to be smaller than theirs? If you think that our situation

is inadequate in this respect, let's have further troops raised as quickly as possible.'

[49] 'My lord,' said Artabanus, 'no intelligent man could find fault with this army or navy as regards their size. In actual fact, if you were to assemble further troops, the two factors I have in mind would became even more of a problem. The two factors are the land and the sea. As for the sea, there's no harbour anywhere, as far as I can tell, with the capacity to shelter this fleet of yours in the event of a storm and so keep your ships safe. In any case, you don't need just one such harbour, but a lot of them, all along the coastline you'll be sailing past. Since there are no adequate harbours, then, it's important to see that chance controls men rather than men controlling chance. So that's one of the two factors I was talking about. What about the other one? The land is your enemy in the sense that if you happen to meet with no resistance, the further you advance the more the land becomes your enemy, as you are enticed ever onward. Men can never get enough success, and so what I am saying is that, if you meet with no opposition, the chances of starvation are increased the more land you gain and the more time you spend getting it. A man of true calibre is one who combines fear when laying his plans, so that he weighs up everything that might happen to him, with courage in carrying out those plans.'

[50] 'That all sounds perfectly reasonable, Artabanus,' Xerxes replied, 'but you still shouldn't be afraid of everything or give everything equal weight. If you were to give everything equal weight in every situation you found yourself in, you'd never do anything at all. It's always better to adopt a positive outlook and experience danger half the time than to worry about everything and avoid experience altogether. You may dispute every proposal, but as long as you can't come up with an alternative course of action which is demonstrably safe, there's nothing to tell between you and the person making the risky proposals, and so your argument should not be regarded as any stronger than his. Anyway, we're only human, so how can we know where safety lies? We can't, in my opinion. Prizes are invariably won, then, by those who are prepared to act, rather than by those who weigh everything up and hesitate.

'You can see how powerful Persia has become. If those who ruled before me had shared your point of view, or even if they hadn't, but had people like you to advise them, you'd never have seen our country make so much progress. In fact, what they did was run risks—that's how they brought Persia to its current position of power, because great achievements are never won without great risks. So we are simply imitating them; we are on the road at the best time of year for campaigning, and by the time we get back home we will have conquered the whole of Europe. Nowhere will we encounter any unwelcome experiences such as shortage of food, because we're taking a good supply of provisions with us on the road, and also because wherever we go we'll get food from the local inhabitants of that land. The people we're attacking have farms—they're not nomads.'

[51] Next Artabanus said, 'My lord, although you don't want me to worry about anything, will you let me give you one piece of advice, on the grounds that complex affairs inevitably require further thought? In my judgement, you shouldn't lead the Ionians against their Athenian fathers, even though the Ionians have been tribute-paying subjects of Persia ever since Cyrus the son of Cambyses conquered the whole of Ionia except Athens. It's not as if the Ionians are essential for us to be able to overcome our enemies, and if they come with us they'll either have to reduce their mother city to slavery or help her win her freedom. In other words, they'll have to choose between committing a terrible crime and behaving with integrity. If they choose the first option, they won't really help us that much, but if they choose the second option they could do a great deal of harm to your army. Under these circumstances you should also bear in mind the truth of the old saying that the end is not obvious at the beginning.'

[52] 'Artabanus,' Xerxes replied, 'this idea of yours is more misguided than anything else I've heard you say. There's really no need for you to worry about the Ionians changing sides. We have irrefutable proof of their worth, and you yourself were there to witness it, along with everyone else who was involved in Darius' Scythian expedition. The annihilation or preservation of the whole Persian army depended on them, and they behaved with proper loyalty, without a hint of iniquity. Besides, they have left their children, wives, and property behind in our country, and that means that they are unlikely even to think about making trouble. So you needn't worry about them either. What I want you to do instead is dismiss these anxieties and protect my household and my kingdom,

because I am choosing you to be the sole guardian of my royal sceptre.'

[53] With these words Xerxes sent Artabanus back to Susa. His next action was to summon the most distinguished Persians to a conference. When they were all there he said, 'Men of Persia, I have convened this meeting to ask you to prove your bravery and avoid disgracing the important and valuable achievements of our predecessors. I want each of us individually, and all of us together, to commit ourselves wholeheartedly to this task; after all, it is the benefits to be won by all of us alike that spur us on. Your orders, then, are to prosecute the war with vigour, because my information is that the men we're attacking are valiant, and this means that if we get the better of them there's no other human force that will resist us. So now let us pray to the gods who are responsible for Persia and then cross over to Europe.'

[54] They spent the rest of the day getting ready for the crossing. The next day, while they waited, because they wanted to see the sun come up, they burnt all kinds of perfumed spices on the bridges and strewed myrtle branches on the road. At sunrise, Xerxes poured a libation from a golden cup into the sea and, facing the sun, asked the sun-god to avert any accidents which might stop him from reaching the outer limits of Europe and conquering the whole continent. At the end of this prayer he threw the cup into the Hellespont along with a golden bowl and a Persian sword—an *akinakes*, as they call it. I cannot tell precisely whether these objects were thrown into the sea as offerings to the sun or whether he had come to regret having lashed the Hellespont and was trying to make amends by giving them as gifts to the sea.

[55] Once Xerxes had finished, the crossing began. The foot-soldiers and all the cavalry contingents used the bridge nearest the Euxine Sea, while the yoke-animals and the camp-followers used the other bridge, the one nearest the Aegean. The brigade of ten thousand Persian soldiers went first, with every single one of them wearing a garland; the rest of the army followed with all the different peoples and tribes mixed up together. The day passed with these two groups making the crossing. On the next day the first contingents to cross were the horsemen and, also wearing garlands, the battalion who carried their lances pointing towards the ground. They were followed by the sacred horses and the sacred chariot, then came Xerxes himself with his personal guard of spearmen, and

then the troop of a thousand horsemen, followed by the rest of the army. While the land army was crossing, the fleet too made its way over to the opposite coast. I also once heard a version in which the king was the very last person to make the crossing.

[56] Over on the European side, Xerxes watched his army crossing the Hellespont under the whip. It took seven days and seven nights of unbroken activity for his army to finish the crossing. There is a story that after Xerxes had crossed the Hellespont a local Hellespontine man said, 'Why, Zeus, do you disguise yourself as a Persian man and take the name of Xerxes instead of Zeus? If you want to devastate Greece, why do you bring the whole of mankind with you, when you could do it by yourself?'

[57] Once the whole Persian army had crossed over into Europe, they were just setting off on their journey when a really extraordinary thing happened: a horse gave birth to a hare. Xerxes dismissed it as insignificant, though its meaning was transparent. It meant that although Xerxes would walk tall and proud on his way to attack Greece, he would return to his starting-point running for his life. There had been another omen for him in Sardis: a donkey had given birth to a foal with both male and female genitals, the male set above the female ones.

[58] Xerxes dismissed both these omens as unimportant and carried on his way, accompanied by the land army. The fleet sailed west along the coast out of the Hellespont with Cape Sarpedon as their destination, where their instructions were to wait for Xerxes' arrival. The foot-soldiers, however, headed east, in the opposite direction from the fleet; they marched overland through the Chersonese with the tomb of Helle the daughter of Athamas on their right and the town of Cardia on their left, and right through the middle of a town called Agora. But after rounding what is called the Black Gulf and crossing the river after which the gulf is named, the Black River (which was not large enough to avoid being drunk dry by the army), they travelled west past an Aeolian settlement called Aenus and Lake Stentoris, until they reached Doriscus.

[59] Doriscus is a part of Thrace consisting of a coastal region and an extensive plain, through which a large river called the Hebrus flows. A royal fortress had been built there—the one called Doriscus—and a Persian garrison posted by Darius ever since the time of his Scythian expedition. This struck Xerxes as a suitable place for him to order and count his troops, and he proceeded to

do so. Once the whole fleet had arrived in Doriscus, Xerxes had the captains bring their ships to the coast by Doriscus. This coastline, which ends at the famous Cape Serreium, was inhabited by Cicones a long time ago, but now there is a Samothracian settlement called Sale and another town called Zone there. The ships were beached along this coastline and hauled up out of the water to dry. And so Xerxes spent this time at Doriscus counting his troops.

[60] I cannot give an exact breakdown of how many men each contingent contributed to the total, because not one person has recorded this information, but it turned out that there were 1,700,000 men altogether in the land army. The census was conducted as follows. Ten thousand men were assembled in a single area and packed as closely together as possible; a circle was drawn round the outside of the body of men (who were then dismissed) and a waist-high wall was built around the circle. Then more men were introduced into the enclosed area, and so on until everyone had been counted. After the census, the men were organized into contingents based on nationality.

[61] Here are the peoples which made up Xerxes' army. First, there were the Persians, dressed as follows. On their heads they wore *tiaras*, as they call them, which are loose, felt caps, and their bodies were clothed in colourful tunics with sleeves ⟨and breastplates⟩† of iron plate, looking rather like fish-scales. Their legs were covered in trousers and instead of normal shields they carried pieces of wickerwork. They had quivers hanging under their shields, short spears, large bows, arrows made of cane, and also daggers hanging from their belts down beside their right thighs. They were commanded by Otanes, whose daughter Amestris was Xerxes' wife. In times past the Greeks used to call Persians Cephenes (even though both they and their neighbours called them Artaei), but then Perseus, the son of Danaë and Zeus, came to Cepheus the son of Belus, married his daughter Andromeda, and had a son, whom he called Perses. Cepheus had no male children, so Perseus left Perses there, and as a result the Persians are named after Perses.

[62] The Median contingent wore the same clothes as the Persians, since it was in fact a Median style of clothing, rather than a Persian one. Their commander was an Achaemenid called Tigranes. Medes used to be called Arians by everybody, but when Medea of

Colchis left Athens and arrived in their country—this is what the Medes themselves say—they too changed their name.

The Cissian contingent was clothed and equipped in the Persian style, except that they wore turbans instead of caps. They were commanded by Anaphes the son of Otanes.

The Hyrcanians also had the same equipment as the Persians, and were commanded by Megapanus, who later became the governor of Babylon.

[63] The Assyrian contingent wore on their heads either bronze helmets or plaited helmets of a peculiarly foreign design which is hard to describe. Their shields, spears, and daggers resembled Egyptian ones, and they also carried wooden clubs with iron studs, and wore linen breastplates. These are the people the Greeks call Syrians, but they were called Assyrians by the Persian invaders. Their commander was Otaspes the son of Artachaees.

[64] The Bactrian contingent wore headgear which was very similar to that of the Medes, and were armed with native cane bows and short spears. The Sacae, a Scythian tribe, had as headgear *kurbasias* whose crowns were stiffened into an upright point, and wore trousers. They carried native bows and daggers, and also battleaxes called *sagareis*. They were in fact Scythians from Amyrgium, but they were known as Sacae because that is what the Persians call all Scythians. The commander of both the Bactrian and Sacian contingents was Hystaspes, the son of Darius and Cyrus' daughter Atossa.

[65] Indian gear consisted of cotton clothing, cane bows and cane arrows with iron heads. For the duration of this expedition they were assigned to the command of Pharnazathres the son of Artabates.

[66] The Arians were equipped like the Bactrians, except that their bows were in the Median style. Their commander was Sisamnes the son of Hydarnes.

Also fitted out like the Bactrians were the Parthians and Chorasmians, commanded by Artabazus the son of Pharnaces; the Sogdians, commanded by Azanes the son of Artaeus; and the Gandarians and Dadicae, commanded by Artyphius the son of Artabanus.

[67] Caspian equipment consisted of jackets, native cane bows, and *akinakeis*. Their commander was Ariomardus the brother of Artyphius.

The Sarangae were conspicuous for their coloured clothing. They wore knee-high boots and carried bows and Median-style spears. They were commanded by Pherendates the son of Megabazus.

The Pactyes wore jackets and were armed with native bows and daggers. Their commander was Artayntes the son of Ithamitres.

[68] The Utians, Mycians, and Paricanians were fitted out like the Pactyes. The Utians and Mycians were commanded by Arsamenes the son of Darius, and the Paricanians by Siromitres the son of Oeobazus.

[69] The Arabians wore belted *zeiras* and carried on their right sides long, reflexible bows. The Ethiopians were dressed in leopard skins and lion pelts, and were armed with bows made out of palm fronds. These bows were long, at least four cubits in length, and their arrows were short and tipped not with iron but with a head made from sharpened stone—the kind of stone they also use to engrave signet-rings. They carried spears as well, whose heads were made out of gazelles' horns sharpened like the head of a lance, and also studded clubs. When they go into battle they paint half of their bodies with chalk and half with ochre. The commander of the Arabians and the Ethiopians from south of Egypt was Arsames, the son of Darius and Cyrus' daughter Artystone, who was his favourite wife. He had a statue of her made out of beaten gold.

[70] So Arsames was the commander of the Ethiopians from south of Egypt, as well as of the Arabians, but there were two lots of Ethiopians in the army. The eastern Ethiopians were assigned to the Indian contingent; these Ethiopians are exactly the same as the others to look at, but they speak a different language and their hair is different. The eastern Ethiopians have straight hair, while the Libyan ones have curlier hair than any other people in the world. The Asian Ethiopians were equipped more or less in the same fashion as the Indians, except that they wore a head-dress consisting of a horse's scalp, including the ears and mane. The mane acted as a crest, and the horse's ears were stiffened into an upright position. Instead of regular shields they had targes made out of crane skins.

[71] The Libyans came wearing leather clothing and armed with javelins whose ends had been burnt into sharp points. Their commander was Massages the son of Oärizus.

[72] The Paphlagonian contingent wore plaited helmets on their heads and were armed with small shields, medium-sized spears, and

javelins and daggers as well. On their feet they wore native boots which reached halfway up their shins. The Ligyan contingent had the same equipment as the Paphlagonians, and so did the Matieneans, Mariandynians, and Syrians (whom the Persians call Cappadocians). Dotus the son of Megasidrus was in command of the Paphlagonians and the Matieneans, and Gobryas the son of Darius and Artystone was in command of the Mariandynians, Ligyes, and Syrians.

[73] The Phrygians' equipment was very similar to that of the Paphlagonians, with only minor differences. According to the Macedonians, the Phrygians were called Briges for as long as they lived in Europe next to the Macedonians, but then when they moved to Asia they changed their name along with their country. The Armenians were fitted out just like the Phrygians—but then they were originally emigrants from Phrygia. Artochmes, who was married to one of Darius' daughters, was in command of both the Armenians and the Phrygians.

[74] The Lydians' equipment was not very different from Greek. A long time ago, the Lydians were known as Maeonians, but they changed their name when they named themselves after Lydus the son of Atys. The Mysians wore a native style of helmet on their heads and were armed with small shields and javelins whose ends had been burnt into sharp points. They were originally emigrants from Lydia, and are also known as Olympieni, after Mount Olympus. The Lydians and the Mysians were under the command of Artaphrenes the son of Artaphrenes, who was jointly responsible, with Datis, for the invasion at Marathon.

[75] The Thracian contingent wore fox-skin caps on their heads and were dressed in tunics with colourful *zeiras* on top; their feet and lower legs were covered in boots made out of fawn-skin. They also carried javelins, bucklers, and small daggers. After they moved from Europe to Asia they were called the Bithynians, but, as they say themselves, before that they were called the Strymonians, because they lived on the River Strymon. They say that they were driven out of their original homeland by the Teucrians and the Mysians. These Asian Thracians were commanded by Bassaces the son of Artabanus.

[76] ⟨The Pisidae⟩† carried small shields of untreated oxhide. Every man among them was armed with two hunting-spears in the Lycian style, and wore a bronze helmet on his head. Each helmet

had the ears and horns of an ox, also in bronze, attached to it, and had a crest as well. They wore red cloths wrapped around their lower legs. There is an oracle of Ares in their country.

[77] The Cabalians (who are known as Lasonians, despite being of Maeonian stock) were fitted out in the same way as the Cilicians, and so I will describe their equipment when I come to the Cilician contingent in my account.

The Milyans carried short spears and wore cloaks fastened with a brooch. Some of them had Lycian-style bows and wore on their heads helmets made out of leather. The whole Milyan contingent was under the command of Badres the son of Hystanes.

[78] The Moschians wore wooden helmets on their heads and carried shields and spears which were short, but with long points. The Tibarenians, Macrones, and Mossynoecians had the same equipment as the Moschians. The Moschians and Tibarenians formed a single contingent under the command of Ariomardus, the son of Darius and Parmys, who was the daughter of Smerdis and granddaughter of Cyrus. The Macrones and Mossynoecians together formed another contingent under the command of Artayctes the son of Cherasmis, who was the governor of Sestus on the Hellespont.

[79] The Mares wore plaited native helmets on their heads, and carried small shields of animal skin and javelins. The Colchians wore wooden helmets on their heads, carried small shields of untreated oxhide and short spears, and were armed with knives as well. Pharandates the son of Teäspis was in command of the Mares and the Colchians.

The Alarodian and Saspeiran troops were equipped like the Colchians, and commanded by Masistius the son of Siromitres.

[80] The tribes who had come from the islands in the Red Sea to take part in the expedition—the islands where the Persian king settles the people known as 'the Dispossessed'—closely resembled the Medes in respect of both clothing and weaponry. These islanders were commanded by Mardontes the son of Bagaeus, who was one of the Persian commanders a year later at the battle of Mycale, where he died.

[81] These were the tribes and peoples who marched by land and were organized into infantry contingents. I have already given the names of the commanders of this division, whose job it was also to organize and count the troops, and to appoint officers to

take charge of the brigades of 10,000 and the battalions of 1,000; the leaders of the companies of 100 and the sections of 10 were appointed by the brigade-commanders. There were also other officers in command of the various regiments and tribal units. Anyway, the commanding officers were as stated.

[82] The High Command, in charge of these officers and of the whole infantry division, consisted of Mardonius the son of Gobryas, Tritantaechmes the son of Artabanus (the Artabanus who had been opposed to the Greek expedition), both of whom were nephews of Darius and cousins to Xerxes,† Smerdomenes the son of Otanes, Masistes the son of Darius and Atossa, Gergis the son of Ariazus, and Megabyzus the son of Zopyrus.

[83] These people were the supreme commanders of the whole infantry division except for the Ten Thousand. This brigade of ten thousand picked Persian troops was commanded by Hydarnes the son of Hydarnes, and was known as the Immortals. The reason for this name was that as soon as a place in the battalion became vacant, as a result of death or illness, it was immediately filled by someone else, so that the battalion remained at exactly ten thousand, no more and no less. In the whole army, the Persians were turned out best, and physically they were the bravest fighters as well. Their equipment has already been described, but they were also conspicuous for the huge amount of gold they wore about their persons. They also brought covered wagons for their concubines, sizeable and well-equipped retinues of slaves, and their own personal provisions, separate from those of the other soldiers, transported by camels and yoke-animals.

[84] These nations were all horsemen, but they did not all provide cavalry units. Here is a list of those that did. The Persian cavalry were fitted out in the same fashion as their infantry, except that some of them wore headgear of beaten bronze and iron.

[85] The Sagartians, a nomadic people who are ethnically Persian and who speak Persian, but dress in a combination of styles from Persia and Pactyice, supplied eight thousand horsemen, who were armed, as is the custom in their country, with no bronze or iron weapons except daggers. The main weapons they rely on in battle are ropes plaited out of leather thongs. What they do when they engage an enemy is throw these ropes, which have a noose at one end, and then pull in to themselves whatever it is they hit, which might be a man or a horse. Their opponents are entangled

in the coils and dispatched. That is how the Sagartians fight. They were detailed to join the Persian contingent.

[86] The Medians and Cissians both had the same kind of equipment as their infantry units. The Indians were fitted out in the same way as their countrymen on foot, but rode war-ponies and chariots, to which they harnessed both horses and wild donkeys. The Bactrians and Sacae† both had the same kind of equipment as their infantry equivalents. The Libyans were also equipped, as far as their bodies were concerned, no differently from their countrymen on foot, and they too all drove chariots. The Pactyes† and the Paricanians also had the same equipment as their infantry equivalents. The Arabians too had the same equipment as their infantry, but they all rode camels, which were just as fast as horses.

[87] These were the only peoples that were mounted. The total number of horsemen in the army was eighty thousand, not counting the camels and the chariots. The horsemen were all organized into regiments, with the Arabians detailed to bring up the rear, because horses cannot abide camels, and in that position their camels would not alarm the horses.

[88] The field commanders of the cavalry division were two sons of Datis called Harmamithres and Tithaeus. Illness had kept the third cavalry commander, Pharnouches, in Sardis. Just as they were about to set out from Sardis, he had an unfortunate accident. A dog ran under the feet of the horse he was riding and the horse, which had not seen the dog coming, took fright, reared up, and unseated him. After his fall he began to vomit blood and developed consumption. His house-slaves lost no time in carrying out their master's orders about what to do to the horse: they took it to the place where it had thrown him and cut off its legs at the knees. So this is how Pharnouches came to lose his command.

[89] The total number of triremes was 1,207, supplied by various nations as follows. The Phoenicians and the Palestinian Syrians supplied three hundred triremes; their equipment consisted of helmets very similar in style to Greek ones, linen breastplates, rimless shields, and javelins. According to their own tradition, these Phoenicians used to live a long time ago on the Red Sea, but then they moved to the coastal region of Syria which they currently occupy. This part of Syria, all the way to the border with Egypt, is known as Palestine.

The Egyptians supplied two hundred ships. They wore plaited helmets on their heads and carried curved shields with wide rims, naval spears, and large battleaxes. Most of them also wore breastplates and carried long knives.

[90] Next, the Cyprians contributed a hundred and fifty ships. Their outfit basically resembled Greek gear—tunics and so on—but members of their royal families wore turbans wound around their heads. People on Cyprus have a variety of ethnic origins, according to their own traditions: Salamis, Athens, Arcadia, Cythnus, Phoenicia, and Ethiopia are all mentioned.

[91] As for the Cilicians, who supplied a hundred ships, they wore native helmets on their heads, carried bucklers made out of untreated oxhide instead of shields, and wore woollen tunics. Every man was armed with two javelins and a sword which closely resembled the Egyptian knife. Cilicians were originally known as Hypachaeans, but then they were named after a Phoenician called Cilix the son of Agenor.

The Pamphylians came with thirty ships and Greek arms and armour. These Pamphylians are descended from people who accompanied Amphilochus and Calchas during the Trojan diaspora.

[92] The Lycians contributed fifty ships. They wore breastplates and greaves, and carried cornel-wood bows, cane arrows without flights, and javelins. They also had goatskin capes slung around their shoulders, and on their heads felt caps trimmed with feathers. They were armed with daggers and billhooks. The Lycians originally came from Crete and were called Termilae, but then they were named after an Athenian called Lycus the son of Pandion.

[93] The Dorians from Asia supplied thirty ships. They had Greek equipment and originally came from the Peloponnese.

The Carians supplied seventy ships and were equipped in the Greek style, except that they also had billhooks and daggers. In an early section of my work I have already mentioned what the Carians used to be called.

[94] The Ionians contributed a hundred ships and had Greek clothing and weaponry. According to the Greeks, while the Ionians lived in the part of the Peloponnese now called Achaea—that is, before Danaus and Xuthus came to the Peloponnese—they were called Aegialian Pelasgians, but later they were named after Ion the son of Xuthus.

[95] The Aegean islanders supplied seventeen ships and were dressed and equipped like Greeks. They too were Pelasgian in origin, but were called Ionian for the same reason that the Ionians from the twelve communities were, who were originally from Athens.

The Aeolians (who according to Greek tradition are another Pelasgian people) contributed sixty ships and had Greek clothing and weapons.

All the communities of the Hellespont except Abydus (whose inhabitants had been given by Xerxes the job of guarding the bridges, which meant that they had to stay at home) contributed a hundred ships to the expedition. Their clothing and weapons were Greek. They were Ionian and Dorian colonists.

[96] There were Persian, Median, and Sacian marines on board every ship. The best ships were those the Phoenicians supplied, and the best of these were the ones from Sidon. Every naval unit was under officers native to the country supplying the ships, as was also the case with the infantry contingents, but I am not going to give the names of these officers, because they are not required by this account of my investigations. In the first place, none of the officers in charge of any of the units of the various peoples was particularly distinguished, and in the second place, there were as many officers as there were communities in every country. Besides, they were not there as military commanders, but were just as much slaves as all their fellow soldiers, since all power and authority over the various national units was invested in the Persian commanders I have already mentioned.

[97] The commanders of the fleet were Ariabignes the son of Darius, Prexaspes the son of Aspathines, Megabazus the son of Megabates, and Achaemenes the son of Darius. Ariabignes (whose parents were Darius and Gobryas' daughter) was in command of the Ionian and Carian squadrons, Achaemenes (who was a full brother of Xerxes) was in command of the Egyptians, and the other two were in command of the rest of the navy. Counting triaconters, pentaconters, light vessels, and small horse-transport ships, the fleet was found to consist in total of 3,000 ships.

[98] After the commanders, the most notable men in the fleet were Tetramnestus the son of Anysus, from Sidon; Matten the son of Siromus, from Tyre; Merbalus the son of Agbalus, from Aradus; Syennesis the son of Oromedon, from Cilicia; Cyberniscus the son

THE HISTORIES

of Sicas, from Lycia; Gorgus the son of Chersis and Timonax the son of Timagoras, both from Cyprus; and from Caria Histiaeus the son of Tymnes, Pigres the son of Hysseldomus, and Damasithymus the son of Candaules.

[99] I pass over all the other officers, because there is no need for me to mention them, except for Artemisia, because I find it particularly remarkable that a woman should have taken part in the expedition against Greece. She took over the tyranny after her husband's death, and although she had a grown-up son and did not have to join the expedition, her manly courage impelled her to do so. Artemisia was her name, and she was the daughter of Lygdamis; her father's family came from Halicarnassus, and her mother's was Cretan. She came with five ships and with men from Halicarnassus, Cos, Nisyros, and Calydna under her command. Hers was the second most famous squadron in the entire navy, after the one from Sidon. None of Xerxes' allies gave him better advice than her. All the places I have listed as being under her command were Dorian in nationality, since the Halicarnassians were originally from Troezen and the others from Epidaurus.

[100] So much for the fleet. When the army had been counted and organized into units, Xerxes decided that he would like to ride among them in person and review them. Later, then, that is exactly what he did. He rode on his chariot past each and every tribal unit and asked questions, with his scribes taking notes, until he had gone from one end of the army to the other and reviewed both the cavalry and the infantry. Then he had the ships hauled back down into the water and he exchanged his chariot for a Sidonian ship; he sat under a golden canopy and sailed past the prows of the ships, asking the same kinds of questions about each group of ships as he had done with the land army, and having notes taken. The ships' captains had sailed about four plethra from the shore and were riding at anchor, all in a row, with their prows facing land and their marines armed and ready for battle. Xerxes reviewed them while his boat passed between the prows of the ships and the shoreline.

[101] Once he was back on land afterwards, he sent for Demaratus the son of Ariston, who had accompanied him on the expedition against Greece, and when he arrived he said, 'I have a mind now, Demaratus, to question you about something I want to know. You are Greek, and from what you and other Greeks I've spoken

to have told me, you come from one of the most important and
powerful Greek cities. So tell me: will the Greeks stand their ground
against me? Will they resist? It seems to me that all the Greeks, and
even the combined forces of the entire western world, would be
incapable of withstanding my advance, unless they formed a unified
front. But I want to hear what you have to say about this.'

In response to this question Demaratus asked, 'Would you like
a truthful answer, my lord, or a comforting one?' Xerxes told him
to be honest and promised that he would not find himself in a less
favourable situation than before.

[102] So Demaratus said, 'My lord, you have asked me to tell
the whole truth—the kind of truth that you will not be able to
prove false at a later date. There has never been a time when
poverty was not a factor in the rearing of the Greeks, but their
courage has been acquired as a result of intelligence and the force
of law. Greece has relied on this courage to keep poverty and despotism at bay. I admire all the Greeks who live in those Dorian lands,
but I shall restrict what I have to say to the Lacedaemonians alone.
First, then, there's no way in which they will ever listen to any proposals of yours which will bring slavery on Greece; second, they
will certainly resist you, even if all the other Greeks come over
to your side. As for the size of their army, there's no point in
your asking how, in terms of numbers, they can do this. If there
are in fact only a thousand men to march out against you (though
it may be fewer or it may be more), then a thousand men will fight
you.'

[103] Xerxes' response was to laugh and say, 'Demaratus, how
can you say such a thing? The very idea of a thousand men fighting an army the size of mine! Now, come on. You say you used to
be these people's king, so tell me: would you be prepared to fight
ten men, for example? Of course not, but if everything you've told
me about your political system is true, it is right that you, their
king, should take on twice as many men as anyone else: that is in
keeping with your customs. If each of them is worth ten men from
my army, I'd expect you to be worth twenty. That would fit in with
what you've been telling me. I suppose they are men like you and
the other Greeks I've met, with the same qualities as you, and
bodies of the same size. But if that's so, are you sure these proud
boasts you Greeks make are not just nonsense? Look, let's be completely rational about this. How could a thousand men—or ten

thousand or fifty thousand, for that matter—when every man among them is as free as the next man and they do not have a single leader, oppose an army the size of ours? After all, let's suppose there are five thousand of them: we will then outnumber them by more than a thousand to one! If they had a single leader in the Persian mould, fear of him might make them excel themselves and, urged on by the whip, they might attack a numerically superior force, but all this is out of the question if they're allowed their freedom. As a matter of fact, it is my belief that the Greeks would find it hard to take on just the Persians, even if they had the same number of troops as us. No, we're the only ones who have the quality you're talking about—at least, a few of us do. After all, there are men in my personal guard who would be prepared to fight three Greeks at once. But you're just talking rubbish from a position of ignorance.'

[104] 'My lord,' Demaratus replied, 'I knew from the start that I wasn't going to endear myself to you if I spoke the truth, but you insisted on absolute honesty, so I told you how things stand with the Spartans. How much I love them at the moment you know perfectly well, since they deposed me, robbed me of my ancestral rights, and made me a stateless exile, while your father took me in and gave me a home and an income—the sort of act of kindness it would be sheer stupidity for anyone to reject rather than appreciate. I'd rather not take on a single opponent, let alone two or ten—an ability I'm certainly not claiming to have. If I had no choice in the matter, however, or if so much was at stake that I was motivated to do so, I'd gladly fight—especially one of those men who claims to be a match for three Greeks. That's how the Lacedaemonians are: they're as good as anyone in the world when it comes to fighting one on one, but they're the best when it comes to fighting in groups. The point is that although they're free, they're not entirely free: their master is the law, and they're far more afraid of this than your men are of you. At any rate, they do whatever the law commands, and its command never changes: it is that they should not turn tail in battle no matter how many men are ranged against them, but should maintain their positions and either win or die. If this seems nonsense to you, I shall hold my peace from now on. I only spoke because you insisted. I only hope that everything goes satisfactorily for you, my lord.'

[105] Xerxes laughed and made a joke of this reply by Demaratus. He was not at all angry, but dismissed him civilly. After this conversation with Demaratus, Xerxes made Mascames the son of Megadostes governor of Doriscus, where they were, to replace the man Darius had appointed. Then he continued marching through Thrace towards Greece.

[106] Mascames, whom Xerxes left in Doriscus, was a man of such calibre that he was the only one who regularly received rewards from Xerxes, year after year, for being the best of all the governors appointed by either himself or Darius. Xerxes' son Artaxerxes continued the honour by rewarding Mascames' sons in the same way. Before Xerxes' campaign governors had been appointed to posts all over Thrace and the Hellespont, but afterwards all of them were expelled by the Greeks except Mascames in Doriscus. No one ever succeeded in getting rid of him, although there were plenty of attempts to do so. That is why the Persian king, whoever it may be at any given time, still sends gifts.

[107] The only one of the governors expelled by the Greeks who was considered a good man by King Xerxes was Boges, the governor of Eïon. In fact, Xerxes never stopped singing his praises, and he heaped honours on his surviving sons, who lived in Persia. And Boges certainly deserved nothing less than high praise. During the siege of Eïon by the Athenians under Cimon the son of Miltiades, he could have left under a truce and returned to Asia, but instead he stuck it out to the bitter end, because he did not want the king to gain the impression that he had survived through cowardice. When there were no provisions left within the stronghold, he made a huge pyre, cut the throats of his children, wife, concubines, and house-slaves, and threw their bodies on to the fire. Next he stood on the wall and flung all the gold and silver there was in the town into the Strymon, and finally he threw himself on to the fire. For this his memory is still held in high esteem among the Persians even today, as it should be.

[108] So Xerxes set out from Doriscus towards Greece. On the way he conscripted everyone he came across into his army. He was able to do this because, as I explained earlier, the whole country as far as Thessaly had been conquered first by Megabazus and then by Mardonius, who between them enslaved it and reduced it to the status of a tribute-paying subject. After leaving Doriscus the first

places he passed were the walled towns owned by Samothrace, the most westerly of which is a place called Mesambria. Near Mesambria is a Thasian settlement called Stryme, and between them flows the River Lisus, which did not have an adequate supply of water for Xerxes' army, but was drunk dry. A long time ago this region was called Gallaïce, but nowadays it is known as Briantice; strictly speaking, however, it within the territory of the Cicones, as is Doriscus.

[109] Having crossed the now-dry bed of the Lisus, Xerxes passed the Greek towns of Maronea, Dicaea, and Abdera. His route also took him past a couple of famous lakes—Ismaris, which is situated between Maronea and Stryme, and Bistonis, which is near Dicaea and is fed by two rivers, the Trauus and the Compsatus. There was no well-known lake near Abdera for him to pass, but he crossed the River Nestus, which flows into the sea there. His route next took him past the mainland towns founded by Thasos. The territory of one of these towns, Pistyrus, includes a lake of about thirty stades' circumference, which teems with fish and is very brackish indeed; the yoke-animals were the only ones to drink from it, but they drank it dry. So these were the Greek coastal towns which Xerxes passed on his left.

[110] Here are the Thracian tribes through whose territory he travelled: the Paeti, Cicones, Bistones, Sapaei, Dersaei, Edonians, and Satrae. Some of them lived on the coast, and they went along with their ships, while the inland tribes from this list of mine were all forcibly conscripted into the land army—all except the Satrae, that is.

[111] The Satrae have never been subject to anyone, as far as we know; they are the only tribe in Thrace to have retained their independence all the way up to my day. They live in a region of high mountains which are thickly wooded with all kinds of trees and covered with snow; they are also extremely good fighters. They are the ones who have the oracle of Dionysus in the highest part of the mountain range in their country. The pronouncements at this shrine are interpreted by the Bessians, a sub-tribe within the Satrae, and as at Delphi it is a prophetess who is the mouthpiece, and her utterances are no more elaborate than those of her counterpart at Delphi.

[112] After skirting this region, Xerxes next passed the strongholds of the Pierians, one of which is called Phagres and the other

Pergamus. He made his way right past the walls of these towns with Mount Pangaeum on his right; this is a massive, lofty mountain where there are both gold- and silver-mines, which are worked by the Pierians, the Odomantians, and especially the Satrae.

[113] North of Mount Pangaeum live the Paeonians, Doberes, and Paeoplae, whose lands Xerxes skirted as he continued west. In due course he reached the River Strymon and the city of Eïon, where Boges (whom I mentioned a short while ago) was the governor, since he was still alive at this time. The country around Mount Pangaeum is called Phyllis; its western border is formed by the River Angites, which is a tributary of the Strymon, and its southern border is formed by the Strymon itself. The Magi sacrificed white horses to the Strymon, looking for a favourable omen.

[114] These were far from being the only magical rites they performed at the river. Afterwards, they crossed the river at Nine Ways (a place in Edonian territory), where they found the Strymon bridged. When they learnt that the name of the place was Nine Ways, they buried alive nine local boys and girls in the ground there. The practice of burying people alive is a Persian custom, because I hear that in her old age Xerxes' wife Amestris too had fourteen children, whose parents were distinguished Persians, buried alive as a gift on her behalf to the god who is supposed to live underground.

[115] To the west of the route the army took after the Strymon is a stretch of shoreline where the Greek town of Argilus is situated. This shoreline and the district inland of it are called Bisaltia. Xerxes marched past Argilus and then, with the bay off Posideium to his left, crossed the plain of Syleus, bypassing the Greek town of Stagirus, until he fetched up at Acanthus. Along the way he drew into his army men from every single one of these places, as well as from the places around Mount Pangaeum. The pattern was the same as the one I have already described: he added ships to the fleet from the people living in coastal regions and gained contingents for the land army from those living inland. The road taken by King Xerxes and his army is still in my time an object of reverence in Thrace: the Thracians avoid ploughing it up or sowing crops on it.

[116] On arriving at Acanthus, Xerxes proclaimed a pact of guest-friendship between himself and the Acanthians. He presented

them with a set of Median clothing and complimented them on
their enthusiasm for the war, which he could see, and on their work
on digging the canal, which he was told about.

[117] During Xerxes' stay in Acanthus Artachaees, who had
been in charge of the construction of the canal, happened to die
of disease. Artachaees was an Achaemenid who was very highly
regarded by Xerxes; he was the tallest of the Persians (being only
four fingers short of five royal cubits) and he had the loudest voice
in the world. Xerxes was deeply upset at his death and gave him a
magnificent funeral and burial; the whole army helped to raise his
burial mound. On the advice of an oracle, the people of Acanthus
have instituted a hero-cult of Artachaees, which involves calling on
him by name. So King Xerxes grieved for the death of Artachaees.

[118] The Greeks who received the troops and provided hospitality for Xerxes were so completely ruined that they lost their own
homes. For instance, when the Thasians entertained and fed
Xerxes' army on behalf of their mainland settlements, they gave
the job to Antipater the son of Orgeus, who was as distinguished
a man as any on the island, and he showed that the meal had cost
four hundred talents of silver.

[119] More or less the same figures were produced by those
from other towns and cities who were responsible for entertaining
the army. The meal was ordered a long time in advance and was
taken very seriously. As soon as they heard from the agents who
were travelling around delivering the message, the inhabitants of
the towns would spend many months dividing up their grain and
preparing wheat-meal and barley-meal; they would also locate the
best cattle money could buy and fatten them up. They kept birds
in cages and waterfowl in ponds for the entertainment of the
troops. They had gold and silver cups, bowls, and tableware in
general made—although these were for the king himself and those
who shared his table, while for the rest of the army they only had
to provide food. By the time the army arrived, they would have
a pavilion pitched and ready, which Xerxes himself could use as a
staging-post on his journey, while the rest of the army stayed out
in the open. When it was time for the meal to be served, all the
hard work fell to the hosts, while their guests ate their fill. Then
they would spend the night there, and on the next day they used
to take down the pavilion and appropriate all the movables before
marching off, leaving nothing behind, but taking it all with them.

[120] This was the occasion of a *bon mot* by Megacreon of Abdera. He put it to the people of Abdera that they should go in full force to the city's sanctuaries, taking their wives as well, to beg the gods to avert half the troubles that might be waiting for them in the future, and to offer heartfelt thanks for the past, because it was not King Xerxes' habit to eat twice a day! His thinking was that if the people of Abdera had been ordered to prepare a midday meal as well as an evening meal, they would either have had to leave before Xerxes' arrival or, if they had stayed put, would have been crushed more miserably than anyone had ever been.

[121] Anyway, despite the pressing difficulties, the various townspeople did what they were required to do. Next, after Acanthus, Xerxes sent the fleet on ahead and told his commanders to have it wait for him at Therma, because he had found out that this town lay on his most direct route. Therma is situated on the Gulf of Therma, and has, in fact, given its name to the gulf. As for the land army, during the journey from Doriscus to Acanthus, it had been divided at Xerxes' orders into a formation consisting of three columns. He had detailed one of these columns, under Mardonius and Masistes, to march along the coast, keeping pace with the fleet; he had another third of the army, commanded by Tritantaechmes and Gergis, take an inland route; and the final column marched between the other two, with Smerdomenes and Megabyzus in command, and with Xerxes himself in their midst.

[122] However, the fleet was now sent on ahead by Xerxes. It sailed along the canal that had been excavated on the peninsula of Athos and through to the gulf where Assa, Pilorus, Singus, and Sarte are situated. Additional troops were recruited from these places, and then the fleet steered for the Gulf of Therma. It rounded Ampelus, the headland in Toronian territory, and sailed past Torone, Galepsus, Sermyle, Mecyberna, and Olynthus—Greek towns from which they recruited both ships and troops. Sithonia is the name of the district where these towns are.

[123] Xerxes' fleet cut across from Cape Ampelus to Cape Canastra, which is the part of Pallene that projects furthest into the sea. Next they recruited both ships and men from Potidaea, Aphytis, Neapolis, Aege, Therambus, Scione, Mende, and Sane, which are the settlements on Pallene (or Phlegra, as it was formerly known). They sailed on past this region towards their destination, and took on additional troops from the communities near Pallene

and bordering the Gulf of Therma—namely, Lipaxus, Combreia, Haesa,† Gigonus, Campsa, Smila, and Aeneia. The region where these towns are situated is still called Crossaea. After the last of the places on this list of mine, Aeneia, the fleet sailed into the actual Gulf of Therma and came to the region called Mygdonia. Finally they reached their destination; they put in at Therma, and also Sindus and Chalestra on the River Axius, which forms the border between Mygdonia and Bottiaeis, where two settlements, Ichnae and Pella, occupy a narrow strip of land on the coast.

[124] So Xerxes' fleet was lying at anchor off the coast from the River Axius to the town of Therma, including the settlements in between, waiting for the king to arrive. Meanwhile Xerxes and the land army were making their way from Acanthus, taking the direct route overland to their destination, Therma. They marched through Paeonia and Crestonia to the River Echeidorus, which rises in Crestonia, flows through Mygdonia and issues by the marshes of the River Axius.

[125] As they were making their way through these regions, night after night lions used to come down from their usual hunting-grounds and attack the camels in their baggage train. They did not harm anything else, man or beast, but savaged only the camels. I wonder what it was that made the lions ignore everything else and attack the camels, when this was a type of creature that was completely unfamiliar to them—one they had never seen or come across before.

[126] There are large numbers of lions in these parts, and also wild oxen, whose enormous horns are imported into Greece. The lions' territory is bounded by the River Nestus, which flows through Abdera, and the Acheloüs, which flows through Acarnania. No lions are found anywhere in eastern Europe east of the Nestus or in the rest of the continent west of the Acheloüs; they only ever occur in the region between these two rivers.

[127] After reaching Therma, Xerxes had his troops bivouac there. The camp spread out all along the coast from Therma and Mygdonia to the Lydias and Haliacmon, two rivers which combine and form the boundary between Bottiaeis and Macedonia. While the invaders were encamped in those parts, of all the rivers mentioned only the Echeidorus, which flows from Crestonia, failed to provide enough water for the army, and was drunk dry.

[128] From Therma Xerxes could see the vast bulk of Mount Olympus and Mount Ossa in Thessaly. He found out that half-way between them there was a narrow ravine, with the River Peneius flowing through it, and was told that there was a way into Thessaly there. This made him want to sail to see the mouth of the Peneius, because his plan was to take the inland route through the peoples living in northern Macedonia and past the town of Gonnus to Perrhaebia, which was the safest route, according to the information he had. Having conceived this desire, he acted on it. He boarded the Sidonian ship he always used for this sort of occasion and gave the signal for the rest of the fleet to put to sea as well, leaving the land army where it was. Once he got to the mouth of the Peneius, Xerxes was greatly astonished at what he saw. He summoned his guides and asked them if it was possible to divert the river and to have it enter the sea elsewhere.

[129] There is a story that Thessaly, which is completely surrounded by vast mountains, was long ago a lake. To the east Mount Pelium and Mount Ossa form a barrier because their foothills merge; the barrier to the north is Olympus, to the west Pindus, and to the south Othrys. Thessaly consists of a basin in the middle of these mountains. A large number of rivers enter this basin, five of which—the Peneius, Apidanus, Onochonus, Enipeus, and Pamisus—are particularly well known. They descend from the mountains surrounding Thessaly, each with its separate name, and meet on this plain, where they all join to form a single river; then they issue into the sea through a narrow ravine. As soon as they have joined together, the name of the Peneius takes over and the others all lose their names. The story goes that in ancient times this ravine—this outlet—did not yet exist; so these rivers, and Lake Boebeis as well, which did not yet have their modern separate names, but still channelled the same volume of water as they do nowadays, flowed down and made the whole of Thessaly an inland sea. According to native Thessalian tradition, the ravine through which the Peneius flows was made by Poseidon. This is not implausible, because the sight of this ravine would make anyone who thinks that Poseidon is responsible for earthquakes, and therefore that rifts formed by earthquakes are caused by him, say that it was the work of Poseidon. For it seems to me that this rift in the mountains was caused by an earthquake.†

[130] When Xerxes enquired whether there was any alternative outlet for the Peneüs into the sea, the guides knew the answer and said, 'No, my lord, there is no other way for this river to reach the sea. This is the only exit there is, because Thessaly is entirely surrounded by mountains.' To this Xerxes is supposed to have replied, 'The Thessalians are no fools. Now I see why they took the precaution a long time ago of conceding to me. The main reason, as it turns out, is that it would take hardly any time or effort to gain control of their country. All one would have to do is dam the ravine so as to divert the river away from it and alter its course, and that would let the water loose on their land, until the whole of Thessaly apart from the mountains would be flooded.' He was referring to the fact that the Aleuadae of Thessaly had been the first Greeks to surrender to him—a move which Xerxes took to be an offer of friendship from the whole country. Having made this remark, he finished looking the site over and then sailed back to Therma.

[131] He stayed in Pieria for quite a few days, because a third of his men were engaged in cutting through the Macedonian mountains to enable the whole army to pass through them and reach Perrhaebia. During this period the heralds he had sent to Greece to demand earth arrived back, some empty-handed, some with earth and water.

[132] The following Greek peoples gave the king earth and water: the Thessalians, Dolopians, Enienians, Perrhaebians, Locrians, Magnesians, Malians, Achaeans of Phthiotis, and, led by the Thebans, the rest of the Boeotians except the Thespians and Plataeans. These peoples were the object of an oath sworn by those of the Greeks who resisted the Persian invasion to the following effect: that after the successful conclusion of the war all those who had surrendered of their own free will to the Persian, despite being Greeks, were to have a tenth of their property made over to the god of Delphi. These were the terms of the oath sworn by the Greeks.

[133] No heralds were sent by Xerxes to Athens and Sparta with a demand for earth because Darius had done exactly that earlier, and the heralds had been hurled into the Pit in Athens, and into a well in Sparta, with the suggestion that they fetch earth and water from there to take to the king. That is why Xerxes did not send men to demand earth and water from Athens and Sparta. I am not in a position to say what happened to the Athenians as a result of

their treatment of the heralds. It is true that their land and their city were devastated, but in my opinion that was not due to their treatment of the heralds.

[134] The Lacedaemonians, however, felt the force of the anger of Talthybius, Agamemnon's herald. In Sparta there is a shrine of Talthybius, and his descendants, called the Talthybiadae, live there and have the right to act as heralds for Sparta whenever the state needs to send an official message. Following the business with the Persian herald the Spartiates could not receive favourable omens from any of their sacrifices. This went on for quite a time, until the Lacedaemonians became annoyed and alarmed. After a large number of general assemblies, they issued a proclamation to find out whether any of the Lacedaemonians was prepared to die for Sparta. Two aristocratic and wealthy Spartiates, Sperthias the son of Aneristus and Bulis the son of Nicolaus, volunteered to let Xerxes punish them for the deaths in Sparta of Darius' heralds, and so they were sent to Persia by the Spartiates to be executed.

[135] Their remarkable bravery was matched by equally impressive words. On their way to Susa they went to Hydarnes, a Persian who was the military commander of the coastal peoples of Asia, who put them up and gave them dinner. During the course of the meal he asked them, 'Why, men of Lacedaemon, do you refuse to be on good terms with the king? Look at me and my situation: you can see that the king knows how to reward good men. The same goes for you too, because he already thinks well of you: if you were to surrender to him, he would probably grant both of you domains to rule in Greece.'

'This recommendation of yours, Hydarnes,' they replied, 'is not based on a balanced assessment of the situation. You have only half the picture. Although you know what it's like to be a slave, you've never experienced freedom and you have no idea whether or not it's a pleasant state. If you had experienced it, you'd be advising us to wield not spears, but even battleaxes in its defence.'

[136] That was their reply to Hydarnes. From his house they made their way up to Susa. The first thing that happened, once they gained an audience with the king, was that Xerxes' guards ordered them, and tried to force them, to fall down and prostrate themselves before the king. Their response to this was to declare that even if the guards were to hurl them headlong down on to the ground they would never do any such thing, not only because

it was not the Greek way to prostrate oneself before another human being, but also because that was not what they had come for. Having overcome this obstacle, they then said, 'King of Persia, the Lacedaemonians sent us to pay the penalty for the death of the heralds in Sparta.' That was more or less what they said. In reply Xerxes magnanimously said that he was different from the Lacedaemonians: whereas in murdering the heralds they had broken a code of practice followed by the whole of mankind, he would not behave in the very way he was criticizing them for, or release them from their guilt by killing them in return.

[137] So for the time being the anger of Talthybius died down because the Spartiates had taken the appropriate action, even though Sperthias and Bulis returned home. However, it awoke again many years later, during the war between the Peloponnesians and Athens, according to the Lacedaemonians. What happened does seem to me to be a particularly clear case of divinity at work. That it was heralds who bore the brunt of Talthybius' anger, and that it did not finally die down until it had worked itself out, was only right; but what makes me certain that it was the work of the gods is that it fell on the children of the men sent to the Persian king to appease this anger in the first place—on Nicolas the son of Bulis and Aneristus the son of Sperthias (this was the Aneristus who captured Halieis, a colony of Tiryns, by landing there in a merchant ship filled with men). Nicolas and Aneristus were sent with a message from Lacedaemon to Asia, but were betrayed by the Thracian king Sitalces the son of Tereus and by a man from Abdera called Nymphodorus the son of Pythes; they were taken prisoner at Bisanthe on the Hellespont and shipped back to Attica, where they were executed by the Athenians, along with a Corinthian called Aristeas the son of Adeimantus. But this happened many years after Xerxes' expedition, and I now resume my earlier narrative.

[138] Although the ostensible target of Xerxes' expedition was Athens, it was in fact the whole of Greece. The Greeks had been aware of this for a long time, but they did not all react in the same way. Some of them had given earth and water to the Persian king and so were confident that he would not harm them. Others, however, had not given these tokens of submission and so were terrified, first because there were not enough ships in Greece to con-

front the Persian advance, and second because most of them did
not want to take an active part in the war, and were therefore
eagerly collaborating with the Persians.

[139] At this point I feel impelled to express an opinion which
I am not going to keep to myself, despite the fact that it will offend
a great many people, because I believe it to be true. If the Athenians had taken fright at the danger that was bearing down on them
and had abandoned their country, or if they had stayed put where
they were but had surrendered to Xerxes, no one would have tried
to resist Xerxes at sea. What would have happened on land, then?
Even if the Peloponnesians had built wall after defensive wall across
the Isthmus, the Lacedaemonians would still have been let down
by their allies, not out of deliberate treachery, but because they
would have had no choice, in the sense that they would have fallen
one by one to the Persian fleet. So the Lacedaemonians would have
been left all alone, and in that situation they would have shown
their mettle and fought bravely and well—and died nobly. Or an
alternative scenario, instead of this one, is that before matters
went this far they would have seen that the rest of Greece was collaborating with the Persians and so they would have come to terms
with Xerxes. But in either case Greece would have come under
Persian rule, because I cannot see what good the defensive wall
built across the Isthmus would have done with Xerxes controlling
the sea.

As things are, however, anyone who claims that the Athenians
proved themselves to be the saviours of Greece would be perfectly
correct, because the scales were bound to tilt in favour of whichever
side Athens joined. Once they had decided that their preference was
for Greece to remain free, it was they who aroused the whole of
the rest of Greece (except those places which were already collaborating with the Persians) and, with the help of the gods, repelled
the king's advance. Not even the fearsome and alarming oracles
that came from Delphi persuaded them to abandon Greece; they
held firm and found the courage to withstand the invader of their
country.

[140] For when some emissaries sent from Athens to Delphi
entered the temple and took their places (after having performed
the prescribed rites in the sanctuary and generally prepared
themselves to consult the oracle), the Pythia, whose name was
Aristonice, gave them the following prophecy:

Fools, why sit you here? Fly to the ends of the earth,
Leave your homes and the lofty heights girded by your city.
The head is unstable, the trunk totters; nothing—
Not the feet below, nor the hands, nor anything in between—
Nothing endures; all is doomed. Fire will bring it down,
Fire and bitter War, hastening in a Syrian chariot.
Many are the strongholds he will destroy, not yours alone;
Many the temples of the gods he will gift with raging fire,
Temples which even now stand streaming with sweat
And quivering with fear, and down from the roof-tops
Dark blood pours, foreseeing the straits of woe.
Go! Leave my temple! Shroud your hearts in misery!

[141] These words completely disheartened the Athenian emissaries. The doom foretold for them plunged them into utter despair, but then Timon the son of Androbulus, who was one of the most distinguished men in Delphi, suggested that they should go back, this time with branches of supplication, and consult the oracle again, as suppliants. The Athenians took his advice and said to the god, 'Lord, please respect these branches with which we come before you as suppliants, and grant us a more favourable prediction for our country. Otherwise we will never leave your temple, but will stay right here until we die.' At this request of theirs the oracle's prophetess gave them a second prophecy, which went as follows:

No, Pallas Athena cannot placate Olympian Zeus,
Though she begs him with many words and cunning arguments.
I shall tell you once more, and endue my words with adamant:
While all else that lies within the borders of Cecrops' land
And the vale of holy Cithaeron is falling to the enemy,
Far-seeing Zeus gives you, Tritogeneia, a wall of wood.
Only this will stand intact and help you and your children.
You should not abide and await the advance of the vast host
Of horse and foot from the mainland, but turn your back
And yield. The time will come for you to confront them.
Blessed Salamis, you will be the death of mothers' sons
Either when the seed is scattered or when it is gathered in.

[142] This oracle was less harsh than the previous one, and that is certainly what the emissaries thought, so they had it written down and then returned to Athens. Back in Athens, they gave their report to the people, and various interpretations of the meaning of

the oracle were proposed. The two which clashed most strongly were as follows. Some of the more elderly citizens argued for the view that the god was predicting the survival of the Acropolis; in times past the Athenian Acropolis had been surrounded by a defensive stockade, so they came to the conclusion that the 'wall of wood' referred to this stockade. Others, however, maintained that the god was talking about ships, and tried to get the Athenian people to abandon everything else and concentrate on preparing a fleet. But those who claimed that the 'wall of wood' meant ships failed to make sense of the last two lines of the Pythia's prophecy:

> Blessed Salamis, you will be the death of mothers' sons
> Either when the seed is scattered or when it is gathered in.

The view that the 'wall of wood' was a fleet was confounded by these words, because the official interpreters of oracles took them to mean that if the Athenians took steps to engage the enemy at sea off Salamis, they were bound to lose.

[143] Now, there was in Athens a man called Themistocles the son of Neocles who had just recently risen to a position of prominence. He claimed that the conclusion the interpreters had come to was not quite right. His argument was that if the oracle had really been directed against Athens it would have been phrased in harsher terms; rather than 'Blessed Salamis', it would have said 'Cruel Salamis' if the inhabitants were doomed to die there. No, the true interpretation of the oracle, he argued, was that the Persians, not the Athenians, were the target of the god's words. So he advised them to get the fleet ready for a battle at sea, on the grounds that the 'wall of wood' referred to the fleet. The Athenians decided that Themistocles' explanation of the oracle was preferable to that of the official interpreters who would rather they did not prepare for battle—whose advice, in fact, was that the Athenians should not resist at all, but should abandon Attica and find somewhere else to live.

[144] This was not the first time that Themistocles' point of view had prevailed at an important moment. Once before, when there were huge surpluses of public funds generated by the mines at Laurium and the Athenians were planning to divide it among themselves at the rate of ten drachmas a man, Themistocles had persuaded them to drop this idea of sharing the money out and to use

it instead to build two hundred ships for the war, by which he meant the war against Aegina—a war which, at the time in question, proved to be the salvation of Greece, because it forced the Athenians to turn to the sea. In fact, the ships were not deployed in the war for which they had been built, but they were available at Greece's hour of need. So Athens had already built these ships, and they felt obliged to undertake a further programme of ship-building as well. After due consideration, prompted by the oracle, they decided to go along with the god's advice and commit all their personnel to meeting the Persian invasion of Greece at sea, with the assistance of any other Greeks who were prepared to join them.

[145] So much for the oracles received by the Athenians. All the Greeks who had the best interests of Greece at heart held a meeting at which they exchanged opinions and pledges. The first concrete result of the debate was that they decided to lay aside all mutual antagonism and end any wars that were currently being fought among themselves. There were a number of these conflicts outstanding, but the most serious one was the war between Athens and Aegina. Once they learnt that Xerxes and his army were at Sardis, they also decided to send spies to Asia to keep an eye on Persian affairs. Other messengers were to be dispatched to Argos, to see if they would join the league against Persia, and to Sicily (specifically to Gelon the son of Deinomenes), Corcyra, and Crete to ask for help for Greece. The idea was to try to find a way to unite the whole of the Greek world—to get everyone to think and act in concert—on the grounds that all Greeks were equally threatened by the imminent danger. Gelon was supposed to have enormous resources, far greater than those available to anyone else in Greece.

[146] Their first step, once they had formed these plans and patched up their feuds, was to send three spies into Asia. These men went to Sardis and carefully observed Xerxes' army, but they were caught and interrogated by the commanders of the land army. They were condemned to death, and were just being taken away for execution when Xerxes found out what was happening. He disapproved of the commanders' decision and sent some of his personal guards with instructions to bring the spies back to him, if they found them alive, which they did. They brought them before the king, and so he found out why they had come to Sardis. His reaction was to tell his guards to take the men on a guided tour of

the whole of his infantry and his cavalry, and when they had feasted their eyes on everything to send them unharmed on their way to any country they wanted.

[147] The reason he made these arrangements, he explained, was that the execution of the spies would have deprived the Greeks of the opportunity to gain advance notice of the incredible size of his forces. The loss of three men would hardly have hurt his enemies, but if the spies got back to Greece, he said, the news of his immense power would in all probability make the Greeks give up their own freedom without the expedition even taking place, so that the Persians would not have to trouble themselves with undertaking a campaign.

There was another occasion when his thinking ran along similar lines. When he was in Abydus he saw supply ships carrying grain through the Hellespont from the Euxine Sea, on their way to Aegina and the Peloponnese. When some of his courtiers realized that these were enemy ships, they were prepared to seize them and they glanced at the king, waiting for him to give the order. Xerxes asked them where the ships were sailing to. 'To your enemies, master,' they said, 'with a cargo of grain.' And he replied, 'Well, isn't our destination the same as theirs? And isn't grain included among our supplies? So they're taking the grain there for us—what's wrong with that?'

[148] So the spies were sent home to Europe after having a good look around. The next thing the Greeks in league against the Persians did, after sending the spies off on their mission, was send a delegation to Argos. Now, according to the Argives, they had already been informed at the beginning about the Persian initiative against Greece, and they realized that the Greeks would try to enlist their support against the Persians, so they sent emissaries to Delphi to ask the god what would be the most advantageous course for them to take, considering that the loss of six thousand men, killed by Lacedaemonian troops under Cleomenes the son of Anaxandridas, was still in the recent past. It was this loss, in fact, they say, that prompted them to consult Delphi. The reply they received to their question from the Pythia was as follows:

> Argos, loathed by your neighbours, but dear to the immortal
> gods—
> Keep your spear indoors, take up a defensive position.
> Defend the head, and the head will preserve the body.

This statement by the Pythia had been made some time before. When the Greek delegation arrived in Argos, they presented themselves before the Council and delivered the message they had been entrusted with. The Argive reply was that they were ready to comply, as long as they got Lacedaemonian agreement to a 30-year peace treaty with them and as long as they were given the command of half the allied forces. They claimed that it would be only fair, in fact, for them to have full command, but that they would still be satisfied with half.

[149] Now, the oracle had forbidden the Argives from entering into an alliance with the Greeks, but despite that, in this Argive version of events, the Council gave this reply to the messengers. Their desire for a 30-year treaty outweighed their anxieties about the oracle, because they wanted their sons to be able to reach adulthood in this period. They were worried, they said, in case without such a treaty they might find themselves under Lacedaemonian control for ever, if on top of the calamity that had already befallen them they met with another disaster, this time at the hands of the Persians. The Spartan members of the Greek delegation replied to the Council's proposals by saying that they would refer the matter of the treaty back to a more numerous body than they constituted, but they had been authorized to respond on the question of leadership. And so they pointed out that they had two kings, whereas the Argives had only one, and that while this made it impossible for either of the two Spartan kings to lose his command, there was nothing to stop the Argive king's views carrying the same weight as those of their two kings. Faced with this situation, the Argives claim, they were so disgusted by the Spartiates' selfishness that they preferred to be ruled by the Persians rather than give way to the Lacedaemonians; so they told the Greek delegation that they had to leave Argive territory before sunset, or else be treated as enemies.

[150] So much for the Argive version of these events. Throughout Greece, however, one hears a different version, to the effect that Xerxes sent a herald to Argos before committing himself to the invasion of Greece. On arriving in Argos the Persian herald is supposed to have said, 'Men of Argos, here is the message from King Xerxes to you: "According to our traditions, we are descended from Perses, whose father Perseus was the son of Danaë, and whose mother was Andromeda the daughter of Cepheus—which means

that we are descended from Argive stock. It follows that it would be wrong for us to make war on you, since you are our ancestral line, and it would be wrong for you to take up arms against us by siding with others; instead you should keep yourselves to yourselves and stay where you are. After all, if everything goes according to plan, you will be second to none in my estimation." '

According to this version of events, the Argives were so taken by Xerxes' message that they did not put themselves forward or make any demands on the Greeks at the time, but later, when the Greeks tried to enlist their support, they made the demands mentioned above because they knew that the Lacedaemonians would refuse them any share in the leadership and so they would have an excuse for doing nothing.

[151] There are people in Greece who claim that the following story, which concerns events that happened many years later, confirms this alternative version. An Athenian delegation consisting of Callias the son of Hipponicus and several colleagues happened to have gone to the Memnonian city, Susa, on other business, and they coincided with an Argive delegation which had been sent to ask Artaxerxes the son of Xerxes whether the pact of friendship they had entered into with Xerxes was still in place, or whether Artaxerxes regarded them as enemies. King Artaxerxes assured them that the pact was definitely still in place, and that there was no city which found more favour with him than Argos.

[152] Now, I am not in a position to say with absolute certainty that Xerxes did send this message to Argos and that an Argive delegation did go to Susa to ask Artaxerxes about their friendship. The only version of events I am prepared to affirm is the one told by the Argives themselves. I do, however, know this much: if everyone in the world were to bring his own problems along to market with the intention of trading with his neighbours, a glimpse of his neighbours' problems would make him glad to take back home the ones he came with. In other words, there are worse things in the world than what the Argives did. I am obliged to record the things I am told, but I am certainly not required to believe them—this remark may be taken to apply to the whole of my account. After all, one can also hear it said that it was actually the Argives who invited the Persians to invade Greece, since they had come off badly in their conflict with the Lacedaemonians and felt that any situation was preferable to their present distress.

[153] So much for what was said about the Argives. The allies also sent another deputation (which included Syagrus, who was the Lacedaemonian representative) to Sicily, to meet with Gelon. Now, Gelon was descended from a man who was born on the island of Telos, off Triopium, but who settled in Gela. When Gela was colonized by emigrants from Lindos in Rhodes, led by Antiphemus, this ancestor of Gelon's went with them. In time this man's descendants came to hold, as a hereditary post, the priesthood of the chthonian goddesses. The first of their forebears to gain the office was a man called Telines. What happened was that some Geloans came off worst in a political dispute and were banished to the town of Mactorium, inland from Gela, and Telines managed to restore them to Gela without relying on force of arms, but only the implements sacred to the goddesses. I cannot say where he got these implements from, or whether they were actually his already, but in any case he used them to restore the exiles, on the condition that his descendants should hold the priesthood of the goddesses. This is the information I was given, but it seems remarkable to me that Telines managed to achieve such a difficult feat—the kind of feat that is normally achieved only by men of exceptional bravery and manly strength—when according to the inhabitants of Sicily Telines was, on the contrary, a rather soft and effeminate person.

[154] So that is how Telines gained this office. When the tyrant of Gela, Cleander the son of Pantares, died (or rather, was killed by a Geloan called Sabyllus), after a reign of seven years, his brother Hippocrates became tyrant. On his accession Gelon, who was a descendant of Telines the priest, served among his personal guards—a sizeable unit which also included Aenesidemus the son of Pataïcus.† A short while later, however, he was promoted to the command of all the cavalry in recognition of his bravery, because whether they were besieging Callipolis and Naxos or Zancle and Leontini, or fighting a combined force of Syracusans and large numbers of native non-Greeks—wherever Hippocrates went to war, Gelon fought with the highest distinction. Apart from Syracuse, none of the places I have mentioned avoided being brought under Hippocrates' dominion. The Syracusans were defeated at the battle of the River Elorus, but the Corinthians and Corcyrans saved them by negotiating a deal whereby Syracuse had to give Hippocrates the town of Camarina, which was originally a Syracusan settlement.

[155] Hippocrates had been tyrant for the same number of years as his brother when he met death at the town of Hybla during a war against the Sicelians. Gelon then pretended to support Hippocrates' sons Euclides and Cleander against the Geloans, who wanted an end to their subjection, but in fact, once he had defeated the Geloans in battle, he usurped the kingdom from Hippocrates' sons and installed himself as tyrant instead. After this piece of good fortune, a coup at Syracuse resulted in the expulsion of the Landowners, as they are called, by the general populace and the Landowners' own slaves (who are known as the Cyllyrians); Gelon engineered the return of the Landowners from their new base in Casmene to Syracuse and added Syracuse to the places under his control, because no sooner had he set out against them than the Syracusan people surrendered both themselves and the city to him.

[156] Now that he had Syracuse, he was less interested in the government of Gela; he let his brother Hiero take care of Gela while he proceeded to strengthen Syracuse, which was the only place he cared about. In no time at all Syracuse shot up and began to flourish. In the first place, he demolished the town of Camarina and moved all the inhabitants to Syracuse, where he enrolled them as citizens, and then he did the same to half the inhabitants of Gela. Also, when the Megarian community in Sicily agreed to terms after being besieged by him, he took the men of substance, and instead of killing them as they expected, because it was they who had started the war, he moved them to Syracuse and added them to the citizen body. As for the general Megarian populace, who were not to blame for the war and therefore expected to remain unpunished, he brought them to Syracuse too—and sold them for export from Sicily. He treated the Euboean community in Sicily in exactly the same way, with the same distinction between rich and poor. The reason for this, in both cases, was that he regarded the general populace as extremely annoying to live with. So these tactics had enabled Gelon to become a tyrant of considerable importance.

[157] To resume: when the Greek deputation arrived in Syracuse, they met with Gelon and said, 'The Lacedaemonians and their allies have charged us with trying to enlist your help against Persia. You have heard, of course, about the threat to Greece, and how a Persian is planning to bridge the Hellespont, bring an army drawn from all over the east out of Asia, and invade Greece. He claims that Athens is his target, but in fact he intends to gain control over

the whole of Greece. Now, you have gained a position of great power, and your rulership of Sicily means that quite a large portion of Greece is in your hands, so we are asking you to support those of us who are fighting for the freedom of Greece and join our struggle. With all Greece united, we form a powerful body of fighting men and we become a match for the invaders, but if some of us sell out and others refuse to help, and if the sound part of Greece remains small, then there is a distinct danger of the whole of Greece falling into hostile hands. If Xerxes defeats *us* in battle and makes us his subjects, you should not expect him not to pay *you* a visit. No, you should take precautions: by helping us you are helping yourself. Well-planned action invariably wins a favourable outcome.'

[158] In response Gelon laid into them. 'It is only self-interest,' he said, 'that has made you Greeks dare to come here and ask me to join forces with you against Persia. But I asked you, some time ago, to help me take on a foreign enemy, when I was locked in combat with the Carthaginians; I urged you to avenge the murder of Dorieus the son of Anaxandridas by the Segestans; I offered to help you liberate the trading-centres which have proved highly advantageous and profitable to you. But did you come to help? No, not for my sake or to avenge the murder of Dorieus. For all you care, the whole of Sicily might be in foreign hands. As it happens, though, things went well for us, and our position even improved. But now it's your turn: war has come to you, and now you think of Gelon. Still, although your treatment of me was disgraceful, I will not reciprocate. I am in fact prepared to help you by providing 200 triremes, 20,000 hoplites, and contingents, each 2,000 strong, of archers, slingers, and light-armed horsemen. I also guarantee to supply the whole Greek army with grain for the duration of the war. There is one condition, however: that I should be the supreme commander of the Greek forces against Persia. If this condition isn't met, I won't come myself and I won't send any troops either.'

[159] This was too much for Syagrus. ' "Surely he would groan aloud",' he said. 'Agamemnon the son of Pelops would groan long and loud, if he heard that Spartiates had been robbed of their leadership by Gelon and Syracusans. Enough! Let's hear no more of this idea that we should surrender the command to you! If you want to help Greece, fine—but rest assured that it will be under

Lacedaemonian leadership. If you can't stand taking orders from others, you'd better not join in.'

[160] Faced with the hostility evident in Syagrus' words, Gelon came up with his final offer. 'My Spartiate friend,' he said, 'when insults descend on a man his anger tends to rise. However, although your words were patently insulting, you haven't persuaded me to be rude in return. Given how strongly attached to the leadership you are, it's hardly surprising that I should be even more attached to it, since I have under my command an army many times the size of yours and a much larger fleet. But in view of your antagonism, we will moderate our original proposal. If you lead the land army, I will have the fleet; or if you prefer the naval command, I am perfectly prepared to take the land army. It's up to you: you must either be content with this proposal or leave here without gaining the kind of reinforcements I have offered.'

[161] It was the Athenian representative who replied to this offer of Gelon's, cutting in before Syagrus had a chance to speak. 'Syracusan king,' he said, 'Greece sent us on this mission to you because we needed an army, not a leader, but you seem to be refusing to send an army unless you achieve your goal of winning a position of authority over Greece. As long as† you were asking for the supreme command of the Greek forces in their entirety, we Athenians were happy to keep quiet, because we knew that the Laconian representative would be capable of replying for us as well. But now that you have withdrawn to a position of asking for the command of the fleet rather than all the Greek forces, we should tell you how things stand. Even if the Laconian representative were prepared to let you gain control of the navy, we would not. The navy is ours, unless the Lacedaemonians themselves want it. If they want this command, we won't stand in their way, but we won't let anyone else have it. It would make a nonsense of our having acquired the largest seagoing force in Greece if we were to concede the command to Syracuse. After all, we are Athenians, the most ancient race in Greece, the only ones to have remained in the same homeland for all our history. Even the epic poet Homer declared that at Ilium there was no one better at deploying and marshalling troops than an Athenian, so there is no blame attached to us for saying it.'

[162] 'Yes, my Athenian friend,' Gelon replied, 'it looks as though you have the commanders—but you won't have the men

for them to command. Since you obstinately refuse to give anything away, but want it all, the sooner you leave, the better. Go home and tell Greece that the spring has been taken from her year.'

[163] After conducting this business with Gelon, the delegation set sail for Greece. The situation did cause Gelon some alarm, in case Greece might not have the resources to overcome Persia, but he could not stand the idea of going to the Peloponnese and having to take orders from Lacedaemonians, when he was the tyrant of Sicily; he found that prospect intolerable. So having ignored that path, he took another one. As soon as he heard that Xerxes had crossed the Hellespont, he sent to Delphi a man from Cos, Cadmus the son of Scythes, with an escort of three penteconters. Cadmus carried with him a great deal of money and words of friendship, and his instructions were to wait and see which way the war went. If Xerxes won, he was to give him the money, and also earth and water on behalf of Gelon's subjects, whereas if the Greeks won, he was to return to Sicily.

[164] Some time earlier, Cadmus had become the tyrant of Cos on his father's death. Although his reign was secure and he was in no danger, from a sense of justice he voluntarily handed the reins of government over to the Coan populace. He then emigrated to Sicily, where he took over the city of Zancle from the Samians and settled there, changing its name to Messana. So this was how a sense of justice brought Cadmus to Sicily, and it was because Gelon knew him as an honest man from personal experience as well that he gave him this mission. Perhaps the most significant testimony Cadmus left to his morality, in a lifetime of moral behaviour, was that although he could have seized the enormous sum of money Gelon had entrusted to him, since it was his to dispose of, he did not choose to do so, and after the Greek victory at sea and Xerxes' retreat, he returned to Sicily with the full amount of money.

[165] Another story one hears from the inhabitants of Sicily is that even though it would have involved taking orders from the Lacedaemonians, Gelon would have helped Greece if it had not been for the actions taken by Terillus the son of Crinippus after his expulsion from Himera by the king of Acragas, Theron the son of Aenesidemus. At more or less the same time as the events we have been talking about, Terillus brought to Sicily an army of 300,000 Phoenicians, Libyans, Iberians, Ligyes, Elisyces, Sardonians, and Cyrnians, under the command of the Carthaginian king, Hamilcar

the son of Hanno. One of the things which persuaded Hamilcar to support this invasion was that he was a guest-friend of Terillus, but the decisive factor was the enthusiasm for the project displayed by Anaxilaus the son of Cretines. Anaxilaus, who was married to Terillus' daughter Cydippe, and who was the tyrant of Rhegium, gave Hamilcar his own children as sec rity and brought him in to support his father-in-law's attack on Sicily. It was because of this situation, they say, that Gelon could not help the Greek war effort, and so sent the money to Delphi instead.

[166] The Sicilians also say that the day on which Gelon and Theron beat Hamilcar of Carthage in Sicily happened to be the very same day that the Greeks beat Xerxes at Salamis. Hamilcar—a Carthaginian on his father's side, but his mother was from Syracuse—had become the king of the Carthaginians thanks to his courage. My information is that during the battle, when defeat was imminent, he vanished and was never seen again, alive or dead, anywhere on earth, although Gelon searched for him everywhere.

[167] The Carthaginians themselves have a plausible explanation for this. They say that throughout the battle between their non-Greek troops and the Greeks (in other words, from early in the morning until late in the evening, because that is how long the engagement lasted), Hamilcar stayed in the camp burning sacrificial animals whole on a huge pyre and seeking favourable omens; he happened to be pouring libations on the victims when he saw that his troops were being repulsed, and he threw himself into the flames. So the reason he was never found, on this account, is that he was burnt to ashes. In any case, whether this Phoenician explanation for Hamilcar's disappearance is correct, or whether something else happened, as the Carthaginians and Syracusans say,† the Phoenicians offer him sacrifices and have built monuments in his memory throughout their colonies, including their most important colony, Carthage itself. Anyway, so much for events in Sicily.

[168] Here is what the Corcyrans said and did in response to the Greek delegation. They were visited by the same group of messengers as had gone to Sicily, and the arguments used to appeal for their assistance were identical to the ones used on Gelon. Their immediate reaction was to promise to send reinforcements and to help the war effort, on the grounds that they could not just stand by and watch Greece being destroyed. After all, they said, the fall of Greece would inevitably be followed the very next

day by the loss of their own freedom, so they had to do all they could to help.

This response of theirs had a specious attractiveness, but their sympathies lay elsewhere, and when it came to actually sending help they did man sixty ships, which eventually set sail, but then they put in at the Peloponnese and rode at anchor off Pylos and Taenarum in Lacedaemon, while they too waited to see how the war would turn out. They did not anticipate a Greek victory, but expected that the Persians would easily win and would gain control over the whole of Greece. So their actions were deliberately designed to enable them to say to Xerxes, 'My lord, because of our considerable resources, and because we could have supplied a good number of ships—more than anyone else except Athens, in fact— the Greeks tried to enlist our help in the war, but we did not want to oppose you or do anything that might displease you.'

They hoped that this speech would win them better treatment than the other Greek states, and I imagine that is exactly what would have happened. But they also prepared an excuse they could offer to the Greeks, which they did in fact resort to later, because when the Greeks accused them of not sending help, they said that they had manned sixty ships, but then found it impossible to round Cape Malea because of the Etesian winds. That, they said, was why they had failed to reach Salamis; it was certainly not cowardice that had made them miss the battle. This was how they deflected the Greeks.

[169] The response of the Cretan communities to the Greeks appointed to try to enlist their help was jointly to send emissaries to Delphi to ask the god whether it was to their advantage to help Greece. The Pythia's reply was as follows: 'Fools, are all the tears Minos has made you shed for the help you gave Menelaus not enough for you? And what was the reason for Minos' anger? Because you helped the Greeks avenge the abduction of the woman from Sparta by a foreigner, while they did not help avenge his death in Camicus.' When the Cretans heard this reply, they refrained from providing any assistance.

[170] For there is a story that Minos' search for Daedalus took him to Sicania (now called Sicily), where he met a violent death. After a while, at the god's urging, all the Cretans except the Polichnians and the Praesians launched a major military strike against Sicania. For five years there they besieged the town of Camicus

(which is inhabited nowadays by people originally from Acragas), but they were unable to take it, and could not stay any longer either since they were faced with starvation, so they eventually abandoned the siege and set off back home. During their return voyage, when they were off Iapygia they met a heavy storm and were driven ashore. Their boats were wrecked and they could no longer find any way of getting back to Crete, so they stayed where they were, founded the community of Hyria, and became Messapians of Iapygia instead of Cretans, exchanging life on an island for life on the mainland. Now, various colonies were founded from Hyria, and it was these colonies that the people of Tarentum were trying to lay waste, many years later, when they suffered a major defeat. In fact, this is the greatest slaughter of a Greek population that we know of. It was not only the people of Tarentum who were involved in the disaster, but the citizens of Rhegium too, who went to support the Tarentines, at the insistence of Micythus the son of Choerus. Three thousand died from Rhegium, and there was no counting the number of Tarentines who lost their lives. Micythus, a former house-slave of Anaxilaus, had been left in charge of Rhegium; he was the man who was banished from Rhegium, moved to Tegea in Arcadia, and set up all those statues in Olympia.

[171] However, this incident involving Rhegium and Tarentum is an addendum to my account. According to the Praesians Crete, which was now depopulated, was colonized by others, especially Greeks. Then, two generations after Minos' death, the Trojan War took place, and it is clear that Menelaus received help of high quality from Cretans during the war. But when they got back from Troy their payment was that both they and their domestic animals were stricken with starvation and disease, until Crete was once again depopulated. Present-day Cretans are a third wave of immigrants, and share the island with the remnants of the previous inhabitants. So that is what the Pythia was reminding them of when they were planning to help the Greek war effort.

[172] The Thessalians originally collaborated with the Persians only because they had no choice in the matter. They made it plain that they did not like what the Aleuadae were up to, because as soon as they learnt that Xerxes was poised to enter Europe, they sent messengers to the Isthmus, where representatives from all over Greece—at least, from those Greek states which had the best interests of Greece at heart—had gathered for a conference. When the

Thessalian messengers got there they addressed them as follows: 'Men of Greece, if you want to shelter not just Thessaly but the whole of Greece from war, you have to guard the pass through Mount Olympus. We're ready to help you in this, but we can't do it alone: you must send a good-sized army. Otherwise, you can be sure that we will come to terms with Persia, because we don't feel that we should stand alone and die for you just because we're in such an exposed position compared to the rest of Greece. If you refuse to come to our help, there's no other pressure you can bring to bear on us, because we are already under the strongest pressure there is—impotence. We will try on our own to find some means of saving ourselves.' That was the Thessalians' speech.

[173] In response, the Greeks decided to send a land army by sea to Thessaly to guard the pass. The army duly assembled and set off by sea through the Euripus, to Alus in Achaea, where they disembarked and left their ships. From there they made their way to Thessaly and arrived at Tempe, where they pitched camp at the pass which runs beside the River Peneius from coastal Macedonia into Thessaly, between Mount Olympus and Mount Ossa. There were approximately ten thousand Greek hoplites assembled there, reinforced by Thessalian horsemen. The division commander who had been chosen to lead the Lacedaemonian troops, despite not being of royal lineage, was Euaenetus the son of Carenus, while the Athenians were under the command of Themistocles the son of Neocles. However, they stayed there only a few days, because a message arrived from Alexander of Macedonia, the son of Amyntas, advising them to pack up and leave the pass, without waiting to be trampled underfoot by the advancing army, whose size and naval capacity were detailed in the message. Now, this message seemed to them to contain good advice, and Alexander appeared sympathetic to the Greek cause, so they did as he suggested. It seems to me, however, that the deciding factor was fear, induced by the fact that they had found out that there was another route into Thessaly from inland Macedonia, running through Perrhaebia via Gonnus—which was in fact the route Xerxes' army took. So the Greeks returned to their fleet and made their way back to the Isthmus.

[174] So much for the expedition to Thessaly, which took place when Xerxes was on the verge of crossing over into Europe from Asia, and was already in Abydus. Given that they had been aban-

doned by their allies, the Thessalians did collaborate with the Persians—so wholeheartedly in fact, and with so little trace of their former hesitancy, that they turned out to be more useful to Xerxes in the war than anyone else.

[175] On arriving back at the Isthmus, the Greeks tried to decide, in view of what Alexander had said, how and where to wage war. The point of view that won the day was that they should defend the pass at Thermopylae. It looked narrower than the pass into Thessaly, and it was also nearer home.† They certainly did not know of the existence of the path which led to the downfall of those Greeks who fell at Thermopylae until they arrived there and heard about it from the Trachinians. So they decided to prevent the Persians from entering Greece by defending this pass. Meanwhile the fleet was to sail to Artemisium in Histiaeotis, so that each of the two forces would be close enough to learn the other's situation.

[176] The terrain in these two places is as follows, taking Artemisium first. The expanse of the Thracian Sea narrows down to a sound between the island of Sciathos and Magnesia on the mainland, and after this sound comes Artemisium, a beach on the Euboean coast, with its sanctuary of Artemis. As for the pass through Trachis, it is, at its narrowest point, only half a plethron wide. In actual fact, though, this is not the narrowest part of the region thereabouts; both before and after Thermopylae the pass narrows even further, until at Alpeni, which is after Thermopylae, it is no more than a cart-track, and before it, at the Phoenix River near the town of Anthela, it becomes a mere cart-track again. The western part of Thermopylae is a tall, sheer, inaccessible cliff which stretches away to Mount Oeta, while to the east of the road there is only marshland and the sea. In the pass there are warm bathing-pools, which the local inhabitants call the 'Pots', and an altar to Heracles is located there. There was once a wall built across the pass, with a gate added a long time ago. The Phocians built the wall, prompted by fear, when the Thessalians came from Thesprotia to live in Aeolis, which they now hold. So because the Thessalians were trying to conquer them, the Phocians took this precautionary measure, and also at roughly the same time let the warm water run down into the pass so as to corrugate the ground with gullies, and did everything they could to prevent the Thessalians invading their territory. The original wall had been built a

long time ago, and most of it was by now lying in ruins as a result
of the passage of time, but the Greeks decided to restore it there,
to keep the Persians out of Greece. There is a village lying very
close to the road, called Alpeni, and the Greeks reckoned on being
able to supply themselves with provisions from there.

[177] These, then, were the places that the Greeks thought
would suit them. They looked at all the possibilities and realized
that the Persians would be unable to take advantage of their superior numbers or make use of their horsemen there, so they decided
that this was the place to meet the invader on his way into Greece.
When news came that the Persians were in Pieria, they brought
their meeting to an end and set out from the Isthmus—the land
army for Thermopylae and the fleet for Artemisium.

[178] So the Greek forces went their separate ways to war, with
due speed. Meanwhile, the people of Delphi were busy consulting
the god because they were frightened about their own future and
that of Greece as a whole; the oracular response was that they were
to pray to the winds, which would prove to be important allies of
Greece. The first thing the Delphians did, having accepted the validity of the oracle, was communicate its details by messenger to the
Greeks who wanted freedom, and thereby earn the undying gratitude of these Greek states, who had been terrified of the invaders.
The next thing the Delphians did was build an altar to the winds
in Thyia (the place is named after Thyia, the daughter of Cephisus,
who has a precinct there), and offer propitiatory sacrifices to
them—a practice initiated by that oracle which has continued right
up to today.

[179] Xerxes' fleet was ready to set out from Therma, but first
their ten fastest ships headed for Sciathos, where there was an
advance guard of three Greek ships, one from Troezen, one from
Aegina, and one from Attica. At the sight of the Persian ships in
the distance, the Greeks fled.

[180] The Persians gave chase and the ship from Troezen, whose
captain was Praxinus, fell into their hands straight away. They then
took the best-looking marine on board up to the prow and slit his
throat, since they counted the best-looking of the first batch of
Greek prisoners they captured an auspicious sacrificial victim. The
name of the man who was slaughtered was Leon—a name which
was perhaps partly responsible for his fate.

[181] However, things did not go so smoothly for the Persians in the case of the Aeginetan trireme, under the command of Asonides. This was due to one of the marines, Pytheas the son of Ischenoüs, whose bravery was unsurpassed that day. Even after the capture of his ship, he fought on until his whole body had been hacked to pieces. At last he fell to the deck, but he was not dead. There was still breath in him, and the marines from the Persian ships were so impressed by his courage that they took a great deal of care to keep him alive. They dressed his wounds with myrrh and wrapped them in bandages made out of fine linen cloth, and when they got back to their encampment they proudly showed him off to the whole army and treated him well, while the rest of the prisoners from the Aeginetan ship were treated as slaves.

[182] So two of the Greek ships had been captured. As the third one, whose captain was an Athenian called Phormus, was trying to escape it ran aground on the silt-banks at the mouth of the Peneius, so that only the ship fell into Persian hands. None of the Athenian crew did, because as soon as they had run the ship aground, they leapt out and found their way back to Athens via Thessaly.

[183] Beacons on Sciathos let the Greeks who were stationed at Artemisium know what had happened. The news made them afraid, and they changed their anchorage from Artemisium to Chalcis so that they could guard the Euripus, but they left lookouts on the Euboean hills. Three of the ten Persian ships were dispatched† to the reef called Myrmeca, which lies between Sciathos and Magnesia. Once the Persians had taken a stone pillar out there and set it up on the reef, the whole fleet set out from Therma, now that the way was clear. It was eleven days since the king had marched out of Therma. The pilot who was particularly responsible for showing them the way through the reef in the sound was a man from Scyros called Pammon. After a full day's sailing the Persians reached Sepias in Magnesia—or rather the beach which lies between the town of Casthanaea and Cape Sepias.

[184] Now, so far, up to the time they reached Sepias and Thermopylae, the Persian forces had been unharmed. My estimate is that their numbers at this point were still as follows. First, on board the 1,207 ships from Asia, there was the original complement drawn from over Asia of 241,400 men, allowing for two hundred men per ship. Each of these ships also carried, in addition to their

native crew, thirty marines—Persians, Medes, and Sacae—who made up an additional complement of 36,210. I shall add on to these two figures the crews of the penteconters, on the assumption that there were more or less eighty men per penteconter. Since there were, as I mentioned earlier, three thousand of these boats, then there were presumably 240,000 men on board them. So the total naval force that was drawn from Asia comes to 517,610. There were 1,700,000 in the infantry and 80,000 in the cavalry. I shall also add the Arabian camel-riders and Libyan charioteers, of whom there were 20,000, by my calculations. The total number of men, therefore, from both the fleet and the land army comes to 2,317,610. And so far I have mentioned only the armed forces Xerxes brought from Asia itself, and I have not taken into account the camp-followers or the supply ships and their crews.

[185] Then there were the men brought from Europe; their numbers must still be added to this total, but only an estimate is possible. The Greeks from Thrace and the islands off Thrace provided a hundred and twenty ships, with 24,000 men on board. Then 300,000 would be my guess as to the number of men recruited into the land army from Thrace, Paeonia, Eordia, Bottiaeis, Chalcidice, Brygia, Pieria, Macedonia, Perrhaebia, Enienia, Dolopia, Magnesia, Achaea, and the communities on the Thracian coast. When all these tens of thousands are added to the figures from Asia, the total number of fighting men comes to 2,641,610.

[186] Given a fighting force this large, I imagine that the camp-followers and the crews of the light vessels for grain transport and also of all the other ships that accompanied the armed forces would surpass rather than fall short of the number of fighting men. But suppose I assume that there was exactly the same amount, neither more nor less. In that case, for every ten thousand fighting men, there will be ten thousand of the others. It follows that the number of men led by Xerxes the son of Darius up to Sepias and Thermopylae was 5,283,220.

[187] This is the grand total of men in Xerxes' expeditionary force; as for the women—cooks and concubines—and eunuchs, no one can possibly know how many of them there were. The same goes for the yoke-animals and other beasts of burden, and the Indian dogs: again, no one could possibly give a reliable estimate of their numbers. In short, it does not surprise me in the slightest that the waters of some rivers should have failed; what I find far

more astonishing is the logistics of feeding all those tens of thousands of people. Suppose each person was given a choenix of wheat a day and no more, then 110,340 medimni would be used up every day, not counting the food consumed by the women, eunuchs, draught-animals, and dogs. Nevertheless, among all these thousands upon thousands of men, there was not one who had more of the looks or the height to deserve the position of supreme power than Xerxes himself.

[188] So the fleet set sail and put in at the beach between the town of Casthanaea and Cape Sepias in Magnesia, with the leading ships moored just offshore and the rest riding at anchor behind them. It is not a large beach, and so there were eight rows of ships at anchor projecting from the shore into the sea. They passed the night in this formation, but early in the morning there was a change in the clear, calm weather. The sea became choppy and they were lashed by a violent storm coming from the north-east on a strong wind—the wind called the Hellespontine by those living in the region. Some of the men noticed that the wind was rising and, if their mooring made it possible, they hauled their ships ashore before the storm struck; these were the crews and the ships that survived. All the ships which the storm found out at sea, however, were either driven on to the so-called Ovens of Mount Pelium or the beach, or wrecked on Cape Sepias itself or at the town of Meliboea, or run aground at Casthanaea. It was a monster of a storm, quite impossible to ride out.

[189] There is a story that the Athenians had appealed for help to Boreas, the north wind, as a result of receiving another oracle, this time urging them to appeal for help to their son-in-law. Now, according to Greek legend, Boreas, the north wind, is married to Orithyia, the daughter of Erechtheus—that is, a woman from Attica. The Athenians, it is reported, interpreted this as a marriage connection and concluded that Boreas was their son-in-law. So there they were, at battle stations off Chalcis in Euboeoa. At some point, either when they noticed that the storm was rising or before that, they performed sacrifices and called on Boreas and Orithyia to come to their aid and to destroy the Persian fleet, as they had before off Mount Athos. Now, whether or not this was why Boreas struck the Persians as they were lying at anchor, I cannot say. In any case, the Athenians say that Boreas had come to their help in the past and that on the occasion in question what happened was

his doing, and when they got home they built a sanctuary to him on the banks of the River Ilissus.

[190] The most conservative estimate of how many ships were lost in this disaster is four hundred, along with innumerable personnel, and so much valuable property that a Magnesian called Ameinocles the son of Cretines, who owned land near Sepias, profited immensely from this naval catastrophe. In the following days and months gold and silver cups were washed ashore in large numbers for him to pick up; he also found Persian treasure-chests, and in general became immeasurably wealthy. However, although he became very rich from all that he found, he was unlucky in other respects; like other people, he had his share of grief—in his case the horrible accident of killing his own child.

[191] An untold number of supply vessels, such as those carrying grain, were lost. In fact, the commanders of the fleet became worried about the Thessalians attacking them while they were vulnerable from the disaster, so they built a tall, protective palisade, made out of the remains of wrecked ships. The storm raged for three days. Finally, the Magi performed sacrifices and set about soothing the wind with spells, and also sacrificed to Thetis and the Nereids, until the storm died down on the fourth day—or maybe it did so of its own accord. They offered sacrifices to Thetis because the Ionians told them that this was the place from where she had been abducted by Peleus, and that the whole of Cape Sepias was sacred to her and her fellow Nereids.

[192] On the fourth day the storm stopped. The day after the start of the storm the look-outs on the Euboean hills raced down from their posts and let the Greeks know all about the wrecking of the fleet. When the Greeks heard the news, they gave prayers of thanks and poured libations to Poseidon the Saviour, and then sailed back as fast as they could to Artemisium, on the assumption that there would now be few ships to oppose them. Back in Artemisium, they remained at battle stations. This was the origin of the worship that still goes on at Athens of Poseidon as the Saviour.

[193] Once the wind had abated and the sea had grown calm, the Persians hauled their boats back down to the water and sailed along the coast of the mainland, around the Magnesian headland, and then straight into the gulf at the end of which Pagasae is situated. On this gulf in Magnesia there is a place where Heracles is

supposed to have been left behind by Jason and his companions
from the *Argo* during their voyage to Aea to fetch the fleece. He
had been sent ashore in search of water, because they were planning to stock up on water and then steer for the open sea—which
is why the place is called Aphetae. It was here that Xerxes' men
dropped anchor.

[194] Now, for some reason fifteen ships from the Persian fleet
put to sea long after the rest, and they somehow spotted the Greek
fleet at Artemisium. In fact, they thought it was their own fleet, and
they sailed right up to them—and fell into enemy hands! This
Persian squadron was under the command of a man from Cyme
who was the governor of Aeolis, Sandoces the son of Thamasius.
King Darius had once had him crucified, having found him guilty
of accepting a bribe to adjudicate a case unfairly when he was one
of the royal judges; but he continued to ponder the matter while
Sandoces was actually hanging on the cross, and he came to the
conclusion that his crimes against the royal house were outweighed
by the good he had done. At the same time he realized that he
had acted with more haste than wisdom, so he released him. So
Sandoces escaped death at the hands of King Darius and lived on,
but it was his fate not to escape a second time, when he sailed
into the Greek fleet. As soon as the Greeks saw the Persians
approaching them, they realized their mistake; they put to sea and
easily captured the enemy ships.

[195] On board one of these ships, and therefore captured by
the Greeks, was Aridolis, the tyrant of Alabanda in Caria. On
another ship was the commander of the Paphian troops, Penthylus
the son of Demonoüs, who had brought twelve ships from Paphos,
but had lost eleven of them in the storm off Sepias. Now he sailed
with his one remaining ship into Artemisium and was taken prisoner. The Greeks questioned these men, extracted all the information they wanted about Xerxes' army, and then sent them in chains
to the Corinthian Isthmus.

[196] So the Persian fleet (all except the fifteen ships under
Sandoces' command that I have mentioned) reached Aphetae, and
three days later Xerxes and the land army arrived at Malis, having
passed through Thessaly and Achaea. While he was in Thessaly,
Xerxes had set up a horse-race, pitting his own horses against the
local Thessalian stock, because he had heard that Thessalian horses
were the best in Greece. As a matter of fact, though, the Greek

horses were easily beaten. The only Thessalian river which proved insufficient for the army's needs and was drunk dry was the Onochonus, but in Achaea even the largest river, the Epidanus, was reduced to a trickle.

[197] While Xerxes was at Alus in Achaea his guides, who wanted to be generally informative, told him a local story, 'The Affair of the Sanctuary of Zeus the Devourer', to the effect that some time after Athamas the son of Aeolus had conspired with Ino and brought about Phrixus' death, an oracle instructed the Achaeans to impose on Phrixus' descendants the following ordeals: the senior member of the clan had to keep away from the People's House (as the Achaeans call their town hall), where they had guards posted. If he entered, he could not leave except to be sacrificed. Furthermore, the guides went on, the potential sacrificial victims fled out of fear in large numbers to another country, but as time went on they returned and, if they were captured entering the town hall, the guides explained how the one who was to be sacrificed was decked all over with garlands and accompanied out of the town hall with a ceremonial procession. It is the descendants of Phrixus' son Cytissorus who endure this rite, and the reason is that when an oracle told the Achaeans to make Athamas the son of Aeolus a scapegoat for their country and they were about to begin the ritual slaughter, Cytissorus came from Aea in Colchis and protected Athamas, and thereby brought the anger of the god down on his descendants. When Xerxes came near the sacred grove, after hearing this story, he not only kept away from it himself, but also gave orders that no one in his army was to go near it either, and he treated the house of the descendants of Athamas with the same reverence he showed the precinct.

[198] That is what happened in Thessaly and Achaea. After these regions, Xerxes came to Malis and followed the coastline of the gulf, where the sea rises and falls every day. The gulf is surrounded by a strip of low-lying land which varies in width from broad to narrow, and then there are the so-called Rocks of Trachis—tall, inaccessible mountains which enclose the whole of Malis. As one approaches the gulf from Achaea, the first community one comes to is Anticyra, on the River Spercheius, which rises in Enienian country and issues into the sea. About twenty stades further on there is another river called the Dyras; this is the river which, in legend, sprang out of the ground to help Heracles when

he was on fire. Another twenty stades away there is a third river, called the Black River.

[199] Five stades away from this Black River is the town of Trachis, built where the strip of land between the mountains and the sea is at its broadest; the plain here is 22,000 plethra in extent, in fact. South of Trachis the mountain range enclosing the area is broken by a gorge through which the River Asopus flows past the foothills of the mountains.

[200] South of the Asopus there is another river, not a large one, called the Phoenix, which rises in these mountains and joins the Asopus. This is where the strip of land is at its narrowest; a cart-track has been made there. Thermopylae is fifteen stades away from the Phoenix, but between the two lies the village of Anthela, which is on the Asopus where it issues into the sea. Here, where the strip of land is broad, there is a sanctuary of Demeter of the Amphictyons, with a meeting-place for the Amphictyons, and a shrine to Amphictyon himself.

[201] So King Xerxes took up a position at Malis in Trachis, while the Greeks were encamped in the pass at the place whose usual Greek name is Thermopylae, although the local inhabitants and their immediate neighbours call it just Pylae, the Gates. With the two armies in their respective positions, Xerxes was in control of everywhere from Trachis northwards, and the Greeks were in control of the whole Greek mainland to the south.

[202] The Greeks who stood against the Persian king at Thermopylae were as follows. As regards heavy infantry, there were 300 Spartiates, 500 from Tegea and another 500 from Mantinea, 120 from Orchomenus in Arcadia, and 1,000 from the rest of Arcadia; then there were 400 from Corinth, 200 from Phleious, and 80 from Mycenae. These were the Peloponnesian contingents, and then Boeotia supplied 700 from Thespiae and 400 from Thebes.

[203] Further heavy infantry was supplied by the Opuntian Locrians and Phocians; when summoned, the Locrians sent every available man and the Phocians sent a contingent of a thousand, since the allies sent messengers to them, appealing for help. In the message they claimed that they were no more than the advance guard of the Greek alliance and that the rest were expected any day; they added that the sea was being guarded and defended by the Athenians, Aeginetans, and other naval contingents. 'There is nothing for you to fear,' the message went on. 'After all, it is no

god, but a mortal human being who is advancing on Greece. At birth, for every man there is or ever shall be, misfortune is part of the mixture—and the greater the man the greater the misfortune. The invader is mortal, and therefore in his case too results will fail to live up to his expectations.' When they heard this the Locrians and Phocians sent help to Trachis.

[204] Each of these contingents had its own commander, supplied by the respective communities, but the supreme commander, and the most impressive man among them, was the Lacedaemonian, Leonidas the son of Anaxandridas. From Anaxandridas he traced his ancestry back to Heracles via Leon, Eurycratidas, Anaxander, Eurycrates, Polydorus, Alcamenes, Teleclus, Archelaus, Hegesilaus, Doryssus, Leobotes, Echestratus, Agis, Eurysthenes, Aristodamus, Aristomachus, Cleodaeus, and finally Hyllus, who was the son of Heracles. Leonidas had come to rule over Sparta as a result of an unforeseeable situation.

[205] Leonidas had no designs on the kingship because he had two elder brothers, Cleomenes and Dorieus. But then Cleomenes died without a male heir, and Dorieus was already dead too, having lost his life in Sicily, and so the kingdom devolved on to Leonidas, who was the natural choice because he was the older remaining son (Anaxandridas had another son, Cleombrotus, but he was the youngest) and also because he had married Cleomenes' daughter. So he went to Thermopylae then, with the traditional unit of three hundred select fighting men, all of whom already had sons. On his way he also recruited the Thebans I mentioned in the above list, whose commander was Leontiadas the son of Eurymachus. Leonidas singled these Thebans out and made a particular point of recruiting them, because they were strongly suspected of collaborating with the enemy. So he appealed for their help in the war because he wanted to find out whether they would supply men for him to take or whether they would shy away from such open support of the Greek alliance. They did send troops, but in fact their sympathies lay elsewhere.

[206] The Spartans sent Leonidas and his men on ahead in the hope that the sight would inspire the rest of the allies to arms, and discourage them from joining the ranks of those who were already collaborating with the enemy, as they might if they got the idea that the Spartans were holding back. Later—that is, after celebrating the festival of Carnea, which was holding them up—they planned

to waste no time in sending every available man to join Leonidas, leaving behind in Sparta only a defensive unit. In fact, the rest of the allies were also planning to do more or less the same: the Olympic festival happened to coincide with these events, so they all sent only an advance guard, because they did not expect the battle of Thermopylae to be decided so quickly.

[207] That was their intention, but meanwhile the Persians drew near the pass, and the thoughts of the terrified Greeks at Thermopylae turned to escape. The Peloponnesians in general were beginning to think that they should return to the Peloponnese and hold the Isthmus, but this idea made the Phocians and Locrians furious, so Leonidas voted in favour of their staying where they were, but at the same time sending messengers around the various towns and cities, ordering them to send aid, since there were not enough of them to resist the Persian army.

[208] The Greeks were busy trying to decide what to do when Xerxes sent a scout on horseback to see how many men he was up against and what they were doing. While still in Thessaly he had received a report that a small force, led by the Lacedaemonians and the Heraclid Leonidas, had assembled at the pass. So the scout approached the Greeks' camp and kept them under close surveillance; but he could not see the whole force, because some of them were out of sight behind the now-repaired wall, where they had taken up defensive positions. Others, however—and it happened at this time to be the Lacedaemonians—were posted outside, where their arms and armour lay in front of the wall, and he was able to take stock of them. He watched them in a variety of occupations, such as exercising naked and combing their hair; this surprised him, but he took careful note of their numbers and then made his way back to Xerxes, without meeting any opposition. No one set out after him, and in fact he met with total indifference. When he got back he gave Xerxes a thorough report on what he had seen.

[209] Xerxes listened to what the scout had to say, but he could not understand that in actual fact the Greeks were getting themselves ready to kill or be killed to the best of their ability. Their behaviour struck him as laughable. He sent for Demaratus the son of Ariston, who had accompanied the expedition, and asked him about everything in the scout's report, item by item, in an attempt to understand what was going on with the Lacedaemonians. 'I told you about these men before,' Demaratus said, 'when we were

setting out for Greece. You laughed at me then, and found my ideas about what would happen in this war absurd, just because I take pride in nothing so much as in trying to be honest to you, my lord. But listen to me now. These men have come to fight us for the pass and they are getting ready to do just that. It is their custom to do their hair when they are about to risk their lives. But you can rest assured that if you defeat these men and the force that awaits you in Sparta, there is no other race on earth which will take up arms and stand up to you, my lord, because you are now up against the noblest and most royal city in Greece, and the bravest men.'

Xerxes found what he was saying completely unbelievable and asked him again how such a small body of men was going to resist his army. 'My lord,' Demaratus replied, 'if things do not turn out as I say, you can treat me as you would any other liar.'

[210] Xerxes still did not believe him. He let four days go by, because he expected the Greeks to run away at any moment, but they did no such thing. What seemed to him to be their stupid impudence in staying stung him to anger, and on the fifth day he sent his Median and Cissian troops against them, with orders to bring some prisoners back alive to him. The Medes rushed the Greek position and died in large numbers, but more men pressed forward, and despite the heavy losses the attack was not driven back. They made it plain to everyone, however, and above all to the king himself, that although he had plenty of troops, he did not have many men. And so the battle continued all day.

[211] After a while the Median troops were withdrawn, badly mauled, and their place was taken by the Immortals, as Xerxes called them—the Persian battalion commanded by Hydarnes. It was expected that they would easily finish the job, but when they came to engage the Greeks, they were no more successful than the Medes had been. The result was no different, because the factors were the same: they were fighting in a restricted area, using spears which were shorter than those wielded by the Greeks, and could not take advantage of their numerical superiority. The Lacedaemonians fought a memorable battle; they made it quite clear that they were the experts, and that they were fighting against amateurs. This was particularly evident every time they turned tail and pretended to run away *en masse*; the Persians raised a great cry of triumph at the sight of the retreat and pressed forward after them, but the Lacedaemonians let them catch up and then suddenly

turned and faced them—and cut the Persians down in untold numbers. However, a few Spartiates would be lost as well during this manoeuvre. Once their attempt on the pass had proved a complete failure and they had not gained the slightest foothold in it, whether they sent in regiment after regiment or whatever tactics they used for their attack, the Persians withdrew.

[212] During this phase of the battle, as he watched his men attacking the Greek positions, it is said that fear for his army made the king leap up from his seat three times. The next day, after the first day of fighting had passed as described, the conflict went no better for the Persians. They went into battle in the expectation that the Greeks would no longer be capable of fighting back, given that there were so few of them and that they had already taken so many casualties. But the Greeks formed themselves into units based on nationality which took turns to fight, except for the Phocians who were posted on the heights above to guard the path. On finding that things had not changed from their experiences of the previous day, the Persians pulled back.

[213] Xerxes did not know how to cope with the situation, but then a Malian called Ephialtes the son of Eurydemus arranged a meeting with him, with information for which he hoped the king would pay him handsomely. Ephialtes told him about the mountain path to Thermopylae, and so caused the deaths of the Greeks who had taken their stand there. Later, he went into exile in Thessaly because he became afraid of reprisals from the Lacedaemonians, and while he was there the Amphictyons met at Pylaea and the Pylagori had him proclaimed a wanted criminal, with a price on his head. Later still, he was killed by a man from Trachis called Athenades—at some point he had returned from Thessaly and was living in Anticyra—and although Athenades' reasons for killing him, which I will explain later, had nothing to do with the battle of Thermopylae, the Lacedaemonians still honoured him for it. In any case, Ephialtes did die later.

[214] There is another story according to which Onetas the son of Phanagoras of Carystus and Corydallus of Anticyra were the ones who gave the king this information and showed the Persians the way around the mountain, but personally I do not believe it. In the first place, one must bear in mind that the Pylagori, representing the Greeks, did not put a price on the heads of Onetas and Corydallus, but on Ephialtes of Trachis, and they had presumably

carried out a thorough investigation of the facts. In the second place, we know that this was the reason for Ephialtes' exile. It is true that even though Onetas was not from Malis he could have known about this path, if he had often visited that part of the country, but in fact it was Ephialtes who showed the Persians the way around the mountain along the path, and I hereby record his guilt.

[215] Xerxes was delighted with Ephialtes' offer, which was just what he needed. He lost no time in sending Hydarnes and his men on this mission. They set off from the Persian camp at dusk. It was the local Malians who discovered this path. They once guided the Thessalians along it to attack the Phocians (this was the occasion when the Phocians built the defensive wall across the pass to guard against military incursion); in other words, the pernicious use of this discovery of theirs has been known to the Malians for a long time.

[216] Here is a description of the path. It begins where the River Asopus flows through the gorge, proceeds along the ridge of the mountain—the Anopaea, which is also what the path is called— and ends at Alpeni (which is the first settlement in Locris after the border with Malis), at the rock called the Melampygus, where the seats of the Cercopes are and the pass is at its narrowest point.

[217] So this is what the path is like. The Persians crossed the Asopus and made their way along the path throughout the night, with the heights of Oeta on their right and those of Trachis on their left. By daybreak they had reached the peak of the ridge where, as I said earlier, a thousand Phocian hoplites were on guard, with the job of protecting their own country and defending the path. Down below, the pass was being held by the Greeks already mentioned, but the path across the mountain was being guarded by Phocian volunteers who had put themselves forward to Leonidas for the job.

[218] The Phocians did not notice the Persians as they were on their way up, because an oak forest entirely covers the slopes of the mountain. However, they perceived their presence once they were at the top because it was quiet and calm and the Persians naturally could not avoid making a great deal of noise by stepping on the leaves under their feet. The Phocians had only just got to their feet and were still arming themselves when the Persians reached them—and were astonished at the sight, because they had not

expected to meet any opposition, and here were men arming themselves for battle. Hydarnes asked Ephialtes what country the enemy force was from, because he was worried in case the Phocians might be Lacedaemonians. Ephialtes put him right, and then Hydarnes got his men into battle formation. The Phocians came under fire from a hail of arrows and retreated up to the top of the mountain; they were convinced that the attack was aimed exclusively at them, so they prepared to fight to the death. It was this conviction that prompted their retreat, but Ephialtes, Hydarnes, and the Persians just ignored them and quickly got on with climbing down the mountain.

[219] The first warning the Greeks in Thermopylae got was when the diviner Megistias inspected the entrails of his sacrificial victims and declared that death would come to them at dawn; secondly, and also while it was still dark, some deserters told them that the Persians were circling around behind them. Thirdly, after daybreak, the look-outs ran down from the heights to warn them. The Greeks discussed what they should do, but there was no unanimity: some argued for not abandoning their post, others put the opposite case. Subsequently, after the meeting had broken up, some of the Greeks began to trickle away back to their various home towns all over Greece, while others prepared to stay where they were with Leonidas.

[220] One also hears it said that Leonidas himself told them to leave because he wanted to spare their lives, but believed that it would be wrong for him and the Spartiates who were there to desert the post they had originally been sent to hold. On this version of events, which I myself strongly incline towards, when Leonidas saw that his allies were demoralized, and unhappy about facing the coming danger with him, he told them that they could go, but that it would not be right for him to leave. Staying there would, he felt, win great renown, and would also preserve Sparta in its prosperity. For in the very early days of the war the Spartiates had consulted the oracle at Delphi about the coming conflict, and the Pythia had predicted that either Lacedaemon would be laid waste by the Persians or their king would die. The prediction, in hexameters, went as follows:

Here is your fate, inhabitants of spacious Sparta:
Either your great and glorious city will be destroyed
By men descended from Perseus, or that will not be,

But the borders of Lacedaemon will mourn the death
Of a king descended from Heracles. For neither the might
Of bulls nor yet that of lions will check the foe head on,
Since he has the might of Zeus. Nor, I declare, will he
Be checked until one of the two has been thoroughly rent asunder.

So I think it was reflection on this prophecy, combined with his
desire to lay up a store of fame for the Spartiates alone, that
prompted Leonidas to let the allied personnel go. I prefer this to
the view that those who left went in disarray after a difference of
opinion.

[221] I have a telling piece of evidence to support this view too,
which is that Leonidas made no attempt to hide the fact that his
reason for sending Megistias away was so that he might avoid
sharing their fate. Megistias of Acarnania (who is said to trace his
ancestry back to Melampus) was the diviner who was attached to
this Greek force; it was he who foretold what was going to happen
by inspecting the entrails of his sacrificial victims. However,
although he had permission to go, he stayed, but sent away his only
child, a son, who had come along on the expedition.

[222] So off went the allied personnel Leonidas had told to
leave, in obedience to his wishes. Only the Thespians and the
Thebans stayed behind to support the Lacedaemonians. The
Thebans did so reluctantly and unwillingly (in fact, Leonidas kept
them there as hostages, as it were), but the Thespians, under the
command of Demophilus the son of Diadromes, were very glad to
stay; they refused to go off and leave Leonidas and his men, but
stayed and died with them.

[223] At sunrise Xerxes performed libations and, about the
middle of the morning, he launched his attack. Ephialtes had told
him to wait only until then, because the way down the mountain
is more direct and far shorter than the path he had taken up and
around the mountain. So Xerxes' forces moved forward, and so
did Leonidas and the Greeks; in fact they advanced far further into
the broader part of the neck of land than they had at first, since
they were taking to the field to meet death. On previous days, they
had been trying to hold the defensive wall, and they had made
sorties into the narrows of the pass, but now they engaged the
enemy outside the narrows. Persian casualties were high, because
their regimental commanders wielded whips and urged every single
man ever onward from behind. Quite a few of them fell into the

sea and died there, but even larger numbers were trampled alive
underfoot by their comrades, until the dead were beyond counting.
For the Greeks knew they were going to die at the hands of the
Persians who had come around the mountain, and so they spared
none of their strength, but fought the enemy with reckless disregard for their lives.

[224] By now most of their spears had been broken and they
were using their swords to kill the Persians. Leonidas fought to the
death with the utmost bravery during this mêlée; and with him fell
other famous Spartiates too, whose names I was told as men who
proved their worth. In fact, I learnt the names of all the three
hundred. A number of eminent Persians fell there too, including
two of Darius' sons, Abrocomes and Hyperanthes. They were his
sons by Phratagoune, the daughter of Artanes, who was the brother
of King Darius, and whose father was Hystaspes the son of
Arsames. Artanes arranged his daughter's marriage to Darius and
later bequeathed her his whole estate, because she was his only
child.

[225] So two of Xerxes' brothers fell during the battle there. The
Persians and Lacedaemonians grappled at length with one another
over the corpse of Leonidas, but the Greeks fought so well and so
bravely that they eventually succeeded in dragging his body away.
Four times they forced the Persians back, and the contest remained
close until Ephialtes and his men arrived. With their arrival, the
battle changed: as soon as the Greeks realized they had come, they
regrouped and all (except the Thebans) pulled back past the wall
to where the road was narrow, where they took up a position on
the spur—that is, the rise in the pass which is now marked by the
stone lion commemorating Leonidas. Here the Greeks defended
themselves with knives, if they still had them, and otherwise with
their hands and teeth, while the Persians buried them in a hail of
missiles, some charging at them head on and demolishing the wall,
while the rest surrounded them on all sides.

[226] For all the courage of the Lacedaemonians and Thespians,
a Spartiate called Dianeces is said to have proved himself the
bravest. Before battle was joined, they say that someone from
Trachis warned him how many Persians there were by saying that
when they fired their bows, they hid the sun with the mass of
arrows. Dianeces, so the story goes, was so dismissive of the Persian
numbers that he calmly replied, 'All to the good, my friend from

Trachis. If the Persians hide the sun, the battle will be in shade rather than sunlight.' This is a typical example of the quips for which Dianeces of Lacedaemon is remembered.

[227] The next bravest Lacedaemonians after Dianeces are said to have been two brothers, Alpheus and Maron, sons of Orsiphantus. The most distinguished Thespian was a man called Dithyrambus the son of Harmatides.

[228] They were buried on the spot where they fell, and a memorial has been set up there to them and to those who died earlier in the battle, before Leonidas sent some of the Greeks away. The inscription on the memorial reads:

> Here once were three million of the foe
> Opposed by four thousand from the Peloponnese.

Apart from this general inscription, the Spartiates have their own separate one:

> Stranger, tell the people of Lacedaemon
> That we who lie here obeyed their commands.

And there is one for the diviner as well:

> This is the memorial of famed Megistias,
> Cut down when the Persians crossed the Spercheius,
> A seer who clearly saw the approach of his doom,
> But could not stand to leave the leader† of Sparta.

The Amphictyons commissioned these epigrams and pillars in honour of the dead, with the exception of the one for Megistias the seer, which Simonides the son of Leoprepes wrote because they were guest-friends.

[229] There is a story about two of the three hundred, Eurytus and Aristodamus. Apparently, they had been released from active service by Leonidas and were laid up in Alpeni with extremely severe eye infections. Under these circumstances, they could have opted for joint action and either been evacuated together to Sparta or have died along with their comrades, if they chose to stay. Either course of action was open to them, but they ended up disagreeing and coming to different decisions. When Eurytus heard that the Persians had found a way round the mountain, he called for his weapons, buckled them on, and told his helot to take him to join the fighting. The helot guided him there, but then fled,

while Eurytus charged into the fray and was killed. Faint-hearted Aristodamus, however, stayed away from the fighting. Now, if Aristodamus had been the only one who had been sick and had gone home to Sparta, or if they had both made the journey together, I think the Spartiates would not have been angry; but since one of them died while the other avoided death, even though he had no better excuse for doing so, they were bound to be furious with Aristodamus.

[230] However, it is only in one version of the story of Aristodamus' safe return to Sparta that he used his illness as an excuse. Others say that he had been sent out of the camp as a messenger, and although he could have got back in time for the battle, he did not want to; he prolonged his journey instead, and so survived, whereas the other messenger with him arrived back while the battle was still being fought and met his death.

[231] Anyway, back in Lacedaemon, Aristodamus met with abuse and disgrace—the latter in that no Spartiate would give him a light for his fire or talk to him, the former in that he was nick-named Aristodamus the Coward. But he completely redeemed himself at the battle of Plataea.

[232] Another one of the three hundred, a man called Pantites, is also said to have survived because he was away carrying a message to Thessaly, and when he got back to Sparta, the story goes on, he met with such dishonour that he hanged himself.

[233] The Thebans under Leonidas' command fought for a while alongside the Greeks against the Persian forces because they had no choice in the matter. However, as soon as they saw that the Persians were gaining the upper hand, they seized the opportunity afforded by Leonidas and the rest of the Greeks charging off to the hill to part company with the others. Then they held out their hands in surrender and approached the Persians. They explained—and this was nothing but the truth—that they had collaborated with the Persians and had been among the first to give the king earth and water, but had then been forced to come to Thermopylae; they could not, then, be held responsible for any set-backs the king had incurred. The Thessalians verified the truth of what they were saying, and so the Thebans were spared. However, things did not go perfectly for them; some of them were killed as they were approaching the Persian lines, and at Xerxes' orders quite a large number of them, beginning with their commander Leontiadas, were

branded with the king's mark. This was the Leontiadas whose son
Eurymachus, many years later, was murdered by the Plataeans after
he and the four hundred Thebans under his command had captured their city.

[234] So much for the Greeks who fought at Thermopylae.
Xerxes had a question for Demaratus, so he summoned him and
began as follows: 'You're a good man, Demaratus. It is your
honesty that has convinced me of this, for things turned out exactly
as you said they would. So tell me: how many Lacedaemonians are
there left? And how many of them are as good at fighting as the
ones we have just met? Or are they all that good?'

'My lord,' Demaratus replied, 'Lacedaemon consists of a number
of communities, and its total population is therefore very large.
But—to tell you what you want to know—there are about eight
thousand men in the city of Sparta in Lacedaemon, and while all
of them are the equals of the ones who fought here, the rest are
good, but not up to the same standard.'

'Demaratus,' Xerxes went on, 'what can I do to defeat these
people with the least amount of trouble? Please tell me. After all,
you were once their king, so you know their plans inside and out.'

[235] 'My lord, if you're seriously consulting me,' Demaratus
replied, 'here is the best advice I can give you, which is what you
deserve. You should consider sending a convoy of three hundred
ships from your fleet to Laconia. There's an island off the coast
called Cythera, and Chilon, the wisest man ever born in Lacedaemon, once remarked that the Spartiates would be better off with
the island at the bottom of the sea rather than sticking out of it.
He was always expecting trouble from it—in fact, exactly the kind
of trouble I'm describing. I don't mean that he foresaw *your* expedition, but he was worried about *anyone* sending a convoy, no
matter who. So your men should use the island as a base from
which to make that worry real for the Lacedaemonians. With their
own private war on their doorstep, there's no danger of them
coming to help while the rest of Greece is being conquered by your
land army, and once the rest of Greece has been enslaved, Laconia
will be isolated and vulnerable. Now, what will happen, in all probability, if you don't do this? There's a narrow isthmus on the
Peloponnese; all the Peloponnesians will form a confederacy
designed to resist you, and then this isthmus will be the place where
you should expect to meet far fiercer fighting than you have met

so far. If you take my advice, though, this isthmus and the Peloponnesian communities will surrender without putting up a fight.'

[236] Now, Xerxes' brother Achaemenes, the commander of the fleet, happened to be there during this conversation and was afraid that Xerxes would be won over to Demaratus' suggestion, so he spoke up next. 'It looks to me, my lord,' he said, 'as though you are allowing yourself to be influenced by someone who resents your successes and may even be sabotaging your whole enterprise. Actually, that's the kind of behaviour Greeks relish; it's typically Greek to envy success and hate being outdone. If on top of our present disasters, when we've just had four hundred ships wrecked, you send another three hundred away from the main body of the fleet on a mission to the coast of the Peloponnese, our enemies will be a match for us in battle. On the other hand, if you keep the fleet intact, it will prove very awkward for them and they'll have nowhere near our capacity. Besides, the fleet as a whole will support and be supported by the land army if they advance together, whereas if you separate them, your army will be no use to the navy and the navy will be no use to you. What you should do, I think, is come up with a plan that serves your own interests well, without taking the enemy's side of things into consideration—without thinking about where they're going to wage war, what they'll do, and how many of them there are. They can be left to worry about their own business, while we do the same with ours. Any battle in which the Lacedaemonians confront the Persians is not going to heal the wound they have just received at all.'

[237] 'I think you're right, Achaemenes,' Xerxes said. 'I'm going to follow your advice. Demaratus genuinely thought that his plan was in my best interests, but your ideas are better than his. But I don't believe that he doesn't have my best interests at heart. I base this assessment not only on previous advice he has given me, but also on the fact that when someone resents a colleague's success, his hostility manifests itself in silence; if his colleague seeks his advice, he wouldn't suggest what seems to him to be the best course of action—unless he is one of those rare individuals, a man of exceptional virtue. On the other hand, no one feels warmer towards another person's success than a guest-friend, and he will do the best he can to help if asked for his advice. Demaratus is my guest-friend, and so in the future I order everyone to refrain from speaking ill of him.'

[238] After this discussion Xerxes made his way through the bodies of the dead. When he came to Leonidas' corpse and was told that this was the Lacedaemonian king and commander, he told his men to cut off his head and stick it on a pole. This, to my mind, is the most convincing piece of evidence (although there is plenty more) that during his lifetime Leonidas had been more of an irritation to King Xerxes than anyone else in the world. Otherwise he would never have acted with such abnormal violence towards his corpse, because the Persians are normally the last people in the world, to my knowledge, to treat men who fight bravely with disrespect. Anyway, the men who were given the job carried out his orders.

[239] I shall now return to a point in my account where something was omitted before. The Lacedaemonians were the first to find out that Xerxes was mounting a campaign against Greece, and so they sent a deputation to the Delphic oracle, where they received the prophecy I mentioned a short while ago. But the way they learnt about the impending campaign was remarkable. Demaratus the son of Ariston, who was living in exile in Persia, did not, I imagine (and it stands to reason too), feel affection for the Lacedaemonians, but one might still wonder whether he did what he did out of affection or actually to gloat over them. As soon as Demaratus, who was in Susa, heard of Xerxes' decision to march on Greece, he wanted to tell the Lacedaemonians. This was very risky—what if he should be caught?—and the only way he could find to get the message to them was to take a folding writing-tablet, scrape off the wax, and write about the king's decision on the bare wood of the tablet. Then he covered the message up again with melted wax, so that during its journey the tablet would not arouse the suspicions of the guards on the route. When it reached its destination, the Lacedaemonians did not know what to make of it. Eventually, however, according to what I heard, it was Gorgo, the daughter of Cleomenes and wife of Leonidas, who guessed the tablet's secret by herself. She suggested that if they scraped off the wax they might find a message on the wood. They took her advice, found the message and read it, and then passed the message on to all the other Greek states. Anyway, that is what is supposed to have happened.†

BOOK EIGHT

[1] The fleet consisted of the following Greek contingents. The Athenians provided 127 ships, with crews of Plataeans as well as Athenians; the Plataeans compensated for their lack of nautical expertise with their courage and determination. The Corinthian contingent was 40 ships, and the Megarians provided 20. The crews of another 20 were supplied by Chalcis, although the Athenians gave them the ships. The Aeginetans provided 18, the Sicyonians 12, the Lacedaemonians 10, the Epidaurians 8, the Eretrians 7, the Troezenians 5, the Styrians 2, and the Ceans 2 triremes and 2 penteconters. The contribution of the Opuntian Locrians consisted of 7 penteconters.

[2] These were the crews who went to fight at Artemisium, and I have also stated the number of ships each people provided.† Not counting the penteconters, then, there were 271 ships in all assembled at Artemisium. The supreme commander of the fleet was Eurybiades the son of Euryclidas—a Spartiate, because the allies refused to follow Athenian leadership and said that they would wreck the projected campaign unless there was someone from Laconia in overall command.

[3] There had been talk right at the start, even before the delegation was sent to Sicily to try to arrange an alliance, to the effect that the Athenians should be in charge of the fleet. But when the allies protested, the Athenians gave way, because what was important to them was the survival of Greece and they knew that if they made leadership a point of dispute, Greece was lost. And they were right, because internal dissension is worse than a united war effort to the same degree that war is worse than peace. So it was appreciation of this fact that made the Athenians give way without making a fuss—but, as they later demonstrated, only for as long as they badly needed the rest of the Greeks. Once Xerxes' invasion had been repulsed and they were fighting for his territory rather than their own, they deprived the Lacedaemonians of the

leadership, using Pausanias' arrogant behaviour as a pretext. But all this happened later.

[4] At the time in question, when the Greeks stationed at Artemisium saw how many ships were moored at Aphetae and saw Persian troops spread out everywhere, they were terrified, because this was not the condition they had expected the Persians to be in, after what had happened, and they began to contemplate a retreat from Artemisium back into Greece. However, the Euboeans realized what was going through their minds and asked Eurybiades to stay for a short while, just until they had removed their children and households to a place of safety. When he refused, they turned instead to Themistocles, the Athenian commander, and won his compliance with a bribe of thirty talents to ensure that the Greeks stayed where they were and engaged the Persians at sea in defence of Euboea.

[5] Themistocles got the Greeks to stay at Artemisium by giving five talents of the money to Eurybiades as if it were his own personal money. With Eurybiades won over, the only remaining person who continued to feel uncomfortable was the Corinthian commander, Adeimantus the son of Ocytus, who insisted that he would not stay, but would withdraw his ships from Artemisium. But Themistocles made him a promise. 'I'm sure you won't be leaving us, Adeimantus,' he said, 'because I'll give you more money for staying than the Persian king would send you for leaving.' And with these words, he sent three talents of silver to Adeimantus' ship. So Adeimantus and Eurybiades were bribed to change their minds, and the Euboeans got their way. Moreover, Themistocles himself made a healthy profit. No one knew that he had the rest of the money; the people who had been given some of it assumed that it had come from Athens just for the purpose to which it was put.

[6] So the Greeks stayed in Euboea and took on the enemy at sea there. Here is what happened. It was early in an afternoon when the Persians reached Aphetae. Although they had already heard that there were a few Greek ships stationed at Artemisium, they now saw them for themselves, and they were eager to attack, to see if they could capture them. However, they decided that this was not the time to make a frontal assault, in case the Greeks turned and fled at the sight of them coming, and night came down while they were trying to escape. If that happened, the Greeks would

presumably get away, but as far as the Persians were concerned no one, not even a fire-bearer, should escape alive.

[7] Under these circumstances, then, here is what they did. They sent a detachment of two hundred ships from the main fleet to sail around the far side of Sciathos, and then around Euboea and into the Euripus via Caphereus and Geraestus, thus staying out of sight of the enemy all the way. The idea was that with the detachment arriving from that direction and blocking off the Greeks' retreat, and with the main fleet making a frontal assault, they would have the Greeks caught in a trap. In accordance with this plan, then, they sent the detachment of two hundred ships on its way, while the rest of them waited, because they had no intention of attacking the Greeks that day, or until they saw the signal indicating the arrival of the squadron they had sent around Euboea. So the detachment was sent on its way, and the Persians occupied themselves with counting the ships that were left in Aphetae.

[8] While they were counting the ships, there was in the Persian camp a man from Scione called Scyllias, who was the best diver of the time; in fact, after the fleet had been wrecked off Mount Pelium he had rescued a great deal of valuable property for the Persians, and also gained a lot for himself. Now, apparently Scyllias had been intending to defect to the Greek side earlier, but no opportunity had presented itself until now. Precisely how he got from the Persian camp to the Greeks, I cannot now say for certain, but I doubt the truth of the story that he dived into the sea at Aphetae and did not surface until he reached Artemisium, having swum underwater a distance of about eighty stades. This is not the only implausible tale that is told about Scyllias (although there are some true stories too), but as far as this incident is concerned I hereby state that in my opinion he went to Artemisium by boat. As soon as he got there, he provided the Greek commanders with the details of the wrecking of the fleet and told them about the ships that were sailing around Euboea.

[9] The Greeks held a meeting and discussed what to do in the light of Scyllias' news. After a lengthy discussion the prevalent view was to stay put for the rest of the day and even to pitch camp ashore for the night, but then to set out after midnight and go to meet the ships that were trying to take them in the rear. Later, however, when no one tried to attack them, they waited until

late afternoon and then sailed against the main Persian fleet. It was time to test the enemy's battle skills and their own skill at the diecplous.

[10] When Xerxes' troops and their commanders saw the small number of Greek ships bearing down on them, they were certain that the Greeks must have gone mad. They too put to sea, expecting an easy victory—not an unreasonable hope, since they could see that their ships far outnumbered the Greeks' and were more manoeuvrable too. And so they confidently set about encircling the Greek fleet. However, some of the Ionians in the Persian fleet, who were pro-Greek and had joined the expedition against their will, were very concerned at the sight of the Greeks being surrounded. They were sure that, given the apparent weakness of the Greek forces, none of them would return home. All the others, though, were delighted with the situation and competed with one another to see which of them would be the first to earn a reward from the king for capturing an Attic vessel, because every contingent of the Persian forces considered the Athenians to be the most formidable of their opponents.

[11] At a pre-arranged signal, however, the Greeks first formed a circle, with their prows facing the enemy and their sterns close together in the middle, and then, at a second signal, they set to work, even though they were hemmed in tightly and had to engage the Persians head on. In this engagement they captured thirty ships, and among their prisoners was Philaon the son of Chersis, who was the brother of King Gorgus of Salamis and a very high-ranking officer. The first Greek to capture an enemy ship was an Athenian, Lycomedes the son of Aeschraeus, and this earned him the prize for valour. Night fell on the combatants while the battle was still in the balance, and they went their separate ways, the Greeks back to Artemisium and the Persians back to Aphetae. The battle had certainly not gone according to Persian expectations. During the battle Antidorus of Lemnos deserted to the Greeks; he was the only one of the Greeks serving in Xerxes' forces to do so in this battle, and the Athenians rewarded him for this with a plot of land on Salamis.

[12] After dark there was a heavy rainstorm which lasted all night, and violent peals of thunder from Mount Pelium, even though it was the middle of summer. Dead bodies and bits of wrecked ship drifted to Aphetae, where they clustered around the

prows of the ships and became entangled with the blades of the oars. The troops there were terrified when they heard about this, and were sure they were going to die, given all the troubles that were besetting them. After all, before they had caught their breath from the wrecking of the fleet and the storm which had occurred off Mount Pelium, they had put up with a tough battle, followed immediately by torrential rain, swollen streams pouring into the sea, and violent peals of thunder.

[13] But if it was a bad night for this lot of Persians, it was far more cruel for those who had been detailed to sail around Euboea. It was not that the night-time conditions were any different, but they occurred while they were out on the open sea. The upshot was disastrous. The rainstorm struck when they were off a place in Euboea called Coela; they were driven off course by the wind, without any idea where they were heading, and were wrecked on the rocky coast. This all happened by divine will, to reduce the Persians' numerical advantage and bring their forces down to the level of the Greeks.

[14] So that was the end of this contingent, at Coela in Euboea. The Persians at Aphetae were delighted to see daybreak, and left their ships idle. They had been so badly mauled that they were content just to keep quiet for the time being. Meanwhile, fifty-three Attic ships arrived to reinforce the Greeks, which boosted their morale—and then at the same time came the report about the loss in the storm of all the Persian ships that were sailing around Euboea. They waited until late afternoon again, just like the day before, before attacking and destroying some Cilician ships. Afterwards they sailed back to Artemisium.

[15] The Persian commanders were angry at the harm done them by such a small number of ships, and they were also afraid of how Xerxes would react, so on the third day they stopped waiting for the Greeks to initiate the fighting and instead, at midday, when their preparations were complete, they put to sea. It so happened that the days on which these naval engagements were fought were exactly the three days of the land battle at Thermopylae. Moreover, the Euripus was the focus of the conflict at sea, just as Leonidas and his men were trying to hold the pass. In both cases the Greeks' rallying cry was to stop the foreigners entering Greece, and the invaders' was to destroy the Greek forces and win the strait.

[16] At first, when Xerxes' fleet formed up and sailed into the attack, the Greeks stayed at Artemisium without reacting. But when the Persians took up a crescent formation, with a view to encircling the Greeks and catching them in a trap, the Greeks sailed out against them and battle was joined. The two sides were evenly matched in this battle, because there were so many ships in Xerxes' enormous fleet that it kept falling foul of itself, as ships were thrown into disarray and collided with one another. Nevertheless, the Persians fought on without giving way, to avoid the disgrace of being routed by so few enemy ships. Many ships were lost on the Greek side, and many men too, but the Persians came off far worse. The battle ended when the two sides separated.

[17] Among Xerxes' troops, battle honours went to the Egyptians, for various notable achievements, but particularly for capturing five Greek ships, crews and all. On the Greek side, battle honours went that day to the Athenians, and among the Athenians to Cleinias the son of Alcibiades, who provided two hundred men and his own ship, all at his own expense, for the war effort.

[18] Once they had disengaged, both sides were glad to make their way back to anchorage, and did so with all speed. The Greeks were at least in possession of their dead and their disabled ships after breaking off from the battle and pulling back, but they had been badly mauled (especially the Athenians, half of whose ships were damaged), and they decided to retreat down into Greece.

[19] It occurred to Themistocles, however, that if they could detach the Ionian and Carian contingents from the Persian forces, they could overcome the rest. He convened a meeting of the Greek commanders, just at the time of day when the Euboeans were driving their flocks down towards the coast, and told them that he thought he had come up with a plan, which stood a good chance of success, for depriving the king of his best men. But he revealed no more of the plan than that, saying only that in the present circumstances they should slaughter as many of the Euboean sheep and goats as they felt like, on the grounds that it was better for their men to have them rather than for the enemy to get their hands on them. He suggested that each commander should tell the men under him to light a watch-fire, and asked them to leave the precise timing of their withdrawal up to him, promising that they would get back to Greece safe and sound. This sounded good to them,

and once the fires were lit they turned their attention to the sheep and goats.

[20] This happened because the Euboeans regarded an oracle of Bacis they had received as nonsense, and had not taken any of their property to a place of safety or stocked up on provisions for a forthcoming war. As a result, they brought disaster down on themselves. The relevant oracle of Bacis went as follows:

> When a man without Greek casts on the sea his yoke of papyrus,
> Be sure to remove your bleating goats from Euboea.

Since they had learnt nothing from these words, then at the time in question, with trouble at hand and more expected, misfortune was their teacher about what is really important.

[21] While the Greeks were occupied with these matters, their scout arrived from Trachis. They had a scout posted at Artemisium—a certain Polyas of Anticyra—whose job it was to tell the Greeks at Thermopylae if the fleet was defeated, and to this end he had a light oared boat ready to go. Likewise, Abronichus of Athens, the son of Lysicles, was stationed with Leonidas, ready to board a triaconter and tell the troops at Artemisium of any setback the land army suffered. It was Abronichus, then, who arrived with news of what had happened to Leonidas and his men. After hearing his report, the Greeks were ready to consider withdrawal, and they proceeded to set out in the order they were stationed in, with the Corinthians first and the Athenians last.

[22] Themistocles picked the fastest Athenian ships and made his way around the various places where there was drinkable water, where he cut a message on the rocks for the Ionians to read when they came to Artemisium the next day. The message was: 'Men of Ionia, it is wrong of you to fight against your ancestral line and to enslave Greece. Ideally, you should join us; failing that, even now adopt a position of neutrality, and ask the Carians to do the same. If neither of these courses of action is feasible, and the Persians have too great a hold on you for you to revolt, in the battle you can remember that you are descended from our stock and that you were the original cause of the enmity between us and Persia, and deliberately fight below your best.' In my opinion, Themistocles was covering both alternatives with this message. Either Xerxes would not get to hear about it and it would induce the Ionians to

change sides, or, if somebody informed and he was told about it, he would stop trusting the Ionians and would keep them out of any battles.

[23] Just after Themistocles had left this message for the Ionians, a man from Histiaea sailed over to the Persians and told them about the Greek withdrawal from Artemisium. At first they did not believe him and they kept him under guard while they sent a squadron of fast ships to have a look, who confirmed the truth of the report. So at sunrise the next day the whole fleet set sail *en masse* for Artemisium, where they stayed until midday, before sailing on to Histiaea. On arriving there they took control of the main town and the district of Ellopia, and overran all the coastal villages in Histiaeotis.

[24] While they were there a man arrived with a message from Xerxes for the fleet. Now, Xerxes had made some prior arrangements as regards the bodies of the men from his army who had died at Thermopylae. About twenty thousand men had fallen there, but he left about a thousand of the corpses and buried the rest in mass graves, which he covered with earth and leaves to disguise them from the fleet. So the messenger sailed over to Histiaea, assembled all the men, and addressed them as follows: 'Friends and allies, there are some people in the world who are foolish enough to think they can overcome the might of King Xerxes. If any of you want to go and see how we deal in battle with such people, the king grants you permission to leave your station and do so.'

[25] On hearing this message, so many people wanted to go and see the battle-site that boats became a scarce commodity. They crossed over to Thermopylae, walked among the corpses, and looked around. Everyone was convinced that all the enemy corpses lying there were Lacedaemonians and Thespians, but in fact they were also seeing helots. None of the men who had come over from Euboea were taken in by Xerxes' ridiculous ploy with the bodies of his men. There were a thousand corpses from their army lying in plain view, while all the enemy corpses, four thousand of them, were lying piled in a heap in a single spot. That day was given over to sightseeing, and then on the next day the men from the fleet returned to their ships at Histiaea, while Xerxes and his army set out on their journey.

[26] Some men from Arcadia deserted and went over to the Persian camp, but there were only a few of them, mercenaries who

needed an income and employment. They were taken before the king, and the Persians—or rather, a single Persian on behalf of the rest—asked them what the Greeks were doing. The Arcadians replied that the Greeks were celebrating the Olympic festival, and watching an athletic competition and a horse-race. The Persian next asked what the usual reward was for winning,† and they told him about the garland of olive that was given as a prize. At this, Tritantaechmes the son of Artabanus made a remark that showed his quality—but one which the king viewed as the mark of a coward. When Tritantaechmes heard that no money was at stake, but a garland, he could not stop himself blurting out in front of everyone, 'Well, Mardonius, what sort of men are these you have brought us to fight? They make excellence rather than money the reason for a contest!'

[27] That was what Tritantaechmes said. Meanwhile, straight after the disaster at Thermopylae, the Thessalians sent a herald to Phocis. They had been feuding with the Phocians from time immemorial, but the latest defeat they had suffered at Phocian hands had made them particularly angry. Just a few years before Xerxes' campaign, the Thessalians and their allies invaded Phocis in full strength, but were beaten by the Phocians and took heavy losses. This came about because when the Phocians were trapped on Mount Parnassus, a diviner called Tellias of Elis was there with them, and he devised a cunning plan. He had the six hundred best Phocian fighters rub themselves and their weapons with chalk and attack the Thessalians at night, with instructions to kill anyone they saw who was not all white. First the Thessalian sentries and then the main army became terrified at the sight of the Phocians, and thought they were seeing something supernatural and ominous. The upshot was that the Phocians took possession of the bodies and shields of four thousand Thessalians. They dedicated half of these shields at Abae and the rest at Delphi. A tenth of the wealth they gained as a result of this battle went towards the group of huge statues in an aggressive pose around the tripod in front of the temple in Delphi, and a similar group was dedicated at Abae as well.

[28] As well as defeating the Thessalian infantry in this way, despite being besieged by them, the Phocians also did irreparable harm to the invading Thessalian cavalry. In the pass near Hyampolis, they dug a wide trench, put empty jars in it, and then piled

earth back on top until it looked like the rest of the ground. Here they met the Thessalian assault. The Thessalians charged, convinced that they would make short work of the Phocians, but the horses' legs sank into the jars and were broken.

[29] These two incidents rankled with the Thessalians, so the message their herald carried was as follows: 'Men of Phocis, now more than ever you must admit that you are no match for us. In times past, while we chose to be on the side of the Greeks, we always meant more to them than you did, and now that we have sided with the Persians we have so much influence that we could have robbed you of your land and reduced you to slavery as well. We could do anything we liked with you, but we do not hold the wrongs you have done us in the past against you, except that they will now cost you fifty talents of silver, and then we guarantee to divert the approaching invasion from your country.'

[30] The context of this offer from the Thessalians was that the Phocians were the only people in that part of the country who were not collaborating with the Persians—and the conclusion I have come to is that this was simply because of their feud with the Thessalians. In other words, if the Thessalians had supported the Greek cause, the Phocians would, I am sure, have collaborated with the Persians. Anyway, in response to this offer from the Thessalians the Phocians refused to pay any money; they also said they could match the Thessalians as collaborators, if for some reason they chose to, but that they would not deliberately betray Greece.

[31] This response so enraged the Thessalians when it was reported back to them that they took it upon themselves to guide the Persians there themselves. So the invasion proceeded from Trachis to Doris, where, between Malis and Phocis, there is a narrow tongue of land about thirty stades wide which was called Dryopis in the old days and was the original homeland of the Peloponnesian Dorians. Doris was left unharmed by the invading Persians, for two reasons: the people were colloborating with them, and the Thessalians thought they should be left alone.

[32] Having passed through Doris, they invaded Phocis, but they failed to catch the actual inhabitants. Some of the Phocians made their way up to the heights of Parnassus (one of whose peaks, called Tithorea, which is situated off by itself near the town of Neon, can accommodate a whole crowd of people, so they took themselves and their belongings up there), while the majority left their homes

and made their way to the territory of the Ozolian Locrians, to the town of Amphissa which overlooks the Crisaean Plain. The Persian army, guided by the Thessalians, overran the whole of Phocis; everywhere they went, they cut everything down and put it to the torch, and set fire to the settlements and the sanctuaries.

[33] To be precise, in the course of their journey through Phocis they laid waste to the entire Cephisus River valley. Drymus, Charadra, Erochus, Tethronium, Amphicaea, Neon, Pedieës, Triteae, Elateia, Hyampolis, Parapotamii—all these places were burnt to the ground, as was Abae, where there was a rich sanctuary of Apollo, well stocked with treasuries and many votive offerings. In those days there was also (as there still is) an oracle there, whose shrine they plundered and burnt down. They chased one group of Phocians as far as the mountains, where they caught up with them; some of the women from this party were gang-raped until they died.

[34] The next place the Persians came to after Parapotamii was Panopes, where the army split. The largest and most powerful contingent set out with Xerxes for Athens and entered that part of Boeotia which belongs to Orchomenus. Now, the whole population of Boeotia were collaborators, and the safety of their towns and cities was ensured by the presence in them of Macedonians, who had been sent there by Alexander for that purpose. The reason they were protecting the Boeotian communities was to make it clear to Xerxes that the Boeotians were on the side of Persia.

[35] While Xerxes' division of the Persian army was heading in this direction, the rest of them set out with their guides towards the sanctuary at Delphi, keeping Mount Parnassus on their right. They continued to devastate every part of Phocis they came to, and in the course of their journey burnt down the towns of the Panopeans, Daulians, and Aeolians. Their mission—the reason they had been split off from the main body of the army and were taking this direction—was to plunder the sanctuary at Delphi and bring before King Xerxes all the property they took from it. My information is that Xerxes had heard so often about everything of note that was to be found in the sanctuary that he was more familiar with them (and especially with the offerings made by Croesus the son of Alyattes) than he was with the things back in his own home.

[36] When the inhabitants of Delphi found out what was happening they became absolutely terrified. They were in such a state

of panic that they asked the oracle whether they should bury the sacred property in the ground or take it away somewhere else. The god said that they should not disturb it, and assured them that he was perfectly capable of protecting his property by himself. On hearing this, the people of Delphi next began to worry about themselves. They sent their women and children across the gulf to Achaea, while most of the men made their way up to the crags of Parnassus and left their property in the Corycian Cave, and the rest withdrew to Amphissa in Locris. The only people left in the town were sixty men and the god's prophet.

[37] Just when the Persians were approaching and had the sanctuary in sight, the god's prophet (whose name was Aceratus) saw that the weapons, the sacred ones which it is sacrilege for any human being to touch, had been brought out of the temple and were lying in front of the building. He went and told the Delphians who had stayed about the miracle. Meanwhile, the Persians pressed on and came to the sanctuary of Athena Before the Temple—only to be greeted by miracles even more remarkable than the one that had already occurred. It is truly amazing that weapons of war should of their own accord appear on the ground outside the temple, but what happened next was quite astonishing, even given all the marvellous things that have happened in the world. Just as the Persians were approaching the sanctuary of Athena Before the Temple, thunderbolts crashed down on them from the sky, and two crags broke off from Mount Parnassus, hurtled towards them with a terrible noise, and hit a large number of them, and at the same time the sound of a loud shout and a war-cry emerged from the sanctuary.

[38] The combination of all these events filled the invaders with fear, and they began to run away. When the Delphians found out about this, they set off in pursuit and killed quite a few of them. The survivors fled straight to Boeotia. I have learnt that the Persians who made it back claimed to have witnessed further miracles, over and above the ones already mentioned; they said they were followed by two heavily armed men of superhuman height, who harried them and killed them.

[39] The Delphians say that these two were the local heroes of Delphi, Phylacus and Autonoüs, whose precincts are located near the sanctuary. The precinct of Phylacus is by the road above the sanctuary of Athena Before the Temple, and that of Autonoüs is

near the Castalian Spring under the Hyampean Cliff. The rocks that fell from Parnassus were still preserved in my day, lying in the precinct of Athena Before the Temple, which is where they came to rest after sweeping through the Persians. So that is how this contingent of Persians came to leave the sanctuary of Delphi.

[40] After leaving Artemisium, the Greek fleet put in at Salamis, at the request of the Athenians. The Athenians asked them to do so because they wanted to evacuate their women and children from Attica, and also because they wanted an opportunity to decide what to do next. The situation was such that they felt they had been misguided in their judgement, and they needed to discuss their concerns. They had been expecting to find every available Peloponnesian in Boeotia, waiting for the invader, but in fact they found nothing of the sort; instead they heard that the Peloponnesians were building a defensive wall across the Isthmus, since all that mattered to them was the survival of the Peloponnese. They were protecting the Peloponnese and abandoning everything else. When the Athenians heard this they asked the Greek fleet to anchor at Salamis.

[41] So the main fleet put in at Salamis, while the Athenian contingent docked at home. Following their arrival, they issued a proclamation that everyone in Athens should see to the safety of his children and household as best he could. Most people sent their families off to Troezen, but others preferred Aegina or Salamis. The evacuation proceeded apace, and only partly because they wanted to obey the oracle. The main reason was as follows. The Athenians say that a large snake, the guardian of the Acropolis, lives in the sanctuary. This is not just something they talk about; they also act on it, by serving the snake a monthly quota of food— honey-cake, to be specific. Now, although in times past this honey-cake had always been consumed, on this occasion it was left untouched. When the priestess told them, the Athenians were even more committed to their abandonment of the city, on the grounds that even the goddess had left the Acropolis. After getting everything away to safety, they rejoined the main fleet.

[42] Once news that the ships from Artemisium were moored at Salamis reached the rest of the Greek fleet (who were at Pogon, the harbour of Troezen, where they had been told to assemble), they began to stream into Salamis to join them. So the total fleet assembled at Salamis now consisted of many more ships than had been

involved in the battle of Artemisium, and there were contingents from a larger number of towns and cities too. The command of the fleet remained with the Spartiate, Eurybiades the son of Euryclidas, as at Artemisium, despite the fact that he was not of royal lineage. The Athenian contingent was the largest, by a long way, and their ships were the best too.

[43] Here is a list of the contingents, starting with those from the Peloponnese. The Lacedaemonians provided sixteen ships, the Corinthians provided the same number as they had at Artemisium, the Sicyonians gave fifteen, the Epidaurians ten, the Troezenians five, and the Hermioneans three. The inhabitants of all these states apart from Hermione are of Dorian and Macedonian stock; they were the most recent arrivals from Erineus, Pindus, and Dryopis. The people of Hermione are from Dryopis; they were evicted from what is now called Doris by Heracles and the Malians.

[44] So much for the Peloponnesian contingent. Those supplied by states from the mainland beyond the Isthmus were as follows. Athens provided a hundred and eighty ships, more than anyone else, and did so with no help this time, since the Plataeans did not support them at the battle of Salamis. The reason was that on the way back from Artemisium the Plataeans left the Greek fleet at Chalcis, crossed over to Boeotia, and set about evacuating their families. So they missed the battle because they were busy saving their families. The Athenians were originally Pelasgians, at the time when the Pelasgians occupied the whole of what is now called Greece; first they were known as Cranaï, and then Cecropidae during the reign of King Cecrops; later, when Erechtheus became king, they changed their name to Athenians, and when Ion the son of Xuthus became their war-leader they were called Ionians after him.

[45] The Megarians supplied the same number of ships as at Artemisium, while the Ambraciots and the Leucadians (both originally of Dorian stock, from Corinth) came with seven ships and three ships respectively.

[46] Turning to the islands, the Aeginetan contingent consisted of thirty ships. These were not the only ships they had ready and available, but they used the rest to protect their own island, while committing their thirty best ships to the battle at Salamis. The Aeginetans are originally Dorians from Epidaurus; the island had previously been called Oenone. Then the Chalcidians provided

the same twenty ships as at Artemisium, and the Eretrians the same seven; these are both Ionian peoples. The contingent from Ceos was also the same size as at Artemisium; the Ceans are Ionian stock, originally from Athens. Naxos provided four ships, which had actually been sent by their government to join the Persian fleet, along with the rest of the Aegean islands, but at the insistence of a man called Democritus (one of the foremost men on the island and at the time the captain of one of the triremes) they disregarded their instructions and went over to the Greeks. The Naxians are Ionians, of Athenian stock. Styra sent the same number of ships as at Artemisium, and Cythnos sent one trireme and a penteconter; the inhabitants of both these places are originally Dryopians. There were also contingents from Seriphos, Siphnos, and Melos, which were the only Aegean islands not to have given earth and water to the Persian king.

[47] All these contingents came from places on the Greek side of Thesprotia and the River Acheron (Ambracia and Leucas, the most remote places to send contingents, share a border with Thesprotia). From elsewhere, the only place to send help to Greece in her time of peril was Croton, which sent a single ship under the command of a man called Phayllus, a three-time victor at the Pythian Games. The people of Croton were originally from Achaea.

[48] Every contingent consisted of triremes, except that Melos, Siphnos, and Seriphos supplied penteconters. The Melians, originally of Lacedaemonian stock, sent two, while the Siphnians and Seriphians (both Ionians, originally from Athens) sent one each. The total size of the fleet, not counting penteconters, was 378.

[49] Once the commanders had assembled on Salamis from all these states, they held a council of war. Eurybiades proposed that everyone should feel free to speak his mind about where, among the territories the Greeks controlled, he thought would be the best place to engage the enemy at sea. He was looking for suggestions outside of Attica, which had already been given up for lost. The majority view was that they should sail to the Isthmus and fight in defence of the Peloponnese. The thinking behind this idea was that if they remained at Salamis and lost the battle, they would be blockaded on an island where no help could reach them, whereas if they were near the Isthmus they could get ashore to friendly territory.

[50] This was the way the minds of the Peloponnesian commanders were working, when an Athenian arrived with the news

that the Persian army had reached Attica and that the whole country was being destroyed by fire. Xerxes and his army had made their way through Boeotia, where they had burnt down Thespiae and Plataea (the inhabitants of both of which had been evacuated to the Peloponnese), and then reached Athenian territory and started to devastate it. The reason Xerxes set fire to Thespiae and Plataea was that the Thebans told him about their refusal to support the Persian cause.

[51] Taking the crossing of the Hellespont as the starting-point of the Persians' journey, they spent one month there, while they crossed over into Europe, and then reached Attica three months later, during the archonship of Calliades at Athens. The city fell to them, but it was deserted. The only Athenians they came across were a few temple-stewards and paupers in the sanctuary, who had made barricades out of doors and planks to defend the Acropolis against the invaders. It was not just poverty that had stopped them going to Salamis; they also reckoned they had understood what the Pythia meant by her prediction that a wall of wood would not fall to the enemy. They were convinced that the place of safety to which the oracle had been referring was not a fleet, but this barricade of theirs.

[52] The Persians stationed themselves on the knoll the Athenians call the Areopagus, which lies opposite the Acropolis, and started on the siege. They tied some tow on to their arrows, set them alight and shot them at the barricades. The besieged Athenians carried on defending the Acropolis, even though they were in desperate trouble and their barricade had failed them. They also refused to listen to the terms proposed by the Pisistratidae for their surrender. One way or another—for instance, by rolling boulders down on the Persians as they approached the gates—they fought back in defence of the Acropolis so well that for a long while Xerxes was stuck and did not know how bring the siege to a successful conclusion.

[53] Eventually, however, the Persians resolved their difficulties by finding a way on to the Acropolis. After all, the whole of mainland Attica was destined to fall to the Persians, according to the oracle. At the front end of the Acropolis, away from the gates and the main road up, was a spot by the sanctuary of Aglaurus the daughter of Cecrops where no one was on guard, and indeed it was so steep that no one could have expected a human being to climb

up that way. Nevertheless, some Persians did just that. At the sight of them up on the Acropolis,† some of the Athenians threw themselves from the wall to their deaths, while others sought sanctuary in the temple. The Persians who had completed the ascent first made their way to the gates and opened them, and then murdered the suppliants. When there was no one left standing, they plundered the sanctuary and set fire to the whole Acropolis.

[54] Now that Athens was completely in his control, Xerxes sent a horseman to Susa with a message telling Artabanus how well things were going for them at present. The day after the messenger left, Xerxes summoned all the Athenian exiles in his party to a meeting and told them to climb the Acropolis and sacrifice victims in their own manner. Perhaps he had been told to do so in a dream, or perhaps his burning of the sanctuary was weighing on his mind. Anyway, the Athenian exiles carried out his orders.

[55] My reason for mentioning this incident is as follows. There is on the Athenian Acropolis a temple of Erechtheus under the title 'the Earth-born', within which there is an olive-tree and a source of salt water, which in Athenian legend were placed there by Poseidon and Athena as their tokens when they were in competition for authority over the land. Now, it so happened that this olive-tree was burnt down along with the rest of the sanctuary by the invaders, but on the day after the sack of the temple, the Athenians who, at Xerxes' instigation, climbed up to the sanctuary to perform sacrifices saw a shoot about a cubit long, which had already sprouted from the stump. They reported the phenomenon to Xerxes.

[56] When news of the events on the Athenian Acropolis reached the Greeks on Salamis, they were so panic-stricken that some of the commanders did not even wait for a final decision on the proposal about what action to take, but rushed for their ships and began to hoist their sails with the intention of beating a hasty retreat. Meanwhile, those who remained on land ratified the decision to fight in defence of the Peloponnese. At nightfall the meeting broke up and they went on board their ships.

[57] On his ship that night an Athenian named Mnesiphilus asked Themistocles what decision the commanders had reached. When Themistocles told him that the plan was to set sail for the Isthmus and fight in defence of the Peloponnese, Mnesiphilus

said, 'Better not—once the fleet leaves Salamis, there'll no longer be a country you can fight for. Each contingent will disperse to its native state, and no one, not even Eurybiades, will be able to stop the fleet falling apart. This is a stupid plan, which will spell the destruction of Greece. You have to find a way to reverse the decision—to persuade Eurybiades to change his mind and stay here.'

[58] Themistocles liked this idea a great deal. Without saying a word in reply, he made his way over to Eurybiades' ship. When he got there, he said that he had something of general importance to communicate. Eurybiades told him to come on board, if he wanted. So Themistocles sat down and repeated Mnesiphilus' arguments as if they were his own, and added some new points as well, until his pleas persuaded Eurybiades to go back ashore and convene a meeting of the commanders.

[59] Once the commanders were in session, and before Eurybiades had a chance to open the meeting by explaining why he had asked them there, Themistocles began to address the others in urgent entreaty. The Corinthian commander, Adeimantus the son of Ocytus, interrupted him and said, 'At the games, Themistocles, those who are too quick off the mark earn themselves a flogging.' But Themistocles countered with: 'Those who get left behind win no prizes.'

[60] At this stage of the proceedings, his response to the Corinthian was moderate. When he came to address Eurybiades, he did not mention his earlier point, that the fleet would disperse once they left Salamis, because it would have been inappropriate for him to cast aspersions with the allies there. Instead he tried a different approach. 'Eurybiades,' he said, 'you have the opportunity to prove yourself the saviour of Greece, if you agree with me and engage the enemy here, where we are now, rather than listen to the others and move the fleet to the Isthmus. Let me explain the consequences of the two options, so that you can compare them. If the battle takes place by the Isthmus, you'll be fighting in the open sea, which puts us at a distinct disadvantage, since our ships are heavier and we are outnumbered. Secondly, even if things basically go well for us, you'll lose Salamis, Megara, and Aegina. Moreover, the enemy's land army will go wherever their fleet goes, and so you'll be drawing them down into the Peloponnese and then the whole of Greece will be at risk.

'However, there are a number of advantages to staying here as I am suggesting. In the first place, our few ships will be taking on a larger fleet in a confined space, and this means, if the battle goes as one may reasonably expect it to, that we will win a convincing victory. I mean, fighting in a confined space favours us, but fighting in the open favours them. In the second place, Salamis will survive—and Salamis is where we have taken our women and children. The final point to note about my plan, which concerns what you all take to be the crucial issue, is that by staying here, Eurybiades, you'll be defending the Peloponnese just as effectively as if you were stationed off the Isthmus, and you won't be drawing the enemy into the Peloponnese either, if you're sensible and adopt my plan. If the outcome is as I expect and we're victorious at sea, the Persians won't appear at your Isthmus; in fact, they won't get any further than Attica. They will retreat in disorder, and we will profit by the safety of Megara, Aegina, and Salamis—which is, after all, the place where it has been foretold that we will overcome the enemy. It is sound planning that invariably earns us the outcome we want; without it, even the gods are unlikely to look with favour on our designs.'

[61] Once again it was Adeimantus of Corinth who protested during this speech by Themistocles. He told him that since he had no state to represent he should keep quiet, he tried to stop Eurybiades letting a stateless person propose a motion, and he suggested that Themistocles should find himself a state before contributing his ideas. He said these things because Athens had fallen and was occupied. This time Themistocles responded with a series of insults about Corinthians in general and Adeimantus in particular, and went on to make it clear that the Athenians still had a city and a country—and one greater than theirs—as long as they had two hundred ships ready for action, since there was no Greek state that could repel an attack from them.

[62] Once he had got this point across, he transferred his attention back to Eurybiades, this time speaking more insistently. 'As for you,' he said, 'if you stay here you are a man of courage, but if not you will destroy Greece. The fleet is vital to the outcome of the war. You *must* do as I suggest. If you don't, we will immediately collect our families and take them to Siris in Italy; after all, it is ours and has been for a long time, and there are oracles claiming that it is destined to be colonized by us. When the rest of you

have lost the quality of military support we provide, you'll remember my words.'

[63] Eurybiades was won over by Themistocles' arguments—or rather, in my opinion, by his fear that the Athenians would pull out if he took the fleet to the Isthmus, because the Athenian presence was critical to the fleet as a whole: without it, they would be no match for the enemy. So he came down in favour of Themistocles' plan of staying and fighting the decisive sea battle there.

[64] After this verbal skirmishing, and once Eurybiades had made up his mind, the Greeks at Salamis prepared to do battle there. At sunrise one day an earthquake occurred, which disturbed the sea as well as the land. The Greeks decided to offer prayers to the gods and to ask the Aeacidae for help, and they immediately put this plan into effect. They prayed to all the gods, called on Ajax and Telamon from Salamis itself, and sent a ship to Aegina to fetch Aeacus and the Aeacidae.

[65] There was an incident reported by an Athenian called Dicaeus the son of Theocydes, who had been banished from Athens and had risen to a position of prominence among the Persians. During the devastation by Xerxes' land army of Attica (now emptied of Athenians), he happened to be on the Thriasian Plain with Demaratus of Lacedaemon, he said, and he saw coming from the direction of Eleusis the kind of dust-cloud that about thirty thousand men might raise. He and Demaratus were wondering who could possibly be causing all that dust, when suddenly they heard the sound of human voices, and it seemed to Dicaeus that the sound was the cry of the mysteries, 'Iacchus!' Now, Demaratus was unacquainted with the Eleusinian rites, so he asked what the sound was. 'The king's forces are going to suffer a major disaster, Demaratus,' Dicaeus replied. 'They can't avoid it. Look, there are no people left in Attica, so this voice is clearly of divine origin, coming from Eleusis to help the Athenians and their allies. If it settles on the Peloponnese, it is Xerxes in person and his land army that will be in danger; but if it heads towards the Greek ships at Salamis, the king will probably lose his fleet. The festival in question is one in honour of the Mother and the Maiden that is celebrated every year by the Athenians, and anyone from Athens or elsewhere in Greece can be initiated if he wants to. During the course of the festival they cry out "Iacchus!", which is the sound you can hear.'

'You'd better keep quiet about this,' Demaratus said, 'and not tell anyone else. If the king hears the news, you'll lose your head, and it will be beyond me or any other human being to protect you. So if I were you, I'd keep silent. The fate of Xerxes' army is in the hands of the gods.'

That was Demaratus' advice, according to Dicaeus. Out of the dust with its sound of voices emerged a cloud which rose high into the air and was carried towards the Greek forces at Salamis. And so they realized that Xerxes' fleet was destined to be destroyed. This is the story told by Dicaeus the son of Theocydes, and he used to claim that various people, including Demaratus, could vouch for its truth.

[66] The crews of Xerxes' fleet left Trachis after viewing the evidence of the Laconian defeat and returned to Histiaea. Three days later they set out through the Euripus, and it took them another three days to get to Phalerum. It seems to me that there were as many men involved in the combined land and sea invasion of Athenian territory as there had been when they arrived at Sepias and Thermopylae. I offset the numbers of those who were killed by the storm or at Thermopylae or in the sea battles at Artemisium by those who had at that time not yet joined the king's forces— namely the Malians, Dorians, Locrians, and Boeotians (who came with every available man, except for the people of Thespiae and Plataea), and also the people of Carystus, Andros, Tenos, and all the other Aegean islands, except for the five states named earlier. For the further into Greece the Persians advanced, the more peoples joined them.

[67] When all his forces were on Athenian soil—all except the Parians, that is, since they had been left behind on Cythnos and were waiting to see how the war would turn out—and the fleet reached Phalerum, Xerxes paid them a personal visit, because he wanted to talk to them and find out what they were thinking. On arriving, he took a seat on a dais in front of an invited group consisting of the rulers of the various peoples and the officers from the fleet, whose seating arrangement was determined by how highly regarded each of them was by the king; the king of Sidon sat closest to him, then the king of Tyre, and then all the rest. When they had sorted themselves out and were all sitting in their proper places, Xerxes sent Mardonius to test each of them by asking whether or not he should meet the enemy at sea.

[68] So Mardonius went around the whole group, starting with the king of Sidon, asking this question. The unanimous view was that he should engage the enemy at sea, with only a single

dissenter—Artemisia. She said, 'Mardonius, please take this message to the king for me, reminding him that I did not play a negligible or cowardly role in the sea battles off Euboea: "Master, it is only right that I should tell you what is, in my honest opinion, the best course of action for you. So here is my advice: do not commit the fleet to a battle, because at sea your men will be as far inferior to the Greeks as women are to men. In any case, why should you have to run the risk of a sea battle? Have you not captured Athens, which was the point of the campaign? Do you not control the rest of Greece? There is no one to stand against you. Everyone who did so has met with the treatment he deserved. I will tell you what I think the future holds in store for our enemies. If you do not rush into a sea battle, master, but keep your fleet here close to shore, all you need do to gain all your objectives without any effort is either wait here or advance into the Peloponnese. The Greeks do not have the resources to hold out against you for any length of time; you will scatter them, and they will retreat to their various towns and cities. You see, I have found out that they do not have provisions on this island of theirs, and if you march overland towards the Peloponnese, it is unlikely that the Greeks from there will remain inactive or will want to fight at sea in defence of Athens. However, if you rush into a sea battle straight away, I am afraid that the defeat of the fleet will cause the land army to come to grief as well. Besides, my lord, you should bear this in mind too, that good men tend to have bad slaves, and vice versa. Now, there is no one better than you, and you do in fact have bad slaves, who are supposed to be your allies—I mean, the Egyptians, Cyprians, Cilicians, and Pamphylians, all of whom are useless." '

[69] These words of Artemisia's to Mardonius upset her friends, who assumed that the king would punish her for trying to stop him committing himself to a sea battle, while those who envied and resented her prominence within the alliance were pleased with her reply, because they thought she would be put to death. But when everybody's opinions were reported back to Xerxes, he was delighted with Artemisia's point of view; he had rated her highly before, but now she went up even further in his estimation. Nevertheless, he gave orders that the majority view was the one to follow. He believed that his men had not fought their best off Euboea because he had not been there, and so now he prepared to watch them fight.

[70] So the order was given to put to sea. They set sail for Salamis, where they had plenty of time to divide into squadrons and take up their battle formation. Night was beginning to draw in, so there was not enough daylight left for them to fight that day, and they got ready to engage the enemy on the following day. The Greeks were seized by terror. The Peloponnesians were particularly afraid, because there they were on Salamis, about to fight for Athenian territory, and if they lost the battle they would be trapped and blockaded on an island, leaving their own territory undefended.

[71] Meanwhile, that same night, the Persian land army marched towards the Peloponnese. However, everything possible had been done to prevent the Persians entering the Peloponnese by land. As soon as the Peloponnesians had heard about the death of Leonidas and his men at Thermopylae, they had flocked from their various communities and stationed themselves at the Isthmus, with Leonidas' brother, Cleombrotus the son of Anaxandridas, in command. While in position at the Isthmus, they destroyed Sciron's Road and then built a wall across the Isthmus, which was something they had discussed and decided to do. And they did succeed in completing the job, thanks to the fact that there were thousands upon thousands of them, and every single man did his share of the work. Stones, bricks, logs, and sandbags were constantly being brought to the site, and the work never stopped, night or day.

[72] The allied forces at the Isthmus consisted of every available man from the following Greek states: Lacedaemon, every community in Arcadia, Elis, Corinth, Sicyon, Epidaurus, Phleious, Troezen, and Hermione. These were the places which contributed troops in their terror over the danger facing Greece; no one else in the Peloponnese bothered to do anything, even though the Olympic and Carnean festivals were over by now.

[73] The Peloponnese is inhabited by seven peoples. Two of them—the Arcadians and the Cynurians—are indigenous and still occupy the land they originally inhabited. One people, the Achaeans, have moved from their homeland to elsewhere, but still within the Peloponnese. The remaining four peoples—the Dorians, Aetolians, Dryopians, and Lemnians—are immigrants. There are plenty of notable Dorian settlements, only a single Aetolian one (Elis), two for the Dryopians (Hermione and Asine—the Asine which is near Cardamyle in Laconia), and the Lemnians have all

the Paroreatae. The Cynurians, who live in Orneae and thereabouts, appear to be the only Ionians among the indigenous
Peloponnesians, although as a result of being ruled by Argos, and
of the passage of time, they have become thoroughly Doricized. So
apart from the places I have mentioned, all the rest of the communities of these seven peoples adopted a position of neutrality—
but, if I may speak bluntly here, remaining neutral was the same
as collaborating with the Persians.

[74] So the Greeks at the Isthmus undertook the task of building a defensive wall, because the race they were running was an
all-or-nothing affair, and because they did not expect great things
from the fleet. Although their colleagues on Salamis heard what
they were doing, it did not alleviate their fear (which was for the
Peloponnese rather than for themselves). For a while men stood
together whispering their incredulity about Eurybiades' foolishness,
but eventually their concern erupted into the open and a meeting
was convened. The same arguments came up as before, and at
considerable length. Some argued that they should sail for the
Peloponnese and take their chances fighting for it, rather than stay
there and fight for a country that had already fallen to the enemy.
But the Athenians, Aeginetans, and Megarians put the case for
staying and resisting the enemy where they were.

[75] In this debate, Themistocles was being beaten by the
Peloponnesians. He quietly slipped away from the meeting, briefed
one of his men (a house-slave of his—his children's attendant, to
be precise—whose name was Sicinnus), and sent him over to the
Persian camp in a boat. Subsequently, when the war was over,
Themistocles had him enrolled as a citizen of Thespiae, which was
accepting new citizens, and made him a wealthy man too. At the
time in question, Sicinnus sailed over and said to the Persian commanders, 'I am on a secret mission for the Athenian commander,
who is in fact sympathetic to Xerxes' cause and would prefer you
to gain the upper hand in the war rather than the Greeks. None of
the other Greeks know that I am here. The message from my master
is that the Greeks are in a state of panic and are planning to retreat.
Unless you just stand by and let them escape, you have an opportunity here to achieve a glorious victory. They are disunited, in no
postion to offer you resistance; in fact you'll see them pitting their
ships against one another, those who are on your side fighting those
who are not.' After delivering this message, Sicinnus left.

[76] The Persian reaction to the message, which they felt to be reliable, was first to send a sizeable body of troops ashore on the little island that lies between Salamis and the mainland, and, second, to have two sections of the fleet put to sea in the middle of the night. The first section, the western wing of the fleet, sailed on a wide curve for Salamis, while the second section, consisting of the ships stationed near Ceos and Cynosura, blocked the whole channel all the way to Munichia. The reason they put to sea was to stop the Greeks escaping; they wanted to trap them on Salamis and make them pay for the battles at Artemisium. And the reason they landed Persian troops on the little island (which is called Psyttaleia) was that it lies in the straits where the battle was due to take place, and so it would be the main place where men and disabled ships would be washed ashore after the battle; with troops there, then, they could save the lives of their own men and kill everyone else. All these preparations (which they carried out in silence, to prevent the enemy finding out) meant that they got no sleep that night.

[77] I cannot argue against the truth of oracles, because when they speak clearly I do not want to try to discredit them. Consider the following lines:†

> But when they have used their ships as a bridge to link
> The holy shore of gold-bladed Artemis with sea-girt Cynosura,
> Their hopes raised to fever pitch by the sack of gleaming Athens,
> Then shall bright Justice quench Pride's son, mighty Excess,
> For all his fearsome lust and purpose to devour the earth.†
> Weapon shall clash with weapon, and with blood shall Ares
> Crimson the sea. Then freedom will dawn for Greece,
> Brought on by far-seeing Zeus and noble Victory.

Faced with the clarity of this kind of statement (from Bacis, in this instance), I hesitate to challenge the validity of oracles myself, and I do not accept such challenges from others either.

[78] So the commanders at Salamis were furiously hurling arguments at one another. They were still unaware that they had been surrounded by the Persian fleet, and continued to assume that the enemy had remained where they had seen them stationed during the day.

[79] While the commanders were locked in argument a man called Aristides the son of Lysimachus crossed over to Salamis from

Aegina. Aristides was an Athenian who had been ostracized by the democratic government. In my considered opinion, from all I hear about his character, he was the best and most honourable man in Athens. He presented himself at the meeting and asked Themistocles to come outside with him. Now, he was no friend of Themistocles—in fact, they were bitter enemies—but the scale of the trouble facing Athens at the time made him overlook this. So he asked Themistocles to leave the meeting because he wanted to have a word with him; he already knew that the Peloponnesian contingents could hardly wait to sail back to the Isthmus. When Themistocles joined him outside, Aristides said, 'The rivalry between us should only be about which of us will do our country more good— that goes not just for now, but for any other occasion too. Now, I can tell you that it doesn't make any difference whether the Peloponnesians go on about sailing away from here or spend hardly any time discussing the matter, because they won't be able to do so anyway. I can assure you of that, because I've seen the reason for myself. Neither the Corinthians nor Eurybiades will be able to sail away from here, because we are surrounded by the enemy. You'd better go back into the meeting and tell them the news.'

[80] 'That's a very good idea,' Themistocles replied. 'And you've brought good news. That's exactly what I wanted to happen—and you've seen it with your very own eyes. I should explain that this move on the part of the Persians was instigated by me. The Greeks didn't want to join battle, so I had to force them into it. But since you are the one who has brought this good news, why don't you deliver the message yourself? If I tell them, they'll think I'm making it up and they won't believe me, on the grounds that the Persians couldn't be doing any such thing. Go in and explain the situation in person. They may believe what you're saying, which would be best, but even if they don't, that won't make any difference, since they still won't be able to run away if we're completely surrounded, as you say.'

[81] So Aristides went in to the Greek commaders. He told them that the Greek navy was entirely surrounded by Xerxes' fleet—so much so that on his way from Aegina he had only just managed to slip past the enemy blockade—and he advised them to get ready to face an attack. Afterwards, he left the meeting. Then the arguments began all over again, because most of the commanders did not believe the news.

[82] Just then, while they were still inclined to disbelieve Aristides' report, a crew of Tenian deserters, commanded by one of their countrymen called Panaetius the son of Sosimenes, brought their trireme into Salamis. They were able to give the Greeks a complete and accurate account of the situation. It is because of this action of theirs that the Tenians are named on the inscribed tripod in Delphi among those who were responsible for the defeat of the Persian invader. With the desertion of this ship to the Greek side at Salamis, and the earlier Lemnian ship that had come over to the Greeks at Artemisium, the Greek fleet made up the deficit of two that it lacked to consist of a total of exactly 380 ships.

[83] Now that the Greeks had accepted the Tenians' report, they prepared themselves for battle. At daybreak they assembled all the marines and gave them their orders. Themistocles put things better than anyone else. He spent the whole of his speech contrasting all the better and the worse aspects of human nature and temperament, and encouraging the marines to choose the better course; he ended by sending them off to their ships. Just after they had boarded their ships, the trireme which had been given the mission of fetching the Aeacidae arrived from Aegina. Then the Greeks launched their whole fleet, and no sooner had they done so than the Persians attacked them.

[84] Most of the Greek ships began to back water and head back to shore, but an Athenian called Ameinias of Pallene sent his ship headlong into the attack. His ship became inextricably entangled with an enemy ship—and so the rest of the Greek fleet joined in by coming to help Ameinias. This is the Athenian version of the start of the battle, but the Aeginetans say that it was the ship which had been sent to Aegina to fetch the Aeacidae that started it. Yet another account claims that a ghostly woman appeared and, in a voice that reached every man of the fleet, gave the Greeks their orders, first telling them off with the words: 'Fools, when are you going to stop retreating?'

[85] In the direction of Eleusis, the Phoenicians made up the western wing of the Persian fleet, and so were drawn up opposite the Athenians; in the direction of the Piraeus, the Ionians, who formed the eastern wing, faced the Lacedaemonians. However, only a few of the Ionians complied with Themistocles' instructions and deliberately fought below their best; the rest of them fought as normal. I could list the names of a lot of Ionian captains who

captured Greek ships, but I will restrict myself to mentioning only two Samians—Theomestor the son of Androdamas and Phylacus the son of Histiaeus. The reason I mention them is because it was as a result of this achievement that Theomestor was instituted by the Persians as the tyrant of Samos, while Phylacus' name was entered on the list of the king's benefactors and he was rewarded with a large estate. The Persian word for these 'king's benefactors' is *orosangai*.

[86] That is how these two fared in the battle, but most of the Persian ships at Salamis were destroyed by either the Athenians or the Aeginetans. This happened because the Greeks fought in a disciplined and tactical manner, while the Persians became disorganized and lost their battle plan. As a result, what happened to them was entirely predictable. Nevertheless, they displayed and acted with far more courage that day than they had off Euboea: every single one of them fought with determination, spurred on by his fear of Xerxes, and each of them imagined that the king's eyes were on him.

[87] I am not in a position to say for certain how particular Persians or Greeks fought, but Artemisia's behaviour caused her to rise even higher in the king's estimation. It so happened that in the midst of the general confusion of the Persian fleet, Artemisia's ship was being chased by one from Attica. She found it impossible to escape, because the way ahead was blocked by friendly ships, and hostile ships were particularly close to hers, so she decided on a plan which did in fact do her a lot of good. With the Attic ship close astern, she bore down on and rammed one of the ships from her own side, which was crewed by men from Calynda and had on board Damasithymus, the king of Calynda. Now, I cannot say whether she and Damasithymus had fallen out while they were based at the Hellespont, or whether this action of hers was premeditated, or whether the Calyndan ship just happened to be in the way at the time. In any case, she found that by ramming it and sinking it she created for herself a double piece of good fortune. In the first place, when the captain of the Attic ship saw her ramming an enemy vessel, he assumed that Artemisia's ship was either Greek or was a defector from the Persians fighting on his side, so he changed course and turned to attack other ships.

[88] So the first piece of good fortune was that she escaped and remained alive. The second was that although she was quite the

opposite of the king's benefactor, her actions made Xerxes particularly pleased with her. It is reported that as Xerxes was watching the battle he noticed her ship ramming the other vessel, and one of his entourage said, 'Master, can you see how well Artemisia is fighting? Look, she has sunk an enemy ship!'

Xerxes asked if it was really Artemisia, and they confirmed that it was, because they could recognize the insignia on her ship, and therefore assumed that the ship she had destroyed was one of the enemy's—an assumption that was never refuted, because a particular feature of the general good fortune of Artemisia, as noted, was that no one from the Calyndan ship survived to point the finger at her. In response to what his courtiers were telling him, the story goes on, Xerxes said, 'My men have turned into women and my women into men!' That is what Xerxes is supposed to have said.

[89] During this mêlée Xerxes' brother Ariabignes the son of Darius, who was one of the Persian military commanders, lost his life; a great many other famous men, from Persia, Media, and every country in the enemy alliance, also died. A few Greeks lost their lives too—but only a few, because they knew how to swim, and so when their ships were destroyed those who remained alive after the close fighting swam over to Salamis. Most of the casualties on the Persian side were men who drowned because they did not know how to swim. The largest numbers of lives were lost during the phase of the battle when the first line of Persian ships were turning to flight, because the crews of the ships behind them were still trying to get past the ones in front and show the king that they too could perform well, so they fell foul of the ships from their own side which were withdrawing.

[90] Another thing that happened in the thick of the battle was that some of the Phoenicians, whose ships had been destroyed, came to the king and insinuated that the loss of their ships was due to the Ionians having failed in their duty. But as things turned out it was not the Ionian commanders who lost their lives over this, but their Phoenician accusers who received their just deserts. While they were in the middle of registering their complaint with the king, a Samothracian ship rammed an Attic ship, which started to sink, whereupon an Aeginetan ship sailed into the attack and sank the Samothracian one. But the Samothracians hurled the javelins with which they were armed, mowed down the marines on the ship that had sunk them, boarded the vessel, and took it over. It was this

episode that saved the lives of the Ionians. When Xerxes saw the Samothracians achieve such a heroic feat, he turned to the Phoenicians in a rage and put the blame for what was happening on all of them. He ordered their heads cut off, so that never again would they traduce their betters. (Xerxes was watching the battle from the foot of the hill called Aegaleos which faces Salamis, and whenever anything went well for his side, he asked who the captain of the ship in question was, and his scribes wrote down the name of the man, his father, and the town he came from.) The fate of the Phoenicians was also helped to a certain extent by the presence of Ariaramnes, a Persian who was friendly towards the Ionians.

[91] So Xerxes' men turned to deal with the Phoenicians. Meanwhile the Persian fleet was in full flight towards Phalerum, but the Aeginetans were waiting for them in the straits and won a notable victory. The Athenians were in the thick of the battle, destroying ships whether they were offering resistance or merely trying to escape, and the Aeginetans were doing the same to any ships that tried to make it through the straits. If a Persian ship managed to escape the Athenians, it sailed right into the middle of the Aeginetans.

[92] At this juncture there was an encounter between Themistocles' ship, which was in pursuit of an enemy vessel, and the ship commanded by an Aeginetan called Polycritus the son of Crius. Polycritus' trireme had rammed a Sidonian ship—in fact, the very Sidonian vessel that had captured the Aeginetan advance-guard ship off Sciathos, on board which was Pytheas the son of Ischenoüs, who had so impressed the Persians with his courage that after hacking him to pieces they kept him on their ship. So the capture of the Sidonian ship and its Persian crew who had been travelling around with Pytheas on board meant that Pytheas got back safe and sound to Aegina! Anyway, when Polycritus saw the Attic ship, he recognized by its insignia that it was the flagship, and he called out to Themistocles, taunting him with the fact that the Aeginetans were supposed to have collaborated with the enemy. So he used his ship to ram an enemy vessel, and then hurled this mocking reminder at Themistocles. The crews of the Persian ships which survived the withdrawal reached Phalerum under the protection of their land forces.

[93] Acclaimed with the highest honours in this battle were the Aeginetans, followed by the Athenians; particular individuals who

earned names for themselves were Polycritus of Aegina and, from Athens, Eumenes of Anagyrus and Ameinias of Pallene. Ameinias was also the one who had chased Artemisia. If he had realized that Artemisia was on board, he would not have stopped until he had either captured her or been captured himself, not just because all the Athenian captains had orders to that effect, but also because a reward of ten thousand drachmas had been offered for capturing her alive, since the Athenians were furious that a woman was attacking their city. In any case, as I explained earlier, she escaped, and she and the others whose ships survived the battle were now at Phalerum.

[94] According to the Athenians, it was right at the beginning of the battle when Adeimantus, the Corinthian commander, was so overcome by panic that he hoisted his sails and beat a hasty retreat, followed—when they saw their flagship withdrawing—by the rest of the Corinthian contingent. In the course of their retreat they had just reached that part of Salamis where the sanctuary of Athena Sciras stands when they came across a boat which must have been sent by divine providence, because no one has even been found who sent it there, and before the encounter the Corinthians were completely unaware of what was happening with the rest of the fleet. This is what led them to conclude that it was a miracle. When the boat drew near the Corinthian ships the crew called out, 'You're betraying the Greeks, Adeimantus, by turning your ships around and running away, but they're winning just the kind of victory they wanted over the enemy.' Adeimantus did not believe what they were saying, so they spoke again, this time offering themselves as hostages and saying that Adeimantus could take them along and kill them if he found that the Greeks were not winning the battle. So he turned the whole squadron around again and arrived back at the main fleet only to find that it was all over. This is the rumour spread by the Athenians about the Corinthians, but the Corinthians disagree and say that they were, on the contrary, among the first to join battle, and the rest of Greece backs them up in this claim.

[95] As for Aristides the son of Lysimachus (the Athenian I mentioned a short while ago as being a man of outstanding merit), while the battle was raging off Salamis, he took a number of hoplites from the Athenian contingent which had been posted along the coastline of Salamis and put them ashore on the island of Psyttaleia, where they massacred all the Persians on the island.

[96] When the battle was over, the Greeks pulled ashore on Salamis all the wrecks which had not drifted away and generally got themselves ready for another sea battle, because they did not think that the king had finished: he still had the rest of his fleet. But a westerly wind carried most of the wrecks to Attica, where they ended up on Colias beach. And so every prediction about the battle came true—not only the ones made by Bacis and Musaeus, but also the statement made in an oracle many years previously about the wrecks which came ashore there, and published by Lysistratus, an Athenian oracle-monger. No one in Greece had been able to interpret the prediction, which went like this: 'The women of Colias will do their roasting with oars.' But this was still in the future, after Xerxes had marched away.

[97] When Xerxes realized the extent of the disaster that had taken place, he became afraid. What if the Greeks got the idea (or had it suggested to them by one of the Ionians) of sailing to the Hellespont and demolishing his bridges? In that case, he would be trapped in Europe, and would probably be wiped out. And so Xerxes' thoughts turned to flight. However, he did not want to let either the Greeks or his own troops know what was going through his mind, so he tried to build a causeway across to Salamis, which involved tying Phoenician merchant ships together to act as both a pontoon bridge and a barrier. He also made other military preparations, as if he were going to instigate another sea battle. The sight of all this activity convinced everyone that he had every intention of staying and fighting—everyone except Mardonius, that is, who knew Xerxes' mind better than anyone and was not deceived.

[98] At the same time, Xerxes also dispatched a messenger to Persia with news of their defeat. There is nothing mortal that is faster than the system the Persians have devised for sending messages. Apparently, they have horses and men posted at intervals along the route, the same number in total as the overall length in days of the journey, with a fresh horse and rider for every day of travel. Whatever the conditions—it may be snowing, raining, blazing hot, or dark—they never fail to complete their assigned journey in the fastest possible time. The first man passes his instructions on to the second, the second to the third, and so on, in the same kind of relay found in Greece in the torch-race which is run during the festival of Hephaestus. The Persian word for this postal system involving horses is *angareion*.

[99] The first report that reached Susa, that Xerxes had taken Athens, caused the Persians who had stayed at home so much pleasure that they spread myrtle over all the roads, burnt perfumed spices, and spent their time performing sacrificial rites and feasting. However, the arrival of the second message on top of the first so overwhelmed them that they all tore their tunics and gave themselves over to unending weeping and wailing. They blamed Mardonius for the disaster. But these displays of grief by the Persians came not so much from their distress about the fleet as from their fear about Xerxes himself.

[100] From then on, until Xerxes actually got back to Susa and put an end to it, the Persians remained in this state. Meanwhile, Mardonius could see how terribly upset Xerxes was as a result of the sea battle and suspected that he was thinking about running away from Athens. He was also worried about himself; he expected to be punished for having persuaded the king to march on Greece, and he thought it would be better for him to take his chances on either subduing Greece or dying a noble death for great stakes. However, it seemed to him that of these two alternatives the conquest of Greece was the more likely. Having come to these conclusions, then, he put the following proposal to Xerxes. 'Master,' he said, 'don't let what has happened distress you or upset you; it's not as bad as all that. After all, this conflict depends, in the final analysis, not on planks of wood, but on men and horses. These Greeks may think that they have already won the ultimate victory, but none of them is going to come ashore from his ship and offer you any resistance, and the same goes for everyone else from this whole continent. Besides, those who did put up some resistance paid for it. So if you think it's a good idea, let's attack the Peloponnese straight away. Or if you'd rather wait a while first, we can do that too. But whatever you decide, don't lose heart, because there is no way out for the Greeks: they are bound to pay for what they've done to us just now and for what they did earlier, and they cannot escape becoming our slaves. This is really what you should do. However, if you've already decided to withdraw and pull the army back, I've got a plan to cover this option too. What you must avoid, my lord, is giving the Greeks the opportunity to mock the Persians. The hurt you have incurred has not been due to the Persians at all; you cannot point to any occasion when we proved ourselves to be cowards. It may be that the Phoenicians, Egyptians,

Cyprians, and Cilicians were cowards, but the Persians had nothing to do with this defeat. Since your Persian troops are not to blame, then, here is my advice. If you've decided not to stay, by all means take most of the army back to your homeland; but let me pick 300,000 men and I'll make you the master of Greece.'

[101] These words of Mardonius' cheered Xerxes up, and he became as happy as anyone could be in such a dire situation. He told Mardonius that he would consult his advisers and then let him know which of the two possible courses of action he would take. He convened a meeting of Persians, and while he was listening to their advice it occurred to him to invite Artemisia along too, to see what she would suggest, because of the earlier occasion on which she had turned out to be the only one with a realistic plan of action. When she came, he dismissed everyone else—his Persian advisers and his personal guards—and said, 'Mardonius says I should stay here and attack the Peloponnese. He thinks the Persians and the land army in general are not to be held responsible for the defeat I have incurred, and says they would gladly show me what they're capable of. Alternatively, if I don't put this plan into effect, he is prepared to pick 300,000 men and enslave Greece for me, while I take the rest of the army and withdraw to my homeland. Now, before the sea battle which has just taken place, you advised me to avoid it, and that was good advice, so I want you now to tell me which of these two courses of action I would be best advised to follow, in your opinion.'

[102] In response to this request for advice, Artemisia said, 'My lord, it isn't actually easy for me to say what's best, but things being as they are I think you should pull back and leave Mardonius here with the troops he's asking for, since he's offering to do that of his own free will. My thinking is that if he succeeds in the conquests he says he has set himself and things go as he intends, the achievement is yours, master, because it was your slaves who did it. But if things go wrong for Mardonius, it will be no great disaster as regards your survival and the prosperity of your house. I mean, if you and your house survive, the Greeks will still have to run many a race for their lives. But if anything happens to Mardonius, it doesn't really matter; besides, if the Greeks win, it won't be an important victory, because they will only have destroyed one of your slaves. The whole point of this campaign of yours was to burn Athens to the ground; you've done that, so now you can leave.'

[103] Xerxes was happy with this advice of hers, since it coincided with his own intentions. But I think he was so frightened that he would not have stayed even if every man and every woman had told him to. So he complimented Artemisia on her advice and gave her the job of taking his children to Ephesus (some illegitimate children of his had come along on the expedition).

[104] The man he sent along to look after these children of his, Hermotimus, came from Pedasa and was his most highly prized eunuch.†

[105] No one we know of has ever exacted a more total retribution for a wrong done to him than Hermotimus. He was taken prisoner in a war, put up for sale, and bought by a man from Chios called Panionius. Now, Panionius made a living in the most atrocious way imaginable. What he used to do was acquire good-looking boys, castrate them, and take them to Sardis and Ephesus, where he would offer them for sale at very high prices; in foreign countries eunuchs command higher prices than whole men on account of their complete reliability. One of Panionius' victims— one among a great many, because this was the way he made a living—was Hermotimus. In fact, however, Hermotimus' luck was not all bad: he was sent from Sardis to Xerxes' court as one of a number of gifts, and eventually became the king's most valued eunuch.

[106] Now, when Xerxes was in Sardis, in the course of setting out with his army against Athens, Hermotimus went down on some business or other to the part of Mysia called Atarneus, where people from Chios live, and he met Panionius there. He entered into a long, friendly conversation with him, first listing all the benefits that had come his way thanks to Panionius, and then offering to do as much good to him in return; all he had to do, he said, was move his family to Atarneus and live there. Panionius gladly accepted Hermotimus' offer and moved his wife and children there. So when Hermotimus had Panionius and his whole family where he wanted, he said, 'Panionius, there is no one in the world who makes a living in as foul a way as you do. What harm did I or any of my family do to you or any of yours? Why did you make me a nothing instead of a man? You expected the gods not to notice what you used to do in those days, but the law they follow is one of justice, and for your crimes they have delivered you into my hands. As a result, then, you should have no grounds for complaint about

the payment I am going to exact from you.' When he had finished this rebuke, he had Panionius' sons brought into the room and proceeded to force him to castrate all four of them. The deed was done, under compulsion, and afterwards Hermotimus forced the sons to castrate their father. And that is how vengeance and Hermotimus caught up with Panionius.

[107] Once Xerxes had entrusted Artemisia with the job of taking his sons to Ephesus, he summoned Mardonius and told him to take his pick of men from the army, and to do everything he could to make sure his actions matched his words. That was as far as things went that day, but during the night, acting under instructions from Xerxes, the commanders began the voyage back from Phalerum to the Hellespont. Each of them made as much speed as he could, with the object of bringing his ships back to guard the pontoon bridge for the king's return journey. At one point in the course of the voyage, the Persian fleet found itself near Zoster. Now, there is a series of small promontories there, jutting out into the sea; the Persians mistook these rocks for ships and fled a considerable distance. It was only when they finally realized that they were rocks and not ships that they re-assembled and continued on their way.

[108] The next day the Greeks saw that the land army had remained in place and assumed that the fleet too was still at Phalerum, so they prepared to defend themselves in the sea battle they anticipated. As soon as they found out that the fleet had left, they decided to set out in pursuit, but by the time they were off Andros they still had not caught sight of the Persians. They put in at Andros and talked things over. Themistocles expressed the view that they should make their way through the Aegean islands after the Persian fleet and head straight for the Hellespont in order to try to demolish the bridges. Eurybiades, however, was in favour of the opposite plan. He argued that demolishing the bridges would be the worst possible thing to do for Greece. His reasoning was that if Xerxes was trapped in Europe and forced to stay there, he would go on the rampage for all he was worth, since inactivity would not further his plans, and would also not help him find a way back home; at the same time, his men would start dying of hunger. But if he put his mind to it and applied himself to the task, the whole of Europe could fall to him, city by city and people by people, as they were either defeated by him or came to terms with

him in order to avoid defeat, and then the Persians would be able
to live off the Greeks' annual crops. In fact, Eurybiades went on,
he considered it unlikely that Xerxes would stay in Europe now
that he had been defeated at sea. It therefore followed that they
should let him escape all the way back to his homeland. And from
then on, he told them, it would be Xerxes' country that was at risk.
The commanders of the rest of the Peloponnesian forces agreed
with Eurybiades' point of view.

[109] The Athenians were particularly annoyed by the Persians'
escape and were perfectly prepared to sail to the Hellespont on their
own if the others refused to join them, so when Themistocles realized that he was not going to persuade a majority of the commanders to go to the Hellespont, he changed tack and addressed the
Athenians. 'Eurybiades is right,' he said. 'In cases I've seen and even
more I've heard about, cornered men fight back after a defeat, and
even make amends for their earlier cowardice. Now, we Athenians
and the whole of Greece have already benefited from our luck in
repelling such an immense swarm of men; they have already taken
to their heels, so why should we go after them? In any case, it was
not we who accomplished this, but the gods and heroes, who did
not want to see a single man ruling both Asia and Europe—and a
man who commits terrible atrocities too. A man who does not distinguish between sacred and profane things, but burns and topples
the statues of the gods; a man who even thrashed the sea and sank
shackles into it. Under the present circumstances let us stay in
Greece now and take care of ourselves and our families. The foreign
invader has been pushed back right beyond our borders, so now is
the time for rebuilding homes and for sowing our fields. Spring will
be the time for us to sail for the Hellespont and Ionia.' His reason
for saying this was to earn credit with Xerxes, so that if he ever
got into trouble with the Athenians, he would have somewhere to
turn to. And in fact this is exactly what happened.

[110] The Athenians were won over by Themistocles' disingenuous speech. He already had a reputation as a man of some ability,
but now that his competence had been demonstrated beyond a
doubt, and his advice had been proved sound, they were ready to
do anything he said. As soon as they had been won over, Themistocles sent off in a boat some men whose silence he knew he could
rely on; even if they were being tortured to death, they would not
reveal the contents of the message he was sending to the king. His

house-slave Sicinnus was again one of this group. When they reached Attica, Sicinnus went ashore and met with Xerxes while the rest of them stayed on the boat. 'I am here', Sicinnus told Xerxes, 'on a mission from Themistocles the son of Neocles, the commander of the Athenian forces, and the bravest and ablest man in the Greek army. Here is my message: Themistocles of Athens, wishing to do you a favour, has stopped the Greeks from carrying out their plan of pursuing your fleet and demolishing the bridges over the Hellespont. You can now make your way home in peace.'

[111] Once the message had been delivered, Themistocles' men returned. Now that the Greeks had decided against following the Persian fleet any further or sailing to the Hellespont to dismantle the causeway, they proceeded to besiege the town of Andros with the intention of taking it. For Themistocles had asked the Aegean islanders to provide financial support, and had started with the Andrians, but they refused. The argument Themistocles put forward to the Andrians was that the Athenians had come with two great gods in their train called Persuasion and Compulsion, and so they had really better give them some money. The Andrians replied to this by saying: 'Of course Athens is so important and prosperous, seeing that she is so well endowed with useful gods. However, there is no one on earth who is worse off for land than we are on Andros, and we have two cruel gods here, who never leave our island but are our constant and loyal companions. These gods are Poverty and Insufficiency, and since they are the gods we possess, we will not give you any money. However strong the might of Athens, it will never be stronger than Andrian impotence.' This was their reply to Themistocles. And so, because they refused to give any money, they found themselves besieged.

[112] This did not put an end to Themistocles' greed, however, and, using the same messengers as he had for Xerxes, he sent threatening demands for money to the other islands. If they did not give him what he was asking for, he said, he would bring the Greek army against them and blockade them into submission. This message enabled him to collect a great deal of money from the Carystians and Parians, because they found out that Andros was under siege for having collaborated with the Persians and that Themistocles' standing among the Greek commanders was particularly high, and this scared them into sending money. I am not in

a position to say for certain whether or not any of the other islands made a contribution, but I think some of them did and not only the Carystians and Parians. Nevertheless, the Carystians, at any rate, did not win any postponement of their troubles by this means, although the Parians managed to bribe Themistocles to keep the Greek forces away from their island. And so, from his base on Andros, Themistocles was extorting money from the Aegean islanders without the rest of the Greek commanders knowing about it.

[113] Xerxes and the land army let a few days pass after the sea battle before retracing their steps back into Boeotia. The whole land army was involved, because Mardonius had decided to escort the king on his way; given that it was not the right time of the year for warfare, he also thought it would be better to establish winter quarters in Thessaly and then to attack the Peloponnese at the beginning of spring. After they had reached Thessaly, Mardonius chose his men. He first picked all the Persians known as the Immortals, with the exception of their commander Hydarnes, who refused to be separated from the king. Next, from the remaining Persian troops he chose the ones with heavy armour and the 1,000-strong troop of horsemen, and then he picked all the infantry and cavalry the Medes, Sacae, Bactrians, and Indians had supplied. He chose every man from these peoples indiscriminately, but he took only a few at a time from the other allied contingents, making either stature or proven worth the basis of his selection. The largest contingent in his élite force was made up of Persians—men who wear necklaces and arm-bands—and then there were the Medes, who did not fall short of the Persians in terms of quantity, but lacked their strength. Counting the horsemen, the whole army consisted of 300,000 men.

[114] While Mardonius was selecting his army and Xerxes was in Thessaly, an oracle reached the Lacedaemonians from Delphi, telling them to demand compensation from Xerxes for the murder of Leonidas and to accept whatever he offered. The Spartiates sent a herald straight away, and he caught up with the Persian army in Thessaly. He came before Xerxes and addressed him as follows: 'King of Persia, the Lacedaemonians and the Heraclidae of Sparta demand compensation from you for the murder of their king who died defending Greece.' Xerxes burst out laughing and then, after a long pause, he pointed to Mardonius, who happened to be

standing by his side, and said, 'All right, then, here's Mardonius. He'll pay them what they deserve.'

[115] The Lacedaemonian herald accepted this reply and left. Xerxes left Mardonius in Thessaly, made his way at some speed towards the Hellespont, and reached the bridge forty-five days later, with what can without exaggeration be described as an insignificant fraction of his army. On their way from Thessaly to the Hellespont, wherever they went and whatever people they encountered, they stole and ate their crops. If there were no crops to be had, they ate grass and herbs they found growing in the ground, and bark and leaves they peeled or pulled off both wild trees and cultivated ones. They were so hungry that they left nothing untried. Moreover, they were ravaged by disease, and men were dying of dysentery throughout the journey. Xerxes also left sick troops in the care and maintenance of whichever community they had reached at that particular point of the march; this happened in Thessaly, in Macedonia, and at Siris in Paeonia.† On his way back, he failed to get back the sacred chariot of Zeus from Siris; in the course of marching on Greece, he had left the chariot and horses there, but the Paeonians had handed them over to the Thracians, so when he asked for them back, they told him that the horses had been stolen while at pasture by some Thracians from the interior, near the source of the Strymon.

[116] This was also the point at which the king of Bisaltia and Crestonia, who was a Thracian, did something particularly inhuman. He had refused to surrender his freedom voluntarily to Xerxes, preferring to take refuge on Mount Rhodope, and he had forbidden his sons from marching against Greece either, but they had paid no attention, or perhaps they just wanted to see the war, and had joined Xerxes' expedition. All six of them returned without a scratch from the war, but their father made them pay for their crime by gouging out their eyes.

[117] Meanwhile, the Persians left Thrace and made their way to the bridge. When they got there, they crossed the Hellespont over the ships to Abydus as quickly as possible, because they found that the pontoon bridge had been shaken loose by a storm. During their time at Abydus there was more food available than there had been on the road, but their undisciplined gorging and the change of water caused further deaths in the already reduced army. The remainder went on to Sardis with Xerxes.

[118] Another story about Xerxes' retreat from Athens claims that from Eïon on the Strymon onwards he gave up travelling by land; instead he made Hydarnes responsible for getting the army to the Hellespont, while he himself made his way to Asia on board a Phoenician ship. The story goes that in the course of the voyage a strong wind—the Strymonian wind—arose and whipped up the sea. The ship was overladen with all the Persians who were travelling with Xerxes on its deck, and the danger from the storm was increasing. Xerxes was overcome by fear and called out to the helmsman to ask what their chances were of surviving. 'None at all, master,' the helmsman replied, 'unless we get rid of this crowd of passengers.'

On hearing this, the story continues, Xerxes addressed his men. 'My life is in your hands, it seems, gentlemen of Persia,' he said. 'Now you have an opportunity to show how much you care for the safety of your king.' In response to his words the men prostrated themselves before him and then jumped into the sea. The ship, now lightened, reached Asia safely. As soon as he went ashore, Xerxes gave a garland of gold to the helmsman, for saving the king's life—and then cut off his head for causing the deaths of so many Persians!

[119] The whole of this alternative version of Xerxes' return seems to me to be suspect, with its most unbelievable aspect being what happened to the Persians. If the helmsman really had told Xerxes what he is supposed to have said, I do not think even one person in ten thousand would doubt that the king would have sent the passengers—who were, after all, not just Persians, but the leading lights of Persian society—down into the ship's hold from the deck, while he cast an equal number of the oarsmen, who were merely Phoenicians, overboard into the sea. But my earlier description of his journey was the true one: he returned home to Asia by road along with the rest of the army.

[120] There is substantial evidence to support this, since it was evidently during his return journey that Xerxes stopped in Abdera and made a pact of friendship with them, sealing the agreement with gifts of a golden *akinakes* and a *tiara* shot through with gold. (The Abderans add the feature, which personally I do not believe in the slightest, that it was only when Xerxes reached Abdera that he felt safe enough for the first time since retreating from Athens to undo his belt.) Abdera is closer to the Hellespont than the

Strymon and Eïon, which is where he is supposed to have taken ship.

[121] Once the Greeks had found it impossible to take Andros, they turned their attention to Carystus, where they laid waste to the land before leaving and returning to Salamis. First they set aside victory-offerings for the gods, including three Phoenician triremes, one of which they dedicated at the Isthmus (where it remained till my day), and another at Sunium, while the third was dedicated on Salamis itself to Ajax. Then they divided up the spoils and sent their victory-offerings to Delphi, which paid for a statue, twelve cubits tall, with the beak of a ship in its hand; this statue is situated in the same place as the golden statue of Alexander the Macedonian.

[122] The Greeks next jointly asked the god whether the victory-offerings they had sent him at Delphi were sufficient and met with his approval. He replied that he was satisfied with what the rest of the Greeks had given, but not with the Aeginetan contribution; he required from them the prize they had won for valour at the battle of Salamis. On hearing this response, the Aeginetans dedicated three golden stars which are fixed on to a bronze mast which occupies a corner very near the bowl dedicated by Croesus.

[123] Next, after dividing the spoils, the Greek fleet set sail for the Isthmus where they planned to award a prize for valour to the Greek whose conduct throughout the war had proved that he was best qualified to receive it. On arriving at the Isthmus, the commanders cast their votes on the altar of Poseidon. Each of them had to make a first and second choice from among their number. Every single one of them judged himself to have been the bravest and voted for himself, but Themistocles won a majority of the second votes. So while they each won at least a single vote, Themistocles was the clear winner of the second round.

[124] Out of envy, the Greeks refused to come to a decision, and they dispersed back to their various homelands without having awarded the prize. Nevertheless, the name of Themistocles was on everyone's lips and throughout the land he acquired the reputation of being by far the most competent man in Greece. But since no reward was forthcoming, despite his having won the vote, from the Greeks who fought at Salamis, he immediately went to Lacedaemon in the hope of finding recognition there. And in fact the Lacedaemonians did make him very welcome, and heaped honours upon him. It is true that they gave the olive-wreath prize for valour

to Eurybiades, but they also gave an olive wreath to Themistocles, in recognition of his skill and ingenuity. They also presented him with the most handsome chariot in Sparta. They praised him highly, and when he left they gave him as an escort a unit of three hundred élite Spartiate troops—the Knights, as they are known—who accompanied him as far as the border with Tegea. No one else, as far as we know, has ever had a Spartiate escort.

[125] When he got back to Athens from Lacedaemon, a man called Timodemus of Aphidnae, whose only claim to fame was his hostility towards Themistocles, was so insanely jealous that he picked a quarrel with him, criticizing his visit to Lacedaemon and saying that it was thanks to Athens, not to his own merits, that he had been honoured by the Lacedaemonians. Timodemus kept on and on at him in this vein, until Themistocles replied, 'It's true that if I came from Belbina the Spartiates wouldn't have honoured me as they did, but they wouldn't have honoured you, my friend, even though you come from Athens!' And that was the end of that.

[126] Artabazus the son of Pharnaces (who was already highly thought of by the Persians before the business at Plataea, which enhanced his reputation even more) escorted the king as far as the bridge with sixty thousand men from Mardonius' picked army. Once the king was in Asia, he started back. On the way, when he reached Pallene, he found the people of Potidaea in revolt; they and the rest of the inhabitants of Pallene had come out in open revolt against the invaders as soon as Xerxes' army had passed by on its retreat from Greece and after the flight of the Persian fleet from Salamis. So under these circumstances, and since he was not yet in any hurry to meet up with the rest of the army, which was wintering with Mardonius in Thessaly and Macedonia, Artabazus thought it appropriate to reduce the population of Potidaea to slavery.

[127] So Artabazus proceeded to put Potidaea under siege. He also began to besiege Olynthus, which he suspected of joining the rebellion against the king. Some Bottiaeans had taken possession of the town after being driven out of the Gulf of Therma by the Macedonians. After besieging the town into submission, Artabazus took the Bottiaeans to a nearby lake and slaughtered them there. Then he handed the government of the town over to Critobulus of Torone and the Chalcidians—which is how the Chalcidians got Olynthus.

[128] After the capture of Olynthus, Artabazus concentrated on Potidaea, and his determination was rewarded, since Timoxenus, the commander of the troops from Scione, agreed to betray the town to him. I cannot say anything about how their negotiations got started, because there is no record of that, but by the end, whenever one of them wanted to send a letter he had written to the other, he would wrap the letter around the shaft of an arrow, next to the slits for the feathers, cover the letter with the feathers, and then shoot the arrow to a pre-arranged location. Timoxenus' treachery was found out, however. Artabazus' shot once missed the pre-arranged spot and hit a Potidaean man in the shoulder; as is usual in times of war, a crowd of people ran to help the wounded man, and in no time at all, when they had got hold of the arrow, they noticed the letter. They took it to the commanders (the Potidaeans had allies from other communities in Pallene fighting there), who read it and discovered the identity of the traitor. However, for the sake of the town of Scione they decided not to publicize Timoxenus' guilt, on the grounds that if they did people from Scione would in the future always have the reputation of being traitors.

[129] So that is how Timoxenus was found out. Now, after the siege had been going on for three months, there happened to be a very low tide, and the water stayed out for a long time. When the Persians saw this, they passed through the shallows that had been created towards Pallene, but they were less than half-way across, with more than half their journey still to go before they were on Pallene, when the tide came back up. According to the local inhabitants, it was the biggest tide ever, although there had been plenty of big ones previously. Those of the Persians who did not know how to swim were drowned, while the Potidaeans took to their boats and killed the swimmers. The people of Potidaea attribute the flood-tide and what happened to the Persians to the fact that the Persians who were killed by the sea were precisely the ones who had desecrated the cult statue in the temple of Poseidon on the edge of the town. Personally, I think that this explanation of events is correct. Artabazus took his remaining troops away to Mardonius in Thessaly.

[130] So much for the king's escort and their subsequent exploits. Once the remnants of Xerxes' fleet reached the shores of Asia in their flight from Salamis, they ferried the king and his army over from the Chersonese to Abydus, and then wintered at Cyme

before assembling at the very beginning of spring at Samos, where some of the ships had spent the winter. Most of the marines on board were Persians and Medes. There they were joined by their commanders, who were Mardontes the son of Bagaeus, Artayntes the son of Artachaees, and, at Artayntes' request, his nephew Ithamitres. They had been too severely battered to advance further west, not that anyone was requiring them to do so, but they— including the Ionian squadrons, the fleet consisted of three hundred ships—remained at their station off Samos to guard against a possible Ionian revolt. They certainly did not expect the Greeks to come to Ionia. On the basis of the fact that the Greeks had not come after them during their flight from Salamis, but were content to be rid of them, the Persians assumed that they would do no more than protect their own country. The Persians were completely demoralized as far as their prospects at sea were concerned, but they anticipated an easy victory from Mardonius on land. So during their time on Samos they discussed possible ways they might hurt the enemy and also kept their ears open for news of how things would go for Mardonius.

[131] However, the arrival of spring and the presence of Mardonius in Thessaly stirred the Greeks to activity. It was too early for the land army to have mustered, but the fleet of 110 ships went to Aegina. The commander of the fleet, who was also the commander-in-chief of the Greek forces, was Leotychidas the son of Menares. From Menares he traced his ancestry back to Heracles, via Hegesilaus, Hippocratidas, Leotychidas, Anaxilaus, Archidamus, Anaxandridas, Theopompus, Nicander, Charilaus, Eunomus, Polydectes, Prytanis, Euryphon, Procles, Aristodamus, Aristomachus, Cleodaeus, and finally Hyllus, who was the son of Heracles. He was from the second of the two royal houses. All of his ancestors, except for the seven closest to Leotychidas in the list, had been kings of Sparta. The commander of the Athenian forces was Xanthippus the son of Ariphron.

[132] The whole fleet had assembled at Aegina when an Ionian delegation (which had also visited Sparta a little earlier and asked the Lacedaemonians to liberate Ionia) came to the Greek forces there. One of these Ionians was Herodotus the son of Basileïdes. There had originally been seven of them, forming a political cabal with the intention of assassinating Strattis, the tyrant of Chios. But the conspiracy had been found out when one of the members of

the group had betrayed the project, and so the remaining six had surreptitiously escaped from Chios and gone to Sparta—and, now, to Aegina. They came to ask the Greeks to sail to Ionia, but they only just managed to get them to go as far as Delos. Everything beyond Delos held terrors for the Greeks; it was unfamiliar territory, and they imagined it all to be filled with armies. As far as they knew, Samos was as distant as the Pillars of Heracles. And so it happened that the Persians were too frightened to venture west of Samos, and despite the pleas of the Chians the Greeks did not dare to sail east of Delos. In this way, fear held the middle ground between them.

[133] So the Greeks sailed to Delos, and Mardonius spent the winter in Thessaly. While he was based there, he sent a man from Europus called Mys around the oracles, with instructions to go everywhere and consult all the oracles he could, to see what answers they gave him. What he hoped to learn from the oracles when he gave these instructions I cannot say for certain, since it is not reported, but I think that the mission can only have been concerned with the matter at hand.

[134] It appears that this Mys went to Lebadeia (where he paid a local man to go down into Trophonius' cave) and to the oracle at Abae in Phocis. But the first place he visited was Thebes. He not only consulted the oracle of Ismenian Apollo there (where the same method of consultation by means of entrails is used as at Olympia), but also paid someone—a stranger, not a Theban—to go and sleep in the sanctuary of Amphiaraus. No Theban is allowed to consult the oracle there, because Amphiaraus once told them through his prophecies that they had to choose one of two options: they could have him either exclusively as an oracle or exclusively as an ally. They chose to have him as an ally, and that is why no one from Thebes is allowed to sleep in his sanctuary there.

[135] Anyway, back to the story of Mys, the man from Europus. According to the Thebans, something happened which I find very odd. Among all the various oracular sites he visited here and there was the precinct of Apollo of Ptoüs. This shrine, called the Ptoüm, lies within Theban-controlled territory, on a hill overlooking Lake Copaïs, very close to the town of Acraephia. On his visit to the Ptoüm the man called Mys was accompanied by three Thebans, who had been delegated by the Theban authorities to write down the oracle's statement. Suddenly, the oracle's prophet began to

speak in a foreign language! The Thebans who had come with Mys were astonished to hear a foreign language instead of Greek, and they did not know what to make of it, but Mys of Europus snatched the writing-tablet they had brought from their hands and began to write down on it the prophet's words, explaining that he was speaking Carian. Then Mys went back to Thessaly.

[136] After Mardonius had read all the various oracles' statements, he sent a Macedonian, Alexander the son of Amyntas, off to Athens with a message. One reason he chose Alexander for this mission was because Alexander had family ties with Persia, since his sister Gygaea, the daughter of Amyntas, was married to a Persian called Bubares; their son, Amyntas of Asia (he had the same name as his maternal grandfather), received from Xerxes an important Phrygian city called Alabanda as his own domain. Another reason Mardonius chose Alexander was because he knew that Alexander was Athens' diplomatic representative and an officially recognized benefactor of the city. So he considered Alexander his best bet for winning over the Athenians, which he wanted to do because he had apparently heard that they were a populous and warlike race, and he was aware that the defeat the Persians had met with at sea was due mainly to them. With the Athenians on his side, Mardonius was sure—an entirely justified confidence—that he would have no difficulty in gaining control of the sea, while he already had a considerable advantage on land, as far as he could see. So this was his plan for overcoming the Greeks. It may well be that the oracles he had consulted had made a prediction along these lines, and had recommended seeking an alliance with Athens, so that he was following their advice in sending Alexander off on his mission.

[137] Now, Alexander was a seventh-generation descendant of Perdiccas, who had gained the kingdom of Macedonia in the following way. There were once three brothers descended from Temenus—Gauanes, Aëropus, and Perdiccas—who were banished from Argos and went to live in Illyria. They crossed over the border from Illyria to inland Macedonia and came to the town of Lebaea, where they hired themselves out as labourers to the king; one of them was a horseherd, another a cowherd, while the youngest brother, Perdiccas, looked after the sheep and goats. Now, in the old days, it was not just the common people who were poor, but the rulers too. The three brothers' food was actually cooked by the

king's wife, and every loaf of bread she baked for the young workman Perdiccas grew to twice its normal size. This happened every time, and eventually she told her husband about it. As soon as he heard the news, it occurred to him that this was an important and meaningful omen, so he summoned the labourers and told them to leave his land. They agreed to do so, once they were paid the wages they were owed. Now, the sun was pouring into the house through the smoke-hole, and when the king heard them mention wages, he pointed to the sunlight and said in his delusion, 'There are your wages. That's all you deserve.' The two elder brothers, Gauanes and Aëropus, just stood there in amazement at his words, but the boy said, 'My lord, we accept your gift.' He traced the circle of sunlight on the floor of the house with a knife that he happened to have on him, scooped the sunlight three times into his lap, and then left with his brothers.

[138] After they had gone, one of the king's advisers explained the meaning of what the boy had done and argued that, despite being the youngest of the three brothers, he had known perfectly well what he was doing in accepting the king's gift. On hearing this, the king angrily sent horsemen after the three brothers to kill them. Now, there is a river thereabouts which the descendants of these men from Argos regard as a saviour and at which they perform sacrificial rites, because no sooner had the three Temenidae crossed it than it became too deep and strong for the horsemen to cross. So the brothers came to another part of Macedonia, where they settled near the place known as the Garden of Midas the son of Gordias, where wild roses grow and every single bush bears sixty blooms, with the sweetest scent of any flowers anywhere. This is the garden where, the Macedonians say, Silenus was caught; it lies at the foot of Mount Bermium, which is impassable in winter. Once they had gained control of this district, the three brothers expanded from there until they had conquered the rest of Macedonia too.

[139] The line of descent from this Perdiccas to Alexander was as follows: Alexander was the son of Amyntas, Amyntas of Alcetes, Alcetes of Aëropus, Aëropus of Philippus, and Philippus of Argaeus, whose father was Perdiccas, who gained the kingdom of Macedonia.

[140] This is the lineage of Alexander the son of Amyntas. When he reached Athens on his mission from Mardonius, he delivered the

following speech: 'Men of Athens, here are the words of Mardonius: "I have received the following message from King Xerxes: 'I hereby grant the Athenians an amnesty from all the wrongs they have done me. Now, Mardonius, here is what you must do: return their land to them, but also let them add to it. Let them choose any extra territory they want—and let them have self-government. Moreover, if they are prepared to accept my terms, I want you to see to the rebuilding of all the sanctuaries of theirs I burnt down.'

' "This is the order which arrived, and I must obey it, unless you prevent me. I must ask you: why are you currently resisting the king? Are you insane? You can't defeat him and you won't be able to hold out for ever either. You know how large an army he has, and you know how much it has achieved. You are also aware of the forces at my disposal. What this means is that even if you overcome and defeat us—which is entirely unlikely, as you will appreciate if you have any sense—another far larger force will appear. You are no match for the king, and you should not think you are, when that means you must lose your country and be on the run for the rest of your lives. No, make peace with us instead. You can do so on very favourable terms, because the king is already inclined in that direction. Be free, by making a treaty with us, without treachery and deceit, and joining our military alliance."

'So much for the message Mardonius instructed me to deliver,' Alexander went on. 'Now, I'm not going to mention my goodwill towards Athens, because it would not be the first time that it has come to your attention, but I do beg you to do as Mardonius suggests. If I thought you had the ability to keep fighting Xerxes for ever, I'd never have come to you with these words; but I can't see that it's a realistic possibility. The king has incredible power at his command and a very long reach. If you don't enter into an agreement with the Persians now, with favourable terms on offer as the conditions under which they are prepared to do so, I fear for your future. After all, you have the most vulnerable country in the Greek alliance: you live right on the main route, you're always the only ones to suffer in defeat, and the terrain you occupy could have been specially designed as a battlefield. So please don't refuse this offer. It is worth a great deal to you that you are the only people in Greece whose wrongs the Great King is prepared to forgive and with whom he wants to be on good terms.'

[141] This was Alexander's speech to the Athenians. The Lacedaemonians had heard that Alexander had gone to Athens with the intention of inducing them to come to terms with Xerxes, and they remembered that there were oracles to the effect that they and the Dorian people as a whole would be expelled from the Peloponnese by a combined force of Persians and Athenians, so they were terrified at the prospect of the Athenians entering into an agreement with the Persians, and they decided to send a delegation to Athens straight away. Now, it so happened that the Lacedaemonian messengers' appointment coincided with that of Alexander, because the Athenians had slowed the proceedings down and procrastinated. They were sure that the Lacedaemonians would hear that a messenger had come from the Persians with a treaty in mind and that once they found out they would waste no time in sending messengers, so they delayed things on purpose, so that the Lacedaemonians could hear what they had to say.

[142] After Alexander had finished speaking, it was the turn of the messengers from Sparta. 'The Lacedaemonians sent us', they said, 'to ask you not to do anything that might harm Greece and not to listen with approval to the words of the Persian king. There are many reasons why it would be particularly wrong and inappropriate for you to do so—not that there is anything that would make it right for any other Greek state either. But it was you who started this war, while it was the last thing we wanted, and right from the start it was your land that was at stake, even if now the whole of Greece is involved. Besides, it would be intolerable for Athens to be responsible for enslaving the rest of the Greeks, when in the past you have always been known to free others from slavery. However, we do sympathize with your difficulties: you have lost two harvests already and your finances have been ruined for a long time now. To compensate for this, the Lacedaemonians and their allies are prepared to maintain your womenfolk and all the members of your households who do not contribute to the war for as long as this war lasts. Don't let Alexander of Macedonia's smooth presentation of Mardonius' offer win you over. He was bound to act as he did: he is a despot, and despots support one another. But you do not have to follow his example, and if you have any sense, you won't, because, as you know, these foreigners are completely unreliable and dishonest.' That was what the messengers said.

[143] The Athenians replied to Alexander as follows: 'In actual fact, we were already aware of the disparity between the resources at our disposal and Xerxes' enormous power, so there was no need for your pointed reminder. Nevertheless, we are so focused on freedom that we will fight for it however we can. Don't try to persuade us to come to terms with Persia; we are not going to do so. Go and take this message from the Athenians to Mardonius: as long as the sun keeps to its present course, we will never come to terms with Xerxes. On the contrary, we will take to the field and fight against him, confident of the support of the gods and heroes for whom he felt such utter contempt that he burnt their homes and statues. If you ever come to Athens in the future, make sure that you come without this kind of proposal; never disguise an inducement to commit sacrilege as an offer of a favour. We wouldn't like to see you come to any harm at the hands of the Athenians, when you are their representative and friend.'

[144] This was the Athenian reply to Alexander. To the messengers from Sparta they spoke as follows: 'It may have been natural for you to worry in case we came to terms with Xerxes, but we still think your fear reflects badly on you, because you are perfectly well aware of the Athenian temperament. You should have known that there isn't enough gold on earth, or any land of such outstanding beauty and fertility, that we would accept it in return for collaborating with the enemy and enslaving Greece. Even if we were inclined to do so, there are plenty of important obstacles in the way. First and foremost, there is the burning and destruction of the statues and homes of our gods; rather than entering into a treaty with the perpetrator of these deeds, we are duty-bound to do our utmost to avenge them. Then again, there is the fact that we are all Greeks—one race speaking one language, with temples to the gods and religious rites in common, and with a common way of life. It would not be good for Athens to betray all this shared heritage. So if you didn't know it before, we can assure you that so long as even a single Athenian remains alive, we will never come to terms with Xerxes. However, we would like to thank you for your thoughtful offer to look after our families during our time of economic ruin. Your kindness leaves nothing to be desired, but we'll find some way to hold out, without troubling you. So there we are, then; what you must do now is get an army in the field as quickly as possible. It looks as though it won't be long

before the Persian comes and invades our country; he'll do so just
as soon as he receives our message and finds out that we are turning
him down flat. It would be a good idea for us† to have an army in
Boeotia to pre-empt his attempt to invade Attica.' After listening
to the Athenian reply, the messengers returned to Sparta.

BOOK NINE

[1] When Mardonius received the Athenians' message, which Alexander brought back with him, he lost no time in setting out from Thessaly at the head of his army to attack Athens, and he gained extra conscripts from every place he passed through. So far from regretting their earlier actions, the Thessalian leaders lobbied the Persians even more. Thorax of Larisa not only accompanied Xerxes during his retreat back to Asia, but now blatantly encouraged Mardonius to invade Greece.

[2] In due course, the army reached Boeotia, where the Thebans tried to persuade Mardonius to stay. They said that there was no better place for him to pitch camp, and they advised him to go no further, but to make Boeotia his base and to work towards the complete subjugation of Greece without striking a blow. They argued that it was not easy for anyone at all to get the better of the Greeks by force of arms when they were united, as they had been before. 'But if you do as we suggest,' they went on, 'it will be no problem for you to influence their thinking. In order to destroy their unity, all you have to do is send money to all the leading men in the various cities. They will come over to your side, and then, with their help, you will easily overcome the ones who oppose you.'

[3] However, Mardonius did not listen to this advice of theirs, because he was in the grip of a terrible longing to take Athens for a second time. In this, he was motivated partly by obstinacy and partly by the fact that he could see himself using beacons placed on successive islands to let Xerxes in Sardis know that he had captured Athens. But when he reached Attica he once again found no Athenians there. Most of them were on Salamis, he found out, or serving in the fleet, and so he captured an empty city. There had been a gap of nine months between Xerxes' capture of Athens and this later invasion by Mardonius.

[4] During his time in Athens, Mardonius sent a Hellespontine man called Murichides to Salamis with the same message that

Alexander of Macedonia had already conveyed to the Athenians. He was aware that the Athenians were not well disposed towards him, but he still sent this message all over again, because he assumed they would give up their obstinacy now that the whole of Attica had fallen and was under his control. This was what prompted him to dispatch Murichides to Salamis.

[5] On arriving in Salamis, Murichides delivered Mardonius' message to the Council. One of the members of the Council, Lycides, argued that in his opinion they ought to welcome Mardonius' proposals and refer the matter to the people. He did this either because he had been bribed by Mardonius, or because he actually approved of the proposals. The immediate response from the Athenians (not only the members of the Council, but also those outside, when they heard about it) was furious anger. They surrounded Lycides and stoned him to death, although they let the Hellespontine go unharmed. The uproar in Salamis over Lycides alerted the Athenian women to what was happening. With every woman arousing and enlisting the support of her neighbour, they spontaneously flocked to Lycides' house, where they stoned his wife and his children to death.

[6] The circumstances of the Athenian exodus to Salamis were as follows. They stayed in Attica for a while, because they were expecting an army to come from the Peloponnese to help them. But the Peloponnesians kept on delaying and putting things off, and once the Athenians heard that the invader had already reached Boeotia, they gathered up all their belongings and crossed over to Salamis. They sent a delegation to Lacedaemon to complain that the Lacedaemonians had allowed Mardonius to invade Attica instead of combining with them and confronting him in Boeotia, and also to remind them of all the incentives the Persians had promised them for changing sides; the delegation was to warn the Lacedaemonians, then, that if they refused to help the Athenians, the Athenians too would find their own way of avoiding danger.

[7] Now, the Lacedaemonians were on holiday at this time; they were celebrating the Hyacinthia, and nothing was more important to them than catering to the god's requirements. Moreover, the defensive wall they were constructing on the Isthmus had reached the stage of having the parapets built on it. When the delegation (which consisted of Megarians and Plataeans as well as Athenians) arrived in Lacedaemon, they came before the ephors and said: 'The

Athenians have sent us to say that not only is the Persian king offering to return our land, but he also wants to enter into an alliance with us, on fair and equal terms and without treachery and deceit, and he is prepared to give us any extra territory we choose, over and above what we already have. Out of reverence for Zeus, the god whom all Greeks worship, and because we find the idea of betraying Greece intolerable, we rejected and refused his offers, despite the fact that we are being criminally betrayed by the rest of the Greeks, and even though we know it would be more advantageous for us to come to terms with the Persians than to fight them. But we will never voluntarily come to terms with the Persians.

'All our dealings with the Greeks have been sincere. As for you, however, although on the occasion we have referred to you were so petrified that you came to beg us not to enter into an agreement with the Persians, now you're ignoring us. And why? Because you're fully aware of our determination never to betray Greece, and also because the wall you're building across the Isthmus is near completion. You had promised to come to Boeotia to confront the enemy, but you have let us down and allowed the Persians to invade Attica. At the moment, then, the Athenians are furious with your dishonourable behaviour, but they hereby ask you to get an army out into the field as quickly as possible to join us, so that together we can meet the Persians in Attica, since the loss of Boeotia means that the best place for us to fight is the Thriasian Plain, in our country.'

[8] The ephors asked for a day's grace before replying to this speech—but then on the next day they postponed their reply for a further day. They went on doing this for ten days, putting their response off from day to day! Meanwhile all the Peloponnesians were very busy fortifying the Isthmus, and had more or less finished the job. Why, at the time of Alexander of Macedonia's mission to Athens, was it so important to the Lacedaemonians that the Athenians should not go over to the Persian side, and why were they then completely unconcerned on this later occasion? I do not know the answer, except to say that they had completed the wall across the Isthmus and thought they had no further need of the Athenians. At the time of Alexander's mission to Athens, they had not yet completed the building programme, but their terror of the Persians was making them work at it.

[9] However, the Spartiates did eventually give the Athenians a reply and send an army. This is how it happened. On the day before what was to be the final audience of the Athenian delegation, a man from Tegea named Chileus, who was the most influential foreigner in Lacedaemon, heard from the ephors the whole of the Athenians' speech. 'Here is how things stand,' he told the ephors afterwards. 'If we fall out with the Athenians and they side with the Persians instead, then however strong a wall we have built across the Isthmus, there will be great gates to the Peloponnese open wide for the Persians. No, you had better do what the Athenians are asking you to do, before they reach a different decision—one which would threaten Greece with catastrophe.'

[10] That was his advice to the ephors, who took his point. Without saying anything to the delegates from the cities, they immediately—before daybreak—sent out five thousand Spartiates, with seven helots assigned to each man. Command of this expeditionary force was given to Pausanias the son of Cleombrotus. The right of leadership actually belonged to Pleistarchus the son of Leonidas, but he was still a child, and Pausanias was his guardian, as well as being his cousin, because Cleombrotus (who was Pausanias' father and the son of Anaxandridas) was no longer alive. He had died shortly after bringing back from the Isthmus the army which had built the wall; the reason Cleombrotus had pulled the army back from the Isthmus was that as he was offering sacrifices in regard to the Persians darkness obscured the sun in the sky. Pausanias chose as his fellow commander a relative of his, Euryanax the son of Dorieus. So off these troops went from Sparta, with Pausanias in command.

[11] The next day the delegates, who were completely unaware of the departure of the army, came before the ephors. They too had every intention of leaving, each man back to his own city. Once they were in the presence of the ephors they said, 'Men of Lacedaemon, why don't you just stay here, then? Celebrate your Hyacinthia and have fun—even at the expense of failing your allies. This injustice of yours and lack of military support will force the Athenians to negotiate the best possible deal with the Persians. It goes without saying that we will then be on the Persian king's side, and we will join his forces in invading any country they lead us against. Then you'll discover what the consequences are.' The ephors responded by assuring the delegates under oath that the

Spartiates had probably already got as far as Orestheum in their march against the 'strangers' (as they called the foreign invaders). The delegates, who of course knew nothing about the expedition, asked the ephors what they meant, and then the ephors told them the whole story. As a result, the delegation set out in astonishment after the Spartiates as quickly as possible. They were accompanied by an élite force of five thousand Lacedaemonian perioeci.

[12] So they went racing towards the Isthmus. As soon as the Argives found out that Pausanias and his men had left Sparta, they sent the fastest courier they could find to Attica, since they had previously promised Mardonius that they would stop the Spartiates leaving the Peloponnese. The courier arrived in Athens and said, 'Mardonius, I have come on a mission from Argos to tell you that the men of military age have left Lacedaemon and taken to the field, and that the Argives could not stop them doing so. Under these circumstances, good luck to you, and good planning.'

[13] After delivering this message the courier took his leave. Mardonius now felt altogether disinclined to stay in Attica. Before receiving this information he had been waiting, to see what the Athenians would do. In fact, he assumed throughout that they would come to terms with him, and so he had neither harmed nor ravaged Attic territory. But when they refused to come to terms, and once he had found out the true state of affairs, he set the evacuation of his forces in motion before Pausanias and his invading force had reached the Isthmus. First, however, he put Athens to the torch and tore down any remaining upright bits of city wall, house, or shrine, until they were all just rubble. There were two reasons for his withdrawal: first, the terrain of Attica was unsuited to cavalry manoeuvres, and, second, if he lost the battle, he could get out of the country only via a narrow pass, which would mean that even a small force could prevent him doing so. His plan, then, was to pull back to Thebes, where he could fight with a friendly city near by and on terrain suitable for cavalry.

[14] Mardonius began to evacuate Attica, then, but while he was actually on the road he received a report that another force of one thousand Lacedaemonians had reached Megara, in advance of the main army. This information caused him to make new plans, because he wanted to defeat this advance guard first, if he could, so he turned his army round and led them back towards Megara. His cavalry went on ahead and overran the territory of Megara.

This was the most westerly point in Europe reached by the Persian army.

[15] Next Mardonius heard that the Greeks had gathered in force on the Isthmus, so he turned back again and marched through Decelea, because that was the route his guides suggested. These guides were neighbours of the Thebans from the River Asopus, and they had been called up to do the job by the Boeotarchs. They took him first to Sphendaleis and then on to Tanagra, where he bivouacked for the night before making his way the next day to Scolus, which was within Theban territory. At Scolus, despite the fact that the Thebans were on the Persian side, he cut down all the trees on cultivated plots of land, not out of hostility, but because he really had no choice, since he wanted to have a defensive stockade built for his troops as a place of refuge in case the battle did not go well for him. His army was posted along the River Asopus, occupying an extensive stretch of land from Erythrae, past Hysiae, and all the way into Plataean territory. However, the actual stronghold which he built was not of course as large as that; it was square in shape, with each side being about ten stades long.

While the Persians were busy with this building work, a Theban called Attaginus the son of Phrynon prepared a magnificent banquet and invited to it not only Mardonius himself, but also the fifty most eminent Persians, who all came in response to the invitation. The banquet was held in Thebes.

[16] I heard what follows from Thersander of Orchomenus, who was one of the most distinguished men of his home town. Thersander told me that he was one of the people invited by Attaginus to this banquet, along with fifty Thebans, and that rather than having the two sets of people—Persian and Theban—reclining on separate couches, Attaginus placed one of each on every couch. After the meal, while they were still drinking, the Persian who was sharing a couch with Thersander asked him in Greek where he was from. When he answered that he was from Orchomenus, the Persian said, 'Since we've shared a table and poured a libation from the same cup, I want to leave you a record of my opinion. Then, with advance warning, you'll be in a position to decide what to do to ensure your own safety. Look at these Persians here at the banquet, and consider also the army which we have left encamped on the river. Before much time has passed you'll see few of them left alive.'

The Persian was weeping as he spoke, Thersander said. He was astonished at his words and said to him, 'Shouldn't you be telling this to Mardonius and the next highest-ranking Persians?'

'My friend,' the Persian replied, 'an event which has been decreed by the god cannot be averted by man, for no one is willing to believe even those who tell the truth. A great many Persians are well aware of what I've just said, but we follow our leaders because we have no choice. There's no more terrible pain a man can endure than to see clearly and be able to do nothing.'

This is what I was told by Thersander of Orchomenus, and he added that he lost no time in telling others the story—that is, that he did so before the battle of Plataea took place.

[17] While Mardonius was encamped in Boeotia all the Greeks living in those parts who had embraced the Persian cause supplied contingents for his army, and indeed they all took part in the invasion of Athens—all, that is, except for the Phocians, who were the only ones not to join the invaders. It is true that they too were staunch collaborators, but only because they had no choice, not of their own free will. A few days after the arrival at Thebes of the Persian army a battalion of a thousand Phocian hoplites came too, led by a very eminent Phocian called Harmocydes. Following their arrival at Thebes Mardonius sent horsemen† to tell them to fall in by themselves on the plain. No sooner had they done so than the whole of the Persian cavalry appeared. Next the rumour spread throughout the Greek contingents of the Persian army that Mardonius was going to have the Phocians cut down by his men's javelins. The same rumour spread among the Phocians too, and then the Phocian commander Harmocydes made a speech to rouse his men. 'Phocians, there can be no doubt', he said, 'that the Persians are intending to wipe us out, and have planned the whole thing in advance—in response, I imagine, to some lies told about us by the Thessalians. Now is the time, then, for every single one of you to prove his courage. It is better to die in action, fighting for one's life, than to submit to the utter disgrace of presenting oneself meekly for slaughter. No, we must teach every one of them what it means for foreigners to plot the murder of Greek men.'

[18] This was Harmocydes' advice to his men. The horsemen surrounded the Phocians, and then advanced as if they were going to kill them. They brandished their weapons just as they would have done if they were going to throw them, and it is even

possible that a few weapons were released. Meanwhile the Phocians stood their ground against them, and presented as firm and compact a formation as possible on all fronts. At that point the horsemen wheeled around and pulled back. It is possible that the horsemen had come, at the request of the Thessalians, to kill the Phocians and then became afraid of being defeated when they saw the Phocians adopt a defensive formation, and so withdrew when Mardonius instructed them to do so; and it is also possible that Mardonius wanted them to test the Phocians to see if they were brave enough. I am not in a position to say which of these alternatives is true. But after the horsemen had pulled back, Mardonius sent them the following message: 'Don't worry, men of Phocis. You have demonstrated your valour, which I had not been led to expect. So now commit yourselves to prosecuting this war, because however many favours you do us, you will be more than repaid by myself and by the king.' That was the end of the incident involving the Phocians.

[19] Once the Lacedaemonians had reached the Isthmus, they established their camp there. When the rest of the Peloponnesians (that is, the ones who were on the right side) heard what the Lacedaemonians were doing, they decided that they should not be left behind—although some of them did so only when they actually saw the Spartiates taking to the field. Once they had obtained favourable omens, the combined forces made their way from the Isthmus to Eleusis, where they once again offered up sacrifices. The omens were favourable, and so they continued on their way, accompanied now by the Athenian troops, who had crossed over from Salamis and joined them at Eleusis. It was when they were at Erythrae in Boeotia that they found out about the Persian encampment on the Asopus, and then, in the light of this information, they took up a position opposite the Persians on the spurs of Mount Cithaeron.

[20] The Greeks persistently refused to come down from the hills to the plain, so Mardonius sent the whole of his cavalry against them. The cavalry was commanded by an eminent Persian called Masistius (though the Greeks know him as Macistius), who rode a Nesaean horse, magnificently caparisoned, with equipment that included a golden bit. The horsemen advanced towards the Greeks and then attacked regiment by regiment. During these attacks, which inflicted severe losses on the Greeks, they taunted them by calling them women.

[21] Now, as it happened, it was the Megarians who were positioned at the most vulnerable point of the whole area, and bore the brunt of the cavalry assaults. They were so hard pressed by the Persian cavalry that they sent a message to the Greek commanders. When the messenger arrived he said to them: 'I bear a message from the Megarians to their allies: "We do not have the resources to resist the Persian cavalry unassisted here in the position we took up at the start of the battle. So far, despite the pressure, we have held out, although it has taken perseverance and courage. But now, unless you send further troops to relieve us at our post, we will abandon it."' Once the messenger had finished speaking, Pausanias questioned the Greeks to see whether any of them would volunteer to go there and relieve the Megarians. All the others refused, but the job was taken on by the Athenians—or, to be precise, by an élite company of three hundred Athenians, under the command of Olympiodorus the son of Lampon.

[22] These were the men who volunteered to be deployed in defence of all the other Greeks at Erythrae. With the support of the archers they took along, they fought long and hard, and the battle was eventually resolved as follows. The Persian cavalry continued to attack regiment by regiment, and during one such attack Masistius' horse, which was out in front of the rest, was hit in the side by an arrow, and the pain of the wound made it rear up and unseat him. As soon as Masistius landed on the ground, the Athenians sprang forward, seized the horse and killed Masistius, although he fought back. At first, in fact, they failed to kill him: next to his skin he was wearing a breastplate made of gold scales, with a red tunic on top, so the Athenians' blows kept hitting the breastplate and achieving nothing. Eventually, however one of them realized what was happening and struck Masistius in the eye. Only then did he fall to the ground and die. Now, somehow the other Persian horsemen failed to observe all this; they did not see him fall from his horse and they did not see him being killed either, because they were too busy wheeling round and pulling back to notice what was going on. As soon as they halted, however, they missed him, because there was no one there to give them orders. Once they understood the situation, they passed the word around and charged forward *en masse*, with the intention of recovering the body.

[23] When the Athenians saw that the horsemen had abandoned the tactic of attacking regiment by regiment and were all charging at once, they shouted out for the rest of the army to come to their

assistance. In the time it took for the general mass of the infantry to reach them, a fierce struggle took place over the body. Before the reinforcements arrived, the three hundred were coming off worst by a long way, and were in danger of losing Masistius' corpse, but once the main body of the Greek army had arrived to help them, the cavalry found it impossible to maintain their impetus. Not only did they fail to recover the body, but they sustained further losses, in addition to Masistius himself. They pulled back two stades, reined their horses in, and tried to decide what they should do. Since they were leaderless, they thought they had better withdraw from the battlefield and find Mardonius.

[24] When the cavalry got back to the Persian encampment, Mardonius and the whole of his army were deeply upset to hear of Masistius' death. They shaved off not only their own hair, but also that of their horses and their yoke-animals, and gave themselves over to unending lamentation. The whole of Boeotia echoed with the sound of mourning, since, after Mardonius, there was no one in Persia who was more highly respected by the Persians in general and the king in particular. So the Persians honoured Masistius on his death in their own fashion.

[25] Greek morale was considerably raised by the fact that they had not only withstood the assaults of the Persian cavalry, but had actually managed to push them back. The first thing they did was load the corpse on to a cart and parade it past their lines. Masistius had been remarkably tall and good-looking (which is in fact why they did this with the body), and the men broke ranks to go and see him. Next, they decided to come down off the hills and go to Plataea, because the land around there was clearly far more suitable than Erythrae as a place for them to establish themselves, for a number of reasons, including the fact that it had a better supply of fresh water. So they decided to move their camp down to Plataea, and in particular to the spring called Gargaphia which rises in that region, and to take up a position there in separate units. They picked up their gear and marched through the spurs of Cithaeron, past Hysiae, and into Plataean territory, where they formed up into various units based on their places of origin. The land they occupied by the Gargaphian Spring and the precinct of the hero Androcrates consisted of knolls and level ground.

[26] A fierce quarrel arose between the Tegeans and the Athenians during the disposition of the troops. There was only one wing

available, and both sides thought they deserved to have it. To support their case, they brought up all their achievements in the recent and distant past. The Tegeans argued as follows: 'This position has been our constant prerogative. Whenever the Peloponnesians have taken to the field together, we've been assigned this position by our allies. This isn't just a recent phenomenon; it has been going on ever since the Heraclidae tried to return to the Peloponnese from exile after the death of Eurystheus. That was the occasion when our actions earned us the privilege. What happened was that we left our country and went to the Isthmus to fight alongside the Achaeans and the Ionians who were living in the Peloponnese in those days. Our forces took up a position facing the returning exiles, and then (so the story goes) Hyllus declared that the two armies shouldn't run the risk of a battle, but that the Peloponnesians should choose from their army the man whom they considered to be their best fighter to meet him in single combat on conditions agreed by the two sides. The Peloponnesians decided to go ahead with this plan, and the two sides swore to abide by the condition that if Hyllus beat the Peloponnesian champion, the Heraclidae could return to the land of their fathers, whereas if he lost, the Heraclidae would leave again, taking their army with them, and wouldn't try to come back to the Peloponnese for a hundred years. The volunteer who was chosen from among all the allied forces was Echemus the son of Aëropus and grandson of Phegeus, who was our military commander, as well as our king. He took on Hyllus in single combat and killed him. As a result of this achievement of his we were awarded by the Peloponnesians of the time various important privileges which we continue to hold, and one of them is the right of always leading the second wing when a joint expedition is undertaken. Now, we're not going to stand in the way of you Lacedaemonians: you can choose either of the two wings, whichever one you want, and we'll let you have it. But what we're saying is that it is our right to lead the other one, just as it has been in the past. Besides, apart from this achievement of ours, the one we've just mentioned, we deserve this position more than the Athenians. We've proved ourselves by our successes in combat time and again not just against you Spartiates, but against others as well. In short, then, it's only fair for us to have the second wing, rather than the Athenians. They don't have the same record of achievements in the recent or distant past that we do.'

[27] The Athenian response to this speech from the Tegeans was as follows: 'We're aware that the object of this gathering of forces is to fight the invaders, not to make speeches, but since the Tegean representative has proposed that we should each mention the brave deeds done by us throughout history, in the recent past as well as long ago, we have no choice but to explain to you how, because of our courage, it came to be our ancestral right, not the Arcadians', to take the leading position. Let's start with the Heraclidae, whose champion the Tegeans remind us they killed on the Isthmus; all the Heraclidae were doing was trying to avoid being enslaved by the Mycenaeans, but every Greek state to which they came refused them shelter, until we took them in; and then with their help we put an end to the brutal reign of Eurystheus, once we had defeated the armies of the people who inhabited the Peloponnese in those days. In the second place, let's take the Argives who had marched against Thebes with Polynices, and who lay there dead and unburied; it is our proud claim to have marched against the Cadmeans, recovered the bodies, and buried them in our own land, in Eleusis. Then there was the successful campaign of ours against the Amazons when they came from the River Thermodon and invaded Attica; and our contribution to the struggle at Troy was as good as anyone else's. But what is the point in mentioning these episodes? People who were brave in those days might be relatively useless now, and vice versa. So that's enough ancient history. In fact, of course, we have† as many successful exploits to our credit as any other Greek state, if not more, but even if we had no others, what we achieved at Marathon would earn us a number of rights and privileges, including the one in dispute at the moment. After all, without any support from other Greek states we single-handedly took on the Persians and, despite the immensity of the undertaking, defeated forty-six peoples to emerge victorious. Doesn't this achievement alone qualify us for the second wing? But this is hardly the time and place for us to be quarrelling about what station we are to hold. We will carry out our orders wherever you Lacedaemonians decide to position us and whichever units of the enemy you think it best for us to face. It makes no difference where we are stationed: we'll still endeavour to prove our worth. Just tell us what to do, and rest assured that we will obey.'

[28] At this reply from the Athenians the cry went up from every man in the Lacedaemonian camp that it should be the Athenians rather than the Arcadians who held the wing. And that is how the Athenians gained the wing and got the better of the Tegeans.

Afterwards the Greeks—the late arrivals as well as the original members of the expedition—formed up at their posts. The disposition of the forces was as follows. A brigade of 10,000 Lacedaemonians held the right wing; 5,000 of these were Spartiates, and they were protected by 35,000 light-armed helots, seven for each man. The Spartiates reserved the place next to them for the Tegeans, in recognition of their prestige and their courage; the Tegean contingent consisted of 1,500 hoplites. The position next to the Tegeans was taken by the 5,000-strong contingent of Corinthians, who gained Pausanias' permission to have the 300 from Potidaea in Pallene stand alongside them. Next came 600 Arcadians from Orchomenus, then a contingent of 3,000 from Sicyon. Next to the Sicyonians came 800 men from Epidaurus, then 1,000 from Troezen, 200 from Lepreum, 400 from Mycenae and Tiryns, and then 1,000 from Phleious. Alongside the Phleiasians stood 300 men from Hermione, then there was a contingent of 600 from Eretria and Styra, then 400 from Chalcis, and then 500 from Ambracia. Next to the Ambraciots stood 800 men from Leucas and Anactorium, and then 200 from Pale in Cephallenia. The next contingent consisted of 500 from Aegina, then there came 3,000 Megarians, 600 Plataeans, and finally, in the forward position on the left wing, there were 8,000 Athenians under the command of Aristides the son of Lysimachus.

[29] The sum total, then, was 38,700, all of whom were hoplites, except for the seven assigned to each of the Spartiates. This was the number of hoplites in the army assembled to confront the Persians, and the total number of light-armed troops was as follows. There were 35,000 men stationed with the Spartiates (seven for each man), every single one of whom was equipped for fighting, and 34,500 light-armed troops from Lacedaemon and elsewhere in Greece, at the rate of one per heavy-armed soldier. So the total number of light-armed men serving in the army was 69,500.

[30] The total number of armed men in the Greek army which assembled at Plataea, then, counting both hoplites and light-armed

troops, was 1,800 fewer than 110,000. Including the Thespians who were there, however, the total number was exactly 110,000, because there were 1,800 survivors from Thespiae in the Greek camp, but they did not actually have any weapons.

[31] So much for the arrangement of the Greek forces on the Asopus. Once Mardonius and his Persians had finished mourning the death of Masistius, they came to Plataea, where they had heard that the Greeks were, and they moved up to the part of the Asopus which flows through that region. There Mardonius disposed his troops as follows. He placed the Persians opposite the Lacedaemonians. In actual fact, though, the Persians outnumbered the Lacedaemonians so much that their line not only had greater depth, but also covered the Tegeans as well. The way Mardonius deployed the Persians was to choose the strongest units to face the Lacedaemonians, while the weaker ones were placed next to them and opposite the Tegeans. This arrangement had been suggested and taught to him by the Thebans. Next to the Persians he deployed the Medes, who covered the Corinthians, Potidaeans, Orchomenians, and Sicyonians. Next to the Medes he deployed the Bactrians, who covered the Greek contingents from Epidaurus, Troezen, Lepreum, Tiryns, Mycenae, and Phleious. Next to the Bactrians he placed the Indians, who covered the troops from Hermione, Eretria, Styra, and Chalcis. Next to the Indians he deployed the Sacae, who covered the Greeks from Ambracia, Anactorium, Leucas, Pale, and Aegina. Next to the Sacae, and facing the Athenians, Plataeans, and Megarians, he posted the Boeotians, Locrians, Malians, Thessalians, and Phocians. There were only a thousand Phocians, because not all the Phocians collaborated with the enemy; some of them, who were pinned in the region of Parnassus, supported the Greek cause by using Parnassus as a base from which to raid and plunder not only Mardonius' army, but also the Greeks who were on his side. Mardonius also positioned opposite the Athenians the Macedonians and those who lived around Thessaly.

[32] Among the peoples deployed by Mardonius only the most important ones have been mentioned by name—the ones which were particularly prominent and famous—but men from other countries were included among them. There were troops from Phrygia, Mysia, Thrace, Paeonia, and elsewhere; there were also Ethiopians and, from Egypt, the Hermotybies and Calasiries, as

they are called, who were armed with knives and who are the only warriors in Egypt. These Egyptians had been serving as marines, but Mardonius transferred them out of the fleet while he was still in Phalerum; they had not been assigned to the land army which came to Athens with Xerxes. As I explained ealier, there were 300,000 men in the Persian army, but no one knows how many Greeks fought alongside the non-Greeks in Mardonius' army, because no tally was made of them. Relying on guesswork, however, I would estimate that there were about 50,000 of them assembled there. This disposition of the Persian troops involved only the infantry; the cavalry was deployed separately.

[33] The day after they had all taken up their positions, people by people and regiment by regiment, both sides offered up sacrifices. Tisamenus the son of Antiochus, who had joined the Greek army as a diviner, was the one who performed the sacrifices for the Greeks; although he came from Elis, from the family of the Iamidae, the Lacedaemonians had enrolled him as a full citizen. This came about because once, when Tisamenus was consulting the oracle in Delphi about whether he would have any children, in the course of her reply the Pythia said that he would win five crucial contests. He misunderstood the meaning of the oracle and applied himself to athletics, on the assumption that those were the kind of contests he would win. He specialized in the pentathlon and only missed out on winning at the Olympic Games by losing a single wrestling-match against his rival, Hieronymus of Andros. The Lacedaemonians, however, realized that the oracle he had received was referring not to athletic contests but to warfare, and they offered him financial inducements to become a war-leader of theirs along with their Heraclid kings. When Tisamenus realized how much the Spartiates wanted his goodwill, he raised the stakes: he told them that the cost of his compliance was for them to make him a fellow citizen of theirs and give him full rights, and that this was not negotiable. At first the Spartiates were angry at his demand and completely stopped asking him, but eventually, with their terror at this Persian invasion hanging over their heads, they went to fetch him and agreed to his conditions. Seeing that they had changed their minds, he declared himself no longer satisfied with these conditions alone, and insisted on his brother Hagias becoming a Spartiate too, on the same terms as his own citizenship.

[34] In making this demand he was imitating Melampus, if one may compare the demand for kingship with the demand for citizenship. When the women of Argos went mad, the Argives went to Pylos to try to hire Melampus to come and cure their wives of their sickness, but Melampus asked for a half share in the kingship as his payment. The Argives thought this was outrageous and left, but later, after more of their women had gone mad, they agreed to his terms and went back to Pylos, fully prepared to give him what he had asked for. But when he saw that they had changed their minds he asked for more; he said that he would do what they wanted only if they also gave his brother Bias a third share in the kingship. The Argives were so desperate that they had to agree to this extra demand as well.

[35] The Spartiates were in the same situation. They needed Tisamenus so badly that they agreed to all his terms. And once the Spartiates conceded, Tisamenus of Elis, now a Spartiate, used his skill as a diviner to help them win five crucial contests. He and his brother were the only people in the world ever to be enrolled by the Spartiates as fellow citizens. The five contests in question were, first, this one at Plataea; second, the battle of Tegea which they fought against the Tegeans and Argives; third, the battle at Dipaees where their opponents were all the Arcadians except for the Mantineans; fourth, the conflict with the Messenians which took place near Ithome; and finally the battle of Tanagra which was fought against a combined force of Athenians and Argives. After this the series of five contests was over.

[36] So at the time in question this man Tisamenus performed the divination for the Greeks at Plataea, where he had been brought by the Spartiates. The entrails gave favourable omens for the Greeks if they remained on the defensive, but not if they crossed the Asopus and took the fight to the enemy.

[37] Although Mardonius wanted to be the one to attack, the entrails also gave him omens that were favourable for defence but unsuited to attack. He too used the Greek method of divination by examination of the entrails, since his diviner, Hegesistratus, came from Elis and was in fact the most distinguished of the family of the Telliadae. Hegesistratus had once been arrested and imprisoned by the Spartiates to await execution for the terrible and horrific treatment they had suffered at his hands. In this desperate situation, because his life was in danger and he was prepared to suffer

gruesome agonies rather than die, he did something that defies description. He was being kept in stocks made of wood bound with iron, and somehow got hold of a blade which had been smuggled into the prison. What he then immediately set about doing must have taken more courage than anything else we have ever heard of. He worked out that the rest of his foot would get free of the stocks if he cut off the bulk of his foot, so he proceeded to do so. Then, since he was under guard, he dug a hole through the wall and ran away to Tegea, travelling by night and resting by day under the cover of woodland. Although the Lacedaemonians were out looking for him in full force, he managed to reach Tegea two nights after escaping. The Lacedaemonians were amazed by his courage when they found half of his foot lying there, but they could not find him. For the time being, then, he managed to escape the Lacedaemonians in this way and take refuge in Tegea, which was at that time not on good terms with Lacedaemon; and when he recovered (although he wore an artificial wooden foot), he made no secret of his hostility towards the Lacedaemonians. But eventually the permanence of his hatred for the Lacedaemonians proved to be his undoing, because he was captured by them while serving as a diviner at Zacynthos and put to death.

[38] Many years were to pass after the battle of Plataea, however, before Hegesistratus died. Now, though, he was on the Asopus, well paid by Mardonius for his services, and he was glad to perform the sacrificial rituals not only because of the money he was making, but also because of his hatred for the Lacedaemonians. Since the omens received not just by the Persians themselves but also by the Greeks in the Persian army (who had their own diviner, a Leucadian man named Hippomachus) warned against engaging the enemy, and because there was a constant influx of men into the Greek army, which was consequently increasing in size, a Theban called Timagenidas the son of Herpys advised Mardonius to patrol the passes over Cithaeron, on the grounds that a great many of the Greeks who were constantly flooding in every day could be caught there.

[39] The two sides had been facing each other for eight days when Timagenidas put this suggestion to Mardonius. Realizing that it was a good idea, Mardonius sent his cavalry that night to the pass on Cithaeron which leads towards Plataea—the pass known to the Boeotians as Three Heads, and to the Athenians as Oak

Heads. This was an effective mission for the Persian horsemen, because they captured fifty yoke-animals (along with their carters) as they were coming down on to the plain with food from the Peloponnese for the Greek army. But once they had taken this prey the Persians turned to indiscriminate murder, slaughtering humans and animals alike. When they had had their fill of killing, they rounded up the remnants of the baggage train and drove them back to Mardonius and the Persian encampment.

[40] Two more days passed after this incident, with neither side being prepared to start the battle. The Persians advanced right up to the Asopus to test the Greeks, but neither side actually crossed the river. Mardonius' cavalry, however, was constantly attacking and harassing the Greeks, because the Thebans (who were staunch and belligerent supporters of the Persian cause) kept guiding the cavalry to within striking distance of the enemy, at which point the Persians and Medes would take over and perform deeds of valour.

[41] That was all that happened for the first ten days. By the end of the eleventh day, however, with the two sides still facing each other, the Greek numbers had considerably increased and Mardonius was chafing at the inaction. Then Mardonius the son of Gobryas and Artabazus the son of Pharnaces, who was one of Xerxes' particular favourites, held a meeting and discussed the situation. It was Artabazus' opinion that they should strike camp as soon as possible and withdraw the entire army to the shelter of the walls of Thebes, where there was a good stock of supplies for them and plenty of fodder for the yoke-animals. They should simply stay there without being drawn into battle and complete the business they had come for by distributing money unstintingly among the Greeks, concentrating above all on the leading citizens in each community. After all, he pointed out, they had plenty of gold, in both coined and uncoined form, and also plenty of silver and cups. Before long, he said, the Greeks would surrender their freedom, and there would be no need for a battle with all its attendant risks. His argument was the same as the one the Thebans had used before, and it suggests that Artabazus too had particular foresight, but Mardonius argued for more forceful, uncompromising, and stubborn measures. Since he had the impression that the Persian army was far stronger than the Greeks, he was all for engaging them in battle as soon as possible, without letting their

numbers increase beyond what they had already reached; as for Hegesistratus' sacrifices, he was prepared to ignore them and, rather than forcing the issue, to follow the Persian custom and just engage the enemy in battle.

[42] This argument of his went unopposed, so he got his way. After all, it was he and not Artabazus who had been given control of the army by the king. So he sent for the officers in charge of the regiments and for the commanders of the Greeks who were on his side and asked if they knew of any oracle predicting the destruction of the Persian army in Greece. The assembled officers said nothing, some because they genuinely did not know of any such oracles, and others because, although they were aware of oracles to that effect, they did not consider it safe to mention them. Finally Mardonius himself broke the silence. 'It may be that you are unaware of any such oracles,' he said, 'or it may be that you are too afraid to speak up. In any case, I'm perfectly well aware of them and I'll tell you what I've heard. There is an oracle to the effect that the Persians are fated to come to Greece, sack the sanctuary at Delphi, and afterwards perish to a man. Armed with this knowledge, we'll bypass the sanctuary without making any attempt to sack it, and so avoid this occasion for destruction. This should please those of you who are loyal to the Persian cause, since it means that we will get the better of the Greeks.' He then told them to get everything organized and ready for joining battle at dawn the following day.

[43] Now, I happen to know that the oracle which, according to Mardonius, referred to the Persians was not designed for them, but for the Illyrians and the army of the Encheleis. However, there was an oracle of Bacis which refers to the battle in question:

> On the Thermodon and the grassy banks of the Asopus
> A gathering of Greeks, and a shout of foreign babble.
> There, before their time, before their fate, many bow-bearing
>   Medes
> Will fall, when the day of their death comes upon them.

I know that these lines refer to the Persians, and there are also similar oracles of Musaeus which refer to them too. The River Thermodon flows between Tanagra and Glisas.

[44] After Mardonius' question about the oracles and his words of encouragement night fell and guards were posted. Late at night,

when both camps had apparently fallen quiet and almost everyone was asleep, Alexander the son of Amyntas, the commander and king of the Macedonians, rode up to the Athenian sentries and asked to meet with their commanders. Leaving most of their comrades on guard, a few of the sentries ran to the commanders and told them that a man had come on horseback from the Persian camp; all he had revealed about his purpose, they said, was that he wanted to meet the commanders, whom he had asked for by name.

[45] On hearing this report the Athenian commanders lost no time in following the sentries back to their posts, where they met up with Alexander. 'Men of Athens,' Alexander said, 'please take what I have to say to you as a token of my good faith. You must keep it to yourselves and tell no one except Pausanias, because otherwise you might destroy me. I wouldn't be telling you this if I didn't care so deeply for Greece as a whole. My family background makes me a Greek myself, and I would hate to see Greece lose its freedom and become enslaved. So I'm telling you that Mardonius and the Persian army have found it impossible to receive favourable omens from their sacrifices; if they had, battle would have been joined long ago. But now he has decided to ignore the omens and to attack at dawn—I imagine because he is afraid of your army increasing any further in size. Get ready to face an attack, then. In fact, even if he puts it off and doesn't join battle, you should just maintain your position and be patient, because he only has enough supplies left for a few days. After the war, if things have gone your way, you must remember me and think of my freedom too. Bear in mind the risk I have run for the sake of Greece; I have done so out of goodwill towards you, because I wanted you to be aware of Mardonius' intentions and to make sure that the Persian attack does not take you by surprise. I am Alexander the Macedonian.' With these words he rode back to his post in the Persian camp.

[46] The Athenian commanders went straight to the right wing and passed on to Pausanias the information Alexander had given them. His response to their report, because he was afraid of the Persians, was to say, 'So battle is to be joined at dawn. You Athenians had better take on the Persians, while we meet the Boeotians and the other Greeks who are currently ranged against you. You're familiar with Persian tactics, because you've already fought them at Marathon, while we are untried and ignorant of them. On the other hand, while we may have no experience of the

Persians, we are experts in Boeotians and Thessalians. So go and collect your gear, and then move over to this wing, while we swap with you and take the left wing.'

'Right from the start,' the Athenians replied, 'ever since we saw the Persians being deployed opposite you Lacedaemonians, we've been wondering whether we should raise precisely the proposal you've just made, but we were afraid you might not like the suggestion. Now, however, you've beaten us to it and brought it up yourselves. We're happy to accept your proposal and are ready to do as you suggest.'

[47] Since both parties liked the arrangement, they set about exchanging positions as day began to break. The Boeotians, however, realized what was going on and told Mardonius, who immediately tried to make changes within his forces too, by bringing the Persians across to face the Lacedaemonians. When this came to Pausanias' attention, he realized that his manoeuvre had been detected, so he led the Spartiates back to the right wing, and Mardonius followed his example with regard to his left wing.

[48] So the original deployment of the troops was restored. At this point Mardonius sent a herald to the Spartiates with the following message: 'Men of Lacedaemon, you are held by everyone in this part of the world to be the bravest of men. They boast that you never retreat and never break ranks, but keep to your post until you either kill your opponents or are killed yourselves. But this is all a pack of lies, apparently. Before the battle has even started, before we have got to close quarters, you've already pulled back and left your post—we saw you do it! You're putting the Athenians out in front, while you yourselves take up a position facing mere slaves of ours. These aren't the actions of brave men: we have been badly deceived in your case. Your reputation led us to expect that you would send a herald to challenge us and declare your willingness to settle the fight by taking on the Persians alone. We were prepared to accept, but instead we find you shrinking away from the fight rather than issuing any such challenge. Since you have failed to take the initiative here, it is now up to us. Why don't our two forces fight each other, with equal numbers on both sides? You can represent Greece, since you're supposed to be the best fighters in Greece, and we can champion Asia. The rest of our armies can fight as well, if you want, but later, after we've finished with each other. But if you don't like that idea and you'd be satisfied with

single combat between just our two forces, then let's fight it out and victory will go to the winning side as a whole.'

[49] The herald waited a short while after delivering this message, but no reply was forthcoming, so he returned and told Mardonius what had happened. Mardonius was delighted. Encouraged by this empty victory he ordered his cavalry to charge the Greek lines. Every unit of the Greek army took casualties from the javelins and arrows of the Persian cavalry as they bore down on them, since they were faced with expert mounted archers to whom they could not get close. The Persian cavalry also churned up and blocked the Gargaphian Spring, which had been supplying the whole Greek army with fresh water. The Lacedaemonians were the only ones posted right by the spring; all the other Greeks had some way to go to reach it (exactly how far depending on where each contingent was deployed). They did not have far to go to the Asopus, but the Persian cavalry with their bows and arrows had made it impossible for them to fetch water from the river, and so, with the Asopus denied them, they had been going to the spring.

[50] Under these circumstances the Greek commanders met with Pausanias on the right wing to discuss various matters, including the loss of the army's water supply and their harassment by the Persian cavalry. There were other items on the agenda because these events were not the only or even the main problems facing them: they had also run out of provisions, and the retainers of theirs who had been dispatched to the Peloponnese to bring them fresh supplies had been cut off by the cavalry and could no longer get through to the Greek camp.

[51] The upshot of the commanders' conference was that they decided to move their forces to the island, if the Persians refrained from joining battle that day. This island is located in front of the town of Plataea, ten stades away from the Asopus and the Gargaphian Spring, where they were based at the time. It is a kind of inland island: a river—the River Oëroë, which the locals hold to be the daughter of Asopus—divides further upstream on its way down from Cithaeron to the plain and the two branches of the river remain separate from each other for about three stades before merging again. So they decided to move here, because then they would not only have plenty of water, but also the cavalry could not inflict the casualties on them that they could when they were able to come straight at them. They decided to make the move during

the night, at the time of the second watch, so that the Persians would not notice them setting out and also so as to avoid having the cavalry on their heels harassing them. They decided as well that once they had reached this new site—the island formed by the splitting of Asopus' daughter Oëroë as she flows down from Cithaeron—they would dispatch half their troops to Cithaeron under cover of darkness to meet up with the retainers of theirs who had gone to fetch supplies and were trapped on Cithaeron.

[52] After they reached these decisions, the whole of the rest of the day was taken up with the constant burden of cavalry attacks, until the horsemen disengaged late in the afternoon. Night fell and the time agreed for departure arrived. The bulk of the army broke camp and left, but they had no intention of going to the appointed place: as soon as they started out, all they wanted to do was get away from the Persian cavalry, so they headed for the town of Plataea. On the way, however, they came to the temple of Hera, which stands in front of the town, twenty stades away from the Gargaphian Spring, and took up a position in front of it.

[53] So they established themselves by the temple of Hera. Now, when Pausanias saw them leaving the camp he assumed that they were going to the appointed place, so he instructed the Lacedae-monians to collect their gear as well and follow the others' lead. Most of his officers were prepared to obey Pausanias, but Amom-pharetus the son of Poliadas, who was the commander in charge of the company from Pitana, declared that as long as he had any say in the matter he would never bring shame to Sparta by retreat-ing from the 'strangers'. In fact, he was puzzled by what he saw going on, since he had not been present at the earlier discussion. His refusal to obey orders made Pausanias and Euryanax furious, but they found even more disturbing the prospect of abandoning the Pitanate company (which they would have to do, if Amom-pharetus remained stubborn,† in order to comply with the plan they had agreed with the rest of the Greeks), because they would then be abandoning Amompharetus and his men to their deaths. These considerations led them to keep their men where they were while they tried to persuade Amompharetus to change his mind.

[54] So Pausanias and Euryanax were trying to win over Amom-pharetus, since the Lacedaemonians and Tegeans had been left behind on their own.† Meanwhile, the Athenians had also not moved from their post, because they were well aware of the

Lacedaemonian tendency to say one thing and plan something quite different. Once most of the army had decamped, they sent one of their men on horseback to see if the Spartiates were making any effort to set out, or whether they had absolutely no intention of leaving, and also to ask Pausanias for instructions.

[55] When the Athenian messenger reached the Lacedaemonian lines, he found that they had not moved—and he found their leaders involved in a quarrel. Euryanax and Pausanias had failed in their attempt to convince Amompharetus of the danger he and his men would be in if they remained there without the support of the rest of the Lacedaemonians, and eventually, just as the Athenian messenger arrived in their midst, they fell to quarrelling. In the course of the dispute Amompharetus picked up a rock with both hands and put it down in front of Pausanias' feet, saying that this was his vote against retreating from the strangers. Pausanias then called Amompharetus mad and out of his mind, turned to the Athenian,† who had asked the question he had been sent with, and told him to let the Athenians know the difficulty of his situation; he requested that they link up with the Lacedaemonians and, as far as the withdrawal was concerned, that they follow the Lacedaemonian lead.

[56] The messenger returned to the Athenian lines. As day began to break, the Lacedaemonians had still not resolved their differences. All this time Pausanias had stayed put, but now he judged—rightly, as it turned out—that Amompharetus would not let himself be left behind if the rest of the Lacedaemonians marched away, so he gave the order and began to lead all the Lacedaemonians except for Amompharetus and his men away through the hills, and the Tegeans fell in behind them. As instructed, the Athenians took the alternate route from that taken by the Lacedaemonians: whereas the Lacedaemonians kept to the hillocks and the spurs of Cithaeron because they were afraid of the Persian cavalry, the Athenians made their way down to the plain.

[57] At first Amompharetus refused to believe that Pausanias would go so far as to leave him and his men behind, so he insisted that they stay put and not desert their post. But when Pausanias' troops were some way off, he saw that they really were abandoning him, so when his company had collected their gear he led them at a slow pace towards the other column, which had opened up a gap of about four stades and had halted on the River Moloeis, at

a place called Argiopius (where there is also a sanctuary of Demeter of Eleusis), to wait for Amompharetus' company. They were waiting so that they could go back and help Amompharetus and his company if they actually refused to leave their post and stayed put. Just as Amompharetus and his men met up with the rest of the Lacedaemonians, the Persian cavalry attacked in full force. The cavalry had been following their usual practice, but found the position the Greeks had occupied for the last few days deserted, so they kept riding forward until they caught up with them, and then they charged into the attack.

[58] When Mardonius found out that the Greeks had left under cover of darkness and saw that their positions had been abandoned, he summoned Thorax of Larisa and his brothers Eurypylus and Thrasydeius. 'Well, sons of Aleuas, what do you have to say now?' he asked. 'You can see that the place is deserted. "The Lacedaemonians never flee from battle," you told me. "Their military prowess is unsurpassed." And they are neighbours of yours. You've already seen them swapping their positions around, and now, as we can all see, they have used the cover of darkness last night to run away. They have now come up against the people who are genuinely the best fighters in the world, and they have proved themselves to be nonentities after all, who used to show off before their fellow nonentities in Greece. It's perfectly comprehensible to me that *you*, who had never come across Persians before, should have been impressed by the Lacedaemonians since you knew something of them, but I am much more surprised at Artabazus' fear. He was so afraid of them, in fact, that he was led to make the thoroughly cowardly suggestion that we should strike camp, withdraw to Thebes, and let ourselves be besieged there. In due course, the king will hear about this from me, but that's a topic for later. Our immediate task is not to let the Greeks get away with this manoeuvre; we must catch up with them and make them pay for all the wrongs they have done Persia.'

[59] With these words he led the Persians at the double across the Asopus and after the Greeks, who he believed were trying to run away. In actual fact it was only the Lacedaemonians and Tegeans that he went for, because the knolls blocked his view of the Athenians, who had headed for the plain. As soon as the officers in charge of the remaining units of the invading army saw the Persians setting out in pursuit of the Greeks, they gave the signal

for their men to join in the chase, and before long an undisciplined and chaotic mob of shouting soldiers was running as fast as they could after the Greeks, convinced that they would make short work of them.

[60] As soon as the cavalry began to attack his men, Pausanias sent a messenger on horseback to the Athenians with the following message: 'Men of Athens, the main battle is about to begin, and the outcome will decide whether Greece is to be free or enslaved. We Lacedaemonians and you Athenians have been betrayed by our allies who ran away last night. It's clear what we have to do from now on, then: we must fight back and defend each other to the best of our abilities. If the Persian cavalry had started out by attacking you, it would of course have been our duty, along with the Tegeans (who are still with us and have not betrayed Greece), to come and help you. In fact, though, they have come in full force against us, so you should come and support us, since we are the ones who are particularly hard pressed. If for some reason you can't come yourselves, please send us your archers. We know that you are totally committed to this war, and so that you will not refuse this request.'

[61] On receiving this message, the Athenians wanted to go and provide all the help they could, but when they were on their way they were set upon by the pro-Persian Greeks who had been deployed against them. This attack put them under so much pressure that they found it impossible to go and help the Lacedaemonians. So the Lacedaemonians and Tegeans were left without any support. Including light-armed troops, there were fifty thousand Lacedaemonians and three thousand Tegeans, who had remained close to the Lacedaemonians throughout. They proceeded to perform sacrifices, since they were about to join battle with Mardonius and as much of his army as was there, but the omens were unfavourable, and many of their men fell, with many more wounded, while the sacrifices were taking place, because the Persians formed their wickerwork shields into a barricade and continuously rained arrows down on the Greeks. In this situation, with the Spartiates under heavy pressure and the omens unfavourable, Pausanias looked towards the Plataeans' temple of Hera, invoked the goddess, and asked her not to let their hopes prove to be false.

[62] Pausanias was in the middle of his prayers when the Tegeans precipitately started forward to attack the Persians, and

then, just as Pausanias finished praying, the Lacedaemonians received good omens. Now that the situation was at last favourable, the Lacedaemonians proceeded to attack the Persians as well, and the Persians laid aside their bows and prepared to meet them head on. The first phase of the battle took place at the wickerwork barricade, until that was knocked down, and then a fierce battle raged for a long time around the temple of Demeter. Eventually the two sides ended up grappling with each other, as the Persians caught hold of the Greeks' spears and broke them off short. In courage and strength the Persians and the Greeks were evenly matched, but the Persians wore no armour; besides, they did not have the skill and expertise of their opponents. They would rush forward ahead of the main body of troops, one by one, or in groups of ten or so, and attack the Spartiates, only to be cut down.

[63] Mardonius rode into battle on his white horse, surrounded by his élite battalion of a thousand first-rate soldiers, and wherever he put in a personal appearance the Persians made things particularly difficult for their opponents. As long as Mardonius was alive, the Persians held their ground and fought back, inflicting heavy casualties on the Lacedaemonians. But after he had been killed and the men of his battalion, the most effective troops on the Persian side, had been cut down, all the others turned and fled before the Lacedaemonians. Their destruction was due more than anything else to the fact that they wore no armour: it was a case of light-armed soldiers taking on hoplites.

[64] Here the process of compensating the Spartiates for the murder of Leonidas was fulfilled by Mardonius, just as the oracle had predicted, and Pausanias the son of Cleombrotus and grandson of Anaxandridas won the most glorious victory of any known to us. (Pausanias and Leonidas had a common ancestry, so the names of Pausanias' ancestors prior to Anaxandridas have already been mentioned in the context of Leonidas.) Mardonius was killed by an eminent Spartiate called Arimnestus, who died some time after the Persian Wars, along with his company of three hundred men, when they took on the entire Messenian army at the battle of Stenyclerus.

[65] When the Persians were routed by the Lacedaemonians at Plataea, they fled in disorder back to their encampment and to the wooden stronghold they had built on Theban land. I find it surprising that although the battle took place by the grove of Demeter

not a single Persian, as it turned out, either entered the precinct or died in there; most of them fell around the outside of the sanctuary on unconsecrated ground. In so far as one may speculate about divine matters, I think the goddess herself kept them away because they had burnt her temple in Eleusis.

[66] Nothing further happened in the battle between the Lacedaemonians and Persians. Now, Artabazus the son of Pharnaces had disapproved of the campaign right from the very start, when Mardonius had been left in Greece by Xerxes, and had often tried, without success, to dissuade Mardonius from joining battle. Since he was unhappy with Mardonius' tactics anyway, then, this is what he did. He was responsible for a sizeable force of about forty thousand men, and because he had no doubts about the final outcome of the battle that was under way, he had them adopt a tight formation and told them to follow his lead wherever he went and at whatever pace he set. Having issued these instructions he marched them out as if they were going to join the battle. When they were some way down the road, however, he saw that the Persians were already in flight. At that point he changed formation and began to run as fast as possible away from the battlefield, but not towards the stronghold or Thebes with its defensive walls. Instead, he made for Phocis, because he wanted to get to the Hellespont without delay.

[67] So Artabazus and his men fled in that direction. Although the rest of the Greeks on the Persian side deliberately fought below their best, the battle between the Boeotians and the Athenians lasted a long time, because those of the Thebans who had collaborated with the enemy were fully committed to the battle and refused to fight below their full capabilities. The outcome was that their three hundred best and bravest men were killed at Plataea by the Athenians. When the Boeotian forces too were beaten back, they retreated to Thebes, but by a different route to the one taken by the Persians and the rest of the allied troops on the Persian side, all of whom—the full complement—fled without having struck a single blow or displayed any courage at all.

[68] It is clear to me that the success or failure of the invasion depended entirely on the Persians themselves. After all, on the occasion in question, Artabazus and his men fled before they had even joined battle, simply because they saw that the Persians had been pushed back. In the end, then, the whole Persian army was beaten

back, except for the cavalry (and especially the Boeotian cavalry), which proved invaluable to those who were fleeing, because they stayed on the side nearest the enemy and so shielded their allies, as they fled, from the victorious Greeks, who gave chase, harrying and slaughtering men from Xerxes' army.

[69] During this rout, word reached the rest of the Greeks (the ones who had taken up a position by the temple of Hera and had not taken part in the fighting) that a battle had taken place which Pausanias and his men had won. As soon as they heard the news, they set out in complete disarray. The Corinthians and the units deployed near them took the high road and headed straight for the sanctuary of Demeter following the foothills and knolls, while the Megarians, Phleiasians, and so on made their way through the level ground of the plain. As the Megarians and Phleiasians drew near the enemy, they were spotted by the Theban cavalry under Asopodorus the son of Timander. The Thebans could see that there was no discipline to their hasty approach, so they charged into the attack, cut down six hundred of them, and chased the scattered survivors back to Cithaeron.

[70] So these men died an inglorious death. The main body of the invading army, including the Persians, had taken refuge inside their wooden stronghold. They managed to climb up the towers before the Lacedaemonians arrived, and then they reinforced its walls as best they could. The Lacedaemonian attack initiated a fairly tough battle for the wall, because until the Athenians arrived the defenders were getting the better of the Lacedaemonians, who did not know how to go about attacking fortified structures. But once the Athenians attacked the stronghold, a fierce and protracted battle took place. Eventually, thanks to their courage and persistence, the Athenians succeeded in scaling the wall and making enough of a breach in it for the Greeks to pour in. The first to enter the stronghold were the Tegeans, and it was they who plundered Mardonius' pavilion, from which they took various objects including the manger Mardonius had used for his horses. This remarkable item of solid bronze was dedicated by the Tegeans as a votive offering in the temple of Athena Alea, but they added the rest of their haul to the common store to which all the Greeks contributed. After the wall had fallen, the foreign troops proved incapable of organizing themselves or thinking of resistance; they were in a complete panic, which was only natural given that there were

thousands and thousands of them, all terrified, trapped in a confined space. The Greeks were afforded such an opportunity for slaughter that out of an army of 300,000 men (discounting, that is, the 40,000 who escaped with Artabazus) not even 3,000 survived. Meanwhile a total of 91 Lacedaemonians from Sparta lost their lives in the battle, along with 16 Tegeans and 52 Athenians.

[71] The Persians were the best of the infantry from the invading army, while the best cavalry unit was that of the Sacae, and the individual prize for valour was held to belong to Mardonius. On the Greek side, although both the Tegeans and the Athenians proved their worth, the Lacedaemonians outshone everyone else. The only evidence I can offer in support of this assessment (because it is true that they all defeated the enemy units opposing them) is that the Lacedaemonians took on the toughest opponents and won. By far the greatest degree of courage was shown, in my opinion, by Aristodamus, who, as the sole survivor of the three hundred at Thermopylae, met with abuse and disgrace. The next most deserving of the prize of valour were also Spartiates: Poseidonius, Philocyon, and Amompharetus. Nevertheless, in conversations about which of their men was the bravest, the Spartiates who had taken part in the battle reckoned that Aristodamus had clearly wanted to die, because of the slur against his name, and so had recklessly broken rank and achieved such heroic exploits, whereas in Poseidonius' case there was no death-wish giving him courage, and so to that extent he was actually the braver of the two. But this argument of theirs may have been motivated by envy. However, among those who fell in this battle, all the men I mentioned, apart from Aristodamus, received special honours. Aristodamus did not, for the reason already mentioned—that he wanted to die.

[72] These were the men who won the most renown at Plataea. Callicrates' death occurred outside the actual battle. He was the best-looking man of his generation in the Greek army—and that takes into account all Greeks, not just Lacedaemonians. Callicrates was sitting in position when he was wounded in the side by an arrow; this was while Pausanias was offering up sacrifices before the battle. By the time battle was joined he had been carried away from the fighting. He struggled against death, and as he was dying he said to Arimnestus of Plataea that he did not mind dying for Greece; what bothered him was that he did not see any action and

so was denied the opportunity to perform as well as he knew he could and as he wanted to.

[73] The Athenian who is said to have distinguished himself most is Sophanes the son of Eutychides, from the village of Decelea. Now, according to local Athenian tradition, the people of Decelea once did something of lasting value. A long time ago the Tyndaridae invaded Attica at the head of a sizeable army to recover Helen, and they laid waste to the country villages because they did not know where she had been hidden. However, the people of Decelea (or, on some accounts, Decelus in person) did not approve of Theseus' high-handed behaviour and were afraid in case the whole of Attica suffered, so they told the Tyndaridae all the facts and showed them the way to Aphidnae, which Titacus, a native of the place, betrayed to them. This deed earned the people of Decelea the right to be exempt from tax in Sparta and to occupy the front seats at festivals there—rights which they have continued to hold all the way down to today. Even during the war which was fought many years later between the Athenians and the Peloponnesians, although the Lacedaemonians devastated the rest of Attica, they left Decelea alone.

[74] This was the village Sophanes came from, the Athenian who displayed the most valour at the battle of Plataea. There are two stories about his prowess there. According to one, he used to carry an iron anchor, attached with a bronze chain to the belt of his breastplate, and whenever he reached a spot near the enemy he would drop anchor, so that as the enemy charged at him from their ranks they could not make him move; if they turned and fled, however, it was his plan to pick up the anchor and go after them. Apart from this story, the other one (which contradicts the first) is that rather than having a real iron anchor attached to his breastplate, there was an anchor depicted on his shield, which was constantly moving from one side to the other and was never still.

[75] Sophanes has another glorious exploit to his credit. During the Athenian siege of Aegina he challenged Eurybates of Argos, a champion pentathlete, to single combat and killed him. Later Sophanes, for all his courage, met his death at the hands of the Edonians, during a battle for possession of the gold-mines at Datus, when he was in joint command of the Athenian forces along with Leagrus the son of Glaucon.

[76] Following the Persian defeat at Plataea, a woman who had been the concubine of a Persian called Pharandates the son of Teäspis escaped from the Persian camp and deserted to the Greeks. When she realized that the Persians were finished and that victory had gone to the Greeks, she decked herself out with a great deal of gold jewellery, dressed both herself and her maids in the finest clothes available to them, got down from her covered carriage, and made her way over to the Lacedaemonian lines while they were still in the middle of the massacre. Now, although she was perfectly familiar with Pausanias' name and had often been told where he came from, she was not in a position to recognize him until she saw him directing all these operations. Once she knew who he was, she went and clasped his knees in supplication. 'Please, my lord, king of Sparta,' she said, 'please save me from the slavery that awaits a prisoner of war. I am grateful to you for what you have already done in killing these men here—men who had no respect for gods or heroes. My birthplace was Cos; I am the daughter of Hegetorides the son of Antagoras. I was captured by the Persians and taken off Cos against my will.'

'Woman, you have nothing to fear,' Pausanias replied, 'not only because you've come to me as a suppliant, but also if you really are the daughter of Hegetorides of Cos, as you claim to be, because he's my closest guest-friend in those parts.' Then he entrusted her, for the time being, to those of the ephors who were there, but later he sent her, at her own request, to Aegina.

[77] Immediately after the arrival of the woman, the next thing that happened was that the Mantineans arrived—after it was all over! They were furious at having missed the battle, and said that they deserved to be punished for doing so. When they found out that Artabazus and his Persians were on the run, they wanted to chase them as far as Thessaly, but the Lacedaemonians refused to let them hunt the fugitives. Afterwards, when they were back home, the Mantineans exiled their military commanders. The Eleans, when they arrived shortly after the Mantineans, were just as upset, and they too returned home and banished their leaders. So much for the Mantineans and the Eleans.

[78] Among the Aeginetan forces at Plataea was Lampon the son of Pytheas, who was one of the leading men of Aegina—and the originator of a really perverted plan, which he rushed up to suggest to Pausanias. 'This victory of yours, son of Cleombrotus,' he said,

'is marvellous—an important and magnificent achievement. The god has allowed you to earn more fame than anyone else we know of, for saving Greece. What you need to do now is follow up this achievement, to enhance your reputation even more and to make any foreigner in the future think twice before committing obscene crimes against Greeks. After Leonidas' death at Thermopylae, Mardonius and Xerxes cut off his head and stuck it on a pole. Pay Mardonius back in the same coin, and all the Greeks, led by the Spartiates, will thank you for it. By impaling Mardonius' corpse you will exact revenge for his treatment of your uncle Leonidas.' He thought Pausanias would be pleased by this suggestion.

[79] 'My friend from Aegina,' Pausanias replied, 'I thank you for your goodwill and consideration, but you're making a bad mistake. First you raise me up high and sing the praises of my country and my achievement, and then you would have me sink to the lowest depths by suggesting that I maltreat a corpse. And according to you it would improve my reputation! It's the kind of deed we would expect from a foreigner, not a Greek, and even in them we find it loathsome. No, I hope no one who finds that kind of behaviour acceptable, whether he comes from Aegina or anywhere else, ever has reason to approve of what I do! It's enough for me if the Spartiates approve of me for the justice of both my words and my deeds. And I say that Leonidas, whom you are telling me to avenge, has been well avenged: he and all the dead at Thermopylae have been repaid in full with the lives of the countless men lying dead here. As for you, I never want to hear any similar proposals or suggestions from you ever again—and you should be grateful to get away without being punished for this one.'

[80] After this, Lampon took his leave. Pausanias issued a proclamation that no one was to keep any of the spoils of war, and he ordered the helots to collect everything of value. They went here and there throughout the Persian camp and found pavilions hung with gold and silver decorations, couches overlaid with gold and silver, various kinds of golden vessels, including bowls and cups; they found carts laden with sacks which turned out to contain gold and silver pots; from the bodies lying on the battlefield they stripped arm-bands and torques, their famous *akinakeis* (if they were made of gold), and gorgeous clothing beyond reckoning. A great deal of valuable property was stolen by the helots and sold to the Aeginetans, but there was also a great deal they could not

hide, and therefore declared. That day proved to be the beginning of great fortunes for the Aeginetans, because they bought the gold from the helots at the price of bronze.

[81] When all the treasure had been collected, they reserved a tenth of it for the god of Delphi, a tenth for the god of Olympia, and a tenth for the god of the Isthmus. From the first tenth was dedicated the golden tripod which sits on the bronze three-headed serpent very close to the altar; from the second tenth was dedicated the bronze statue of Zeus, ten cubits tall; and from the third tenth was dedicated the seven-cubit bronze statue of Poseidon. After separating out these three tenths, the rest of the treasure—the Persians' concubines, the gold, silver, and other valuables, and the yoke-animals—was divided up, with every contingent receiving the amount it deserved. No one has left a record of how much, if anything, was set aside and given to those who excelled in the fighting at Plataea, but I imagine that they did not go unrewarded. Ten of everything of value—women, horses, talents, camels, and so on—were set aside and given to Pausanias.

[82] Here is another incident that is supposed to have taken place at the time. In fleeing from Greece, Xerxes bequeathed his paraphernalia to Mardonius. The story goes that when Pausanias saw all these things, fitted out with gold and silver and embroidered hangings, he told Mardonius' bakers and chefs to prepare the kind of meal they had made for Mardonius. They did so, and then, when he saw the gold and silver couches with their fine coverings, the gold and silver tables, and the magnificent feast, he was amazed at all the good things spread out there and, for a joke, he told his own servants to prepare a typical Laconian meal. When the food was ready, Pausanias was amused to see the huge difference between the two meals, and he sent for the Greek commanders. Once they were all there, he pointed to the two meals and said, 'Men of Greece, my purpose in asking you all here is to show you just how stupid the Persian king is. Look at the way he lives, and then consider that he invaded our country to rob us of our meagre portions!' That is what Pausanias is supposed to have said to the commanders of the Greek forces.

[83] Chests of gold, silver, and other valuables were often found by people from Plataea for some time afterwards. There was also something that came to light even later, after the corpses had lost their flesh: when the Plataeans were collecting all the skeletons and

putting them all together in a single place, they found a skull without any sutures at all, but consisting of solid bone. They also turned up a jaw-bone on which both the front teeth and the molars on the upper jaw† were all a single unbroken bone. And they found the skeleton of a man who was five cubits tall.

[84] As for Mardonius,† his corpse disappeared the day after the battle. I cannot say for certain who took it, though in the past I have heard a number of stories to the effect that so-and-so from such-and-such a place buried Mardonius, and I know of a number of people who were handsomely rewarded by Artontes the son of Mardonius for doing so. I have not been able to find out for certain which of them was the one who stole the body and buried it (though there is also a rumour that it was Dionysophanes of Ephesus), but this is how things stand with his burial.

[85] After the Greeks had divided the spoils at Plataea, each contingent buried its own men in separate graves. The Lacedaemonians made three graves, one for the priests† (such as Poseidonius, Amompharetus, Philocyon, and Callicrates), another for the rest of the Spartiates, and the third for the helots. That is how the Lacedaemonians buried their dead, but the Tegeans buried all their dead in their own common grave, as did the Athenians, and so did the Megarians and Phleiasians with their men who had been killed by the enemy cavalry. The tombs made by these contingents did actually contain bodies, but my information is that all the other national tombs that can be found at Plataea are simply empty mounds constructed to impress future generations by people who were ashamed at not having taken part in the battle. After all, there is even a so-called tomb of the Aeginetans there, which I was told was built as much as ten years after the battle, at the request of the people of Aegina, by a Plataean called Cleades the son of Autodicus, who was the local representative of the Aeginetans.

[86] As soon as the Greeks had buried their dead at Plataea, they held a meeting at which they decided to march against Thebes and demand the surrender of those who had collaborated with the Persians (especially the ringleaders, Timagenidas and Attaginus), and, if the Thebans refused to hand them over, not to leave until the city had fallen. They put this decision into effect, reached Thebes ten days after the battle, and proceeded to lay siege to it. The Thebans refused to comply with their demand to surrender the

collaborators, so they laid waste to their farmland and attacked the
city walls.

[87] On the twentieth day of continuous devastation by the
Greeks Timagenidas addressed his fellow Thebans. 'Men of
Thebes,' he said, 'the Greeks are determined to continue the siege
either until Thebes falls or until you hand us over to them. But let
us not be the cause of any more suffering for Boeotia. It may be
that what they really want is money, and their demand for our surrender is a bluff. If so, let's give them money out of the public treasury; after all, we weren't the only ones to support the Persians, but
did so with public approval. However, if they do genuinely want
to get hold of us and that is why they are besieging the city, we'll
give ourselves up for trial.' The Thebans thought this was an excellent idea, and timely too, so they lost no time in sending a message
to tell Pausanias that they were prepared to extradite the men he
was after, and the two sides agreed to these terms.

[88] At this point Attaginus escaped from the city, but Pausanias had his sons arrested. He acquitted them, however, on
the grounds that they were too young to be guilty of collaboration.
The other men extradited by the Thebans expected to stand
trial and of course were convinced that they would bribe their way
out of trouble. But Pausanias was alert to exactly that possibility,
so once he had the traitors in his hands he dismissed the members
of the allied forces and took the Boeotians to Corinth, where he
executed them. So much for the battle of Plataea and events in
Thebes.

[89] By now, Artabazus the son of Pharnaces, who had escaped
from Plataea, had already covered a good distance. When he
reached Thessaly, the people there invited him to a banquet, at
which they began to question him about the rest of the army,
because they were completely unaware of what had happened at
Plataea. Now, Artabazus was sure that telling them the whole truth
about the battle would be risking death for himself and all his men,
since he thought that anyone at all who knew what had happened
would attack him. (It was because he had come to this conclusion
that he did not tell the Phocians anything either.) So he said, 'As
you can see, men of Thessaly, I am in a hurry to get to Thrace,
where I am marching with all speed. I have been assigned this
army and dispatched from our camp on an urgent mission. But
Mardonius himself is right behind us with his army, and you should

expect him any day. If you lay on a banquet for him too and show yourself his benefactors, you will have no cause to regret it later.' After this, he set off at the double with his army through Thessaly and Macedonia, heading straight for Thrace by the inland route, genuinely in a hurry. Eventually he reached Byzantium, but large numbers of his men had been lost along the way, slaughtered by the Thracians or overcome by hunger and exhaustion. At Byzantium the remainder of his men embarked on ships and crossed over to Asia.

[90] So that is how Artabazus returned home to Asia. It happened that on the same day as the Persian defeat at Plataea, they also suffered another defeat at Mycale in Ionia. For the Greek fleet under the command of Leotychidas of Lacedaemon was based on Delos, and while they were there three men came from Samos with a message. These three men were Lampon the son of Thrasycles, Athenagoras the son of Archestratides, and Hegesistratus the son of Aristagoras. They had been sent by the Samians on a secret mission, which neither the Persians nor their puppet ruler on Samos, the tyrant Theomestor the son of Androdamas, knew about. They presented themselves before the Greek commanders and Hegesistratus spoke at length, coming up with all kinds of arguments to suggest that the mere sight of the Greek fleet would be enough to make the Ionians rise up against Persia, and that the foreigners would not offer any resistance. 'Even if they *do* stay and fight,' he said, 'you'll never find prey as good as this. In the name of the gods worshipped alike by you and by us, I urge you to rescue us, Greeks like yourselves, from slavery and to fight back against the foreign invaders. This won't be a difficult task for you, because their ships are inadequate, and are no match for yours in battle. If you're worried in case we might be leading you into a trap, we'll gladly come with you on board your ships as hostages.'

[91] The Samian visitor put his request with a great deal of intensity, and in due course Leotychidas asked his name. He might have asked this question because he was looking for an omen, or it might even have been just a lucky question, prompted by some god. 'I am Hegesistratus . . .', the Samian began, but Leotychidas cut off whatever else Hegesistratus was going to add, and said: 'I accept this as a valid omen, my friend from Samos. All I ask from you is that you do not sail away until we have your sworn word,

and that of your companions here, that the Samians will be committed to helping us in the war.'

[92] He immediately set about putting his words into effect, because the Samians gave their assurances straight away, and swore a treaty of alliance with the Greeks. When this was done, they began to prepare for the voyage. Leotychidas asked Hegesistratus to sail with the Greeks, because he considered his name auspicious. They waited and the next day they performed sacrifices to seek favourable omens, with their diviner being a man from Apollonia (the Apollonia in the Ionian Gulf) called Deïphonus the son of Euenius.

[93] Here is a story about something that once happened to his father. In this town of Apollonia there is a flock of sheep which is sacred to the sun. By day they graze along the banks of a river which rises on Mount Lacmon and flows through the countryside around Apollonia to the sea by the port of Oricus. At night it is up to the leading citizens, from the wealthiest and noblest families, to look after them; one of them is chosen for the job and does it for a year. The importance of this flock to the people of Apollonia is due to a prophecy they once received. The sheep spend the night in a cave which is some distance from the town.

This was the cave where Euenius was on the occasion in question, when it was his turn to guard the flock. One night he fell asleep during his watch, and wolves slipped past him into the cave and killed about sixty of the sheep. When this came to his attention, he kept it to himself and did not tell anyone, because he planned to replace the dead sheep with others that he would buy. He did not get away with it, however: the people of Apollonia found out what had happened and took him to court. For the crime of sleeping during his watch, he was sentenced to lose his eyesight. No sooner had they blinded Euenius, however, than their sheep and goats stopped giving birth and the land became barren too. Emissaries consulted the oracles in both Dodona and Delphi as to why this calamity had happened to them, and received the same reply—that it was because they had wrongfully blinded Euenius, the guardian of the sacred flock. The gods said that they themselves had sent the wolves, and that they would carry on taking revenge for what had been done to him until the people of Apollonia paid him in compensation whatever he chose and felt was appropriate; when this had been done, the gods said, they would give Euenius a gift which would make many men count him happy.

[94] The Apolloniate emissaries kept the content of these oracles to themselves, and instructed certain of their fellow townsmen to deal with the matter. The way they went about it was this. They came up to Euenius when he was sitting on a bench, sat down by him, and started chatting with him. They steered the conversation around to the point where they could express sympathy for his misfortune, and then asked him what compensation he would choose, if, hypothetically, the people of Apollonia were to undertake to make amends for what they had done. So he made his choice in ignorance of the prophecy. He said that he would be satisfied with certain plots of land (and he named the townsmen who he knew owned the two finest plots in Apollonia) and also a certain house (which was, as he was well aware, the finest in the town); once he was in possession of these things, he said, he would stop being so angry and would feel that he had been adequately compensated. 'Euenius,' his companions on the bench replied, 'the people of Apollonia grant you this compensation for the loss of your sight, in fulfilment of the oracles they have received.' When Euenius heard the truth and realized that he had been tricked, he was enraged, but his fellow townsmen bought the land and house he had chosen from their owners and gave them to him. And from then on he had the natural gift for divination for which he became famous.

[95] So this was the Euenius whose son Deïphonus had been brought by the Corinthians to act as the diviner for the Greek fleet. I have also heard it said that Deïphonus was not really Euenius' son, but usurped his name and used to travel throughout Greece offering his work for hire.

[96] The Greeks put to sea, after obtaining favourable omens, and set off from Delos towards Samos. When they reached the Samian coast off Calami, they dropped anchor there, close to the temple of Hera which is on that part of the island, and got themselves ready for battle at sea. Meanwhile, the Persians had heard of the Greeks' approach and also launched their ships—but headed for the mainland with the whole of their fleet except for the Phoenician ships, which were dispatched elsewhere. Having talked things

over and come to the conclusion that they were no match for the
Greeks at sea, they decided against fighting and instead sailed off
towards the mainland, so as to gain the protection of the land army
of theirs which had been separated off from the main army and left
at Mycale, by order of Xerxes, to guard Ionia. This land army was
sixty thousand strong and was commanded by Tigranes, who was
the best-looking and tallest man in Persia. So the commanders of
the fleet decided to beach their ships under the protection of this
army and to build a defensive stockade as a place of refuge for
themselves and the ships.

[97] This was the plan they had in mind when they put to
sea from Samos. They sailed past the sanctuary of the Reverend
Goddesses at Mycale and came to Gaeson and Scolopoeis, where
there is a sanctuary of Demeter of Eleusis, built by Philistus the
son of Pasicles who went with Neileus the son of Codrus to found
Miletus. There they beached their ships. They cut down cultivated
trees, surrounded the ships with a stockade of stone and wood,
and fixed stakes in the ground around the stockade. Then they
were ready for a siege—or for victory, since they had made their
preparations with both possibilities in mind.†

[98] The Greeks were irritated when they found out that the
Persians had given them the slip and gone to the mainland, and
had no idea what to do next. Should they return home or sail to
the Hellespont? In the end they decided to do neither of these
things, but to sail to the mainland. So they made sure they had all
the equipment—boarding-planks and so on—that they might need
for a sea battle, and set sail for Mycale. As they drew near the
enemy camp, not a single ship was to be seen sailing out against
them; instead, they could see ships beached inside the stronghold
and a large land army drawn up along the shoreline. As a first
response, Leotychidas sailed his ship along the shoreline, steering
as close in as he could, and had a crier call out the following
instructions to the Ionians: 'Men of Ionia, if any of you are listening, hear what I have to say. Don't worry: the Persians won't understand anything of what I'm telling you. When battle is joined, you
must first remember your freedom, and then bear in mind our
watchword, "Hebe".† When you hear this message, pass it on to
anyone who hasn't.' Leotychidas' intention in this exercise was the
same as Themistocles' at Artemisium: either the Persians would not
hear about the message, in which case he might win the Ionians

over, or they would, in which case he might make them distrust the Greeks.

[99] Next, after Leotychidas had put this proposal to the Ionians, the Greeks brought their ships into shore, disembarked on to the beach, and began to form battle lines. The first thing the Persians did, when they saw the Greeks getting ready for battle and realized that they had made an appeal to the Ionians, was disarm the Samians on suspicion of having pro-Greek sympathies. In fact the Samians had freed some Athenian prisoners of war who had been brought over in the Persian fleet after having been stranded in Attica and captured by Xerxes' army; the Samians let them all go and sent them on their way to Athens with supplies for the journey. The fact that they had freed five hundred head of Xerxes' enemies was the main reason they were under suspicion. The second step the Persians took was to order the Milesians to watch the passes which lead towards the heights of Mycale; they pretended that the reason they were giving this job to the Milesians was that they were particularly familiar with the region, but in fact they wanted them away from the camp. So the Persians took these precautionary measures against those of the Ionians whom they actually had good reason to think would, given the opportunity, make trouble for them, and then formed their wickerwork shields into a tight protective barrier for themselves.

[100] The Greeks completed their preparations and set out towards the Persian lines. As they were advancing, a rumour sped its way to the entire army and a herald's wand was seen lying on the beach; the rumour, which spread throughout the ranks, was that the Greeks had defeated Mardonius' army in a battle in Boeotia. There is plenty of convincing evidence that the divine plays a part in human affairs. Consider how on this occasion, with the Persian defeat at Plataea and their imminent defeat at Mycale happening on the same day, a rumour of Plataea reached the Greeks at Mycale, boosting their morale and making them even more willing to face danger.

[101] Another coincidence is that there were precincts of Demeter of Eleusis near both battle-sites. The battle of Plataea took place, as I have already said, right by the temple of Demeter, and the same was true of the forthcoming engagement at Mycale. The arrival of the rumour that Pausanias and his men had been victorious also turned out to be accurate in the sense that the battle

at Plataea took place early in the day, while the one at Mycale took place in the afternoon. That both engagements were fought on the same day of the same month only became apparent to the Greeks a little later, when they looked into the matter. Before the arrival of the rumour they had been afraid, not so much for themselves as for their compatriots in Greece, in case Greece should fall because of Mardonius. But once the mysterious rumour had sped its way to them, they advanced into the attack with more energy and speed. The Persians were just as anxious as the Greeks to join battle, since both the Aegean islands and the Hellespont were at stake.

[102] Now, about half of the Greek forces, consisting of the Athenians and the troops deployed next to them, were advancing over the beach and level ground, whereas the Lacedaemonians and their neighbours in the lines had to make their way via a ravine and some hills. So while they were still on their way around the hills, the other wing had already engaged the enemy. As long as the Persians could fight back with their wickerwork barricade upright, the battle remained evenly balanced; but then, in their desire to win victory for themselves and to deny it to the Lacedaemonians, the Athenians and their neighbours motivated themselves for an extra effort. That was the turning-point. They forced their way through the wickerwork shields and charged *en masse* against the enemy; for a long time the Persians stood their ground and fought back, but in the end they began to retreat towards their stronghold. The Athenians and their neighbours—the Corinthians, the Sicyonians, and the Troezenians, in that order—stayed together as they chased the fugitives and charged into the stronghold. Once even their stronghold had fallen, all the enemy troops gave up fighting and took to flight, except the Persians. Small groups of Persians fought on against the successive waves of Greeks pouring into the stronghold. Of the Persian commanders, two escaped and two died: the naval commanders, Artayntes and Ithamitres, escaped, while Mardontes and Tigranes, the commander of the land army, died fighting.

[103] The Lacedaemonians and their half of the Greek forces arrived while the Persians were still fighting and helped to finish off the remnants. Casualties on the Greek side were very high in this battle, especially among the Sicyonians, who also lost their

commander, Perilaus. The Samians who were serving in the Persian army and had been disarmed saw straight away that the battle was finely balanced and did all they could to help the Greeks. Seeing the Samian initiative, the other Ionians also deserted from the Persian side and attacked the enemy.

[104] It was with a view to their own safety that the Persians had ordered the Milesians to watch the passes, so that if things turned out as they actually did, they would have guides to show them the way to the refuge of the heights of Mycale. That was one reason the Milesians were given this job, and the other was to get them out of the camp where they might cause trouble. But the Milesians did exactly the opposite of what they were supposed to do. They guided the fleeing Persians along the wrong paths—ones which took them into the midst of the enemy—and in the end they turned out to be the Persians' worst enemies in terms of the numbers they killed. And so for the second time Ionia rose up against Persia.

[105] The Athenians displayed exceptional bravery in this battle, and among the Athenians the prize for valour went to Hermolycus the son of Euthoenus, who was a specialist at all-in wrestling. Hermolycus met death some years later, when Athens was at war with Carystus, during a battle in Carystian territory at Cyrnus. He is buried on Cape Geraestus. The next bravest contingents, after the Athenians, were those from Corinth, Troezen, and Sicyon.

[106] After the Greeks had killed most of the enemy, either while fighting in the battle or while trying to escape, they set fire to the Persian ships and to the entire stronghold—but not before they had brought the booty out on to the beach and discovered some caches of money. Once they had burnt the stronghold to the ground, the Greeks set sail for Samos. When they got there, they held a meeting to discuss whereabouts in Greece (as much of it as was under their control) they should resettle the people of Ionia, if they evacuated them and abandoned Ionia to the Persians. It was not feasible, in their opinion, for them to stand guard over Ionia for ever, but failing that they did not hold out any hope that Ionia would get away without being punished by the Persians. The response of the Peloponnesian leaders to all this was to suggest that they should depopulate the trading-centres belonging to those Greek nations

which had collaborated with the Persians and give the territory to the Ionians instead. The Athenians, however, did not think it was a good idea to evacuate Ionia in the first place, and were also not happy to have the Peloponnesians deliberating about Athenian colonists. They put their objections forcefully, and eventually the Peloponnesians conceded. And this is how the Athenians came to enter into an alliance with all the Aegean islands which had supported the Greek war effort, including Samos, Chios, and Lesbos; the terms of the treaty bound the islanders with pledges of honour and with oaths to abide by the conditions of the alliance and not to secede. After entering into this solemn treaty with the islanders, the Athenians set sail to go and dismantle the bridges, which they expected to find still intact. So off they went to the Hellespont.

[107] The few foreigners who escaped and had been enclosed in the heights of Mycale made their way to Sardis. In the course of the journey Masistes the son of Darius, who had been present at the defeat, went on and on at the commander, Artayntes. He heaped all kinds of abuse on him, and at one point said that his style of leadership was more cowardly than a woman's, and that there was no punishment he did not deserve to suffer for the harm he had done the king's house. Now, in Persia to be called more cowardly than a woman is the worst insult there is. Artayntes put up with all this abuse for a while, but then in a rage he drew his *akinakes* against Masistes. He meant to kill him, but a man from Halicarnassus called Xenagoras the son of Praxilaus, who was standing right behind Artayntes, noticed him lunging at Masistes. He caught Artayntes round the middle, lifted him up in the air, and dashed him to the ground—by which time Masistes' personal guards had interposed themselves between their master and Artayntes. This action of Xenagoras' earned him not just Masistes' thanks, but Xerxes' as well, for saving his brother; in fact, it gained him the rulership of the whole of Cilicia, as a gift from the king. This was the only significant event that happened on their journey, and then they reached Sardis, where the king had been ever since he had fled there from Athens after his failure in the sea battle.

[108] During his time in Sardis Xerxes had fallen in love with Masistes' wife, who was also there. She proved impervious to his messages, however, and he did not try force out of respect for his

brother. In fact, this was precisely what was giving the woman strength of purpose: she knew perfectly well that she would not have force used on her. Under these circumstances, with all other options closed off, Xerxes arranged for his son Darius to marry the daughter of this woman and Masistes, since he expected to have a better chance of seducing the woman in this situation. Once he had betrothed the couple and carried out the customary rites he rode off to Susa. However, after he had arrived and had received Darius' wife into his house, he dropped Masistes' wife and began to desire Darius' wife, Masistes' daughter, instead. Her name was Artaynte, and he was successful with her.

[109] After a while, however, the secret got out. What happened was that Amestris, Xerxes' wife, wove a wonderful shawl, long and colourful, as a present for Xerxes. He liked it a lot, and wore it when he went to visit Artaynte. She gave him pleasure too—so much so that he told her he would give her anything she wanted in return for the favours she had granted him; whatever she asked for, he assured her, she would get. It was destined that she and her whole household would come to a bad end, so she asked Xerxes, 'Will you really give me anything I want?' Not suspecting for a moment what she was going to ask for, he promised her that he would and gave her his word—and now that she had his word, she boldly asked for the shawl. Xerxes did everything he could to dissuade her, because he really did not want to give it to her, for one reason and one reason alone: he was afraid that Amestris would have her suspicions confirmed and find out what he was up to. He offered Artaynte cities, unlimited gold, and sole command of an army (a typically Persian gift), but she refused everything. Eventually, then, he gave her the shawl, which she liked so much that she used to wear it and show it off.

[110] Amestris heard that Artaynte had the shawl, but this information did not make her angry with Artaynte. Instead she assumed that her mother was to blame and was responsible for the whole business, and so it was Masistes' wife whose destruction she started to plot. She waited until her husband Xerxes was holding a royal banquet—that is, the banquet which is prepared once a year on the king's birthday. The Persians describe this banquet as *tukta*, which is to say 'complete' in Greek. This is the only time of the year when the king anoints his head with oil, and he also distributes gifts among the Persians. So when the day arrived, Amestris

told Xerxes what she wanted her gift to be—Masistes' wife. Xerxes understood the reason for her request, and was shocked and horrified, not only at the thought of handing over his brother's wife, but also because she was innocent in this matter.

[111] His wife was implacable, however, and he was constrained by the tradition that on the day of the royal banquet no request could be refused, so he agreed, with extreme reluctance. He turned the woman over to his wife and told her to do with her what she liked, and also sent for his brother. When he arrived, he said, 'Masistes, as well as being the son of Darius and my brother, you are a good man. I want you to divorce your present wife, and I'll give you my daughter instead. You can have her as your wife. But get rid of the present one; the marriage displeases me.'

Masistes was astonished at the king's words. 'Master,' he said, 'what a cruel thing to say! Can you really be telling me to get rid of my wife and marry your daughter? I have grown-up sons and daughters by my wife; in fact, you have married your own son to one of our daughters. Besides, she suits me perfectly well. I count it a great honour to be thought worthy of your daughter, my lord, but I refuse to comply with either of your commands. Please don't insist on having your way in this matter. You'll find another husband for your daughter, someone just as good as me. Please let me stay married to my wife.'

This reply of his made Xerxes angry, and he said, 'Do you want to know what you've done, Masistes? I'll tell you. I withdraw the offer of marriage to my daughter, and you're not going to live with your wife a moment longer either. That will teach you to accept what you're offered.'

At these words all Masistes said was: 'You haven't yet killed me, master.' Then he walked out of the room.

[112] In the mean time, during this conversation between Xerxes and his brother, Amestris had sent for Xerxes' personal guards and with their help had mutilated Masistes' wife. She cut off her breasts and threw them to the dogs, cut off her nose, ears, lips, and tongue, and then sent her back home, totally disfigured.

[113] Masistes was still completely unaware of all this, but he was expecting something terrible to happen to him, so he ran back to his house. As soon as he saw how his wife had been maimed, he first sought the advice of his sons and then made his way to

Bactra along with his sons and, of course, others as well, with the intention of stirring up revolt in the province of Bactria and doing the king as much harm as he could. And he would have succeeded in this, in my opinion, if he had managed to reach the Bactrians and the Sacae in time, because they were attached to him and he was the governor of Bactria. But Xerxes found out what he was up to; he dispatched an army to intercept him while he was on his way, and killed him, his sons, and all his troops. And that is the end of the story of Xerxes' desire and Masistes' death.

[114] Driven off course by adverse winds, the Greeks who had set out from Mycale for the Hellespont first anchored off Cape Lectum, but then they reached Abydus. They had expected to find the bridges still intact, and that was the main reason they had gone to the Hellespont, but when they got there they found that they had already been demolished. Leotychidas and his Peloponnesians decided to sail back to Greece, but the Athenians under Xanthippus chose to stay in the area and attack the Chersonese. So the Peloponnesians set sail for home, while the Athenians sailed across from Abydus to the Chersonese and proceeded to besiege Sestus.

[115] Now, Sestus had the strongest fortifications in the region, so when people from the outlying towns heard that a Greek force had come to the Hellespont, they flocked there. Among their number was a Persian called Oeobazus, who travelled from Cardia, where he had been keeping the cables from the bridges. Sestus was inhabited by local Aeolians, but at the time the population also included Persians and vast numbers of people from their various allies.

[116] The ruler of this province was Xerxes' governor Artayctes, a Persian who was both cunning and corrupt. Once at Elaeus, during Xerxes' march towards Athens, he tricked him and stole the treasure of Protesilaus the son of Iphiclus. Protesilaus is buried in Elaeus on the Chersonese, and there is a precinct there surrounding the tomb. Within the sanctuary there used to be a lot of votive offerings, including a great deal of money, gold and silver cups, bronze, and clothing; Artayctes stole all of this, and did so with the king's permission. He tricked Xerxes by saying, 'Master, there's a house here of some Greek who took part in an expedition against your land and got his reward by being killed there. Please give me the house; that will teach people not to invade your country.' This sort of argument was guaranteed to persuade Xerxes to give him

someone's house without any hesitation. He had no suspicion of what was going through Artayctes' mind. When Artayctes said that Protesilaus had invaded the king's land, he was bearing in mind the fact that the Persians regard all Asia as belonging to them and to whoever is their king at the time. After taking possession of the 'house', he transported all the valuables out of Elaeus to Sestus and turned the sanctuary into arable land which he farmed. And whenever he went to Elaeus, he used to have sex with women in the temple. But now he was being besieged by the Athenians. Somehow their attack caught him off his guard: he had not been expecting to see the Greeks there, and so was completely unprepared for a siege.

[117] The siege was still in progress when autumn arrived. Irritated at being away from home and at their failure to capture the stronghold, the Athenian troops asked their commanders to take them back to Athens—which the commanders refused to do until they had either captured the town or been recalled by the Athenian authorities. So the men accepted the current state of affairs.

[118] Meanwhile, inside the stronghold, the situation was so utterly dire that they were boiling the leather straps from their beds and eating them. When there were not even any straps left, the Persians, including Artayctes and Oeobazus, escaped from the town under cover of darkness by climbing down the most remote wall, where there were hardly any enemy troops. The next day the Chersonesites in the town signalled to the Athenians from the towers to let them know what had happened, and then opened the gates. Most of the Athenians went after the fugitives, while the rest occupied the town.

[119] Oeobazus got as far as Thrace, but the Apsinthian Thracians caught him and sacrificed him, after their own fashion, to a local god called Pleistorus; they also killed all his companions, but not by sacrificing them. Artayctes and his men made their break from the town later than Oeobazus and were overtaken just beyond Aegospotami. They resisted for a long time, but eventually were either killed or captured. The prisoners, who included Artayctes and his son, were bound by the Greeks and taken back to Sestus.

[120] There is a story told by the people of the Chersonese of a miracle that happened when one of the men guarding these pris-

oners was roasting his salt fish: the fish were lying in the fire when they suddenly started flopping about and wriggling, like newly caught fish. The people grouped around the fire were puzzled by the phenomenon, but when Artayctes noticed it he called out to the man who was cooking the fish and said: 'You needn't be alarmed by this omen, my Athenian friend. It has nothing to do with you. It is Protesilaus from Elaeus telling me that even though he is dead and mummified like a salt fish, the gods still grant him the power to punish a criminal. Under these circumstances I shall impose the following penalty on myself: in compensation for the property I took from the sanctuary, I'll pay the god a hundred talents, and I'll give two hundred talents to the Athenians for the life of myself and my son, if I am allowed to live.' Xanthippus, the Athenian commander, remained unmoved by these promises. The people of Elaeus had already demanded his execution—this was their way of avenging Protesilaus—and Xanthippus was inclining in the same direction himself. So the Athenians took him down to the shore on which Xerxes' bridge across the straits had ended (or, in another version, to the hill which overlooks the town of Madytus), where they nailed him to a plank of wood and suspended him from it, and then stoned his son to death before his eyes.

[121] They then sailed back to Greece, taking with them various valuable items, including the cables from the bridges, which they intended to dedicate in their sanctuaries. Nothing further happened for the remainder of the year.

[122] This Artayctes, the one who was crucified, was the descendant of Artembares, who was the author of a certain proposal which the Persians passed on to Cyrus for ratification. The proposal went like this: 'Since Zeus has given sovereignty to the Persians and to you in particular, Cyrus, now that you have done away with Astyages, let's emigrate from the country we currently own, which is small and rugged, and take over somewhere better. There are plenty of countries on our borders, and plenty further away too, any one of which, in our hands, will make us even more remarkable to even more people. This is a perfectly reasonable thing for people with power to do. Will we ever have a better opportunity than now, when we rule over so many peoples and the whole of Asia?'

Cyrus was not impressed with the proposal. He told them to go ahead—but he also advised them to be prepared, in that case, to become subjects instead of rulers, on the grounds that soft lands tend to breed soft men. It is impossible, he said, for one and the same country to produce remarkable crops and good fighting men. So the Persians admitted the truth of his argument and took their leave. Cyrus' point of view had proved more convincing than their own, and they chose to live in a harsh land and rule rather than to cultivate fertile plains and be others' slaves.

APPENDIX 1
A Note on Greek Clothing

In this book the standard ways of translating items of Greek clothing have been followed, but since they tend to set up some wrong associations in a modern mind, a corrective note is not out of place. Greek clothing for both men and women consisted basically of two lengths of material draped and fastened around the body—one worn as an under garment and the other, when necessary, as an outer garment. The under garment (*khiton*, or in Herodotus' dialect *kithon*) was an oblong piece of linen or wool, usually worn at knee-length by men and ankle-length by women, fastened on one or both shoulders with a brooch, and tied with a belt around the waist. This has been translated 'tunic'. The outer garment (usually called a *himation*, though Herodotus also uses the Homeric word *heima*) was a much larger length of cloth—perhaps as large as 8 feet by 6 feet (2.4 × 1.8 m.)—and similarly draped and fastened over the body. This has been translated 'cloak'. Of course, for some purposes, such as riding or fighting, shorter cloaks were used (as also by children), and there were variations for gender too: each had its own name (e.g. *tribon, khlamys, peplos, khlaina, khlanis*). An accessible short treatment of Greek clothing may be found in James Laver, *A Concise History of Costume* (London, 1969).

APPENDIX 2
Weights, Measures, Money, and Distances

There was considerable flexibility about these matters in the ancient world. What follows is just one system.

Measuring Distance

16 fingers (breadth)	= 4 palms = 1 foot
12 fingers	= ½ cubit = 1 span (i.e. the distance between the tips of the thumb and the little finger when the hand is fully spread; see 2.149)
1¼ feet	= 1 pygon (i.e. the distance from the elbow to the bottom joint of the middle finger)
1½ feet	= 1 cubit (i.e. the distance from the elbow to the tip of the middle finger; the 'Egyptian' and 'Samian' cubits mentioned in 2.168 are this kind of cubit)
27 fingers	= 1 royal cubit (see 1.178)
6 feet	= 1 fathom (i.e. the distance between the fingertips when the arms are stretched out horizontally)
100 feet	= 1 plethron
600 feet	= 1 stade
30 stades	= 1 parasang = ½ schoenus ('rope'; see 2.6)

In addition, Herodotus uses a square measure: 1 aroura ('field') is defined at 2.168 as 100 square cubits.

In modern absolute terms, 1 foot, on the Attic scale which Herodotus was using, has been estimated to be 29.6 cm. (11.65 in.). Therefore:

1 finger	= 1.85 cm. (0.73 in.)
1 palm	= 7.4 cm. (2.91 in.)
1 span	= 22.2 cm. (8.74 in.)
1 pygon	= 37 cm. (14.57 in.)
1 cubit	= 44.4 cm. (17.5 in.)
1 royal cubit	= 49.95 cm. (19.66 in.)
1 fathom	= 1.776 m. (1.94 yd.)
1 plethron	= 29.6 m. (32.38 yds.)

APPENDIX 2

```
1 stade     = 177.6 m. (194.29 yds.)
1 parasang  = 5.328 km. (3.31 miles)
1 schoenus  = 10.656 km. (6.62 miles)
```

Money, or Measuring Weight

Greek coinage was not on the whole fiduciary, but was worth its weight. Hence the measures of weight are at the same time financial measures.

```
1 talent   = 60 minas = 6,000 drachmas = 36,000 obols
1 obol     = 722 mg. (0.025 oz.)
1 drachma  = 4.332 g. (0.15 oz.)
1 mina     = 433.2 g. (15.16 oz.)
1 talent   = 25.992 kg. (57.31 lb.)
```

This is the scale for the Euboïc-Attic talent (see 3.89); Herodotus there also talks about a Babylonian talent, which is worth 70 Euboïc minas, or 30.324 kg. (66.86 lb.).

There was also in circulation in the east, at any rate, a stater (or 'standard', also sometimes called a daric, after Darius), which Herodotus occasionally mentions, whose weight on the Attic scale was 4 drachmas, or almost 18 g. (0.63 oz.). But it is not absolutely clear, when Herodotus is talking about eastern staters (as at 7.28–9), that he is thinking in terms of the Attic scale.

Measuring Capacity

Liquid measures: 1 amphora ('jar') = 12 choes ('pitchers') = 144 cotylae ('cups') = 864 cyathi ('spoons'). Since 1 amphora = about 39 litres (68.64 pints, 8.58 gallons), then 1 chous = 3.25 litres (5.72 pints), 1 cotyle = 270 ml. (0.48 pint), and 1 cyathus = 45 ml. (0.079 pint, 1.58 fl. oz.). Herodotus refers only to the amphora (1.51, 70, 4.81) and cotyle (6.57). In this latter passage he also refers to a liquid measure he calls the 'Laconian fourth', which F. Hultsch (*Griechische und Römische Metrologie* (Berlin, 1882), 500) says is 'obviously' a quarter of a metretes or amphora—i.e. (on the Laconian scale) about 14 litres (24.64 pints). The 'arister' mentioned at 2.168 was apparently the same as a cotyle.

Dry measures: 1 medimnus = 48 choenixes = 192 cotylae. Since 1 cotyle = 270 ml. (0.48 pint), then 1 choenix = 1.08 litres (1.90 pints), and 1 medimnus = 51.84 litres (91.24 pints, 11.40 gallons).

EXPLANATORY NOTES

In the notes that follow I have tried to keep in mind the general reader's need to know basic background information about names and dates, how the passage at hand fits into the larger ongoing narrative, and something of its more extended significance for Herodotus and the period he describes. The notes have been designed to be read section by section along with the corresponding chapters of the text. The cross-references and more lengthy notes are intended for the reader who is curious to pursue Herodotus' narrative habits and explore his general interests and the historical content more fully; they are not meant to oppress, or to interfere with the reader's ability to hear and enjoy Herodotus' own voice.

Wherever possible, for historical information I have pointed the reader to the second edition of the *Cambridge Ancient History*, volumes iii–v (1982–92), here called *CAH* iii/1, *CAH* iii/2, *CAH* iii/3, *CAH* iv, *CAH* v, because these volumes are widely accessible, and their ample bibliographical references allow further exploration of many topics connected to the *Histories*. Please see the Select Bibliography on pp. xliii–xlv for titles of other works cited by author in the Notes, as well as some other works of general interest published in English. In the Notes, How and Wells (1913, repr. with corrections, 1928) is referred to as H & W; Meiggs and Lewis (1969) is referred to as M-L; Fornara (1983) as Fornara; West (1994) as West; and Jacoby (1957) as FGH. The reader who wants more information on topics of general classical interest (including figures from myth, individuals and authors, peoples, cities, and countries) is encouraged to begin by consulting the *Oxford Classical Dictionary* (third edition, 1996), edited by S. Hornblower and A. Spawforth.

The scholarly reader is encouraged at all points to consult the major commentaries, for instance, the Italian series published by the Fondazione Lorenzo Valla, Lloyd's commentary on Book 2, and among the older works, How and Wells, and Macan. The outlines placed at the beginning of the notes for each individual book below are intended to serve only as a convenience for the reader, not as an analysis of the *Histories'* underlying structure.

Many more scholars have given generously of their time in answering queries than I can thank by name here; S. Burstein, P. Cartledge, S. Cole, J. Marincola, S. Morris, M. Munn, J. Papadopoulos, K. Raaflaub, and R. Woodard have been particularly helpful. J. Appleby, M. Chambers, D. Boedeker, J. Ginsburg, A. Ivantchik, M. Jameson, A. Lloyd, W. K. Pritchett, A. Raubitschek, R. Stroud, W. G. Thalmann, P. Vasunia, and R. Waterfield have read and improved considerable portions of the Introduction or Notes. For efforts going far beyond the call of duty or even friendship, I would like particularly to thank B. T. Jones, D. Lateiner, P. O'Neill, and M. Ostwald. None of them, however, has seen the whole of what follows, or is responsible for the errors that remain therein.

BOOK ONE

Book 1 is very simply structured. It consists of four passages of increasing length that guide the reader gradually towards the theme that will underlie much of the rest of the narrative: the sixth-century growth of the Persian empire, beginning with Cyrus the Great (c.557–530 BCE). The first passage is only a single paragraph long, and sets out Herodotus' name, the fact that the whole of what follows is the product of his own *historiē* or investigation, and the announced purpose of it: to preserve and celebrate great deeds of the past, both Greek and foreign. It ends by declaring that the enmity between Greeks and foreigners, and the cause for that enmity, will be of particular concern. The second passage then plays with this first announced topic by giving a quasi-humorous account several pages in length about a series of mythic abductions of Greek women by foreigners and foreign women by Greeks (1.1–5). The third passage, quite a bit longer still, moves from mythic to historical figures—in this case, Croesus of Lydia, nearest eastern neighbour of the Ionians, the Greeks who lived on the western coast of Asia Minor. Croesus (560–546 BCE) was famous in antiquity for his fabulous wealth, for his conquest of the eastern Greeks, and for his unlooked-for defeat at the hands of Cyrus the Persian, and all of these topics figure prominently in Herodotus' narrative about him (1.6–94). Finally, Cyrus' appearance as a conqueror in the Croesus story necessitates a fourth narrative (1.95–216) that begins by answering the question: who was this Cyrus, who came out of his stony eastern high-lands to conquer Croesus in 546 BCE?

Introductory paragraph We use the textual tradition that calls the author 'Herodotus of Halicarnassus', but Herodotus (hereafter H) may well have written 'of Thurii', where he lived later in life. This is the version Aristotle knew (*Rhetoric* 1409ª). Thurii was a Panhellenic Athenian foundation in southern Italy in the late 440s. Its appearance in H's proem would have emphasized the connection of his *historiē* with the complexities of contemporary mid-fifth century politics and intellectual currents (Thurii's lawgiver was the sophist Protagoras) rather than with the east Greek past of H's original home town, Halicarnassus.

1.1   The first five chapters of Book 1 comprise a formal introduction, a proem markedly different in kind from what will come after. It consists of a tongue-in-cheek survey of a sequence of four mythic abductions of women. The women represent some of the major geographic regions the *Histories* will cover: Io is an Argive Greek who goes to Egypt; Europa is Phoenician taken to Crete; Medea is Colchian, from the region of the Euxine (Black) Sea, and goes first to Greece and then eventually to Media; and Helen is a Spartan who travels to Troy, on the north-west coast of Asia Minor. It is suggestive (though it cannot be pushed too far) that each of the first three becomes symbolically important for the country she ends up in. For the Greeks (though not for H himself), Io the Argive is often assimilated to Isis, a major Egyptian goddess (cf. n. 2.38–41); Europa the Phoenician gives her name to the continent of Europe (4.45); Medea eventually gives her name to the Medes (7.62). Perhaps H is suggesting that it will not be easy, in telling the long story of Greek–barbarian enmity, always to tell the 'Same' from the 'Other'. (The last woman in the sequence, Helen, does not become a symbol of Trojan identity, although H might have expected his audience to see the pun on her name and the Greek verb *helein*, 'to destroy', since the Trojan War which her abduction gave rise to becomes the mythic moment at which enmity between east and west was established. Cf. Aeschylus' pun in *Agamemnon* 687–8.)

   Thus H in this clever proem makes several points at once. He writes an entertaining sketch that he can dismiss at its end as insufficiently factual (a flattened, rationalized version of the sort of tale that appears in literary treatments like a *Prometheus Bound*, an *Argonautica*, or an *Iliad*, unable even when carefully demythologized to overcome the fact that the original events have been transformed out of recognition). H seems to think that this is what happens to accounts of the past, if one doesn't take the trouble to investigate things and write down one's results. At the same time, for those who want to think more deeply, these stories of reciprocal violent abduction, rationalized and stripped of their literary embellishments, present the forcible exchange of women as a model for the ambiguity of resulting cultural identities—how will their children identify themselves, or be identified by others? In the rationalized, non-mythic way these *logoi*, or stories, are presented here, at the beginning of the *Histories*, they serve as a warning that very often in what we are about to read things will not be as simple as they first seem. Greek myth here has become exotic and at the same time rationalized, by being looked at temporarily through Persian and Phoenician eyes.

H has begun by narrating what Persian *logioi*, or 'experts', have told him. One has to decide whether to take him at his word here, or to see this statement as merely part of the joke, since it might well have been obvious to H's audience that the stories the Persian *logioi* tell are Greek ones. Perhaps, however, there really were Persians loosely resembling African griots or professional story-tellers, 'remembrancers', who were interested in telling both Greek and Persian stories; or, alternatively, H may have merely talked to Persians who knew a lot of information and therefore were called *logioi*. Possible candidates would have been knowledgeable and to some extent Hellenized Persian aristocrats who came west, like Zopyrus (3.160) or the families of the two Persian generals Hydarnes and Artabazus, who were given western commands after the Persian Wars and whose descendants continued to rule in H's day.

The Red Sea: H uses this term mostly to mean the Persian Gulf (1.180, 3.30), the 'southern sea' (2.158, 4.37), and the Indian Ocean (2.11). The sea we call the Red Sea is generally called by him the Arabian Gulf (2.11, 102). H & W comment of the Red Sea that 'H means by this all the water SE and E of Asia Minor'.

1.5 Here H presents his first variant version, that is, details in which Phoenicians disagree with the Persian story. Under cover of narrating an amusing set of myths, he is also making a procedural point. He will often cite a source from whom he has heard his version of past events, sometimes indicating its authority and contrasting alternative versions where they differ. By recounting the Phoenician version here—the Phoenicians were, they say, only helping Io escape her parents and an awkward situation—he also serves notice at the beginning of the *Histories* that *everything* told about the past is in fact tendentious, and is merely the version that the person telling it wants you to hear. That is why one needs *historiē*, or investigation, to help decode a story and sift the wheat from the chaff. The abduction sequence as a whole is perhaps mocked in Aristophanes' *Acharnians* 523-9 (produced in Athens, 425 BCE).

'To my certain knowledge': Without naming him, H is referring to Croesus. Here H moves into the *spatium historicum*, that is, the more recent past one can know things about, as opposed to the unrecoverable pasts of myth and legend he has just been discussing.

1.6-92 The story of Croesus of Lydia and his Mermnad ancestors (*CAH* iii/2. 643-55). The Euxine is the Black Sea. The Cimmerians (Gimiraia) were nomadic invaders from southern Russia who arrived in

Anatolia before 679 BCE and stayed in Asia Minor until the early 630s, wreaking havoc on many kingdoms, including Midas' Phrygia (c.675) and Gyges' Lydia (c.645). They are the 'Gomer' of Genesis 10: 2 and Ezekiel 38: 6 and are mentioned in cuneiform sources as early as 714 BCE. See n. 4.11–12 and *CAH* iii/2. 555–60.

1.7   The mythic genealogy of Candaules here does not agree with the genealogy of 7.61, where Andromeda, the granddaughter of Belus, is rescued by Perseus, Heracles' ancestor.

1.8   H begins with a digression that goes back to Croesus' fifth-generation grandfather, Gyges and his usurpation of the Lydian throne. We learn at the end of the Croesus story (1.91) why H begins the story of Croesus here: Croesus will pay for his ancestor's choices. The hapless Gyges is the first of many 'warners' in the *Histories*, wise advisers who try to bring those in power to a realistic sense of their own limitations—usually, as here, without success.

For the notion that misfortune was 'bound to come', see Gould, 72–3. Passages that concern the notion of fate include 2.133, 161, 3.43, 65, 4.79, 5.33, 92, 6.135. This is often connected with the theme of *tisis*, divine retribution for past misdoings; see nn. 1.23, 1.86, 1.91, 1.204, 3.126–8, 4.205, the end of n. 8.97–107, and Lateiner, 141–3, 153–5, 203–4. Genealogy will also be an important connecting narrative thread throughout the *Histories*. If someone has an interesting descendant or ancestor, H often interrupts his narrative to comment on the details. Gyges was a real seventh-century Lydian king (c.680–645 BCE; *CAH* iii/2. 644–7, iii/3. 197); there is a (probably Hellenistic) papyrus fragment of a tragedy based on the Gyges story found in H; cf. the more mythic version of Plato, *Republic* 359.

1.12   Archilochus of Paros: 'Gyges and all his gold don't interest me. I've never been prey to envy, I don't . . . yearn for great dominion' (Archilochus, fr. 19 West). Archilochus was an iambic and elegiac poet, the son of Telesicles of Paros, and took part in the colonization of Thasos in the early seventh century BCE (*CAH* iii/3. 255). His poetry celebrated (apparently autobiographically) the life of a wild and woolly poet and mercenary soldier.

1.13   Delphi: the most important oracular centre of archaic mainland Greece; see *Iliad* 9.404–5. (*CAH* iii/3. 305–20 reviews Delphi's involvement in the archaic period in the affairs of neighbouring states, culminating in the embarrassment of Delphi's pro-Persian stance in the Persian Wars.) Delphi and the priestess of Apollo's oracle appear many times in the *Histories*, and Delphic tradition will be an important source for many of H's stories of past events (see e.g. the story of the colonization of Cyrene, esp. 4.155–9). The end of 1.13 anticipates the end of the Croesus story and sets the stage for Apollo's explanation in 1.91. As Gould points out (pp. 67 ff.), the religious explanations advanced at the beginning and end of the story do not render inconsequential all the ordinary, secular mis-judgements that bring about Croesus' downfall. Both levels of causation count.

1.14 Ancient sanctuaries were religious centres but were also like museums, where trophies and dedications were displayed and important states had their own treasuries. H is often interested in the current visible remains of past events; see, for instance, his comments about other treasures at Delphi at 1.25, 50–1, 4.162, 8.27 (see *CAH* iv. 385–8 for the financial operations of Greek religion). H is also interested in inventors and first instances of achievements (cf. Arion as the first producer of the choral dithyramb in 1.23), and he will often note them, as here in his comment about Midas and Gyges, since they are part of the 'important and remarkable achievements' he has promised in his introductory paragraph to record. See further n. 2.65–76. 'Thirty talents': see App. 2. For Midas' Phrygia, see *CAH* iii/2. 622–43. Like Gyges, Midas the Phrygian became a figure of Greek myth and literature (Ovid, *Metamorphoses*, 11.90–193).

1.16–18 The war between Alyattes the Lydian and Cyaxares the Mede in the 580s BCE will be told at greater length in 1.74. For the historical achievement of the Mermnad dynasty from Gyges to Alyattes, see *CAH* iii/2. 643–51. Alyattes waged war on Miletus *c.*617–612 BCE.

1.20 See 5.92 for more connections between the two tyrants Thrasybulus of Miletus and Periander of Corinth; there Periander asks Thrasybulus for advice. Periander came to power about 627 BCE. The treasury of Corinth at Delphi is mentioned in 1.14 and 1.50, and is evidence for the wealth and importance of Corinth under the Cypselids. See *CAH* iii/3. 341–51 and n. 5.90–3 for tyrants as agents of social, economic, and cultural change in the archaic Greek world.

1.23 This is the first real pendant or parenthetical digression in the *Histories*, a story about the poet Arion, apparently included here only because at the end of his adventure Arion appears in the court of Periander of Corinth. This account of Arion and his production in Corinth of the dithyramb, a choral song in honour of Dionysus, figures as part of the scanty evidence for the origins of tragedy (see also n. 5.67–8). H implies that the story of Arion is told here simply because it is remarkable, but there are clear thematic resonances linking it to the more important narratives of Book 1 as well. In particular, the story of Arion illustrates a favourite move of H's, similar to Aristotle's notion of 'recognition' (*anagnōrisis*, *Poetics* 1452ª29): leaping out to confront the astonished sailors, Arion provides the datum, inconvenient but true, that gives the lie to the Corinthian sailors' self-serving version of events and makes the onlookers quickly revise their previous assumptions. It is also another example of *tisis*, retribution: attempted murder will out (cf. n. 1.8). The cape of Taenarum is the southernmost point of the Peloponnese.

1.26–94 The story of Croesus (560–546 BCE) now officially begins. H first reverts to the theme of 1.6, Croesus' subjugation of Greek cities. Croesus' story introduces or develops themes that will be repeated throughout the *Histories*, in particular the tendency for those in power to engage in wishful thinking and to fail in their schemes because they have overestimated their own comprehension and control of events. For Croesus as a historical personage, see *CAH* iii/2. 651–3.

1.27 Bias of Priene, Pittacus of Mytilene are two of the famous Seven Wise Men of archaic Greece (cf. Plato *Protagoras* 343a); a third, Solon of Athens, appears in 1.29. As H & W comment, their connection with Croesus is not likely to have been historical. Six of those later named among the seven appear in H's first book: to Solon, Bias, and Pittacus add Thales of Miletus (1.74, 170, with Bias), Chilon of Lacedaemon (1.59), and Periander of Corinth (1.20, 23, 27). Two others often found in the list appear later: Anacharsis (4.46, 76) and Pythagoras (2.81, 4.95). For the spirit of Ionian rationalism and problem-solving with which these figures were often associated, see *CAH* iii/3. 220 ff.

1.29 Solon, archon of Athens *c.*594 BCE. For Solon's historical importance, see *CAH* iii/3. 375–91. H largely ignores both his poetry (although see 5.113) and his political role in Athens' constitutional history (although H has him borrowing a law from Egypt, 2.177). It is not impossible but it is unlikely that Solon visited Croesus at the very beginning of Croesus' reign (560 BCE); it was not within ten years of his archonship. The meeting between Solon and Croesus has immense thematic importance for H's *Histories*. It sets up Croesus to become an example of 'small becoming big and big small' (1.5) and introduces the complementary traditional Greek theme of the uncertainty of human life, summed up in Solon's warning to count no man happy until he is dead (1.32). Solon, like the Scythian sage Anacharsis (4.76), learns about the world by *theōriē*, sightseeing. Although H does not use the same word for his own travels, it is hard not to read Solon here as somehow suggestive of H himself, a Greek traveller seeing the world and making sense of it.

1.31 Two statue bases have been found with archaic inscriptions which probably refer to the dedication of Cleobis and Biton. Two sixth-century Argive statues of young men (*kouroi*) that are often associated with these bases were discovered by the French excavation of Delphi in 1893; they can still be seen in the museum at Delphi. Note that, although they were not wealthy like Croesus, Tellus and the two Argive brothers were all memorialized concretely and publicly after their deaths.

1.32 The gods begrudge happiness to humans: see Gould, 78 ff., and in the *Histories*, 3.40, 7.10, 46, 8.109. The idea is always expressed not by H himself but by characters speaking in the narrative. (Note, however, that in 1.34 H states that a divine *nemesis* or vengeance fell on Croesus, possibly because he assumed that he was the happiest man alive.) This whole cluster of ideas has less to do with Greek ideas about the personality of divinity than with the observed fact that human life is very difficult. Solon's calendar reforms for Athens were well known, so it is not surprising that H here allows him a little pedantic arithmetical calculation about the number of days in a human life. The intercalary month did not occur every other year, but was sometimes inserted into the Athenian and many other ancient calendars to make the solar and lunar years (365.25 days versus 354 days) agree more closely; without this adjustment, the lunar year quickly lost all connection with the four seasons. For the general treatment of numbers in the *Histories*, see Lateiner, 32. For the notion that the world is an interlocking and balanced whole, see the Introduction, pp. xxxvii–xxxviii, 3.106, 108, and 116, and the end of n. 1.142–51; Immerwahr, 306–26; Gould, 93 ff.; Lateiner, 194 ff.

1.34 Solon had used the word *atē* to denote disaster in 1.32 (and the same term is found in the historical Solon's poetry, although not elsewhere in H); Croesus' son is called Atys. Atys, however, is also a recognized Lydian name (1.7, 7.27), and may be linked to the myth of Attis, the companion of the Phrygian goddess Cybele or Cybebe, another young man killed by a wild boar (cf. 5.102 for Cybebe's temple in Sardis and n. 4.76–81 for her worship in the Propontis region). Was the story told to H merely rationalized myth? (The name Adrastus, 'inevitable, inescapable', has some of the same problems. There was a Mysian city Adrasteia, but in 1.43 H probably emphasizes the name because of its connections with a Greek cult title for the goddess Nemesis, divine vengeance.)

1.46 The seven shrines (significant number? cf. 1.98) consulted here do not, according to Asheri, match sixth-century realities. Note that in 1.92 Croesus is said to have rewarded Branchidae too, although we are not told why. Delphi will play an important role in the narrative of the Persian Wars: 7.140, 220, 8.36–9.

1.51 An amphora holds as much as nine gallons (*c*.39 litres), so this was a very large silver bowl, as extraordinarily large as the Scythian bowl at Exampaeus (4.81). We do not know enough about ancient metallurgy to say that such sizes were impossible; consider the famous oversize crater found in a tomb at Vix in France (*CAH* iii/3. 141). Theodorus was a renowned ancient craftsman; he also made Polycrates' ring (3.41). H notes here that the inscription on one of the aspergilla, or sprinkling bowls, is misleading; visual evidence often needs to be supplemented with other kinds of investigation (cf. the statues of 2.131 or the tomb of the Aeginetans in 9.85). This is the first inscription mentioned in the *Histories*; cf. n. 5.57–61. On its engraver: H not infrequently refrains from stating something he knows, for religious reasons, or because it is unnecessary, or from general disapproval, as here (Lateiner, 64–9).

1.55 For Croesus' tender feet in the oracle, cf. n. 1.79.

1.56–68 This is the second common type of digression in the *Histories*, not a complete interruption like the Arion episode, but a long parenthesis that adds background information only tenuously related to the main narrative. This particular digression concerns who the most important Greeks are, and how they got to be the way they were when Croesus investigated which Greek state to take for an ally in the early 540s. Until after the battle of Salamis in the Persian Wars proper (8.40–82), the main narrative thread continues to concern eastern initiatives. Other important stretches of Greek material appear in 3.39–60, 139–49, 5.39–96, 6.49–94, 7.132–78, as well as in briefer treatments of individuals or families, like Arion, Polycrates, Miltiades, or the Alcmaeonidae. Much Greek material in the *Histories* occurs in digressions like this one (Immerwahr, 34–42).

1.56–7 Pelasgians. Historians agree with H that Greece itself had originally been home to a pre-Greek population. In its material culture Athens was Greek from the Mycenaean period on; unlike H here, many historians distinguish at least two waves of Greek migration into the Balkan peninsula: an earlier, Mycenaean invasion that had taken place *c.*2000 BCE, and possibly a much later set (*c.*900–800?) that brought Dorians (the 'children of Heracles', n. 4.147–8) down into the Peloponnese. (Increasingly, however, historians doubt that a 'Dorian invasion' was responsible for an apparent decline in population and living standards in the eleventh to ninth centuries.) For the Greek concept of 'Pelasgians', see also n. 6.137–40 and Lloyd, ii. 232 ff. For the Hellenes, Deucalion was the Greek mythic equivalent of Noah, survivor of the flood. Cadmus the Phoenician was the mythic son of Agenor, brother of Europa, and founder of Thebes (n. 5.57–61 and Lloyd, ii. 226–31). The Cadmeans of Illyria claimed descent from Cadmus in his old age (5.61); those in Boeotia had come with him originally from Phoenicia (5.58). Cadmus, his sister Europa, and the Cadmeans will reappear many times, implicitly linking many parts of the earliest Greek world together (1.2, 146, 173, 2.49, 145, 4.45, 147, 5.57–61, 9.27). By Creston H probably means the area in Thrace called Crestonia; on nearby Lemnos inscriptions have been discovered in a language resembling Etruscan (*CAH* iv. 725; see however n. 1.94).

1.59 For Pisistratus, the famous tyrant of Athens (561–527 BCE), see *CAH* iii/3. 392–416 and iv. 287–302. This passage is an important piece of evidence for the history of the tyranny. It is placed here because of the importance Athens will have in Books 7–9; as a piece of sixth-century history it is anachronistic, because Corinth was more powerful than Athens in the 540s BCE, and other states were arguably as powerful. Chilon the famous sixth-century Spartan ephor was one of the Seven Sages; cf. n. 1.27.

1.61 The curse of Megacles' family, the Alcmaeonidae, is explained in 5.71. For the Alcmaeonidae see n. 5.62–3 and for the founding of

NOTES TO PAGES 26-32

the family's fortunes see 6.125. The Alcmaeonidae were important in H's own day because Pericles of Athens was through his mother an Alcmaeonid (6.131); Thucydides describes the tactical uses to which the Lacedaemonians put the ancient curse at the beginning of the Peloponnesian War, trying to discredit Pericles as Athens' political leader (Thucydides 1.126–7).

1.62 For Hippias' return as an old man in 490 BCE to Marathon as a landing-site for the Persian attack against Attica, see 6.102, 107 ff. (The family of the Pisistratids, like the Philaids (n. 6.102–7), originally came from Brauron, just south of Marathon.)

1.65–8 This passage is the earliest extant mention of Lycurgus, the (mythic? eighth-century?) lawgiver of Sparta (*CAH* iii/1. 736–7, 741–3). Tyrtaeus (c.650) seems not to have mentioned him in his elegies, but according to Plutarch (*Life of Lycurgus* 1), Aristotle saw a bronze discus at Olympia with Lycurgus' name on it that connected him with the establishment of the first Olympic Games in 776 BCE. All full Spartan citizens are Spartiates and in this translation are called either Spartans or Spartiates. (The other two classes of inhabitants of Laconia were perioeci, citizens but without full legal rights, and helots, land-based slaves. Cf. nn. 3.46–7, 6.58–60.)

For sixth-century Spartan history, see *CAH* iii/3. 351–9 (355 for the Tegean War). The treaty between Sparta and Tegea occurred c.550 BCE. Tegea is on the main road from Sparta to the Isthmus and therefore strategically important; Tegea will play an important role as Sparta's ally in the battle of Plataea, 9.9, 26–8, 62, 70. (Greek heroes bring protection after their deaths; see n. 5.108–17. For the skeleton's height, see n. 7.105–27.)

1.70 Another set of alternative versions, with both Lacedaemonians and Samians reporting versions of the story that reflect well on their own actions (n. 1.5). This will be one of H's most important tools for instilling in his readers a healthy scepticism about stories from the past (Lateiner, 76–90). The Lacedaemonians arrive too late to help Croesus; they also arrive late for Marathon (6.106, 120), but do finally bestir themselves to march to Plataea (9.7–11; H however gives them full credit for Thermopylae: 7.209, 211, 224). For Sparta as a member, together with Croesus and Amasis, in a defensive alliance against Persia in the 540s, see *CAH* iv. 464.

1.71 Sandanis is another wise adviser (n. 1.8 above). He prefigures such important advisers to Xerxes as Artabanus (4.83, 7.10) and Demaratus (7.101, 234). Notice the tension here between the vigorously uncivilized Persians and the overcivilized Lydians (cf. 1.55), as later between the overcivilized Persians and the poor but vigorous Scythians or Greeks. The very end of the *Histories* (9.122) has Cyrus the Great drawing the same contrast as a generalization.

1.72 H makes the time for the journey from Sinope on the shore of the Euxine (Black) Sea to the Mediterranean (about 350 miles or 560 km.) much too short, both here and in 2.34. Cf. the astonishing speed of Philippides (6.106), who ran about 140 miles (225 km.) in two days. The interest in geography evinced here will be displayed many times in the *Histories*; see Gould, 86–109, and e.g. nn. 1.93, 2.6–12, 2.30–1, 4.37–45.

1.73 The prehistory of Croesus' alliance with the Medes. Notice the multiple causation for Croesus' decision, and how the behaviour of Gyges is here entirely omitted by H as a cause. It comes in only at the end, when Croesus himself learns of it (cf. 1.13). For more on the Scythians, see nn. 1.103, 1.105, and Book 4.

1.74 Two possible candidates for the eclipse: 28 May 585, or 21 September 582 BCE. Although H rejects Thales' engineering feats in 1.75, he accepts the prediction of the eclipse. Cf. n. 1.27 for the Seven Sages.

1.75 H looks forward here to 1.107. Authorial cross-references dot the *Histories*, sometimes to passages at a considerable remove: 7.93 refers back to 1.171. Three of them remain unfulfilled: 1.106, 184, 7.213.

1.77 Amasis of Egypt was also alarmed by Cyrus (*CAH* iii/2. 721, 725; cf. n. 3.44); it is not clear that Labynetus (= Nabonidus) was actually part of Croesus' alliance (*CAH* iii/3. 23–4). The Nabonidus Chronicle perhaps dates Cyrus' conquest of Lydia to April 547 (*CAH* iii/3. 401).

1.78 Portents, along with dreams and oracles, are the most important ways in which the gods foreshadow to human beings what will happen. Croesus' story contains all three. Cf. 3.10, 6.27, 7.57.

1.79 The Lydians are more cultivated than the Persians (1.71), but they are warlike until Croesus effeminizes them, 1.156. The Lydians' warlike nature is also mentioned in 2.167.

1.80 Harpagus the Mede will figure crucially in Cyrus' coming-of-age story, esp. 1.109, 117–19, 123, 129. Later he also subdues Ionia, 1.164–77. Camels are the object of H's attention in 3.102–3 for the strangeness of their behaviour in India and their odd physiology; Xerxes will bring them down into Greece, 7.125.

1.82 The Spartans do not help; cf. the end of n. 1.70. The battle of Thyreatis between Sparta and Argos (*c*.546 BCE) consolidated Sparta's place as the leading power in Greece (*CAH* iii/3. 356).

1.86–7 Cyrus understands something here that he forgets later (1.204), that as a human being he is not inherently exempt from the kind of *tisis* that befalls Croesus here. The tradition of Croesus' last-minute rescue from the pyre is not attested before H, although Croesus on his pyre was a theme of earlier poetry and vase-painting. Cf. Bacchylides 3.23–62, where Croesus is transported by Apollo to the Hyperboreans. The Babylonian Chronicle seems to record that Cyrus killed Croesus in the sack of Sardis (*CAH* iv. 33–4).

1.89 Croesus has become a wise adviser himself, though his advice does not always continue to be as good as it is here (1.207, 3.36; cf. n. 1.71).

1.91 This is a full statement of the theme of *tisis*, or divine retribution; see n. 1.8. Ring composition (see pp. xxii–xxvii) brings us back to the topic that originally introduced the long narrative of Croesus and his family. Apollo does not entirely exonerate Croesus from responsibility, however; Croesus should have enquired more carefully concerning the oracle he received.

1.92 The first conquest of Ionia: this looks forward to the second submission in 1.169 and the third in 6.32. Cf. the two Ionian revolts in 5.30 and 9.104. Asheri notes that the same enumeration is made of Spartan campaigns in Asia (3.56, looking ahead to 9.96) and the first and second Persian conquest of Babylon (1.192, 3.159). Cf. 5.76, for the enumerations of Dorian invasions of Attica. For Croesus' dedications, see n. 1.14 above.

1.93 Ethnography, biology, geography, and a report of local *thōmata*, wonders, will be a regular feature in the *Histories* (Immerwahr, 317–23; Gould, 86–109; Lateiner, 143–62). The Persians are described in 1.131–40, the Babylonians in 1.178–87 and 192–200, the Egyptians in 2.2–182, Indians in 3.98–106, Scythians and their neighbours in 4.5–82, and Libyans in 4.168–99. Smaller passages reflecting the same interests are scattered throughout the *Histories*. In such narratives H may sometimes be borrowing from earlier writers of *periploi* or travel narratives, like Hecataeus of Miletus (n. 5.36) or Scylax of Caryanda (4.44). On Alyattes' tomb, see *CAH* iii/2. 650–1.

1.94 Whether Lydian colonists came to Etruria to become the Etruscans (H's Tyrrhenians) is very doubtful; see *CAH* iv. 639. Coinage was indeed a Lydian invention, from as early as the reign of Alyattes, *CAH* iii/2. 649.

1.95–216 H now moves from lower to upper Asia, by going on to the second major narrative, the story of Cyrus the Persian (*c.*557–530 BCE). Cyrus' campaigns will not be treated until 1.141; first, as in the earlier Croesus story, H gives background: the rise of the Medes, the reign of Cyrus' Median grandfather, Astyages, the story of Cyrus' miraculous rescue as a child, and his defeat of Astyages. Finally, a brief ethnography of the Persians precedes the account of Cyrus' reign. At the end, Cyrus, like Croesus, will fall (214).

For the Medes and their dislocation by the Persians in *c.*550 BCE, see *CAH* iv. 1–33, esp. 24–33. H's account seems to be 'a potpourri of Median and non-Median legends which have been woven into a national folk-epic' (p. 17). For a historical summary of the rest of Cyrus' career, see *CAH* iv. 33–46.

1.96 Media is a rural society in the process of urbanization or, more precisely, synoecism, as a Greek would see it. The Median story and chronology of H do not completely fit the current state of eastern evidence. Working backwards from 550 as the defeat of Astyages gives the following chronology: Deioces (700–647), Phraortes (647–625), Cyaxares (625–585), Astyages (585–550). For H, Deioces is a paradigm of the absolute monarch who grows more inaccessible and tyrannical as his power increases (cf. 3.80); see also the portraits of Cambyses (3.30–7) and Darius (3.84, 118), and even Xerxes' lack of sober judgement (7.11, 39, 8.69, 118, 9.108–13).

1.98 The circuit of Athens was about sixty stades (6.62 miles or 10.66 km.). Cf. 2.7 and 4.99 for other attempts to interpret foreign measurements for Greeks.

1.103 See n. 1.74 for the eclipse that dates the battle between Medes and Lydians. Cyaxares gave the Medes real hegemony; he is attested in the Babylonian Chronicle as Umakistar, who finally conquered Nineveh in 612 BCE. The sudden invasion of the Scythians is difficult to date; A. Ivantchik believes that it occurred late in the seventh century (c.630–615?) and did not result in a continuous period of domination (cf. CAH iii/2. 564 ff. and iv. 19–20). H's Protothyes might have been Partatua (mentioned in a text of c.672 BCE), ally and probably son-in-law of the Assyrian king.

1.104 Lake Maeetis is the Sea of Azov.

1.105 Cf. n. 1.131 for the 'Heavenly Aphrodite'. Again in 2.44 H is interested in the connections that link various temples of the same god. The Scythian *enareis* are mentioned again in 4.67 as a caste of androgynous diviners who owe their powers to Aphrodite. The fifth-century Hippocratic *Airs, Waters, Places* 22 claims that both the Scythians' excessive equestrianism and their habit of wearing trousers led to their effeminization. The Scythians were not remembered with fondness in Asia Minor; they may be the enemy from the north mentioned in the Bible as a scourge of apocalyptic proportions (Jeremiah 1:14, 5:15–17, 50:41–2, Ezekiel 38:15), and the Ashkenazim of Genesis 10:3, 1 Chronicles 1:6, Jeremiah 51:27 (cf. cuneiform Ash-gu-za-a). H's Scythians enter the *Histories* most fully in H's account in Book 4 of Darius' attempt (c.513 BCE) to conquer them in their homeland.

1.106 Cyaxares' trick here is later used also by Cyrus against the 'uncivilized' Massagetae, though with less success (1.207, 211). H's comment that he will elsewhere tell of the fall of Nineveh is the first of three notorious unfulfilled promises in the *Histories* (1.184, 7.213). Both 1.106 and 1.184 refer to an 'Assyrian *logos*' that seems not to have been written. See 1.178–200 for H's treatment of Babylon.

1.107 Astyages is the Istumegu of the Babylonian Chronicle's report on the conquest of the Medes by the Persians in 550 BCE, CAH iv. 17. Asheri comments that urine in Assyrian sources seems to be linked to the birth of a son.

1.110 H has already commented (1.95) that of all the stories about Cyrus the one he tells is the most plausible. The rescue and rearing of the king by a sacred animal, as in the Romulus legend at Rome, has here been rationalized (Cyno in Greek, Spaka in Median, means female dog or bitch). Cf. the connection of Mitradates' name with the god Mitra, 1.131; the privileged status of dogs among the Persians, 1.140; and the widespread Indo-European notion of the warrior as a dog or wolf, n. 4.102–9.

1.114 For the office of the King's Eye, see also Aeschylus, *Persians* 979.

1.119 The Scythians had done the same to one of the Median boys entrusted to them by Astyages' father, Cyaxares (1.73). Dining can be problematic in H; see e.g. 1.106, 211, 2.100, 107, 5.18–20. See also his other mentions of cannibalism: 3.25, 38, 99, 4.18, 26, 106.

1.123 See 5.35, 7.239 (if it is genuine), and 8.128 for other secret written messages. Writing is often associated with cleverness, and even the excessive cleverness of tricks and tricksters: cf. 1.187, 3.40, 128, 5.14, 29, 8.22.

1.127 For the conflict between Cyrus and Astyages, we have the Babylonian Chronicle and the Dream Text of Nabonidus as well as the story in H, *CAH* iv. 30–3. In both the Babylonian Chronicle and the Dream Text it is not clear whether Cyrus is a vassal of the Medes. When he entrusts Harpagus with a command, Astyages is *theoblabēs*, deluded by the gods, the same word that is used of the Macedonian king in 8.137.

1.129 H enjoys creating a sudden shift in perception, a 'recognition' (Aristotle's *anagnōrisis*, *Poetics* 1452ª29), either on our part as we read or on the part of the participants in events. Cf. the revelation of Astyages' responsible loyalty here to Arion's sudden appearance to the sailors (n. 1.23), and to Croesus' exclamations on his pyre (1.86); see also the middle of n. 4.121–32 (on 4.132 and 134). Astyages is not exonerated from the charge of cruelty, however (1.130).

1.131–40 Persian ethnography, cf. n. 1.93 above, and *CAH* iv. 79–111 for a modern survey.

1.131 Mitra. Mithra is the ancient male Iranian sun-god. Anahita is the Persian mother goddess mentioned with him in the Avesta, an ancient Persian collection of religious texts, and in Persian inscriptions. It is not clear that Cyrus was a Zoroastrian or that H here describes the Persian religion of his time accurately. H does not mention the most important god, Ahura Mazda, by name but rather seems to call him Zeus, the Greek equivalent (n. 1.181). It is true, however, that mountain sacrifices are still practised by present-day Zoroastrians in rural Iran. For the syncretism of Persian religion under the Achaemenids, see *CAH* iv. 99–103. The 'Heavenly Aphrodite' is the great Semitic queen of heaven Ishtar, some of whose titles are here given: Mylitta = 'lady', and Alilat = 'goddess'. Here, as throughout in discussions

of religion, H is interested in religious practices, and in cultural borrowings from one people to another but not in stories about the gods
or in what we would call dogma (2.3).

1.133 See 9.110 for another, more sinister, account of a Persian royal
birthday. The Roman historian Tacitus (*Germania* 22) ascribes the
same custom of alternating sobriety and inebriation to the Germans.
In 1.71, Sandanis the Lydian calls the 'uncivilized' Persians water-
drinkers; cf. the Ethiopian's assessment of Persians and wine (3.22).

1.134 Prostration, *proskunēsis*, was a habit that filled Greeks with dismay
(7.136); much later, Alexander the Great notoriously required it of,
among others, Aristotle's nephew (Arrian, *Anabasis* 4.10.5 ff.). The
method of governing by proximity seems to have been modified by
Cyrus and especially Darius, 'the retailer' (3.89), who finally established a complete system of administrative units (satrapies) and
regular payment of taxation in the empire. See *CAH* iv. 41-3, 87-91,
129-33.

1.135 It is odd that H here does not mention that Persians wear trousers
(1.71, 7.61-2). The tolerance for foreign customs seems genuine
(*CAH* iv. 103-4, 111, 475-6; cf. n. 1.156). Cyrus is celebrated in
Isaiah 40-8 for returning the Jews to Jerusalem in the 530s BCE, after
their fifty-year exile in Babylon; his decree authorizing the rebuilding of the Temple and providing for its funding is found in Ezra
1:1-11 (cf. Ezra 6:2-12). Cambyses pays for the obsequies to bury
the Apis bull in Egypt (n. 3.27-9). See also n. 6.97 for Delos and
Darius' respect for the 'sacred gardeners' of Apollo.

1.136 Horsemanship, archery, honesty: H will make ironic implicit reference back to this general observation with Cambyses' skill at the bow
(3.35) and Darius' verbal virtuosity (3.72). See also the sarcastic
comment of the Ethiopian concerning Persian archery and honesty
(3.21). Archery and cavalry against Greek heavy-armed troops will
play a part both at Marathon (6.112) and at Plataea (9.49 f., 62-3),
CAH iv. 512, 599 f.

1.137 Cf. the treatment of Sandoces (7.194).

1.139 The observation is only valid for the Greek forms of masculine
Persian names; many see this as proof that H did not know
Persian.

1.140 Only in H are the Magi Medes. They have disastrously interpreted
Astyages' dream (1.120), and later they will attempt to take the government away from the Persians, between the reigns of Cambyses
and Darius (3.61-79). *CAH* iv. 103 notes, however, that they are
present in the depiction of rituals at Persepolis. H says that on one
day of the year, a great festival day for Persians, they are persecuted
by the Persians for their attempt at revolt in Cambyses' reign (3.79).

1.141 After the conquest of Croesus (546 BCE), H moves to Cyrus' reign
and (the subject of most interest to Greeks) his conquest of Ionia (cf.
1.26); the narrative takes up where 1.94 left off. Before conquering

Croesus, Cyrus had attempted to get Asiatic Greeks as allies (1.76). The anecdote about the fish is also found among Aesop's fables. Cyrus makes a treaty with Miletus because of its record of successful earlier resistance to Alyattes (1.17–22).

1.142–51 As usual, H begins with a background of the major players. Here the Ionians, Dorians, and Aeolians of east Greece are very generally surveyed before we hear of the outcome of their embassy to Sparta in 545 BCE. See *CAH* iii/3. 196–221 for the eastern Greeks. There seems to have been no aristocratic and politically oriented oral tradition that H could have drawn on to make his account more specific, and this tendency might have been exacerbated by competitiveness between cities and a general feeling of defeat after the collapse of the Ionian revolt and the later imposition of Athenian rule: *CAH* iv. 470–1.

Cf. the Hippocratic *Airs, Waters, Places* 16 for the mildness of Asian men and countryside and Aristotle, *Politics* 1327ᵇ for climate as responsible for making the Greeks a mean between northern Europeans and Asians. For H's further thoughts on geography and natural balance, see the Introduction, pp. xxxvii–xxxviii and 3.106, 116.

1.143 We do not know how accurately H is portraying Ionians here. Is he a witness to real demoralization, or is he, a Dorian from Halicarnassus, expressing an unjust bias? Cf. 4.142, 5.69, 88, 105, 6.13. H does hold the Ionians and Athenians responsible for stirring up the enmity of the Great King (5.97). No traces of archaic building have been found at the Panionium, the Ionian meeting place near Priene; there is little archaic evidence of the formal organization or membership in an exclusive league mentioned by H for both Ionians and Dorians (*CAH* iii/3. 217).

1.146 H often pricks the pretensions of founders of lineages with claims to importance: cf. n. 6.125–30. Whether 1.146 is more of the same, or a restatement of the themes discussed in the abduction sequence in 1.1 f., or a prejudice against Ionians *per se* must be left to the reader to decide. H's own (originally Dorian) home town of Halicarnassus had a large Carian element.

1.147 The Athenians did retain the four Ionian tribes as the basis for their political organization until the Cleisthenic reorganization of 508/7 BCE (see n. 5.66), and as religious and kinship units after that. They also celebrated the Apaturia (a three-day Ionian festival), and used a dialect close to Ionian. All of this testifies to earlier kinship, and the likelihood that Athens sponsored the original settlement of Ionia (*CAH* iii/3. 361). That said, H's protest that all of these eastern Greeks show a considerable admixture of foreign blood is no doubt justified.

1.150 In an extant fragment the seventh-century poet Mimnermus writes, 'and from there (Colophon) we . . . took Aeolian Smyrna by God's will' (Strabo 14.634 = Mimnermus, fr. 9 West).

1.152 The story resumes from 1.141. Lacedaemonian suspicion of luxury, long-windedness, and involvement in foreign adventures probably plays an implicit part here; cf. 3.46, 148, 5.50–1, 9.91. For Phocaea's leadership, see n. 1.163–4 below. For Sparta's uncompromising and long-standing hostility to the extension of Persian domination into Greece, see *CAH* iv. 464 f., 497–8, and nn. 3.44, 3.148. It will culminate in the Spartan resistance to Persia narrated in Books 7 to 9 (see esp. 7.102, 104).

1.153 Cyrus' gnomic powers, and the hardy simplicity that go with them, are also displayed in 1.141 and 9.122. The Lacedaemonians have their own pretensions in this sphere (4.77).

1.156 Croesus' advice here has the same odd flavour as his later advice to trick the Massagetae (1.207). Notice that two Medes, Mazares and Harpagus, are Cyrus' agents in the west, demonstrating the co-operation with other peoples that made Persian administration of the empire possible and Cyrus' approach so welcome later in places like Babylon (n. 1.188–91; see also. nn. 1.35, 6.97; *CAH* iv. 42–3, 475–6). It backfires with Pactyes the Lydian as it does later with Psammenitus the Egyptian (3.15).

1.163–4 This siege took place *c*.540 BCE. The Phocaeans were the founders of Massalia (Marseilles) about 600 BCE and traded in Italy, southern France, and Spain, *CAH* iii/3. 139–43, 214; the Mediterranean Sea south of Italy was called 'Ionian' because of Phocaean and Samian activities there. The remnant who stay in Phocaea will retain their naval skills but they will only have three ships and a talented general to give later to the Ionian cause, 6.11–12.

1.165 Cyrnus is Corsica. This anecdote poignantly displays some of the terrors of colonization. H is interested in cities being founded and destroyed, as part of 'great becoming small' and vice versa (1.5). For a general description of Greek colonization, see *CAH* iii/3. ch. 37. Cf. n. 4.150–3.

1.166 Tyrrhenians (Etruscans) and Carthaginians are the principal powers in the western Mediterranean at this time. For the commercial and geopolitical implications of the battle of Alalia (*c*.535 BCE), see *CAH* iv. 750 f. A Cadmean victory is one where the cost is too high, as in the war fought between Cadmus' descendants, Polynices and Eteocles, over Thebes, in which both brothers died (see 5.59 for a Theban genealogy).

1.167 For Delphi's role in founding colonies, see *CAH* iii/3. 144 f. Here Delphi's original advice was apparently misunderstood, as in the colonization of Cyrene; there also those who sailed off were not supposed to come back (4.156). At Hyele (Elea) the Phocaeans finally flourished. (A philosophical school was later founded there whose most famous members were Parmenides and Zeno.)

1.168–9 For the Greek hero, see n. 5.108–17. This second conquest of Ionia occurred in 546 BCE. For the first conquest (and H's fondness for enumeration), see n. 1.92, and for the third, 6.32. The Milesians' bargain has already been mentioned (1.141).

1.170 See n. 1.27 for the Seven Sages. H resumes here his irony about 'pure' Ionians (1.147), but is probably referring not to Thales himself but to the tradition that the Milesians originally descended from Cadmus. Cf. a 'Cadmean' Lacedaemonian (4.147), the Gephyraei of Athens (5.57), or the Phoenicians supposed to have settled Boeotia (2.49). This advice rounds out the section on Ionian resistance to Cyrus much as Cyrus' advice ends the *Histories* as a whole in 9.122.

1.171–5 As earlier (n. 1.142–51), a brief review of peoples to the south-west before Harpagus attacks them. For the Carians, cf. n. 5.117–21. The Lycians in inscriptions do refer to themselves as Trmli (Termilae); cf. 7.92 and *CAH* iii/2. 655–65. Delphi does not counsel resistance to Persia, now or later (7.140, 148). A slightly different story of the priestess of Pedasa (175) is found in the MSS of H at 8.104. Such repetition is rare in H; much more common is deliberate cross-referencing, even across many books; e.g. 7.93 (regarding the Carians) refers back to 1.171.

1.176 The last several chapters have, as Asheri notes, shown several different types of response to the invader: submission, reasonable resistance, and suicidal resistance.

1.178–200 A survey of Babylon is broken into two parts by the chapters on Cyrus' capture of the city (188–91). Chs. 178–87 survey Babylon itself (giving information useful for understanding the narrative of the siege in 188–91), while chs. 192–200 give a brief description of its taxable wealth, agriculture, boats, clothing, customs, and food.

1.178 In 612 BCE Cyaxares the Mede, father of Astyages, in alliance with Babylon, had captured Nineveh, the Assyrian capital city (*CAH* iii/2. 180). H does not distinguish the (Chaldean) neo-Babylonian rulers from the earlier Assyrians. Between 612 and 539 the Chaldean overlords of Babylon controlled the Fertile Crescent; they were responsible for the 'Babylonian captivity' of the Jews, massive deportations from Jerusalem in 597, 586, and 582 BCE (*CAH* iii/3. 22–3, 2 Kings 24–5).

1.178–83 Eyewitness account is mixed with hearsay. In the description of Babylon's fortifications and temples, H makes Babylon too big, and his description does not conform to our current archaeological understanding, since now, at least, the monuments are on the east bank of the Euphrates. He is trying to describe a huge non-Greek city to Greeks. He is correct that it was mostly built of baked brick, and about the breadth of the walls. For Babylon at this time, see *CAH* iii/2. 236–9, 261–4.

1.179 Natural asphalt is a petroleum by-product, from a region that is still petroleum-rich today. The Red Sea in ch. 180 is the Persian Gulf.

1.181 Zeus as Bel (Baʿal). Bel-Marduk was the most important god of the Babylonians who, on the evidence of the Babylonian Chronicle, welcomed Cyrus' coming to supplant the Chaldean Nabonidus (H's Labynetus, 1.188), *CAH* iv. 37 f. H tends to call the chief male god of various peoples Zeus; cf. 1.44, 131, 171, 2.29, 42, 54, 4.59, 127, 180, 5.119, 8.115.

1.183 For Babylonian rebellion in Darius' and Xerxes' reigns, see *CAH* iv. 129–38 (cf. 3.159).

1.184–7 Semiramis and Nitocris. Semiramis was the wife of a late ninth-century Assyrian king around whom legends were collected (H & W say 'a sort of Assyrian Catherine II' of Russia), later embroidered by the Greek historians Ctesias and Arrian. Nitocris does not seem to have existed (cf. 2.100 for an Egyptian Nitocris), but may be H's misunderstanding of the role played by Nebuchadrezzar II, the strong predecessor of Nabonidus at Babylon, who built the fortifications north-west of Babylon known as the 'Median Wall'. The waterworks served as irrigation as well as a secondary line of defence. Nebuchadrezzar's wife was a Median princess and perhaps to her in the Persian period was given the achievement of her husband (confused with the strong, priestess mother of Nabonidus?). The later historian Berosus makes the Median princess responsible for the famous hanging gardens of Nebuchadrezzar, which H does not mention, *CAH* iii/2, 236–9. Darius' portrayal in ch. 187 reminds us of his Persian appellation, 'the retailer' (3.89). He reconquered Babylon in *c*.521, at the beginning of his reign (*CAH* iv. 130; 3.159).

1.188–91 See *CAH* iv. 36–41 for Cyrus' conquest of Babylon in 539 BCE. Nabonidus (H's Labynetus) was disliked and the city fell without effort. Aristotle (*Politics* 1276ᵃ) says Babylon was so big it took three days for all the inhabitants to hear it had been conquered. According to the Babylonian Chronicle, vigorous fighting occurred at Opis, north of Babylon in October 539 BCE. The account H gives of the complex punishment of the Gyndes (cf. 7.35, even though Persians respect water, 1.138) may be a 100-year-old echo of real engineering feats performed to lower the rivers to make them fordable to Cyrus' army. Babylon itself fell though treachery, not the diversion of the Euphrates (191). The Red Sea in 1.189 is the Persian Gulf. For the general history of Babylonia through the period covered by H, see *CAH* iv. 112–38.

1.192 Tritantaechmes may have been the satrap or governor of Babylon when H was there. If his father was H's Artabazus, he brought the Persian land forces home safely from Greece after the disastrous battle of Plataea in 479 BCE (8.126, 9.89). Cf., however, a Tritantaechmes son of Artabanus in 7.82 and 8.26. For H's weights and measures, see App. 2.

1.193 With regard to the width of the grain, H is sensitive to the possible incredulity of his audience (cf. 6.43 with reference to 3.80).

1.194 This recalls H's pledge in the introduction to talk of 'important and remarkable things'—clearly he thinks the boats that ply the Euphrates remarkable. His interest in such matters, in Book 2 in particular, led earlier scholars to guess that H was at some point a merchant; it is certain he had a lively curiosity about how things worked. Cf. 2.40, 86–7, 96, 4.61, 7.36.

1.196 H may have heard of the Eneti (Lat. Veneti), who lived on the Adriatic coast (5.9), in Thurii. He enjoys making cross-cultural comparisons: see the beginning of 1.198, 4.195, 6.58, 59, and, more ambitiously, 2.104. The conquest referred to at the end of the chapter is probably that under Darius (3.150f.), although Babylon continued to give trouble (*CAH* iv. 129, 133).

1.199 For the cult of Aphrodite on Cyprus, cf. 1.105.

1.201–16 Cyrus' final campaign. Nothing is known of this historically. As usual, H begins with the background of the people to be conquered (201–4). He confuses several great rivers in the part of Cyrus' empire towards central Asia, to the north-east. See *CAH* iv. 41–6 and 170–1 for other speculations on Cyrus' last years. He seems to have been buried at Pasargadae, with or without his head.

1.203 H's figures for the Caspian are small; it is actually 750 miles long (1,210 km.) and 130–300 miles wide (209–480 km.). Unlike many other Greeks H knew it was self-contained. H & W call it 'one of his geographical triumphs'.

1.204 Although not explicitly identified as such here, this is the resumption of a theme already introduced in the Croesus episode (1.32, 34). Cyrus here forgets something he once knew about human vulnerability and divine *tisis*, 'retribution' (1.86). See also nn. 1.8, 1.91, 4.205.

1.207 Croesus remembers his own experiences, but it doesn't help much. He refers to the Massagetae in much the same terms as Sandanis had used for the Persians themselves (1.71). He does not, however, draw the same wise conclusion, but counsels Cyrus to use their 'uncivilized' ignorance to trick them, just as Cyaxares had tricked the uncivilized Scythians in 1.106. His use of the theme of men versus women is taken up again later by Persians in defeat (8.88, 9.107). Cf. 4.162 for a Greek example.

1.209 Darius will not appear until 3.70, after Cambyses has died and the Magi have taken over Persia, *CAH* iv. 53–8, 172. This episode looks like justification for Hystaspes and Darius, but we don't know who told it or why it was necessary.

1.214 H enjoys reporting 'firsts' and 'bests' as part of the record of the remarkable he promises in his introduction to include; cf. 1.14, 23,

94, 2.68, 3.122, 4.42, 58, 152, 183, 6.112, 8.105. For the most savage Greek battle, see 7.170. H ends the Cyrus account by assuring his audience that he is interested in reporting facts, not myths (cf. n. 1.193). Cyrus died in 530 BCE.

1.215–16 As in the Babylonian account above, H sandwiches the account of Cyrus' deeds between two more generally descriptive passages. For comparable sexual customs, see 1.203, 3.101, 4.104, and 172. For dining habits, cf. 3.99, 4.26.

BOOK TWO

All of Book 2, H's giant excursus on Egypt, is structurally a pendant designed to give the background that introduces and explains the importance of Cambyses' invasion of Egypt, narrated in Book 3. Cambyses, Cyrus' son, will reign only for eight years (530–522 BCE), and conquering Egypt will be his great achievement. Paradoxically, Cambyses' success in Egypt will also create the conditions for his own growing instability and death. By devoting Book 2 to Egypt itself—the multiple astounding facts about its land, river, peoples, monuments, flora and fauna, and history—H shows rather than tells how important Egypt was in the growth of Persian power. Book 2 may well have been a separate treatise, originally written to stand alone and only integrated later into H's massive study of the growth of the Persian empire and Persia's defeat in Greece. Its tone is often paradoxical, argumentative, and even critical—here H is more willing than in the rest of the *Histories* to display the secrets of his workshop, the nature of his judgement, and the kinds of critical thinking encompassed by *historiē*. In the notes to this book I have relied heavily upon the commentary by A. Lloyd.

2.1   Notice some formal similarities between 2.1, 1.26, the beginning of
       Croesus' reign, and 7.2–5, the beginning of Xerxes' reign; all three
       accession *logoi* include the topic of military aggression against
       Greeks. Ch. 2.1 does not resemble the beginning of the Cyrus story
       because the conquest of Lydia rather than the transmission of power
       from his father brings Cyrus to our notice (1.46; some formal ele-
       ments of an accession moment occur in 1.130). The narrative of
       Persian conquest resumes in 3.1.

2.2   The narrative of Egypt begins with Egyptian investigations of their
       own distant past undertaken by Psammetichus I (664–610 BCE), the
       king who first introduced Greeks into Egypt (2.152). This account
       sets a tone that will prevail throughout the book; Egyptians are
       learned themselves, and understanding Egypt will require real learn-
       ing from others in turn; H will be on his mettle. The story about the
       children is Ionian, but it is one that Egyptian priests in Memphis
       could have heard by H's time. The story surely hinges on the bleat-
       ing sound made by the goats (that is why the Greek version about
       the woman without a tongue seems so stupid to H). Thus it is com-
       parable to the abduction stories that begin Book 1, in that it is a
       research-driven narrative, but it also
       contains a warning about the limitations of scientific research, since
       the data produced lead to a faulty conclusion. On what grounds does
       Psammetichus decide at the end that the Egyptians are the *second*
       oldest people in the world? For the Phrygians, cf. the end of n. 1.14.
          Memphis was built by the first human king of Egypt, Min or
       Menes (2.99). It was the site of the temple of Ptah, and the seat
       of royal power for much of the Old Kingdom. The priests of Ptah
       (H's Hephaestus) at Memphis were H's most important sources
       of Egyptian information, especially for the Egyptian kings: cf. 2.99,
       110f., 121, 136, 141–2. The word 'Egypt' itself is perhaps derived
       from one of the Egyptian names for Memphis, Hwt-Ka-Ptah, 'House
       of the Spirit of Ptah'. The ruins of Memphis were used for building
       modern Cairo near by.

2.3   H gives two other main sources for his information on Egypt: Thebes
       and priests at Heliopolis. Thebes was the capital of Egypt during the
       most powerful Eighteenth Dynasty (the Mycenaean period in
       Greece), but it was sacked by the Assyrians in the seventh century
       and in H's time held provincial status. The priests of Amon-Re were
       his informants there (2.54). Heliopolis was not an important politi-
       cal centre, but was the major cult centre of Re, the sun-god, located
       close to Memphis and connected to the Nile by a canal. See Lloyd,
       i. 89–116 on H's Egyptian informants.
          Here H makes a general statement to which he will adhere
       throughout the *Histories*: he will tell about the gods only when he
       has to because they are part of the account of human affairs; see
       further, 2.53. This presents a particular challenge in a land so theo-
       centric as Egypt (2.37), and results in a picture of Egypt which would
       have seemed very foreign to the Egyptians themselves (Lloyd, i. 96).

2.4   H emphasizes the Egyptians' claims to cultural priority over other ancient civilizations. Lloyd comments (ii. 20, 30) that the Sumerians were probably literate before the Egyptians were, and there were Mesopotamian altars as early as c.4200 BCE. The Egyptians did face 'the problem of the incommensurate nature of the solar year and lunar month' and created a solar year of 365 days. As H himself knows (2.50), Egypt did not give their names to all twelve of the Greek Olympians; here the priests are probably talking of the nine main Heliopolitan gods, whose only identifiable Greek equivalents are Helios, Heracles, Dionysus, Demeter, and Typhon. For the Olympian gods of the Greeks, see n. 6.108.

2.5-34   The geography of Egypt: formation by sedimentation (5, 10-14), measurement (6-7, 9), physical layout (7, 8), boundaries and definitions (15-18), the Nile (17, 19-34); this whole section owes a great deal to Ionian science.

2.5   H is not correct about the sounding; even today, eleven fathoms is much nearer than H thinks, about fifteen miles (24 km.) from the coast. H here calls the land 'a gift from the river', using the same expression as his Ionian predecessor Hecataeus (n. 5.36); for a detailed discussion of Hecataean borrowings in Book 2, see Lloyd, i. 127-39. H is right about the alluvial nature of the Nile valley, even far south of the Delta. (Lloyd, ii. 90: 'The commonest name for Egypt is Kmt "The Black Land" i.e. the land made up of black alluvial silt as distinct from Dsrt "The Red Land" i.e. Desert.')

2.6-7   The actual length of an Egyptian schoenus is uncertain; it was a practical measure and seems to have varied from 30 to 120 stades. H always calculates it as 60 stades (6.62 miles or 10.66 km.); this plus the fact that he measures by calculating the number of days taken to pass between two points (a long day by sea is 700 stades or about 77 miles or 124 km. (4.86); the standard is 500 stades) means that his measurements are not exact by modern standards. This particular measurement is quite a bit too long; the actual length of the Egyptian coastline is 297 miles (478 km.), not 396 (637 km.). Lateiner (p. 33) comments, 'The difficulties of getting *any* numbers right in his circumstances should not be underestimated.' For H's measurements in general, see App. 2.

2.7   Pisa is a district near Olympia, conquered c.570 BCE by Elis. H is approximately correct to compare the distance between Pisa and Athens (c.150 miles or 241 km.) with that between the Egyptian coast and Heliopolis (c.165 miles or 266 km.). (Cf. 1.98, 192, 4.99 for H's interest in interpreting foreign measurements for Greek readers; see n. 6.108 for the Altar of the Twelve Gods in Athens.)

2.8-9   H's observations on distance here have given rise to much discussion (Lloyd, ii. 47-59). Two months for crossing the mountains westward to the Red Sea is much too long; it is not clear what feature made H think that Egypt narrows in the middle and widens suddenly again to the south; the distance between the Arabian range and the Libyan plateau is considerably shorter than H says (12 miles or 19.2 km. as opposed to his approximately 22 miles or 35 km.). (H generally thinks of our Red Sea as a gulf branching off the larger body of water he calls the Red Sea, cf. the end of n. 1.1 and n. 2.11–12.)

Both the time and the distance in 2.9 are incorrect. The actual distance between Thebes and Heliopolis is about 450 miles (720 km.); H seems to make it about 535 miles (861 km.), and also to think it can be travelled in less time than would actually be required. Cf. n. 4.85–6. (The stade used in App. 2 is 177.6 m.; Lloyd calculates it at 198 m. but cautions that all modern equivalents of ancient measurements are necessarily approximate.)

2.10   H is correct about the alluvial nature of the west coast of Asia Minor; he lists the relevant sites from north to south. The silting of the Cayster has left the ancient city of Ephesus 6 miles (9.6 km.) inland.

2.11–12   The 'gulf which is an extension' is our Red Sea. At its widest its width is c.220 miles (354 km.), which would take well over three days to sail. H's basic point is that Egypt was once a gulf like the Red Sea, and that if the Nile could be diverted into the Red Sea, it would soon be filled up too. In 2.12 he goes on to give as evidence the marine fossils found in Egypt (though Lloyd thinks most of these go back to the earlier Eocene period when the whole plateau was submerged; the sea came about as far south as modern Cairo in the Pliocene).

2.13–14   Still arguing the alluvial nature of Egypt, H moves on to the evidence of what others have told him. He argues that since the time of Moeris (probably Amenemhet III, 1842–1797 BCE (cf. 2.101)) the land has risen considerably, since it now takes fifteen cubits to flood what eight cubits used to flood. In fact, H is probably using two contemporary measurements of flooding, both good but taken at different parts of the river; the length of time between Moeris and his own day (actually about 1,400 years) was not sufficient to explain the rise in height he posits.

Rain does fall in Egypt, although on average 0.4 in (1 cm.) a year. Lloyd (ii. 74) notes that H 'failed to recognize the backbreaking toil required by the irrigation system' of ancient Egypt.

2.15–18   Here H argues with the older Ionian view (perhaps that of Hecataeus) that Egypt is only the Delta. He argues that the people who now inhabit the Delta must have come from the Thebaïd, which originally constituted Egypt, before the water built up the rest of the country. (H does not know that the name Egypt was originally given only to a part of Memphis, n. 2.2.) In ch. 16 he takes on a problem of definition in Ionian geography; if the Nile is the dividing line between Asia and Libya, the Egyptian Delta must be a separate continent!

2.19-34 The Nile: the causes of its flooding (19-27); its source (28-34).

2.19-27 H is right, the Nile floods in summer, and he wants to know why. H's approach is scientific, in the spirit of the Hippocratic corpus: he states the problem, discusses other theories and gives reasons for not accepting them, and offers his own theory with a clear statement of its difficulties. Chs. 24-6 give H's theory: he thinks it has to do with solar powers of evaporation and the apparent seasonal movement of the sun.

As Lloyd (ii. 104-5) notes, both H's own ideas and his refutations of other theories are based on the false conviction of contemporary geography that the earth was a disc 'over which the heavens extended in a hemisphere to meet the disk at the edge. The sun and other heavenly bodies passed across this dome and . . . could be affected by storms in rather the same way as clouds are blown about.' In reality two groups of winds of different temperatures collide over the Ethiopian highlands and cause torrential downpours (*pace* H & W, melting snow has nothing to do with it). Given the scientific knowledge of his day, H's arguments here are very intelligently marshalled.

H also wants to know why the Nile does not give off breezes from its surface (19); he answers this (27) with the idea that the Nile flows through such hot lands that the water becomes warm.

2.28-34 The source of the Nile. The actual sources of the Nile are complex 'since the R. Nile draws water from several quarters—the Atbara, Blue Nile and White Nile—each of which, in turn, has several sources' (Lloyd, ii. 110).

2.28 Saïs was until the reign of Amasis the capital of the kings of the Twenty-sixth Dynasty and, being close to Naucratis (2.178-9), was well known to the Greeks. H's informant was probably the 'scribe of the treasury of Neith'. Crophi and Mophi are probably rocks in the Cataracts south of Elephantine rather than between Syene (Aswan) and Elephantine; before the damming of the Nile there was a violent southward-running counter-current above Aswan more than fifty miles (80 km.) long (Lloyd, ii. 112-14). Psammetichus is again testing hypotheses (2.2); although there are Twenty-sixth-Dynasty inscriptions in the Cataract area, the story probably arose because of Psammetichus' mystique.

2.29 Those who doubt H's integrity especially doubt that he came south all the way to Elephantine since he does not make it clear that it lies on an island, and does not describe the spectacular buildings at Thebes, which he must have passed; Lloyd does not give these objections much weight (ii. 116). Elephantine translates the Egyptian name, since the city was the end-point of the ivory road from the Sudan. Tachompso was almost certainly Djerar, now inundated by the waters of the Aswan Dam. H's Meroë is either Napata, below the Fourth Cataract, or Meroë, below the Sixth Cataract; Lloyd thinks it is the latter. Amun and Osiris (Zeus and Dionysus) were certainly worshipped in Ethiopia, but they were not the only gods worshipped there.

2.30–1 Lloyd says the distance (56 days, about 1,120 miles or 1,790 km.) is not far from the truth, and that 'the evidence points very strongly to the Blue Nile and Gezirah as the Land of the Deserters, but that in this case the fifty-six days is from Elephantine, not from Meroe'. *Asmakh* seems etymologically related either to the Egyptian 'left' (as opposed to right) or to 'forget'. In the Twenty-sixth Dynasty, troops were certainly needed at Elephantine to guard against the Meroitic kingdom to the south. Pelusium was the most dangerous post (guarding against the Assyrians), and the one to which Psammetichus assigned his Greek and Carian mercenaries (2.154, 3.11). In ch. 31 the river is seen as turning west on analogy with its mirror image, the Ister (the Danube, 2.33). According to H's geography, the desert forms the outermost zone of the disc that is the world, and just inside it live the peoples of fable, like Arimaspians and Hyperboreans; inside these dwell the four peoples on the edges: Celts in the west, Scythians in the north, Indians in the east, and Ethiopians of Libya in the south.

2.32–4 For Cyrene, a Greek city in North Africa, see 4.151 ff. The oracle at Ammon was in the oasis of Siwa; Zeus Ammon was the major god at Cyrene in H's time. For the geography of the young Nasamonians' journey, see Lloyd, ii. 137 ff. The Niger might be involved, or the Bodele Depression.

It 'makes sense' to H that the river they reached was the Nile (although it is much to the west of the Nile's course), both because it contained crocodiles and because H was still susceptible to the arguments from symmetry advanced by the Ionian thinkers Anaximander and Hecataeus. With the Mediterranean as the east–west axis, it 'makes sense' that just as the Ister (Danube) flows east across Europe and bends on a right angle south towards its mouth, so the Nile flows west across Africa and bends north towards its mouth. (In fact, H's placement of the source of the Danube in the far west shows only how little fifth-century Greeks knew of the geography of northern Europe.)

2.35–98 The customs of Egypt. This is some of the most valuable material in Book 2, since H relies extensively on his own considerable powers of observation.

2.35–6 This is one of the most famous passages in the *Histories*; in it H claims that Egyptian customs and practices (perhaps following the behaviour of their river?) are the opposite of those in other countries. (Sophocles in the *Oedipus at Colonus* 337 ff. makes the same point.) Men almost certainly bought and sold goods as well as women and both sexes carried loads on their heads, but H is probably correct about the weaving, about men squatting to urinate (it is less clear that women stood), about indoor facilities (for Egyptian toilets, see Lloyd, ii. 150), and about male priesthoods. It seems also to have been true that women were bound to support their fathers, while men were exempt from this duty if the parents were irresponsible (Lloyd, ii. 151–2). The practices of ch. 36 seem to be accurately reported as well, although Lloyd comments that Egyptian medical papyri contain a number of recipes for making hair grow, so baldness may not have been universally admired.

H's problem is one of over-schematization; both bread and clay for brickmaking, for instance, seem to have been kneaded both with the feet and with the hands. Dung was probably necessary in Egypt for fuel, while in Greece it was used only for fertilizer. Circumcision was certainly practised; the other peoples who use it are listed in 2.104, though H's notion of cultural diffusionism (with its emphasis on one originator) was certainly wrong (see Lloyd, i. 149–53). While H is correct about the direction of Greek and Egyptian writing, he omits a third Egyptian script, hieratic.

2.37–64 Egyptian religion: priests (37), sacrifices, victims, and festivals (38–49), Greek and Egyptian gods (50–3), divination (54–7), festivals (58–64).

2.37 H is correct that cleanliness was crucial to the Egyptians as a matter of ritual purity. Their daily rations consisted of bread, beer, and meat; Lloyd (ii. 315) states that in hieroglyphic texts the notion of impurity is generally signified by a fish. Beans were certainly known in Egypt but Lloyd thinks (ii. 169) that (like the priests of the Eleusinian mysteries and the Pythagoreans and Orphics) Egyptians avoided beans, probably because demons were connected with flatulence, and beans 'were considered unusually efficient demon-carriers'. See Lloyd, ii. 169 f. for Egyptian grades of priest.

2.38–41 The sacrifice of cattle. Epaphus was the Greek name of Apis, the sacred bull of Memphis; in Greek myth it was assimilated to the offspring of Io (e.g. in Aeschylus' *Prometheus Bound* 850–1). The stress here on the Apis bull becomes relevant to the main narrative later (3.28–30), in that it emphasizes the extent of Cambyses' impiety in killing the bull. The living Apis had his own dwelling-place in Memphis (2.153), and was chosen because of sacred markings (cf. 3.28); the priests checked before sacrificing a bull to make sure it was not an Apis bull. For details of the sacrifice, see Lloyd, ii. 172–83: 'The seal bore the representation of a man on his knees with hands bound behind his back and a sword at his throat' (p. 173). Isis is the goddess mentioned in 2.40.

2.42–6 Ram- and goat-cults; the problem of Heracles. Goats (and cattle and antelope) were sacrificed in Thebes but not sheep, because of the worship of Amun the ram-god. Heracles was probably identified as Chonsu, son of Amon-Re, and in 43 as Shu, one of the nine Heliopolitan gods. (Chonsu was frequently assimilated to Shu.) H then digresses to discuss Heracles, displaying in the process his own investigatory processes. The problem is that the Egyptian Heracles seems to be a full-fledged divinity, not a hero, and to have been around much earlier than the Greek Heracles, son of Amphitryon.

As Lloyd (ii. 201) notes, of H's proofs that the name and divinity of the Greek Heracles came from Egypt four are a matter of evidence and one of reasoning. For evidence, H cites the fact that the Greek Heracles' parents had Egyptian ancestors (since they were descendants of Perseus, 2.91); the Egyptian god is very ancient indeed; Tyrian priests (of the Phoenician sea god Melqart) speak of the foundation of a temple of Heracles c.2750 BCE; and the temple of Heracles in Thasos was built by Phoenicians five generations before the birth of the (human) Greek Heracles. For reasoning, H comments that if the Egyptians had borrowed Greek gods, they would have borrowed gods of the sea, Poseidon and the Dioscuri. The 'silly story' about Heracles that H criticizes in 2.45 appears to have been treated by Pherecydes and Panyassis, H's older relative and an Ionian epic poet (Lloyd, ii. 212 and *CAH* iii/3. 53). In 46 Pan is Mendes, who was depicted both as a ram and as a goat; the connection between bestiality and the Mendesian nome (district) was well known to the Greeks. Lloyd (ii. 216) comments that near Mendes a mould has been found which represents bestiality between a woman and a goat.

2.47-9 The pig in Egypt was connected with Seth, the arch-enemy of Osiris, and both Isis and Osiris are connected with the moon. Representations of ithyphallic Osiris are common in Egypt (Dionysus, the Greek equivalent, himself is never depicted as ithyphallic, though he is surrounded by ithyphallic satyrs and sileni). As in Greece, he is honoured in Egypt by song (though not, apparently, by choral dancing); for Melampus, see 9.34. H is reticent about a story in which Osiris' phallus was the only part of his body not recovered after Seth had dismembered it. When Isis reconstituted the body she used a model phallus to replace the original, and this is why it was carried in ritual procession. On Cadmus of Tyre and his Theban and Phoenician connections, see nn. 1.56-7, 4.147, 5.57-61, and Lloyd, ii. 226-31.

2.50-3 An aside on Greek gods. H (incorrectly) sums up the sources of the Greek gods as Pelasgian (the Dioscuri, Hera, Hestia, Themis, the Graces, and the Nereids), Libyan (Poseidon), and Egyptian (all others known to the Greeks), Lloyd, ii. 232-51. For Pelasgians see n. 1.56-7; H seems to use the term generally to mean pre-Greek peoples. Note particularly H's false etymology of the gods (*theoi*) in 52, from a form of the verb *tithenai*, 'to set, place' and his comment in ch. 53 that Homer and Hesiod gave the Greeks their gods. Dodona was the oracular shrine *par excellence* in Homer (*Iliad* 16.233) and was associated with Zeus Pelasgicus, i.e. reflecting a pre-Greek population stratum. Homer is conventionally dated c.750, Hesiod c.700; H was writing c.440. For the Cabiri, see n. 3.37.

2.54-7 H's discussion of the origins of the oracles at Dodona and the oasis of Siwa, from the abduction of two priestesses from Egyptian Thebes. The connections between the two oracles were known before H's time at Dodona; see Lloyd, ii. 253-4 for the various ways in which the story might originally have been concocted. (Other female

founders of religious practices occur in 2.171, 182, 4.33; other
women who are abducted but have a strong influence on the country
to which they are brought occur in 1.1–3, 146, 4.110f., 6.138.)

2.58–64 For the principle of cultural diffusionism, see Lloyd, i. 147–9. H
thinks that since Egyptian festivals, religious processions, and
parades were earlier than those of Greece, the Greeks must have
learned from the Egyptians. The Egyptians did keep many religious
festivals, including calendar festivals, royal festivals, and festivals of
the dead. In ch. 61 it is Osiris whose death they lament. H's account
of various festivals is important because it gives detailed descriptions
of Lower Egypt where the Egyptian evidence favours Upper Egypt;
moreover, H's interests were in the behaviour of worshippers rather
than in the liturgy and processions emphasized by the Egyptian tradition. The verb used of Ares' intentions in 2.63 may mean 'communicate with' as well as 'have sexual intercourse with', and H's use
here is ambiguous.

2.65–76 Animal worship and the zoology of Egypt. Lloyd is right (ii. 291;
cf. i. 141–7) to introduce this section by referring to H's interest in
thōmata, wonders. (This is part of his larger interest in the remarkable: see especially the account of India and Arabia, 3.98–116, but
also nn. 1.14, 1.23, 1.93, 1.194, 1.214, 2.147–57, 5.16, and the
bottom of n. 8.97–107.) The animals H emphasizes here are all
strange to Greece: cats, crocodiles, hippopotamuses, other aquatic
animals, the phoenix, horned snakes, flying serpents, and ibises. H
begins his discussion of animals by commenting that the Egyptians
regard animals as sacred (65); because he does not want to discuss
the gods (2.3), he is going to pass over this topic, even though it has
enormous significance for the Egyptians themselves. Animals worshipped in cult throughout the country include the cow (Hathor), the
jackal (Anubis), and the ibis and hawk (Thoth and Horus).

General points of some interest include the fact that the cat did
not arrive in Europe until the first century CE; it did not become
common until the twelfth century, as a result of the spread of rats
from southern Russia and Asia. 'Dogs' seem in Egypt to include wild
dogs, foxes, and jackals (67). The passage on how to hunt the crocodile (70) is partly derived from Hecataeus (*FGH* 1, fr. 324); the
crocodile's maximum length is only about twenty feet (6 m.). The
whole of the peculiar description of the hippopotamus (71) also
derives from Hecataeus, and probably means that H did not see one
at very close range; it is the most inaccurate piece of zoology in Book
2. (On the other hand, ch. 66 may contain genuine observation: in
late March of 1996 a cat named Scarlet in Brooklyn, New York,
became a media heroine because she had repeatedly re-entered
a burning building to save her kittens.) Both the crocodile and the
hippopotamus were worshipped in some regions. They were exe-
crated in others, particularly if they were connected with Seth, the
enemy of Osiris (Lloyd, ii. 308–9).

H makes it clear that he did not see the mythical bird, the phoenix (73), but only its pictures. Its Egyptian pictures seem to represent the purple heron or grey heron; most of the marvels H recounts are a Greek reworking of Egyptian mythology (Lloyd, ii. 320). The winged snakes (75) are something of a mystery; they recur in 3.107. H claims to have seen skeletons and to have talked to Arabians, the inhabitants of the Isthmus of Suez where the snakes tried to enter Egypt. Perhaps they were locusts, or *draco volans*, a flying lizard now living in south-east Asia (Lloyd, ii. 326–7); cf. the 'flying serpent' of Isaiah 30: 6. Because of the disappearance of the papyrus no species of ibis now breeds in Egypt.

2.77–91 Customs of Egyptians who live in the arable part of the country. These are the Egyptians H calls *logiōtatoi*, 'the most learned people I have ever come across'. Lloyd (ii. 330) comments that 'Annals such as the Palermo Stone and King Lists like the Abydos, Saqqara and Karnak Lists and the Turin Canon provided a chronological perspective stretching back to the beginnings of Egyptian History and beyond to the Dynasties of the Gods millennia before Gk. traditions began. . . .'

H discusses their personal regimes, customs, clothing, practices of prediction and divination, medicine, burial practices (including embalming), and their reluctance to use Greek customs but also their celebration of the Greek hero Perseus. The 'ale made out of barley' (77) was very similar to beer; some vineyards existed but wine was a drink of the upper classes. There are no independent Egyptian sources for the practice of carrying around a wooden corpse at parties (78), though small carved figures similar to those H describes have been found (Lloyd, ii. 336). The 'Linus' song (79) was a song of lamentation sung in Greece and the Near East (perhaps from a Semitic phrase like the Hebrew *oi lanu*, 'woe to us'). For extensive discussion of Egyptian burial and mummification practices, see Lloyd, ii. 351–65. Chemmis (91) was very close to the Greek trading settlement near Neapolis and presumably held Greek games because of intermarriage and a population that was partly Greek in consequence. It is probable that Perseus was identified by H or his predecessors with an Egyptian deity, probably Horus (cf. the footprint of Heracles in Scythia in 4.82, of the same length as Perseus' here). H is interested in Perseus, like Cadmus, as an ancient alleged founder of a variety of peoples (cf. nn. 6.52–4, middle of 7.60–83, 7.148–52).

2.92–8 Customs of the marshy parts of the Delta. The marshes were a refuge for those expelled from Egypt (2.137, 140, 151). H emphasizes the food, animals, plants, and insects that are different from those in the rest of Egypt, and discusses the boats and boat-culture of the region. H has observed the fish of the Delta but has not completely understood what he saw (Lloyd, ii. 377–9): 'Pools and mud holes become filled with fish so quickly because the fish come along the canals which bring the first waters of the inundation.' Egyptian seine nets had a mesh sufficiently small that, when folded several times, they might well have kept out most mosquitoes; certainly much of the population of the Delta were fishermen and there were lots of mosquitoes. H's description of how the boats are made to move (96) is well documented in Egyptian sources. On the appearance of Egypt in times of flood (97), Lloyd (ii. 391) quotes the Arab writer Massoudi: 'It is like a white pearl . . . when, submerged by the river, it forms a vast sheet of whitish water above which the farms situated on the mounds and hillocks shine like stars.'

2.99–182 Ch. 99 is important as a window into how H thought of his investigations, at least in the writing of Book 2. It also begins the section on the history of Egypt. This divides into two parts: (*a*) the pre-Greek period of the rulers from Min to Sethos (99–142); (*b*) the period of the twelve kings to Amasis (147–82), during which Greeks were in the country. Lloyd (iii. 1–4) discusses the various factors that affect the reliability of H's account, especially in the first part: his dependence on oral traditions, contamination of these by Greek traditions, the absence of a clear and fixed chronology, overschematization, imaginary analogies between Greece and Egypt, and H's own historiographic and moral assumptions. He concludes: 'In view of these obstacles it was quite impossible for H to produce a history of Egypt acceptable to the modern Egyptologist. To his credit he was aware of some of his difficulties and does his best to cope with them. . . . The main value of II, 99–142 is as a record of the historical traditions on the distant past which were generally current in Egypt during the 5th Century B.C. [II, 147–182] is still the most important extant source on Saite history.'

2.99–142 (*c.*3100–700 BCE) Lloyd (iii. 5) comments: 'The major source is Egyptian oral tradition, probably channelled through the priests of Memphis . . . compounded of ingredients of widely differing origins and character: historical reminiscence . . . the Egyptian ideal of kingship which tends to assimilate historical figures . . . folklore elements . . . confusion between rulers of different periods . . . nationalist propaganda . . .' Egypt had no historiography of its own at this time.

2.99 Min (Menes) probably embodies elements from the reigns of a number of the First-Dynasty kings (*c.*3100–2890 BCE), perhaps especially Narmer.

2.100 Manetho, an Egyptian priest of the Ptolemaic period, believed that there were 323 kings between Min and Sethos (probably Shabataka of the Twenty-fifth Dynasty), so H may be reflecting an Egyptian tradition here. Nitocris was a common Egyptian woman's name (cf. n. 1.184–7) but it is difficult to identify a specific queen (Manetho thought she was from the Sixth Dynasty (*c.*2300 BCE); see Lloyd, iii. 13–14). H refers back here to 1.185, evidence that at least in its final redaction H envisioned Book 2 as an integral part of his long work.

2.101 H seems to think of Moeris as Amenemhet III of the Twelfth Dynasty (1842–1797 BCE). In 2.13, however, he says that Moeris lived less than nine hundred years before his own time, placing him five hundred years too late. He has also left the pyramid builders (c.2686–2181) out of their proper place in the chronology (Lloyd, i. 188–9, iii. 60).

2.102–10 The reign of Sesostris, with an excursus on Colchians (104–6). Sesostris was used by the Egyptians for capping foreign achievement, in particular the achievements of the Persians. His accomplishments blend memories of Senwosret I and Senwosret III of the Twelfth Dynasty (c.1800 BCE) and Ramesses II of the Nineteenth Dynasty (c.1300); according to *CAH* iv. 264, some of Darius' accomplishments in Egypt may have been added in as well. See Lloyd, iii. 20–1, 26–8 for the foreign pillars and statues in Ionia and 'Syrian Palestine' (102, 106); these were Hittite rather than Egyptian. If the statues involved are correctly identified, H's description of them is somewhat imprecise. Cf. n. 5.57–61 for H's use of inscriptions in general. On the Colchians (104), Lloyd thinks a dark skinned Khazar people might well have lived east of the Caucasus, practised circumcision, and been close enough in appearance for H to have drawn the conclusion that they were Egyptian in origin. For the very loose use of 'Syrian' in ch. 104, see Lloyd, iii. 24. H is correct in ch. 108 that Egyptian conquerors used their subjects for massive building projects; the Twelfth Dynasty was particularly interested in land-reclamation schemes, and digging canals was one of the duties of the ideal king. Some Greek notions enter H's description of Egyptian land allocation (109); Egyptian procedures emphasized precision and justice, not equality (Lloyd, iii. 33). Ch. 109 is the first Greek reference to the sundial and hours ('the twelve divisions of the day').

2.111 'Pheros' is merely the word pharaoh; the story is folk-tale.

2.112–20 The name Proteus comes from Homer (*Odyssey* 4.383 ff.). H's interest in Proteus' reign has to do with its involvement in the Helen–Menelaus story. See Lloyd, iii. 46–52 for a detailed consideration of this alternative version of the legend of Helen. H is tapping post-Homeric Greek traditions; cf. also Euripides' *Helen*. A stele bearing a Phoenician dedication to Astarte (the foreign Aphrodite) has been found south of the temple of Ptah in Memphis. The quotation in ch. 116 is from *Iliad* 6.289–92 (omitted as interpolations are *Odyssey* 4.227–30 and 351–2, found after the lines from the *Iliad* in some manuscripts of H). There is no reason to doubt that by the time H talked to the priests of Memphis they knew quite a bit about Helen and Menelaus; Greeks had been in Egypt at least since the 660s.

2.121–3 Rhampsinitus and his treasury, his voyage to the underworld, and Egyptian beliefs about death. Rhampsinitus is a composite based on the Ramesses-Pharaohs of the Nineteenth and Twentieth Dynasties (*c*.1320–1069 BCE), transmuted into a figure of legend. Its style suggests that the long story of the thief is probably Egyptian in origin, as are the tale of the descent and the ritual connected to it. H warns us in ch. 123 that his own approach to such stories (and much else that he heard) was sceptical.

The game in ch. 122 was an Egyptian board-game called *snt*, connected to the mortuary-cult, played like chess but with the moves determined by the cast of the dice. See Lloyd, iii. 58–60 for the ritual of ch. 122 and the theology of ch. 123. Transmigration was apparently not an Egyptian belief; in H's time it was associated with Pythagoras, Empedocles, and the Orphics, some of whom may be alluded to at the end of ch. 123.

2.124–35 The pyramid builders: Cheops and Chephren (124–8), Mycerinus (129–34), Rhodopis (134–5).

The classic age of pyramid-building occurred in the Third to the Sixth Dynasties (2686–2181 BCE); H makes the building of the pyramids take place much later, only a few generations before Psammetichus I (664–610 BCE; Lloyd, i. 188). See Lloyd, iii. 60 ff. for a detailed discussion of the pyramids themselves. Cheops ruled *c*.2596–2573 BCE; the hostility of the account may contain some historical memory of an actual brutal corvée or forced labour, but the figure of 100,000 (124) probably refers only to the total work-force during the inundation season, with a much smaller permanent crew in place for the rest of the year (Lloyd, iii. 64). The account in hieroglyphs of how much was spent on radishes, onions, and garlic for the workers (125) seems improbable (for one thing, the implicit notion of money is anachronistic); Lloyd (iii. 71) comments that H's translator was 'either an extremely bad philologist or a bare-faced liar, probably the latter'. The story of Cheops' daughter (126) recalls similar stories in 1.93 and 2.121, and again contains an anachronistic reference to money; the small pyramid referred to was actually built for one of Cheops' queens. Chephren was actually Cheops' son (129). For the measurements of the first three pyramids, especially the measurement of the base, H acquits himself rather well; he is less good on height (unless the loss of the ancient casings accounts for the difference), and he makes the base of Mycerinus' pyramid considerably too short (134). For the notion that his misfortune was inevitable, see n. 1.8. Cf. 2.161.

Lloyd (iii. 76) does not think the mention of Philitis (128) contains any reference to the Hyksos invaders that ended the Middle Kingdom (*c*.1650). For the problems of the relationship between Cheops, Chephren, and Mycerinus and the possible reasons for Mycerinus's favourable press, see Lloyd, iii. 78. In popular folklore he evidently became the model of the Solomon-like just king. The story of the cow is likely to be highly heterogeneous in its sources, and the cow itself is perhaps a Saite ritual object connected with an annual Osiris festival. The story that follows, about Mycerinus' indignation at the gods and his systematic drunkenness, Lloyd thinks typically Egyptian in its elements (iii. 82).

It is not clear why the Greek courtesan Rhodopis (135) became connected with the building of a pyramid, Lloyd, iii. 84–7. Two of Sappho's (c.612–550 BCE) fragments (Sappho, frs. 5, 15 West) reproach her brother, and fr. 15 names the woman he was smitten with as Doricha; Rhodopis was perhaps an earlier courtesan (*CAH* iii/3. 43) or Doricha's nickname.

2.136 Asychis was Sheshonk I of the Twenty-second Dynasty (c.945–924 BCE). He was a lawgiver, reunified the country, and had an extensive building programme at Memphis and elsewhere; Josephus (*Jewish Wars* 6.10) says that Asychis conquered and sacked Jerusalem, a feat of Sheshonk I, c.930 (1 Kings 14:25–6; cf. 2 Chronicles 12:1–9).

2.137–40 Anysis seems to represent the kings of the Twenty-third Dynasty (c.818–715 BCE). Sabacos is the Nubian pharaoh Shabaka of the Twenty-fifth Dynasty. He invaded Egypt c. 716 BCE and ruled until 702. The Ethiopian kings were models of the pharaonic ideal: they built temples, they were scrupulous in religious observance, they respected the traditions of the past, and they staved off the Assyrians, whom the Egyptians dreaded. In Greek myth also from the eighth century Ethiopians were a semi-fabulous and just people with whom the gods partied (*Iliad* 1.423–4, 23.206–7; *Odyssey* 1.22–3, 5.282). See Lloyd, iii. 94–5 for the temple and grounds of Bastet/Hathor at Bubastis (cf. 2.60). We may note that Sabacos is the one ruler in the *Histories* who, faced with a choice between the extension of his power and *dikē*, justice, simply gives up power. This is not a concept that occurs to other rulers except perhaps Demaratus, and he does it less gracefully (6.67–70, 7.235). Cf. the story of Gillus in 3.138.

Amyrtaeus (140; cf. Thucydides 1.110) was an anti-Persian rebel of the northern marshes of the Delta in H's own day (c.450 BCE). Anysis the blind king is placed more than four centuries too early in ch. 140, and the Assyrians' role in eventually expelling the Ethiopians is ignored; see Lloyd, iii. 98.

2.141 Sethos was actually the Ethiopian Shabataka (702–690 BCE); the events described here took place in 701. Lloyd speculates that H's informants wanted to make an Egyptian, not an Ethiopian, responsible for expelling the Assyrian. For other sources for the campaign, see Lloyd, iii. 102–5. The Assyrians were apparently weakened by disease; cf. Isaiah 37:36. See Lloyd, iii. 104–5 for Horus' part in the Egyptian victory; the statue was in the temple of Ptah.

2.142–6 Before going on to the Egyptian history for which there are Greek sources, H makes a chronological excursus that stresses the extreme antiquity of Egyptian history and the precision of Egyptian accountability and record-keeping over vast stretches of time. For the problem of the four reversals of the sun's course and the 341 statues

H saw as opposed to the 345 that Hecataeus saw, see Lloyd, iii. 106-8. H counted only the statues to the time of Sethos; Hecataeus was counting up until his own day. For Hecataeus' appearance as a historical actor in the *Histories*, see n. 5.36; here H seems to find amusing Hecataeus' genealogical pretensions, cf. n. 1.146. Horus was the last of the Egyptian divine kings (144); the pharaohs after him ruled as his incarnations on earth. Typhon was the Greek figure who most closely resembled Seth, the enemy of Osiris. In chs. 145-6 H defends the position that Heracles, Dionysus, and Pan are Egyptian gods who have been imported into Greece. Cf. 2.43-6.

2.147-82 The Twenty-sixth or Saite Dynasty from Psammetichus I down to the end of the reign of Amasis (664-526 BCE). For this part of his Egyptian history H is an important source. His reign lengths are more accurate and the connection with historical reality much greater than in his narrative of previous reigns (although the labyrinth (148) was built more than 1,100 years earlier than H says it was). The account remains dependent on oral tradition with a large infusion of Greek interpretation and emphasis on issues of interest to Greeks. This is surely true for other books of the *Histories* as well, but we can see it clearly here.

2.147-57 The twelve kings and Psammetichus I (664-610 BCE). H's twelve kings symbolize the internal political fragmentation of the Ethiopian and Assyrian periods, in which the authority of the central government was often nominal. The labyrinth of ch. 148 was actually built by Amenemhet III of the Twelfth Dynasty; both the labyrinth and the lake near it are described at length because they are *thōmata*, wonders (n. 2.65-76). For their accurate description, see Lloyd, iii. 121-7. The lake (149) was a natural formation, watered by the Nile, and considerably smaller than H says, with a circumference of c.170 miles (272 km.), not the c.400 miles (640 km.) that would make it equal the coastline of Egypt in H's reckoning (cf. n. 2.6). Nineveh was destroyed in 612 BCE by a Median/Babylonian combined force (150; cf. n. 1.178); H here is relating a confused tradition with folk-tale elements in it. Psammetichus was, like his father, pro-Assyrian and began his reign as an Assyrian vassal (Lloyd, iii. 132). Gyges of Lydia may have helped Psammetichus win independence from Assyria by sending him Carian and Greek mercenary troops; Psammetichus controlled all of Egypt by 656 BCE. On the Apis cult (153), see 2.38. The description of the shrine at Buto (155) is added as a *thōma*, 'wonder', to the end of Psammetichus' reign because Psammetichus had consulted it (152). For the description of the shrine and the lake near it, see Lloyd, iii. 140-5, and 146-9 for the historicity of the siege of Azotus (Ashdod, 2.157). Control of Ashdod meant control of the route to Syria-Palestine; it was a rich prize commercially.

2.158-9 Necho II reigned from 610 to 595 BCE. See Lloyd, iii. 150-8 for the canal and its military and commercial benefits to Egypt. The chauvinism expressed at the end of 2.158 is entirely Egyptian (Lloyd, iii. 157–8). Lloyd concludes that Egyptian power and prestige were drastically curtailed between 605 and 595 BCE, but that 'Necho must at least get the credit for preventing the Chaldaean occupation of his country—and that, we have every reason to believe, was the ultimate aim of his policy' (iii. 159).

2.160–1 Psammis was Psammetichus II (595–589 BCE). He did invade Ethiopia, but the account of the Olympic games contains unhistorical elements, since the Eleans did not gain control of the games until about 570 BCE. Diodorus of Sicily (1.95) places the anecdote in the time of Amasis. For the notion that an evil fate was sometimes inescapable, see n. 1.8.

2.161–71 The account of Apries' reign (589–570 BCE) contains two episodes from his campaigns, the expedition against Cyrene, and his deposition by Amasis. The rest is a series of pendants: the warriors and other classes (164–8), the royal tombs at Saïs (169), and the Sanctuary of Athena at Saïs and rituals connected to it (2.170–1). His operations against Tyre and Sidon (161) probably are to be dated late in his reign; H thinks that the military revolted because of resentment at the defeat of the Cyrene campaign in c.571 BCE (cf. 4.159), but on a deeper level Lloyd connects it with resentment at the favoured status given Greek mercenary troops. See Lloyd, iii. 178–9 for discussion of the Amasis stele and the modifications of H's account of the end of Apries' reign it suggests; Apries at the head of Asiatic troops attacked Amasis and was killed in battle, perhaps three years after the end of his reign. It is true that Amasis changed the capital to Memphis (Lloyd, iii. 181); early in his reign he was not yet the famous philhellene he later became (2.178, 3.39).

See Lloyd, iii. 182–96 for the excursus on Egyptian class structure, its concentration on the military class, and the geographical assignment of the nomes (2.164 ff.). The priests and the warriors are the only two classes about whom there is wide agreement; they were the only two that controlled land and were also the most likely to impinge upon the attention of foreign observers. H's notions of the *makhimoi*, or warriors, are almost certainly affected by Greek assumptions about warriors and Spartans in particular (167); warriors in Egypt seem originally to have been mainly Libyans. In ch. 170 H is reluctant to mention the tomb of Osiris at Saïs; the sacred lake was a standard feature of Egyptian temples. In ch. 171 H again expresses his (mistaken) belief that most Greek religious institutions derived from Egypt (cf. 2.43–64 passim). The Thesmophoria was a three-day festival celebrated by Greek women before the autumn sowing of crops; its details were kept secret.

2.172–82 The reign of Amasis (570–526 BCE). Three stories of his reign are given in 2.172–5. In ch. 172 he educates the Egyptians to honour him as king despite his low birth; Lloyd (iii. 212–13) thinks it likely that in the Persian period the legitimacy of his family line as well as

his rule was denied. The other two stories (173–4) are more likely
to contain Egyptian motifs retold by Greeks.

In chs. 175–6 Amasis' building activities in Saïs and Memphis are
described, and in chs. 177–82 his reign's stability and prosperity.
Lloyd thinks his status as a lawgiver has to do with the reorganization of the country after the civil war with Apries. In chs. 177–82
his connections with the Greeks are emphasized; Amasis was a
famous philhellene, but his reign was too late for him to have
inspired Solon's laws (c.594 BCE). For Naucratis (178), see Lloyd, iii.
222–30 and CAH iv. 455–6. Most of the Greeks in Egypt, except for
the mercenaries employed by the pharoah, lived there, but cf. 2.39,
41 and Lloyd, i. 13–38. For more on the reconstruction of the temple
at Delphi c.548 BCE (180), see n. 5.62–3, and App. 2 for monetary
values. For the relations between Amasis and Cyrene, see Lloyd, iii.
234–5. Amasis' whole energy in foreign policy would have gone into
defending against the growing threat of Persia, and this shaped his
relations with Cyrene, Rhodes, Cyprus, and Samos. For his relations
with Polycrates of Samos, see further 3.39–43. We do not know
which of the two actually ended the alliance, but it seems more probable that Polycrates did; see n. 3.44 below.

BOOK THREE

So far the narrative structure has been quite simple. Book 1 consists of the stories of Croesus and Cyrus; Book 2 concerns Egypt. Book 3, however, reminds us that the books were almost certainly not H's own divisions, but an Alexandrian invention probably designed to produce roughly comparable units of papyrus that could easily be stored and handled. It contains a short and lurid account of the eight-year reign of Cambyses (530–522 BCE), and a longer account of the beginning of the reign of Darius, as he begins to assert control over the huge and unwieldy empire he has taken on. Several themes run through this book: the complexities of power, and the ease with which it is abused; the way that apparently quite disparate events impinge on each other; the way each new person who becomes the focus of the account (Cambyses, Darius, but also Polycrates, Periander, Oroetes, Maeandrius, and even Democedes and Charilaus) has his own ideas about how to get what he wants, and how these schemes fit into the larger geopolitical account. Small does become big and big small in Book 3; the personal delusions of Cambyses and Charilaus and the private desires of Syloson the exile and Democedes the slave physician have considerable consequences.

Cambyses and Darius demonstrate two different aspects of the problems inherent in empire: Cambyses is an unstable, perhaps sick, man at the helm of something too powerful for him to handle, while Darius, though intelligent and competent, begins his reign by killing one of his co-conspirators and is manipulated first by his wife and his slave physician, and then (in a more distant fashion) by the ambitious brother of Polycrates and the mad brother of Polycrates' *de facto* successor. Around the transition from Cambyses' reign to that of Darius, H interlaces several episodes that explain how the Persians first became interested in Greece through the story of Samos and its foreign affairs. Vividly demonstrated here is the impact of imperial power on the fortunes of small islands far away, and how imperial power is subverted by local and regional ambitions. Finally, implicit in the story of Babylon's fall is both a comparison and a contrast with Cyrus' earlier achievement; while, according to H, the army of Cyrus had won Babylon by an engineering feat, drawing off the water of the Euphrates and entering along the river-bed (1.191), Darius reconquers it by a trick involving the grotesque self-mutilation and ambitious duplicity of one of his subordinates—whose grandson, H notes, deserted later to Athens (3.160).

3.1 For a different and more sympathetic portrayal of Cambyses' accomplishments see *CAH* iv. 47–52. Neither the Egyptians nor Darius had an obvious interest in portraying Cambyses as a competent military commander or ruler, but we may note that as crown prince he had been entrusted with the rule of Babylon by his father, Cyrus, and had apparently kept it loyal; as king (530–522 BCE) he did plan and achieve the conquest of Egypt (525 BCE). The three stories H gives that begin his reign and give his apparent motivations for invading Egypt are all personal, concerning a woman in his household—no hint of plans previously laid by his father, abstract geopolitical considerations, or even the will of the gods (all of which figure, for instance, in Xerxes' comparable decision at the beginning of Book 7). For what might have been some of Cambyses' actual considerations, see *CAH* iv. 254–5. Control of Egypt was necessary if the coastline of Syria-Palestine was to remain under Persian rule.

3.2 Cassandane, Cambyses' mother, has also been mentioned in 2.1. Her brother (according to H at least) is Otanes, the hero of Darius' accession story (3.68–72, 80). Cambyses is extremely involved with the women of his own family; he later marries a cousin, Otanes' daughter, as well as a couple of his own sisters (3.31, 68). Note that here as in Book 2 Egyptians are praised for their knowledge (cf. 2.77).

3.4 A large bowl has been found at Naucratis dedicated by Phanes son of Glaucus; *CAH* iii/3. 52 notes that this may be the same Phanes (cf. 3.11). One of Psammetichus' significant problems was that important and trusted underlings like Phanes and Udjahorresne, the keeper of the temple of Neith at Saïs and commander of the fleet, betrayed him for the Persian invader in 525 BCE, *CAH* iv. 49, 258. See more broadly *CAH* iii/2. 725–6 for the isolation of the Egyptian navy after Cyrus won over the Phoenicians and Polycrates of Samos.

3.8–9 A brief excursus on Arabians, following H's custom of describing a people as the Persians encounter them. They will recur (3.88, 107–13). For the definition of Arabs and Arabia in the Achaemenid period, see *CAH* iv. 162–4. For Alilat, see n. 1.131; perhaps Orotalt is a form of Ba'al. There is no known river corresponding to the Corys in 3.9.

3.10 Rain at Thebes is defined as a portent. Cf. n. 1.78.

3.12 The mention of the battle of Papremis (459 BCE, *CAH* iv. 276) dates H's sightseeing in Egypt at least later than the mid-450s. Inaros and Amyrtaeus with Athenian help attempted to free Egypt from Persian rule, Inaros was defeated, and a substantial Athenian fleet was lost (about 250 ships, according to Thucydides 1.104, 109–10, 112). Cf. 3.69 for another instance of the (mistaken) belief that Persians wear hats all the time, 2.36 for Egyptian baldness.

3.14–15 This is the first real anecdote about Cambyses, and first sign of behaviour that becomes increasingly pathological. For Persian tolerance, cf. nn. 1.135 and 1.156. The end of ch. 14 reminds the reader of the end of 1.86; no wonder Croesus weeps here.

3.16 Amasis' cartouches must have been obliterated at this time, although the testimony of Udjahorresne the collaborator (whose statue in the Vatican bears a brief autobiography in hieroglyphs) acquits Cambyses of outraging Egyptian religious sensibilities. Foreign troops were quartered in the temple precincts at Saïs (*CAH* iv. 258).

3.17–26 Cambyses' three expeditions. *CAH* iv. 49 discusses the improbability of such massive incompetence on Cambyses' part, given his past record. There is some evidence that Egypt's southern borders were successfully defended and at least northern Nubia brought under Persian rule: in 3.91 Libya, Cyrene, and Barca are all part of Darius' tribute-bearing empire; in 7.70 Ethiopians form part of Xerxes' army. See Asheri.

Much in the report of Ethiopia is highly imaginative; for the Table of the Sun (18), see earlier Greek fantasies of a just people who dine with the gods, n. 2.137–40. H distinguishes the Ethiopians of Africa from the Ethiopians of Asia (cf. 3.94, 101, 7.69–70). Among the southern, African Ethiopians he includes a variety of African peoples.

3.19 The willing surrender of the Phoenicians to Persia was of considerable military and political significance, since the Phoenicians became the backbone of Persia's navy (under Darius: 5.108, 112, 6.6, 14; Thucydides 1.16; under Xerxes: 7.89, 96, 8.67; Thucydides 1.100). See further *CAH* iv. 156–7, and for the effect of isolating the Phoenician colony, Carthage, and making it turn its attention westwards, *CAH* iv. 749–50. Cf. n. 1.166. Cyprus joins the Greek side in the Ionian revolt of the 490s but is crucial to Persian maritime control and will be reconquered (5.104, 108–16, 6.6).

3.21 Another story of the strong and less civilized versus the overcivilized; cf. n. 1.71. The king of the Ethiopians echoes some of the observations of Tomyris the Massagete in 1.206; to both of them the Persian compulsion to conquer seems odd. The notion of the attraction of the fruits of civilization finds its ironic completion in Pausanias' juxtaposition of a Spartan and a Persian dinner in 9.82, after the battle of Plataea. The Persians are called water-drinkers in 1.71, but cf. 1.133 and, for Cambyses himself, 3.34. Cf. n. 1.136.

3.23–4 The Ethiopians in Xerxes' army (7.69) are archers. Parts of this passage are a mixture of fantasy and misunderstood or mistranslated travellers' tales (cf. the 'feathers' of 4.31). For the crystal coffins, see Strabo 17.3 and Diodorus 2.15.

3.25–6 The Ammonians lived at the famous oasis of Siwa, in Egypt's western desert. The cannibalism of Cambyses' main army is not a matter of vengeance, as in the Astyages story (1.73), or a part of

culture (3.99, 4.26), but foolishness brought on by Cambyses' mad
impetuousity. Lloyd (i. 118) singles out the Greek (Samian) inhabitants of the oasis in 3.26, El Khargeh, as possible Greek sources of
H's information on Egypt. Asheri notes that Phanes the Halicarnassian of 3.4 and 11 is another possible candidate. For Egyptian
sources, see n. 2.2.

3.27–9 Hieroglyphic records do not bear out the story H reports, *CAH*
iv. 260. One Apis was born in 543 and died in September 525, and
the following Apis was born in 526 and died in 518, in the reign of
Darius. Egyptian hieroglyphic records in the Memphis Serapeum
testify that Cambyses financed the construction of the Apis sar-
cophagus and performed the traditional burial rites. Cambyses' constraints on Egyptian temple revenues may have been responsible
for his later bad press from the temple priesthoods. Memphis was
the seat of government and important cults, esp. that of Apis. Cf.
2.38, 153 for the Apis cult in Egypt; in 2.38 H refers ahead to this
passage for the description of the marks of the animal. Ch. 29 foreshadows the wound on the thigh that will cause Cambyses' own
death (3.64). The extensive description of Egyptian religiosity in
Book 2 has helped the reader understand how shocking Cambyses'
behaviour is here.

3.30–2 Cambyses' mistreatment of his family. A long trilingual inscription
exists at Bisiton (mod. Behistun), carved in Old Persian, Elamite, and
Babylonian, in which Cambyses' successor, Darius, confirms the gist
of what is said here, that Cambyses had his brother Smerdis (Persian,
Bardiya) killed. None the less, it is a very peculiar story (*CAH* iv. 53
f.); for its continuation in H, see 3.61 below. Asheri notes the
similarity between Astyages' dream in 1.107, Cyrus' dream in
1.209, and Cambyses' dream in 3.30. The 'Red Sea' here is the
Persian Gulf.

For the royal judges see also 3.14 above. *CAH* iv. 82–3 doubts
that there was a fixed body or number, but H believes they were
appointed for life; cf. 5.25 and 7.194 for the strenuousness of the
position. Persian royal decrees were written down and kept (*CAH*
iv. 87), whence the famous immutability of the 'law of the Medes
and the Persians' in Daniel 6:8 and 15. Atossa, the elder of the two
sisters Cambyses marries, will go on to an influential career as
Darius' most important wife (3.133, 7.3). (A third daughter of
Cyrus and Cassandane, Artystone, does not marry her brother
Cambyses but will become Darius' favourite wife: 3.88, 7.69.) As
often, the variants in ch. 32 contain a common kernel of meaning,
here that the sister is unhappy at Cambyses' murder of their brother.
For the 'first atrocity' cf. n. 5.96–7. Cf. more generally H's habit
of keeping track of the numbers of times something happens,
n. 1.92.

3.33 Epilepsy. The Hippocratic *On the Sacred Disease* 1 also claims that
the causes are physical rather than religious.

3.34–6 Cambyses has proved to his own satisfaction that he is not too drunk to shoot his cupbearer accurately. Prexaspes' courtier-like behaviour reminds one of Harpagus (1.119), but Prexaspes will decide at the end to remain faithful to the Achaemenids (3.74–5). Burying people alive (35) is something Persians do (7.114). This is the last time Croesus figures in the continuous narrative (36), scuttling out of the room in fear of Cambyses (there are incidental anecdotes in 6.37 and 125 and some later monuments and temple dedications).

3.37 The temple of Ptah at Memphis had a privileged position, exempt for instance from financial restrictions, *CAH* iv. 260. For the temple, see 2.99, 101; for its priests as H's most important Egyptian informants, see n. 2.2. It is not clear what ancient connections existed among the Greek metalworking god Hephaestus and the helping figures of the Phoenician Pataïci, the Cabiri of Egypt, and the Cabiri of Lemnos or Samothrace (2.51). Cabiri were also part of seventh-century Boeotian cult, although connected with agriculture rather than craft.

3.38 An important and rare passage of H's own judgement on religion and custom; cf. 2.3. The Callatiae may be the Callantiae of 3.97 (cf. 3.99). Plato, *Gorgias* 484b also quotes the Pindar passage (fr. 169 Snell), but the gist of the Platonic quotation is that the strong hand of custom dominates both god and man, justifying violence. Other vivid expressions of H's personal opinion occur in 2.43–5, 53, 143, 3.106, 108, 6.27, 7.139, 8.13.

3.39–60 An excursus on Samos and in particular on the foreign policy of Samos' famous tyrant Polycrates (*c.*535–522 BCE); cf. *CAH* iii/3. 218–19. H probably follows here the principle noted by Immerwahr (p. 61) that 'the place between logoi forms a pause'. H discusses the complicated story of Samos at the end of his account of Cambyses' reign, thus using it to mark a pause before embarking on the continuous account of Cambyses' downfall and Darius' accession; it also lays the background necessary for understanding the two subsequent Samian narratives of 3.120–5 and 139–49. The fate of Polycrates reminds the reader of the impossibility of evading one's assigned destiny (cf. n. 1.8). H's treatment of Samos in the *Histories*, as well as the much later biographical tradition, suggests that he knew Samos well and may be recording reasonably good information here.

3.39–43 The story of Polycrates' ring; Amasis' pessimism turns out to be well founded (3.125). The struggle between Samos and Miletus for dominance of the Aegean trade routes was ongoing and traditional. Syloson will reappear in 3.139. Theodorus (41) is also the craftsman H thinks made the giant silver bowl Croesus sends to Delphi (1.51).

3.44 There is a possibility that Polycrates broke off his alliance with Amasis and went over to Persia, perhaps when the Phoenicians became part of the Persian empire, *CAH* iv. 464, cf. n. 3.19. This must have intensified the Lacedaemonian hostility to Polycrates, since Sparta was determined to keep Greece independent of Persian overlordship (1.152; cf. n. 3.148).

3.46-7 Spartans are indeed laconic; see n. 1.152. The bowl had been stolen in 547 BCE (1.70). Sparta's seventh-century struggles with Messenia (47) ended with the subjection of Messenia and the enslavement of its population c.620; cf. n. 6.58-60.

3.48-53 Corinth was part of the Peloponnesian League from about 550 BCE (*CAH* iii/3. 356-7), and no doubt joined Sparta for that reason. H uses the fact of Corinth's presence in the war against Polycrates to interrupt the Samian narrative to tell the earlier story of Periander, Corinth's famous tyrant (c.627-587 BCE; for Periander and other tyrants, see *CAH* iii/3. 346-51). Political motivations in H are often personal, but this is one of the most peculiar. It is highly improbable that the Corinthians were still angry in the 520s that their tyrant two long generations earlier had been foiled by the Samians in his attempts to castrate 300 Corcyran boys. The relevance of the story here is thematic, in a narrative replete with instances of tyrannical behaviour. In 5.92 H again inserts the story of the Corinthian tyranny into a context that seems strained to a modern ear.

3.55 H rarely names his interlocutors; cf. 2.55, 4.76, and 9.16. Only here and probably at 2.28 does he expressly say where the interview took place; cf. 2.44 for another rare glimpse of research as a part of H's travels.

3.56 This is record-keeping; the second expedition was in 479 BCE, to Mycale (9.96). Cf. n. 1.92 for other enumerations in H.

3.57 Asheri notes that four of H's five instances of the verb 'to flourish, be prosperous' are of cities which later are destroyed: here and also 1.29, 5.28, 6.127. The one human who 'flourishes' is the courtesan Rhodopis, 2.134. The island of Siphnos was famous in the archaic period for its mineral resources of silver, lead, and gold, and the Siphnian treasury in Delphi was famous for its wealth (cf. n. 1.14). The Siphnians only supplied one penteconter or fifty-oared ship, however, to the Greek cause in the Persian Wars (8.48).

3.59 This whole set of events probably took place about 524-519 BCE. A chief cause for hostility between Samos and Aegina was probably rivalry for the markets of Libya and Egypt. Aegina was the only non-east Greek state with a presence in the Egyptian trading-centre of Naucratis, and a Samian base established in north-west Crete threatened the Aeginetan trade route southwards. Cf. n. 4.152 and *CAH* iv. 364.

3.60 The temple was begun about 570 BCE, before Polycrates' time; Rhoecus, its builder, was also said with Theodorus to have invented smelting and casting metal (Pausanias 8.14.8, 9.41.1). This temple burned down and an even larger one was begun under Polycrates, which H saw and was impressed by (but cf. 2.148 for an even more impressive building in Egypt). One can still today get a good idea of the aqueduct, the mole, and the temple H admired on Samos.

3.61–87 The story of Cambyses resumes from 3.38. Structurally, it is interesting that this section of narrative about the transfer of power from Cambyses to Darius is framed by the long excursus on Samos before it (3.39–60), and by an equally long survey of the extent of the Persian empire after it (3.88–116).

3.61–7 The story of Cambyses resumes from 3.38. The Medes seize power; Cambyses dies. H's story stays fairly close in its major out-lines to Darius' own account in the Bisitun inscription, although Darius calls the rebel Mede Gaumata and mentions no second Median brother; he gives another name, Bardiya, to H's other Smerdis, the brother Cambyses had killed (3.30; *CAH* iv. 53–7). Cambyses' speech (65) refers again to a theme of the Croesus and Astyages stories, a fate foretold in a dream that he could not and should not have tried to avoid. Cf. n. 1.8.

3.68–79 The conspiracy of the seven. H accurately names all but one; in the Bisitun inscription Darius calls H's Aspathines Ardumanish (*CAH* iv. 54). The conspirators remain close to the centre of power (except for Intaphrenes in H, 3.118; Darius' inscription, however, names Intaphrenes as reconquering Babylon near the beginning of Darius' reign). Otanes is the brother of Cambyses' wife, Cassandane (3.2), and the father of another of his wives, Phaedymia; his descen-dants become the rulers of Cappadocia. He argues for a democratic government in Persia (3.80), and yet ironically he subdues Samos for Darius (3.141, 147, 149). Aspathines is the father of Prexaspes, one of Xerxes' officers in the expedition to Greece (7.97). Gobryas is both Darius' brother-in-law and father-in-law (7.2, 5); he is one of Darius' councillors in Scythia (4.132); his son, Mardonius, becomes Xerxes' brother-in-law, the most fervent supporter of his invasion of Greece (7.5), and the invasion's military commander. Megabyzus, who argues for oligarchy in 3.81, is the father of Zopyrus, in H's version the conqueror of Babylon for Darius (3.153, 160). Hydarnes is the father of two of Xerxes' military commanders (7.66 and 83) and his son of the same name becomes the governor of the Asian coastal region (7.135); his family later become the rulers of Armenia.

Darius' rule meant return of control to the Persian Achaemenid military and administrative élite (perhaps to a different branch of it from that of Cyrus); in his inscription Darius claims that he returned pastures, herds, household slaves, and houses to 'the people' and re-established 'the people on its foundations' in both Persia and Media. His emphasis on Gaumata as a Magus and on the restora-tion of destroyed sanctuaries perhaps indicates a degree of attempted religious revolution as well; cf. 3.79 where H says that an annual

Persian festival is still held in his day celebrating the 'murder of the Magi' (Magophonia).

3.70-2 In the Bisitun inscription Hystaspes the father of Darius is satrap of Parthia. Ch. 72 highlights without editorial comment Darius' carelessness about basic Persian values (cf. 1.136). Like Amasis (2.173-4), Darius is something of a trickster figure at the beginning of his reign.

3.80-3 As Asheri notes, this tripartite typology of governments is found already in Pindar (*Pythian Odes* 2.85 ff.), and later in Plato, Aristotle, Isocrates, and Polybius. Although H emphasizes here and again in 6.43 the fact that this debate really occurred, his account of it owes a great deal to fifth-century Greek sophistic thought. It is highly structured, so that each speaker contradicts the previous one, and it is the most theoretical discussion of political systems in the *Histories*. See Lateiner, 167-86 for the large bibliography on the subject and the issues entailed. The aftermath of the debate makes it clear that Darius' strongest argument is the (unspoken) one of self-interest; except for Otanes, everyone hopes himself to become king. H's own sympathy for Otanes' position is patent; cf. his depiction of Sparta (7.104) as governed by law, and Athens (5.78) as successful when its citizens become free from despotism. He respects *isonomiē*, 'equality before the law' or, more generally, 'political equality', but remains somewhat ambivalent about democracy as practised in Athens (5.97). Cf. H's irony towards Samos in 3.142-3.

3.84-7 Darius makes no mention of his groom's odd trick; he credits his success to the will of Ahura Mazda, in the Bisitun inscription, *CAH* iv. 54. The rule about access to the king except when he is with a woman (84) will figure in the Intaphrenes story (3.118).

3.88 Darius reigned from 521 to 486 BCE. For Arabians cf. n. 3.8; they control the spice trade (3.107) and are valuable friends, but their independence is perhaps less absolute than H supposes, since they will serve in the army that marches to Greece (7.69). Darius had married a daughter of Gobryas before becoming king (7.2); Artystone daughter of Cyrus was his favourite wife while she lived (7.69; cf. n. 3.30-2).

3.89-97 This seems to be a development from the system of government described in 1.134 and remains a valuable survey of the organization into satrapies of the Persian empire and the revenues of each. Cf. *CAH* iv. 87-91, 96-9, and the individual discussions of taxation and tribute for Babylonia, central Asia, Europe, India, and Syria-Palestine. H perhaps has misunderstood the 360 talents of gold-dust he assigns to India in 3.94. *CAH* iv. 204 thinks it is much more likely to have been the weight in silver equivalent to the value of the assessed gold-dust. See Asheri, H & W, and Legrand, *ad loc.* for efforts to make H's arithmetic in ch. 95 come out correctly. The last chapter (97) discusses the parts of the empire that gave 'gifts' instead of a fixed tribute.

3.98–105 H gives a brief ethnography of India as a pendant to the subject of the Indian gold-dust paid as tribute. It ends with an elaborate traveller's tale about how the gold is collected; see Asheri for the long afterlife of the story of ants as big as foxes. (In the *New York Times* of 25 Nov. 1996 a French ethnologist, Michel Peissel, is quoted as claiming that the Persian word for marmot was the equivalent of 'mountain ant', and that marmots have been recently observed on the Dansar plain, near the border between India and Pakistan, engaging in behaviour resembling that described here. The camels, however, are missing from the modern story.)

3.102 Caspatyrus was the origin of the remarkable voyage of Scylax of Caryanda (4.44); its geographical location remains uncertain (*CAH* iv. 201 f. thinks it is Peshawar).

3.103 H may have mistaken the hock of the camel for a second knee, given the odd way in which the camel kneels down; Aristotle tacitly corrects H (*Historia Animalium* 499ᵃ).

3.104 Since the earth is seen as a flat disc and the sun travels westwards in an arc across it, logically in the extreme east it is hottest in the morning. See n. 2.19–27.

3.106–16 H's survey of the amazing things found at the ends of the earth; cf. n. 2.65–76. H & W comment that the stories of horrific dangers and difficulties associated with the harvesting of spices may have been invented by his sources to dissuade potential competitors from the lucrative spice trade. The 'wool from trees' (106) is cotton. For the flying snakes (107), cf. 2.75.

3.108 See Immerwahr, 307 for the notion of a divine balance as one that controls the political sphere as well as the natural one in H.

3.115–16 Eridanus is a mythic river in Hesiod, *Theogony* 338. In Pherecydes, *FGH* 3, fr. 74 and Euripides, *Hippolytus* 732 ff. it is the Po, to others the Rhône, and it may be connected in myth to memories of an early amber route from the Baltic. The griffins and Arimaspians come from the *Arimaspea* of Aristeas of Proconnesus (cf. n. 4.13–16). The Cassiterides (literally, the Tin Islands) are commonly identified as the Scilly Isles, or possibly Britain itself. H ends ch. 116 with ring composition, a repetition of the thought with which this geographical excursus begins in 3.106.

3.117 This chapter provides a transition back to the topic of Darius and the subsequent narratives that detail his efforts to control his huge empire. Central Asia did have a developed irrigation system dating back to the Late Bronze Age, but this particular plain does not exist, *CAH* iv. 183–4. 3.117 may be read as an ominous thematic indication of what Persian conquest means, but H does not force this interpretation on us. Without comment he instead embarks on the long narrative of Darius' reign, which will last down to the beginning of Book 7.

3.118–60 The large outlines of H's narrative for the rest of Book 3 show a progression with some thematic coherence: Darius first kills a trusted confidant (118), then removes a powerful satrap (126), conquers Samos (149), and finally resubdues Babylon, the most important western capital of the empire (150). Much is excluded: for instance, many of the revolts around the empire put down by Darius in the early years of his reign, as well as a conquest of the eastern Scythians, the Sacae (*CAH* iv. 57–66). See n. 3.150–60, end.

3.118–19 In the Bisitun inscription Intaphrenes (Vindafarnah) is listed first among the conspirators, and is said to have put down a revolt of Babylon on 27 Nov. 521 BCE (*CAH* iv. 130). The story of Intaphrenes may suggest an attempted revolt by other high-ranking Persians against Darius' rule, but H is our only source for it.

Many think that the story of Intaphrenes' wife in H is the source of Sophocles' *Antigone* 905–12. If this is true, it suggests a date in the mid-440s for this part of the *Histories*' composition, although H could have been narrating the story long before finishing the *Histories* as a whole. Alternatively, a common earlier source might lie behind both passages. In H the point of the story seems to be Darius' recognition of the woman's cleverness in expressing her tacit loyalty, by choosing to save a member of her natal family rather than her politically compromised husband. H enjoys narrating witty retorts and paradoxical observations: cf. 1.71, 2.30, 172, 4.142, 144, 7.120, 226, 8.26.

3.120–49 Here begins a narrative thread demonstrating how small becomes big and vice versa (1.5). A squabble in Darius' antechamber between two rival satraps from the west (120) leads by a circuitous route to the destruction of a famous Greek tyrant (125), the turning of Darius' attention towards the conquest of Greece (138), and the brutal subjugation of the island of Samos (149).

3.120–6 Oroetes is a powerful and ambitious satrap in the western part of the empire, ruling from Sardis, Croesus' old capital. He takes advantage of the confusion surrounding the end of Cambyses' reign to kill both Mitrobates, a rival satrap from the region of the Hellespont, and Mitrobates' son (126). But first, in this episode (the continuation of 3.39–60), Oroetes destroys Polycrates, whom H calls the most magnificent of all Greek tyrants except for the rulers of Syracuse (125). H's comment on Polycrates here forms part of his interest in 'firsts' and 'bests'; cf. n. 1.214.

Anacreon (*c.*570–485 BCE) was a poet of love and wine at the court of Polycrates, who went to the court of the Pisistratidae in Athens after Polycrates' death and then perhaps to Thessaly. At the end of Polycrates' story (125) H makes an oblique reference back to the story of Amasis and the ring (3.40–3); in defining Polycrates as the first real person to aim at control of Ionia and the islands, H again separates off the *spatium historicum*, the time of real history, from the myths that antedate it (122). Cf. 1.5 and 2.147 where he also demarcates an earlier period from a later one that seems more securely known. In his treatment of Minos H is more cautious than Thucydides (1.4).

3.127–8 The theme of *tisis* or divine retribution recurs here; cf. n. 1.8. The word itself occurs in the Greek text in 1.13, 86, 2.152, 3.109, 5.56, 79, 6.72, 84, 7.8a, 8.76, 105, 106, and twice in this passage. The ability of writing to do crafty, unexpected, or long-range harm intrigues H: cf. n. 1.123 and passages cited there.

3.129–38 The confusion of the domestic and the political (sometimes called 'harem politics'), suggested as a theme in Cambyses' reign (3.1–3, 30–2), recurs here with a vengeance. Democedes, although he is only now a Greek slave, inveigles the queen, Atossa, to become his mouthpiece and influence the shaping of Persian foreign policy (134). Repeatedly, underlings give Darius or Xerxes partial or misleading information designed in reality to further private aims of their own: Megabazus, Aristagoras, and Histiaeus do so successfully in Book 5 and Mardonius influences the whole of the campaign in Greece in Books 7–9 (H also enjoys showing such thinking backfire, as in the case of the ambitious Paeonian brothers in 5.12–15). Darius does receive useful and impartial advice from his brother, Artabanus (4.83), and Xerxes will receive it from Artabanus (7.10f., 46f.), Artabazus (9.41), and two Greeks, Demaratus (7.101 f., 209, 234 f.) and Artemisia (8.68, 8.102) as well, but good advice is usually not taken; cf. nn. 1.8, 1.71, 9.41–3.

Atossa's speech in ch. 134 is intelligently argued; it raises some of the same issues later contained in the speeches of Xerxes and his ambitious cousin, Mardonius, in 7.5, 7.8, and 7.9. Mardonius himself in Books 7 to 9 is an example of the kind of Persian Atossa warns Darius against here; a prudent ruler finds wars a useful way to distract excessively ambitious subordinates.

3.137 Milo the late sixth-century wrestler was one of the most famous athletes of the ancient world, six times an Olympic victor, six times at the Pythian games, ten times each at the Isthmian and Nemean games. The Pythagoreans in Croton were said to have met at his house.

3.138 Like the Ethiopian Sabacos (2.139), the Athenian Aristides (8.79), and the Persian Otanes (3.80), Gillus is a rare example of someone who does not at all costs cling to power. His forbearance implicitly highlights by contrast the very different story of another exile that immediately follows (3.139–49). The formulaic sentence at the end of the chapter indicates that the account begun in 3.129 is ending. By its emphasis on 'firsts' it also indicates the importance of this account to the larger theme of the *Histories*, East–West hostilities, despite the apparent triviality of many of the motives involved (cf. n. 1.92). This is the first in a series of westward-turning Persian military expeditions that will dominate the remaining narrative of the *Histories*.

3.139-49 The third and final episode of the Samian story. Samos is destroyed after Darius' establishment of Syloson as its tyrant goes awry (*c*.521 BCE). Syloson's initial banishment by his brother Polycrates had been noted in 3.39. The story here is full of bitter ironies; cf. Otanes' interest in *isonomiē* for the Persians (3.80) with his behaviour in Samos as Darius' henchman (144, 147, 149). On the other hand, H remarks that the aristocrats in charge of Samos 'did not want to be free'. The abusive behaviour that Argives and Scythians use successfully towards men they call former slaves (4.3, 6.83) backfires when used on the Samian Maeandrius (142-3); he is not cowed into submission. In its largest outlines, this account, like the story of Democedes before it, signals how little control even a conscientious ruler like Darius has over the events unfolding under his jurisdiction.

3.142 It is curious that the brother of Maeandrius responsible for his initial acts of violence is later found ruling Lemnos under the Persians, unchanged in character (5.27, unless the current text refers instead to Otanes).

3.148 This is the second time a Samian has asked for Spartan help, and the theme of Ionian eloquence vs. Spartan simplicity is again raised (3.46; cf. 1.152). For Cleomenes, the energetic king of Lacedaemon (*c*.520-490 BCE), see *CAH* iv. 356-67. He resisted embroiling Sparta in overseas adventures: in H, in 517 he refuses aid to Maeandrius, in 513 to the Scythians (6.84), and, most significantly, in 499 to the Ionians revolting against Persia (5.49 f.). At the same time we see him throughout Books 5 and 6 trying to maintain control over the other member states of the Peloponnesian League and to extend its power, interfering in the government of Athens (5.64-74), trying to mount war against Aegina (6.50), demolishing the Argives at the battle of Sepeia (6.77 ff.), and driving his fellow king, Demaratus, from office (6.61 f.); like Cambyses he goes mad. His gruesome death is attributed by other Greeks to a variety of transgressions (6.75). A systematic desire to check the growth of Persian influence may have inspired some of his activity. On the other hand, much of it also led to increased ill will and disunity among the various Greek states of the mainland (cf. nn. 5.49-51, 6.73-84, 6.108).

3.149 Asheri notes that this is the first of a number of wholesale interferences with European populations by Darius; he deports Barcans (4.204), Paeonian Thracians (5.15), Milesians (6.20), Eretrians (6.119). For Otanes' disease, cf. 1.105, but also 1.19, 4.205, and perhaps 3.32 and 6.75. For a fuller description of 'trawling' cf. 6.31.

3.150-60 This account of Babylon's revolt early in Darius' reign is connected as a synchronism to the Persian take-over of Samos. Darius' Bisitun inscription records two revolts in Babylon in Darius' first year, and revolts in Persia, Elam, Media, Assyria, perhaps Egypt, Parthia, Margiana, Sattagydia, and Scythia as well (*CAH* iv. 58-63 and 129 f.). What Darius tells us in the Bisitun inscription cannot be reconciled with the twenty-month siege described here, and Zopyrus's role is known only from H. The account of this revolt was perhaps designed as part of the 'Assyrian *logoi*' which H promises in 1.106 and 184 but does not include in his *Histories*. H never distinguishes Babylonia from Assyria.

3.153 Cf. 1.55 (1.91) and 7.57 for other unlikely mules. For portents generally, cf. n. 1.78. The portent starts Zopyrus thinking, much as the dropped helmet starts Cyrus' men thinking in 1.84, as they besiege Sardis.

3.154 The king's benefactors are indeed rewarded abundantly; see the end of this story in 3.160 and 8.85. (For a Greek example of expedient self-mutilation, cf. 1.59.) The story of Zopyrus ends with a twist, however, since H concludes the whole account of the capture of Babylon by remarking that Zopyrus' grandson much later deserts to Athens—perhaps to become one of H's informants or even one of the Persian *logioi* mentioned in 1.1? Other rewards the king gives for service turn out oddly as well: cf. 3.139 f. and 5.11, which lead respectively to the destruction of Samos and the Ionian revolt. It is not a good idea to count on lasting gratitude from the king; cf. 7.29 and 38. (For a Greek example of expedient self-mutilation, cf. 1.59.)

3.158 For the temple of Zeus-Bel, cf. 1.181.

3.159 The Babylonians must here marry non-Babylonian women; cf. n. 1.1. In 1.146 also H emphasizes that blue-blooded Ionians are actually half-Carian, but in 3.159 the tone is less paradoxical and amused. Cf. the end of 1.196 for a description of contemporary Babylonian hardship.

BOOK FOUR

Up until now the story of Persia has been one of military success and imperial growth. Despite the problem of Cambyses' madness and death and
the confusing interregnum that follows, by 515 or so Darius has put
things back together again. In terms of effective governance, Darius' reign
(521–486 BCE) will turn out to be the acme of the Achaemenid empire.
His prompt and rather ruthless disciplining of Intaphrenes, Oroetes, and
Babylon in Book 3 has indicated how resourceful he will be; the geographical and financial survey of his vast empire in 3.89–97 has tacitly
confirmed how vast and well organized is the power he wields.

Book 4, however, introduces a new element: it shows what happens to
Darius' army and his imperial ambitions when he ventures out of Asia into
Europe, and encounters a people quite different from the highly civilized
populations heretofore encountered. Structurally, the first and longer part
of Book 4 reminds one of Book 2: it starts with a survey of the exotic land
and people of Scythia before they are attacked, and then it recounts the
Persian war against them. But Scythians are not Egyptians, and this war
goes quite differently.

Book 2 has shown us that Egypt is organized into an intricate agricultural and highly civilized society; even the land is criss-crossed with man-
made canals. H thinks that the Egyptians are among the oldest, most
learned, most highly developed people in the world, and according to
H the Greeks have acquired most of their religion and many kinds of
learning from them. The picture is an organized and rather static one:
Egyptians are categorized within functional classes and carry out a variety
of specified and elaborate rituals. The Scythians of Book 4, on the other
hand, claim to be the youngest people in the world. They want nothing to
do with outsiders and have only one real skill—but it is worth a great
deal—the art of not staying where their enemy can attack them. They move
rapidly across their vast grasslands with their herds and their families in
wagons, and they practise the art of war from horseback with a single-
minded tenacity. Scythians make clothing, napkins, and quiver-covers out
of the skin of their enemies, drink from their skulls, and build no shrines
to any gods but Ares, god of war. Their sacrifices, from a Greek point of

view, are sketchy. Where the Egyptians build elaborate stone pyramids, the Scythians bury their kings in huge pits in the ground and cover them with mounds of earth.

Scythians are nomads, and as F. Hartog has recently pointed out, in some respects H's account of the Scythian expedition is an extended meditation on nomad power: 'As Darius learns to his cost, throwing a bridge across the Ister does not suffice for truly entering Scythia' (p. 61). The initial, long, ethnographic description shows us what Darius will encounter: a vast territory stretching north of the Euxine (Black) Sea and mostly consisting of grassland steppes, broken by a series of gigantic rivers, from the Ister (Danube) in the west to the Tanaïs (Don) in the east. Across these steppes ride the Royal Scythians, warrior nomads. Darius does not see how little he has understood them until the wonderful moment where he finally meets them army to army—and the Scythians, just as battle is about to be joined, catch sight of a hare and ride off *en masse* after it! (4.134) So Darius gives up his plans of conquest and retreats, back to the Ionians waiting to ferry him across the Ister.

Although the parallel cannot be pushed too far, in a number of ways the account of Scythia foreshadows the war Xerxes, Darius' son, will fight in Greece in Books 7 to 9. There too Artabanus will warn the king, the king will kill the offspring of a man who had sought their release from the army, the king will contemplate his army on its passage from Asia to Europe on a throne, the relatively poor and disorganized European enemy will take pride in their freedom, the Europeans will have problems reconciling their differences and fighting the Persians together, the Persians will have problems provisioning their army, and the enemy will prove elusive—when their cities are burned, the Greeks will take to their ships, their 'wooden walls'. Finally, the Persians will flee homeward, the king fearing for his life.

(For the discussion of Libya, see below, 4.145–205.)

4.1 It is curious that as Darius' intentions/attentions are depicted, no reference is made back to the conversation with Atossa in which she apparently persuades him to turn his attention from Scythia to Greece (3.134). The Scythians in Scythia in 515 BCE are unlikely to have been the same peoples who terrorized Asia Minor with their lengthy and destructive incursions in the seventh century (1.15, 73, 103–6), although both were mounted élite war-bands originating in the eastern parts of the steppe (*CAH* iii/2. 555).

4.2–4 H begins with a story that performs some of the same functions as the story of King Psammetichus and the children without language that begins the story of Egypt in Book 2, in that it tries through story to characterize the people being introduced. The Scythians drink horses' milk (cf. *Iliad* 13.5–6) and need slaves to do the complicated job of milking the mares. Since the Scythians are nomads or people on the move all the time, they cannot just lock the slaves up or shackle them as a Greek would do, but must blind them to keep them from running away. *CAH* iii/2. 568 suggests that behind 4.3–4 may lie a dim historical memory of one group of nomadic steppe peoples returning from Asia Minor to find another group inhabiting their previous territory. In any case, as well as taking up the narrative thread of the Scythians from 1.106, this story highlights several of the oddest salient characteristics of Scythians in a single picture: their nomadism, their use of milk (very strange to Greeks), their use of the whip (cf. the later Cossack or Tatar *nagaica*), and above all their ruthless single-minded logicality, given their premises. We will meet it again in their efficient use of their enemies' physical remains (4.64) and their judgement of Ionians as slaves at the end of the Scythian narrative (4.142). Slave rebellions are also the point in 6.83 and 138 and were a commonplace fear in the Greek world.

Lake Maeetis (3) is the Sea of Azov, and H refers again to the trench coming into it as the eastern boundary of the Royal Scythians (4.20). It is not clear what geographical feature he is describing, but it is unlikely to have been dug by rebellious slaves. The end of ch. 4 restates the topic of ch. 1; Darius' invasion will not be narrated until ch. 83.

4.5–13 Four stories about the origins of the Scythians. As often with variant versions, some underlying features remain the same: in this case, common to two versions are the three brothers, of whom the youngest becomes king (cf. the Egyptian emphasis on being oldest, 2.2); common to two other versions are successive waves of nomads coming from the East and compelling their predecessors to move westwards. The Indo-European tripartite division of function into farming, fighting, and religion is suggested by the nature of the four gold objects falling from the sky in the native Scythian story (two of them are agricultural). The Scythians of H's own day were of Iranian stock, *CAH* iii/2. 552. In 4.120 reference is made to three Scythian kings in charge of the army marshalled against Darius, but they are all from the Royal Scythians; there is no indication that they correspond to the lineages of the three sons sketched here.

4.7 For the feathers, cf. ch. 31.

4.8–10 For the Greeks who live on the shores of the Euxine (Black) Sea, see *CAH* iii/3. 122–30. They are almost certainly H's main source of information for 4.1–82. The Greek version has three brothers also, but these now represent the Scythians as an undifferentiated whole, their neighbours to the north-west towards the Carpathian mountains, the Agathyrsians, and those to the north-east, the Gelonians; cf. chs. 104 and 108. Heracles' odd route from Gibraltar back home via Scythia makes more sense if we remember that for H the Ister (Danube) has its origins in Spain and flows eastwards across all of Europe before emptying into the west or north waters of the Euxine (Black) Sea—it reveals a great deal about the state of geographical knowledge for H's contemporaries that H has to emphasize that Spain lies west of the Euxine (Black) Sea. H criticizes the notion of the circumambient Ocean also in 2.21 and 23, and 4.36 (cf. 3.115); the criticism is perhaps directed at Hecataeus. The snake-lady (9) perhaps owes something to Hesiod (*Theogony* 297 ff.), but there are also Scythian representations of a goddess with snake legs and snakes protruding from her shoulders. Her confident bluntness and easy ways with Heracles' property in H's story anticipate the behaviour of the Amazons who later become founding mothers of the Sauromatae (4.110–17).

4.11–12 For the Massagetae, see 1.201. The Araxes cannot be clearly identified; it is perhaps the Volga. According to A. Ivantchik, the Cimmerians were also probably, like the Scythians, in origin an Iranian people; the Tyras, near which the royal Cimmerians are buried, is the modern Dniester. Judging from archaeological remains, the Cimmerians inhabited Ukraine, south Russia, and the north Caucasus. See also n. 1.6–92.

4.13–16 If Aristeas is a historical figure, he probably lived in the sixth century BCE, *pace* H who places him more than 240 years before his own time. Aristeas' home, Proconnesus, was an island in the Propontis. The fragments of his hexameter poem, the *Arimaspea*, that survive are a mixture of tales from Ionian geographical exploration and fable. H seems to think of the Issedones as a real people living far east and north of the Scythians near the Massagetae (1.201, 4.25–7, 32), but they do not come into the account of Darius' Scythian campaign. Some have seen in Aristeas and other figures mentioned in Book 4 echoes of shamanistic practices (cf. Abaris in 4.36, the *enareis* in 1.105 and 4.67, Salmoxis and Pythagoras in 4.94–6). Metapontum (15) was a Pythagorean community in the Gulf of Tarentum in southern Italy close to Thurii, and H may have heard the story of Aristeas' reappearance there. The story of Aristeas is a pendant that wraps up the mythic/historic account of Scythian origins; at the end of 4.16 H launches into a survey of the real peoples north of the Black or Euxine Sea.

4.17–36 This is the first of several narratives that catalogue the vast lands in which the Scythians and their neighbours live; H takes up the rivers again more systematically in 4.47–58, the shape and distances of Scythia in 4.99–101, and the various outlying peoples in 4.102–17.

4.17–27 A survey of land and peoples. H here begins not at the Ister, the most westerly point of the later narrative, but where the Scythian land begins, near the Greek coastal trading town of Olbia/Borysthenes on the Hypanis (Bug). From there he arranges his narrative much like a *periplous* or Greek travel narrative; he moves east and north clockwise around the north shore of the Euxine (Black) Sea, describing each river in turn and describing each people one would encounter moving upstream as far as one can go, before moving on to the next river eastward. The Hypanis (Bug), the Borysthenes (Dnieper), and the Tanaïs (Don) are the major identifiable rivers; the Gerrhus and the Panticapes do not seem to match current rivers in

the area. This may be due to error (is the Panticapes the Ingul, on
the other bank of the Borysthenes? is the Gerrhus merely a part
of the Borysthenes?) or to changes in the terrain. The territory of the
Royal Scythians (20) stretches from the steppe east of the Dnieper
to the Donets and some parts of the Don (Tanaïs), as well as the
Crimean Steppe. The steppe as a whole stretches about 4,350 miles
(6,960 km.), from the foot of the Carpathian mountains east to
Mongolia.

For a matching of H's descriptions with the cultures unearthed in
Soviet archaeological investigations of lower Ukraine, see *CAH* iii/2.
573-90; the problem is complicated by the migratory habits of the
populations involved, the conservatism of the Scythian lower classes
that sometimes makes dating of artefacts difficult, and clear evidence
(judging from artefacts and skeletal remains) of mixing and blending of different population groups at different times. Both long- and
round-skulled Europid skeletons have been found and, in greater
numbers moving east, Mongoloid skeletons as well, sometimes as
part of the same family group. Human bones have been found mixed
with animal bones and kitchen refuse in the area east of the middle
Dnieper where H puts the *Androphagoi* or Cannibals (18; cf. 4.106).
The fourteen days' journey from the Panticapes to the Gerrhus in
ch. 19 cannot be reconciled with the ten days altogether from the
Borysthenes to Lake Maeetis in 4.101; Legrand thinks it should
perhaps be 'four' instead. From ch. 22 H moves off north and eastwards, perhaps reflecting an ancient trading-route, and the stories
become increasingly improbable; H reassures us (24) that he is
reporting accounts he has heard. In ch. 25 he is much less sanguine
about the possibility that real information is being conveyed but
nevertheless reports what he has been told. The Argippaei (23) may
be a Mongolian people; the Kalmucks call a similar drink 'atschi'.
H shows no clear knowledge of the Urals or the Volga.

4.28-31 The climate of the steppes is for a Greek worth mentioning. There
is in fact a hot, dry period in July and August, when the steppes dry
up, but by late August fog and rain have begun again, and the winter
lasts from late October until March. For another Greek's dismayed
account of the steppes and their effect on Scythian physiognomy, cf.
the Hippocratic *Airs, Waters, Places* 19. Skeletons of hornless cattle
have indeed been found in Scythian graves, probably introduced
from the East, although H's account of the cause is of course incorrect; the Homeric verse is *Odyssey* 4.85. Plutarch (*Moralia* 303b)
confirms the absence of mules in Elis, due (he says) to an ancient
curse from King Oenomaus. Ch. 30 is a valuable indication of H's
desire to attach as much information as he can to his ongoing
account, whether or not it is strictly relevant. In ch. 31 H explains
the mysterious 'feathers' of ch. 7.

4.32-6 With the journey of the Hyperboreans, legendary Apollo-
worshippers from the far north, H may be recalling early archaic

trade routes of amber from the Baltic, or grain from the Pontic regions. Delos (33), along with Delphi, is one of the two most important Greek cult centres for the worship of Apollo; cf. 1.64 for its sixth-century purification by Pisistratus (*CAH* iii/1. 769–70). Olen (35) is a name connected with early cult hymns, like Musaeus, Orpheus, Melampus, Pamphos; others call him too a Hyperborean. Abaris the Hyperborean (36), the Greek Aristeas (4.13), and the Thracian Salmoxis (4.95) are all later connected with the Pythagorean tradition. See n. 4.94–6.

4.36 As in 2.21, 23, and 4.8, the notion of an all-encircling Ocean is attacked. (Both the maps of Anaximander and Hecataeus (*FGH* 1, frs. 36, 18, 302) had included it, Lloyd, i. 129.) Here H goes further and promises a description of the known world that is not based on a theoretical symmetry but on the observed relationship of land masses.

4.37–45 H tries to lay out the world as an irregular set of contiguous land masses, like a large jigsaw puzzle with five pieces. The first and central piece (37), a rectangle longer (north–south) than it is wide (east–west), consists of the territory of four peoples, moving bottom to top (south to north): the Persians, the Medes, the Saspeires, and the Colchians. This column represents the block of land from the Persian Gulf northward to the area south of the Caucasus.

He grafts to the top-left side of this column an irregular, horizontal, long piece extending west, and to the bottom-left side he grafts another, even longer and more irregular roughly horizontal piece also extending west, so the whole looks like an irregularly shaped backwards C with the south-eastern corner of the Mediterranean lying between its two arms. The top or more northerly of these two horizontal pieces roughly comprises our idea of Asia Minor (38). The bottom, longer piece (39) heads west from Persia to include Assyria and Arabia west as far as the Arabian Gulf (our Red Sea) but also includes Phoenicia and the Levantine coast. This is where Asia ends, but to H's thinking (41) this lower peninsula continues down into Egypt (where it narrows), and finally Libya (where it broadens out again).

A fourth piece of the puzzle (40) stretches off to the right (east) of the original (Persian) piece to India, with what he calls the Red Sea (here the Indian Ocean) forming its southern border. This is of course part of Asia. Finally (42), up on top or north of the original piece, stretching from an unidentified eastern boundary to the Pillars of Heracles in the extreme west, lies what H calls Europe. H's notion of Europe included much of what we think of as northern or northwestern Asia.

The excursus on Phoenician, Persian, and Carian geographical explorations (42–4) seems designed principally to prove Europe the greatest mass of land, since both Libya and East Asia have been circumnavigated, and Europe has not. In the process of disbelieving what he has been told, H gives us a clear indication that the

Phoenicians probably did sail around Africa, since they claim to have
had the sun on their right while sailing west around the bottom of
'Libya', what we call the Cape of Good Hope (42).

The Persian Sataspes, who rapes Zopyrus' daughter (43) is the
brother of Pharandates, the Persian whose concubine will be returned
to Cos by Pausanias after the battle of Plataea (9.76), and the cousin
of Xerxes and Mardonius. The woman Sataspes outrages is from a
family almost as powerful as his own; in H, Zopyrus achieves the
conquest of Babylon for Darius (3.153) and is the son of one of the
original seven conspirators, Megabyzus (3.81).

For Caspatyrus and Scylax's voyage (44), cf. 3.102; the Indus does
not flow eastwards. Scylax might have left from Pascapyrus (now
Peshawar) where the Kabul flows east into the Indus (CAH iv.
201–3), but there are also other candidates for his starting-point.
Some few fragments of his account of his voyage remain as well as
a later forgery; Caryanda is in Caria, north of Halicarnassus; cf. n.
5.117–21.

The whole description of the way the continents fit together is of
considerable interest; it has the same kind of associative logic behind
it as H's narrative style does, in which a number of different *logoi*
are arranged as pendants off one main *logos*—which is (like the original Persian land-block) not necessarily the biggest one. In 4.45 H
ends this geographical excursus by emphasizing the arbitrary and
culture-bound way human beings designate land masses. H comments on the oddness of naming Europe after a woman, Europa, who
was born in Tyre, was taken to Crete, and ended in Lycia with her
son Sarpedon (1.2, 173 and 4.147). This restates a theme introduced
at the very beginning of the *Histories*, the highly ambiguous connection that links countries and women from whom they take their
names (cf. n. 1.1). Both as a narrator and as a geographer H's priority is empirical, mapping, clarifying, and connecting up what he
has been given as data, rather than seeking to make a rationalized
and more systematic pattern from it. He inserts this geographical
overview of the earth as a whole into the Scythian narrative at the
point where the furthest northerly point of his knowledge has been
reached.

4.46   For Anacharsis, cf. n. 4.76–81. H sums up the people through whose
       territory Darius will march, and again introduces the central fact
       about the Scythians: they are nomads. How does one fight nomads?

4.47–58   H reverts to the subject of rivers (cf. 4.17–35), this time begin-
       ning from the Ister (Danube) at the extreme west shore of the Euxine
       (Black) Sea. He uses the same principle of organization as before,
       moving north–east around the north shore of the Euxine, this time
       treating each river in turn without including much on resident popu-
       lations. The thought that connects this river survey to 4.46 is prob-
       ably that the rivers create the grasslands that allow the Scythians to
       live as nomads off their herds; certainly in conclusion to the whole

narrative (58) he mentions the tendency of the grass to make the cattle bilious. (It is not clear from the Greek of ch. 58 whether dissection of dead animals is involved, or the observation of the orifices of living animals.) Apart from Heracles' footprint (4.82), the rivers themselves are Scythia's only remarkable natural feature (cf. n. 2.65–76). The Ister (49–50; cf. 2.33) does not of course rise in the extreme west of Europe; Aristotle (*Meteorologica* 350b) follows H here, although he makes 'Pyrene' no longer a city but a mountain (the Pyrenees). H is right that the Ister (Danube) does not flood in its lower reaches but he is (as in 2.24 for the Nile) wrong about the reasons. The flooding occurred farther upstream, in the Hungarian plains. In the rivers Carpis and Alpis (49) may be some echo of the Alps and the Carpathians, neither of which H overtly recognizes.

The Panticapes, Hypacris, and Gerrhus cannot be identified today. It is more puzzling that, after the fording of the Ister, not once do the rivers play a part in the actual narrative of Darius' invasion of Scythia that all this is designed to introduce (4.83–142).

4.59–75 Scythian customs. H seems only to describe the customs of the Royal Scythians and perhaps the nomad Scythians here; the tribes to the south-west are more agrarian and some of them farm and live in houses, a fact he here ignores. He describes the Scythians' gods (59), sacrifices (60–3), war (64–6), divination and oaths (67–70), and burial practices (71–5). The archaeological exploration of Ukraine over the last fifty years and more has largely substantiated H's picture of Scythian nomad culture.

4.59 H does not even implicitly criticize the Scythian gods; cf. 2.3. The most important god is Hestia (Tabiti), the goddess of the hearth, and the most powerful Scythian oath is the one taken 'by the king's hearth' (4.68). The list ends with Ares, the god of war, the only god to receive image, altar, or shrine in Scythia. (According to H, the Persians, another Iranian people, have no images, temples, or altars (1.131); the Egyptians, on the other hand, say that they invented these and gave them to the Greeks (2.4).)

4.60–3 Sacrifice among the Scythians is presented through a lens that assumes knowledge of normal, i.e. Greek, sacrificial customs (Hartog, 178–86). There are no fire, first-fruits, or libations, no consent of the victim, or cutting of the throat, and finally no setting apart of the portion for the gods, ceremonial consumption of the viscera, roasting of the meat, or distribution to the participants. The bones are burned when necessary, and the meat cooks inside the animal's own stomach; H's fascination with the tidiness of the 'self-cooking ox' (Hartog, 185) is comparable to his delight in Babylonian boats (1.194). The Scythians, like the Egyptians, avoid swine (2.47, 4.63).

4.64–6 Rolle (p. 64) comments: 'no other people in history have provided archaeologists with so many objects of weaponry as have the Scythians.' Scythian weapons include the composite bow, razor-sharp arrowheads with thorns attached, the lance, spear, axe, long and short sword, the miniature chain-flail, and the whip. The body armour is often metal, consisting of thousands of bronze or iron scales attached to a leather jerkin, and the shield can be worn on the back, with the arms left free for riding and shooting. The beheading of an enemy (cf. Tomyris the Massagete, 1.214) is a normal part of warfare, and the act of carrying about the severed enemy head by hand or fastened to the reins of one's horse is one of the scenes from daily life found depicted on Scythian cups and belts. *Aposkythizein*, 'to de-Scythianize', is the normal Greek term for scalping; in the excavated fortified settlement at Bel'sk there has been found a skull-cup 'workshop', with the cup-handles made from temple-bones. Some skulls found in the kurgans (burial-mounds) show the marks of scalping; one beautifully tattooed warrior buried ceremonially in a Pazyryk kurgan had had a scalp sewn back on his head, with horse-hair attached to it; perhaps his family had reclaimed his body after his death and scalping (Rolle, 83).

4.67–70 A similar divination by yarrow sticks is still practised in the East. The *enareis* (67) are perhaps connected with shamanism (cf. Lloyd, i. 78 and 1.105). The Scythian people as a whole is attached to the hearth of the king and there is an organic connection between the king's health and the honesty of his subjects (68; Hartog, 125–33). This means the Scythians are not able to understand the selfish concerns of the Ionian tyrants at the bridge (4.140) and in consequence dismiss them as merely servile (4.142).

4.71–5 The kurgans or burial-mounds that dot the Ukrainian and south Russian steppes and the forest steppes bear testimony to H's accuracy here. Sixth- and fifth-century royal tombs were as H describes, rectangular shafts between 33 and 49 feet deep (10–15 m.), within a raised mound above. Some later mounds are as high as a three-storey building, and the base of a mound can extend to a diameter of over 328 feet (100 m.). Branching off the central shaft inside the mound are the burial chambers. The mounds themselves are built out of cut sod with the surface grass attached, often brought to the site from a considerable distance (Rolle, 19, 22, 32). H is correct that buried with the dead king are large numbers of human retainers and animals, particularly horses; some tombs have been found with hundreds of horse skeletons schematically arranged around the central chamber. The elaborate and beautiful golden objects taken from the Scythian tombs and stored in the Hermitage Museum in St Petersburg have made the term 'Scythian gold' well known in the western world.

The forty days during which the royal corpse visits his realm is a traditional Indo-European length of time between death and burial (73); tents and rugs for the purifying cannabis (hemp) sweat-lodge and hemp-inhaling equipment have been found in the Pazyryk kurgans far to the east, in the Altai mountains (Rolle, 94). Cf. 1.202 for a similar though less elaborate custom among the Massagetae;

there the smoke is inhaled for amusement rather than hygiene or ritual purification.

4.76–81 Scythians and foreigners. H ends his account of the Scythian way of life with two stories, presumably both told by Tymnes, the deputy of Ariapithes, king of Scythia. Both show the Scythian dislike of Greek customs. Anacharsis eventually (though not expressly in H) becomes in some accounts one of the Seven Wise Men (cf. 4.46, n. 1.27) and is said to have held conversations with Solon. He is the uncle of Idanthyrsus, the king who replies to Darius (127). Scyles is the much later half-Greek son of Ariapithes, Tymnes' former employer. Both worship foreign gods (the Mother of the Gods, Dionysus); both are slain by their countrymen for doing so. Cyzicus (76), where Anacharsis first celebrated his rites, is the city of the Propontis where the story of Aristeas' initial resuscitation came from (14) and a great centre for the worship of Cybebe (the Mother of the Gods, n. 1.34); Olbia/Borysthenes (78) is the important Greek trading city at the mouth of the Hypanis (Bug) on the Euxine (Black) Sea. The variant version of the Anacharsis story complimenting the Lacedaemonians (77) is not to be taken very seriously. In this respect it is similar to the Greek version of the story of the Egyptian children's speech in 2.2; H implies that it misses the whole point of Anacharsis' life, that he was killed for consorting with Greeks and adopting Greek ways.

4.81–2 H finds the idea of population interesting as part of the Scythians' general elusiveness in their huge territory; in contrast, he does not report investigating the number of Egyptians. The peculiar simplicity and visual concreteness of the Scythian way of life is shown by their pointing at the giant bowl that embodies the number of Scythians; for the bowl itself, n. 1.51. Cf. the message they send Darius in 4.131, which they also refuse to decode. (For Pausanias (81), see n. 9.9–11, and for his stay at Byzantium after the Persian Wars, see *CAH* v. 46.)

4.83–4 Darius probably marches from Susa about 513 BCE, although this westward expedition against the Scythians cannot be dated or even confirmed from Persian records. Artabanus will also later advise his nephew, Xerxes, at much greater length, expressly referring to the advice given here (7.10–12, 15–18, 46–52). Oeobazus (84) is also paralleled in the Xerxes story by Pythias (7.27, 38); H implies in passing that Darius has paid assassins in his employ. Cf. the conclusion of the Deioces story, 1.100, Otanes' comments in 3.80, and Thrasybulus' advice described in 5.92.

4.85–6 For the 'wandering' rocks at the opening of the Euxine (Black) Sea, see *Odyssey* 12.61. Not surprisingly, given the lack of precise tools and standards of measurement, H's figures for the length and breadth of the Euxine, Bosporus, Propontis, and Hellespont are somewhat off; he tends to overestimate the speed of the sailing ship. The Euxine is c.700 miles long (1,120 km.) and c.300 miles wide

(480 km.); he exaggerates the width somewhat, but makes it about twice as long as it really is; cf. 2.6–7. The Bosporus he makes a little shorter than it is, the Propontis longer and wider. The Hellespont is 290 stades long (about 32 miles or 51 km.) rather than 400. For H's distances and measurements, see App. 2.

4.87–8 The pillars look like good circumstantial evidence that Darius at least made the expedition; the figures for his troops, however, are a conventional number and probably exaggerated (cf. 6.9 and 95, the battles of Lade and Marathon, also assigned six hundred Persian ships each). The relative permanence of the pontoon bridges at the Bosporus and the Ister suggest that Darius' real aim was the creation of new satrapies or parts of his empire to the west and the north rather than just an invasion in retribution for depredations a century earlier by the Scythians. H had probably seen Mandrocles' painting at Samos.

4.90–3 In Europe now, Darius subdues Thrace before marching with his army up to the Ister (Danube) to cross into Scythia; the Getae are the only Thracians who resist him, and they must therefore become part of his army (4.96).

4.94–6 The Hellespontine Greeks rationalize the Thracian Salmoxis as a slave and pupil of Pythagoras. Pythagoras, a contemporary of Polycrates of Samos, lived in the later sixth century BCE, obviously (as H points out) much later than Salmoxis; he migrated west to southern Italy, where he founded influential philosophical communities at Croton and Metapontum. This is the final reference in Book 4 to something like shamanistic practices, one of the remarkable things that fascinated H and that he considered it his duty to mention (cf. 4.13, 32–6, 67, and n. 2.65–76). It is not clear, however, that H considered Aristeas, Abaris, the Hyperboreans, and Salmoxis as aspects of a single phenomenon, or what he meant to imply by mentioning the Pythagorean connection. In the fourth century, Plato's *Charmides* 156d–158b depicts Socrates in conversation with a Thracian physician who calls Salmoxis his king and god and practises a form of psychosomatic healing.

4.97–8 It is not usually possible to discern H's source for a particular story, but here and at the end of the bridge story (4.133, 136–42) we can safely claim a Greek contribution. Darius is not inexperienced in fighting nomads from the East; he had fought and subdued the eastern Sacae in c.519 BCE (they fight as part of the Persian army at Marathon in 490 (6.113)). Given this experience, it is most unlikely that in 513 Darius, a skilled and seasoned campaigner, leaves his supply lines and return route untended; it is almost as unlikely that he has recourse to the primitive system of a knotted leather strap to count off the days until his return, or tells the Ionians to disband after sixty days.

Coës does later receive from Darius the tyranny of Mytilene but is killed by the Mytileneans (5.37–8). In the story of the bridge as a whole the Ionians play an unlikely central role in determining Darius' overall strategy; see also n. 4.133-42 below for Miltiades the Athenian, and nn. 5.23-4, 5.105-7, 5.124-6, 6.1-5, 6.26-30 for Histiaeus the Milesian.

4.99-101 H measures off Scythia, making it a square of twenty days' march on each side. The left side and top are inland; the bottom and the right side are both coastlines. He makes the Ister (Danube) come down to the north shore of the Euxine (Black) Sea from the north (forming the western border), he gives the Sea of Azov a long, straight coastline running north–south, and he has no understanding of how the Crimea is shaped. He visualizes the Crimea as simply the lower right-hand corner of the big square, and comments how odd it is that the triangle comprising that corner is inhabited by the non-Scythian Taurians—as though some foreign people inhabited Cape Sunium in Attica, or the heel of Italy (99). The double comparison suggests both the scope of H's own geographical imagination and its necessary limitations—regional maps did not yet exist that might have shown how different the Crimea, Sunium, and southeast Italy looked (for Anaximander's famous map, see n. 4.36 and the bottom of n. 5.49-51). This part of H's *Histories* might have been delivered orally in both southern Italy and Athens. The principles on which this picture is constructed do not seem to be the same as those of the previous geographical descriptions of Scythia in 4.17-27 and 47-58; those are constructed around the observed course of the rivers (cf. the very different course of the Ister in 4.49-50) and this is instead a schematic overview, perhaps taken from an earlier written source.

4.102-9 The Scythians decide to ask neighbouring tribes for help (cf. 7.144 f.), so H describes them, beginning with the Taurians who inhabit the Crimea, and then the others, who mostly live north of Scythia proper, beginning again in the west and moving east. The locations of the Neurians, Cannibals, Black Cloaks, Sauromatae, and Budinians have been mentioned in H's first geographical description (4.17, 18, 20, 21), those of the Agathyrsians, Neurians, and Sauromatae in the second (4.49, 51, 57). Euripides' *Iphigenia in Tauris* later makes use of a version of the story H tells about the religion of the Taurians (103). Concerning the Neurian werewolves (105), A. Ivantchik comments that the idea of bands of warriors as savage dogs or wolves was an old and widespread Indo-European notion that was particularly important to the Scythians and their descendants, the Ossetes. As mentioned above (n. 4.17-27), east of the middle Dnieper, where H puts the Cannibals (106), human bones have been found mixed with animal bones and kitchen refuse. Gelonus, the city of the Budinians (108), may be one of the hundred or more fortified settlements found in the forest steppe region, the largest of which is at Bel'sk (Rolle, 117; Bel'sk, however, is on a tributary of the Dnieper, not beyond the Don, where H puts the Budinians); the wooden ram-

parts are 20½ miles (32.8 km.) long, in the form of an irregular triangle. Darius burns Gelonus down (4.123).

4.110–17 The Amazons are a foreign band of warrior women who appear
regularly in Greek myth. They are the ancestresses of the Sauromatae, who appear at the end of H's list of the Scythians' neighbours,
and whose half-Amazon origins H relates, again developing his interest in the blending of cultures through marriage (nn. 1.1, 3.159). The
Sauromatae are the eastern neighbours of the Royal Scythians.
According to Rolle (p. 88), graves of women warriors are found
throughout the steppe region. They are buried with armour and
weapons, and the skeletons bear evidence of wounds taken in battle.
In Sauromatia, the region of the lower Volga, 20 per cent of graves
containing weapons and harness are those of women, but sizeable
numbers have been found in western Scythia as well.

4.118–20 The narrative resumes from 4.102, and the Scythians decide on
a strategy; a number of their hoped-for allies reject them. Cf. 7.144,
148, 157, 168, 169, 172—the Greek neutrals in 480 BCE are both
less honest and more variously resourceful in their explanations than
the neighbours of the Scythians. The strategy of retreat, for which
the Scythians become so famous (4.46), is here presented as a counsel
of desperation. The Tanaïs (Don; ch. 120) comes in from the north
to the northern tip of the Maeetian Lake (Sea of Azov), and it and
its tributaries roughly form the eastern border of Scythia; the Scythians intend to draw Darius to the extreme north and east of their
territory.

4.121–32 The campaign proper: Persian aggression. H makes it about two
months total in length, but the giant loop north and east and then
back to the Ister again covered by Darius was more than 2,000 miles
(3,200 km.) in all, and for an army consisting of both horse and foot
surely more like three months was required, *CAH* iv. 242. Darius
and his army march east from the Danube all the way to the Don,
north and east of the Sea of Azov. The four rivers in 123 have not
clearly been identified; they may be tributaries of the Don or the
Volga (which flows into the Caspian Sea but at its westernmost bend
is *c*.50 miles (80 km.) from the Don). The eight forts (124) have not
been identified, and scholars generally doubt that Darius built them;
perhaps they were earlier kurgans, or funeral mounds, on the banks
of the Volga.

  The Scythians loop back into Scythia (124), and Darius pursues
them westwards all the way to the land of the Agathyrsians, north
of the Ister, and then back through the land of the Neurians (north
and east of the upper Tyras (Dniester)) and back into Scythia
proper (125). Finally Idanthyrsus gives Darius a rationale for the
puzzling behaviour of the Scythians (127); cf. the retort of Demaratus to Xerxes (7.102 and 209), that of Tomyris to Cyrus (1.206),
that of the two Spartan heralds to Hydarnes (7.135)—even, a little
further afield, that of Astyages to Harpagus (1.129). Here as elsewhere H enjoys showing the incommensurability of different people's

basic assumptions. The thought here is very similar to the one expressed more gnomically in 4.197: 'Most of them are not now and were not then concerned in the slightest about the Persian king.' Darius has encountered a people he cannot control with the threat of arms, because he cannot hold their towns and families hostage. Darius' wishful thinking affects his common sense in ch. 132; he finally realizes this when he sees the Scythians chase off after the hare.

In Moscow in 1812, Napoleon is supposed to have exclaimed in horror, 'Quels hommes! Ce sont des Scythes!' as he watched the Muscovites burning down their own city. The looming threat of an intolerable winter without normal housing was an implicit but important part of both the Scythian and the later Russian strategy to force the invader's withdrawal. Notice how ch. 129 makes a brief cross-reference back to 4.29; the long ethnographic survey has been designed to underlie and support the narrative of the Persian campaign, even if they look like two completely discrete narratives.

4.133–42 The campaign: Scythian countermoves. Here the division of Scythians sent to the Ionians left at the Ister (4.98) make their approach and are rebuffed (137) but also deceived (140). Cf. the Scythians' own feeling of organic attachment between king and people (4.68) and H's interest in the incommensurability of different people's assumptions commented on just above. According to H's narrative, Darius does not realize until the end of ch. 140 the degree to which his fate has been left in the hands of the Ionians; this is an echo of a theme developed in Book 3, where relatively marginal actors in affairs effect large changes; cf. n. 3.129–38.

Ch. 137 is the first appearance in the *Histories* of the adventurous Athenian and tyrant of the Hellespontine Chersonese, Miltiades the younger. Miltiades' advice to the other tyrants to accept the Scythian offer was almost certainly invented years after the fact (perhaps in Athens?), because otherwise Darius would not have left him in place after the Scythian campaign, as he seems to have done; cf. 6.39–41 for his story. Miltiades will later play a decisive role as one of the ten Athenian generals at Marathon (6.109), and will come to grief after a dubious conquest of Paros (6.136). His son, Cimon, becomes a famous Athenian politician and general of the early fifth century, and the historian Thucydides is almost certainly a later collateral member of the same family.

The consequences of Darius' decision to reward Histiaeus of Miletus for his role in Scythia (5.11, 23, 35) are not particularly emphasized here, but H makes it clear later that they will play a large part in Histiaeus' decision to help foment the Ionian revolt (the narrative of Books 5 and 6).

4.143–4 Megabazus is left behind (cf. 5.1, 10, 12) as Darius returns to Asia. Cf. the role of Mardonius later (8.115), although Megabazus is much more successful in subduing the Thracians c.513 BCE than Mardonius will be in Greece in 479 (*CAH* iv. 67–8).

4.145–205 The story of Cyrene and Libya. The basic structure is much like that of the Scythian narrative: H begins with an announced Persian expedition, then spends a great deal of time describing the people and land against whom the expedition is sent; the actual Persian expedition is recounted briefly at the end (200–4, with 205 as a pendant). Here, however, the population against which the Persians march is Greek. In the story of Cyrene we see a Greek colony in Africa negotiating relations with other Greek cities and drawing on the powers of Egypt and Persia when convenient. At the end, Darius' army in Egypt is called on to prosecute the vengeful designs of an angry Greek queen mother, whom the gods punish for her excessiveness (205). That is, whereas the Scythians successfully band together against the Persians, the Greeks' dissensions among themselves draw Persian attention to Cyrene and Barca (c.512 BCE) and bring about the eventual treacherous and bloody downfall of Barca, with the population dispersed to Bactria in Central Asia. This episode provides a fitting transition between the Scythian narrative and the story of the Ionian revolt to come in Books 5 and 6, since it is a foretaste of what Persian imperial power can do to a Greek population.

H's decision at this point to focus on North Africa and the founding of Cyrene is of enormous value for our understanding of the process of Greek colonization. For H's views on Libya as a continent, cf. 4.42.

4.145–53 The prehistory of Cyrene: the founding of Thera and the Theran version of the founding of Cyrene.

4.145–6 In myth, Jason and the Argonauts helpfully repopulated Lemnos after the murder of its men by the women; the sons of Tyndareus from Sparta, the twin brothers of Helen of Troy, were among the Argonauts (see also 5.75, 6.127, and 9.73). For the later story of Lemnos, and the abduction of Athenian women by Pelasgians who had by then expelled the Minyans and settled Lemnos themselves, see 6.137. For Pelasgians, see n. 1.56–7.

4.147–8 Thera, modern Santorini, was in fact founded from Lacedaemon, probably in the tenth century BCE. (The much earlier culture, perhaps Minoan, had been destroyed in a volcanic eruption c.1500 BCE). According to the mythic genealogy used by H, Theras, the founder of Thera, is the brother-in-law of that Aristodamus, the great-great-grandson of Heracles, who led the Spartans back to the southern Peloponnese (in the 'return of the children of Heracles', 6.52, 9.26; cf. n. 8.133–44), and thus he is the maternal uncle of the twins who begin the Spartan royal line. The mythic genealogy used here is in approximate agreement with the genealogies of 5.59 and 6.52. For Cadmus and his sister Europa as peripatetic Phoenicians see n. 1.56–7. Theras and his sister are Cadmeans descended from Oedipus' son Polynices, a fact which mythically helped explain the rivalry of the two royal families of Sparta in the historical period (cf. 6.52). Note that Theras (148) intends in Calliste or Fair Isle to make the same claim that the Minyans have just made in Sparta, that as distant family he has the right to settle. The six towns settled by the Minyans who do not sail with Theras are located in the north-west Peloponnese.

4.149 The Aegeidae were a famous Dorian clan who held the priesthood of Apollo Carneus, with branches in Boeotia, Sparta, Thera, Acragas, and Cyrene (*CAH* iii/1. 737); the Theban poet Pindar claimed descent from them (*Pythian Odes* 5.75-6).

4.150-3 The Theran version of the founding of Cyrene, *c.*630 BCE. Here the Theran paternity of Battus is emphasized, while, in the version from Cyrene that follows, his maternal descent is more important; like Archilochus on Paros, Battus is the son of a concubine and a member of the local aristocracy. (Euphemus, from whom Battus' Theran ancestors are descended via the Minyans of Lemnos, was for Pindar (*Pythian Odes* 4.23 ff.) the particular mythic Argonaut to whom land in Libya had been promised; cf. 4.179, where he is not specifically identified.) The drought on Thera (151) seems to have happened around 640 BCE. Both the version from Thera and the version from Cyrene below make clear how difficult and risk-filled it actually was to found a successful colony; cf. 1.164-7 and 5.42-8. For a general description of Greek colonization in the archaic period, see *CAH* iii/3. ch. 37.

4.152 For Colaeus of Samos and Sostratus of Aegina as vastly successful Greek traders, see *CAH* iii/3. 20 and 428, and iv. 364-5 and 456-8. Colaeus journeyed to Spain *c.*638-6 BCE, and H would have seen his dedication in the temple of Hera at Samos. In recent years a stone anchor dedicated by Sostratus *c.*500 BCE has been found in the Greek sanctuary at Gravisca, the port of Tarquinia; the first letters of his name also occur on late sixth-century Attic pots found extensively in Etruria. Sostratus' prominence as a sixth-century trader is the kind of odd fact, not part of the literary tradition, that H sometimes preserves and that we unexpectedly later find independent confirmation for; it should give pause to those who claim that the *Histories* are a tissue of pure invention by H himself.

4.153 A fourth-century inscription from Cyrene claims to transmit the original settlement decree passed in the seventh century at Thera (M-L, 5, and Fornara, 18).

4.154-64 The history of Cyrene from the reign of Battus I (*c.*632 BCE, according to Eusebius), down to that of his great-great-great grandson, Arcesilaus III (*c.*525-520 BCE); cf. *CAH* iii/3. 134-8. As the oracle (163) implies, Cyrene had four kings named Battus, alternating with four named Arcesilaus (*c.*630-*c.*440); Pheretime (162) is the wife of Battus III, the mother of Arcesilaus III, and the grandmother of Battus IV.

Cyrene owed its great prosperity to the export of natural resources, in particular silphium (4.169), a plant perhaps connected to the modern asafoetida but extinct already in the Roman imperial period; it was valued in the ancient world for its medicinal properties. Cyrene was also famous for its horses. Battus II, the Prosperous, seems to have invited settlers in from Greece, c.580 (159); this created the strains with the local Libyan population that led to the battle at Irasa, c.570. H has already mentioned that Apries' massive loss of Egyptian troops against Cyrene was in large part responsible for the disaffection of the army that led to Apries' downfall; in 2.161 he explicitly sends the reader ahead to this passage.

Note that dissension in the royal family of Cyrene is responsible for the foundation of Barca, probably before the middle of the sixth century (160), and civic dissension of various kinds leads to the decision to call upon outside powers, Greek, Egyptian, and Persian (2.181, 4.161, 162-3, 165). In 3.91 both Cyrene and Barca are included in the survey of tribute-paying parts of the Persian empire under Darius.

Demonax (161) is one of a number of sixth-century adjudicators and lawgivers; cf. the more famous (much earlier or mythic) Lycurgus (1.65), Solon (1.29), Periander (5.95), and also the anonymous Parians in Miletus (5.28-9). (For the origins of the institution in the seventh-century Greek colonies of the western Mediterranean, see CAH iii/3. 236.) The Delphic oracle in 163 was surely produced after the fall of Arcesilaus IV, the last Battiad in Cyrene, c.440 BCE.

4.165-7 Aryandes was the satrap placed in charge in Egypt when Cambyses left to quell the revolt at home in 522 BCE (3.64). Aryandes was deposed by Darius, probably in about 496 (CAH iv. 64-5, 266). This narrative is resumed in 4.200. For the 'daric', see App. 2.

4.168-99 The formal pretext for this long excursus on Libya is H's statement at the end of 4.167 that in aiding Pheretime the Persians actually hoped to subdue Libya. Like the description of Scythia in the first half of Book 4, the Libyan chapters come as a series of smaller essays that have not been entirely integrated with one another. The backbone of the account is the survey of Libyan peoples from east to west (cf. H's description of Scythia, n. 4.17-27), from the Egyptian border (168) to beyond the Pillars of Heracles (196). This account, however, is split into two halves, 168-80 and 191-6 (cf. the account of the history of Cyrene, just above, interrupted for this narrative and resumed in 4.200, or the description of Babylon, split between 1.178-87 and 192-200). In the description of Libya H takes his main account westwards to Lake Tritonis (perhaps a little west of where the border between Tunisia and Libya is today, though the lake cannot now be identified). There (180) two smaller narratives are inserted. First H describes a chain of oases that, he claims, stretch from east to west all the way across the continent, at more or less regular intervals of ten days' journey each, south of the coastal region previously described (181-5). Next he launches into a more general description of nomad Libyan mores (186-90), presumably because

Lake Tritonis marks in his opinion the end of nomad Libya and the beginning of cultivated Libya.

At ch. 191 he resumes the second or western half of the survey of Libyan peoples. He integrates into this description of Libya's more westerly parts a description of the animals in Libya (191–2) and detailed descriptions of five western Libyan peoples, only three of whom are named. H concludes this account with some general observations on the fertility of the region of Cinyps and of Cyrene's harvests. The whole passage begins (167) and ends (197) ring-composition style, with the thought that at the time that the narrative concerns, most Libyans neither knew nor cared at all about Darius king of Persia.

Like the descriptions of Egypt in Book 2 and Scythia in the first part of Book 4, this passage offers us a chance to observe H at work as a naturalist, geographer, and ethnographer. For Libya he draws more on the reports of others than on his own observations, and it is clear that his information came from a variety of sources; Hecataeus was probably one of them. As usual, H's basic geographical assumptions show a tendency to over-schematization, especially in describing the chain of oases in chs. 181–5 (which he does not name as such; 'Oasis' is used once, as a proper noun, in 3.26). The oases really begin on the latitude of Memphis, not Thebes, and H has clearly not seen them. H does not recognize the unevenness of the North African coast or the extent of the Syrtis, and has no notion of sub-Saharan Africa. He largely presupposes here the reader's familiarity with the geographical descriptions already set out in 2.28–34 and 4.37–45: 'Libya' (Africa) is longer east–west than it is north–south, is smaller than Europe, and surrounded by seas, and the Nile is assumed to run from its extreme west towards the east until, in Egypt, it bends sharply north and heads towards the coast. It is odd that the Nile does not come into the geographical description of Libya in Book 4.

It is also puzzling that Carthage is omitted from this description, although H uses Carthaginians as sources for Libyan material (explicitly in 4.43, 195–6); see *CAH* iii/2. 490–8. No Lake Tritonis or River Triton (178, 186) can now be found where H indicates they should be; they were either entirely mythological (cf. Pindar, *Pythian Odes* 4.20) or a phenomenon of the shifting coastline of the western Syrtis. H does not actually say he has been to Cyrene, and is vague in his description of the surrounding region. Some of the names of tribes are either doublets (Atlantes, Atarantes of ch. 184), confused with each other (the Garamantes of ch. 174 are not the same people as those of ch. 183, based on H's own description), or otherwise nicknamed or unknown (ch. 169, the Giligamae; ch. 177, the 'Lotus-eaters'); most of the others are mentioned by other ancient writers on Libya. Much of the ethnographic description is no doubt accurate, although also subject to Greek interpretations of what was seen and reported. The oracle of chs. 178–9 was clearly circulated by sixth-century Sparta to encourage the colonization of Libya by Greeks; the story of the tripod was invented to explain why the colonization did not take hold.

4.200–5 This is the continuation of the story of Pheretime and the Persian expedition to Barca (4.167); H has made it contemporaneous with Megabazus' reduction of Thrace (4.145), that is, *c*.512–510 BCE.

4.201 H thinks it relevant to report people ruthlessly juggling with conventions of oath-taking and religious practice; cf. 1.160, 4.154, 5.71. Cleomenes the king of Sparta is notorious for his creative behaviour in this realm: 6.66, 75, 76, 79, 82; his co-conspirator against Demaratus, Leotychidas, gives a long speech on the subject of keeping one's word and respecting one's oaths in 6.86. H often, as here, reports the breaking of the oath or promise without much comment on its morals.

4.203 Not much credence is given to this tale as history; more likely, Cyrene was firmly under Darius' sovereignty in the 510s but by H's day found it politic to downplay the fact.

4.204 Euesperides has been mentioned in 4.171; it will later be renamed Berenice by Ptolemy III, *c*.246 BCE, whence the modern Libyan name of Benghazi. For conquered people transplanted by Darius, see n. 3.149; a threatened transplant occurs in 6.3.

4.205 *Tisis*, the gods' repayment for human excess, is the focus of this pendant. H plays with the term since he does not mention *tisis* itself here, but uses the participial form *tisamenē*, 'having taken revenge'; by taking excessive revenge, Pheretime has usurped the gods' function. See nn. 1.8, 1.91, 3.127–8, and Lateiner, 141–3, 193–5, 203–4.

BOOKS FIVE AND SIX

In Books 5 and 6, the narrative begins to focus on the Greek world, although it is still structured as an account of Persian expansion. Darius the imperialist turns his sights in dead earnest on the north-west corner of his kingdom, in his desire to expand into Europe. The basic outline of these two books (certainly in H's mind one single stretch of narrative) is quite simple. It comes in three stages. First Darius' henchmen subdue Thrace and generally try to establish Persian supremacy over the area around the Hellespont (5.1–27; c.513–510 BCE). Then Aristagoras, cousin and son-in-law of Histiaeus the tyrant of Miletus, who has been left in charge while Histiaeus is away in Susa, inveigles Artaphrenes, the local Persian satrap, into trying to conquer the island of Naxos in the Cyclades (Ionia itself has been under foreign domination since its conquest by Croesus, 1.26). The attempt to take Naxos fails, and Aristagoras, rather than account to his superiors, mounts a rebellion against Persia, and virtually all the Ionians and many of their neighbours join in. The campaign lasts six years (5.28–6.42; 499–494 BCE), and at its disastrous conclusion the great cultural efflorescence of Ionia that has defined the most advanced trade, art, and politics of the Greek seventh and sixth centuries has come to an end; Miletus for instance, one of the most powerful cities in the eastern Mediterranean, will become henceforth a sleepy, backwater town. After the battle of Lade (494 BCE) some of the population of Ionia is enslaved; Greek boys are castrated and girls sent in slavery east (6.9, 32). The third portion of this narrative (hard to separate cleanly from the narrative of the revolt proper) involves mop-up operations in the northern Aegean on the Persian side and the flight of the Athenian Miltiades back to Athens just in time to mount an Athenian resistance to Persia at Marathon. Book 6 ends with Miltiades' death (489 BCE) and earlier exploits gaining Lemnos for Athens (490s?).

If H was himself writing in the 440s, the battle of Lade was about as far removed from his own day as the conclusion of the Second World War is from the late 1990s. Men of H's father's and grandfather's generation vividly recalled the Ionian revolt; H was undoubtedly able to talk to survivors of this terrible six-year effort to resist Persian imperial domination. The descriptions of individual moments in these books capture some of that eyewitness immediacy, as far as times of day, details of the battles, and so on are concerned, but, perhaps because H's informants were not themselves high up in the chain of command (they would have been young soldiers and sailors at the time), there remains a certain frustrating vagueness about Greek strategic and tactical decisions, compared with the narrative of Books 7 to 9.

Up to this point in the *Histories* the Greek world has always been a matter for the margins, parenthetical remarks or small essays inserted into the larger narrative; the main focus of the narrative has alternated between Persian aggression and an ethnographic approach to whichever people H shows the Persians to be attacking. But now the new people being attacked are Greeks; from 5.27 on the rest of the *Histories* will mostly consist of an account of Persian–Greek hostilites. H takes for granted that many things about the Greeks are already known to his Greek audience, although he does add local information about Ionia that a Greek from, say, southern Italy might not know. This makes the narrative of these later books more rapid but also sometimes a little harder to follow, since he is assuming a more intense and educated interest on his audience's part about the matters being narrated.

What also makes the narrative bones of 5 and 6 somewhat harder to perceive is the enormous amount of additional background material inserted into the main story and the rapidity with which the narrative focus switches back and forth between two or more scenes. In the first stage (5.1–27), Darius' activities in the Hellespont, the scene alternates between activities at the front and Darius' own activities at Sardis and Susa. In the second, longest, stretch, the revolt proper, we follow Aristagoras of Miletus to Sparta and Athens asking for help against Persia; in each place H pauses to give extensive background on local developments. (The Athenian narrative, 5.55–96, is our first and most detailed account of the beginning of Athenian democracy under Cleisthenes in 508/7 BCE.) When he turns to narrating the campaigns of the revolt itself, H alternates between events on the Aegean coast and those in Cyprus, much further south and east. In the last section (6.34–140), the story of Miltiades begins and ends the account, but within it occurs a long excursus on Aeginetan–Athenian enmity (6.49–93) leading to a discussion of (among many other things) the career of King Cleomenes of Sparta. It is designed in part to show why some of the most important Greek cities acted as they did in the years between the Ionian revolt (499–494 BCE) and the Persian invasion of mainland Greece (480 BCE).

5.1–10 Megabazus and the Thracians. Darius' army has first crossed the Hellespont to the northern Aegean region of Thrace on the way to Scythia (4.89–93), and on his return to Persia he has left the excellent Megabazus behind with 80,000 men to consolidate his control of the region (4.143–4). Megabazus' sons also play an active part in Darius' and Xerxes' armies (5.21, 6.33, 7.22, 67). For historical background on Thrace and Thracians, see *CAH* iii/2. 591–618; for the question of how much European territory Darius controlled by 510 BCE, see *CAH* iv. 243–53. The Persian presence on the northern Aegean coastline in the late sixth and early fifth centuries considerably shifted the balance of power among local tribes and certainly benefited Macedonia.

5.1 H does not always point the moral when wrongdoing leads to divine retribution (cf. nn. 1.8, 4.205); the story of the Perinthians and Paeonians implicitly serves as background explanation for Darius' outrageous treatment of the Paeonians in 5.12–15 (the Paeonians live in the upper valleys of the Strymon and Axius rivers). In the *Iliad*, resolution by duel is common (*Iliad* 3.15 ff., 7.22 ff.); for another resolution of crisis by limited combat in H, cf. 1.82. Exoticism is added here by the use of animals (cf. 3.32).

5.3 The Greeks were divided over what people was the most numerous; they were all quite clear that it was not Greek. (H himself also mentions Indians in 3.94.) Nenci comments that Ctesias (*FGH* 3c, 688 fr. 45, 2) names Thracians; Thucydides (2.97), Scythians; the much later Pausanias (1.9.5), Celts.

5.4 The Getae have been described in 4.93–4, in the context of Darius' first invasion into the region. The evils of human life are a literary conceit; cf. *Iliad* 15.132, *Odyssey* 5.207, and Euripides' *Cresphontes*, fr. 449 Nauck. (Cf. n. 5.96–7 for another Homeric idea, the 'beginning of evils'.) 'Homerisms' dot the *Histories*; Longinus 13.3 calls H the 'most Homeric' of ancient writers.

5.7 The Thracian gods are even more limited in number than those in Scythia, 4.59.

5.9 The Ligyes (to the Romans, Ligurians) are the people of the region around Marseilles (Massalia); in 7.165 they help in the army of Terillus of Himera. Strabo (11.11.8) puts the 'Sigynnae' further east, in the region of the Caucasus, and Aristotle in the *Poetics* (1457[b]) uses 'sigynon' as an example of a word that is strange to Greeks but normal in Cyprus. For the Eneti (Veneti) cf. n. 1.196.

5.10 For another climatological improbability cf. n. 4.7; here, however, H does not rationalize the 'bees', which may be gnats or mosquitoes.

5.11 Myrcinus is in the region of Thrace where the Athenians will later found Amphipolis (Thucydides 4.102; cf. n. 5.124–6). Histiaeus' request (a reward for his actions in 4.137) may be a tacit recognition of how much the Persian/Phoenician conquests of the late sixth century have blocked traditional Ionian trade routes and opportunities for expansion in the southern and western Mediterranean. The story continues in 5.23.

5.12–15 There is an odd mixture of humour and horror in this story. The two brothers are almost a parody of a theme noticed before in the *Histories*, of ambitious underlings seeking personal advancement with the king (cf. n. 3.129–38). Here most in play is the incommensurability between the scope of Darius' plans and anything these two rustics from the Thraceward region can imagine. The fate of the Paeonians (15) resembles what happens to the Eretrians in the coming war (6.119), although Aristagoras will later give at least some of the unfortunate Paeonians a return to the coast (5.98). Cf. other removals of whole populations, n. 3.149.

5.16 For H's delight in other efficient and exotic ways of doing things, cf. for example the boats of 1.194 and the 'self-cooking ox' of 4.61. These are no doubt among the 'remarkable things' he has promised to report in the introductory paragraph to the *Histories*.

5.17–22 Most scholars are sceptical of this exciting tale, cf. *CAH* iv. 495–6. Macedonia prospered under Persian control, *CAH* iv. 246, 248–53, although it was found convenient in H's day to downplay this fact. Alexander himself may well have been H's informant; he ruled from *c*.498 to 454 BCE and was also a friend and patron to Athens (despite H's claims (22), he is not found on the official list of Olympic victors). He plays an active role in the Persian Wars of Books 7 to 9 (7.173, 8.140, 9.44.) As H promises in ch. 22, he later argues the Greek descent of the Macedonians (8.137–9); Thucydides (2.99) also accepts their claim to Argive ancestry, but Demosthenes (9.31) contests it. The demand for earth and water (18), signifying formal submission to Persia, was probably made within a few years of the Scythian expedition, *c*.510 BCE. Bubares (21) is still in royal favour as one of the two men in charge of the Athos project in 7.22. The whole episode shows the philomacedonism of H (cf. 7.173, 8.143, 9.44). Some reports say that H himself died at Pella, the capital of Macedonia.

5.23–4 Darius' decision to remove Histiaeus from Thrace and send him to Susa is one of the causes of the Ionian revolt; cf. 5.35 (cf. 5.106–7, 6.1–5, 26–30). As Book 3 shows extensively, part of the problem of empire is the way talented individuals are constrained by its structures and try in consequence to manipulate and even subvert its *raison d'être* (i.e. to provide basic stability and equity, cf. 1.96–100). Hence the advice Thrasybulus gives the young Periander in 5.92: to be a successful ruler, lop off the tallest ears of grain if you want things to go smoothly. The weakness of the system is the unspoken secret of the narrative of 3.80 ff.—everybody (or almost everybody) wants as much personal power as possible, and competent, energetic people are the hardest to keep subservient. From Darius down to Democedes the slave physician or Charilaus the madman, almost every actor in the *Histories* wants to have autonomy and opportunity for advancement for himself or herself and manipulates the system to get them; cf. n. 3.129–38.

5.25–7 The rapidity with which the Persians are establishing themselves in the northern Aegean is impressive and Aristagoras, Histiaeus' ambitious son-in-law (5.30), will try to exploit the process for his own purposes. For the Otanes of chs. 25–6 see n. 5.117–21; he is different from the Otanes of 3.80 and 3.144. For Pelasgians, cf. nn. 1.56–7 and 6.137–40. We do not know why the brother of Maeandrius (3.143) is placed in charge of Lemnos in the last decade of the sixth century; it suggests that some aspects of the earlier Samian story remain untold. Lemnos does not stay Persian; Miltiades takes it for Athens during the Ionian revolt or the years leading up to it, although H mentions this fact only in telling of Miltiades' later exploits and death (6.137, 140), *CAH* iv. 298. For Miltiades, cf. n. 4.137. In general, Otanes completes the conquest of the northern Aegean, which will stay Persian until the Ionian revolt begins in 499 BCE.

5.28–9 The prehistory of the Ionian revolt. A city at its acme, or height of prosperity, is in a dangerous position; cf. n. 3.57. Alone of the cities of Ionia, Miletus has preserved a measure of autonomy from before the time of Croesus' and Cyrus' initial conquests of the region *c.*546 BCE (1.22, 141, 169). For the beginning of evil mentioned in ch. 28 and restated in 5.30, cf. nn. 5.4, 5.96–7.

5.30–6.33 At this point the *Histories* largely abandon ethnography and begin to narrate a fairly continuous historical account of hostilities between Persia and the Greeks, having to do with the Persian imperial move westwards, *c.*499–479 BCE. Even though the Ionian revolt of Books 5 and 6 fails, its lessons will help us understand the narrative of the attempts of the mainland Greeks to mount a more successful defence against Xerxes in Books 7 to 9. Certainly the implications of the story H tells here—the consequences of disorganization and treachery, seen in the ruthless punishment Persians mete out afterwards to rebels—help organize our readerly perception of what the Greeks do right later and how acute the danger facing them in 481 BCE really was. The Ionian campaign shows how easily mainland Greece too could have fallen.

For a historical analysis of the revolt, see *CAH* iv. 68–9, and esp. 461–90. H narrates the Ionian revolt as a foolish and ill-organized catastrophe (and war is always worse than peace, 8.3), but the speed with which other states joined Aristagoras suggests that Aristagoras was only exploiting an already precarious situation, not creating it wholesale. See n. 5.37–8.

5.30–4 The attempt to subdue Naxos. H depicts Aristagoras as the evil genius of the narrative of the Ionian revolt; his arrival here in Sardis and then later in Sparta (5.49) and Athens (5.65) structures the whole plot of Books 5 and 6 as stemming from his self-interested machinations. Artaphrenes (usually called Artaphernes in modern scholarship) is Darius' brother and the satrap of Lydia (5.25). He will supervise the foiling of a plot to unseat him by Histiaeus, the suppression of the revolt, and the reorganization of Ionia afterwards (5.100, 123, 6.1–4, 30, 42). It is possible that an important part of the initial revolt was a regional contest between Sardis and the Ionians (who would get the spoils of Naxos?). *CAH* iv. 475 suggests that the reforms on Naxos leading to the exile of their 'men of substance' (30) may have been inspired by the Athenian example of Cleisthenes in 508/7 BCE (5.66).

5.32 H refers parenthetically here to a later scandal, the behaviour in the 470s, after the end of the Persian Wars, of Pausanias, victor of the battle of Plataea (cf. n. 9.9–11). In Thucydides (1.128–35) Pausanias' downfall is treated at length, although there he is said to aspire to the hand of a daughter of Xerxes himself. On the whole H treats Pausanias more respectfully (9.76, 79, 82; cf. 8.3).

5.33 For the notion of destiny or fate, cf. n. 1.8. Here it seems to mean little more than that Naxos in fact did not fall. Myndus is on the west coast of Caria, a region familiar to H. The controversy here between Megabates and Aristagoras (499 BCE) implicitly highlights differences in the way Persians and Greeks treat people of lesser rank, a theme that will become more prominent in Books 7 to 9; cf. Xerxes' diatribe against Pythias the Lydian at the outset of his campaign (7.39). It is unlikely that the Naxians had to wait for Megabates' treachery to learn of the preparations against them. A Persepolis treasury tablet names Megabates as a high official (admiral?) some time between 492 and 486, so he did not suffer for the failure to take Naxos (*CAH* iv. 473).

5.36 H considers some synchronisms significant; cf. 9.90 for the synchronism of Plataea and Mycale, and 7.166 for that of Himera and Salamis. This episode and a similar one in 5.125 are the only times the geographer Hecataeus of Miletus enters the *Histories* as a historical agent, although H mentions him as a source of information in 2.143 and 6.137, and probably used him as a source for ethnographic information elsewhere (Lloyd, i. 127–39). H's treatment of Hecataeus' judgement is respectful: because Hecataeus knows useful information, he is not swayed by the enthusiasms of the moment. He is another Herodotean wise adviser (cf. nn. 1.8 and 1.71) and H implies that his advice ought to have been heeded; Hecataeus here acts in the role of a Herodotus to his fellow conspirators. Myous is at the mouth of the Meander River, north of Miletus.

The cross-reference back to the mention of the treasures at Branchidae 'in the first of my narratives (*logoi*)' suggests that H thinks of the *Histories* as a sequence of separate narratives that have been carefully dovetailed into one another through numerous either implicit or explicit interconnections. The reference is to 1.92.

5.37–8 For the role of despots in Ionia at this time and their relations with Persia, see *CAH* iv. 474–6. Histiaeus has already pointed out to the other Ionian tyrants in Scythia that the Ionian cities would choose democracy if they could (4.137). Dissatisfaction with Persian rule did not just involve the Persian maintenance of tyrants at a time when tyranny was becoming unpopular; Persian military levies and disruption of traditional Ionian trade routes in the Mediterranean were also seriously affecting the prosperity of the Ionian cities, and regional rivalries (esp. with Sardis) may have been involved. Cf. nn. 5.11, 30–4.

   Isonomiē, 'political equality', is not strictly speaking democracy (it is also used by H in 3.80, 83, 142). For its Athenian implications under Cleisthenes, see *CAH* iv. 323–4; in Athens it seems to have been a slogan for the new form of government adopted in 508/7 BCE but even in Athens it principally meant that legislation was valid only if ratified by the people as a whole in council and assembly. In H's day *isonomiē* was an ambiguous concept in Ionia, because in its name the Athenians had taken over and were controlling the Ionian cities much as the Persians had earlier, *CAH* iv. 474.

   Darius gave Mytilene to Coës for his advice at the outset of the Scythian expedition, 4.97, 5.11.

5.39–48 Aristagoras goes to Sparta, and H takes the opportunity of inserting material on the early years of King Cleomenes of Sparta and the colonizing adventures of his half-brother Dorieus. Fraternal tensions dog the Spartan kingship; cf. n. 4.147 and the longer account of the origins of the Spartan dual kingship in 6.51–2. Dorieus' son Euryanax will serve as his cousin Pausanias' joint commander at Plataea (9.10, 53, 55); both of them are grandsons of King Anaxandridas and his second wife. H is in error that Cleomenes' reign was short (48); Cleomenes seems to have reigned from c.520 to 490 BCE (cf. n. 3.148).

   For Dorieus' attempts to found a colony first in North Africa and then in Sicily in about 514 BCE, see *CAH* iv. 751–3; cf. the end of n. 4.150–3. Thera was itself a colony of Lacedaemon (4.147 ff.) and from Thera Cyrene had been successfully founded (4.150 ff.), so Dorieus' choice of Therans to guide him in settling North Africa is a reasonable one. Sybaris in southern Italy was destroyed in 510 BCE (44) and refounded in the late 440s as Thurii, the Panhellenic colony in southern Italy where H himself is supposed to have lived as a citizen. H refers briefly again to the destruction of Sybaris when Miletus falls, 6.21.

   Croton figures in the story of Democedes the famous doctor (3.137) and is the only western Greek city to support mainland

Greece against the Persians in 480–479 (8.47). One of the Iamidae of Elis (44) will also serve as a diviner for Lacedaemon at the battle of Plataea (9.33) and four important battles thereafter (9.35). As often when the narrative turns to the western Mediterranean, the Phoenicians and their colonists, the Carthaginians, are part of the story (42, 46; for the role of Phoenicians in Sicily in this period, see *CAH* iv. 742–53).

5.49–51 Aristagoras' attempt to persuade King Cleomenes of Sparta, probably in 498 BCE. Cf. n. 3.148 for Cleomenes' other rejections of the opportunity for Lacedaemonian overseas engagement; his reappearance throughout Books 5 and 6 also testifies, however, to his willingness extensively to meddle in the affairs of other Greek cities. Cleomenes here is typically Spartan in his brief reply to Aristagoras' long-winded arguments; cf. n. 1.152 (in 1.152 the purple coat is expected to entice; here the object is a map). The humour of this account comes in part from the way the map, the physical object, transmits truths its owner wants kept hidden, under Cleomenes' acute questioning. Cleomenes' acuity also stands in sharp contrast to the later credulity of '30,000 Athenians', who will fall for Aristagoras' optimistic pitch (5.97). Cleomenes' daughter, Gorgo, will marry King Leonidas, her half-uncle, who dies at Thermopylae (7.205). She has something of her father's ability to decipher objects (7.239).

In 3.148 Cleomenes' character is portrayed as unblemished; here it is shaky but still virtuous, but cf. the difficulties the other Greeks have in deciding which of his many moral transgressions have brought about his gruesome death in 6.75. There clearly was a divided tradition (perhaps even in Sparta itself) about Cleomenes, and H draws on both strands without trying to make them cohere into a single consistent portrait.

Some scholars think the map here is Hecataeus' improvement on the famous map of Anaximander. H calls it a *gēs hapasēs periodos*, perhaps an allusion to the title of Hecataeus' great written work. Cf. 4.36 for H's criticism of Ionian maps in general. (Nenci mentions a Babylonian document, known in three versions, that tells of Semitic merchants who ask Sargon to embark on an expedition against Nur Dagan, king of Purushanda, who is oppressing them; they show him a map. Such a scene may have already been an old literary topos in the Near East; it may also have been a recognized way of being persuasive that Aristagoras actually adopted.)

5.52–4 H uses the opportunity offered by the map to give his own account of the posting-stages of Darius' Royal Road. Aristophanes may be parodying it in *Acharnians* 68 ff. (425 BCE); he also has Strepsiades in *Clouds* 515–16 (423 BCE) make the same error in reading a map that Aristagoras here hopes Cleomenes will make.

Like the list of satrapies in 3.89–97 and of the various contingents in Xerxes' army in 7.61–99, the description in 52–4 may well come

from Persian documents. A parasang is 30 stades or about 3.3 miles
(5.3 km.), so H's total for the length of the road, taking into account
the distance from Ephesus to Sardis as well as that from Sardis to
Susa, is just under 2,000 miles (3,200 km.). The extensive description of the route to Susa from the sea helps to make it clear how
very optimistic and misleading Aristagoras' original presentation is
(not to mention the underlying notion that an empire of such vastness in its western half alone could be easily defeated!). For Cyrus'
division of the Gyndes see 1.189.

There are problems matching H's account here with actual geographical data. Macan's app. XIII (pp. 289–303), and H & W and
Nenci, ad loc. discuss them extensively. There may be textual corruption (the totals in ch. 53 do not agree with the figures H gives as
he goes along for the number of stages and of parasangs), there are
major dislocations in the placement of several rivers (perhaps because
of textual corruption), and a number of individual difficulties arise
both in locating the course of H's road and in confirming the accuracy of his reporting. None the less, it is clear that H is making use
of actual and detailed information in compiling his account.

For the historical implications of the great network of royal roads
that held Darius' empire together and allowed the movement of
information, armies, and goods across the empire, see CAH iv. 90–1,
178–9, 216–17. As the account in Book 7 of Xerxes' preparations
for his invasion of Greece will make clear, the Persians are skilled
highway engineers, CAH iv. 526–32. If the road from Sardis to
Susa described in chs. 52 ff. really did make the pronounced bend
northward that H describes, however, it was probably built originally for the use of the earlier Hittite empire in the late second mil-
lennium BCE.

5.55–96 Without more ado, H follows Aristagoras to Athens and launches
into a massive background pendant on the formative years of the
Athenian democracy. Within this long and rather complicated tale of
the relations of Athens with its Greek neighbours occur several
further substantial pendants: the Phoenician background of the
slayers of Hipparchus (58–61), the deeds of Cleisthenes' grandfather,
the tyrant of Sicyon (67–8), the background of Athens' long-
standing hostility towards Aegina (82–8), and a long speech by the
Corinthian Socleas about the Corinthian tyrants, Cypselus and
Periander (92). The narrative is very well organized but makes confusing reading if one does not take into account how a Herodotean
pendant works; cf. the Introduction, p. xxii.

5.55 Here H takes up the story of Athens roughly where 1.59–64 leaves
off. Hipparchus was killed in 514 BCE. Thucydides treats the
episode twice (1.20, 6.54 ff.); both Thucydides and H believe that
Hippias was the elder brother and succeeded to the tyranny on
Pisistratus' death in 527 BCE. Hippias was ousted in 510. Cf. 6.123,
where H claims that the family of the Alcmaeonidae was much
more influential in getting rid of the tyrants than were Harmodius

and Aristogiton. Harmodius and Aristogiton, however, quickly became legendary figures to conjure with, in the young Athenian democracy (6.109).

5.56 The Athenian tyrants take dreams, oracles, and the like very seriously; cf. 5.90, 6.107, 7.6. The Panathenaea here mentioned is the great festival held in Athens in the third year of each four-year Olympiad (in the other three years a simpler festival was held). It was made quite elaborate by the Pisistratidae, presumably in order to strengthen civic identification among the Athenian population with Athens itself, rather than with their local cult centres.

5.57-61 The alphabet probably did come to the Greeks through Phoenicians but not precisely as H says; cf. *CAH* iii/1. 794-833 for the development of the Semitic and Greek alphabets, and *CAH* iii/3. 1-7, 24-31 for cultural connections between Phoenicians and Greeks in the archaic period. H puts the introduction of the alphabet into Greece at least four centuries too early.

For H's use of inscriptions, cf. S. West (1985). In the *Histories* H uses 13 Greek inscriptions (1.51, 4.87, 4.88, 5.59-61 (3), 5.77, 6.14, 7.228 (3), 8.22, 8.82); 2 Lydian (1.93, 7.30); 1 Babylonian (1.187); 3 Persian (3.88, 4.87, 4.91); and 5 Egyptian (2.102, 106, 125, 136, 141). The serpent-column mentioned in 8.82 and 9.81 may be found in M–L 27 (Fornara, 59), and the Athenian epigram of 5.77 in M–L 15 (Fornara, 42). H's method of using inscriptions is certainly not that of the trained modern historian and epigrapher (see nn. 2.102–10, 8.22, and 8.82), but he does use them as evidence to answer historical questions. In this passage it is not clear what relation H understands to have existed between Cadmus the Phoenician in Boeotia and the Ionians who, he says, first adopted Phoenician letters into the Greek language.

Thucydides (1.12) dates the Phoenician migration to Boeotia to sixty years after the Trojan War; H places it six generations before the Trojan War. Amphitryon (59) was the human father of Heracles. H here gives the mythic genealogy linking Cadmus, the Phoenician founder of Thebes, to the house of Laius, father of Oedipus. For Cadmus and the Cadmeans, see n. 1.56–7. Laius lived in H's chronological system three generations before the Trojan War. Scaeus (60) was killed by Heracles for helping his father Hippocoön drive Tyndareus, father of Helen, Clytemnestra, and the Dioscuri, from Sparta. He had no connection with Thebes, as H himself sees. The third couplet, in ch. 61, has to do with Oedipus' grandson; the Encheleis are in southern Illyria (cf. 9.43). H may well have seen some very old tripods with peculiar inscriptions on them at Thebes, but from what we know of the history of early Greek writing, the inscriptions were not added to the tripods earlier than the mid-eighth century BCE.

5.62-3 The family of the Alcmaeonidae was intimately connected to the establishment of Athenian democracy. Its most famous members were Cleisthenes (5.66 f.) and, in H's own generation, Pericles (through his mother, 6.131). For the founder of the family's fortunes,

Alcmaeon (*c*.550 BCE), see 6.125, for their connection with the
temple at Delphi burnt in 548 BCE (cf. 2.180), see *CAH* iv. 301, and
for their hereditary curse, see n. 5.71. H also presents the Alcmaeonid
Megacles and his family as enemies of the Pisistratidae at 1.60 and
64. However, 1.61 presents a picture of ambiguous opportunism,
and an archon-list fragment (M–L 6) shows that a Cleisthenes,
son of the Alcmaeonid Megacles, was archon 525/4, and thus the
Alcmaeonidae were not exiled throughout the later years of the
tyranny, as they claimed. Leipsydrium is in northern Attica near
Mount Parnes.

It is possible that the Lacedaemonians took much more of an
initiative than H claims here, alarmed by Pisistratid friendships
with Persia and Argos, *CAH* iv. 301. Cf. nn. 1.152, 3.44, 3.148 for
Lacedaemonian hostility to Persian influence in Greece. The sons of
Pisistratus were in power from 527 to 510 BCE, and Anchimolius'
expedition took place about 511.

5.64-5 The second and successful Lacedaemonian expedition in 510 BCE.
The 'Pelasgian Wall' was a Mycenaean fortification wall around the
Acropolis. The thirty-six years of the rule of the Athenian tyrants
were from *c*.546 to 510, dating from Pisistratus' second and final
return from exile to Athens (1.64). Sigeum is near Troy. For the
careers of Pisistratus and the Pisistratidae, see *CAH* iii/3. 392–416
and iv. 287–302. Nestor son of Neleus was the famous king of Pylos,
Agamemnon's senior adviser at Troy in the *Iliad*.

5.66-96 The exploits of the young Athenian democracy, from 510 down
to 499 BCE, when Aristagoras of Miletus arrives in Athens to ask for
help, having been rejected at Sparta.

5.66 For a modern historical account of the events leading up to the establishment of Athenian democracy in 508/7 BCE, see *CAH* iv. 303–6.
Probably Cleisthenes initially 'allied himself with the
common people' only to gain the edge in his struggle for political dominance
with Isagoras; 'It was not a contest between opposing principles of
government', *CAH* iv. 305. The abandonment of the old traditional
Ionian four tribes as the basis for government (family units, perhaps
originally organized by function: *geleontes* (cultivators), *aegikoreis*
(herdsmen), *argadeis* (workers), *hopletes* (warriors)) and the invention of ten new Athenian tribes based on geography will have had
revolutionary consequences many of which were unintended by
Cleisthenes himself; see n. 5.69. Ch. 66 is the first time the demos of
Athens is presented as a political entity in H.

Ajax is included as one of the ten new Athenian tribal heroes
because the Athenians have laid claim to Salamis from the seventh
century, *CAH* iii/3. 372–3; cf. the notorious interpolated line in the
Iliad which places Salaminian Ajax's ships next to the Athenian contingent (*Iliad* 2.558). According to the Aristotelian *Constitution of
Athens* (21), the Delphic oracle was given a list of a hundred heroes,
and picked the ten that would identify the new Athenian tribes. For

heroes in general, see n. 5.108–17 below; for the battle order of the
ten Athenian tribes, n. 6.111–17.

5.67–8 The family of Cleisthenes of Sicyon, the Orthagoridae, ruled
Sicyon in the northern Peloponnese from c.665 to 565 BCE, and
Cleisthenes himself ruled from c.600 to 570. For the famous occasion of his choice of an Athenian and Alcmaeonid husband for his
daughter, see 6.126–31.

Adrastus was an important character in the lost Cyclic epic the
Thebaïs and was the Argive father-in-law of Oedipus' son Polynices;
Cleisthenes' treatment of Adrastus testifies to the seriousness with
which the Greeks regarded their poetry and the celebration of dead
and mythic heroes (cf. n. 5.108–17). Melanippus was a local Theban
hero who was one of Adrastus' opponents in the war of the Seven
against Thebes. H's comment about 'tragic choruses' at the end of
5.67 is suggestive of some sixth-century developments that may have
led in Athens to the invention of Attic tragedy.

It is hard to believe that the official names of the three Dorian
tribes were terms of contempt in Sicyon, particularly because they
were maintained for a number of years after Cleisthenes' death.
Perhaps they were nicknames; perhaps they were not originally
derogatory but merely rustic in nature. The story suggests an enduring division in Sicyon between the pre-Dorian and Dorian population, one that Cleisthenes perhaps exploited to maintain his tyranny.

5.69 The thinking seems to be that Cleisthenes the grandson changed the
Athenian political system because he despised Ionians as his grandfather had despised Dorians; it is improbable. In 6.131 H acknowledges Cleisthenes as the founder of Athenian democracy, but he is
not interested in the details of how the system he devised worked or
the remarkable breakthrough in human political economy it represented. (The year 1993 CE was widely noted as the 2,500th birthday
of democracy, dating from Cleisthenes' reforms in 508/7 BCE.)

For a detailed account of the new, Cleisthenic constitution, see
CAH iv. 309–46. Cleisthenes' reforms established *isonomiē* (cf. n.
5.37–8) and *isēgoriē*, 'equality of speech' (5.78), in Athens (*CAH* iv.
309, 323). In order to break the regionally based power of the traditional aristocratic clans and to stop the factional fighting which
had previously crippled Attica (cf. 1.59 for earlier Attic factions),
each of the new ten tribes drew its membership from all three different regions of Attica: from the city, from the coast, and from the
inland regions. Thus neighbouring villages or demes which had previously served their own regional interests or a particular locally
powerful family's interests now frequently found themselves scattered into different tribes. The 139 or possibly 140 demes (not ten
per tribe, as H claims) became centres for local cults, and one's deme
was the place where citizenship was registered and military service
organized. The council of Five Hundred (50 members from each
tribe, drawn by lot and changed annually) was the administrative

body which prepared the agenda for the assembly and handled various civic business. The system lasted, essentially unchanged, for about 300 years.

5.71 Eusebius' list of Olympic victors dates Cylon's victory to 640 BCE (*CAH* iii/3. 369). Thucydides (1.126) gives a fuller account than H. Cylon's father-in-law was tyrant of Megara, and with the encouragement of the oracle at Delphi and help from his father-in-law he tried to seize the Acropolis in an Olympic year (636? 632? 628?). In Thucydides' account Cylon and his brother escaped and the others were killed although they had been promised life; Megacles the Alcmaeonid was one of the nine archons of the city responsible (perhaps tacitly correcting H, who calls him one of the presidents of the naucraries or naval boards, Fornara, 22) and was exiled in consequence. This was the origin of the hereditary curse on the Alcmaeonidae. The fact had particular relevance in H's day because the Lacedaemonians invoked the curse against Pericles in 432, on the eve of the Peloponnesian War (Thucydides 1.127).

5.72–4 Timesitheus (72) was twice an Olympic victor and three times a Pythian victor in the pancration (Pausanias 6.8.6). On the banishment: the population of Attica in the late sixth century was probably about 120,000 (30,000 adult males), so seven hundred families represents a substantial part of the city. The demos or people as a whole show loyalty to the new Cleisthenic reforms but are not willing to accept Persian overlordship as the price of their freedom from Sparta. The behaviour of Cleisthenes' supporters in Persia (73) may help explain why the Alcmaeonids' loyalty was suspected by other Athenians after the battle of Marathon (6.115, 121–4), *CAH* iv. 340, 521–2.

Cleomenes' invasion came in the spring of 506 BCE; Oenoe is on the Boeotian border. Chalcis is on the island of Euboea, facing Attica.

5.75–8 For the continuing story of Demaratus' lack of loyalty to Cleomenes, his fellow king, see 6.50–1 and 61 ff.; Cleomenes ultimately has him removed from the kingship, and he flees to Persia in about 490 BCE. He will be one of Xerxes' advisers in the war on Greece (7.3, 101–4, 209, 234–7). For the Tyndaridae, see nn. 4.145–6, 5.80.

For H's habit of enumerating important repeating events, cf. n. 1.92. The first Peloponnesian invasion of Attica was in the distant past, the second and third in 511 and 510 BCE, and this fourth some four years later. The enumeration had topical importance in H's own day, given the invasions of Attica in 446, 431, 430, and 428 BCE, in the Peloponnesian War.

The victory over Chalcis and Boeotia (77) is the first victory of democratic Athens. Cleruchies, or settlements of Athenian citizens abroad, were subsequently used extensively by the democracy during the heyday of the Athenian empire; the cleruchs, or settlers, both guarded Athenian interests locally and often became more prosperous themselves while relieving Athens of the pressures of overpopulation.

Fragments of two monument-bases bearing the epigram celebrating Athens' victory over Chalcis and Boeotia in 506 have been found on the Acropolis (the original and a later copy) and both the text and a discussion of the site can be found in M–L 15 (Fornara, 42). H celebrates the strength of the young democracy in ch. 78; this is one of his most important personal statements, on the power of *isēgoriē*, 'freedom of public speech', and *eleutheriē*, 'freedom'.

5.80 The Asopus is a Boeotian river whose daughter Aegina gave birth by Zeus to the Aeacidae. Like the Tyndaridae of 5.75 the Aeacidae are cult figures, images, to be carried as talismans into battle. Aeacus had as sons Telamon and Peleus, who in turn had as sons Ajax, Teucer, and Achilles. The Thebans use the mythological connection to draw the Aeginetans into their quarrel with Athens.

5.82–9 The prehistory of hostility between Athens and Aegina, dating back perhaps to the early seventh century (*CAH* iii/3. 372). Damia and Auxesia were obviously fertility deities, 'Earth', and 'Increase'. The story as H reports it is aetiological, meant to explain why the two carved statues are kneeling, and it also explains in passing why contemporary Athenian women use no brooches while Argive and Aeginetan women use very large ones (88). Historically it is relevant only in suggesting the length of time and the complexity of the ill-feelings that divided Athens and Aegina by about 500 BCE.

H does not mention it, but surely commercial rivalry played a large part in this war, especially for control over the Saronic Gulf. Corinth and Athens at this time were united in mutual hostility towards Aegina (cf. 5.92 and 6.89). The Aeginetans were famous traders; H describes the merchant Sostratus of Aegina as the richest Greek of all time (4.152). For Aegina's aggressive trading policies and an overview of this controversy, cf. *CAH* iv. 364–7. The narrative of Aeginetan–Athenian hostilities is taken up again by H in 6.87.

5.90–3 The Athenians are distracted from their desire to punish Aegina by a Lacedaemonian attempt to restore Hippias the son of Pisistratus to power in Athens, *c.*504 BCE. The Lacedaemonians are foiled by their allies the Corinthians because Corinth wants an independent Athens as a counterweight to Aegina and also to the power of Sparta. Ch. 92 tells as a cautionary tale the story of the growth of Corinthian tyranny; cf. the story of Periander, his wife Melissa, and his children in 3.48–53, also attached as a pendant to the main narrative.

The lion was a symbol of royal power but not, in ancient Greece, of the restrained majesty that we associate with it; a lion was a ravening, bloodthirsty beast (cf. *Iliad* 5.782). In H the lion is also connected in dreams with the Athenians Hipparchus (5.56) and Pericles (6.131). A 'cypselus' was a chest; Pausanias in the second century CE claimed to have seen at Olympia the cedar-wood 'chest of Cypselus' (5.17.5). Cypselus reigned *c.*657–627 BCE and his son, Periander, *c.*627–587.

For Greek tyrants, cf. n. 1.20 and *CAH* iii/3. 341–51. Trade and commerce led from the seventh century onwards to changes in the balance of power within and among Greek cities. The infusion of new and somewhat redistributed wealth, plus the invention of hoplite warfare (requiring a committed phalanx of trained soldiers), weakened traditional structures of aristocratic authority. Often tyrants came to power with the support of the ordinary citizenry and new money behind them. By the late sixth century, however, they were seen as a reactionary, oppressive force; cf. the dissatisfaction of the Ionians with their tyrants (n. 5.37–8) and H's comment on Athens' growth of power after getting rid of her tyrants (5.78).

The long speech of Socleas in ch. 92 is especially ironic for H's audience, since in the second half of the fifth century Athens and Corinth were enemies (Thucydides 1.31–55). The narrative here implies that Hippias from his study of the oracles has some idea of what will come some sixty or seventy years later (93).

5.94–5 Sigeum, in the Troad, probably became Athenian in about 600 BCE, too early for the bastard son of Pisistratus to be its first ruler. He may, however, have had to win it back when he came to Sigeum sometime before Pisistratus' death in 527. The Athenians and Mytileneans had a long-standing rivalry in the Troad. The area was vital to maintaining the Athenian grain route from the Euxine (Black) Sea, although control could not be exercised from Sigeum, *CAH* iii/3. 374.

Alcaeus' fr. 401B West celebrates the loss of the poet's shield at Sigeum: 'Alcaeus is safe, but his fine armour and shield the Athenians have hung up in the shrine of the pale-eyed goddess.' Much of the poetry of Alcaeus (b. *c.*620 BCE) has to do with contemporary aristocratic politics and his hatred of the Lesbian tyrant Pittacus (alongside whom, however, he fought the Athenians at Sigeum). Alcaeus was a contemporary of Sappho, another famous lyric poet of Lesbos (n. 2.124–35).

5.96–7 Here H tacitly shows why he has taken us through this long (55–96) excursus on late sixth-century Athenian politics: we now understand why the Athenians are so willing to embark on the foolhardy project proposed by Aristagoras the Milesian in 498 BCE. They need friends; they fear the return of their tyrants, who are sitting up in the Troad and conspiring with Persia, and they also have the Lacedaemonians, the Aeginetans, and the Thebans to worry about. Twenty ships was almost half the Athenian fleet, before Themistocles built it up in the late 490s and the 480s; cf. 7.144 and *CAH* iv. 343, 367.

For these ships as 'the beginning of misfortune', cf. 3.30, 5.28 and 30, and 6.67, as well as 1.5, 5.82 and 89. (Cf. *Iliad* 1.6, 5.62, and esp. 11.604, and Thucydides 2.12. Cf. n. 5.4.)

5.98 H returns to the unfortunate Paeonians of 5.15.

5.99 H refers here to the so-called Lelantine War fought by Chalcis and Eretria, the two major cities in Euboea, in about 700 BCE; cf.

Fornara, 7, *CAH* iii/1. 760-3 and iii/3. 308-9. Eretria may also be helping Athens in the Ionian revolt because Athens has recently defeated Chalcis (5.77).

5.100-2 *CAH* iv. 466 comments: 'The burning of Sardis and its temple was a symbolic act which justified the Persian burning of Ionian temples after the revolt and of the Athenian Acropolis in the Great War (5.102): this led in turn to the demand for vengeance and reparations incorporated in the Delian League, and to the use of League funds for the Periclean building programme; the hereditary curse was only finally laid to rest with the burning of Persepolis by Alexander the Great. Seldom has such a symbol reverberated though history with such consequences.' The Athenians lose their enthusiasm for the revolt; they pull out and go home immediately, and two years later (496/5 BCE) they elect as archon Hipparchus son of Charmus, almost certainly the brother-in-law of Hippias, their exiled tyrant. For Cybebe cf. the end of n. 1.32.

For Simonides the poet, see the end of n. 7.201-33.

5.104 Cyprus is crucial to the control of the Levant and has been under Persian control since the 520s (3.19). The story of the revolt of the Greek cities of Cyprus continues in 5.108-16. Salamis is the major city on Cyprus, not here the island off Attica where the naval battle of 480 was fought.

5.105-7 For H's critical view of Ionians, cf. n. 1.143. Darius here asks who the Athenians are; in 5.13 he has asked who the Paeonians are, and has shipped them *en masse* to Phrygia (cf. 1.155, where Cyrus asks who the Spartans are). In ch. 106 Histiaeus makes the same argument as Creon in line 590 of the *Oedipus Tyrannus* of Sophocles, but here it is intended to fool Darius and does so; cf. n. 5.23-4. In H's view, of course, Histiaeus is lying; cf. 5.35. The largest Mediterranean island is Sicily, not Sardinia.

5.108-17 The revolt of Cyprus, resumed from 5.104. *To koinon tōn Ionōn*, 'the Ionian authorities' (109), implies a common Ionian decision-making body, probably based at the Panionium (1.141, 148, 170, 6.7), *CAH* iv. 481, 488, 543. The paired land and sea battles in Cyprus (112-13) probably occur in the summer of 497 BCE. See *CAH* iv. 484 for a description of the archaeological excavations of the Persian siege of Paphos in this campaign. Salamis and Soli are the two biggest and most hellenized cities on Cyprus. In Cyprus, as later at Lade, treachery on the Greek side wins the campaign for Persia, despite Greek victory at sea (113).

Onesilus is made a hero by his former enemies (114); cf. 1.168, 5.47, 7.117. The Greeks (unlike Persians or Egyptians, 2.50, 143) honoured dead heroes and believed that they wielded powers that would continue to protect a community and its territory—a belief that becomes very important as the Persians invade Greek territory (8.39, 109, 143). Cf. also the implications of this belief in 1.67-8, 168, 5.66-7, 6.69.

5.117–21 The revolt of Caria. Halicarnassus lies on the Carian coastline, and H's own family, like that of many Dorian Halicarnassians, may contain a Carian element (cf. the names of his father and probable uncle, Lyxes and Panyassis). H notes activities of Carians (1.171, 2.152), emphasizes their valour (1.175, 5.118–19, 121, 8.105), and suggests the possibility of Carian local information and informants (e.g. 1.175, 2.61, 4.44, 8.104–5). The Hecatomnidae, the rulers of Caria in the fourth century (they include the famous Carian king Mausolus (377–353 BCE), whose elaborate tomb was one of the Seven Wonders of the ancient world and gives us the word mausoleum), were probably descendants of the Carian royal family of the 490s; Artemisia, the queen regent of Halicarnassus (7.99, 8.68–9, 87, 103) during the Persian Wars, may be related to them also; her name reappears in the dynasty.

The shrine of Labraunda (119), half-way between Miletus and Halicarnassus and a little inland, was supported by the Hecatomnidae and remained active into the third century BCE and beyond, as a spectacular discovery of inscriptions attests; cf. Strabo 14.2.23 for the Roman period.

Myrsus son of Gyges, whose death is briefly noted (121), is the messenger Oroetes employed to trick Polycrates into coming to Magnesia, where Polycrates met his gruesome and treacherous death (3.122). H does not here note the connection; it suggests to us how many other stories and connections between stories he knows but does not tell us in the *Histories*.

Two of Darius' sons-in-law, Daurises and Hymaees, die on this campaign (116, 121, 122). The third, Otanes, survives. This is not the Otanes who was one of the seven conspirators (3.68, 80, 88, 144) but is the Otanes whose chair as a royal judge was strung with his own father's skin (5.25). We do not know if he is the Otanes (7.61) active later in the Persian Wars and the father of Xerxes' ferocious queen, Amestris (7.114, 9.109). One wishes that the Persian nobility had been more inventive in their names and less inclined to marry their close relatives.

Sisimaces (121) is one of the many Persian names from the Ionian campaign and the Persian Wars later who has now shown up on the Persepolis tablets, as Zissamakka, for December of 500 BCE, a fact that suggests the general reliability of H's sources for the Persian prosopography of this period, *CAH* iv. 469–70.

5.124–6 Myrcinus lay at the root of the Ionian revolt, since it was Histiaeus' ambition there that originally led Darius to remove him to Susa (5.11, 24). It is an area of interest to H's contemporary public, since in 437/6 BCE the Attic colony of Amphipolis was founded near by, after earlier failed attempts; cf. Thucydides 4.102–8. (Thucydides himself was banished from Athens after he failed as a naval commander to prevent Athens' loss of Amphipolis to the Spartan Brasidas in 424/3 BCE, Thucydides 5.26.) Leros is a small island 30 miles

(48 km.) south-west of Miletus; as in 5.36, here again Hecataeus the *logopoios* gives advice that is ignored.

The town in which Aristagoras dies may well be 'Nine Ways', Enneaodoi (7.114), close to the later site of Amphipolis. H has some sympathy for Histiaeus as a competent and inventive tyrant (4.137–9, 5.23, 6.26–30), but the only good thing he has to say about Aristagoras is his refusal to accept the Persian mistreatment of his friend in 5.33—and even that Aristagoras mishandles. Cf. 5.30, 35, and 124 for his personal ambition, lack of judgement, and cowardice.

6.1–5 The story of Histiaeus, continued from 5.35 and 106. It is unlikely that we, or even H himself, can discern Histiaeus' true motives. At this point they probably have to do with survival, since he is in a tight place. Persia has become uncomfortable for him, with Artaphrenes hostile (6.1, 30) and awaiting an increasingly improbable satisfactory resolution to troubles in the west; to cap it off, the Milesians do not want Histiaeus back, and he is betrayed by his agent, Hermippus of Atarneus. (Atarneus, on the Aeolian coast, is connected with two other tales of perfidy, in 1.160 and 8.106; it is also where Histiaeus is finally captured, 6.28.)

Given Darius' record of transporting populations, Histiaeus' lie is not altogether unbelievable; cf. 3.93 and n. 3.149.

6.6–18 The battle of Lade, 494 BCE. The Persians now mount a massive response that is aimed at Miletus, the heart of the rebellion, *CAH* iv. 487–90. For the catalogue of combatants, cf. 7.61 ff., 89 ff., 8.1 ff., 43 ff., 9.28 ff. Such lists are traditional; cf. *Iliad* 2.484 ff. The 'diecplous' (12) was a manoeuvre of sailing through the enemy's line and then turning and ramming from the rear. For a judgement on the larger Ionian strategy, see *CAH* iv. 488: '(T)he power and the unity of the Ionians were triumphantly demonstrated; but so was their lack of organization. The appointment of a commander had not been made by the *koinon* [cf. n. 5.108–17], but was left to a council of war on the actual campaign: it was perhaps a basic weakness of the Ionians that their cities were too equal in power to make questions of leadership easy to settle, whereas for the mainland Greeks there was an obvious choice. On this occasion the solution was ingenious . . . rivalries between the great states were avoided.' The strength of the contingents from Samos, Chios, and Miletus testifies to the power and wealth of Ionia in the late archaic period. *CAH* iv. 490 points out that the two great naval powers of mainland Greece in the archaic age, Corinth and Aegina, only provided forty and thirty triremes respectively at the battle of Salamis fourteen years later.

The problem of the bias of H's informants, noticeable throughout the story of the Ionian revolt (e.g. in the consistently unfavourable picture of Aristagoras, n. 5.124–6), becomes critical here. Some elements in the account (e.g. the story of Ionian laziness and failure of discipline (12); H's inability correctly to assign blame and praise for

performance in the battle itself (14)) suggest that some of H's sources
may have been interested in mitigating the picture of Samian treachery (13–14) as the cause of defeat. (Other factors that might influence the account: the long-standing rivalry between Samos and
Miletus, principally over control of Aegean trade routes (cf. 3.39);
the desire in contemporary Athens to justify Athenian control over
an Ionia defined by them as undisciplined and uncourageous (Thucydides 1.99).) See *CAH* iv. 466–73 for an assessment of sources, and,
more generally, the lack of Ionian aristocratic family traditions, and
the kinds of oral account preserved by a defeated people.

6.16 For the Thesmophoria, cf. 2.171. This festival dates the battle to the
autumn of 494.

6.19–20 The other part of the oracle is given in 6.77 and seems to refer to
the battle of Sepeia fought between Lacedaemon and Argos. The
temple of Apollo at Didyma to which the oracle refers is the famous
shrine of the priests called the Branchidae (1.46, 92, 157, 2.159, 5.36),
one of the three great sanctuaries of Ionia along with the Heraeum at
Samos and the Artemisium at Ephesus. Here Darius makes good his
threat of 6.9. The Red Sea here is the Persian Gulf, cf. n. 1.1.

6.21 Sybaris was captured c.510 BCE (cf. 5.44 and n. 5.39–48). Phrynichus was an older contemporary of Aeschylus' in Athens; he also
wrote a *Phoenissae*, or *Phoenician Women* (performed in 476 BCE
with Themistocles as producer or *choregus*), on the theme of the
battle of Salamis, and a number of plays with mythological themes.
In the fifth century a drachma was a skilled labourer's daily wage,
and a slave could be bought for less than 100 drachmas, so this fine
represented a very substantial sum. In the same spring, 493/2 BCE,
Miltiades probably arrived back in Athens with his four surviving
ships, only to face prosecution at the hands of his political enemies
for having established a tyranny in the Chersonese (6.104; *CAH* iv.
339); cf. n. 6.132.

6.22–4 Zancle, later called Messana (modern Messina), is in the north-
east corner of Sicily. Rhegium is across the straits on the western
coast of the toe of Italy; Locri, its rival, is on the eastern coast of the
toe. Anaxilaus of Rhegium will support the Carthaginian invasion
of Sicily timed to take place as Xerxes launches his attack on Greece
(7.165–6). For the various political machinations of the tyrants
Hippocrates and Anaxilaus, see 7.154–5, 164–5; *CAH* iv. 760–4,
771, 775.

6.25 Aeaces has been rewarded for his services before the battle of Lade
(6.13). His father, Syloson, brother of Polycrates, had given Darius
his red cloak and received in return the tyranny of Samos (3.139–40,
144). Aeaces had presumably been deposed with the other tyrants at
the beginning of the Ionian revolt (5.37, 6.9).

6.26–30 For Histiaeus' career, see 4.137 (an unlikely scene, at least for
Miltiades' role in it) and nn. 5.23–4, 5.105–7, 5.124–6. His calcu-

lations and his fate remind us of the relatively even-handed judgements that H believes the Persian king makes (1.137, 7.194; see also n. 1.156), but also of the ability to subvert royal plans exercised by the king's ambitious and powerful underlings (cf. n. 3.129–38).

6.27 Altogether the Chians have had an exceptionally difficult time of it; cf. 6.15–16. The accident to the Chian schoolhouse is one of the earliest mentions of formal education in Greece. Here H makes one of his rare personal comments on the pattern formed by human events; cf. n. 3.38.

6.32 Cf. nn. 1.92 and 5.75–8 for enumeration as a marker of the importance of an event. *CAH* iv. 490: 'The ruin of Chios and the sack of Miletus mark the end of the archaic period more definitely than any other political event: the two greatest cities of the Greek world, with populations perhaps double that of Athens, never recovered.'

6.34–8 The story of Miltiades, the founder tyrant of the Chersonese (*c*.555 BCE), whose nephew, also named Miltiades, has been active with Darius in Scythia *c*.513 BCE (n. 4.133–42). For the elder Miltiades' complex relationship with the Pisistratidae, see *CAH* iii/3. 404–5. Despite the improving story of the Doloncians, the initiative for Miltiades' removal northwards may well have come from Pisistratus himself, who would have found a powerful, energetic Athenian aristocrat more useful in the Chersonese, keeping an eye on the grain route and the local grain supplies (n. 7.145–7), than in Athens. Note that the events at Lampsacus (37) must have taken place before Croesus' removal (*c*.546 BCE); the old name of Lampsacus, on the Asiatic side of the Hellespont, was Pityusa (*pitus* is pine).

6.39–41 Miltiades the younger may have come to the Chersonese *c*.516 BCE; this is the first recorded Athenian trireme. (For the death of his father Cimon see 6.103.) His Thracian wife, Hegesipyle, was the mother of Cimon the later Athenian commander and statesman; her father's name was the same as that of the Athenian Olorus, father of Thucydides the historian. (She may be the Athenian Olorus' grandmother; Thucydides' burial monument was in Cimon's family graveplot.) The 'now' of ch. 41 is 493 BCE, as the Phoenicians approach the Chersonese after the failure of the Ionian revolt. For more on the younger Miltiades and his family, see nn. 4.133–42, 6.103–4, 132–40.

6.42 Artaphrenes sets up the system of taxation that lasted, H says, until his own day; note that Thales had already (1.170) suggested the desirability of political unity for the region more than half a century earlier. In H's own day, tribute was paid to Athens by the Ionians; the implication here may be that the Athenian tribute was virtually the same as the earlier, Persian assessment.

6.43–5 Mardonius, the nephew, brother-in-law, and son-in-law of Darius, appears on the scene; his father Gobryas was one of the original seven conspirators in 3.70–9, and Mardonius himself will feature largely as the commander-in-chief of his cousin Xerxes in Books 7 to 9. In 6.43, as in 3.80 itself, H assures his reader that, incredible as it may seem, Otanes really did argue for democracy in 521 BCE, and he sees Mardonius' dismantling of tyrannies in 492 as confirmation of a sort.

Mardonius marches on Athens and Eretria because these two cities had helped in the Ionian revolt (5.99). Xerxes will spend three years digging a canal to avoid having to round Mount Athos in 480 BCE (7.22), because of the disaster Mardonius' fleet suffers (44). Mardonius' expedition may have had as its main object not conquering central Greece but solidifying Persian control of the Thraco-Macedonian area (*CAH* iv. 494–6); if so, it was a larger success than H thinks it was; 'When he withdrew with part of his forces in 491, he left a well-organized and prosperous satrapy, which was to serve as a base for further operations' (*CAH* iv. 496). Macedonia is not a new addition to the Persian empire (5.18), but has just received a new king, Alexander (*c.*498–454 BCE), and perhaps for the first time substantial numbers of Persian troops.

6.46–9 In 491 BCE Darius demands that the Thasians tear down their walls. *CAH* iii/3. 6–7 is sceptical of Phoenician activity in archaic Thasos (Thucydides the Athenian historian later possessed rights to work mines in this region of Thrace, presumably in part because of his family connections in the area (cf. n. 6.39–41 and Thucydides 4.105)). Darius then demands earth and water from the Greek cities of islanders and mainlanders alike. We understand more of the significance of Aeginetan compliance here because of the complicated account of Athenian–Aeginetan relations H has already given us in 5.82–9. The Athenians and Cleomenes have cause to be alarmed.

6.50–93 This passage is designed to explain the complicated Greek political background of the events of the late 490s BCE, as mainland Greece sees evidence building of massive Persian military preparations against Greece itself. An account can be constructed of many of Cleomenes' activities that has as one of its principal aims securing mainland Greece from Persian conquest (61), but his enemies both at home and abroad figure among H's sources; cf. n. 3.148. His fellow king, Demaratus, is a serious thorn in his side (51; cf. 5.75, 6.61 f).

The story of Crius the Aeginetan (50) can be pieced together from its continuation in 6.73, 8.92. Cleomenes has a reputation for snappy repartee; cf. 5.72, 6.76. Crius' name means 'ram'.

6.51–60 A pendant on the history of the Spartan kingship. Sparta is the only Greek state whose customs H extensively describes, as if Spartans were as foreign as Lydians or Persians (1.93–4, 131–40).

6.52–4 The account in ch. 52 is an aetiology, designed to account for the origin of the Spartan dual kingship; cf. n. 4.147–8, for more on the maternal, Cadmean connection. The genealogy in ch. 53 refers to the fact that the Dorians through Hyllus and his father Heracles were descendants of Perseus (ignoring the troublesome mythic complications of 1.7). In 7.61 and 150 Perseus is assumed even by the Persians to be Argive through his mother Danaë, not Assyrian as is claimed here (cf. n. 2.91); in 2.91 he is claimed by the Egyptians. H does not take most pretensions of racial purity very seriously; cf. nn. 1.1, 1.146, 6.125-30.

6.57 For H's weights, measures, and distances, see App. 2. In the most common Greek system of measurement, one choenix was a modest day's ration of grain.

Thucydides 1.20 is very severe on 'someone' who claimed the Lacedaemonian kings, had two votes each, but here H may be merely (somewhat sloppily) implying that each relative cast one vote for the relevant king and one for himself.

6.58-60 Solon had forbidden extravagant displays of emotion as signs of mourning at Athens, and supposedly Lycurgus had done the same for the funerals of private people at Sparta (Plutarch, *Life of Solon* 12; *Life of Lycurgus* 27); cf. 1.198, 2.79, 85, 4.71. In Sparta the perioeci (*perioikoi*), or inhabitants of the surrounding region, were considered Lacedaemonian citizens, though with lesser rights than the Spartiates; the helots were slaves attached to the land, descended from the Laconian and Messenian populations enslaved by Sparta and now farming for the Lacedaemonians the land their ancestors had owned. The existence of helot labour made the Spartiate way of life possible, but also created real anxieties about potential revolt (cf. Thucydides 1.101-3). Both perioeci and helots will figure among the forces Sparta brings to the war with Persia (8.25, 9.10, 11, 28, 80, 85).

In Sparta (unlike Athens) daughters with no brothers could inherit. In the fourth century, according to Aristotle (*Politics* 1270ᵃ), two-fifths of Spartan land was in the hands of women; Lacedaemonian women were famous among other Greeks for their oddly independent ways. For H's comparison of Spartans with Persians and Egyptians, cf. n. 6.51-60 (and 3.67 for an instance of release from debt at a royal accession, 2.164 for Egyptian castes).

6.61-72 Demaratus, son of Ariston, was king at Sparta c.515-491 BCE. His opposition to Cleomenes in 506 (5.75, 6.65), and again here in the later 490s, no doubt persuades Cleomenes to remove him.

As H indicates (61), Helen of Troy was worshipped at Sparta; she may have originally been a faded pre-Indo-European tree-goddess. The Gymnopaedia or Festival of Unarmed Dancing (67; literally 'Festival of Naked Youths'), took place just after midsummer; it was one of the three major Spartan festivals, along with the Hyacinthia in late spring (9.7, 11) and the Carnea in August or September (7.206, 8.72).

On Demaratus' mother's reply (68): Astrabacus was in Spartan myth a hero and the great-grandson of Agis, founder of the senior, Agiad royal house at Sparta; Demaratus is a descendant of the other, Eurypontid, house. An *astrabē* is a mule's saddle, hence the insult about the muleteer (68). Demaratus leaves post-haste for Persia, so perhaps he did not find his mother's answer an entirely satisfactory one. It is not easy to judge whether Demaratus as king initially had a more friendly attitude towards Persians than did Cleomenes (cf. Demaratus' friendship with the Aeginetans) or whether he was driven into their arms by his intense dislike of Cleomenes (61) and, like Hippias of Athens, by the economic necessities of his expulsion from power. Later he is one of Xerxes' major advisers on things Greek (cf. n. 5.75–8).

On Leotychidas, Demaratus' successor as Eurypontid king: H skips ahead to the late 470s to describe his disreputable end (71–2). Leotychidas' initial hostility to Demaratus is entirely understandable (65); he will, moreover, play a vigorous role in the Greek offensive against Persia at the battle of Mycale (9.90–2, 98; *CAH* iv. 611–16). None the less, H implies that his later career emphasizes the same lack of character as does his initial accession to the kingship; perhaps (though he does not say so here (cf. n. 5.1)) he believes Leotychidas' later fate to be a punishment for going along with Cleomenes' scheme.

Leotychidas' grandson, Archidamus, is the Spartan king who plays a role in the first years of the Peloponnesian War in H's own day (Thucydides 1.79–85, 2.19–20); the first ten years of it are called 'the Archidamian War' after him although he dies in 427 BCE. Some have read H's unflattering portrait of Leotychidas as evidence for contemporary bias on H's part.

6.73–84   For Cleomenes' career, see n. 3.148. H disrupts the chronological order, perhaps to highlight underlying moral connections. We see first Cleomenes' prosecution of his quarrel with Aegina and Crius the Aeginetan in 491 BCE (H describes the consequence, open hostility between Athens and Aegina in the 480s, in 6.85–93; cf. 8.92 for the long memory of Crius' son). H implies that the events leading to Cleomenes' death happen shortly thereafter; he may well have died in 490, the year of the battle of Marathon. In chs. 75–84 the narrative is organized around the various things Cleomenes did in his earlier career that might have brought upon him his horrible end. (Some scholars find the Lacedaemonian account of that end very suspicious; others find it plausible, given the degree to which Cleomenes' character and actions did not fit the usual Spartan mould, and the sense of strain and even madness that might have ensued, *CAH* iv. 366–7.) For the helot (75), see nn. 1.65–8, 6.58–60.

6.76–80   H backtracks to Cleomenes' most notorious act, after the corruption of the Pythia: his sacrilegious murder of the Argives in *c*.494 BCE after the battle of Sepeia, near Tiryns. The Argives themselves later cite their huge losses (6,000 men, 7.148) as a principal reason for withholding their aid to the Greek side in the forthcoming Persian invasion of Greece. For the prehistory of the Spartan–Argive struggle for dominance in the Peloponnese, see *CAH* iv. 353–6 and n. 1.82.

In the oracle's opening line (77) the female is Sparta and the male
is Argos. A *seps* is a dangerous snake; the presence of snakes proba-
bly gave the mountain, and hence the battle near by, the name Sepeia.
The serpent is a national symbol of Argos (Sophocles, *Antigone* 125).
For the confusion of Argus the hero and Argos the city in ch. 80, cf.
Cambyses' oracle about his death at Ecbatana (3.64).

6.83 Tiryns sent a force to the Greek cause at Plataea (9.28, along with
Mycenae) and so was clearly independent from Argos in 479 BCE.
The ensuing wars that H mentions here (*c.*470 BCE) were an attempt
by Argos to establish control over its neighbours and ended in the
destruction of Tiryns and the weakening of Argos, *CAH* v. 106-7,
500(3).

6.86 Macan's comment, *ad loc.*: 'One hardly knows which more to admire
in the speech of Leotychides at Athens, the perfection of the narrative or the inconsequence of the logic. The Athenians doubtless were
charmed by the one, but easily evaded the other.' Leotychidas is in
Athens in the first place because of a Lacedaemonian vote of no-
confidence; the oracle delivered at Delphi in his speech points a larger
moral than he intends, and H does not expect the irony to be lost
on the reader. (Note that the fact of a Milesian in the time of Croesus
coming to Sparta for his banking needs tacitly points up the far
greater power of Sparta than of Athens, even for Ionians, in the mid-
sixth century.)

6.87-93 The narrative of enmity between Athens and Aegina, resumed
from 5.81. H does not make clear whether all the events recounted
here happen before Marathon or whether he includes hostilities of
the 480s as well. In *c.*483 BCE Themistocles tells the Athenians
that the navy to be built will be used against Aegina (7.144); here
(89) the Athenians are hampered by their lack of ships. H comments
that the greatest cause of disunity on the Greek side at the time of
the first meeting of the Greek league against Persia (481) is the war
between Athens and Aegina (7.145).

On the irony for H's contemporaries of the friendship between
Corinth and Athens, united in hostility to Aegina, cf. the end of n.
5.90-3. The mention of Aeginetans being driven off their island (91)
may refer to the Athenian expulsion of the population of Aegina in
431 BCE (Thucydides 2.27). If so, it is one of the latest events cited
by H in the *Histories*; he does not refer to their subsequent destruction at Thyreae in 424 (Thucydides 4.57).

Sophanes (92) from the Athenian deme of Decelea will reappear
in 9.73-5, winning a reputation for wonderfully improbable feats at
the battle of Plataea. Pausanias 1.29.5 sees Sophanes' grave in the
great Athenian cemetery, the Ceramicus, and also comments on his
slaying of Eurybates. H may have seen the same monument.

6.94-120 The Marathon campaign, 490 BCE. After the burning of Sardis
in 498, Darius had shot his arrow and appointed the slave to remind
him of Athens every time he sat down to dinner (5.105). After the

NOTES TO PAGES 386–8

defeat of the Ionians, he had begun building warships and horse transports to punish the Athenians and Eretrians in 491 (6.48). The disaster suffered by Mardonius' forces at Athos (95) had happened in 492 (6.44–5); the consequent decision of the Persian fleet in 490 to go straight across the Aegean from Samos probably took the Greeks by surprise. The number of six hundred Persian ships is a conventional one; cf. 4.87, 6.9.

6.96 The Persians remember the events of 499 BCE (5.30–4). Cf. Aristagoras' arguments about the stategic value of Naxos, 5.31.

6.97 Delos is the birthplace of Apollo and Artemis. Despite their reputation for autocratic cruelty, the Persians also have a reputation for fairness (cf. n. 6.26–30), even-handedness to subject peoples, and respect for their gods (nn. 1.135, 1.156; *CAH* iv. 103–5, 111, 475–6). Apollo may get special consideration; cf. the letter of Darius to Gadatas, perhaps satrap of Ionia (M–L 12; Fornara, 35), threatening to punish him for taxing the gardeners sacred to Apollo and forcing them to work non-sacred land. See also 6.118.

6.98–9 Artaxerxes reigned after Xerxes, 465–424 BCE. H refers to the Peloponnesian War of his own day, fought between Athens and the Peloponnesians but eventually involving the whole of the Greek world (Thucydides 1.1). Thucydides 2.8 mentions an earthquake on Delos shortly before 431, also called unique. Carystus is on the southern tip of Euboea, and later sends ships with Xerxes and runs foul of Themistocles (8.66, 112, 121). Modern students of Old Persian interpret the three Persian names somewhat differently: The stem of Darius is *Dārayavahu-*, and means 'holding firm the good', from *dar-* ('to hold') and *vau-* ('the good'); that of Xerxes is in OP *Xshayārshan-*, 'a real man among kings,' from *xshaya-* ('king') and *arshan-* ('man, hero, bull'). Artaxerxes is *Artaxshaça*, 'having a kingdom of justice,' from *arta-* ('justice') and *xshaça-* ('kingdom').

6.100–1 This report looks as if it may come from Athens. For the cleruchs, or Athenian settlers, see n. 5.75–8. The Eretrians themselves will later be transported *en masse* to Asia, 6.119. For the Persian numbers, and the tactics of the first part of this campaign, see *CAH* iv. 502–6; Burn, 236–41; Lazenby, 45–50.

6.102–17 The battle of Marathon, 490 BCE. H begins with the story of Cimon, half-brother of Miltiades the elder and father of Miltiades the younger. H has promised in 6.39 to treat of Cimon's death, and does so in ch. 103. Cimon was killed, according to rumour, by the Pisistratidae; his three Olympic victories were in the 530s and 520s BCE. After the Ionian revolt, his son Miltiades the younger flees the Chersonese just in time to come home to Athens *c.*493, to stand trial and be acquitted, and to muster the Athenian resistance to Persia (cf. 6.41, 104). He is elected to the Athenian board of ten generals, to serve for a year (103; cf. 109–10). For Miltiades' later career and his earlier capture of Lemnos for Athens, see 6.132–40. Cf. nn.

4.133–42, 6.39–41 for his well-known family, the Philaïdae (6.35 for their claimed descent from Ajax of Salamis).

6.105–6 The story of Philippides who ran about 140 miles (225 km.) in two days. He is called Pheidippides in some manuscripts, but the name is very rare, and Pheidippides, the somewhat slippery son in Aristophanes' *Clouds*, is unlikely to have been given the same name as the hero of Marathon.

In a later legend, told by Lucian (*Pro lapsu inter salutandum* 64.3), Philippides/Pheidippides is at the battle itself, runs the 26 miles (40 km.) back to Athens, with his last breath says *khairete, nikōmen*, 'hail, we're the winners', and dies. Hence the name of the Marathon, the modern 26-mile race. The story was expanded by the nineteenth-century poet Robert Browning ('Pheidippides', 1879), into a long and overwrought narrative poem in which Pheidippides runs to Sparta, runs back to fight at Marathon itself; when asked by Milti-ades to report the victory at Athens, he runs the 26 miles to Athens from Marathon, reports the victory, and finally expires: 'Till in he broke: "Rejoice, we conquer!" Like wine through clay | Joy in his blood bursting his heart, he died—the bliss!'

Religious law at Sparta forbade the Lacedaemonians to leave Laconia until the moon was full in the month of the Carnea at Sparta. They seem to have started at moonset on the first possible day and to have marched the distance from Sparta to Athens with a vanguard of 2,000 men in two days and a night (6.120; *CAH* iv. 514).

6.107 For Hippias' attention to dreams and the like, cf. n. 5.56. He has been making trouble for Athens with the Persians since his banish-ment in 510 BCE (5.96, 6.94), and he will continue to do so (7.6). He has the Persians land at Marathon, the same site where in his own younger days his father Pisistratus had made his final tri-umphant return to Athens, 546 BCE, and where he might hope for some local support (n. 1.62).

6.108 From Thucydides 3.68 we can date the Plataean connection with Athens to 519/8 BCE. The Twelve Gods were Zeus, Hera, Poseidon, Demeter, Apollo, Artemis, Hephaestus, Athena, Ares, Aphrodite, Hermes, Dionysus; the altar was set up in the Athenian agora by Pisistratus the grandson of the tyrant (Thucydides 6.54), and all Athenian distances were measured from it. The ill will that Cleomenes encourages here between Athens and Thebes bears even-tual fruit in the Theban invasion of Plataea in 431 BCE, precipitat-ing the Peloponnesian War (Thucydides 2.2).

6.109 The Archon Polemarch or 'war leader' was one of the nine archons or annual magistrates of Athens; by H's day his responsibilities had become largely ceremonial. Callimachus comes from Aphidna, the deme of Harmodius and Aristogiton (cf. 5.55), so Miltiades' appeal to their example may be particularly effective.

6.111–17 See *CAH* iv. 506–17; Burn, 242–52; and Lazenby, 54–74 for reconstructions of the strategy and tactics of the battle itself drawn

from H, other ancient sources, and archaeological evidence. Cavalry
was part of the Persian force but apparently played no part in the
battle (cf. Fornara, 48). The key on the Athenian side was an infantry
built up heavily in the wings and thin in the centre. When the Persian
infantry centre (where the picked Persian and Scythian forces were)
broke through the Athenian centre, it was isolated from supporting
Persian forces and could be attacked by the victorious Athenian
flanks from the rear. The official Cleisthenic battle order for the
ten tribes of Athens was: Erechtheis, Aegeis, Pandionis, Leontis,
Acamantis, Oeneis, Cecropis, Hippothoontis, Aeantis, Antiochis.
The Athenians approached at a run, in part to minimize the lethal
effect of Persian arrows.

   Cynegeirus (114) was the brother of Aeschylus the Athenian play-
wright, who also fought in the battle. Aeschylus himself chose for
his own epitaph not mention of his dramatic works but the following: 'The grove at Marathon, and the long-haired Mede of his knowledge may speak of the glorious courage of Aeschylus' (trans.
Hammond, *CAH* iv. 515).

   The 192 Athenian dead (117) were buried in the Great Mound,
c.150 feet (45 m.) in diameter at the site of the battle; the Plataeans
and slaves were buried in a separate mound. Some of the scenes H
describes (of Epizelus, Cynegeirus, Callimachus) were perhaps
depicted in the Stoa Poecile or 'Painted Stoa' in Athens (c.460), where
H would have seen them.

6.119 The Eretrians are settled about 24 miles (38.5 km.) from Susa; a
primitive oil well is described here.

6.121-4 H's assessment of the charge of treason against the
Alcmaeonidae. Ch. 122 contains a short passage on Callias (omitted
in this translation), which is often thought to be an interpolation;
like 7.239, it less clearly serves as background for its context than
the normal Herodotean pendant. (This Callias was grandfather of
the Athenian statesman Callias of the fifth century, who was cousin
of Aristides and brother-in-law of Cimon.)

   It is not clear that H's defence of the Alcmaeonidae would have
seemed convincing to an early fifth-century Athenian. They were not
in exile throughout the period of the tyranny (cf. 1.61, n. 5.62-3),
and they seem to have been implicated in an earlier Athenian
approach to Persia (n. 5.72-4). Xanthippus, married to the niece of
Cleisthenes, prosecuted Miltiades, the victor of Marathon, seeking
the death penalty on his return from Paros (6.136; *CAH* iv. 340-2,
521-2). Xanthippus' brother-in-law, the Alcmaeonid Megacles, was
ostracized (that is, required to leave Athens for a ten-year period) in
487/6 BCE, during a time when Athens was clearing itself of Persian
sympathizers (a year after the ostracism of Hipparchus son of
Charmus, the leader of the Pisistratidae in Athens). Xanthippus was
ostracized in 485/4.

   The Alcmaeonidae may well have engineered the removal of the
tyrants from Athens (123) and have created the Athenian democra-

tic constitution (5.66) without being automatically anti-Persian. They were more likely anti-Lacedaemonian (5.70, 72–3)—or simply, in their own eyes, pro-Athenian. For the Athenian politics of the period and the use of ostracism, see *CAH* iv. 334–46, 521–4. It is impossible to say, however, whether a shield was flashed at Marathon as a signal to the Persians, or, if so, who did it and what they meant by it.

6.125–30 H is irreverent towards the founders of important lineages; cf. the story of Gyges (1.8–12), of the dual Spartan kingship (6.51–2), and of the family of the tyrants at Gela (7.153). Cf n. 1.146 and more generally the end of n. 6.52–4. (That H habitually refuses a reverent or even respectful attitude towards important people, particularly Greek, greatly exasperated the second-century CE essayist Plutarch: see Pearson (ed.), *On the Malice of Herodotus = Moralia* 854–74.) The chronology of the Alcmaeon story is difficult; as H & W point out, Croesus reigned in Lydia *c.*560–546 BCE, but by about 550 Alcmaeon's granddaughter was old enough to be married to Pisistratus (1.61).

For Cleisthenes of Sicyon (126, *c.*600–570 BCE), see n. 5.67–8; and *CAH* iii/3. 346–50 for Cleisthenes as one of a number of sixth-century Greek tyrants. For the chronological difficulties created by the list of suitors, see Macan, H & W, and Legrand, *ad loc.* Missing are suitors from Corinth, Thebes, Sparta, and Ionia; given the story of 5.67 f., it seems improbable that an Argive would think he had a chance. According to Pherecydes (*FGH* 3, fr. 2), Hippoclides of Athens, the chief rival of the Alcmaeonid Megacles, was a Philaid, an older relative of the family of the two Miltiades, nn. 6.34–8, 6.39–41.

6.130–1 Reference to 'Athenian custom' reminds H's contemporary readers of Pericles' citizenship law of *c.*450 BCE, demanding that an Athenian citizen have two Athenian parents. Here Pericles' own great-grandmother is the foreigner involved. H follows up with the genealogy of Pericles himself and a reference to his mother's dream of giving birth to a lion (cf. n. 5.90–3).

6.132–6 Having accounted for the Alcmaeonidae, H now switches back to the later doings of Miltiades, victor of Marathon. H's sources are clearly hostile to Miltiades; *CAH* iv. 518–19 points out that it was sensible strategy to try to secure the Cyclades for Athens in 489 BCE, given what the Persian fleet had done in the previous year. Miltiades may have secured some other islands before turning to Paros; thereafter the campaign clearly misfired. The Hydarnes mentioned in ch. 133 is probably the son of the Hydarnes found among the seven Persian conspirators (3.70); he was commander of the Immortals in Xerxes' invasion (7.83, 211). On Paros: the tribute lists of the Athenian empire attest its wealth, not least because of its marble (5.62).

For Xanthippus, Miltiades' attacker, see n. 6.121–4. Although married into the Alcmaeonid family, Xanthippus quite possibly launched this prosecution independently in 489 BCE, to further his own political career. He fathers Pericles (131), is ostracized (a fact not mentioned by H), and comes back to Athens to participate in the Persian Wars as a naval officer and direct the Athenian occupation of the Hellespont thereafter (8.131, 9.114, 120). Fifty talents (136) is three hundred times what Phrynichus had to pay for his play, *The Fall of Miletus* (6.21; there are 6,000 drachmas in a talent).

6.137–40 For Pelasgians as the pre-Greek indigenous population of Greece, cf. 8.44 and n. 1.56–7 and 8.44. According to Strabo 9.2.3 the Pelasgians mentioned here are not the native Athenian Pelasgians (cf. 8.44 and Macan's note *ad loc.*) but Boeotian Pelasgians driven into Attica by the Thessalian immigration into Boeotia, dated by Thucydides 1.12 to two generations after the Trojan War. The descendants of the Argonauts expelled from Lemnos when the Pelasgians came became part of the Lacedaemonian colony in Thera (4.145–6).

The story of chs. 138–9 seems to be an Athenian 'charter myth', designed to justify the Athenian control of Lemnos and, more generally, the superiority of Athenian blood or at least the upbringing given by an Athenian mother. (Cf. the story of Cyrus' boyhood habits, 1.114–15, but also 1.146 for the transmission of culture through the female line.) Aeschylus refers to the traditional 'Lemnian crime' in *Libation Bearers* 633, that is, the murder of the men of Lemnos by its women before the arrival of the Argonauts.

For the curse (139), cf. 1.167, 3.65, 4.151, 5.82, 9.93. The story of the oracle and its consequences certainly look like a convenient support of Athenian claims in the northern Aegean in about 500 BCE. It is difficult to assign a date to Miltiades' conquest of Lemnos for Athens; it presumably occurred during the time of the Ionian revolt, since it involved Miltiades in an open break with Persia. Lemnos' importance to Athens initially had to do with its position on the grain route from the Euxine (Black) Sea to mainland Greece (cf. n. 7.145–7); it was a part of the fifth-century Athenian empire and with Imbros and Scyros was allowed to remain in the possession of Athens after the King's Peace of 386 BCE (Xenophon, *Hellenica* 5.1.31).

BOOKS SEVEN TO NINE: THE WAR IN GREECE

Books 7 to 9 tell the climax of H's story, the great three-year struggle between Greeks and Persians in Greece itself, and the victory achieved by the Greeks, first in Greece and then also in Ionia (481–479 BCE). H is writing more than thirty years later, when the victory has begun to seem ambiguous to many Greeks—to the Athenians, because they see their great sacrifice and valour in the war disregarded by their erstwhile allies, and their later successes envied and feared (Thucydides 1.73–7); to the rest of the Greeks, because they see the peoples of the Aegean in the 450s and 440s dominated by Athens as they had been by the Persians, and more generally, because many of them view the initiative and energy displayed by Athens in the decades after the Persian Wars as intrinsically dangerous for everybody else. The demos or ordinary Athenian citizen body decisively defeated the Persians in 480 by manning the Athenian fleet; and if we take seriously the picture painted in the early books of Thucydides, we see that Athenian democracy under Pericles—in particular, in its aggressively imperialist ambitions—is regarded by the more conservative Greek states as a dangerous model and one that Athens might try to export elsewhere. As a Corinthian opines in 432 BCE (Thucydides 1.70), '[The Athenians] are by nature incapable of either living a quiet life themselves or of allowing anyone else to do so.'

H's decision sometime about the middle of the fifth century to write a narrative of the Persian Wars, beginning with the growth of Persian power and leaving off at the moment of Greek victory in 479, before the Greeks became overtly divided among themselves, was an act fraught with political significance at the time of writing. Many scholars have assumed that one of H's purposes in writing was to support contemporary Athens. He is, after all, explicit in giving Athens her due, and he emphasizes that she created the conditions under which victory was possible at all. On the other hand, in recent years a more ironic set of interpretive strategies has been discerned running through his narrative as well. H is unequivocally respectful of Pausanias, the Lacedaemonian general at Plataea, despite rumours of Pausanias' later collaboration with Persia and moral downfall, while he is grudging in his praise of Themistocles, the architect of Athenian victory and has scarcely anything to say at all about other Athenian commanders. One of the most eloquent spokesmen for the Greek values of freedom and law is the exiled Spartan king in Xerxes' entourage, Demaratus.

H emphasizes that the victory was almost a defeat; repeatedly in the last books of the *Histories* the Greeks only barely manage to come together in time to stave off disaster for the moment. What undoes the Persians is not the resources ranged against them by the Greeks (although these were necessary)—it is rather their own inability to look closely at how to use their resources efficiently and a lack of strategic vision. Although the sentiment is expressed by the self-serving and even actively duplicitous Themistocles, H's most fundamental assessment seems to be the one articulated by Themistocles after Salamis (8.109): 'It was not we who accomplished this, but the gods and heroes, who did not want to see a single man ruling both Asia and Europe.' If we go back through the earlier books of the *Histories*, we understand what Themistocles is talking about: there is an economy, a natural order to the world, that makes it necessary to check the Persian ambition to conquer everything—as Xerxes puts it, to 'make Persian territory end only at the sky, the domain of Zeus, [so that] the sun will not shine on any land beyond our borders' (7.8). In H's understanding, that is not the way the world works; something that gets too big will in its turn become the focus of *tisis*, 'retribution', and become small again. In his narrative of Books 7 to 9 we see how the sequence of events in Greece from 481 to 479 BCE illustrates this principle in action.

In the more confident scholarship of the earlier twentieth century, the theme of aggression, reciprocal violence, and consequent divine retribution in H's narrative was often viewed as an archaic survival, a rather sentimentalizing and religious patina spread over a more neutrally realistic narrative of events that could be discerned underneath. Today, however, much of what in H's narrative is expressed in religious terms can be put instead in terms of a political ecology: the sense (certainly understood by the ancient Greeks) that the resources of the earth are finite, and that the balancing that will inevitably occur is a natural one—those who try to discern the underlying balance fare better in the long run than those who follow their own compulsive agendas to the end.

Xerxes is (as his uncle Artabanus points out) a young king, with an unrealistic view of the scope of his power, and unrealistic expectations for his great expedition. We see him at the end retreating from Greece back to Asia and there embroiling himself in a disastrous affair with his own daughter-in-law. Xerxes was in fact killed in a palace revolt in 465 BCE—an event H does not mention but assumes that we know. H is quite clear that as human beings Persians are on the whole no better and no worse than Greeks. Structurally, however, Xerxes' great expedition to Greece stands as a monument to the dangerous blindness of massive empires and grandiose thinking—but it is also the backdrop against which H has been able to present to us the Greeks' love of their homeland, their valour against incredible odds, and their deep desire to preserve their freedom.

BOOK SEVEN

Book 7 again shows that H did not plan his narrative around our book divisions, since the battle of Artemisium at the beginning of Book 8 is the natural continuation of the battle of Thermopylae in Book 7. Apart from that, however, Book 7 has some coherence as the narrative of the preparatory movements of the Persians and the Greeks, those taken prior to the great battles that will decide the war. The first half of the book is taken up with Persian preparations and transport of the huge Persian army and navy down into Greece during the spring and summer of 480 BCE. H emphasizes the care of Xerxes' preparations and the numbers of his army and navy. The Greek efforts to come together are then recounted, with most of the emphasis laid on the various excuses and evasions of important Greek states who do not join the league against Persia. The Greeks abandon Thessaly, since it is clear they cannot defend it. Leonidas and his valiant band of about five thousand (300 Spartiates, 3,100 Peloponnesians, and additional helots, Thespians, and Thebans) hold the pass at Thermopylae for as long as possible, but they receive no reinforcements and those who remain all die when Xerxes is shown a way around the pass. The only consolation the Greeks can find at this point is that several days earlier the Persians have lost perhaps up to a third of their fleet in a huge storm off Cape Sepias in Magnesia.

7.1–19 Persian reactions to Marathon and decisions leading up to the campaign in Greece.

7.1 Darius dies in 486 BCE, and revolt in both Egypt and Babylon in the 480s complicates the Persian plan to punish Greece for Sardis and Marathon (*CAH* iv. 72–5). The revolt in Babylon was suppressed by Megabyzus. It is not mentioned by Greek authors, although Xerxes' removal of the statue of Bel-Marduk (cf. 1.183) may well date to this time. The necessity of quenching revolts in these other important provinces probably bought the Greeks crucial time to begin settling their own differences; if Darius or Xerxes had been able to march on Greece in the mid-480s, the outcome might have been very different, especially given the bad relations between Athens and Aegina at the time. Notice that H essentially omits the complicated rivalries of the Greek states in the 480s as a main focus of his narrative.

7.2–4   Xerxes was born c.518 BCE and Darius probably made him crown prince even earlier than H thinks (CAH iv. 72), but the addition of Demaratus to the scene adds a piquant element for H's Greek audience, particularly given Demaratus' own problems of lineage in Sparta and the notorious difficulties of the Spartan dual kingship, 6.61–6, 52.

7.5   Gobryas was one of the original seven conspirators (3.70, 78). He was Darius' father-in-law before Darius became king, and he also married Darius' sister. His son by that sister, Mardonius, is therefore the nephew of Darius and cousin of Xerxes; he is also Darius' son-in-law (6.43). Mardonius is ambitious to become the satrap of Greece, and so argues for conquest with a mixture of reasonable and silly arguments (cf. 9.82 for the poverty of Greece). For the Persian love of trees, cf. 7.31; 'paradise' is originally a Persian word for an enclosed garden or orchard.

7.6   Other proponents of a war against Greece. The rest of the Thessalians are not as enthusiastic about the prospect of Persian invasion as the Aleuadae are (7.172). For the susceptibility of the Pisistratidae and Hippias himself to dreams and oracles, cf. n. 5.56; for their collection of oracles, cf. 5.90, 93. Musaeus was a mythic singer connected to Orpheus; H refers to his oracles also at 8.96 and 9.43. Since their expulsion from Athens in 510 BCE the Pisistratidae have lived at Sigeum in the Troad, as clients of Persia (cf. 5.94).

7.7   Persian rule over Egypt becomes much harsher, possibly precipitating the revolt of Inaros c.463–2 BCE. Achaemenes the satrap dies in the battle of Papremis, 459 (n. 3.12).

7.8–11   As he has already done in the constitutional debate of 3.80 ff., H uses the speeches of Xerxes and his courtiers here to elucidate the arguments that figure prominently in the Persian thinking to invade Greece; it also makes something of the temper of the principal actors clear. Cf. Atossa's conversation with Darius in 3.134. It is a narrative technique that Thucydides after him will use to great effect.

Note in Xerxes' speech his desire to equal his father; cf. Aeschylus' Persians 753 f. and CAH iv. 76. Pelops was in myth the son of Tantalus of Lydia, the father of Atreus, and the grandfather of Agamemnon, victor at Troy. He gave his name to the Peloponnese. Mardonius in his flattering reply (9) exaggerates considerably; only some of the Indians, Sacae, and Ethiopians are subjects of Persia. For his previous expedition, see n. 6.43–5. The rest of those present fear to oppose him (10).

Artabanus (10) has already advised his brother, Darius, wisely in c.513 BCE (4.83), a fact of which he reminds his nephew, Xerxes, here. He will hold more conversation with Xerxes about the brevity of human life at Abydus, 7.46–52. Here he raises themes that remind us of Solon's advice to Croesus; both elaborate on aspects of the Delphic motto, *mēden agan*, 'nothing in excess'; the gods bring down those with pretensions. For the notion of the envy of the gods, see n. 1.32. The pathos of bodies torn apart by birds and dogs is more Greek than Persian (*Iliad* 1.4; cf. *Histories* 1.140, where it is presented as a normal Persian custom). The allusion to 'staying with the women' in Xerxes' angry retort (11) will be developed later: 8.88, 9.20, 107, 108–13.

7.12–19 In ch. 13 Xerxes refers to his youth; if he was born about 518 BCE, he was still under 40 at the time of the Greek campaign. The point of the dream sequence is that the gods do intend the Persian invasion of Greece to happen, just as they intended the death of Croesus' son, 1.34. The fact that the gods intend the invasion does not render Xerxes himself guiltless, cf. n. 1.13.

7.20–5 From the spring of 484 to the spring of 480 BCE Xerxes prepares for war. For Darius' invasion of Scythia, see 4.83–144; for the Scythians' invasion of Asia in the early seventh century, see n. 1.103. H believes the Trojan War to be about eight hundred years before his own time (2.145).

Acte (on which Mount Athos is located) is the easternmost of the three peninsulas of Chalcidice (22); excavation of the Persian canal began c.483 and was designed to avoid the dangerously stormy tip of the peninsula (6.44). The canal was 2,400 yards (2,200 m.) long and at least 65 feet (20 m.) wide (*CAH* iv. 526). The charge levelled by H in ch. 24 does not hold, for the portage of a fleet as large as Xerxes' (together with its support convoys) would have been practically impossible. Xerxes was aiming moreover at permanently attaching Greece to his empire, and the convenience of the canal would continue into the future. The moral issue is another matter (7.35; also, for making peninsulas into islands, cf. 1.174). See Lateiner, 126–35 for the importance of geographical boundaries and the notion of transgression in H.

7.26–32 The march from Critalla to Sardis. In myth Marsyas was a satyr who challenged Apollo to a musical contest with his Phrygian pipe and lost; Apollo skinned him alive. The end of the story of Pythius the Lydian, told at 7.39, may be compared to that of Oeobazus in 4.84, at the outset of Darius' Scythian expedition. Such events, along with the ample mention of the Persian lash (e.g. 7.22, 35, 56, 103, 223), suggest to the reader what is expected to happen to Greece if Xerxes triumphs.

For Pythius' enormous wealth (28): one (silver) talent was 6,000 drachmas and one drachma was a skilled Greek labourer's daily wage. The gold daric stater was particularly pure, cf. 4.166. Cf. App.

2. For Xerxes' Immortals (31), cf. 7.83. On the demand for earth and water: Xerxes does not send messengers to Athens and Sparta (32), because they had killed Darius' earlier emissaries (6.48; cf. 7.133); earth and water are the normal tokens of submission to Persian rule (4.126, 5.17, 6.48, 7.131). Xerxes and the army spend the winter of 481–480 BCE in Sardis.

7.33–6 The reference to Artayctes, the Persian governor of Sestus, looks forward to events at the end of the war (9.116–21); Artayctes will be crucified overlooking the site where Xerxes' army marches into Greece via the bridge, and the general who orders this will be the Athenian Xanthippus, father of Pericles, in the winter of 479/8 BCE. Xanthippus then takes the captured remnants of Xerxes' bridge-cables home and dedicates them in sanctuaries that H does not specify, possibly on the ruined Acropolis and also in the Athenian stoa at Delphi (9.121). In referring briefly to the fate of Artayctes here, H anticipates the final undoing both of Xerxes' literal bridge and of his more general attempt to bridge the separation of Europe and Asia and import Persian ways into Greece. Protesilaus was the first Greek who had leapt ashore at Troy (*Iliad* 2.695 ff.) and if one adds that to the presence of Pericles' father at Artayctes' death, the implicit ironies are multiple. They lend an ominous tone to the next narrative, the report of bridge-building in chs. 34–6; that narrative begins by emphasizing not the incredible feat of building the bridge itself, but rather Xerxes' violence in punishing the Hellespont— again, a tacit reminder of what may happen in Greece if Xerxes triumphs.

For a detailed description of the construction of the pontoon bridge, see *CAH* iv. 527–32. The ships beneath are designed to support the weight of the bridge and reduce the strain on the cables. The distance across of seven stades (34) is some three-quarters of a mile, or 1.24 km. (The modern Hellespont is wider.)

7.37–43 Xerxes marches from Sardis in the spring of 480 BCE. His progress to the coast and down the European side from Thrace is deliberate; he will not reach the scene of serious fighting until late August or September. This will badly affect his campaign because the weather and the approach of winter will limit his choices. There was no solar eclipse at this time (37), although there had been one visible at Susa in the spring of 481 and there would be one visible at Sardis in February 478; local tradition perhaps conflated these to make an eclipse coincide with Xerxes' departure. The connection of Apollo with the sun explains the thinking of the Magi, at least for a Greek audience. (The story is unlikely to come from a Persian source, since Mitra also is a god of light.)

Xerxes' treatment of Pythius here suggests a certain instability in Xerxes himself (cf. 7.44–7 below). His act is the same as his father's in 4.84, but the coupling of it with the earlier effusive praise and grand gesture is not. Again, the army's departure through the two halves of the severed body of Pythius' son strikes an ominous note.

The sacred chariot (40) will be given to the Thracians and the horses stolen (8.115) while Xerxes is campaigning down south in Greece. Xerxes' charioteer is probably also his brother-in-law, since Otanes is the father of his wife Amestris and commander of the Persian forces of his army (7.61), and two other sons of Otanes are ranking officers (7.62, 82). Cf. the end of n. 5.117–21. Note Xerxes' interest in tourism at Troy and elsewhere on his trip into Greece; a brisker timetable with a leaner army might have affected the outcome.

7.44-56 Just before Xerxes crosses the Hellespont into Europe, he gazes at his army and holds another conversation with his uncle Artabanus. Xerxes likes to look at his army (7.56, 59, 100), and he associates value with large numbers (7.103). Here (49) Artabanus tells Xerxes that the very massiveness of his force will also be his greatest weakness, since it will be difficult to find safe anchorage for the fleet and food for the land army. These strategic factors certainly play a part in the forthcoming campaign.

In ch. 51 Artabanus also worries about the loyalty of the Ionians; Xerxes reassures him, citing their loyalty during his father's Scythian campaign, misunderstanding their motives as much as the Scythians did (4.142; cf. 4.137). Cf. n. 8.19–26. In chs. 53 and 54 Xerxes' determination to conquer all of Europe is again emphasized. The image of his army being whipped across the Hellespont for seven continuous days and nights is a very vivid one, but the time is probably compressed, *CAH* iv. 537. This theme stands in ironic counterpoint to the sycophantic exclamation of the Hellespontine man addressing Xerxes as Zeus (56). Cf. the oracle in 7.220.

7.57-9 Xerxes travels from the Hellespont to Doriscus in Thrace. First he has to march north-east through the Chersonese (the Gallipoli peninsula) and then turn west. In mythology Helle was escaping from a wicked stepmother with her brother Phrixus and rode on the golden ram's back over the Hellespont; she fell off and had the strait named after her in consequence, while the ram's golden fleece ended up in Colchis to be taken by Jason (cf. 1.2). For Darius' stay in Thrace, cf. 4.143; the fortress was probably set up by Megabyzus afterwards (5.2). The Cicones of ch. 59 occur in Homer: *Iliad* 2.846, *Odyssey* 9.39; Ciconian women murdered the legendary Thracian singer Orpheus.

7.60-83 The review of the infantry. The number is undoubtedly exaggerated; cf. for example *CAH* iv. 533–6, where the total is calculated as 220,000 men under arms on land, and another 22,000 for the supply service and so on; others put the total figure as low as 80,000–100,000. Note that the Greeks never encounter the full force of Xerxes' land army, even at Thermopylae.

Like the account of the Persian tax rolls in 3.90 ff. and the description of the stages of the Royal Road in 5.52 ff., this list of infantry units may be based on official Persian information. H arranges his material in a geographical order: the Medes and Persians, then those peoples to the east, those to the south, those of Asia Minor, and finally of the Levant.

The mythological material in chs. 61 and 62 is of course Greek in inspiration. Among other problems, the mythic genealogy of Perseus is inconsistent with that of 1.7, since here Belus is grandfather-in-law to Perseus while Perseus' descendant Heracles is in 1.7 Belus' grandfather. Cf. 6.54. For the fanciful etymology of the Medes from Medea (62), the best that can be said about it is that it is old; cf. Hesiod, *Theogony* 1000 f. 'Arian' (62) is an Indo-European word found in Old Persian and Sanskrit as well, now vitiated by the murderous use to which it was put in the 1930s under its Sanskrit form, Aryan.

The Sacae of ch. 64 are not the (European) Scythians described in Book 4, but a similar nomadic people from farther east; cf. *CAH* iv. 171, 174. For the distinction between southern and eastern Ethiopians in ch. 70, cf. 3.17, 94. The Thracians of ch. 75 are from Asia. The name of the people in ch. 76 is missing; what is given is Stein's conjecture. For the 'Dispossessed' of ch. 80, see 3.93.

7.84–88 Review of the cavalry. For the speed of camels (86) cf. 3.102, although in actuality they move at a rate of about 2½ miles (4 km.) per hour; only the modern dromedary approaches a speed of 10 miles per hour. Cf. 1.80 for their tendency to frighten horses.

7.89–99 Review of the fleet. Like other Persian figures, the number 1,207 is very high; some historians set it more probably at about 600 instead. Aeschylus' *Persians* 341–3, produced in 472 BCE, only eight years after the battle (in which Aeschylus himself fought), also gives 1,207, but he uses it not for the initial size of the fleet but for the number of Persian ships at Salamis later in the summer (September 480). This discrepancy has not been satisfactorily explained. *CAH* iv. 532 says that the proportion of smaller ships to triremes, however, is about right (H says 3,000 ships 'in total' (97)). Note the presence in Xerxes' fleet of those who had fought valiantly to free Ionia from Persian rule in the 490s (90–5).

In 7.99 H singles out Xerxes' one woman naval commander, Artemisia, the queen regent of Halicarnassus. As another Herodotean wise adviser (n. 171), she advises Xerxes before and after the battle of Salamis (8.68 and 101), but she also saves herself by daring and unscrupulous tactics during the battle (8.87). She is the mother or grandmother of the tyrant Lygdamis, who in the ancient accounts was the enemy of H's family in Halicarnassus; none the less, H gives her a role among Xerxes' intelligent counsellors.

7.100–4 For Demaratus the exiled king of Sparta in Xerxes' retinue, see nn. 6.61–72 and 7.2–4. Whereas Artemisia gives tactical advice (8.68), Demaratus is the most eloquent spokesperson for Greek values, and particularly the connections that link Greek poverty, courage, intelligence, and respect for the law. (He, however, talks of

Spartans, not Greeks.) Xerxes will take Demaratus' prescient opinions more seriously after Thermopylae, 7.234–7; here he laughs (103)—almost always a mistake in H (Lateiner, 28).

7.105–27 Xerxes travels from Doriscus to Therma. H violates chronological order in chs. 106–7, to describe the Persian loss of most of Thrace at the end of the war. The Persians were expelled from Sestus in early 478 BCE (9.118), and Thucydides tells of their loss of Byzantium that same year (Thucydides 1.94, 128) and of Eïon in c.476/5 (Thucydides 1.98). Eïon is just north-east of the three-pronged peninsula of Chalcidice.

H has referred to the conquest of Thrace by the Persians in 5.1, 5.26, and 6.44. In 7.111 he compares the oracle of the shrine of Dionysus in the mountains of Thrace to Delphi; evidently he had heard exotically misleading claims made for it. In keeping with the touristic nature of this portion of the campaign narrative, we may note that in ch. 115 Xerxes passes by Stagirus, birthplace of Aristotle ninety-six years later.

Artachaees, the overseer of the canal recently dug across Acte (117; cf. 7.22–4), was according to H's calculations about eight feet (2.4 m.) tall. Other tall people in the *Histories* are the Orestes skeleton (1.68), measuring an improbable ten feet (3.1 m.) tall, the skeleton of 9.83, over seven feet (2.2 m.) tall, and the Athenian woman Phya (1.60), who was just under six feet (1.8 m.) tall. A cubit is some eighteen inches (44 cm.), or the length of a forearm; for H's weights, measurements, and distances see App. 2. For the significance of Artachaees becoming a hero, cf. the end of n. 5.108–17.

For the four hundred talents spent on Xerxes' dinner (118), cf. nn. 6.132–6 and 7.26–32. A talent is about fifty-seven pounds (26 kg.) of silver. H records the witticism of one Megacreon of Abdera (120); cf. the end of n. 3.118–19. On the three routes that Xerxes' land army took and the co-ordination of his fleet and his land army, see *CAH* iv. 537–9. By splitting up and taking three different routes, the army could take the local grain from a larger region, and the animals could graze, since it was summer. Therma (7.127) is in Macedonia, near the site of the later city of Thessalonike.

7.128–31 Here Xerxes is enjoying another spectacle, not now the grandeur of his army but the grandeur of nature; cf. 7.44–56. Just as he has dug a trench at Mount Athos and has whipped the Hellespont (7.22, 35), here he falls to thinking how he might subdue the geography of Thessaly to his purposes. Note H's rationalizing in ch. 129; H does not disbelieve in Poseidon but points out that the person who takes the epithet 'Earth Shaker' seriously, by definition thinks Poseidon is responsible for earthquakes. Xerxes' delays in this early part of his journey may be responsible for pushing the campaign into the dangerous late summer weather that imperils his fleet further on (cf. 7.188–91); *CAH* iv. 539–40, 546 gives Xerxes high

marks, however, for the planning and practical organization underlying this stage of the invasion.

7.132–78 As Xerxes waits for Greek submission (cf. 7.32), the scene shifts
to the Greeks themselves and their efforts at preparation. The notion
of tithing the collaborators probably does not mean to fine them, but
rather to destroy them utterly and give a tenth of the profits to
Delphi. The Lacedaemonians later (9.106) make the proposal to evict
from their lands all the states who have collaborated with Persia and
to resettle the Ionians there, but the Athenians object. H makes it
clear that most of the states who openly collaborate have had virtually no choice (cf. 172).

7.133–7 Darius had sent envoys in the late 490s to Greece (6.48). Pausanias, the later travel writer (3.12.7), knows a version of events that
holds Miltiades responsible for the Athenian mistreatment of Darius'
messengers, but H would probably have included such a story in his
account of Miltiades' end, 6.132–6, if he had heard it. Hydarnes, the
Persian satrap of ch. 135 (and son of Hydarnes the conspirator,
3.70), is in fact part of the Miltiades story also (6.133). For the Greek
horror at *proskunēsis*, voluntary prostration before another person,
cf. n. 1.134; it was a gesture a Greek would perform only before a
god. The episode of ch. 137 is one of the latest events narrated in
the *Histories*; it happened in 430 BCE, early in the Peloponnesian
War (Thucydides 2.67).

7.138–44 The survey of Greek activity begins with Xerxes' demand for
earth and water; not until after the battle of Salamis does the Greek
narrative become something more than a response to Persian aggression (Immerwahr, 34). In ch. 139 H makes his famous defence of
Athens. *CAH* iv. 543 points out that Sparta's role was at least as
crucial; they were the impetus behind the formation of the Greek
league in the autumn of 481 BCE (7.145), and without their presence
at the battle of Plataea in spring 479, the Athenian-led victory at sea
at Salamis would have amounted to relatively little. The Athenians,
however, had many temptations to become collaborators, but did
not, and for that H gives them credit (cf. 8.140–4 and 9.4–5).

In chs. 140–3 H introduces two interrelated topics: Delphi's
extreme pessimism about Greek victory, and Themistocles, the man
'just recently risen to prominence in Athens', who turns Athens'
gloomy oracles into a mandate to develop the Athenian navy. The
Spartans, Cretans, and Argives also receive depressing oracles from
Delphi (7.220, 169, 148). Delphi has had ties to the East throughout the period narrated in the *Histories* (e.g. 1.13, 19, 47, 55, 85),
and had seen the fate of Didyma and other sanctuaries after the
Ionian revolt (6.19). Moreover, many of the states of northern and
central Greece who comprise the majority of Delphi's Amphictyony,
or secular administrative body, are in the path of the invading Persian
army; it is not surprising that Delphi has tacitly medized (*CAH* iv.
540, and more generally for Delphi, iii/3. 312, 318–19). Delphi's

pessimism about Greek victory against Persia does not compromise H's admiration for the oracle or his belief in its powers (8.36-9, although he knows it is not incorruptible: cf. 6.66).

Themistocles was born in the 520s, was eponymous archon in Athens in 494/3 BCE and in 483/2 persuaded the Athenians to use their profits from the silver-mines at Laurium to build their fleet and fortify their port, ostensibly against Aegina. H introduces him into the narrative just before his greatest accomplishment, rallying the Athenians to resist Persia with their new fleet; Themistocles will be the architect of the Greek victory at Salamis (8.56-63, 75, 79-80, 83, 123-5). H is grudging in his praise for Themistocles (here as a new man, and in 8.109-12 for his duplicity and avarice) but avoids describing in detail Themistocles' supposed later escapades, in particular his implication in the crimes of Pausanias and subsequent flight to Asia (where he died c.459, the wealthy governor of Magnesia under Artaxerxes). Thucydides 1.135-8 is more enthusiastic than H about what must have been Themistocles' remarkable intellectual gifts.

7.145-7 H is not specific about the timing of the Greek congresses that meet, perhaps this one in autumn 481 BCE and another in spring 480 (7.172), to organize against the Persian invasion. For details of how the Greek resistance might have been organized, see CAH iv. 540-5. Sparta was given control on land and sea (cf. 8.2), and there was an advisory council consisting of a commander from each contingent, but ultimately the Spartan commander-in-chief had control over strategy. The story of the spies whom Xerxes sends back to Greece (147) shows not just his magnanimity, but also the extent to which he expects the vastness of his resources to overwhelm the Greeks psychologically; cf. 7.56. Ch. 147 is also a particularly vivid piece of evidence for the existence of a grain route from the Euxine (Black) Sea to Greece in operation in the 480s. The grain is going to the Peloponnese and Aegina here; the grain route from the north was also of great importance to Athens, as Athens' earlier foreign policy in the area of the Hellespont suggests (n. 6.34-8).

7.148-52 Argos medizes. H is sympathetic (152) to the plight of the Argives, only fourteen years after their disastrous defeat at the battle of Sepeia (n. 6.77-80). The right of command is not a trivial issue, as any observer of modern multinational military forces can attest; cf. Pausanias' reported behaviour at Plataea, 9.46-7. The rivalry between Lacedaemon and Argos is long-standing; cf. n. 1.82.

The genealogy of Perseus has already figured in the Histories in a variety of connections, in 2.91, 6.53-4, 7.61. Whatever the details of their accord, H reports the Argives actively supporting the Persian cause by pre-arrangement in 9.12. The 'other business' referred to in ch. 151 is thought by some historians to be a reference to a 'Peace of Callias' formally ending the conflict between Persia and Athens perhaps c.450/49 BCE (mentioned by the fourth-century orators

Isocrates, Demosthenes, and Lycurgus but with differing details about the boundaries to be established). Neither Thucydides in the *pentecontaetia* (Thucydides 1.89–117) nor Lysias in 2.56–7 mentions it. Cf. the different view of *CAH* v. 121–7.

H's disclaimer in ch. 152 is helpful in clarifying his relationship to the text he narrates. He presents himself as an investigator who has taken the trouble to ferret out and test stories, and narrate them to us, but part of his task is to remind us that he cannot vouch for all he has been told; cf. 2.123, 125, 3.122, 4.96, 105, 195, and the large number of variant versions of stories, n. 1.70. See the Introduction, pp. xxix–xxx.

7.153–67 The Greek league and Sicily. In chs. 153–6 H usefully narrates as background the growth of the tyranny at Gela and the tyrants' expansion into the control of Syracuse as well. Cleander became tyrant at Gela *c.*505 BCE and was succeeded by his brother Hippocrates in 498, who turned his rule into an empire in eastern Sicily. In 491 Hippocrates died, and his cavalry commander Gelon put down a revolt but made himself tyrant. Syracuse had been founded by Corinth *c.*734 and so Corinth had saved Syracuse from Hippocrates, but it was taken by Gelon working with its own ruling élite in 485. At that point Gelon moved to Syracuse and gave Gela to his brother Hiero. Gelon reigned in Syracuse until 478. See further, *CAH* iv. 757–70. H & W point out that Gelon's creation of a 'great Syracuse', involving the ruthless shifting of populations, probably saved Sicily from conquest by Carthage. It was certainly ruthless: 'more than two generations before the first Carthaginian army destroyed a Greek city in Sicily, three had already been annihilated by a true "panhellenic" Greek tyrant' (*CAH* iv. 770). The detailed narrative of Sicilian conquest prepares us for Gelon's jaundiced view of the role the Greeks want to assign him in the coming struggle; he controls more resources than any of them and has won them by his own efforts.

The debate between Gelon and the Greeks (157–62) is a vivid dramatization of the problems of disunity that will dog the Greek League. It is similar in function to Xerxes' debate with Artabanus (7.46–52), which highlights Persian problems with land, sea, and Ionians. Gelon's assessment, that there are lots of chiefs but no Indians in the Greek force, proves a difficulty that the Greeks barely overcome (8.2, 56, 61, 9.26, 53). It is why Demaratus' or perhaps even Artemisia's advice if acted upon might well have won the war for Xerxes (7.235, 8.68); it should have been easy to scatter the weakly united Greek force.

For Gelon's reference to his war with the Carthaginians and the murder of Dorieus that he wanted avenged (158), see *CAH* iv. 767 and 5.42–6. It seems unlikely that Gelon ever seriously contemplated sending massive resources to mainland Greece, since war with Carthage was looming for him, especially after 482, when Theron of Acragas expelled the pro-Carthaginian tyrant Terillus from Himera (165).

Gelon's simile in ch. 162 is said by Aristotle (*Rhetoric* 1365ᵃ and 1411ᵃ) to have been used by Pericles at Athens, probably in his funeral speech for the Athenians who died in the Samian war in 440 BCE. Syagrus's first reply to Gelon (159) echoes *Iliad* 7.125; the Athenians' Homeric allusion (161) is to *Iliad* 2.552–4.

7.163–4 The Scythes referred to in ch. 163 is perhaps the expelled ruler of Zancle (6.23; *CAH* iv. 760–3). If so, Cadmus has inherited his virtue from his father (6.24). See Macan, H & W, and Burn, 309–10 for the numerous questions raised by chs. 163–4. Macan concludes, 'The total absence of any cross reference here [to 6.23–4] is astounding; it is perhaps the most frappant of all such cases of Hdt.'s insouciance.' There is much about Cadmus and Zancle we are not told and would like to know—particularly if (and how!) Cadmus went from being a henchman of Anaxilaus of Rhegium to becoming the right-hand man of Gelon in the delicate negotiations to be held with Xerxes in the case of a Persian victory in Greece in 480 BCE. Nor is it clear when exactly the name change from Zancle to Messana took place; cf. Thucydides 6.4.

7.165–7 H remarks in passing (166) that the battle of Himera, in which Gelon of Syracuse and Theron of Acragas won decisively against the Carthaginians in the north of Sicily, took place on the same day as the battle of Salamis (probably September of 480 BCE). (The later Greek historian Diodorus 11.24 puts it on the same day as Thermopylae.)

Aristotle in the *Poetics* (1459ᵃ) uses the synchronism of Himera and Salamis to demonstrate the superiority of poetry to history; he claims that poetry can deal with organic developments and their underlying unity, while history perforce has to deal with what happened in a given time, whether there is an underlying connection or not. Aristotle has used an unfortunate example, however, because H does *not* talk about the battle of Himera in its chronological order but places it here, much before the narration of Salamis or even Thermopylae, because of its logical connection with other, earlier events in Sicily. (However, some historians thinking over the coincidence in time find it reasonable to argue that there is in this instance an underlying logical connection: the Phoenicians may have encouraged their colonists, the Carthaginians, to mount a western offensive precisely to keep the great Greek cities of Sicily occupied during the time of the Persian invasion of Greece.) For a fuller account of events in Sicily leading up to and including the battle of Himera, see *CAH* iv. 766–75; Burn, 297–310, 477–87.

7.168 Corcyra is the modern Corfu. In his cynical reading of Corcyraean motives and actions, perhaps H was responding to their role in the early stages of the Peloponnesian War (Thucydides 1.25, 31–44).

Greeks who hoped to avoid war in the 430s would have been exasperated by the traditionally isolationist and self-serving politics of Corcyra. Etesian winds do blow violently off Cape Malea in late summer.

7.169–71 An excursus back into the quasi-mythological history of Crete, to explain why the Delphic oracle counsels non-participation in the Greek League. King Minos of Crete, in his quest for Daedalus, had been treacherously boiled in his bath by the daughters of the king of Camicus.

The mutual slaughter of Tarentines and Rhegians (170) occurred after the Persian Wars, dated to 473 BCE by Diodorus 11.52; Iapygia is south of Brindisi, on the heel of Italy. H would not have called this the greatest slaughter of all if he had known of the Athenian disaster in Syracuse in 413 BCE (Thucydides 7.85, 87). The 'third wave' (171) consists of the Dorians, who, by tradition, arrived in Crete before they conquered the Peloponnese, *CAH* iii/3. 234. Crete in classical times was Dorian.

7.172–4 This is probably the second major meeting of the Greek League (see 7.145 for the first), and the meeting at which they determine their initial strategy for meeting the Persians. Euripus (173) is the strait between the island of Euboea and the mainland stretching north of Attica. For Alexander the Macedonian, see n. 5.17–22. *CAH* iv. 545 thinks that the Greek position at Tempe was certainly untenable, and that by June 480 BCE the Greeks had withdrawn back to the Isthmus. If so, the brief Greek expedition and retreat in chs. 173–4, though it is narrated after Xerxes' entrance into Thessaly (7.128), took place about two months earlier, *CAH* iv. 546. For the political situation (especially of Alexander) see Burn, 341–5.

7.175–7 Thermopylae is chosen as a place to defend because it appears that there is only one route, not several, as in Thessaly; moreover, it is narrow and thus a small force can defend it against a large force. On Artemisium: the Greeks' land and sea forces must stay in contact with each other. H & W (*ad loc.*) quote Munro: 'Thermopylae could not have been held without Artemisium, for it would have been at once turned by the enemies' fleet, but . . . Artemisium was [also] useless without Thermopylae, for the Persians would never have attacked the Greek fleet but simply sailed past it outside Euboea, if the land road to the Isthmus had been open. All they wanted was to get their army and fleet to the Peloponnese at the same time.'

H's directions for the lie of Thermopylae are wrong (the pass goes east–west, not north–south), although his general description is good. H & W: 'The pass between mountain and sea has at either end an extremely narrow gate; the western gate, however, near Anthela, could be easily turned by crossing a projecting spur of the mountain, the eastern near Alpeni is clearly behind the Greek position.' In the three miles (4.8 km.) between them was the middle gate, the nar-

rowest passage between mountain and sea and the crucial position
to defend. This is where the 'ancient wall' was located, built by the
Phocians for protection against the Thessalians (cf. 8.27–9). See
7.210–24 for the actual encounter. For a map and detailed description see *CAH* iv. 556 and Burn, 409–11.

7.178–95 The name 'Thyia' itself means 'raging;' thus H begins the narrative of the Persian navy's descent into Greece with a detail that
looks forward to the disastrous storm to come off the coast of Magnesia, which will cost the Persians as much as a third of their fleet
(188–92). He begins the narrative of the descent, however, with an
account of a preliminary skirmish that shows the clear superiority of
the Persian fleet in speed (179)—in a few weeks the Greeks will win
at Salamis (8.84–95) not because their fleet is absolutely better, but
because of Themistocles' brilliance in choosing conditions that
favour the smaller number of slower, lower, more solid Greek ships.
The name of the sacrificed Greek marine, Leon, means 'lion' in Greek
(180). After the capture of the Greek ships, the rest of the Greeks
take refuge in Chalcis on the inner coast of Euboea (183) and so are
protected from the storm that will batter the Persians off Cape
Sepias.

Before the account of the storm, however, H surveys the full might
of the Persian naval force (184–7). His estimate both of the number
of men per vessel and of the number of Europeans who joined Xerxes
is probably exaggerated, but his arithmetic is correct except for the
calculation of the amount of grain needed to feed the Persian troops.
H & W explain where the error in division occurred.

On Boreas, the north wind, and Orithyia, his Athenian wife, cf.
Plato's reference to the myth in the *Phaedrus* (229b), and Simonides'
poetry on the battle of Artemisium, one fragment of which, if M.
West's restoration is correct, might name the sons of Boreas, Zetes
and Calaïs. For discussion of the important new Simonides fragments
and their relation to the Persian Wars, see Boedeker, ed. (1996), and
for Simonides himself, the end of n. 7.201–33. (For the reference to
Athos in ch. 189, cf. 6.44. Cf. 7.49 for Artabanus' reference to the
combined danger of wind and sea.)

Two themes prominent in Book 1 appear in this passage: big
becomes small (1.5), and, with reference to the story of Ameinocles
(190), no human life is without its share of grief and pain (cf. 1.32).
Thetis (191) is the immortal Nereid mother of the Greek hero
Achilles; a *sēpia* in Greek is a cuttlefish, a relative of the squid—
hence the name of the headland and perhaps the myth of Thetis and
her sisters living along this coast as well. (Sepia or dark-brown ink
originally came from the cuttlefish.) Another mythic story, that of
the voyage of the Argonauts, is referred to in ch. 193. In Apollonius'
later version (1.1207 ff.) Heracles is left behind instead in Mysia on
the Propontis, while hunting for Hylas. For Darius' judgement on
the unfortunate Sandoces (194), cf. 1.137 and 5.25.

7.196–200 *Xerxes' land army.* When last seen, Xerxes was in Thessaly, demanding earth and water from the Greeks (7.131–2); now he moves his land forces southwards from Thessaly into Malis and the coastal town of Trachis (near Mount Oeta, where Heracles died (198), and the setting of Sophocles' *Trachiniae*). On the way Xerxes is interested in local beliefs and scrupulous about not violating local custom. Xerxes pays much more attention to these old myths and the rituals connected to them than he does to the good advice of his Greek advisers concerning the invasion at hand.

There are about 9.1 stades in a mile, so the places named here are very close together. There must be some mistake in the text in ch. 199, because 22,000 plethra (6 plethra in a stade) are about 405 miles (651 km.), and though the coastline has changed since antiquity, this has always been a narrow coastal plain. Some scholars think that H is actually calculating the area of the plain of Trachis, not its width, because that is relevant as the territory covered by Xerxes' encampment.

Xerxes' road, which has taken him south along the coast, here turns sharply east, since the rugged coastline juts eastwards. He is stopped at the west gate of the pass by the Greeks. To the south of the pass are the high mountains, to the north the sea and impassable marshland. As the Greeks saw it, stopping Xerxes from threading his troops east along the narrow coastal pass at Thermopylae would block his entry down into the southern parts of central Greece.

7.201–33 *The battle of Thermopylae.* Thermopylae means 'warm gates'. The Solonian platitudes that persuade the Opuntian Locrians and Phocians to join the Greek force (203) have an odd ring, since they turn out not to be true, or at least not in the short term useful to the Greeks at Thermopylae.

On numbers: H's cross-reference in ch. 205 refers back to the number given in ch. 202; there is some uncertainty about the number of Peloponnesians actually at the first two days of battle, since the epigram in ch. 228 mentions 4,000 Peloponnesians in total, while H's count in ch. 202 is 3,100. (All the Greek dead are by H numbered at 4,000 in 8.25.) The Persian count in the epigram is 3,000,000; H's count for the original infantry forces in 7.60 was 1,700,000, and it is by now swollen with 300,000 European additions (7.185). H says that 20,000 of the invaders died at Thermopylae (8.24). For more realistic numbers for the total Persian land force, cf. n. 7.60–83; there were certainly many more foreign invaders than there were Greeks at Thermopylae, and many fell, including two of Xerxes' own brothers (224). For the battle itself, see *CAH* iv. 555–8; Burn, 407–20; Lazenby, 136–48.

Before describing the battle, H does honour to Leonidas, Cleomenes' younger half-brother and now king of Lacedaemon, by retelling his whole genealogy (204; cf. 8.131, 139, 9.64). For the family and its problems, cf. 5.39–48. Men with sons would leave a family line behind them; they were also thought to care more deeply about their cities than those without families (Thucydides 2.44). The reference to the Carnea (206) helps to date Thermopylae to the full moon of either mid-August or mid-September 480 BCE. (There is much controversy, however: see *CAH* iv. 588–9; Burn, 403–5; Lazenby, 118–19.)

In the four days of waiting (207–9), Xerxes has trouble believing that Leonidas intends to contest his right to the pass, and has another conversation with Demaratus; cf. 7.101–4 and 234–7. The two-day battle that ensues (210–12) leads to a stalemate, until a Greek traitor from Malis betrays to Xerxes the fact that a route exists west of Thermopylae going south into the mountains and east along their ridge that can then bring Xerxes' troops down to the coast road again east of the pass, so that Leonidas' army can be attacked from two sides. Leonidas has set the Phocians to guard the mountain route (212) but either he has not instructed them well, or they betray their charge (218). In any case, when Leonidas discovers that the Persians have found the route around the pass, he sends most of his troops away except for the Thebans and Thespians, and on the third day of fighting at the pass dies valiantly with his whole remaining force (220, 223). For the career at Plataea of the unfortunate Spartan who missed the battle (232), see 9.71.

There is much scholarly debate about the wisdom of Leonidas' strategy and tactics at Thermopylae, but no one disputes the heroism of the last stand. Leonidas' decision to stay and fight may well have saved the Greek alliance, since Athens and the other cities of central Greece in the league would have been furious if he had retreated to the Isthmus and given up central Greece without a fight. Understandably enough, many states in the path of the Persian army (like Thessaly) had already medized and without Leonidas' stand many more might have done so. By the 440s the war was being presented as Greeks versus barbarians; in 480 the individual cities were more interested in their own survival than in defending the abstractions involved in a 'Greek way of life'.

The promise to tell about the death of Ephialtes the traitor (213) is one of three unfulfilled promises in H; cf. 1.106, 184; for the Amphictyons see the middle of n. 7.138–44. The negative portrait of the Thebans (222, 233) undoubtedly has been influenced by Thebes' decision to medize; it seems unlikely that Leonidas would have chosen to retain in the pass a Theban force that was clearly untrustworthy from the start. (As one of the latest dates mentioned in the *Histories*, H notes the role of the Theban commander's son in the Theban attack on Plataea that precipitates the Peloponnesian War almost fifty years later (7.233; cf. Thucydides 2.2–5).)

Simonides of Ceos (228; cf. 5.102, n. 7.178–95, the end of n. 9. 33–40; *CAH* iv. 619–20) was a famous poet of dithyrambs, hymns, dirges, scolia, encomia, epinicians, elegies, and epigrams (*c*.556–468 BCE). It is possible that all of the poems quoted here are his, but that the poem for Megistias was the only one written for free, out of friendship; it is also true that many poems were later attributed to him that he did not write. He was the Greek poet *par excellence* of the Persian Wars; his epitaph on the fallen at Marathon was said to have been selected by the Athenians over that of Aeschylus. He had among his patrons the Pisistratidae of Athens, the Scopadae of Thessaly, and Hiero at Syracuse; he is also said to have been a friend of Themistocles. See Boedeker, ed. (1996).

7.234–8 Demaratus advises Xerxes again, this time to fortify Cythera, an island south of Laconia that was in fact taken by the Athenians during the Peloponnesian War, in 424 BCE (Thucydides 4.53–4). Chilon (235) is the sixth-century Spartan ephor included in the group of Seven Sages; cf. n. 1.59. Demaratus' thinking here is similar to Artemisia's (8.68), although Demaratus' advice is better because it relies on the navy drawing off the Spartans from the Greek force, rather than the Persian land army having initially to fight through all the Peloponnesians massed at the Isthmus.

Achaemenes (236), Xerxes' brother, has been the satrap of Egypt since 486 and is commander of the Egyptian forces in the Persian navy against Greece (7.97); he will die at the battle of Papremis in Egypt in 459 (3.12). Xerxes' wrong-headed but judiciously generous reply to Achaemenes (237), acknowledging Demaratus' worth, stands in stark contrast to his ignominious treatment of Leonidas' corpse. Cf. Pausanias' treatment of Mardonius' corpse after Plataea, 9.78–9.

7.239 Many scholars regard this as an interpolation, in part because it does not follow H's normal practice of inserting pendants where they act as background explanation, in part because the whole transition between Books 7 and 8 is very unsatisfactory for its abruptness, and this anecdote does not improve matters. It is, however, an amusing story.

BOOK EIGHT

Book 8 begins abruptly with an account of the confrontations and accidents at sea that actually took place in late summer of 480 BCE, at about
the same time as the land battles at Thermopylae narrated already at the
end of Book 7. Strategically, the initial positions of the Greek land and sea
forces at Thermopylae and Artemisium have been closely connected:
Leonidas needs Eurybiades and the fleet to stop the Persians from landing
and surrounding him at the pass; the fleet needs Leonidas to hold the pass,
to block Xerxes' land forces from proceeding southwards. If the way had
lain open for the Persian land army at Thermopylae, the Persian fleet could
have simply sailed south around Euboea and rejoined the land army in
Boeotia or Attica. As it is, the Greek decision to block the Persians at Thermopylae forces the Persian fleet to spend time off the dangerous coast south
of Magnesia and leaves them exposed to violent late summer storms, difficult moorage, and confrontations with the Greek fleet off Artemisium.
When the Persians move south after their land victory at Thermopylae, it
is with a substantially diminished and probably demoralized fleet.

After winning through at Thermopylae, Xerxes and his land forces
proceed south, and the Persian fleet moves south also to Phalerum on the
coast of Attica. At Salamis, the large island in the Saronic Gulf between
Athens and Megara, the Greek commanders debate what to do. Attica is
evacuated, Xerxes captures the city and fires the Acropolis, and the Peloponnesian Greeks counsel retreat for the entire Greek force to the Isthmus
and the abandonment of central Greece altogether to Xerxes. At this point
Themistocles the Athenian provides crucial if unconventional leadership
for the Greeks. He cajoles and then threatens Eurybiades, the Spartan naval
commander-in-chief; further, he secretly sends a message to the Persians
which traps both the Greek and Persian fleets into fighting in the straits
off Salamis. The narrow space between Salamis and the mainland gives
the smaller, disciplined fleet of the Greeks a tactical advantage, and their
heavier and slower ships, built for ramming, have a definite advantage over
the faster ships of the invader.

After Salamis, still in the early autumn of 480 BCE, Xerxes is disheartened and flees northwards home with the larger part of his land army,
while his fleet retreats to Samos. Mardonius is left to spend the winter in
Thessaly with a picked force (said to comprise 300,000 men) and to fight
the Greeks on land during the following spring.

8.1–18   Artemisium. H begins with a summary of the Greek fleet that par-
          allels the list of the land forces before Thermopylae (7.202), rein-
          forcing the link between the land and sea battles. Triremes (17) are
          the largest fighting ships, and come with a complement of two
          hundred men (one hundred and seventy oars); penteconters are

smaller ships of war supplied with fifty oars. Here H lists the states in the order of the number of ships supplied, tacitly demonstrating the force of Athens' claim to command of the sea (2–3). In 8.3 H seems to minimize Pausanias' later errors; cf. Thucydides 1.128–34 and *CAH* v. 100–1.

The story of Themistocles' use of bribery (4) and H's general depiction of him as a master of deceit may well have grown up after his later complicated career and departure to Persia (cf. 8.110, 124, the end of n. 7.138–44, and *CAH* v. 62–7). In any case, the main reason the fleet now stays at Artemisium is surely strategic; Eurybiades has to protect Leonidas' position at Thermopylae from the Persian fleet. The Corinthian Adeimantus mentioned in ch. 5 will be Themistocles' main opponent in the councils at Salamis (8.59, 61). The 'fire-bearer' in a Greek army (6) was in charge of keeping alight the fire taken from the city centre for sacrifice and his person was inviolable; it is not clear that a Persian would have used the expression found here. At Artemisium, as its name implies, is a temple of Artemis.

A series of events leaves the Persian fleet weaker. The two hundred Persian ships that have been sent clockwise around Euboea to block the Greek fleet from attempting to escape southwards down the narrow strait separating Euboea from the mainland (7) are caught off Euboea in a storm at night and all perish (13). H doubts (8) that Scyllias of Scione swam the whole way from Aphetae to Artemisium underwater, not surprisingly, since eighty stades is about nine miles (14 km.). In a preliminary skirmish with the rest of the Persian fleet from Aphetae the Greeks acquit themselves well (11) by adopting a circle formation, their prows facing the enemy and their sterns close together, to prevent ramming; in the main battle of Artemisium a couple of days later they prove the match of the much larger Persian fleet (16–18). The single best Greek warrior, Cleinias (17), is the father of the notorious Alcibiades active during the Peloponnesian War (Thucydides 5.43, 6.15–18). H thinks the sea battles at Artemisium happened over the same three days as the land battle at Thermopylae (15); unlike some of the other battle synchronisms in H (9.100, perhaps 7.166) this one is not accidental but the result of Greek strategy. H delivers one of his rare judgements on the gods' role in determining the outcome of events in 8.13; cf. n. 3.38.

8.19–26 Aftermath of Artemisium. Themistocles' inventive tactic during the Greek withdrawal (19 ff.) serves more to make the Persians nervous than to draw many Ionians away from the Persian cause (cf. 8.85); surely the message actually scratched on the rock face (22) was not as long and eloquent as H reports it to be. Many collections of oracles existed in the fifth century under the name of Bacis (8.20, 77, 96, 9.43); at least three different Bacises were known, Boeotian, Attic, and Arcadian. The figure of twenty thousand Persian dead given for Thermopylae (24) is probably too high and it is not clear how H reached the Greek total of four thousand (25); cf. the beginning of n. 7.201–33. Ch. 26 is a wrap-up anecdote, in which Artabanus' son keeps up the family tradition of delivering improving sentiments to Xerxes (cf. 4.83, 7.10, 46).

8.27–39 Cf. 7.176 for the enmity between Thessaly and Phocis and more creative stratagems from the Phocians. H is sympathetic to the Phocians' sufferings (31–3) but not sentimental about their motives (30). For the dedications of Croesus in Delphi (35), cf. 1.50–1 and 92. Not surprisingly, modern scholars doubt the series of miraculous interventions here. Delphi was probably protected from harm because of the oracle's refusal to take an openly pro-Greek stance; cf. the middle of n. 7.138–44. H does not endorse these stories, but rather claims to report what has been said by the Delphians and the invaders themselves (38).

8.40–125 The battle of Salamis. Nine days pass between the end of the fighting at Artemisium and the arrival of the Persian fleet at the Bay of Phalerum in Attica (8.66). During that time the Persian land army marches to Attica. The Greek command is divided, with the Athenians wanting a sea battle off the coast of Attica, and most of the Peloponnesians wanting to retreat to the Isthmus. Themistocles forces the issue, and the Greeks win the battle.

8.40 According to H here, the decision to evacuate the population of Attica is taken only as an emergency measure after the collapse of the Greek position at Thermopylae. However, an inscription (M–L 23; Fornara, 55), dating from perhaps the late fourth or early third century BCE, was found at Troezen and published in 1960 that suggests a different reconstruction of events from that narrated by H. It purports to be a decree proposed by Themistocles to evacuate the Athenians to Troezen and Salamis. In it the Athenians of military age are instructed to man 200 ships, 100 of which are to go to Artemisium, while the other 100 are to remain at Salamis and Attica. If this 'Themistocles Decree' is not a fourth- or early third-century imaginative reconstruction, but the approximate recopying of a genuine decree from before Artemisium, it suggests that the battle of Salamis was not a hurried last-minute improvisation brought on by the collapse of Thermopylae, but part of a long-thought-out plan. H's narrative (8.40–4), on the other hand, stresses the last-minute haste and fear of the Athenians leaving their city before the arrival of Xerxes.

8.42–8 H lists the Greek contingents here (for the Persian forces see ch. 66). There are fifty-four more Greek ships than at Artemisium and nine new states supplying ships. As in 7.61 and 8.73, H inserts some ethnographic material into his list of contingents. For the Pelasgians of Attica (44), cf. n. 1.56–7; the relationship between the Pelasgians who are the autochthonous Athenians here and those expelled in 6.137 is not explained by H. Of the western Greeks, only the Crotonians (47), from southern Italy, supply aid, one ship. For other figures of Athenian ships supplied to the battle, cf. Thucydides 1.74

(*c*.265 ships out of 400), and Demosthenes, *On the Crown* 18.238 (200 ships out of 300). H's total only comes to 366 triremes (and 7 penteconters), not 378 as stated in ch. 48, unless the text is emended.

8.49–55 The Greek commanders opt for retreat, and news comes of the arrival of Xerxes in Attica. Only at ch. 51 does H date by Athenian archon years, and it is the first such extant dating by a historian; the annual archonship began in the late 680s BCE. The scene shifts to Xerxes' attack on the Acropolis, but we see it first through the terrified eyes of the Greeks themselves. For the 'oracle of the wooden wall', probably delivered several months before Xerxes' final descent into Greece, see 7.141. The shrine of Aglaurus (53) was identified in the early 1980s, not where we would expect it from H's description, at the west end of the north slope of the acropolis, but at the east end instead. The portent of the olive-tree (55) will remind the reader of Xerxes' dream at the outset of his expedition (7.19); for Erechtheus, cf. 8.44. In the myth, Athena and Poseidon had a contest over who would claim the city; each had to create a useful gift for it and Cecrops chose Athena as the winner.

Artabanus, to whom Xerxes sends the message of success in ch. 54, has been sent back to Persia from Abydus to govern in Xerxes' absence (7.53).

8.56–64 Greek response to the fall of Athens. Some scholars assume a source hostile to Themistocles behind the detail of the otherwise unknown Mnesiphilus (57–8); the portrait here of Adeimantus the Corinthian may reflect Corinth's unpopularity in Athens in the late 430s when H would have been finishing his *Histories* (59; see also the Athenian story of 8.94).

Themistocles's threat to Eurybiades in ch. 62 is a real one: he has named his daughters Italia and Sybaris, and Athens does in fact found a colony in Thurii in about the same region on the instep of Italy in the 440s (*CAH* v. 141–3; H himself was apparently one of the colonists). Two Athenian expeditions were moreover sent to Sicily in 427 and 415–413. The adventures of the Samians at Zancle after the collapse of the Ionian revolt suggest the sort of life that the Athenians might have had in mind (6.22–4). For the figures of the Aeacidae, or sons of Aeacus (64), cf. n. 5.80.

8.65–9 Notice how the scene shifts back and forth between Greek preparations and Persian ones. Dicaeus (65) is seeing a vision of the great Iacchus procession sacred to Demeter and Persephone, which customarily took place on the fifth day of the Eleusinian mysteries (the 20th day of the month Boedromion) along the Sacred Way from Athens to the city of Eleusis fourteen miles (22 km.) away on the Thriasian Plain. The figure of 30,000 is the standard number of male Athenian citizens (cf. 5.97). The point of this story is the same as in 8.55: there Athena sends forth the olive shoot on the Acropolis; here Demeter and Persephone celebrate the Iacchus procession in the border sanctuary of Eleusis, both events signifying the gods' continuing divine protection of Attica even though the Athenians have left the city for Salamis. H rarely gives the name of an individual as the source for a story; probably Dicaeus is named here to lend additional credence (or at least authenticity for it as a story) to the very unusual account. (Cf. n. 3.55 for H's named interlocutors.) One can well understand Demaratus' lack of enthusiasm for miraculous happenings at this point in his life (cf. 6.68–70).

In ch. 66 the operations of the Persian fleet are resumed from 8.25. (Phalerum, at the time the main harbour of Athens, lay west of where the modern airport is located.) It seems highly improbable that in a couple of weeks Xerxes has made up the enormous losses suffered at Sepias, in the storm off Euboea, and at Artemisium (7.190, 8.13, 16)—H & W calculate that his fleet of 1,327 (7.89, 184, 185) is now down to about six hundred. Aeschylus' *Persians* 341 ff. gives the total at Salamis as 1,207 (the same as H's original total for the Persian fleet at 7.89), and perhaps that is why H thinks Xerxes has brought his fleet up to its original fighting strength (cf., however, *CAH* iv. 566 n. 86; Lazenby, 173–4, 187–8).

Notice that the weaknesses displayed by the Greek council (8.59–63) are those of a loosely organized confederation of independent states, while the Persian weaknesses (68–9) are those of an autocracy. Xerxes' courtiers are thinking only about court politics, not the successful prosecution of this war. For Artemisia's insult (68), cf. 2.102, 8.88, 9.20, 107; for Artemisia herself, cf. n. 7.89–99. In ch. 69 Xerxes again wants to watch something spectacular; cf. 7.31, 43, 44, 100, 128. Here he thinks the fact of his watching the battle will tip the balance in his favour—but H suggests that, though Xerxes' presence inspires zeal, it also contributes to the confusion into which the Persian fleet falls (8.86, 89, 90).

8.70–83 The Persians have reason to expect the Greeks to behave as they did with their land forces at Thermopylae, sending the bulk of their fleet away and perhaps leaving a small and desperate Athenian contingent to fight at Salamis.

The Peloponnesian fortification of the Isthmus is going on apace (8.40, 71, 74). Next spring, 479 BCE, the Athenians will bitterly reproach the Spartans for the choice they have made, to put all their energies into building their new wall (9.7–8). The date of the eclipse, 2 October 480 BCE (9.10), provides a useful *terminus ante quem* for the battle of Salamis.

Just as he has done with the cities of central Greece (7.132), H specifies at ch. 73 which of the cities of the Peloponnese medized. It is hard to be confident of the chronology for the Greek councils described in 8.56, 59, 74, but the gist is clear: Themistocles is finding it difficult to persuade the rest of the Greek fleet to stay at Salamis, as the Persians gather at Phalerum and prepare for battle (70). Themistocles' duplicity and Aristides' integrity together tip the balance and the Tenian deserters (82) carry the day, so that the

Greeks prepare themselves for fighting come the morning. For the tripod at Delphi (82), see. 9.81. Because of Themistocles' secret warning, many in the Persian fleet have been up all night working very hard (76), while presumably it is only the Greek commanders who have stayed up arguing among themselves (81, 83). Rested Greek troops will be fighting exhausted foreigners in narrow straits that the foreigners do not know well.

For the oracle of Bacis mentioned in 8.77 and 96, cf. n. 8.19–26; for H's other expressions of personal authorial opinion (77), especially about religion, cf. n. 3.38. We know from other sources that Athens recalled Athenians previously exiled through ostracism, but probably not immediately before the battle, as 8.79 implies.

8.84–96 There is much dispute about the events of the battle of Salamis. For detailed reconstructions of the battle and the differences between Aeschylus' version of Salamis in the *Persians* and H's, see H & W, app. XXI; *CAH* iv. 573–81; Burn, 450–71; Lazenby, 151–97. The Persians, believing Themistocles' message, may have sent part of their fleet clockwise around Salamis to try to block the Greeks from escaping around the western end of the island, through the narrows of Megara. The Greeks make use of the circumscribed space of the narrows to prevent the Persians from encircling and boarding them with marines; the heavier build of the Greek ships allows them to ram and disable the already crowded and confused Persian line. Themistocles intends wind, wave, and the treacherous coastline of the narrows to work together in the Greeks' favour.

Many Persians lose their lives because they cannot swim (89), and many more that have been stationed on the tiny island of Psyttaleia are slain by Aristides' hoplite troops (95). Artemisia saves herself by attacking and sinking an allied ship, with all hands on board (87), tricking both friends and enemies: Xerxes is impressed with her valour, while the Athenian pursuing her turns away. H enjoys reporting both the insults that the Aeginetan Polycritus, Crius' son (cf. 6.50, 73), hurls at Themistocles (92), and also Polycritus' amazing recovery of Pytheas (92), the Aeginetan taken by the Persians before the storm off Cape Sepias and kept alive as a sort of mascot because of his courage (7.181). H's report is not about Greek or Persian strategy or tactics so much as it is about individual striking episodes. He acknowledges an anti-Corinthian bias in his Athenian informants (94).

8.97–107 Aftermath of the battle on the Persian side. H seems to compress into a single day Xerxes' dismay, his attempt to build the causeway, his sending of the news to Persia, his conversations with Mardonius and Artemisia, his entrusting of his children to Artemisia, as well as Mardonius' selection of the crack 300,000 troops (cf. 9.32) from Xerxes' army, and the sailing of the Persian fleet from Phalerum north to the Hellespont. Xerxes himself leaves with the bulk of his army after only a few days (8.113). *CAH* iv. 582–3 comments that this narrative may point back to a different reality, in which Xerxes' land army probed as far as Pegae in the Megarid and the Isthmus of Corinth, a serious attempt was made at building a causeway to Salamis, and a second sea battle was contemplated, since Xerxes' navy was still considerably larger than that of the Greeks opposing him. It may have been Xerxes' fear of the coming of winter (as well as of being cut off himself at the Hellespont) that caused him finally to abandon his plans (8.113).

H gives no details on the losses of ships. Diodorus 11.19, probably following Ephorus, sets the Greek loss at forty and the Persian at more than two hundred, apart from those captured.

The Persian messenger service (98), of interest in itself as the fastest travel of which mortals are capable (cf. n. 1.214), is described in terms that recall the *Odyssey* (4.566 ff.). H's text about the Persian royal messengers was in turn adapted and inscribed on the 1914 façade of the General Post Office in New York City by one of its architects: '. . . neither snow nor rain nor heat nor gloom of night stays these couriers from the swift completion of their appointed rounds.' It has become the unofficial motto of the US Postal System. The relay torch-race was run at the Panathenaea and at the festivals of Prometheus, Hephaestus, Pan, Bendis, and Theseus. Aeschylus' *Persians* 532 ff. gives a vivid account of the mourning at Susa on the receipt of the news of the sea battle (99).

The conversations between Xerxes and his two counsellors (8.100 ff.) reveal both Mardonius' true objectives and Artemisia's realistic assessment of the risks and opportunities involved. What even Artemisia does not anticipate, however, is the demoralization that apparently will strike Xerxes after his hasty flight back to Asia (9.108–13, described by H without editorializing comment). Xerxes' behaviour in Book 9 certainly continues the man/woman theme H has played with here in portraying Artemisia and Xerxes (7.99, 8.68, 88, 103).

A surprising addition at this point is the pendant on Hermotimus the eunuch (105 ff.), whose name looks suspiciously as if it means 'honour of the herm'. A herm is a statue with genitals prominently displayed (ch. 2.51). His story contains both the theme of the remarkable promised in the *Histories*' introduction, and that of a *tisis*, 'vengeance', long delayed but finally and satisfyingly achieved; cf. nn. 1.8, 1.91. A report of the priestess of Pedasa (104) and her beard-growing proclivities, also mentioned in 1.175, has come into the text of H's manuscripts here, but is generally believed more germane to the context of 1.175, where some of the language looks less suspiciously late as well.

8.108–12 Aftermath of Salamis on the Greek side. This narrative must have made for bitter-sweet hearing or reading by H's audiences in the 440s and 430s BCE, since it looks forward to the behaviour of the Athenians towards islanders and mainland Ionians in the fifty years after the Persian Wars. The opportunism and greed of Themistocles are marked, as well as his readiness to contemplate feathering his own nest later with Persian largess (110; cf. the end of n. 7.138–44). H's sources here are clearly not fans of Themistocles, but Thucydides, who rates Themistocles' gifts and achievements much more highly than H does, accepts as historical the story of the message to Xerxes (Thucydides 1.137).

It is peculiar that two of the most moving assessments of Greek values and the meaning of the Greek cause are expressed by Demaratus, the exiled king of Lacedaemon in Xerxes' camp (7.102), and Themistocles, the master trickster, here (109). Themistocles speaks as he does for the purpose of beguiling his allies and later winning credit with Xerxes. For the thrashing of the sea to which Themistocles refers, see 7.35.

8.113–20 Mardonius picks his army, and Xerxes marches homewards. The troops Mardonius chooses have been described in 7.41, 61, 62, 64, 65. The payment rendered by Mardonius (114) will be his own death and loss of the battle of Plataea the following spring, 9.63–4. Of the sufferings H describes on the return march (and the even more dramatic sufferings described in Aeschylus' *Persians* 480 ff.), *CAH* iv. 585 comments, 'We need to take all this with a cellar of salt.' See also Burn, 470–1 and Lazenby, 205–6. Xerxes takes forty-five days to march the 550 miles (880 km.) or so back to the Hellespont (115), suggesting neither headlong haste nor total breakdown. H does not tell us why he includes the improbable story of the sea captain and the wholesale jettisoning overboard of Xerxes' court (118–19), but it may be for the sake of his own tongue-in-cheek remark that follows, certainly implying a criticism of the way Xerxes has run his war. He has in effect seated overdressed and out-of-shape courtiers at the oars of his ship of state.

For an assessment of Xerxes' campaign as a whole, see *CAH* iv. 587–8. The issue of this war was still very much in doubt at the end of 480 BCE, as the resistance of Andros and Carystus to Themistocles' harassment shows. 'What made Salamis decisive at sea was the change in the plans of Xerxes. Whatever his reasons, he did not return . . .' (*CAH* iv. 588).

8.121–5 Greek dedications and the assignment of honours. Croesus' bowl has been described in 1.51. For Themistocles' further exploits at Sparta after the end of the war, cf. Thucydides 1.90–2, where Themistocles draws out a visit to the Lacedaemonians long enough for the Athenians to get their walls rebuilt, a move Sparta opposes in 478 BCE. The hostility to Themistocles indicated in the anecdote of ch. 125 seems to have been widespread in Athens, since Themistocles was not offered a sea command after 480 (we find Xanthippus in command in 479 (9.114)). Belbina is a rocky and insignificant island off the coast of Sunium.

8.126–9 Artabazus is the commander of the Parthians and Chorasmians in Xerxes' army (7.66); he is perhaps a close relative of Xerxes, since his father Pharnaces has at least the same name as a Pharnaces son of Arsames who was in charge of the royal treasury in Fortification Texts from Darius' reign (*CAH* iv. 85) and may have been Darius' uncle (1.209).

As H says (126), Artabazus will become even more important after he manages to lead forty thousand of Xerxes' troops away from Plataea the following spring (9.66, 77, 89), leaving Mardonius in Greece. Some scholars speculate that H's knowledge of Mardonius' thoughts in Books 8 and 9 may ultimately come from Artabazus, if a Tritantaechmes son of Artabazus is the Persian satrap of Babylon in H's time and possibly one of H's informants (1.192). Artabazus and his family also remain influential in the region of the Hellespont. Artabazus seems to have been blamed by Xerxes neither for the losses in Chalcidice over the winter of 480–479 nor for abandoning Mardonius, since in Thucydides 1.129 we see him become satrap of Dascylium immediately after the war, assigned by Xerxes to the delicate task of dealing with Pausanias. Artabazus' grandson is still satrap in Dascylium during the early Peloponnesian War (Thucydides 2.67, 5.1), and his great-grandson is the Pharnabazus of Thucydides Book 8 and Xenophon's *Hellenica*.

Here (127) Artabazus makes use of the winter lull in fighting to try to reduce Olynthus and Potidaea, cities at the northern end of Pallene, the westernmost tongue of the Chalcidice peninsula, which have taken the opportunity offered by Xerxes' retreat to revolt. He takes Olynthus but is undone by a treacherous tide at Potidaea as he tries to get his army past the city walls on to Pallene proper; the tides of the Aegean normally rise and fall by only a few inches, but a strong current comes into the north-east corner of the Mediterranean from the Euxine (Black) Sea (fed by all those rivers H describes in Book 4), and it may here be complicated by the effects of earthquake. (The Potidaeans are sure that Poseidon, god of earthquakes, is involved (129); the town is named after him and the Persians have desecrated one of his temples on the city's outskirts.) As a Corinthian colony, Potidaea is again of military interest in the initial stages of the Peloponnesian War (Thucydides 1.56–65; cf. a tactic similar to Artabazus' by Aristeas the Corinthian in Thucydides 1.63).

8.130–2 Xerxes' fleet keeps an eye on Ionia from Cyme and Samos; the Greek fleet gathers at Delos. The Athenians have put Xanthippus the former exile in charge of their fleet (for his connections, cf. the middle of n. 6.121–4) and not Themistocles. Themistocles' tactics have saved the Peloponnese from invasion but have not saved Athens itself from being burned and sacked (*CAH* iv. 594).

The Lacedaemonians have now made one of their kings commander-in-chief (signifying the importance they give to the fleet, after

Salamis?). H honours Leotychidas with a genealogy, as he has Leonidas (7.204), although Leotychidas' later career is less glorious; cf. the end of n. 6.61–72. For the energetic prosecution of the war in Ionia under Leotychidas' command later in the spring of 479 BCE, see 9.90–106. An echo of Ionian irritation at the timidity of the mainlanders can be found in the comment about the Pillars of Heracles in ch. 132. Strattis (132) must be getting on in years, at least if he is the same Strattis of Chios who has been tyrant of Chios since Darius' Scythian expedition (4.138). The 110 ships the Greeks muster at Aegina in the spring is about one-third of the number gathered at Salamis in the previous autumn; presumably most of the Athenians are now preparing to fight the Persians by land in Boeotia, and they may also be deliberately withholding most of their navy from the allied cause in order to encourage Sparta to fight in central Greece (cf. the threats of 8.62).

8.133–44 Mardonius' activities in winter and early spring 480–479 BCE. He first consults oracles in central Greece. For the Persian sacking of Abae (134), cf. 8.33; for H's interest in Caria and Carians, cf. n. 5.117–21. Amphiaraus is an Argive, one of the mythic seven heroes led by Polynices, Oedipus' son, against Thebes; Croesus had consulted Abae and Amphiaraus also (1.46, 49, 52, 92).

Alexander is introduced in ch. 136 without acknowledgement of our previous acquaintance with him (and Bubares!), although in 5.22 H sends the reader forward to this passage for proof that the Macedonian kings are Greek; cf. n. 5.17–22. Thucydides 2.99 takes the claim of the Temenids, the Macedonian royal family, to Argive ancestry seriously as well; Temenus was one of the Heraclidae, or sons of Heracles, who in myth returned from the north to claim the Peloponnese (cf. the 'Dorian invasion', with which the Heraclidae are mythically associated, nn. 1.56–7 and 4.147–8). Temenus took Argos for his portion (cf. CAH iii/3. 282–5 for possible real seventh-century connections between Argos and Macedonia).

The story of the three sons (137; cf. 4.5) may go back to Iranian folk-tale. On the Garden of Midas (138): this part of Macedonia for more than three centuries (c.1150–800 BCE) had been the home of the Brygi, most of whom may well then have set off for Asia and become the Phrygians of north-west Asia Minor (7.73; CAH iii/1. 649, 653–4).

Mardonius' choice of Alexander as an ambassador is an astute one. Alexander has already successfully warned the Greeks off defending Thessaly (7.173), and he will play a vital role later in the spring at Plataea, telling them of Mardonius' plans (9.44–6). His arguments are sensible. The two subsequent speeches, those of the Lacedaemonian envoys and of the Athenians themselves, are fascinating, because in them we see articulated the growth of a consciousness that is specifically Hellenic, crystallizing around the issue of the war with Persia. The Spartans represent a paler and more conflicted version of it. They are both sympathetic and irritated; they feel reluctantly implicated in the troubles that, by their way of thinking, the Athenians have brought on themselves (cf. 4.118–19, for the same issues debated by the Scythians and their neighbours). The Athenians in return articulate the principle of a common Hellenism, defined by ties of religion, blood, speech, and custom. It is not clear that before Xerxes' invasion most Greeks would have thought such connections important or would have thought of themselves principally as Greeks rather than as members of an individual tribe or city (cf. Polycritus' behaviour in 8.92). Unlike the Scythians in Book 4, for the moment the Athenians do not articulate the practical threat of what will happen to the Peloponnese should the Athenians decide to collaborate (but see 9.7, 11).

BOOK NINE

In the early spring of 479 BCE it is still not at all clear that the Greeks will succeed in expelling the Persians from Europe. Mardonius has wintered in Thessaly, and the Lacedaemonians are again showing themselves reluctant to venture north of the Isthmus. The narrative gathers speed and moves straightforwardly through Mardonius' abortive attempt to pry Athens out of the Greek alliance, the second firing of Athens, the Peloponnesians' rapid march northwards into central Greece, once they have decided it is in their interest to move, and then the two big moments: first the battle of Plataea and then the battle of Mycale—fought, H reports, on the same day in the late spring or early summer of 479. After the battles there is a brief portrait of Xerxes in Sardis, wreaking havoc on his family, and then a picture of the Athenians conducting siege operations in the region of the Hellespont during the autumn. The Athenians do not show the magnanimous generosity towards the conquered displayed by Pausanias at Plataea; instead they crucify Artayctes, the wicked governor of Sestus, overlooking the spot where Xerxes first brought his army into Europe. The very last episode is a pendant flashback to Cyrus, in which he gives gnomic advice to the Persians of the mid-sixth century: if the Persians wish to rule, they must remain in their rocky homeland and avoid the seductions of luxury: soft lands tend to breed soft men.

In this set of narratives, H resists a picture that unequivocally praises the Greeks or deprecates the Persians. Thus the portrait of Mardonius is complex. On the one hand, he succeeds in drawing the Peloponnesians north of their new fortifications at the Isthmus, and in forcing them to fight in the plains of Boeotia that favour the use of Persian cavalry. He is much less subtle, however, than his fellow general Artabazus; in the grip of a desire to prove Persian military superiority over the Spartans, he loses both his army and his life fighting valiantly at Plataea, when H thinks that he could probably have been successful using Persian persuasion and money to split the Greek alliance and win influential friends for Persia in the major cities. H makes it clear that Mardonius and his troops are a match for the Greeks in valour and strength; they are not equipped, however, to withstand trained and fully equipped Greek hoplites (9.62). Artabazus flees from the battlefield, taking his forty thousand men with him northwards back to Thrace and Asia, an action that H notes but does not judge. Nor are things presented in black and white on the Greek side: rivalries and tensions between the various cities considerably complicate the Greek defence. The Spartiates at Plataea are professional soldiers, not at all interested in the kind of contest for glory Mardonius has in mind, but only in winning the war with whatever is the most efficient means they have to hand. The battle itself, narrated from the Greek side, is a confused affair, with a good number of puzzling incidents, mixed or misunderstood messages, and contingents coming late to the fighting.

Across the sea with the small Greek fleet at Delos (9.90), it is hard not to suspect some irony in H's picture of Ionians asking the Greek navy to come to liberate them; in his own day the Athenian presence in Ionia was bitterly resented by many. There is also irony in the way Athenians, Peloponnesians, and Ionians are depicted during and after the battle. Is the final picture of Pericles' father crucifying the offending Persian, and stoning the son to death before his father's eyes, intended to be read as an ominous portent for the future, or merely a punishment befitting the crimes Artayctes had committed? H does not say.

Burn's comment (p. 489) about the winter preceding Plataea and Mycale is relevant to the whole of Book 9: 'The brilliant fifth-century society of Greece bore within it, from its beginning, the seeds of its own decay; and in this season . . . may be seen already the jealousy and fear of Athens, felt, not without reason, by the smaller and older maritime states; and the tensions within Athens itself, and within Sparta itself, which were to weaken both, and to make each appear slippery and unreliable in the eyes of the other. Herodotos is never more revealing than in his choice of anecdotes to represent these tensions.'

9.1–8 Again it is clear that the boundaries of significant narrative units are not necessarily reflected in the book divisions, since ch. 1 is merely the end of Athens' rejection of Mardonius's offer narrated at the end of Book 8. Thorax is one of the Aleuadae, the ruling family of Larisa in Thessaly; his family has been exhorting Xerxes to the conquest of Greece from the beginning (7.6). The Thebans (2) understand that Mardonius must divide and conquer Greece, here echoing Demaratus (7.235) and Artemisia (8.68). Both Artabazus and the Thebans seem to understand the effectiveness money would have in this process (9.41).

The episode reported in 9.5 is also mentioned by Demosthenes (*On the Crown* 18.202, 204) and Lycurgus (*Against Leocrates* 122). Like the final episode involving Athenians (9.120), it has an ambivalent ring. On the one hand, the Athenians are indeed firmly committed to fighting the Persians, but on the other, a lynch-mob mentality seems to prevail, among the women (cf. 5.87) as well as among the councillors themselves. If we think of Aristagoras' earlier success in Athens (5.97) and this episode as H's two main portraits of Athenian democracy in action, it is hard to view H as its uncritical supporter; cf. the very different picture of Athenian deliberation given in Thucydides' early books (e.g. 2.34, 40). But the episode certainly also shows the pressure the Athenians are under, twice now having to abandon their homes and farms and sit across the straits watching the Persians burn their city down. H is sympathetic to their general situation; the language he uses of the Lacedaemonians (7), that in the early summer of 479 BCE they are 'on holiday' and also getting on with the defensive wall across the Isthmus, makes it clear why he gives Athens significant credit for the final victory (7.139).

9.9–11 Chileus the Tegean (9) is said by Plutarch also to have helped Themistocles with his strategy (*Life of Themistocles* 6). Since the Lacedaemonians fear both helot revolt and problems with their Peloponnesian neighbours at home if they leave *en masse* for central Greece, having a Tegean's assurances of support at this point is valuable for them. One indication of the tensions between Sparta and their neighbours is that the only Arcadian contingents at Plataea are from Tegea and Orchomenus (9.28). Notice that when the Lacedaemonians do march, they take a route that is very far from their traditional enemy Argos, and they leave in secret, taking a large number of helots with them (10–12). Demaratus numbers the whole Spartiate force at eight thousand (7.234), so the five thousand of ch. 10 represent a significant percentage of Sparta's manpower. For the five thousand perioeci (*perioikoi*) of ch. 11, cf. n. 6.58–60; they are citizens, but lack the full hereditary rights of the Spartiates. Plutarch's *Life of Aristides* 10 names either Aristides or Cimon, Xanthippus, and Myronides as the indignant Athenian ambassadors to Sparta (11); it is worth noting that H presents it as an action of the Athenian community, rather than an accomplishment of named individuals.

The eclipse mentioned in ch. 10 occurred on 2 October 480 BCE. It is extremely valuable in helping to date the whole of Xerxes' campaign, and is a *terminus ante quem* for the battle of Salamis. After Leonidas' death at Thermopylae, his nephew, Pausanias, asks Euryanax, another grandson of Anaxandridas (5.39–41), to help lead the campaign. Despite the flattery of the Coan courtesan (9.76), Pausanias remains not king but regent for Leonidas' son Pleistarchus until his own disreputable death. Then (*c.*470) Pausanias was believed by many to be intriguing with the Persians to betray Greece in exchange for a royal Persian marriage alliance. He had earlier been removed from the allied command in Ionia and was ultimately recalled to Sparta, where he was suspected of fomenting a helot revolt. He took sanctuary in a temple, where he was starved to death (cf. Thucydides 1.94–5, 128–35; *CAH* v. 100–1).

9.12–18 The Persian offensive. For Argive–Spartan hostility, cf. n. 6.76, and references to it in 5.49, 9.35. Attica lacks the large, smooth plains that make the use of cavalry efficient (13). For Decelea (15), cf. the end of n. 9.58–75. (Technically H's claim (14) that Megara is as far west as the Persian army goes, is wrong, since central Greece has a pronounced north-west to south-east slant and the invading Persian army has been farther west in its descent through Thermopylae and Delphi in the previous summer; perhaps he means this particular army under Mardonius. This is certainly as close as the Persian land army gets to the Isthmus.)

The Boeotarchs (15) are the eleven aristocratic federal magistrates who claimed supreme authority in Boeotia. There is evidence of a Boeotian confederation from as early as the sixth century (cf. *CAH* iv. 358 n. 11). In the Persian Wars, however, Thespiae and Plataea (both Boeotian cities) remain loyal to the Greeks. Burn (p. 511) calculates that the Persian fort, somewhat more than a mile long on each side, is about nine hundred acres in area; if one uses the figures for a Roman camp for one legion, such a fort would suffice for an army of sixty or seventy thousand men, ten thousand of them cavalry.

For more on Attaginus of Thebes (16), cf. 9.86. Thersander of Orchomenus is one of the few sources H names; see also n. 3.55. The unnamed Persian's intuition (16) is not necessarily a mystical one; intelligent Persians in Mardonius' ranks no doubt did feel gloomy contemplating pitched battle against large numbers of fully equipped Greek hoplites (9.62). For the long-standing enmity of

Thessaly and Phocis that, to the Phocians at least, explains Mardonius' odd behaviour in ch. 17, cf. 7.176, 8.30.

9.19–24 The basic strategy that prevails is for each side to lure the other
from terrain favourable to it. The Persians hold good, flat cavalry
ground north of the Asopus River. The Greek hoplite and light-armed
forces hold the south bank of the Asopus, near the foothills of Mount
Cithaeron. The battle line is unusually long and drawn-out. Perhaps
H himself walked the battlefield, but it is difficult precisely to identify H's carefully named locations because of changes both in land-
marks and terrain through time. There is some implicit irony if
we compare the way the battle of Plataea actually unfolds to
Mardonius' smug assessment of Greek military tendencies in 7.9:
'They seek out the best, most level piece of land, and that's where
they go and fight.'

On the episode of the Persian cavalry commander Masistius (20),
and the taunt of 'women' hurled at the Greeks, the Scotsman Burn
asks, 'Is this the first case recorded of badinage between trousered
and kilted men?' (p. 516 n. 16). But cf. also 8.88, 9.107. The Olympiodorus mentioned in ch. 21 may well be the father of Lampon, the
seer and friend of Pericles whom H might have known at Thurii
(Plutarch, *Moralia* 812d).

9.25–89 Those interested in studying the vexed questions of tactics and
terrain at Plataea are encouraged to consult *CAH* iv. 599–609; Burn,
516–40; Lazenby 217–47; Pritchett, i. 103–21, and v. 92–137. H
portrays Plataea as a series of fortuitous occurrences rather than as
carefully thought-out and successfully implemented strategy and
tactics on Pausanias' part. This may be an attempt long afterwards
on the part of H's informants to deny Pausanias credit for the victory,
or simply a result of the fact that those informants still alive in the
440s or 430s BCE would not have been high up in the chain of
command in 479 and so would not have known the actual tactical
decisions involved. Or it may reflect what really happened; Burn
comments, 'There are many indications that [Plataea] was well
planned; but for a battle to be well planned, and for the plan to be
frustrated by the enemy, and for the troops to win it nevertheless, is
no rarity in the history of war' (pp. 533–4). Both sides play a waiting
game. Reinforcements continue to pour in for the Greeks (38),
swelling their hoplite ranks from about 30,000 to 38,700, with
69,500 light-armed troops as well (29, 30); the Persian forces are
probably of about the same strength. After eight days Mardonius
succeeds in cutting the Greeks off from their supply lines and reinforcements coming over the Cithaeron pass and then later in fouling
their major sources of water.

The sacrifices continue to be unfavourable, and on the night
between the eleventh and twelfth day of waiting, Alexander of
Macedonia comes with the news that Mardonius has decided to
attack. There is some reorganization of the Greek battle lines, and

on the twelfth night Pausanias withdraws his troops from their positions in the foothills (52); on the thirteenth day the battle is fought.
The Greeks acquit themselves well; if Burn's reconstruction is at all
accurate (p. 536), it is not surprising that Artabazus turns and leads
his forty thousand by forced marches back to the Hellespont.

The impression left in the Greek rank and file afterwards was one
of disorganization: a recently formed allied army with twenty-one
contingents might well experience difficulties in deciding on relative
positions in line, alleged disobedience of orders, and a somewhat
chaotic retreat to the final battle positions. Nevertheless, the allied
Greek forces at Plataea, and above all the Lacedaemonians, fought
well enough to win the battle.

9.25–7 Pausanias moves west from Erythrae to Plataea, positioning the
army towards the plain, but remaining on land unsuitable for the
Persian cavalry. The long speeches of the Tegeans and the Athenians
(26–7) are perhaps designed to fill in the reader's sense of many days
of waiting while the sacrifices for battle are unfavourable; they are
unlikely to have been delivered on the field, facing the enemy. They
continue the heroic and even epic flavour that has already been conveyed in the narrative of the death of the Persian cavalry commander Masistius (9.22). The Tegeans mention the return of the Spartans'
ancestors, the Heraclidae or sons of Heracles, to the Peloponnese (cf.
nn. 4.147, 8.133–44) about a hundred years after Heracles' death,
and they emphasize their own valour in opposing them; for the
ancient rivalry between Sparta and Tegea, cf. n. 1.65–6. The
Athenians are craftier. Their speaker mentions instead their support
of the Heraclidae in the mythic past (cf. Euripides' play of the same
name) and then adds other mythic deeds that show magnanimity as
well as valour. The examples adduced, the protection of the children
of Heracles, the aftermath of the battle of the Seven against Thebes,
and the victory over the Amazons, occur regularly, along with
Marathon, in later Athenian encomiastic and funeral speeches
and may reflect H's own sense of favourite Athenian topics for self-
congratulation.

Notice that at the crux of his argument is the battle of Marathon.
The Athenian speaker draws a line of demarcation between the
traditional, mythic past and the hard reality of a battle fought a
decade before the present (the same lines of thought are found in the
speech of the Athenians at Sparta in Thucydides 1.73). This persuades the Spartans to give the Athenians the left wing. In the present
context Marathon is more relevant as an example than Salamis
would have been because, like Plataea itself, it is a hoplite battle
(6.107 ff.). (Through the fifth and fourth centuries Marathon continued to be the Athenians' most often-mentioned victory, in part
because Marathon was much more an Athenian (rather than Greek)
victory, in part because Marathon was a victory of the propertied
class, the hoplites, while Salamis, far more important for achieving

the ultimate repulse of the Persian invaders, was a victory of the upstart Themistocles and the lower class *thētes*, many of whom manned the navy. In terms of traditional Greek aristocratic and military values, Marathon was the more conventionally impressive accomplishment.)

9.28-32 H has very detailed and apparently circumstantial figures here, for the numbers and positions of the Greek line and for the positions of the Persian contingents facing them. Small details (like the positioning of a small band of Potidaeans next to the Corinthians (28)) that do not look like constructions from general probability or as though they have been copied from a post-war monument lead many scholars to think that H here is using sources from those who fought at the battle. His figures, 38,700 for the Greek hoplite forces (29) and 69,500 Greek light-armed troops (30), for a total of 108,200, are perhaps more reasonable than many such numbers in the *Histories*. By the Thespian survivors (30) H means those who had not died at Thermopylae; Thespiae itself has been burnt down by the Persians (7.202, 222, 8.50). For Mardonius' forces, see 8.113; cf. the original description of Xerxes' contingents by nationality in 7.41-100. For the Phocians who had become guerrilla fighters in the mountains for the Greeks, see 8.32. Bactria (31) is roughly modern Afghanistan, and the Sacae are an eastern people (cf. n. 3.118-60 and the end of n. 7.60-83; 1.153, 3.93, 6.113; *CAH* iv. 170-1). For the Egyptian Hermotybies and Calasiries, see 2.164, 168. The number of 300,000 Persians here (32, cf. 8.113) is almost certainly overstated—most scholars assume a rough parity of Greek and Persian forces.

9.33-40 A Greek military campaign or individual battle customarily begins with sacrifice, and the commander waits until the signs from the innards of the sacrificial animal are auspicious before starting the undertaking (cf. 7.134, 219, 9.10 for other inauspicious signs, 9.19, 96 for favourable ones). Pausanias uses sacrifice here as an important way to hold his troops in check until he wishes to give battle; delay favours the Greeks more than the Persians. Given Spartan religiosity, it is unlikely, however, to have been a purely cynical manipulation of the ritual. (The Persians also use a Greek diviner for the occasion, and he does not receive auspicious signs either, so that Mardonius eventually loses patience with the whole process (41).)

The Iamidae (33) claimed descent from Apollo (cf. Pindar, *Olympian Odes* 6.71) and continued to be an important family of diviners at Olympia into the third century CE; cf. 5.44. The pentathlon consisted of jumping, the discus, the javelin, running, and wrestling, with the wrestling decided by the best of three falls; presumably Tisamenus won two events and missed winning a third, wrestling, only by one fall. Three of the five battles mentioned in ch. 33, those at Tegea, Dipaea, and Ithome, involved the Spartans in battles against their neighbours in the Peloponnese in the 470s and 460s BCE. Tanagra was fought in 457 (Thucydides 1.108).

The story of Melampus (34) is inserted as a pendant elaborating on the motivation of Tisamenus; cf. the insertion of the story of Cleisthenes of Sicyon in 5.67 ff. Melampus was the oldest and most famous mythic seer of the Greeks (cf. 2.49 and *Odyssey* 11.285 ff., 15.225 ff.), healer of the Argive daughters of Proetus. M. West has identified a badly tattered fragment of verse (Simonides, *el.* 14) as part of a long elegiac poem by Simonides on the battle of Plataea: it may describe the message that Tisamenus the seer gives the Spartans in ch. 36. For Simonides, cf. the end of n. 7.201–33.

On the Persian side, Hegesistratus (37) is also from a line of diviners o: Elis (cf. 8.27). We do not know what Tegean–Lacedaemonian hostilities are in question in the years before Plataea (they are not mentioned among the Greek feuds resolved in 7.145), or why the Lacedaemonians are so irritated with Hegesistratus. For traditional tensions between Sparta and Tegea, cf. 1.66–8.

Timagenidas (38) along with Attaginus is handed over to the Greeks after the Theban surrender, and is summarily executed at Corinth by Pausanias (9.86–8). His advice to Mardonius (38) certainly leads to one of the most effective Persian tactical moves of the whole stay in Boeotia.

9.41–3 It would be interesting to know how H found out about the debate between Mardonius and Artabazus; for Artabazus' later career, cf. n. 8.126–9. The move Artabazus advocates, of creating at least dissension in the Greek cities by paying influential citizens (cf. the advice of the Thebans, 9.2) is one followed with great success by Philip of Macedonia in the fourth century. Plutarch (*Life of Aristides* 13) mentions a plot during this time of waiting, fashioned by some of the richest and best-born Athenians to overthrow the democracy and betray Greece to the Persians. It is foiled by the judicious magnanimity of Aristides. (A fourth-century inscription exists claiming to be the 'Oath of Plataea' (Fornara, 57), taken by the Athenian forces at some point before the battle, pledging solidarity to the united cause. Its authenticity was denied by the fourth-century historian Theopompus (*FGH* 115, fr. 153) and has been debated by many others since then (Burn, 512–15).)

Mardonius' comments about the oracles (42–3) seem rather behindhand, since his troops have already gone through Delphi (8.36–9), although his knowledge may have come about during the winter investigation of Greek oracles by Mys (8.133). The timidity of his entourage again reflects what H clearly thinks to be a major drawback of autocracy (cf. the end of n. 8.65–9). The tribal army of Encheleis (43) apparently accompanied the mythic Cadmus and Harmonia in their old age (5.61, and the middle of n. 1.56–7). H's statement that he knows Mardonius' oracle to be about the Illyrians and the Encheleis and not the Persians is unusually definite—cf. 1.5, where he states that he knows Croesus to be the first barbarian to perpetrate unjust acts against Greeks, or 4.15, where he knows what happened in Metapontum two hundred and forty years after Aristeas' disappearance in Proconnesus. On the selective use of oracles, cf. 7.6; for Musaeus and Bacis, cf. 8.96 and nn. 7.6, 8.19–26.

9.44–9 Last-minute changes before the battle. Some scholars are inclined to believe that the story of Alexander's secret midnight ride was invented, or at least its motives were changed after the fact, to palliate Alexander's generally pro-Persian stance during the Persian Wars; cf. n. 5.17–22 for the equally tendentious story of his murder of the Persian envoys and the middle of n. 8.133–44 for the alleged Greekness of his family. The picture of the last-minute change in battle order that follows has elements of Keystone Kops comedy in it. It is not likely to have happened as it is narrated, in the first light of dawn with battle pending; 'If the line was nearly three miles long (reckoning eight men to a yard) the operation of marching two divisions of 8,000 and 10,000 men, in column of eights, past each other in rear of the centre, would have taken an hour, and the moment when an attack was expected does not seem the right time at which to do it' (Burn, 528). Nor does the motive reported seem probable, that at the last minute Pausanias was fearful of having Spartiates face Persians, although this part of the story does allow H to develop a highly ironic picture of Mardonius' response, his unrealistic confidence, and his ignorance of Spartan strengths.

In the narrative of events from this point until the end of the episode of Plataea, many peculiar and unexpected things happen. It is possible to think of these happenings in at least two ways, depending on one's predilections. Either they show H to be incapable of understanding or narrating a 'normal' battle (those who think so often mention the unlikelihood that H would himself have fought in a war as a citizen, given his exile at an early age) or, conversely, the very oddness of the way things unfold (narrated, after all, to a series of audiences who do understand war) is some testimony to the efforts H made to talk to people who had been close to events, and to narrate what they say, no matter how odd it looks. That is, arguments from probability cut both ways.

9.50–7 The removal of the Greek forces to Plataea. The path taken in this move, and the locations of the 'island' to which the Greeks were supposed to go and the temple of Hera to which they did go are discussed in detail in the works mentioned at the beginning of n. 9.25–89. The second watch (51) falls between our 11 p.m. and midnight; Plataea had been destroyed by the Persians (8.50), but foundations would have remained. Thucydides 1.20 denies that there was a 'company from Pitana', implicitly attacking H's accuracy in 9.53. H had been in Pitana (3.55), and perhaps here he is reflecting an earlier organization of the Spartan army than the one Thucydides knew, or perhaps he heard that Amompharetus was from Pitana and incorrectly assumed that Amompharetus' command was a local one. The detail about the rock/voting pebble (55) is worth noting, since it is not Spartans but Athenians who vote by casting small stones or potsherds into urns, and an Athenian observer seems to be part of the scene as H describes it.

9.58–75 The battle of Plataea. Mardonius gloats prematurely to the Aleuadae (cf. n. 9.1–8), and crosses the Asopus after the Greeks, who he thinks are fleeing (59; cf. the disorder of the Persian forces at Salamis, 8.86). Even among the probably tendentious and confused reports that go into the battle account that follows, it is possible to discern both intelligence and skill behind Pausanias' actions (ch. 69 must be read in the light of the fact that Megarians were not friendly to Athens in the 440s and 430s BCE when H was writing). There may well have been, as at Thermopylae, a feigned retreat and counter-attack (cf. Plato, *Laches* 191b–c); there was certainly great discipline behind the delay in sounding the call for battle until Pausanias deemed the moment suitable (61–2). For the cavalry a thousand strong around Mardonius (63) and for the oracle requiring compensation for the death of King Leonidas (64), cf. 8.113–14. Leonidas' lineage is given in 7.204 and is referred to here because it is the same as that of his nephew Pausanias.

Notice that in ch. 65 H again reluctantly comments on religious matters (n. 3.38); cf. 9.101 for the coincidence that there was also a sanctuary of Eleusinian Demeter at Mycale. This is the first we hear of the burning of the temple at Eleusis; cf. 9.13 for the burning of Athens.

For Artabazus' retreat, family, and career, see n. 8.126–9. The prosperity of his later career shows that Xerxes did not hold him responsible for failing to support Mardonius at Plataea. The Thebans have a long-standing traditional hostility towards the Athenians that makes them enthusiastic fighters here (67–8; cf. 5.74, 77, 6.108).

The figures for the dead, both Greek and Persian, are particularly improbable (70); clearly more Greeks fell and fewer from the Persian ranks. Of the noteworthy Greek combatants, we have already met Aristodamus the Spartiate (71; 7.229) and Sophanes the Athenian (73–5; 6.92); here H repeats information mentioned in 6.92. Macan (p. 753) thinks that this is one sign among a number of others that Books 7 to 9 were composed before the other books of the *Histories*, although in a work involving this much detail and probably delivered orally over a number of years, it is extremely dangerous to draw inferences from what is or is not given an explicit cross-reference. H refers to Sophanes' deme, Decelea, as spared by the Lacedaemonian invasions of Attica in the first years of the Peloponnesian War; almost certainly H would have mentioned the capture of Decelea by King Agis in 413 BCE if he had known about it at the time of writing (Thucydides 6.91, 7.19, 27). The battle at which Sophanes dies, probably c.465, is in the Thraceward region, near where the Athenians will later found Amphipolis. (For Helen of Troy

(73) and her brothers the Tyndaridae (also known as the Dioscuri), cf. nn. 4.145–6, 5.75. Her brothers found and brought her back to Sparta, after Theseus had abducted her to Athens when she was very young. As heroes, their cult figures accompanied the Lacedaemonian army when it campaigned abroad.)

9.76–85 Aftermath of Plataea on the Greek side. The Coan concubine (76) has been in the entourage of Pharandates, a nephew of Darius and the brother of that Sataspes who attempted the circumnavigation of Africa (n. 4.37–45). She flatters Pausanias by calling him king, not regent. Several episodes have indicated what the Greeks might expect for their women if they lose this war—the aftermath of the Ionian revolt (6.32), the behaviour of Artayctes the satrap of Sestus (7.33), and the treatment of the inhabitants of central Greece (8.33), among others. The return of this one woman to her family on Cos is the first tangible sign of what Greece has gained by the victory at Plataea. (Cos is an island just off the coast of Halicarnassus, so H might have known the story from local report of it.)

Repeatedly in his account of the aftermath of the battle H emphasizes the moderation and good sense of the victorious general Pausanias. He alludes earlier (5.32) to the charges of Medism and worse that were made against Pausanias in the early 470s BCE, but also points out how conveniently such charges fit the Athenians' plans for Ionia (8.3; cf. n. 9.9–11). Two ephors or elected magistrates later regularly accompanied the Spartan king on campaigns away from home (Xenophon, *Spartan Constitution* 13.5); it is not clear if their presence here (76) is part of the same practice. The theme of hardy simplicity and its contrast with luxury occurs here as a point of contrast between Greeks and Persians, but it runs throughout the *Histories*; cf. 1.155, 7.102, 9.122, and nn. 1.71 and 3.21.

The bronze serpent-column (81) was taken by the emperor Constantine to Constantinople (Istanbul) and placed in the hippodrome, *CAH* iv. 616–17 and 618 fig. 51. One can still read incised on its coils the names of thirty-one Greek cities that fought at Plataea (M–L 27; Fornara, 59). Thucydides (1.132) tells us that Pausanias had an ambiguously provocative epigram put somewhere on the original monument (consisting of base, serpent-column, and a tripod of solid gold resting on top of the column): 'Pausanias, Captain-general of the Hellenes, dedicated this monument to Phoebus when he destroyed the army of the Medes.' The couplet was erased at some point afterwards and replaced, Thucydides says, by the names of all the cities making the dedication.

A certain amount of anti-Aeginetan bias is found throughout this passage: Lampon (78) is an Aeginetan who thinks to flatter Pausanias; the wealth of Aegina is attributed solely to their cheating Lacedaemonian helots of the true value of the gold spoils gathered after the battle (80; cf. 2.178, 4.152, 7.142); they have an empty tomb put up ten years after the battle for show (85). For the huge skeleton of ch. 83, cf. n. 7.105–27.

9.86–8 For Timagenidas, cf. the end of n. 9.33–40, and for Attaginus, cf. 9.16. Thucydides 3.62 has a Theban speaker describe the Theban government in this period as a 'rule of a few men'. Plutarch (*Life of Aristides* 21) suggests that a standing Greek army of 10,000 infantry, 1,000 cavalry, and 100 ships was proposed by Aristides and voted on by the other Greek states. Whatever plans were made for a continued Greek league, however, were quickly abandoned in the political, economic, and social complexities of the immediate post-war period (*CAH* v. 27–33, 96–120). The Athenians set up their own Delian League instead, which soon became, at least in the eyes of the other Greeks, an Athenian empire (*CAH* v. 34–61).

9.89 For Artabazus among the Phocians, fleeing Plataea, cf. 9.66. For Artabazus' later very successful career, cf. n. 8.126–9. Demosthenes, *Against Aristocrates* 23.200, claimed that the Macedonians caused much trouble to Artabazus on his retreat.

9.90–7 The focus here shifts to the Greek fleet in Ionia, taking up the narrative thread from 8.132, where an embassy from Chios had already asked for help from the Greeks. The narrative structure itself now portrays the war as virtually won, since H no longer presents Greek action only as a response to Persian aggression. Rather, the initial narrative focus in ch. 90 is on the Greeks themselves, and their desire to rid Ionia of the Persian presence. The name Hegesistratus (91) means 'leader of the army'. The scene of persuasion again plays on the contrast between Spartan taciturnity and Ionian verbosity (cf. n. 1.152); H seems to find this topic amusing, since he has included it a number of times in the *Histories*. Another Spartan, King Cleomenes, also makes a pun on names (6.50).

Xerxes had made Theomestor despot of Samos for his performance at Salamis (8.85); the generous reward of competent and loyal non-Persian subjects was certainly one important way Persia built and controlled its empire (cf. nn. 1.134, 1.156).

In chs. 93–5 H adds a pendant on the background of the Greek seer at Mycale, just as he has done for the seers at Plataea (9.33–7). Apollonia (94) is a Corinthian colony in Illyria, in the north-western part of Greece. The ambivalences of this story (the bitter-sweet gift of the gods, the trick that lets Euenius' countrymen off the hook, the possibility that Deïphonus is not Euenius' son at all) reflect H's refusal at the end of the *Histories* to sing a simple paean of praise to Greek unity or even virtue.

Mycale (96) is a mountainous promontory on the mainland opposite Samos, between Ephesus and Miletus. One would like to know whether the Phoenicians are sent away because they are now deemed ineffective in fighting Greeks at sea (8.90, 100), or because the Persian leadership is pessimistic about fighting in Ionia with untrustworthy Greeks in their force, and wants to spare the best part of their fleet for later. H finds time to comment on Tigranes' looks (96) as part of his emphasis on firsts and bests (cf. n. 1.214), and his (very Greek) interest in good-looking people (cf. 3.20, 114, 5.47, 6.61, 7.180, 187, 9.25, 72).

9.97–101 The temple of the Holy Ones/Reverend Goddesses was probably dedicated to Demeter and Persephone. H comments on the coincidence that the battles of Plataea and of Mycale are both fought at sanctuaries of Demeter of Eleusis (101). Cf. 8.22 for the plot of Themistocles that Leotychidas imitates here. Many modern readers are sceptical of the rumour of victory at Plataea circulating at Mycale, but Mardonius had expected to signal his success at Athens to the king by means of relay beacons of fire (9.3), and it would not be implausible if the Greeks too had signals of some sort, *CAH* iv. 614.

9.102–5 The Athenian contingent has rejoined the Greek fleet by now (cf. the end of n. 8.130–2). The battle is a land one on a narrow strip of beaches and plain, around and in a hastily built Persian stockade (96). The Persian force is most improbably set at sixty thousand (96) but no number is given for the opposing Greeks, presumably because H did not know one. Both Samians and Milesians begin to fight on the Greek side, in the 'second revolt of Ionia' (103–4; cf. 5.30). The Athenians are eager to finish off the fight before the Lacedaemonians arrive (102), a sign of some competitiveness in the Greek camp and perhaps also of what lies ahead for Ionia (8.3, 9.106, 114). Hermolycus the Athenian (105), the best fighter at Mycale, practises the pancration, a mixture of boxing and wrestling; the war in which he later dies was fought in southern Euboea, probably c.472 BCE (Thucydides 1.98; *CAH* v. 42, 45–6). For the battle of Mycale itself, see *CAH* iv. 613–15; Burn, 547–52. For H's habit of marking importance by enumeration, see nn. 1.92, 3.56, 5.76.

9.106–7 The Lacedaemonians are probably following their usual policy of not wanting to be over-extended, arguing that the Ionians should move to mainland Greece (nn. 1.152, 3.148; cf. 9.8–9 for Spartan insularity). Later the Athenians will use their defence of Ionia and their connection with Ionians as their colonists as justification for their fifth-century empire. Breaking the Persian control of the Hellespont and the Thraceward regions is crucial for re-establishing Greek trade northwards and with the Black Sea region; the grain trade is particularly important for Athens with its large population (n. 7.145–7).

While the Greeks argue over their future course of action, the Persian high command falls to bickering (107); for the insult, cf. the end of n. 9.19–24. H says that Xenagoras of Halicarnassus becomes the ruler of Cilicia, but according to Xenophon (*Education of Cyrus* 7.4.2, cf. *CAH* iv. 226–7), Cilicia remains under the rule of a local Cilician prince until c.400 BCE. However, H could be expected to know of a Halicarnassian who had risen as far as Xenagoras apparently has. Thematically, the episode prepares us for the gruesome family drama that follows.

9.108–13 In the mean time Xerxes is imposing upon his brother Masistius' female relatives in Sardis. There are thematic links between this episode and the first major story in the *Histories*, that of Gyges and Candaules' wife (1.8–13). In each case, the ruler involved forgets the power an angry wife can wield, and forgets to keep his eye on the real business at hand. Candaules loses his rule and his life; Xerxes is not paying attention to events in Greece but to the attempted seduction of his own sister-in-law and daughter-in-law, and ends up destroying his brother's family. (Amestris' burial alive of fourteen Persian children has already been described in 7.114, although there it is described as a Persian custom rather than as private pathology.) Darius, Xerxes' eldest son, will be put to death by his brother Artaxerxes after Xerxes' own assassination in 465 BCE (Diodorus 11.69); no doubt H expects his readers to recognize that the palace intrigue of 479 narrated here is also a tacit allusion to later events in the Persian royal family. It is a crushing last picture of Xerxes himself, and a final restatement of the Persian tendency to subsume all power—personal, familial, governmental—under the fallible control of one man (cf. 7.8). For H's connection of despotism with the transgression of normal sexual boundaries, cf. Otanes' judgement of monarchy in 3.80, and Lateiner, 138–9.

9.114–22 Xerxes built his bridge to end very near Sestus (7.33–4; see Lateiner (p. 128) on the theme of the Persian violation of natural boundaries, and how the final restatement of this theme here provides closure for the *Histories*). Sestus is on the Greek side of the Hellespont and of strategic importance to Athens in securing the grain supply from the Euxine (Black) Sea (cf. 7.147 and Miltiades' domination of the Chersonese, 6.34 ff.). Cardia (115) is also on the Chersonese. Protesilaus (116) was the first Greek to fall at Troy, in the Trojan War (*Iliad* 2.701–2); he became a hero and his sanctuary was at Elaeus, at the tip of the Chersonese (n. 7.33–6). Presumably Artayctes was one of the governors of the new Persian province of 'Skudra' (Thrace and Macedonia), ruling from a well-fortified Sestus (*CAH* iv. 246–9). Xanthippus, the father of Pericles and connection by marriage of the Alcmaeonidae, is the general in charge of the Athenian forces at Sestus (cf. the middle of n. 6.121–4). He probably died within a few years of this campaign, since we find Pericles himself the *choregus*, or producer, for Aeschylus' *Persians* in Athens in 472 BCE.

Vengeance for the violation of Protesilaus' sanctuary provides temporal as well as geographical closure for the Persian Wars. Xerxes' bridges are broken, his abusive governor punished, and with Protesilaus the reader is also reminded of one legendary beginning of military hostilities between Asia and Greece, at Troy, referred to at the beginning of H's *Histories* (1.4). The ironies in the episode of

Artayctes' punishment are multiple. Artayctes himself attempts to point a moral, learn from his mistakes, and save his life, but his (unconvincing, even slightly comical) exegesis is rebuffed by Xanthippus, who intends to do as the Elaeusians want instead (120), and so crucifies Artayctes overlooking the spot where Xerxes' army had bridged the strait. As Artayctes is dying the Athenians stone his son to death before his eyes. Xanthippus and the Athenians behave very differently from Pausanias after the battle of Plataea (9.76, 79); there is no magnanimity or moderation here. One final irony of history is not noted by H, presumably because it had not yet happened as he was finishing the *Histories*: Aegospotami, where Artayctes is captured fleeing Sestus, is also the scene of the final battle of the Peloponnesian War and Athenian defeat in 404 BCE (Xenophon, *Hellenica* 2.1.21–30).

9.122 A final pendant, reverting to the time of Cyrus the Great (557–530 BCE) and some good advice Cyrus is said to have given the Persians; it is a very different philosophy from the one Cyrus espouses in 1.125–6. In their prosecution of the war in Greece, the Persians have clearly abandoned the way of life encouraged here by Cyrus (9.82). For the notion that character is conditioned by the environment, cf. the Hippocratic *Airs, Waters, Places* 24. For the association of poverty with political and military success, cf. 1.71, 7.102, 8.26, and 9.82. H's massive work ends by recalling the past greatness of Persia, but does so in a way that encourages us, his readers, to decide what meaning the episode has for the present or the future, in particular, the future of Athens' fifth-century empire. At any rate, it is clear once more that for H change is in the order of things. Because small becomes big and big small, and 'knowing that human happiness never remains long in the same place' (1.5), he has given us a final cautionary tale for our contemplation and a generous measure of both big and small in his *Histories*.

TEXTUAL NOTES

I have translated the Oxford Classical Text of C. Hude (3rd edn., Oxford, 1927), except at the following points, which are marked in the text with an obelus. The names in brackets show the original source of the emendation or conjecture, at least as far as they are known to me.

1.12.2: this last sentence is probably an interpolation
1.38.2: retaining τὴν ἀκοήν (MSS)
1.56.2: reading προκεκριμένα ἔθνεα τὸ ἀρχαῖον, τὸ μέν (Porson)
1.71.3: reading [οὐ] σῦκα (Merkelbach)
1.120.1: reading τότε for ταύτῃ (Powell)
1.132.2: omitting τῷ θύοντι (Powell)
1.148.2: this last sentence may well be an interpolation
1.167.1: filling the lacuna with Stein's suggestion
1.191.1: reading ἀπαναστᾶσαν (Stein)
1.191.2: omitting κατά (Powell)
1.199.1: omitting ἐπὶ ζευγέων (Powell)
1.207.1: reading σφάλμα φέρον (Powell)
2.8.3: omitting Dietsch's addition
2.11.3: retaining the MSS text deleted by Schweighäuser
2.15.3: reading τῷ ὑπὸ Ἰώνων ⟨Αἰγύπτῳ⟩ καλεομένῳ (Powell)
2.36.3: retaining the phrase omitted by some MSS
2.44.2: reading μεγάλως (Wesseling)
2.47.3: retaining κρέα (some MSS)
2.52.1: reading νομάς ⟨νείμαντες⟩ (Powell)
2.75.2: reading στεινή (Stein)
2.77.2: reading στρεφόντων σιτίων (Waterfield)
2.78.1: omitting πάντῃ (Stein)
2.79.3: reading [καὶ] ἀοιδήν (Powell)
2.104.4: retaining κατὰ τὰ αἰδοῖα (MSS)
2.116.2: reading κατὰ ταῦτα γὰρ ἐποίησε (Powell)
2.116.4–5: in the transmitted text there is a longish passage containing further Homeric references, but it is clear from the singular 'this passage' at the beginning of §117 that it is all an interpolation
2.118.3: retaining βασιλεύς (MSS)
2.124.3: reading δεκαέτεα (Powell)
2.126.1: retaining ἐν τοῖς ἔργοισι (MSS)
2.145.4: retaining the transmitted text

2.155.1: reading ⟨ἐν δεξιᾷ⟩ ἀναπλέοντι (Blakesley)
2.175.5: retaining ἐνθυμιστόν (MSS)
2.176.1: reading τοῦ αὐτοῦ (some MSS) for Αἰθιοπικοῦ
3.49.1: reading ἐόντες ἑωυτοῖσι ⟨συγγενέες⟩ (Godley)
3.59.2: omitting καὶ τὸν . . . νηόν (MS S)
3.64.4: omitting ἔτι (Powell)
3.70.2: some of the MSS, some of the time, have the form 'Megabyxus', preferred by Hude, for this name; I have preferred 'Megabyzus', throughout the book
3.89.2: omitting Reiske's addition
3.92.1: reading Παρητακηνοί (How and Wells)
3.125.4: retaining τῇ . . . προεμαντεύσατο (some MSS)
3.140.4: reading ἀλλ᾽ ὧν (Denniston)
3.146.3: reading πάντας (Denniston ap. Powell)
4.6.2: the words τοῦ βασιλέος ἐπωνυμίην look very like a gloss
4.10.3: reading μούνῳ (How and Wells)
4.11.2: reading μηδὲ πρὸ σποδοῦ δὴ μένοντας κινδυνεύειν (Stein, Bredovius, Waterfield)
4.28.1: omitting the second πηλόν (Stein)
4.42.2: omitting ἕως (Powell)
4.85.3: omitting the comma after στόματος (Powell)
4.95.3: reading ἐς χῶρον τ⟨οι⟩οῦτον (Renehan)
4.99.2: reading ἀπὸ Ἴστρου εὐθὺς ἤδη ἄρχ⟨ετ⟩αι ἡ Σκυθίη [ἐστί] (Powell)
4.119.4: reading [οὐ] τείσομεθα (Renehan)
4.133.1: reading φυγέειν instead of φρουρέειν (Powell)
4.149.2: reading ὑπέμειναν (Stein) τὠυτὸ τοῦτο ⟨συνέβη⟩ καί (Reiske)
4.158.1: reading παραφησάμενοι (Madvig)
4.180.3: retaining τὴν λίμνην (some MSS)
5.16.1: retaining the transmitted text
5.27.2: I have made up something to fill the lacuna, without pretending to know what the original Greek might have been
5.31.4: reading ἐξηγητής (MSS)
5.52.3: transposing this sentence with Stein
5.55.1: retaining τῷ ἑωυτοῦ πάθεϊ (MSS)
5.57.2: there seems no good reason for Madvig's addition
5.59.1: reading ἐόντ᾽ (Valckenaer)
5.77.4: reading ἀχνυόεντι (Hecker)
5.78.1: reading ⟨τι⟩ κατεργάζεσθαι (Powell)
5.92β.1: reading οἱ (Madvig)
5.112.2: reading αὐτόν (some MSS)
5.117.1: reading ταύτας μίαν ἐπ᾽ ἡμέρῃ ἑκάστῃ (Powell)

6.64.1: reading διότι (Richards)
6.66.2: reading Περίαλλαν (some MSS), and similarly a few lines later
6.75.1: retaining ἐς Σπάρτην (MSS)
6.75.1: omitting μανίη as a gloss (Waterfield)
6.119.3: filling the lacuna with Stein's conjecture
6.122.1–2: the whole of §122 is undoubtedly an interpolation, since in style and vocabulary it is not Herodotean. It contains a short eulogistic digression on Callias
6.137.3: retaining the transmitted text
7.11.2: the additions to the text are from Macan
7.16γ.2: reading οὐδὲ ἐπιφοιτήσει (some MSS)
7.25.2: adding σῖτον after πλεῖστον (Stein)
7.36.2: reading τριηρέων διχοῦ (Hude)
7.36.4: reading αὐτοὺς for αὖτις (Waterfield)
7.36.5: retaining καὶ οἱ ἵπποι (MSS)
7.42.2: deleting the comma after λαβών (MSS)
7.61.1: filling the gap with καὶ θώρηκας (Biel)
7.76.1: reading ⟨Πισίδαι⟩ δὲ ἀσπίδας (Stein)
7.82.1: adopting How's and Wells's transposition
7.86.1: reading καὶ Σάκαι ὁμοίως (Munro)
7.86.2: reading Πάκτυες (Stein)
7.123.2: reading Αἶσα (Stein)
7.129.4: reading φαίνεται (some MSS)
7.154.1: reading υἱέος (Stein)
7.161.2: reading ὅσον μέν νυν ⟨χρόνον⟩ (Powell)
7.167.2: there seems no compelling reason to delete this clause with Stein
7.175.1: reading ἅμα (some MSS)
7.183.2: reading ἐστάλησαν (O'Sullivan)
7.228.3: reading ἡγεμόνα (Stein)
7.239.4: the whole of this last section may be an interpolation
8.2.1: reading ὅσον τὸ πλῆθος (Reiske)
8.26.2: retaining τὸ ἄεθλον (MSS)
8.53.2: retaining ἐπὶ τὴν ἀκρόπολιν (MSS)
8.77.1: reading ῥήματα (Stein)
8.77.1: reading ἀνὰ . . . πίεσθαι (Düntzer)
8.104.1: two or three sentences follow which are certainly an interpolation since they repeat, almost verbatim, the beginning of 1.175
8.115.3: adopting Stein's transposition
8.144.5: retaining ἡμέας (MSS)
9.17.2: retaining ἱππέας (MSS)
9.27.5: reading οἷσπερ ἐστὶ πολλά (Renehan)
9.53.3: reading ταῦτ' ἀναινομένου (some MSS)

9.54.1: reading μούνων (MS B) . . . λελειμμένων (MS D)
9.55.2: retaining πρός τε and ὁ Παυσανίης (MSS)
9.83.2: reading κατὰ τὸ ἄνω (Stein)
9.84.1: reading ἐπεί γε δή (Stein)
9.85.1: reading ἱρέας (some MSS), and similarly a couple of lines later
9.97.1: retaining the clause and sentence unnecessarily deleted by Krüger
9.98.3: retaining Ἥβης (MSS)

GLOSSARY OF GREEK TERMS

Note: most of these topics are covered more fully in the *Oxford Classical Dictionary*

acropolis the citadel or high point of a Greek city; often the site of the original settlement, and in historic times well stocked with temples and sacred sites

aegis Athena's shield or short cloak, with a fringe of snakes and device of Medusa's head

archon literally 'leader', but in Athens the title of the most important civic office; nine archons were elected annually; one, the eponymous archon, gave his name to the year

chthonian deities the nether or earth gods, regarded as dwelling in or under the earth

cithara a stringed instrument similar to a lyre

deme a township in Attica, but then, after Cleisthenes' reforms (*c.*508/7 BCE) a municipal subdivision: for political and identificatory purposes every Athenian citizen was born into one of 139 demes

diecplous a naval manoeuvre in which a ship of one line aimed to sail between two enemy ships, damaging the enemy's oars (and, presumably, oarsmen), before circling round to take the crippled ship in the rear and board it

dithyramb a choral hymn sung at festivals in honour of Dionysus

Ephor in Sparta, the most important civic office; five Ephors ('overseers') were elected annually, and had supreme administrative power, even over the two kings

hecatomb originally, as the name implies, a sacrifice of one hundred oxen (*hekaton, bous*); then any particularly large number of victims destined for public sacrifice

helots the original inhabitants of Laconia and Messenia, now held in serfdom by their Spartiate masters, whom they outnumbered

hoplite a heavily armed Greek citizen foot-soldier, fighting in a phalanx formation

Iacchus the cry of the initiates into the Eleusinian mysteries, often personified as an associate of Demeter

naucrary forty-eight early subdivisions of the Athenian tribal system, until being supplanted by the demes (q.v.)

ostracism at Athens, a vote with potsherds (*ostraka*) for the expulsion of a political leader. Exile was for ten years, unless recalled, and involved a certain stigma but no loss of status or property

paean a hymn or cry of praise to Apollo, originally, but later with wider application

penteconter a type of ship with fifty oars

perioeci 'dwellers round Sparta', inhabitants of neighbouring towns, who were Spartan citizens, though of lesser status than full Spartiates

polemarch 'war leader', one of the archons in Athens, and in Sparta the commander of a *mora*, the largest unit in the Spartan army, of which there were originally five and later six

rhapsode a professional reciter/chanter of epic poetry, especially that of Homer, on public occasions such as festivals

satrapy in the huge Persian empire, a district ruled with some autonomy by a satrap or governor

silenus a satyr-like creature from Greek mythology, associated with the god Dionysus

Spartiate a full citizen of Sparta; numbers were limited by strict regulations as regards qualifications, which included lineage and submission to the famous Spartan upbringing

triaconter a thirty-oared ship

trireme the classic deckless Greek galley, with about 170 rowers, probably in three banks, allowing a ramming speed of up to four knots

GLOSSARY OF FOREIGN WORDS
USED BY HERODOTUS

Quite early in the processs of translating, I made the decision to transliterate and italicize a certain category of word used by Herodotus—namely, words with a blatant non-Greek origin. It is of course impossible to tell at what stage of familiarity any given word was. When did 'bungalow' stop being a word one had to italicize or surround with apostrophes and become a familiar part of the English language? At which stage of this process was *baris* or *tiara* for Herodotus' audience? Both these words, and several others in the list, certainly became relatively well known in later Greek. However, all the words included in the list below are signalled by Herodotus himself, somewhere in the book—even if not on their first occurrence—as foreign words, and I take this to mean, in most cases, that the word would have struck his audience as somewhat alien. In the list below I include the meaning Herodotus himself assigns to each word, without having the expertise to know in all cases whether or not he is correct.

akinakes a type of Persian and Scythian sword (3.118, 128, 4.62, 70, 7.54, 67, 8.20); not a 'scimitar', which is both medieval and curved, whereas an *akinakes* was short and straight

angaros a mounted courier in Persia for carrying royal messages (3.126, cf. 8.98)

antakaios a type of invertebrate fish found in the Borysthenes River in Scythia (4.53)

arima the Scythian for 'one' (4.27)

artaba a Persian measure of about 55 litres (1.192); cf. the modern Egyptian *ardeb*

askhu a Scythian name for a kind of syrup they make (4.23); cf. the modern Kalmuck drink *atschi*

Asmakh the Egyptian for 'those who stand to the left of the king' (2.30). It is not clear what ancient Egyptian word Herodotus has in mind, but there is a similar word meaning 'left': see Lloyd, ad loc.

baris a kind of barge used on the Nile (2.41, 60, 96, 179)

battos a North African word for 'king' (4.155)

bekos the Phrygian word for 'bread' (2.2). Herodotus is perfectly correct about this: the word occurs in Phrygian inscriptions. See

W.M. Calder, *Monumenta Asiae Minoris Antiqua*, vii (Manchester, 1956), nos. 313, 454, 495

enareis Scythian hermaphrodites (1.105, 4.67); cf. Avestan *a-nar*, 'not a man'

kalasiris an Egyptian undergarment of linen (2.81). It is not certain what Egyptian word Herodotus has in mind; certainly there was no known item of clothing with such a name (see Lloyd, ad loc.)

khampsa the ancient Egyptian word for 'crocodile' (2.69). Herodotus is very close: see Lloyd, ad loc.

kiki the ancient Egyptian word for castor oil (2.94). Herodotus is perfectly correct: see Lloyd, ad loc.

kurbasia a kind of Persian (5.49) and Scythian (7.64) turban-like head-dress, ending in a point

kyllestis an Egyptian word for a kind of barley loaf (2.77). Herodotus is reflecting an Egyptian word for a kind of unleavened bread: see Lloyd, ad loc.

ladanon the Arabian word for rock-rose resin (3.112)

lepidotos a kind of Egyptian fish regarded as sacred (2.72); further information on the fish in Lloyd, ad loc.

lotos the word was perfectly familiar to the Greeks since Homer's time, and hence has not usually been italicized (2.92, 96, 4.177, 178), except that once, in a typical burst of erudition, Herodotus refers to the original Egyptian word (2.92). It is not, however, an Egyptian word

oior the Scythian word for 'man' (4.110)

orosangai the Persian word for the king's benefactors (8.85). Various scholars have variously accounted for Herodotus' word

paprax a kind of fish in Paeonia (5.16)

pata the Scythian word for 'kill' (4.110)

piromis the Egyptian for 'man of rank' (2.143); actually based on the Egyptian for 'man'

pontikos the fruit tree that produces the fruit from which the Scythians make *askhu* (4.23); perhaps a type of cherry

rhadinake the Persian word for petroleum oil (6.119)

sagaris a kind of battleaxe in common use throughout the Persian empire and beyond (1.215, 4.5, 70, 7.64)

sigynna the Cyprian word for 'spear' (well attested), and (unattested) the Ligurian word for 'retailer' (5.9)

spaka the Median word for 'dog' (1.110); cf. e.g. the modern Persian *aspaka*, 'dog'

spou the Scythian word for 'eye' (4.27)

tiara a kind of Persian headgear, *not* a turban (1.132, 3.12, 7.61, 8.120)

tilon a kind of fish in Paeonia (5.16)

tukta the Persian for 'complete' (9.110)

zegeris a kind of mouse found in North Africa (4.192), meaning 'hill mouse'

zeira a kind of long coat worn by Arabians (7.69) and Thracians (7.75)

INDEX OF PROPER NAMES

Place names are assumed to include the names of their inhabitants, where relevant. Thus the entry 'Aeolis' also lists references to 'Aeolians', 'Phocis' includes 'Phocians', and so on.

Numerals refer to book and section of *The Histories*; a bold letter indicates that a place is named on a map.

Aegyptus 2.182
Aeneia 7.123
Aenesidemus 7.154, 165
Aenus 4.90; 7.58
Aenyra 6.47
Aeolis D, H, 1.6, 26, 28, 141,
  149–52, 157, 171; 2.1, 178; 3.1, 90;
  4.89; 5.94, 122–3; 6.8, 28, 98; 7.9,
  58, 95, 176, 194; 8.35; 9.115
Aeolus 7.197
Aëropus (son of Argaeus) 8.137
Aëropus (son of Philippus) 8.139
Aëropus (of Tegea) 9.26
Aesanius 4.150
Aeschines 6.100
Aeschraeus 8.11
Aeschrionians 3.26
Aeschylus 2.156
Aesop 2.134
Aetolia B, G, 6.127; 8.73
Agamemnon 1.67; 4.103; 7.134, 159
Agariste 6.126, 130–31
Agariste (granddaughter of the above)
  6.131
Agasicles 1.144
Agathyrsians A, 4.48, 78, 100, 102,
  104, 119, 125
Agathyrsus 4.10
Agbalus 7.98
Agenor 4.147; 7.91
Agetus 6.61–2
Agis (father of Echestratus) 7.204
Agis (father of Menares) 6.65
Aglaurus 8.53
Aglomachus 4.164
Agora ('Market') 7.58
Agrianes (river) 4.90
Agrianes (tribe) 5.16
Agron 1.7
Agylla 1.167
Ajax 5.66; 6.35; 8.64, 121
Alabanda (Caria) 7.195
Alabanda (Phrygia) 8.136
Alalia 1.165–6
Alarodians 3.94; 7.79
Alazeir 4.164
Alcaeus (of Lesbos) 5.95
Alcaeus (son of Heracles) 1.7
Alcamenes 7.204
Alcenor 1.82
Alcetes 8.139
Alcibiades 8.17
Alcidas 6.61
Alcimachus 6.101

Alcmene 2.43, 145
Alcmaeon 1.59; 6.125, 127, 130
Alcmaeonidae 1.61, 64; 5.62–3, 66,
  70–1, 90; 6.115, 121–31
Alcon 6.127
Aleian Plain 6.95
Aleuadae 7.6, 130, 172; 9.58
Alexander (of Macedonia) 5.17,
  19–22; 7.173, 175; 8.34, 121,
  136–44; 9.1, 4, 8, 44–6
Alexander (of Troy) 1.3; 2.113–18,
  120
Alilat (goddess) 1.131; 3.8
Alizones 4.17, 52
Alopecae 5.63
Alpeni 7.176, 216, 229
Alpheus 7.227
Alpis (river) A, 4.49
Alus 7.173, 197
Alyattes 1.6, 16–26, 47, 73–4, 92, 93;
  3.48; 8.35
Amasis (king) 1.30, 77; 2.43, 134,
  145, 154, 162–3, 169, 172–82; 3.1,
  4, 10, 14, 16, 39–41, 43, 47, 125
Amasis (Maraphian) 4.167, 201, 203
Amathous D, 5.104, 108, 114
Amazons 4.110–17; 9.27
Ambracia B, G, 8.45, 47; 9.28, 31
Ameinias 8.84, 93
Ameinocles 7.190
Amestris 7.61, 114; 9.109–13
Amiantus 6.127
Ammon (god) 1.46; 2.18, 32, 55
Ammonians A, 2.32, 42; 3.17, 25–6;
  4.181–2
Amompharetus 9.53, 55–7, 71, 85
Amorges 5.121
Ampe 6.20
Ampelus ('Vine'), Cape 7.122–3
Amphiaraus 1.46, 49, 52, 92; 3.91;
  8.134
Amphicaea 8.33
Amphicrates 3.59
Amphictyon 7.200
Amphictyons ('Dwellers Round About
  Delphi') 2.180; 5.62; 7.200, 213,
  228
Amphilochus 3.91; 7.91
Amphilytus 1.61
Amphimnestus 6.127
Amphion 5.92
Amphissa G, 8.32, 36
Amphitryon 2.43–4, 146; 6.53
Amun (god) 2.42

Chemmis (city) 2.91, 165
Chemmis (island) 2.156
Cheops 2.124–7, 129
Chephren 2.127–8
Cherasmis 7.78
Chersis 5.104, 113; 7.98; 8.11
Chersonese ('Peninsula') B, 4.137,
  143; 6.33–4, 36–41, 103–4, 140;
  7.22, 33, 58; 8.130; 9.114, 116,
  118–19
Chileus 9.9
Chilon 1.59; 7.235
Chilon (grandson of the above) 6.65
Chios (island) B, 1.18, 25, 142,
  160–1, 164–5; 2.135, 178; 4.138;
  5.33–4, 98; 6.2, 5, 8, 15–16, 26–8,
  31; 8.105, 132; 9.106
Choäspes (river) A, 1.188; 5.49, 52
Choereae ('Pig Town') 6.101
Choerus 7.170
Chorasmians A, H, 3.93, 117; 7.66
Chromius 1.82
Cicones B, 7.59, 108, 110
Cilicia D, H, 1.28, 72, 74; 2.17, 34;
  3.90, 91; 5.49, 52, 108, 118; 6.6,
  43, 95; 7.77, 91, 98; 8.14, 68, 100;
  9.107
Cilix 7.91
Cilla 1.149
Cimmeria D, 1.6, 15, 16, 103; 4.1,
  11–13, 28, 100; 7.20
Cimmerian Straits C, 4.12, 45
Cimmerian Walls 4.12
Cimon 6.34, 38, 39, 40, 103, 137,
  140
Cimon (grandson of the above) 6.136;
  7.107
Cindye 5.118
Cineas 5.6
Cinyps (region) 4.198
Cinyps (river) I, 4.175; 5.42
Cissia H, 3.91; 5.49, 52; 6.119; 7.62,
  86, 210
Cissian Gate (Babylon) 3.155, 158
Cithaeron (mountain) J, 7.141; 9.19,
  25, 38–9, 51, 56, 69
Cius 5.122
Clazomenae ('Screaming Birds') B,
  1.16, 51, 142; 2.178; 5.123
Cleades 9.85
Cleander (of Gela) 7.154–5
Cleander (of Phigalea) 6.83
Cleinias 8.17

Cleisthenes (of Athens) 5.66–7, 69–73;
  6.131
Cleisthenes (of Sicyon) 5.67–9;
  6.126–31
Cleobis 1.31
Cleodaeus 6.52; 7.204; 8.131
Cleombrotus 4.81; 5.32–41; 7.205;
  8.71; 9.10, 64, 78
Cleomenes 3.148; 5.39, 41–2, 48–51,
  54, 64, 70, 72–6, 90, 97; 6.50–1,
  61, 64–6, 73–85, 92, 108; 7.148,
  205, 239
Cleonae 7.22
Cnidos B, 1.144, 174; 2.178; 3.138;
  4.164
Cnoethus 6.88
Cnossus B, 3.122
Cobon 6.66
Codrus 1.147; 5.65, 76; 9.97
Coela ('The Hollows', Chios) 6.26
Coela ('The Hollows', Euboea)
  8.13–14
Coele ('Hollow') 6.103
Coenyra 6.47
Coës 4.97; 5.11, 37–8
Colaeus 4.152
Colaxaïs 4.5, 7
Colchis A, C, H, 1.2, 104; 2.104–5;
  3.97; 4.37, 40, 45; 7.62, 79, 197
Colias 8.96
Colophon B, 1.14, 16, 142, 147, 150
Colossae ('Giant Rocks') 7.30
Combreia 7.123
Compsatus 7.109
Conda 5.63
Contadesdus (river) 4.90
Copaïs (lake) G, 8.135
Corcyra (island; Corfu) B, 3.48–9,
  52–3; 7.145, 154, 168
Coresus 5.100
Corinth E, 1.14, 23–4, 50, 51; 2.167;
  3.48–53, 134; 4.162, 180; 5.75, 87,
  92–3; 6.89, 108, 128; 7.154, 195,
  202; 8.1, 5, 21, 43, 45, 59–61, 72,
  79, 94; 9.28, 31, 69, 88, 102, 105
Corobius 4.151–3
Coronea G, 5.79
Corycian Cave 8.36
Corydallus 7.214
Corys (river) 3.9
Cos (island) B, 1.144; 7.99, 163–4;
  9.76
Cotys 4.45

Couphagoras 6.117
Cranaï 8.44
Cranaspes 3.126
Crannon **G**, 6.127
Crathis (river, Aegae) 1.145
Crathis (river, Sybaris) 5.45
Cremni ('The Cliffs') 4.20, 110
Creston 1.57
Crestonia **B**, 5.3, 5; 7.124, 127;
 8.116
Crete **A, B, D**, 1.2, 65, 171–3; 3.44,
 59; 4.45, 151, 154, 161; 7.92, 99,
 145, 169–71
Cretines (of Magnesia) 7.190
Cretines (of Rhegium) 7.165
Crinippus 7.165
Crisaean Plain 8.32
Critalla 7.26
Critobulus (of Cyrene) 2.181
Critobulus (of Torone) 8.127
Crius ('Ram') 6.50, 73; 8.92
Crobyzan Thracians 4.49
Crocodilopolis ('Crocodile City')
 2.148
Croesus 1.6–94, 130, 141, 153,
 207–8; 3.14, 34–6, 47; 5.36; 6.37–8,
 125; 7.30; 8.35, 122
Crophi (mountain) 2.28
Crossaea 7.123
Croton **I**, 3.125, 129, 131, 136–8;
 5.44–5, 47; 6.21; 8.47
Curium ('Youthful') 5.113
Cyaxares 1.16, 46, 73–4, 103, 106–7
Cybebe (goddess) 5.102
Cyberniscus 7.98
Cyclades (islands) 5.31
Cydippe 7.165
Cydonia ('Country of Quinces') **D**,
 3.44, 59
Cydrara 7.30
Cyllyrians 7.155
Cylon 5.71
Cyme **B**, 1.149, 157–60; 4.138;
 5.37–8, 123; 7.194; 8.130
Cyneas 6.101
Cynegeirus 6.114
Cynesians **A**, 2.33; 4.49
Cyniscus ('Puppy') 6.71
Cyno ('Bitch') 1.110, 122
Cynosarges 5.63; 6.116
Cynosura ('Dog-tail') 8.76–7
Cynurians **E**, 8.73
Cypria (Homer?) 2.117

Cyprus (island) **A, D, H**, 1.72, 105,
 199; 2.79, 182; 3.19, 91; 4.162,
 164; 5.9, 31, 104–16; 6.6; 7.90, 98;
 8.68, 100
Cypselidae 6.128
Cypselus (of Athens) 6.34, 35, 36
Cypselus (of Corinth) 1.14, 20, 23;
 3.48; 5.92, 95
Cyrauis (island) 4.195
Cyrene **A, D, I**, 2.32–3, 96, 161, 181,
 182; 3.13, 91; 4.152, 154–6,
 159–65, 169, 170, 171, 186, 199,
 203; 5.47
Cyrnus (Euboea) 9.105
Cyrnus (hero) 1.167
Cyrnus (island; Corsica) **A, I**, 1.165–7;
 7.165
Cyrus 1.46, 54, 71–3, 75–80, 84,
 86–91, 108–214; 2.1; 3.1, 2–3, 14,
 32, 34, 36, 44, 61, 63, 64, 65, 66,
 67, 68, 69, 71, 74, 75, 88, 89, 120,
 133, 139, 152, 159, 160; 4.165;
 5.52; 7.2, 8, 11, 18, 51, 64, 69, 78;
 9.122
Cyrus (grandfather of the above)
 1.111; 7.11
Cythera (island) **B, E**, 1.82, 105;
 7.235
Cythnos (island) **B**, 7.90; 8.46, 67
Cytissorus 7.197
Cyzicus **B, C**, 4.14–15, 76, 138; 6.33

Dadicae 3.91; 7.66
Daedalus 7.170
Damasithymus (of Calynda) 8.87
Damasithymus (of Caria) 7.98
Damasus 6.127
Damia 5.82–3
Daï 1.125
Danaë 2.91; 6.53; 7.61, 150
Danaus 2.91, 98, 171, 182; 7.94
Daphnae 2.30, 107
Daphnis 4.138
Dardanae 1.189
Dardanum 7.43
Dardanus 5.117
Daritae 3.92
Darius 1.130, 183, 187, 209–10;
 2.110, 158; 3.12, 38, 70–3, 76, 78,
 82–3, 85–9, 90, 95, 96, 101,
 117–19, 127–60; 4.1, 4, 7, 39, 44,
 46, 83–143, 166–7, 204; 5.1–27, 30,
 32, 37, 65, 73, 96, 98, 103, 105–8,

Echeidorus ('Bountiful', river) 7.124, 127
Echemus 9.26
Echestratus 7.204
Echinades (islands) 2.10
Edonia B, 5.11, 124; 7.110, 114; 9.75
Eëtion 1.14; 5.92
Egypt A, D, H, 1.1, 2, 5, 30, 77, 93, 105, 135, 140, 153, 182, 193, 198; 2.1–3.38; 3.44–5, 47, 64, 65, 91, 107, 125, 129, 132, 139; 4.39, 41, 42, 43, 45, 47, 53, 141, 152, 159, 165–7, 168, 180, 181, 186, 203, 205; 6.6, 53–4, 60; 7.1–2, 4–5, 7–8, 20, 25, 34, 69–70, 89, 91, 97; 8.17, 68, 100; 9.32
Egyptian Sea 2.113
Eight (Primal) Gods 2.43, 46, 145, 156
Eileithyia (goddess) 4.35
Eïon B, 7.25, 107, 113; 8.118, 120
Elaeus ('Olives') B, 6.140; 7.22, 33; 9.116, 120
Elateia G, 8.33
Elbo (island) 2.140
Eleon 5.43
Elephantine ('Ivory Town') D, 2.8, 17, 18, 28–31, 69, 175; 3.19–20
Eleusis F, 1.30; 5.74–6; 6.64, 75; 8.65, 85; 9.19, 27, 57, 65, 97, 101
Elis B, E, 2.160; 3.132; 4.30, 148; 5.44–5; 6.70, 127; 8.27, 72, 73; 9.33, 35, 37, 77
Elisyces 7.165
Ellopia 8.23
Elorus (river) 7.154
Encampments, the D, 2.154
Encheleis 5.61; 9.43
Eneti (Venetians) A, 1.196; 5.9
Enienia 7.132, 185, 198
Enipeus (river) 7.129
Eordia 7.185
Epaphus (god) 2.38; 3.27–8; see also Apis
Ephesus B, J, 1.26, 92, 142, 147; 2.10, 106, 148; 5.54, 100, 102; 6.16, 84; 8.103, 105, 107; 9.84
Ephialtes 7.213–15, 218, 223, 225
Epicydas 6.86
Epidamnus 6.127
Epidanus (river) 7.196
Epidaurus E, 1.146; 3.50, 52; 5.82–4, 86; 7.99; 8.1, 43, 46, 72; 9.28, 31

Epigoni (Homer?) 4.32
Epistrophus 6.127
Epium 4.148
Epizelus 6.117
Erasinus (river) 6.76
Erechtheus 5.82; 7.189; 8.44, 55
Eretria G, J, 1.61–2; 5.57, 99, 102; 6.43, 94, 98–102, 106, 107, 115, 119–20, 127; 8.1, 46; 9.28, 31
Eridanus ('Quarrelsome', river) I, 3.115
Erineus ('Woollen') 8.43
Erochus 8.33
Erxander 4.97; 5.37
Erytheia (island) 4.8
Erythrae ('Red Rocks') B, 1.18, 142; 6.8; 9.15, 19, 22, 25
Erythrebolus ('Red Earth') 2.111
Eryx (mountain) I, 5.43, 45
Eryxo 4.160
Etearchus (Ammonian) 2.32–3
Etearchus (of Oäxus) 4.154
Eteocles 5.61
Ethiopia (Africa) D, H, 2.12, 22, 29–30, 42, 86, 100, 104, 106, 110, 127, 134, 137, 139–40, 146, 152, 161; 3.17–26, 97, 101, 114; 4.183, 197; 7.9, 18, 69, 90; 9.32
Ethiopia (Asia) 3.94; 7.70
Euaenetus 7.173
Euagoras 6.103
Eualcides 5.102
Euboea (island) B, G, 1.146; 3.89, 95; 4.33; 5.31, 77; 6.100, 127; 7.156, 176, 183, 189, 192; 8.4, 6–8, 13–14, 19–20, 25, 68–9, 86
Euclides 7.155
Euelthon 4.162; 5.104
Euenius 9.92–5
Euesperides ('West Town') I, 4.171
Euesperitae 4.198
Eumenes 8.93
Eunomus 8.131
Eupalinus 3.60
Euphemus 4.150
Euphorbus 6.101
Euphorion (of Athens) 2.156; 6.114
Euphorion (of Azania) 6.127
Euphrates (river) A, H, 1.179–80, 185–6, 191, 193; 5.52
Euripus (strait) G, 5.77; 7.173, 183; 8.7, 15, 66
Europa 1.2, 4, 173; 2.44; 4.45, 147

MAPS

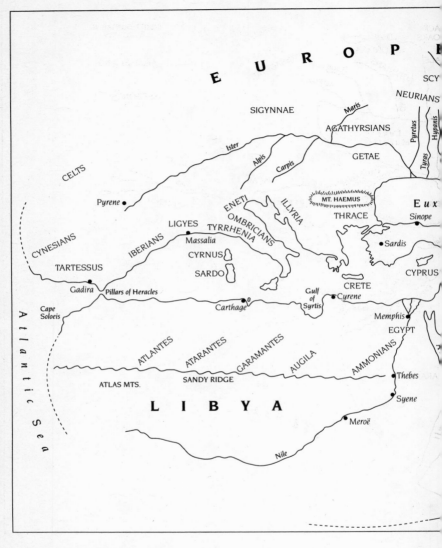

A. HERODOTUS' WORLD

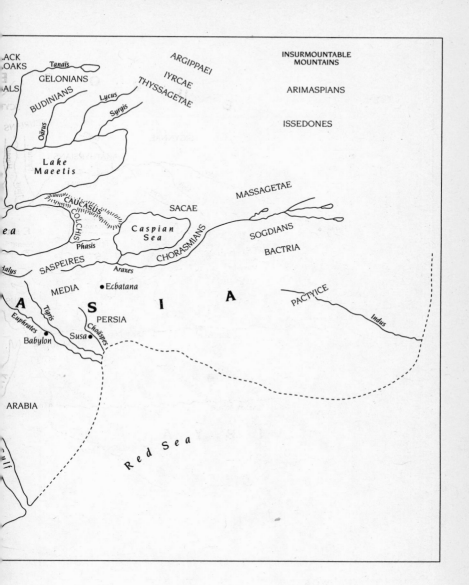

BLACK
CLOAKS

ALS

Tanaïs

GELONIANS

BUDINIANS

Oärus

Lycus

Syrgis

ARGIPPAEI

IYRCAE

THYSSAGETAE

INSURMOUNTABLE
MOUNTAINS

ARIMASPIANS

ISSEDONES

Lake
Maeetis

e a

CAUCASUS

COLCHIS

Phasis

SASPEIRES

dalus

Araxes

SACAE

Caspian
Sea

CHORASMIANS

MASSAGETAE

SOGDIANS

BACTRIA

MEDIA

●Ecbatana

Tigris

A   S   I   A

PACTYICE

Indus

Euphrates

Babylon ●

Susa ●

Choaspes

PERSIA

ARABIA

ulf

R e d   S e a

B. GREECE AND THE AEGEAN

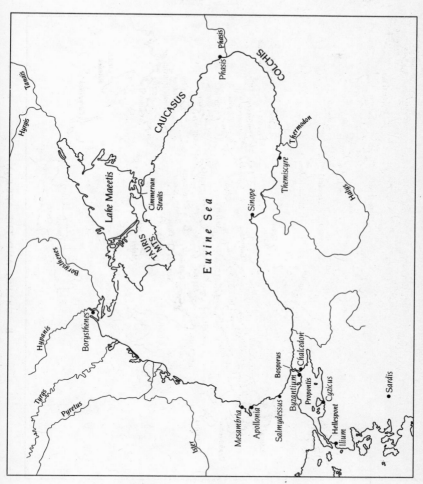

C. THE EUXINE (BLACK) SEA

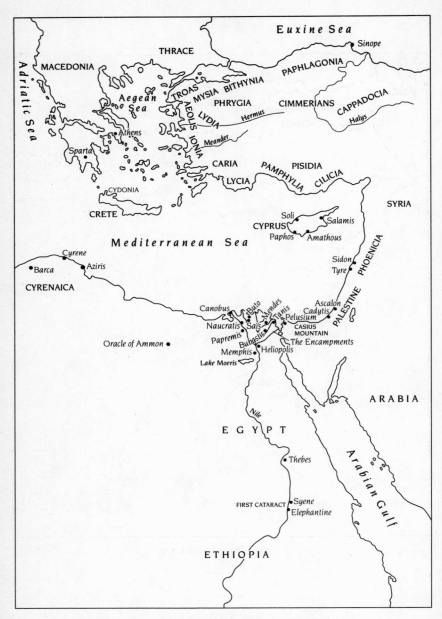

D. EGYPT, CYRENAICA, AND THE NEAR EAST

E. THE PELOPONNESE

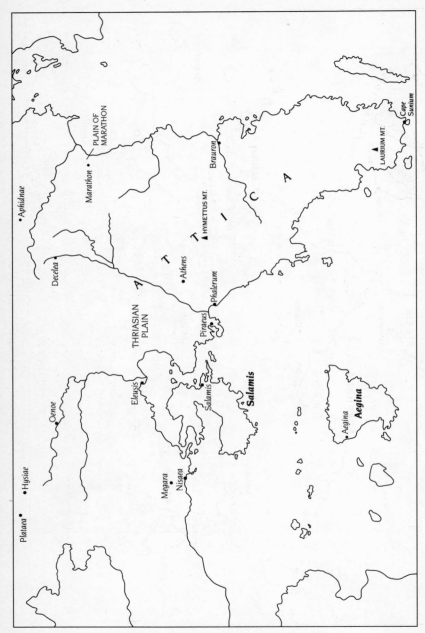

Aphidnae

PLAIN OF
MARATHON

Marathon

Decelea

ATTICA

Athens

HYMETTUS MT.

Brauron

A

LAURIUM MT.

Cape
Sunium

THRIASIAN
PLAIN

Phalerum

Piraeus

Oenoe

Eleusis

Salamis

Salamis

Hysiae

Plataea

Megara

Nisaea

Aegina

Aegina

F. ATTICA

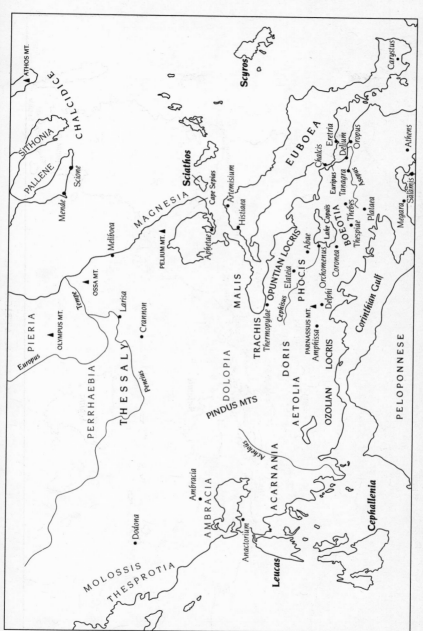

G. CENTRAL AND NORTHERN GREECE

H. THE PERSIAN EMPIRE

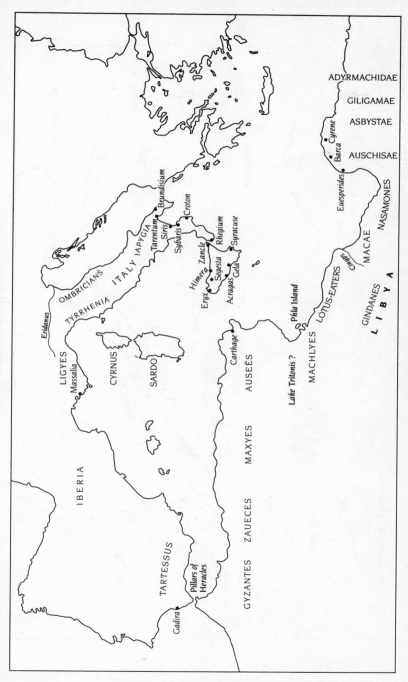

ADYRMACHIDAE

GILIGAMAE

ASBYSTAE

AUSCHISAE

Cyrene
Barca

Euesperides

NASAMONES

MACAE

LOTUS-EATERS

Cinyps

GINDANES

Phla Island

MACHLYES

L I B Y A

Lake Tritonis ?

AUSEËS

Carthage

MAXYES

ZAUECES

GYZANTES

Pillars of Heracles

Gadira

TARTESSUS

IBERIA

LIGYES
Massalia

CYRNUS

SARDO

Eridanus

OMBRICIANS

TYRRHENIA

ITALY IAPYGIA

Brundisium
Tarentum
Siris
Sybaris
Croton

Himera
Zancle
Rhegium
Syracuse
Segesta
Eryx
Acragas Gela

I. THE WESTERN MEDITERRANEAN

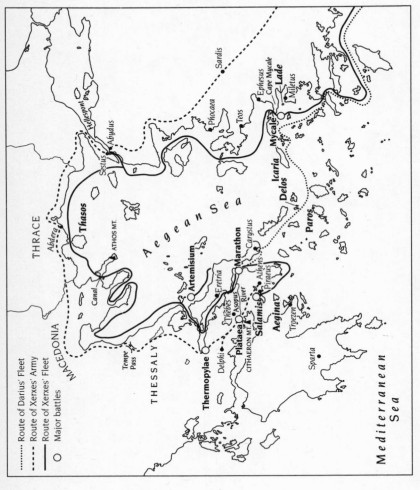

THRACE

MACEDONIA

Aegean Sea

THESSALY

Mediterranean Sea

Sardis

Ephesus
Cape Mycale
Icaria
Delos
Phocaea
Teos
Mycale
Miletus
Lade

Hellespont Pass
Abydus
Sestus

Thasos
Abdera

Canal
ATHOS MT.

Paros

Artemisium
Eretria
Carystus

Marathon

Tempe Pass

Thermopylae

Delphi
Thebes
Asopus River
Plataea
CITHAERON MT.
Salamis
Athens
Piraeus
Aegina
Troezen

Sparta

...... Route of Darius' Fleet
----- Route of Xerxes' Army
— Route of Xerxes' Fleet
○ Major battles